30 Agents Every AI Engineer Must Build

Build production-ready agent systems using proven architectures and patterns

Imran Ahmad, PhD

<packt>

30 Agents Every AI Engineer Must Build

This book was written by Imran Ahmad, Ph.D. Generative AI tools were used only to assist with ideation, phrasing, and diagram drafts, and all technical content and code were created, verified, and tested by the author and Packt's editorial team. Packt does not accept AI-generated content that replaces expert authorship.

Portfolio Director: Gebin George
Relationship Lead: Ali Abidi
Project Manager: Prajakta Naik
Content Engineer: Mark D'Souza
Technical Editor: Riya Agarwal
Copy Editor: Safis Editing
Indexer: Hemangini Bari
Production Designer: Ajay Patule
Growth Lead: Nimisha Dua

First published: March 2026

Production reference: 1300326

Published by Packt Publishing Ltd.
Grosvenor House
11 St Paul's Square
Birmingham
B3 1RB, UK.

ISBN 978-1-80610-901-2
www.packtpub.com

To my family: Naheed, Omar, and Anum, whose patience

and encouragement sustained this work.

And to every engineer who has looked at a language model

and wondered: what if it could not only answer questions,

but pursue goals?

– Imran Ahmad

Contributors

About the author

Imran Ahmad, Ph.D is a data scientist at the **Advanced Analytics Solution Center** (**A2SC**) within the Canadian federal government, where he builds and deploys machine learning systems for mission-critical applications. In his 2010 doctoral thesis, he introduced a linear programming-based algorithm for optimal resource assignment in large-scale cloud computing environments, work that anticipated many of the distributed systems challenges now central to agent deployment. In 2017, he pioneered the development of StreamSensing, a real-time analytics framework that has become the foundation of several research papers on processing multimedia data within machine learning paradigms.

Dr. Ahmad holds a visiting professorship at Carleton University in Ottawa and is an authorized instructor for Google Cloud and Microsoft Azure. He is the author of the bestselling *50 Algorithms Every Programmer Should Know* (Packt Publishing), which has been widely adopted in both academic curricula and industry training programs. His work on intelligent agent architectures reflects a sustained engagement with the algorithmic, distributed systems, and cognitive computing traditions that converge in the emerging discipline of agent engineering. Every pattern in this book has been tested against the production realities of latency, cost, reliability, and security that define real-world deployments.

I owe a heartfelt thanks to my wife, Naheed, my son, Omar, and my daughter, Anum, for their patience and unwavering support through the many long evenings and weekends this book demanded. A special acknowledgment goes to my father, Inayatullah, whose relentless encouragement to keep learning has been a guiding force throughout my life. On the Packt side, I would like to thank Ali Abidi, relationship lead, for his steady guidance; Mark D'Souza, content engineer, for upholding high editorial standards and keeping the project aligned with its vision; and Prajakta Naik, project manager, for orchestrating every moving piece so seamlessly.

About the reviewers

Arjun Chakraborty is an applied scientist working on the benchmarking and evaluation of security agents at Microsoft. His background is in security and AI, with previous experience at Databricks and NVIDIA.

Raju Dandigam is an engineering manager and staff engineer with over 15 years of experience in AI-powered systems, full-stack development, and scalable enterprise platforms. He has led large-scale engineering initiatives across web and cloud-native environments. Raju has served as a technical reviewer for Manning and Packt Publications. He has also authored technology blog posts that have been published on leading platforms and has been a speaker at industry conferences.

Table of Contents

Chapter 6: Information Retrieval and Knowledge Agents 145

Chapter 14: Financial and Legal Domain Agents 391

Chapter 15: Education and Knowledge Agents 421

Preface

The AI landscape is undergoing a profound transformation. We are moving from an era of passive, reactive AI systems to one dominated by autonomous, goal-directed intelligent agents: systems that can perceive their environment, make decisions, and take actions to achieve objectives with minimal human intervention. This shift is not incremental. It represents a fundamental change in how we conceive of, design, and deploy computational systems.

As the author of *50 Algorithms Every Programmer Should Know*, I have observed how understanding the fundamental building blocks of computer science provides engineers with the capabilities to build increasingly sophisticated systems. Just as algorithms form the foundation of traditional software engineering, intelligent agents represent the next evolutionary step in AI development. Understanding these agent architectures gives you the power to create systems that can solve problems of unprecedented complexity.

This transformation is architectural, not merely incremental. The distinction between a system that generates text in response to a prompt and a system that maintains persistent goals, reasons about its environment, selects and invokes tools, and adapts its strategy based on feedback is not a matter of degree. It is a qualitative shift in the kind of computational entity we are building. The closest historical analogue is the transition from procedural to object-oriented programming in the 1980s, which did not simply change how code was written but fundamentally altered how engineers conceptualized the relationship between data and behavior. The shift to agent-based systems carries similar implications for how we conceptualize the relationship between human intent and computational action.

The core thesis of this book is straightforward: mastering a carefully selected set of intelligent agent architectures will give you the capabilities to build transformative AI systems across virtually any domain. These are not theoretical constructs alone. They are practical, implementable patterns that solve real-world problems. The emergence of powerful LLMs has provided the cognitive engine that makes these agent architectures possible at scale for the first time. However, raw LLMs alone are not enough. The key to building effective systems lies in understanding how to architect agents that decompose complex tasks into manageable steps, connect to external tools and data sources, maintain context and memory across interactions, collaborate with humans and other agents, learn from experience, and make ethical decisions aligned with human values.

Consider a concrete example of what this shift means in practice. A traditional software system that processes insurance claims follows a fixed pipeline: validate the form, check the policy, compute the payout, and generate the letter. An agent-based system performing the same task operates differently. It reads the claim, identifies ambiguities, consults the policy database, cross-references historical claims for fraud indicators, escalates edge cases to a human adjuster, and generates a summary that explains its reasoning. It adapts to exceptions it has never encountered before by reasoning from first principles rather than following hardcoded branches. This book teaches you how to build systems like this.

This book bridges the gap between theoretical agent concepts and practical implementation. We will not merely describe what these agents can do. We will show you exactly how to build them. Every chapter includes working code, formal architectural patterns, real-world case studies, and guidance on avoiding common implementation pitfalls.

Who this book is for

This book is written for practitioners who need to implement working systems, and not merely understand concepts. It is ideal for AI and ML engineers looking to move beyond model training to building complete intelligent systems, software engineers expanding their toolkit to include agent-based AI solutions, technical leaders responsible for AI strategy and implementation, product managers who need to understand what is possible with modern agent architectures, and domain specialists looking to apply AI agents in their field.

While some familiarity with ML concepts and Python programming is assumed, the book focuses on architectural patterns rather than low-level implementation details, making it accessible to readers with various technical backgrounds. Each chapter is self-contained enough to be read independently, though reading them in sequence provides the most comprehensive foundation.

This book does not require a background in formal logic, control theory, or cognitive science, though readers with such backgrounds will recognize the theoretical traditions that inform many of the architectural patterns presented. The emphasis throughout is on building working systems informed by sound principles, rather than on proofs or formal verification.

What this book covers

Chapter 1, Foundations of Agent Engineering, introduces the core concepts, terminology, and architectural patterns that underpin all intelligent agent systems. It traces the evolution from simple rule-based systems to modern LLM-powered agents and establishes the cognitive architecture, development lifecycle, and evaluation frameworks used throughout the book.

Chapter 2, The Agent Engineer's Toolkit, surveys the essential frameworks, tools, and development environments for building agent systems. It provides a comprehensive analysis of LangChain, LlamaIndex, AutoGPT, and other frameworks, along with guidance on LLM selection, fine-tuning strategies, and foundational infrastructure including vector databases and observability solutions.

Chapter 3, The Art of Agent Prompting, explores advanced prompt engineering techniques specifically tailored for agent systems. It covers system prompt design for shaping agent cognition, agent-to-agent communication protocols, and iterative prompt development methodologies for testing and refinement.

Chapter 4, Agent Deployment and Responsible Development, addresses the practical considerations of scaling, securing, and ensuring ethical behavior in production agent systems. It covers infrastructure requirements, prompt injection defenses, user data protection, and responsible AI frameworks including bias detection, transparency requirements, and regulatory compliance.

Chapter 5, Foundational Cognitive Architectures, presents the core agents that form the building blocks of all intelligent systems. It covers the autonomous decision-making agent, the planning agent with tree-of-thought reasoning, and the memory-augmented agent with working, episodic, and semantic memory implementations. These patterns provide the cognitive substrate upon which all subsequent domain-specific agents are constructed.

Chapter 6, Information Retrieval and Knowledge Agents, examines how agents connect LLMs to external information sources. It covers advanced retrieval-augmented generation techniques, document intelligence architectures, and scientific research agents for literature review automation and hypothesis generation.

Chapter 7, Tool Manipulation and Orchestration Agents, explores systems that coordinate tools, functions, and other agents. It covers function-calling architecture patterns, chain-of-agents orchestration with task routing and delegation, and agentic workflow systems with human-in-the-loop coordination.

Chapter 8, Data Analysis and Reasoning Agents, focuses on agents specialized in analyzing information and drawing insights. It covers data exploration and visualization recommendation systems, verification and validation agents for factual consistency checking, and general problem solvers with domain-agnostic reasoning frameworks.

Chapter 9, Software Development Agents, covers agents that assist in code creation, testing, and maintenance. It presents program synthesis techniques with LLMs, security-hardened agent patterns for prompt injection defense, and self-improving agents that learn from user feedback.

Chapter 10, Conversational and Content Creation Agents, explores agents that generate, modify, and manage different forms of content. It covers natural dialog management, personality modeling, multi-modal content generation, and recommendation agents with hybrid recommender architectures.

Chapter 11, Multi-Modal Perception Agents, examines agents that process and understand various forms of input data. It covers vision-language agents for image understanding, audio processing agents for speech recognition and sentiment analysis, and physical world sensing agents for IoT data integration.

Chapter 12, Ethical and Explainable Agents, focuses on agents designed with transparency, accountability, and values alignment. It covers value alignment frameworks, ethical decision-making models, reasoning transparency techniques, and decision explanation frameworks for safety-critical applications. The ethical and explainability frameworks established here serve as prerequisites for the regulated-domain agents in Chapters 13 through 16.

Chapter 13, Healthcare and Scientific Agents, explores agents transforming biomedical research and patient care. It covers medical knowledge integration, patient data analysis patterns, clinical decision support frameworks, and scientific discovery agents for literature synthesis and hypothesis generation.

Chapter 14, Financial and Legal Domain Agents, examines agents specialized for regulated industries with complex requirements. It covers market data analysis architectures, risk assessment frameworks, personalized financial planning, legal knowledge base integration, case analysis, and contract analysis frameworks.

Chapter 15, Education and Knowledge Agents, covers agents that facilitate learning, teaching, and knowledge transfer. It presents personalized curriculum planning, adaptive learning techniques, collective intelligence architectures with multi-agent collaboration, and consensus mechanisms for emergent intelligence.

Chapter 16, Embodied and Physical World Agents, focuses on agents that bridge digital intelligence with physical environments. It covers robotics control interfaces, physical world reasoning frameworks, perception-action loops, and cross-domain knowledge synthesis for complex systems modeling.

Epilogue, The Future of Intelligent Agents, examines emerging paradigms including autonomous agent evolution and adaptation, agent societies and emergent behaviors, brain-inspired cognitive architectures, and strategic considerations for building agent capability roadmaps within organizations.

How this book is organized

This book is designed to accommodate three distinct reading approaches:

- **Sequential reading (***Chapter 1* **through the** *Epilogue***)**: This provides the most comprehensive foundation, as each chapter builds deliberately on the patterns and vocabulary established in its predecessors.
- **Domain-focused reading**: This allows practitioners with specific application needs to proceed directly to the relevant domain chapters (*Chapters 13–16*) after completing the foundational chapters (*Chapters 1–5*), which establish the architectural vocabulary used throughout.
- **Reference reading**: This allows experienced agent developers to consult individual chapters as needed for specific architectures, case studies, or design patterns.

Every chapter follows a consistent six-part structure: conceptual foundation, implementation guide with working code, real-world case studies, design patterns and variations, integration considerations for combining agents into larger systems, and common pitfalls that capture lessons from production deployments.

To get the most out of this book

To follow the examples in this book, you will need a computer running macOS, Windows, or Linux (8 GB RAM minimum; 16 GB recommended), Python 3.10 or later, git, and a terminal. A Python virtual environment tool such as venv, conda, or uv is recommended. An NVIDIA GPU with CUDA 12+ is optional but useful for experimenting with local models. The code examples in the book run on CPU by default.

Familiarity with Python programming and basic machine learning concepts will help you get the most from the implementation sections. Experience with frameworks such as LangChain or LlamaIndex is helpful but not required, as the book introduces these tools progressively.

Software/hardware covered in the book
Python 3.10+
LangChain/LangGraph 0.2+
CrewAI/AutoGen (*Chapters 2, 7, and 9*)
LlamaIndex (*Chapters 2 and 6*)
OpenAI API (GPT-4o/GPT-4o-mini)
Anthropic API (Claude 3.5+)
ChromaDB/FAISS

Software/hardware covered in the book
Pinecone/Weaviate/Milvus (*Chapters 2, 4, 5, and 6*)
sentence-transformers/scikit-learn (*Chapters 6 and 8*)
pandas/NumPy/statsmodels (*Chapter 8*)
Matplotlib/Plotly (*Chapter 8*)
Hugging Face Transformers/PyTorch (*Chapters 8 and 11*)
pytest (*Chapters 5 and 9*)
Flask/Pydantic (*Chapter 9*)
Tesseract OCR (*Chapter 6*)
Neo4j (*Chapter 6*)
SHAP/LIME (*Chapter 12*)
FHIR Resources (*Chapter 13*)
Finnhub API/Tavily API (*Chapter 14*)
yfinance/NetworkX (*Chapters 14 and 15*)
ROS2 Humble+ (*Chapter 16*, optional)
Docker/Kubernetes (*Chapters 4 and 9*, optional)
Grafana/LangSmith (*Chapter 4*, optional)
Apache Kafka (*Chapter 4*, optional)
NVIDIA GPU with CUDA 12+, 16 GB VRAM (*Chapter 11*, optional)

Before starting with *Chapter 5*, which introduces the first hands-on code implementations, we recommend setting up a dedicated development environment. Create a Python virtual environment, install the core dependencies (langchain, openai, chromadb), and configure your API keys as environment variables. The README file in the GitHub repository provides step-by-step setup instructions for all major operating systems.

Download the example code files

The code bundle for the book is hosted on GitHub at`https://github.com/PacktPublishing/30-Agents-Every-AI-Engineer-Must-Build/`. We also have other code bundles from our rich catalog of books and videos available at `https://github.com/PacktPublishing`. Check them out!

Conventions used

There are a number of text conventions used throughout this book.

`CodeInText`: Indicates code words in text, database table names, folder names, filenames, file extensions, pathnames, dummy URLs, user input, and Twitter handles. For example: "Initialize the agent by calling `AgentExecutor.from_tools()` with your configured tool list."

A block of code is set as follows:

```
class AutonomousAgent:
    def __init__(self, llm, tools, memory):
        self.llm = llm
        self.tools = tools
        self.memory = memory
```

Bold: Indicates a new term, an important word, or words that you see on the screen. For instance, words in menus or dialog boxes appear in the text like this. For example: " Navigate to the **Settings** panel and select **API Keys**."

Note

Warnings or important notes appear like this.

Tip

Tips and tricks appear like this.

Get in touch

Feedback from our readers is always welcome.

General feedback: If you have questions about any aspect of this book or have any general feedback, please email us at `customercare@packt.com` and mention the book's title in the subject of your message.

Errata: Although we have taken every care to ensure the accuracy of our content, mistakes do happen. If you have found a mistake in this book, we would be grateful if you reported this to us. Please visit `http://www.packt.com/submit-errata`, click **Submit Errata**, and fill in the form.

Piracy: If you come across any illegal copies of our works in any form on the internet, we would be grateful if you would provide us with the location address or website name. Please contact us at `copyright@packt.com` with a link to the material.

If you are interested in becoming an author: If there is a topic that you have expertise in and you are interested in either writing or contributing to a book, please visit `http://authors.packt.com/`.

Free benefits with your book

This book comes with free benefits to support your learning. Activate them now for instant access (see the "*How to Unlock*" section for instructions).

Here's a quick overview of what you can instantly unlock with your purchase:

Complete Code Bundle

Download the full source code for this book's examples and projects.

DRM-Free PDF Version

EPUB PDF

Download DRM-free PDF and ePub copies of this book.

7-Day Packt Library Access

Get 7-day unlimited access to 8,000+ books and videos. No credit card required.

Available for first-time Packt+ trial users only.

Next-Gen Reader Access

Read this book on Packt Reader with progress sync, dark mode and note-taking.

How to Unlock

Scan the QR code (or go to `packtpub.com/unlock`). Search for this book by name, confirm the edition, and then follow the steps on the page.

UNLOCK NOW

Note: Keep your invoice handy. Purchases made directly from Packt don't require one

Share your thoughts

Now you've finished *30 Agents Every AI Engineer Must Build*, we'd love to hear your thoughts! Scan the QR code below to go straight to the Amazon review page for this book and share your feedback or leave a review on the site that you purchased it from.

`https://packt.link/r/1806109018`

Your review is important to us and the tech community and will help us make sure we're delivering excellent quality content.

1

Foundations of Agent Engineering

The future belongs to organizations that can harness artificial intelligence not as a replacement for human intelligence, but as an amplification of it.

— Andrew Ng, AI researcher and co-founder of Coursera

Artificial intelligence (**AI**) stands at a transformative threshold due to the emergence of **autonomous agents**, which represent perhaps the most significant architectural advancement in computing since the transition from procedural to object-oriented programming, a fundamental reimagining of how digital systems operate and interact with their environments. These agents are not merely enhanced algorithms but cognitive entities that perceive their surroundings, maintain persistent state, reason strategically about complex objectives, and adapt their behavior based on experience. The implications of this evolution extend far beyond technical implementation details to challenge our fundamental conception of the relationship between human intent and computational action.

This chapter establishes the conceptual foundation for understanding **agent engineering** as both a theoretical discipline and a practical framework. We explore the evolutionary trajectory from simple reactive systems to sophisticated cognitive architectures, examine the structural components that enable autonomous behavior, and introduce the development methodologies that bridge theoretical principles with production implementations. Through this exploration, we aim to provide both a comprehensive framework for conceptualizing agent systems and practical insights for designing, developing, and deploying them effectively, whether you're a software engineer building autonomous workflows, an enterprise architect integrating intelligent assistants into legacy systems, or a product leader exploring how agent-based platforms can deliver scalable customer support or compliance automation.

The principles outlined here are not merely academic; they represent critical knowledge for organizations seeking to harness the transformative potential of agent-based systems. Whether automating complex workflows, augmenting human capabilities, or enabling entirely new classes of applications, autonomous agents are increasingly becoming essential components of the digital landscape. However, realizing their full potential often involves navigating complex integration challenges, such as robust tool orchestration, secure data privacy, and ethical alignment. Understanding their fundamental nature and architectural requirements provides the foundation upon which successful implementations are built and through which these challenges can be effectively addressed.

In this chapter, we'll be covering the following topics:

- Introducing agents
- Architecture of agents
- Interoperability protocols
- The agent development lifecycle
- The evolution of agent interaction paradigms
- The Agentic AI Progression Framework
- Real-world business impact

Introducing agents

We stand at a pivotal inflection point in the history of computing. The transition from traditional software systems to autonomous agents represents a fundamental paradigm shift that transforms how digital systems operate and interact with their environments. While conventional programs operate within predetermined pathways defined by explicit instructions, agent-based systems exhibit goal-directed behavior, maintain persistent state, and adapt their strategies based on environmental feedback. This transformation challenges established software engineering principles and introduces new frameworks for conceptualizing intelligence in computational systems.

The distinction between traditional software and agent-based approaches is not merely semantic but architectural. While conventional systems process discrete inputs to generate predictable outputs, agents operate continuously within dynamic environments, forming internal representations, making decisions under uncertainty, and learning from experience. For practitioners trained in deterministic programming models, this shift requires not only new technical skills but a reconceptualization of how intelligent systems function and evolve.

Key traits that distinguish intelligent agents from traditional software include:

- **Autonomy**: The ability to operate without continuous human guidance
- **Persistence**: Maintaining state and memory across interactions
- **Reactivity**: Responding to changes in the environment in real time
- **Proactiveness:** Initiating actions based on internal goals, not just external triggers
- **Adaptability**: Learning from experience and modifying behavior accordingly
- **Goal-orientation**: Pursuing objectives through planning and reasoning under uncertainty

In common usage, an agent is *one that acts or exerts power* (Merriam-Webster). Within AI, this definition evolves into a more technical construct: an AI agent is a computational system that perceives its environment, processes internal state, and takes actions to achieve defined goals. These systems exhibit autonomy, adaptability, and reactivity, key attributes that differentiate them from traditional software programs.

An agent operates not merely by reacting to inputs, but by maintaining context, managing goals, and adjusting strategies based on feedback. This dynamic behavior draws from the paradigm of **situated AI**, where intelligence emerges from continuous interaction with the environment. Franklin and Graesser (1997) encapsulated this concept:

> *An autonomous agent is a system situated within and a part of an environment that senses that environment and acts on it, over time, in pursuit of its own agenda.*

This definition laid the groundwork for architectures that incorporate sensing, planning, acting, and learning. In enterprise applications, agents are increasingly deployed as digital workers (handling customer onboarding, processing invoices, managing workflows) each with persistent state, memory, and feedback mechanisms.

The history of AI agent development can be segmented into distinct technological eras:

- **1970s–1980s:** Rule-based expert systems, such as MYCIN (a Stanford-developed system for diagnosing blood infections and recommending antibiotics), used logic-based inference engines to solve narrowly defined problems. Despite deterministic precision, these systems were brittle and inflexible.
- **1990s**: Classical machine learning methods like decision trees and SVMs introduced pattern recognition capabilities. While more adaptive than rule systems, they remained task-specific and stateless.
- **2010s**: Deep learning revolutionized data perception. Speech recognition, image analysis, and translation reached human-level performance. However, these models were largely reactive, designed for input-output prediction rather than autonomous behavior.
- **2020s and beyond**: The advent of **large language models** (**LLMs**), that is, AI systems trained on vast text datasets to understand and generate human language, and **transformers**, neural network architectures that excel at processing sequential data, introduced emergent reasoning, natural language generation, and few-shot learning. Yet early LLMs were limited by context size, lack of memory, and tool integration.

While many recent advances in AI, such as **retrieval-augmented generation** (**RAG**), external tool use, API orchestration, and memory systems, have been pivotal in their own right, they also serve as critical enablers for building more capable autonomous agents. Frameworks such as LangGraph, CrewAI, and AutoGen support planning, decision-making, and real-time interaction, enabling agents to complete multi-step goals in open-ended environments.

For instance, in customer support, the progression has been dramatic:

- **2010**: Static FAQ scripts provided predetermined responses to common questions, requiring human intervention for any deviation

- **2018**: ML-based ticket routing systems could categorize and assign support requests to appropriate departments but still required human resolution
- **2025**: Advanced multi-agent systems now demonstrate resolution rates of 70-85% in production deployments (based on implementations at companies like Zendesk, Intercom, and ServiceNow), integrating LLMs for natural conversation, account systems for personalized context, and live knowledge bases for current information

This evolutionary trajectory, illustrated in *Figure 1.1*, highlights fundamental architectural and philosophical distinctions between conventional AI applications and truly autonomous agent systems; these are differences that extend well beyond technical implementation to how these systems operate, learn, and interact with their environments. These architectural shifts are not just academic; they translate into measurable business outcomes such as reduced support costs, increased first-contact resolution rates, faster onboarding, and greater scalability across customer touchpoints.

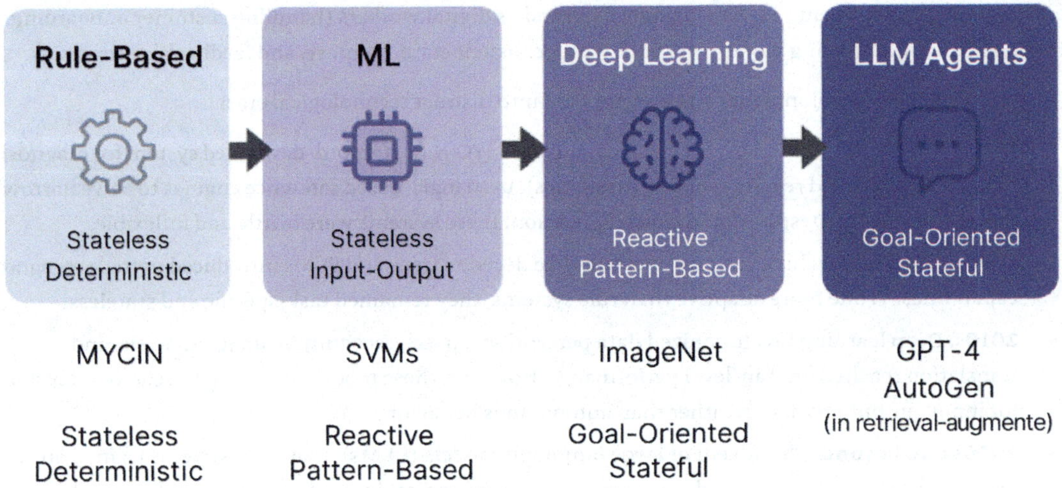

Figure 1.1 – Evolution of AI agent technologies

Having traced the historical evolution of AI agents from rule-based systems to today's sophisticated autonomous entities, we now turn to examine the structural foundations that enable this intelligent behavior. Understanding how agents are architected—the cognitive loops, communication patterns, and design choices that transform computational systems into goal-directed entities—is essential for building effective agent-based solutions.

Architecture of agents

The architectural design of intelligent agents marks a fundamental shift from procedural logic to cognition-driven computation. Unlike traditional software systems that execute static instructions in response to defined inputs, agents operate continuously within dynamic environments, making real-time decisions, maintaining persistent memory, and adapting their strategies over time. At its core, an agent's architecture must integrate key cognitive functions—*perception*, *reasoning*, *planning*, *action*, and *learning*—into a modular, stateful framework that supports both reactivity and deliberation. This often draws inspiration from established AI paradigms: for instance, models like BDI (Belief–Desire–Intention) provide a framework for agents to manage their beliefs about the world, their desires (goals), and their intentions (chosen plans). Similarly, hybrid approaches that combine symbolic reasoning (which processes explicit knowledge and logical rules, often used for planning and decision-making) with neural networks (which excel at pattern recognition and learning from data) enable agents to form robust internal representations, reason effectively about complex objectives, and coordinate sophisticated tool usage in pursuit of long-term goals. In practice, this means designing systems that separate concerns: perception modules interface with sensors or APIs; planning engines decompose objectives; memory subsystems manage historical and semantic context; and execution layers interface with tools, services, or other agents. Frameworks like LangGraph and CrewAI implement these principles by providing composable runtime environments where agents can maintain state across sessions, orchestrate workflows using graphs, and operate autonomously. This architectural cohesion is what transforms agents from reactive bots into intelligent systems capable of navigating open-ended, real-world complexity.

To understand how this architectural vision translates into practical implementation, we examine three foundational elements: the cognitive loop that drives agent decision-making, the communication patterns that enable seamless interaction between components, and the design patterns that determine how agents transform perception into action.

The cognitive loop

The cognitive architecture of intelligent agents defines how perception transforms into purposeful action through structured, repeatable processes. At the heart of this design lies the **cognitive loop**, a continuous cycle of perception, reasoning, planning, action, and learning, which enables agents to operate autonomously in dynamic environments. As illustrated in *Figure 1.2*, this loop forms the backbone of intelligent agent behavior, providing the scaffolding through which decisions are made, actions are executed, and knowledge is accumulated over time.

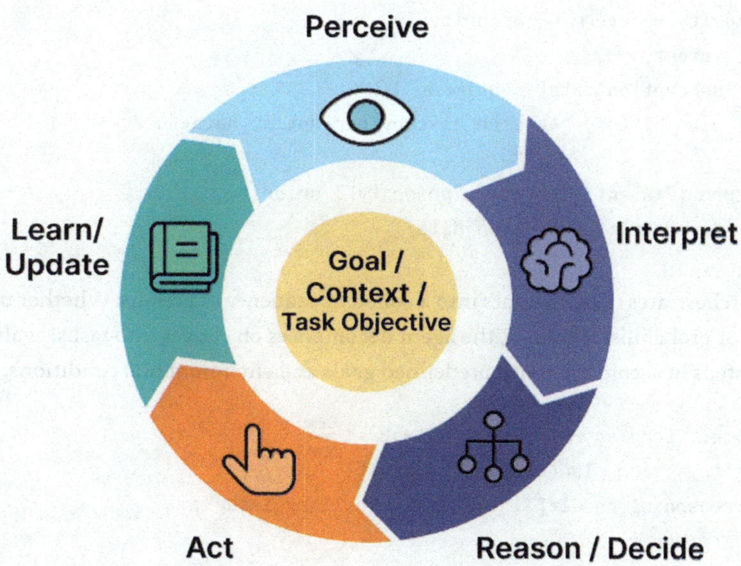

Figure 1.2 – Cognitive architecture of intelligent agents

To understand how this architecture functions in practice, let's explore each phase of the cognitive loop in detail, beginning with *perception*, which is the critical first step that shapes everything that follows:

1. **Perception** initiates the loop by capturing data from the environment, whether through user input, APIs, sensors, or external systems, and converting it into structured formats suitable for processing. This raw input forms the basis for subsequent cognitive steps and determines the scope of the agent's situational awareness.

```
# Example: Perception in a customer service agent
def perceive_input(user_message, context):
    return {
        "message": user_message,
        "timestamp": datetime.now(),
        "user_id": context.get("user_id"),
        "session_state": context.get("session"),
        "sentiment": analyze_sentiment(user_message)
    }
```

2. **Reasoning** follows by contextualizing this perceived information, applying pattern recognition, inference engines, or statistical models to extract meaning and relevance. This stage transforms signals into insights, allowing the agent to understand not just what is happening, but why it matters.

```
# Example: Reasoning about customer intent
def reason_about_intent(perception_data):
    intent = classify_intent(perception_data["message"])
    priority = determine_priority(
        intent,
        perception_data["sentiment"],
        user_history=get_user_history(perception_data["user_id"])
    )
    return {"intent": intent, "priority": priority,
        "context": perception_data}
```

3. **Planning** orchestrates these insights into a coherent sequence of actions. Whether using deterministic rule chains or probabilistic models, the agent decomposes objectives into tasks, evaluates options, and prioritizes steps in accordance with predefined goals and environmental conditions.

```
# Example: Planning response strategy
def create_action_plan(reasoning_result):
    if reasoning_result["intent"] == "billing_issue":
        return [
            "fetch_account_details",
            "analyze_billing_history",
            "generate_explanation",
```

```
            "offer_resolution"
        ]
    elif reasoning_result["priority"] == "urgent":
        return ["escalate_to_human", "log_urgent_case"]
```

4. **Action** then executes the selected steps, interfacing with external tools, APIs, databases, or systems to operationalize the agent's decisions. This phase is often implemented using function-calling frameworks or tool orchestration layers such as those found in LangChain or LangGraph.

```
# Example: Action execution
def execute_action(action_plan, context):
    results = []
    for action in action_plan:
        if action == "fetch_account_details":
            result = billing_api.get_account(context["user_id"])
        elif action == "generate_explanation":
            result = llm.generate_response(context, results)
        results.append(result)
    return results
```

5. **Learning** closes the loop by analyzing outcomes, measuring the success of actions, and updating internal models or memory stores. This feedback mechanism allows the agent to refine its behavior over time, improving performance based on both successes and failures.

```
# Example: Learning from interaction
def learn_from_outcome(interaction_data, user_feedback):
    success_score = calculate_success(user_feedback)
    update_user_preferences(interaction_data["user_id"], success_score)
    if success_score < 0.7:
        flag_for_model_improvement(interaction_data)
```

As seen in *Figure 1.2*, these phases form a feedback-driven system rather than a linear pipeline. Each component influences and is influenced by others, enabling the agent to adapt to new data, unforeseen conditions, and evolving goals. In practice, this architecture supports applications ranging from customer engagement agents that tailor responses based on prior interactions, to supply chain agents that continuously adjust operations based on shifting constraints.

This modular yet interdependent structure, where sensing leads to understanding, planning leads to execution, and learning closes the loop, is what elevates agents from automated scripts to intelligent, adaptive systems. Understanding this architecture is essential for designing agents capable of long-horizon objectives, contextual decision-making, and real-world autonomy.

Communication patterns between components

An intelligent agent is not defined solely by the sophistication of its reasoning engine or the accuracy of its outputs, but also by the integrity of the communication pathways that bind its internal components. These pathways (*Figure 1.3*) form the nervous system of cognition, transforming disjointed subsystems into unified, adaptive intelligence.

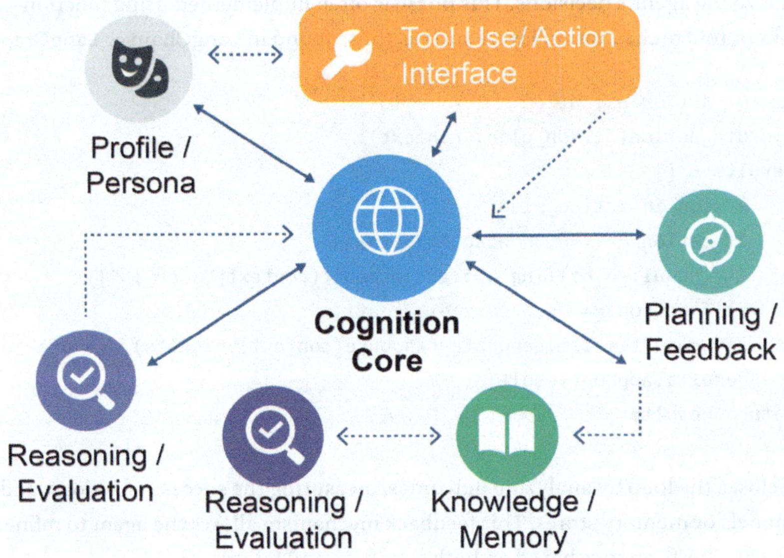

Figure 1.3 – Communication patterns in agent cognitive architecture

At the center of this architecture lies the **cognition core**, the executive coordinator responsible for synthesizing input from other modules, resolving conflicts, orchestrating actions, and maintaining coherence across the agent's state. Every major function (reasoning, planning, memory, and interaction) is mediated through this core, which acts less like a centralized command and more like a dynamic broker of task-relevant signals.

> **Note**
>
> In real-world deployments, this central role can introduce concerns about single points of failure. Robust implementations typically address this through redundancy, distributed coordination layers, and health-check mechanisms that ensure the cognition core can recover from crashes, load spikes, or degraded components. Some frameworks implement fallback nodes, heartbeat signals, or cloud-native orchestration to guarantee uptime and responsiveness in production environments.

Surrounding the core are five foundational communication layers, each representing a distinct functional role:

- **Profile/Persona**: This layer defines the agent's character: its tone, behavioral constraints, and system-level alignment with user intent. In implementation terms, this might take the form of system prompts or role templates, acting as an initialization boundary that informs how the agent interprets ambiguity, enforces guardrails, and communicates with users. Notably, this layer is not static; it responds to evolving context and can be updated during runtime to reflect changes in audience, task, or ethical parameters.

- **Tool use/Action interface**: This connects the agent's internal deliberations with the external world. Reasoned intent is transformed here into tool invocations, API calls, or system commands. This channel handles both the dispatch of actions and the interpretation of their results, feeding execution feedback back into the cognition loop. In production systems, this is often the most latency-sensitive component and requires robust error handling, retry logic, and observability pipelines.
- **Planning/Feedback**: This module provides forward-looking strategy and backward-looking correction. Goals are decomposed into task graphs, prioritized based on constraints, and monitored for success or failure. When an outcome deviates from expectations, say, a hotel booking fails or a response from an API times out, this layer triggers replanning. This feedback loop is essential for long-horizon autonomy and is often orchestrated using frameworks like LangGraph, which model planning workflows as directed acyclic graphs with embedded feedback mechanisms.
- **Knowledge/Memory**: This layer is the agent's temporal substrate. It comprises short-term working memory, long-term knowledge stores, and episodic recall systems. These components allow the agent to ground its behavior in history, recall prior tasks, reuse contextual constraints, and deliver coherent behavior over time. Architecturally, memory is accessed asynchronously, enabling the agent to preserve real-time responsiveness while retrieving deep context in the background. To minimize latency and ensure consistent real-time responsiveness, production-grade agents often employ caching strategies for frequently accessed knowledge (e.g., user profiles or recent interactions), as well as vector index prefetching or approximate nearest-neighbor (ANN) search techniques. Additionally, memory systems may implement time-to-live (TTL) caching, request batching, or tiered memory (e.g., short-term vs. long-term) to balance depth of context retrieval with speed.
- **Reasoning/Evaluation**: These components are strategically distributed around the periphery in *Figure 1.3* to provide multiple validation checkpoints and specialized assessment capabilities. Rather than relying on a monolithic reasoning engine, many systems distribute evaluation across specialized validators, e.g., safety checkers, factual accuracy auditors, or domain-specific reviewers. This distributed approach ensures robustness through multiple validation layers and allows for parallel processing of different reasoning tasks. These reasoning modules exchange structured messages with the cognition core, supporting mechanisms like self-reflection, confidence scoring, and iterative output refinement.

Taken together, these communication layers form more than a functional schema; they represent a philosophy of modular, composable intelligence. The bidirectional flows and dotted-line callbacks in *Figure 1.3* emphasize that cognition is not linear but cyclical, reflexive, and feedback-driven. As conditions change, memory influences planning, evaluation redirects action, and persona shapes interpretation. This networked interdependence ensures that the agent can adapt to complex, dynamic environments without losing coherence or goal alignment.

Robust communication design also supports engineering priorities: modularity allows teams to build components in parallel; observability aids debugging and trust, often implemented using tools like Prometheus, Grafana, or LangSmith in agent ecosystems for tracking agent state, action success rates, latency, and error events; and separation of concerns facilitates scalability and testability. Moreover, by decoupling reasoning from execution and state from strategy, agent systems gain resilience against uncertainty and partial failure, making them suitable for real-world deployments in enterprise automation, adaptive learning, customer service, and beyond.

Ultimately, it is not just what an agent knows or does that defines its intelligence, but how well its internal systems talk to one another. Communication between components is where cognition takes shape, not as a monologue of logic, but as a dialogue of purpose.

Choosing an agent brain: patterns of perception-to-action

The architecture that governs how an agent transforms perception into action defines the core of its intelligence. This **perception-to-action** loop, whether reflexive or reasoned, determines how the agent engages with its environment, processes uncertainty, and balances immediacy with strategy. Unlike traditional software systems, which follow fixed logic pathways, autonomous agents require cognitive scaffolding that supports flexible, context-sensitive decision-making. The choice of "agent brain," that is, its reasoning pattern, is not simply an implementation detail, but a structural commitment that shapes long-term performance, adaptability, and system behavior.

Agent design patterns can be categorized into three dominant paradigms, each representing a different approach to modeling intelligent behavior: reactive, deliberative, and hybrid.

These patterns are not mutually exclusive; rather, they offer developers a design palette for aligning cognitive structure with the demands of specific tasks, user expectations, and operational environments.

Understanding these patterns is critical for building systems that can function reliably under real-world conditions. Agents deployed in customer-facing workflows may rely on reactive models for low-latency interactions, while knowledge-intensive systems require deliberation to ensure contextual accuracy and compliance. In domains where both are needed, such as enterprise automation or healthcare diagnostics, hybrid models provide a resilient middle path. The following sections explore each pattern in depth, offering guidance on when and how to apply them based on architectural trade-offs, environmental complexity, and agentic goals.

Reactive agents: The reflexive response

Reactive agents represent the simplest and most immediate class of intelligent systems. These agents function through direct stimulus-response mechanisms, mapping environmental inputs to predefined actions without maintaining an internal state or engaging in higher-order reasoning. Their design is inspired by the notion of reflexive behavior, that is, rapid, automatic responses that bypass deliberation in favor of efficiency and predictability.

To understand the essence of reactive behavior, consider a thermostat. When the temperature drops below a certain threshold, it instantly activates the heating system. It doesn't evaluate trends, consider external weather data, or optimize for energy efficiency. Instead, it operates on a singular rule: if the temperature is low, turn on the heat. This direct coupling of perception and action is the core principle that governs reactive agents.

These agents are stateless and memoryless. Every decision is based solely on the present sensory input, with no reference to past observations or accumulated knowledge. This lack of internal state makes reactive agents incredibly fast and computationally efficient, enabling real-time responsiveness in environments where delay is unacceptable. Systems like anti-lock braking mechanisms in vehicles or fire detection alarms exemplify the value of immediacy, reacting without hesitation to critical changes in the environment.

Implementation-wise, reactive agents rely on simple condition-action rules. These rules are evaluated continuously, and when a specific environmental condition is met, a corresponding action is triggered:

```
IF stimulus_1 detected THEN execute action_1
IF stimulus_2 detected THEN execute action_2
```

This minimalist architecture results in highly deterministic behavior, which is a significant advantage in contexts requiring robust performance under tight operational constraints.

Of course, the simplicity of reactive agents comes at a cost. They lack the capacity for memory, learning, or foresight. They cannot generalize beyond their rule set or plan ahead in complex, partially observable environments. Their performance diminishes when confronted with unfamiliar situations that don't match their predefined conditions, and they are unable to adapt without external modification. For example, a reactive fire suppression system might repeatedly activate in response to steam from cooking, unable to distinguish between actual fire and false alarms without additional context or learning mechanisms.

Despite their limitations, reactive agents have found widespread application across industries. In robotics, simple bumper sensors enable mobile agents to turn away from obstacles without any need for mapping or localization. In smart home systems, devices like thermostats, motion-sensitive lights, and smoke detectors rely on reactive principles. In games, non-player characters often employ simple rule-based behaviors to create the illusion of intelligence while maintaining performance efficiency. Emergency systems also frequently adopt reactive logic to execute rapid shutdowns or alerts when critical thresholds are breached.

Nonetheless, their deterministic nature makes them exceptionally reliable in scenarios where conditions are well-defined and the cost of delay is high.

While reactive agents occupy the lowest rung in the hierarchy of intelligent architectures, they serve as the foundational building blocks upon which more advanced agent models are constructed. In many practical applications, their speed, simplicity, and robustness remain not just sufficient, but optimal.

Deliberative agents: The strategic thinkers

Deliberative agents embody a model of intelligent behavior rooted in foresight, planning, and structured reasoning. Unlike reactive agents that respond instantly to stimuli, deliberative agents pause, analyze their environment, and project potential outcomes before deciding on a course of action. Their architecture follows the **Sense–Model–Plan–Act (SMPA)** paradigm, enabling them to operate strategically rather than impulsively.

At the heart of a deliberative agent's design is the use of an internal world model, a dynamically updated representation of the environment and goals. This internal state allows the agent to not only react to current stimuli but also to reason about future possibilities and plan accordingly. As shown in *Figure 1.4*, this paradigm is demonstrated through the example of an AI-powered travel assistant.

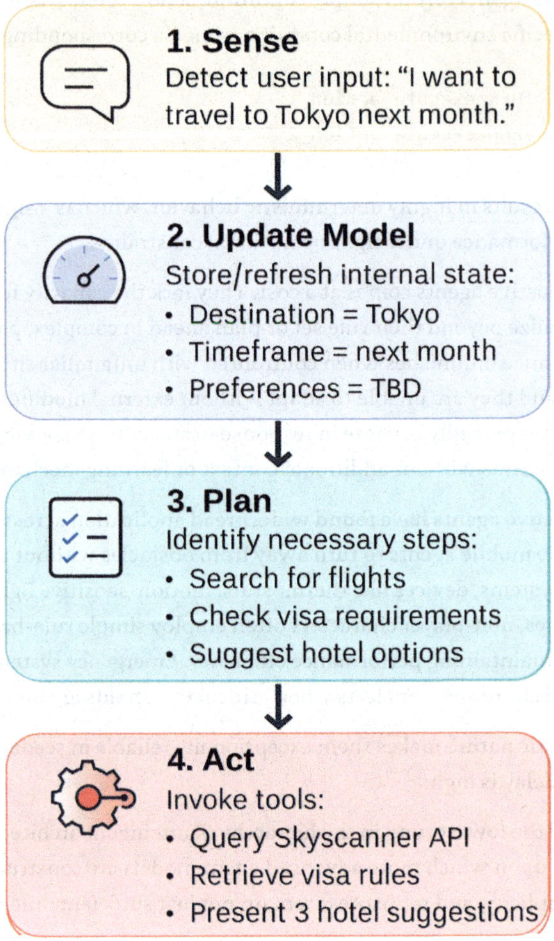

Figure 1.4 – Deliberative agents

The process begins with sensing, where the agent perceives its environment or receives an input. In the figure, this input comes as a natural language instruction: `I want to travel to Tokyo next month`. This marks the starting point for a more involved decision cycle. Instead of reacting immediately, the agent transitions to the modeling phase, parsing the user input into structured data. Key elements such as the destination (`"Tokyo"`) and timeframe (`"next month"`) are extracted and stored. Certain preferences are marked as unknown or to-be-determined, indicating areas where the agent must seek clarification or infer defaults.

Next, the agent enters the planning phase. Drawing on its internal state and the user's intent, it decomposes the high-level goal into actionable steps. As the figure illustrates, the agent identifies the need to search for flights, verify visa requirements, and suggest hotel options. Each subtask is framed within a larger strategy, allowing the agent to evaluate various pathways and choose an optimal sequence of actions that satisfies both constraints and goals.

Finally, the agent acts. This execution step is not a blind trigger but the result of deliberate computation. The agent queries APIs, for example, retrieving flight options through Skyscanner, checking visa policies, and presenting personalized hotel recommendations. These actions are the culmination of a reasoning process, and not simply a reaction to a prompt.

In production environments, these outputs are often subject to monitoring and validation pipelines to ensure they are accurate, policy-compliant, and safe. Techniques like output filtering, post-hoc validation models, and guardrails are commonly employed to detect hallucinations or policy violations before the results are surfaced to users or downstream systems.

This strategic architecture provides several advantages. Deliberative agents can handle temporal reasoning, simulate future states, and adapt to novel situations by generating new solutions rather than relying on predefined rules. As such, they are invaluable in domains requiring complex multi-step decision-making. Applications include autonomous navigation in vehicles, financial planning tools, intelligent personal assistants, and manufacturing robots coordinating intricate assembly sequences.

In real-world deployments, these agents are often equipped with fallback strategies, such as default rule-based routines, escalation protocols to human operators, or simplified decision trees, to handle failures in planning or uncertainty in the environment. These safeguards ensure graceful degradation and continuous service delivery, even when strategic computation breaks down.

However, these capabilities introduce certain limitations. Maintaining and updating an internal model requires significant computational resources, and the planning phase introduces latency. If the agent's internal model is inaccurate or incomplete, its decisions may degrade, and in some edge cases, it may fail entirely when confronted with unfamiliar scenarios beyond its training or assumptions.

Still, in contexts where quality of decision-making outweighs immediacy, deliberative agents consistently outperform simpler architectures. The example in *Figure 1.4* exemplifies how these agents integrate perception, memory, reasoning, and execution to deliver a coordinated response across multiple subsystems. This makes deliberative agents indispensable wherever intelligent, adaptable, and goal-aligned behavior is essential.

Hybrid agents: Layered intelligence in action

Hybrid agents represent a class of intelligent systems that integrate the rapid responsiveness of reactive behavior with the strategic foresight of deliberative reasoning. Rather than relying on a single decision-making model, hybrid agents employ a layered architecture where different subsystems specialize in either fast, context-independent responses or slower, goal-oriented planning.

Figure 1.5 shows a typical hybrid architecture, where input stimuli are routed through both reactive and deliberative processing layers.

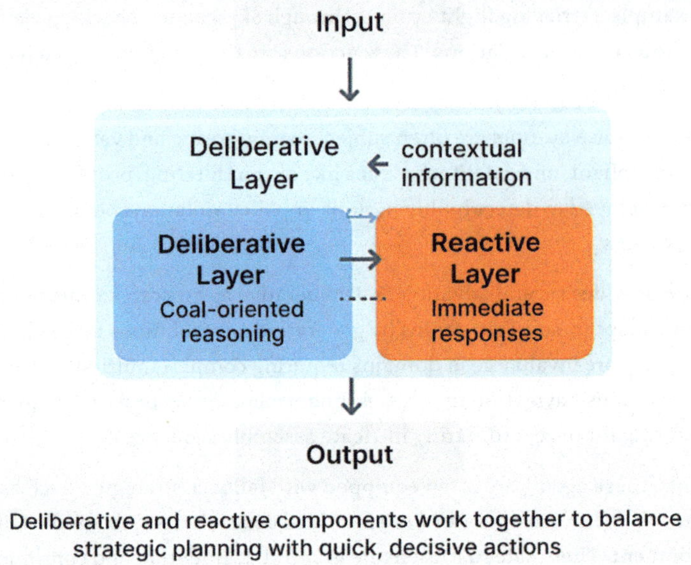

Figure 1.5 – Hybrid agents

Inputs are initially processed and assessed for urgency through priority classification mechanisms that evaluate factors such as time constraints, safety implications, and task criticality. Time-critical events are routed directly to the reactive layer, shown in orange, which executes predefined actions using direct stimulus-response mappings. This enables immediate behavior such as obstacle avoidance, safety shutdowns, or alert handling.

In engineering practice, this routing logic is often implemented using asynchronous patterns such as event buses (e.g., Kafka, NATS) or message queues (e.g., RabbitMQ, AWS SQS), which allow agents to decouple input classification from response execution while ensuring reliable delivery and prioritization under load.

At the same time, the deliberative layer (represented in blue) monitors the environment from a strategic perspective. It maintains internal models of goals, state information, and resource constraints. This layer is responsible for higher-order reasoning tasks such as path planning, multi-step execution, prediction of future states, and optimization across time horizons. It can influence or override the behavior of the reactive layer by adjusting thresholds, modifying routines, or introducing new goals based on ongoing evaluation.

Crucially, the communication between these layers is bidirectional. Consider a warehouse robot navigating to deliver packages: when the robot encounters an unexpected obstacle (like a fallen box), its reactive layer immediately stops movement and initiates avoidance maneuvers. Simultaneously, this obstacle detection triggers an interrupt to the deliberative layer, which reassesses the optimal delivery route, updates its internal map, and may decide to request human assistance if the obstacle represents a persistent blockage. Meanwhile, the deliberative layer continuously updates contextual information, such as delivery priorities or battery levels, that informs the reactive system's parameters, perhaps adjusting movement speeds based on urgency or remaining power. *Figure 1.5* highlights these interactions through feedback arrows and optional dashed pathways that activate under such dynamic situational conditions.

This architecture supports a coordinated output mechanism that balances rapid decision-making with longer-term objectives. Final actions emerge as a negotiated outcome, often synthesized from both layers depending on the current operational context. The warehouse robot example demonstrates how reactive collision avoidance operates in parallel with deliberative route optimization, creating seamless navigation that is both safe and efficient.

Different implementation models exist to realize hybrid behavior. Subsumption-based systems may place reactive control at the core, augmented by strategic planning layers. Other designs use arbitration mechanisms where multiple subsystems propose actions, and a control module selects the most appropriate one based on priorities and environmental conditions. Blackboard architectures (shared memory systems where different reasoning components contribute knowledge to a common workspace) further support hybridization by using shared memory repositories where each layer contributes to a collective decision space.

Hybrid agents are particularly effective in complex environments that demand flexibility. In industrial robotics, they coordinate immediate stop mechanisms with production scheduling. In autonomous vehicles, they manage obstacle avoidance in parallel with navigation planning. In cybersecurity, emerging hybrid agent models aim to block live threats while concurrently evaluating longer-term system integrity, though most current implementations focus on rule-based detection with limited adaptive coordination. The hybrid approach represents a next step toward dynamic, self-adjusting defenses. Even intelligent assistants benefit from this model, providing instant user responses while maintaining contextual continuity and task memory.

In these scenarios, performance constraints are often non-negotiable: response latency must be kept under 100 ms in robotics and autonomous vehicles to avoid safety risks, while cybersecurity agents must detect and act on threats within milliseconds to prevent exploitation. Even intelligent assistants face constraints such as maintaining session coherence under memory limits and balancing accuracy with speed in real-time dialogue.

The modular nature of hybrid architectures also supports maintainability and scalability. Each layer can be designed, tested, and updated independently. However, this flexibility also introduces complexity. The coordination between layers requires careful resource allocation, conflict resolution protocols, and extensive testing to ensure stable behavior across operating conditions. Debugging hybrid systems can be challenging since issues may arise from interactions between layers rather than individual components. Additionally, the overhead of maintaining multiple reasoning systems can impact performance and increase computational costs.

As demonstrated in *Figure 1.5*, hybrid agents represent a deliberate convergence of reactive efficiency and deliberative depth. Their layered structure enables systems to act swiftly without sacrificing the capacity for structured reasoning, an essential capability in modern AI deployments.

Having explored the foundational architectures that enable individual agents to perceive, reason, and act, we now turn to the critical challenge of enabling these intelligent systems to work together and integrate seamlessly with existing enterprise infrastructure.

Interoperability protocols

As agent-based systems mature from isolated tools into distributed ecosystems, their ability to interoperate with both external services and peer agents becomes mission-critical. **Interoperability protocols** serve as the foundation for scalable, modular agent architectures by enabling clean, contract-driven interfaces for communication, delegation, and coordination. These protocols decouple agents from tool-specific logic, support asynchronous orchestration, and allow collaborative decision-making across distributed components, even when those components are independently developed or maintained.

This section explores two foundational protocol categories that underpin agent interoperability:

- **Model Context Protocol (MCP)**: standardizes agent interactions with tools, APIs, and data sources. Rather than hardcoding tool-specific logic into each agent, MCP defines a universal interface layer that enables agents to discover, evaluate, and invoke external services dynamically. Tools are registered with metadata and capability definitions, which agents use to query available operations at runtime. This abstraction makes it possible to swap or upgrade tools without modifying agent logic.
- **Agent-to-Agent (A2A) Protocols**: define message-passing interfaces between collaborating agents in a decentralized system. These protocols specify how agents communicate intent, share state, exchange roles, and synchronize task progress. A2A protocols are especially important in multi-agent environments, where coordination must occur without centralized control.

Together, these protocols allow for dynamic, pluggable, and resilient systems that scale across capabilities and organizational boundaries.

In real-world production systems, **versioning and schema management** are essential to ensure long-term stability. Protocols like MCP and A2A often rely on **contract-based designs**, using technologies such as OpenAPI specifications, Protocol Buffers, or JSON Schema to define message formats and service capabilities. Explicit versioning of these contracts allows systems to maintain backward compatibility, negotiate capabilities between agents and services, and gracefully handle mismatches due to updates. This ensures that newer agent versions can interoperate safely with legacy components and external APIs, critical for maintaining robust, evolving systems over time.

Model context protocol (MCP)

MCP defines a universal framework through which agents discover, evaluate, and invoke external capabilities. As depicted in *Figure 1.6*, MCP introduces a **universal interface layer** that abstracts external services, exposing them through three key operations:

- **Capability description**: Each tool registers its functionality and metadata (inputs, outputs, constraints) in a machine-readable format. For instance, a simple JSON schema could define the capabilities of a weather retrieval tool:

```
{
  "name": "SearchFlights",
  "description": "Retrieve available flight options based on input parameters",
  "input_schema": {
    "type": "object",
    "properties": {
      "origin": { "type": "string" },
      "destination": { "type": "string" },
      "departure_date": { "type": "string", "format": "date" }
    },
    "required": ["origin", "destination", "departure_date"]
```

```
    },
    "output_schema": {
      "type": "array",
      "items": {
        "type": "object",
        "properties": {
          "airline": { "type": "string" },
          "price": { "type": "number" },
          "duration": { "type": "string" }
        }
      }
    }
  }
```

- **Discovery**: Agents query the universal layer to identify the appropriate tools based on current task needs and capability metadata.
- **Invocation**: Once a tool is selected, the agent invokes it through a standardized protocol without requiring tool-specific integrations.

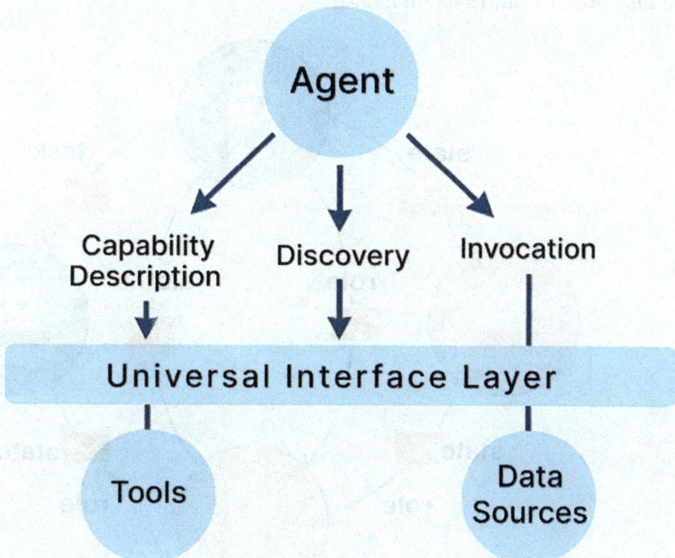

Figure 1.6 – Model context protocol

This architecture enables agents to operate independently of hardcoded service logic, allowing for plug-and-play integration. New tools can be introduced dynamically, and legacy tools can be updated without affecting the core logic of the agent. For example, an agent performing product research could query a market data API, evaluate a sentiment analyzer, or invoke a summarization engine, all through the same interface pattern.

MCP also facilitates cross-agent tool reuse, ensuring that tool registration is not duplicated across the agent network. This creates an organization-wide registry of capabilities that promotes standardization, governance, and faster integration cycles.

Agent-to-Agent (A2A) protocols

While MCP governs vertical interactions between agents and services, A2A protocols facilitate peer-level collaboration. These protocols formalize message exchange among agents that operate in a shared environment, enabling them to share state, assign roles, and coordinate tasks asynchronously. When designing such systems, it's crucial to consider various consistency models (e.g., strong consistency, eventual consistency) to ensure that shared state is synchronized appropriately across agents, balancing data integrity with performance requirements.

As shown in *Figure 1.7*, agents communicate using structured message packets containing:

- **State**: Contains contextual data and intermediate results that agents share to maintain situational awareness across the team
- **Role**: Contains functional designations and responsibilities that define each agent's position and capabilities within the collaborative workflow
- **Status**: Contains lifecycle updates including success, failure, or readiness indicators that keep all agents informed of task progress and system health

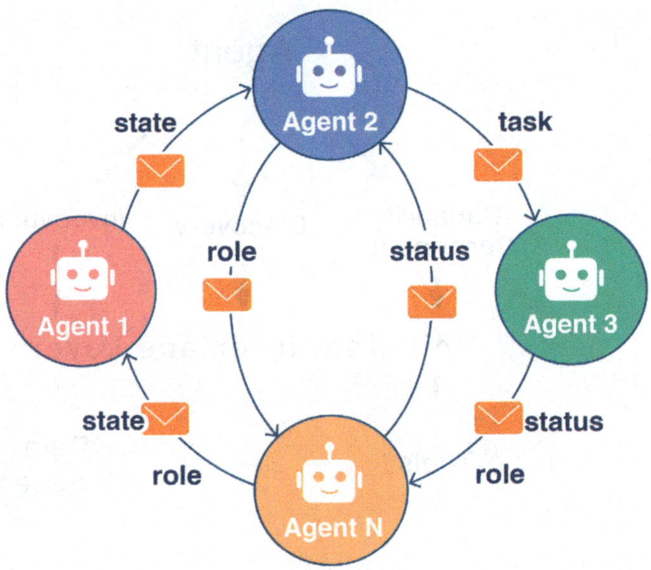

Figure 1.7 – Agent-to-Agent protocols

This architecture allows agent teams to do the following:

- Distribute specialized tasks (e.g., research, validation, QA)
- Operate asynchronously while maintaining coordination
- Recover from failure by dynamically assigning roles to backup agents

For example, in a customer service automation pipeline, a triage agent might pass a ticket to a billing specialist, who then forwards the case to a compliance validator. These interactions occur without centralized orchestration; agents make local decisions using shared protocol rules, promoting fault-tolerance, parallelism, and self-healing workflows.

Frameworks such as **CrewAI** and **LangGraph** provide native support for A2A patterns, enabling structured interactions through actor-based modeling, state channels, and pub-sub messaging. Popular open-source systems like NATS, RabbitMQ, and Apache Kafka are often used to implement these messaging layers, enabling reliable and scalable communication between distributed agents.

With a solid understanding of agent architectures and communication protocols established, we now examine the practical process of bringing these intelligent systems from concept to production through a structured development methodology.

The Agent Development Lifecycle

The development of autonomous agents follows a structured, iterative lifecycle that serves as a roadmap, but one that fundamentally diverges from traditional software engineering practices. Unlike procedural systems that rely on static logic and predefined behavior, intelligent agents must operate within dynamic, uncertain environments. They interpret ambiguous inputs, make decisions under uncertainty, invoke external tools, and continuously refine their behavior through feedback. These evolving, goal-directed behaviors require a lifecycle model that is not just iterative, but also deeply adaptive, supporting reasoning, learning, memory, and orchestration. The **Agent Development Lifecycle** (**ADL**) was designed to meet this need, providing a flexible framework that mirrors the operational complexity of modern agent-based systems.

This section outlines the **ADL**, a practical framework that spans from early conceptualization to post-deployment refinement. It provides developers and organizations with a roadmap for building robust, goal-aligned agentic systems that continuously improve over time.

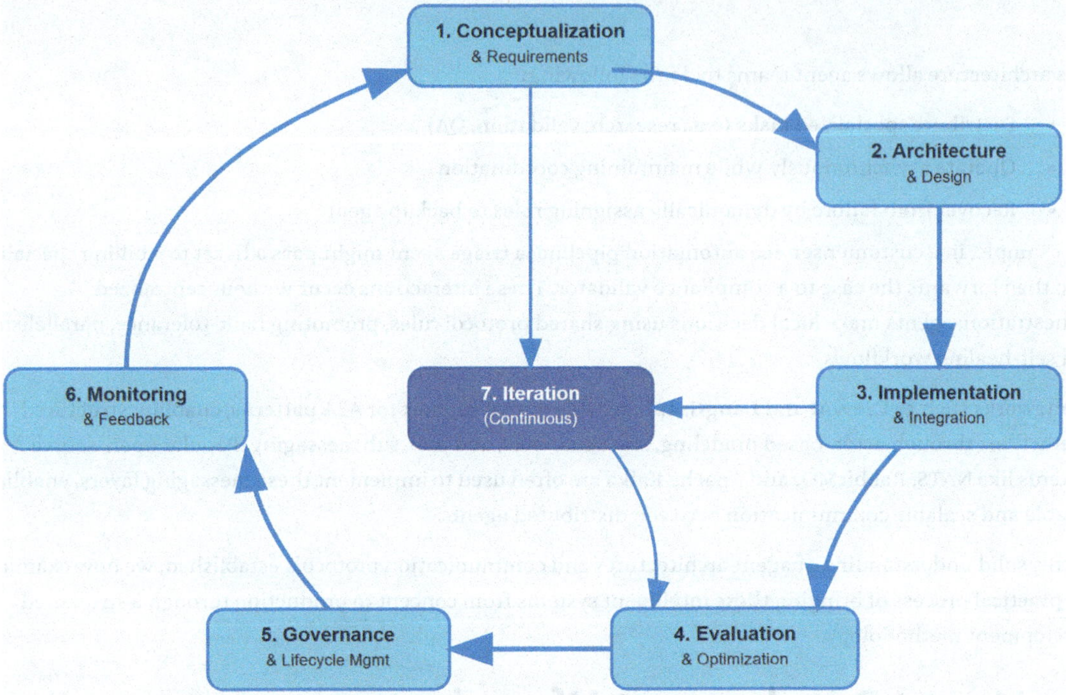

Figure 1.8 – Agent Development Lifecycle

The following subsections explore each phase of this lifecycle in detail, examining the unique considerations and best practices that distinguish agent development from conventional software engineering approaches.

Conceptualization and requirements analysis

Agent development begins with defining the problem space and articulating the agent's goals in context. This is more than requirements gathering; it's an exercise in modeling a cognitive workload, meaning the mental processes the agent must simulate or manage in order to operate intelligently. This includes tracking user intent, interpreting environmental signals, selecting appropriate strategies, and updating plans based on feedback, functions traditionally associated with human cognition. Developers must analyze the domain, understand the user's intent, and assess the capabilities the agent will require to operate effectively. Unlike static applications, agent goals may evolve and must be formulated with sufficient flexibility to accommodate environmental changes and emerging requirements.

In this stage, developers identify the operating environment, map objectives into achievable sub-goals, and determine the ethical, technical, and operational boundaries. For instance, an agent assisting in regulatory compliance may require explicit constraints on behavior that are both encoded into rules and monitored during execution. Importantly, this phase includes evaluating success metrics (performance, alignment, and user trust) all of which guide future decisions in architecture and implementation.

To summarize, key activities in this conceptualization phase include the following:

- Defining clear, high-level agent goals

- Mapping these goals into achievable sub-goals or tasks
- Setting measurable success metrics (e.g., performance, alignment, user trust) to guide development and evaluation

Architecture and design

Once the objectives are well-scoped, the agent's internal architecture is designed to support them. As discussed in *Architecture of agents* section , this includes choosing between cognitive models, such as ReAct, plan-and-execute, or BDI, and specifying components responsible for sensing, planning, acting, and learning. The architecture must balance modularity, autonomy, and extensibility.

In this stage, agent designers define memory strategies (short-term, long-term, episodic), internal communication flows, and interaction points with external systems. Just as importantly, they ensure the agent can interoperate via established protocols and persist state across sessions. Security and safety mechanisms are integrated from the start, not as afterthoughts. This design phase forms the conceptual and technical backbone of the entire system.

To ensure traceability and informed iteration, many teams adopt **Architecture Decision Records** (**ADRs**) to document key design decisions, such as why a particular memory model, orchestration strategy, or protocol framework was selected. This helps future contributors understand tradeoffs, revisit past assumptions, and evolve agent architectures without losing institutional knowledge.

Implementation and integration

Implementation brings the architecture to life using development frameworks such as LangChain, CrewAI, or LangGraph. Developers construct modules for reasoning, perception, planning, and memory, and bind them through workflow graphs or event-driven engines. Function calling APIs, memory databases, and orchestration layers are stitched together using open toolchains.

The focus here is on cohesion and correctness. Modules must interact predictably, and the agent's behavior must match its defined goals. Developers run local simulations or stage deployments to test the interaction of cognitive components under load. It's at this point that real-world constraints emerge (latency, context limits, token usage, etc.) and require engineering trade-offs to balance capability with cost.

To support robust iteration, teams often integrate agent behavior testing into CI/CD pipelines. These pipelines validate cognitive workflows (e.g., reasoning chains, tool calls, memory usage) using automated test harnesses, synthetic prompts, and simulated failure cases, ensuring stability across deployments and catching regressions early.

Evaluation and optimization

After deployment in a testing or controlled environment, agents must be rigorously evaluated. Unlike conventional systems, success is not always binary. Performance metrics include task completion rates, decision quality, and robustness under ambiguity. Evaluation may involve synthetic environments or production shadows, with extensive logging and telemetry pipelines in place.

Feedback from internal reflection mechanisms, such as confidence scoring or critique loops, is coupled with external signals like user satisfaction and tool performance. These insights feed back into the architecture, enabling adaptive changes. Optimization in this phase may include refining planning depth, adjusting context window strategies, or improving memory relevance scoring.

Typical optimization metrics include ***task success rate***, ***average response time***, ***user satisfaction scores***, ***tool invocation latency***, and ***fallback frequency*** (how often the agent defers or fails). Tracking these metrics enables teams to iteratively improve agent quality based on both performance and user trust signals.

Governance and lifecycle management

Deploying an agent is not the end of its development but the beginning of a continuous improvement loop. Lifecycle management includes proactive monitoring, log auditing, model updating, and failure recovery. Governance also encompasses security patching, compliance auditing, and ethical oversight, ensuring the agent remains reliable, transparent, and aligned with human intent.

This phase encompasses both the monitoring and iterative improvement processes. Agents deployed at scale must support observability and incident response. Tools such as LangSmith or Prometheus provide real-time insights into agent performance and health. Furthermore, policies for model retraining, versioning, and rollback ensure that system changes are deliberate and recoverable. Continuous iteration based on performance data, user feedback, and changing requirements ensures that agents evolve and improve over their operational lifetime. This is critical in mission-critical domains like finance, legal, or healthcare, where unexpected behavior can have significant consequences.

For example, logs from LangSmith or Prometheus might reveal a drop in tool invocation success rates or an increase in hallucinated outputs. This can trigger alerts, initiate human review, and lead to adjustments in prompt design, fine-tuning, or even retraining the underlying model. Incorporating this loop—from ***observability to auditing to retraining***—is essential for building resilient agents in production.

The evolution of agent interaction paradigms

As AI systems become more embedded in our daily lives and enterprise workflows, understanding the levels of agent interaction becomes essential for designing robust, scalable, and intelligent architectures. These levels represent a progression in agent capabilities, ranging from basic prompt-response interactions to collaborative, distributed agent networks.

The five-level interaction paradigm framework offers a structured approach for analyzing agent design along three critical dimensions: operational autonomy, contextual awareness, and decision-making authority. It helps system architects, developers, and stakeholders make informed decisions about which type of agent architecture is most appropriate for their use case. The five models that follow illustrate this evolution, each grounded in a representative figure and defined by its interaction pattern, processing capabilities, and architectural complexity.

To help system designers quickly assess and compare different levels of agent complexity, the following table summarizes the five agent interaction paradigms across key dimensions such as autonomy, context awareness, and decision-making authority.

Level	Agent Type	Operational Autonomy	Contextual Awareness	Decision-Making Authority	Typical Use Case
1	Direct LLM Interaction	Stateless/ None	None	Human-led	One-off Q&A, creative generation
2	Proxy Agent	Low	Light contextualization	Instruction-based	API parameterization, semantic translation
3	Assistant System	Medium	Session-based	User-guided	Digital assistants, tool-augmented chat
4	Autonomous Agent	High	Persistent memory	Partial autonomy	Task planning, research assistants
5	Multi-Agent System (MAS)	Very High	Shared + distributed	Distributed autonomy	Supply chains, orchestration, simulations

Table 1.1 – Comparison of agent interaction paradigms across key architectural dimensions

Direct LLM interaction: The stateless conversationalist

This foundational level represents the most basic form of agent engagement, where a user interacts directly with an LLM through natural language prompts. These interactions are stateless, with no memory of prior inputs and no persistent context across turns.

As shown in *Figure 1.9*, a user inputs a query such as "*What's the capital of Canada?*" and the LLM instantly responds with "*Ottawa*." The diagram highlights the absence of memory using a prohibition icon, indicating that the model treats each prompt in isolation. There is no internal context tracking, no task history, and no conversation threading.

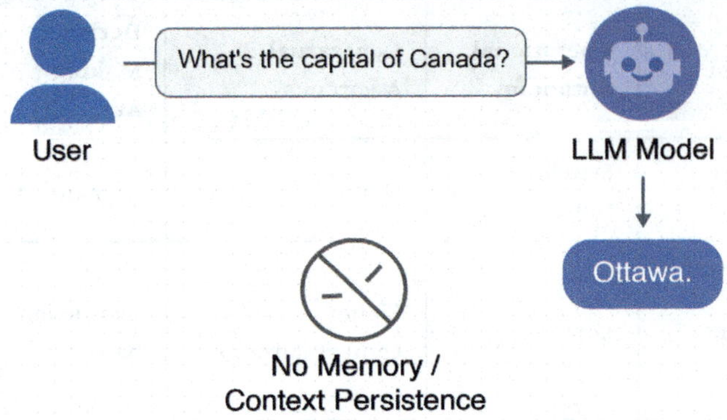

Figure 1.9 – Direct LLM interaction

This approach excels in lightweight scenarios such as factual Q&A, creative content generation, or one-shot assistance. However, it is limited in its ability to manage multi-step interactions, maintain user state, or complete goal-driven workflows. The lack of memory or adaptive feedback mechanisms means these systems cannot build long-term context or engage in truly conversational behavior. A typical stateless LLM interaction looks like a single prompt producing a one-time response, with no memory of previous queries:

```
from openai import OpenAI
client = OpenAI()
response = client.chat.completions.create( model="gpt-3.5-turbo",
    messages=[
        {"role": "user", "content": "What is the capital of Canada?"}
    ]
)
print(response.choices[0].message.content)
```

Real-world examples of direct LLM interaction include:

- **Chat-based QA systems**: For instance, chatbots answering factual questions on a retail website, such as like "What are your opening hours?" or "Where's my order?".
- **Creative writing tools**: Applications like Jasper or Sudowrite that generate single paragraphs or ideas based on prompts.
- **Educational flashcard assistants**: Systems that answer discrete academic questions, such as "Explain Newton's First Law" for quick study references.

Proxy agent: The intelligent intermediary

Proxy agents represent a foundational yet often underappreciated pattern in the architecture of intelligent systems. Unlike autonomous or multi-turn agents that maintain state or invoke external tools, proxy agents focus on a more narrowly defined but crucial responsibility: transforming unstructured user input into a well-structured, executable format suitable for backend systems.

At their core, proxy agents function as semantic intermediaries. When a user submits a request such as "*Find restaurants near me*," the proxy agent doesn't immediately forward this to a service endpoint. Instead, it acts as a translator by injecting additional context, disambiguating vague terms, sanitizing input, and reformatting the query into a structured representation. This design not only enhances precision and reliability but also protects downstream systems that depend on strict schemas or predefined parameter sets.

The proxy agent follows a well-defined processing flow. First, it captures the user's input. This input is typically in free-form natural language, which is inherently ambiguous or incomplete. The agent then integrates this input into a structured prompt template. This template contains both instructions for the underlying language model and placeholders for dynamic data such as the user query or contextual metadata. After completing the prompt, the agent invokes a language model, such as OpenAI's GPT or Anthropic's Claude, and receives a structured response, often in JSON or SQL format. Finally, this structured result is forwarded to the intended service or execution layer.

To better understand how this works, consider the following example scenario:

A user asks: "*Find restaurants near me that are open now.*"

Figure 1.10 – Proxy agent

The proxy agent doesn't relay this message directly to the restaurant discovery API. Instead, it processes the request through a structured transformation pipeline that converts natural language into machine-readable format.

Implementation example

The following code demonstrates how a proxy agent implements this natural language to structured data transformation:

```
from langchain.prompts import PromptTemplate
from langchain.chains import LLMChain

template = """
You are a proxy agent responsible for translating natural language into structured
queries.

User input: "{query}"
```

```
Return a JSON object with the following fields:
- intent: The action to perform.
- location: Inferred or stated location.
- time_filter: Indicate if the query includes time-based constraints.
- format: Response format (e.g., 'list').

Respond ONLY with JSON.
"""

prompt = PromptTemplate(input_variables=["query"], template=template)
chain = LLMChain(prompt=prompt, llm=openai_chat)

response = chain.run({"query": "Find restaurants near me that are open now"})
```

Structured output

When executed, this implementation produces a clean, structured response that downstream systems can reliably process:

```
{
    "intent": "search_restaurants",
    "location": "current_user_location",
    "time_filter": "open_now",
    "format": "list"
}
```

This result is now clean, context-rich, and fully structured, ideal for calling an API or passing to a downstream planner. The template ensures consistency while the language model provides the semantic reasoning to infer missing information such as the location (from user metadata) or the time filter (`"open now"`).

For production deployments, additional considerations are vital:

- **Input sanitization**: Implement robust input sanitization to prevent prompt injection attacks or unexpected model behavior from malicious or malformed user inputs.
- **Logging**: Comprehensive logging of prompts, responses, and execution times is essential for debugging, auditing, and understanding agent behavior in real-world scenarios
- **Monitoring prompt response times**: Continuously monitor the latency of LLM invocations to ensure the agent meets performance SLAs and provides a responsive user experience

The ability of proxy agents to act as a controlled layer between natural user intent and rigid system requirements makes them ideal in safety-critical or schema-bound systems. For instance, they are widely used in financial services platforms to validate and transform client instructions, in healthcare systems to process patient queries into structured triage protocols, and in customer service tools to sanitize requests before executing backend operations.

Importantly, proxy agents also mitigate risks associated with prompt injection or instruction manipulation. Because prompt templates define a clear structure and isolate user content from system directives, developers can enforce strict boundaries around how the model interprets and processes each input.

While proxy agents do not manage memory or initiate long-term plans, their role as input optimizers is fundamental to building robust, trustworthy, and production-grade AI systems. In any architecture where backend services expect strict inputs, but users communicate naturally, a proxy agent bridges the gap with clarity and control.

Proxy agents serve as translators, taking natural language inputs and turning them into structured data for backend execution. Their real-world applications include:

- **Voice-to-command processing**: Virtual assistants like Google Assistant converting "Play my workout playlist" into structured API calls to music services
- **Form-fill and processing bots**: Healthcare bots that take patient free-text symptoms and reformat them into structured triage reports for doctors

Assistant system: The tool-augmented helper

Assistant systems represent a substantial step forward, combining session-level memory, tool invocation, and user-guided autonomy. These agents not only interpret user requests but also have access to external tools or services that they can invoke to complete tasks.

In *Figure 1.11*, a user requests "*Book a flight to Paris.*" The assistant system interprets this instruction and invokes appropriate services, such as flight APIs, booking databases, or calendar tools, to carry out the task. The diagram shows the assistant acting as a **task orchestrator**, capable of interacting with external systems through tool invocation pathways.

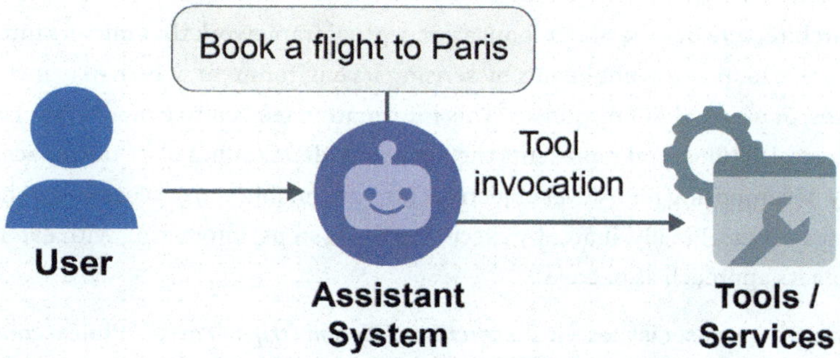

Figure 1.11 – Assistant system

The assistant maintains session state across turns, enabling dialog continuity, clarification handling, and result summarization. However, it typically operates with user-in-the-loop approval, seeking confirmation before taking consequential actions like completing bookings or initiating transactions.

For example, if a user first says, "*I want to fly to Paris next Friday,*" and later adds, "*Also book a hotel near the Eiffel Tower,*" the assistant retains the earlier flight request and destination context while processing the new command. This ability to track and apply session variables (like destination and date) across turns allows the assistant to complete multi-step tasks with continuity and precision.

This model is ideal for enterprise digital assistants, intelligent customer service bots, and personal productivity agents that require controlled autonomy and operational transparency.

Assistant systems combine natural language understanding with tool invocation and limited session memory. Their examples in practice include:

- **Enterprise digital assistants**: Like Microsoft Cortana for Business, which helps schedule meetings, manage emails, and fetch documents across different enterprise systems
- **Customer service bots**: Intelligent virtual assistants in banks that can access user account data, process simple transactions (e.g., balance inquiries, fund transfers), and escalate to human agents when needed
- **Notion AI and similar productivity agents**: These can search databases, summarize project notes, or create structured content templates, extending beyond single-turn interactions to support real productivity

Autonomous agent: The independent problem solver

Autonomous agents mark a pivotal evolution in the design of intelligent systems. Moving beyond reactive tools or assistant-style interfaces that rely on step-by-step user input, autonomous agents possess the ability to act independently, interpreting goals, reasoning about strategy, invoking tools, and adjusting behavior dynamically in response to changes. This independence enables them to perform complex, long-horizon tasks in a manner that closely resembles human cognitive problem-solving.

However, increased autonomy also introduces risks: agents operating without adequate oversight may misinterpret goals, pursue unintended strategies, or trigger undesirable actions. Therefore, safeguards such as policy constraints, human-in-the-loop checkpoints, or behavior monitoring mechanisms are critical to ensuring reliability in sensitive domains.

At the core of their architecture lies the SMPA loop, a conceptual framework that mirrors intelligent decision-making processes. In this loop, the agent begins by sensing its environment, which may include user inputs, internal state changes, or external API responses. This information feeds into a model that maintains contextual memory, tracks historical actions, and represents the agent's understanding of its task space. The agent then formulates a plan by decomposing high-level objectives into actionable steps, sequencing them based on dependencies and constraints. Finally, it acts by executing those steps, interacting with external systems, APIs, or tools, and adapting its approach as needed.

Consider the scenario where a user issues the instruction, "*Plan my trip to Paris.*" While a conventional assistant might respond with a static list of flights or hotel options, an autonomous agent interprets this request as a multi-stage objective. It initiates a process that includes itinerary generation, hotel selection, visa eligibility assessment, and travel insurance procurement. Rather than treating each task in isolation, the agent constructs a coherent plan, identifying dependencies, for example, determining visa requirements before finalizing flight bookings, and executes the workflow end-to-end.

Throughout this process, the agent maintains a persistent internal memory. It remembers user preferences, such as favored airlines or accommodation types, and uses that knowledge to refine decisions. If a preferred hotel is fully booked, it searches for alternative accommodation that meets similar criteria. If a visa application process introduces unforeseen delays, the agent reschedules connected elements of the itinerary accordingly. These adaptations are not hardcoded but emerge from feedback loops that assess success or failure and revise strategy in real time.

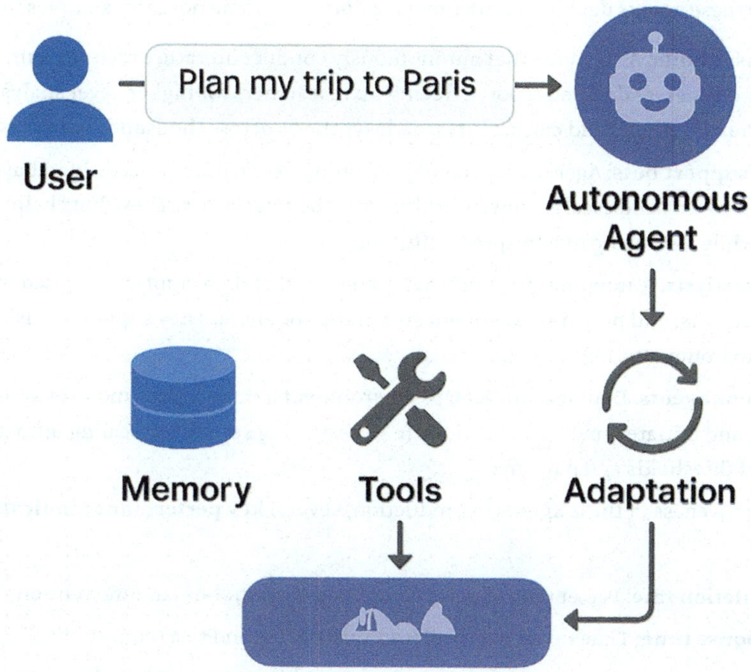

Figure 1.12 – Autonomous agent

Technically, such agents are built using modern frameworks like LangGraph, LangChain, and CrewAI. LangGraph allows developers to structure the agent's reasoning as a directed graph, with state transitions and context retention. LangChain provides abstractions to connect language models with tools, enabling the agent to search the web, make API calls, or interact with databases. CrewAI facilitates collaboration between specialized agents: one handling logistics, another focused on compliance, and yet another managing communications. Together, these frameworks support asynchronous execution, robust error handling, and real-world scalability.

In practical terms, autonomous agents are increasingly deployed across a wide spectrum of domains. In research, they automate literature reviews, generate experimental protocols, and synthesize findings into reports. In business, they coordinate multi-step workflows, manage onboarding processes, or execute marketing campaigns. In adaptive learning environments, they craft personalized learning plans, monitor progress, and adjust pacing based on learner performance. Their ability to persist context and autonomously refine actions makes them particularly valuable in systems that demand sustained attention, dynamic reactivity, and outcome-oriented execution.

Autonomous agents, therefore, are not merely more capable assistants; they are independent problem solvers. With the capacity to plan, reason, act, and adapt over extended timelines and with minimal supervision, they represent a step toward systems that not only follow instructions but also understand objectives. As this capability matures, autonomous agents are poised to reshape the landscape of digital work, transforming how we approach complexity across industries.

Autonomous agents independently create plans, make decisions, and execute tasks over longer workflows. Their capabilities span goal-setting, tool invocation, memory management, and adaptive behavior. In the real world, we increasingly see these agents deployed across diverse domains. Some notable examples include:

- **Research assistants**: AI systems that autonomously conduct literature reviews, summarize key findings, and generate detailed reports, freeing up researchers for higher-level analysis. These agents reduce manual overhead and can scale research synthesis across thousands of papers or sources.
- **Customer support bots**: Agents that classify incoming user requests, access databases or CRM systems to retrieve answers, and escalate unresolved issues when necessary. These bots help reduce human workload while improving first-response efficiency.
- **Financial analysts**: Autonomous agents that gather market data, apply rule-based models or machine learning forecasts, and prepare investment summaries or alerts. They support decision-making in time-sensitive environments.
- **IT operations agents**: Deployed in DevOps environments, these agents monitor system metrics, detect anomalies, and initiate remediation actions (e.g., restarting services or scaling infrastructure) based on pre-learned thresholds and patterns.

To evaluate the effectiveness of these agents in production, several **key performance indicators** (**KPIs**) are used:

- **Task completion rate**: Percentage of tasks completed without human intervention
- **Mean response time**: Time taken to complete a task or respond to a request
- **Factual accuracy/consistency**: Especially important in research and data-intensive domains
- **Escalation rate**: Percentage of tasks that require human fallback
- **User satisfaction score**: Based on surveys, star ratings, or behavioral signals like reuse

These metrics not only help measure success but also inform refinement cycles and trust calibration, ensuring that autonomy is not just powerful, but also reliable, accountable, and user-aligned.

Multi-agent systems: Collaborative intelligence

At the apex of agent interaction is the **multi-agent system (MAS)**, a distributed framework in which multiple autonomous or semi-autonomous agents coordinate to achieve complex goals. These systems distribute cognitive responsibility across specialized agents, each with domain-specific roles, capabilities, and communication protocols.

In *Figure 1.13*, the user submits a task, *Analyze data*, which is distributed across a network of agents: *Agent A* (data retrieval), *Agent B* (data cleaning), and *Agent C* (data visualization). A shared state repository is shown at the center of the diagram, allowing agents to communicate, exchange results, and maintain consistency across the system.

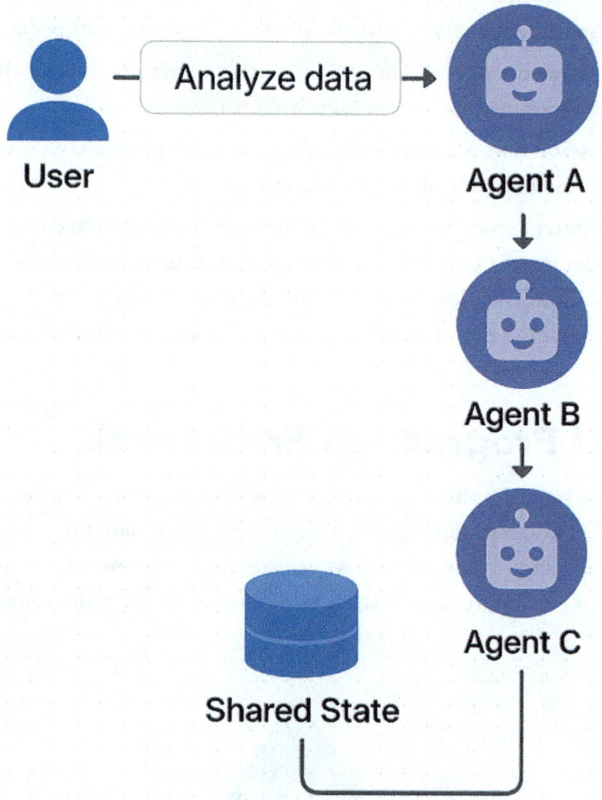

Figure 1.13 – Multi-agent systems

This collaborative model enables parallelism, redundancy, and domain specialization. MAS architectures often rely on **publish-subscribe messaging systems** (where agents broadcast updates to interested subscribers), **shared memory models** (centralized data stores accessible by all agents), or **task dispatch protocols** (systematic methods for assigning work to available agents) to manage interactions. Agents may be coordinated by a central supervisor or operate as fully decentralized nodes depending on the system's design goals.

To ensure robustness, these architectures typically include fault tolerance mechanisms, such as agent health checks, watchdog timers, or automatic reallocation of tasks in case an agent crashes or becomes unresponsive. Some systems employ redundant agents or fallback agents for critical roles, ensuring continuity in long-running workflows. This resiliency is essential in real-world deployments where hardware, network, or software failures can occur unpredictably.

Multi-agent systems are ideal for enterprise orchestration, scientific research platforms, intelligent supply chain networks, and distributed AI infrastructure, where modularity, scalability, and robustness are essential.

Multi-agent systems feature teams of specialized agents collaborating to handle complex tasks that are too broad or dynamic for a single agent. Examples include the following:

- **Self-driving cars**: Systems like those in Waymo's fleet where agents for perception (detecting obstacles), navigation (finding routes), and safety (avoiding collisions) work in tandem.

- **Financial trading platforms**: Hedge funds like Citadel using coordinated AI agents—market analysis, risk management, sentiment analysis—to execute thousands of trades per second.
- **Smart home orchestration**: AI controlling thermostats, lights, and security in unison, adjusting lighting based on temperature changes or security status.
- **Healthcare diagnostics**: IBM Watson for Oncology, where multiple AI agents analyze patient data, suggest treatments, and flag possible drug interactions.

While understanding the different types of agent interactions, from direct LLM conversations to complex multi-agent collaborations, provides insight into what's possible today, organizations need a structured way to evaluate their current capabilities and plan their agent development journey. The framework that follows offers a systematic approach to assessing agent maturity and charting a path toward increasingly sophisticated autonomous systems.

The Agentic AI Progression Framework

As intelligent systems evolve from simple automation scripts to fully autonomous entities, organizations require structured evaluation models to assess capabilities, plan development roadmaps, and align technology investments with strategic objectives. The **Agentic AI Progression Framework** provides this structured approach, categorizing agent capabilities across three critical dimensions: ***autonomy***, ***reasoning***, and ***adaptability***.

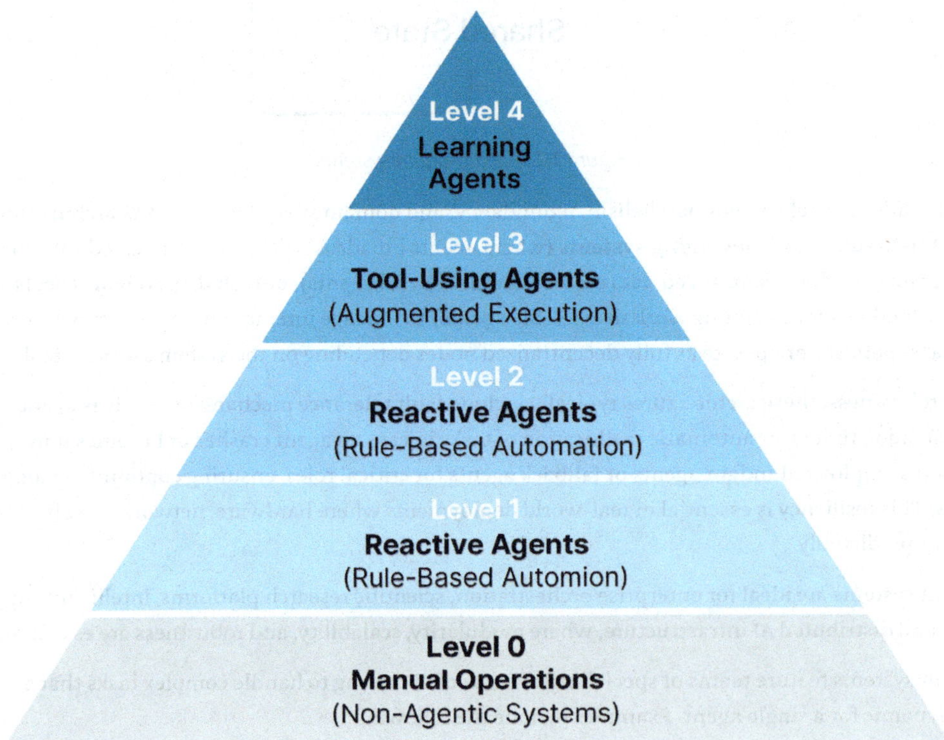

Figure 1.14 – The Agentic AI Progression Framework

This progression model enables technologists and business leaders to assess current implementations, identify capability gaps, and plan strategic advancements toward increasingly sophisticated agent systems. The framework establishes five distinct levels of agent maturity, each representing a qualitative transformation in how intelligent systems operate and the value they deliver.

Level 0: Manual operations – Non-agentic systems

At this foundational level, no intelligence or automation exists within the system itself. All actions require direct human initiation, execution, and oversight. Context interpretation, decision-making, and execution rest entirely on human cognitive effort, with digital systems serving merely as tools rather than active participants in the workflow.

Example: Financial analysts manually preparing monthly reports, HR staff manually entering new employee data, and customer service representatives individually responding to each email.

Level 1: Reactive agents – Rule-based automation

Reactive agents introduce predefined, deterministic behavior governed by simple conditional logic. These systems respond to specific triggers with preprogrammed actions, operating in a stateless, context-free manner. While effective for routine tasks with clear parameters, reactive agents lack adaptability to novel situations or the ability to learn from experience.

Example: Automated email responders that send templated replies, **robotic process automation** (**RPA**) bots that extract and input data into forms, and basic voice assistants like Amazon Echo that control smart home devices based on voice commands.

Level 2: Tool-using agents – Augmented execution

At this level, agents become semi-intelligent orchestrators capable of interfacing with external services and invoking specialized tools. These systems can parse natural language instructions, select appropriate tools based on context, and chain multiple operations to accomplish defined objectives. While still limited to session-based context and explicit instruction, they demonstrate emergent capabilities through tool composition.

Example: Document processing systems that extract information from scanned PDFs and upload it to a database, automated report generators that compile data from multiple sources, and intelligent help desk systems that pull answers from extensive knowledge bases.

Level 3: Planning agents – Contextual and goal-oriented

Planning agents introduce sophisticated reasoning capabilities and goal-oriented behavior. These systems decompose high-level objectives into structured task sequences, incorporate feedback from intermediate steps, adjust plans when encountering obstacles, and maintain persistent awareness across extended operations. This level represents a significant advance in autonomous decision-making and strategic thinking.

Example: Autonomous travel planning agents that book flights, hotels, and activities dynamically; digital onboarding assistants that coordinate document submission and training schedules for new employees; and intelligent project management systems that adapt timelines based on team availability and progress.

Level 4: Learning agents – Adaptive and evolving

Learning agents represent the most advanced tier in the progression framework. These systems not only execute complex plans but evolve their capabilities over time through experience. They incorporate feedback from past interactions, develop personalized models for individual users or scenarios, adapt to environmental changes, and continuously refine their strategies based on observed outcomes and explicit guidance.

This progression framework provides organizations with a structured approach for evaluating current agent capabilities, identifying strategic development priorities, and planning capability roadmaps that align with business objectives. By understanding where systems fall within this maturity model, leaders can make informed decisions about technology investments, development priorities, and implementation strategies for agentic AI.

Example: Personalized recommendation engines that learn user preferences and improve over time; advanced fraud detection systems that evolve with changing attack patterns; and autonomous research agents that design and conduct scientific experiments, refining their hypotheses and methods based on experimental results.

This framework offers both a conceptual foundation for understanding agent evolution and a tactical blueprint for implementation. For researchers, it aligns with paradigms such as reactive systems, hierarchical planning, and reinforcement learning. For practitioners, it provides clear examples and deployment considerations, illuminating a roadmap for transitioning from manual processes to intelligent, adaptive systems. By understanding where systems fall within this maturity model, leaders can make informed decisions about technology investments, development priorities, and implementation strategies for agentic AI.

Having established both the theoretical foundations of agent engineering and a framework for evaluating agent maturity, we now examine how these concepts translate into tangible business value. The following real-world case studies demonstrate that autonomous agents are not future possibilities but present-day revenue drivers, fundamentally transforming how organizations operate and compete in their respective markets.

At the same time, **ethical guardrails**, such as transparency, accountability, fairness, and safety, must guide the deployment of such agents. As autonomy increases, so do the risks of unintended actions, bias propagation, or regulatory violations. Integrating these principles into design and governance ensures that intelligent agents not only deliver impact but do so in a manner aligned with organizational values and societal expectations.

Real-world business impact

Forget theoretical abstractions; autonomous agents are reshaping industries today, driving measurable returns and competitive advantage for early adopters. These aren't experimental prototypes or academic curiosities but revenue-generating systems transforming how businesses operate, serve customers, and scale their capabilities beyond traditional constraints.

Quandri: The automated insurance revolution

Insurance processing once meant armies of humans trudging through paperwork forests. Quandri shattered this paradigm by deploying an autonomous agent network that devours thousands of policies daily. What previously consumed hours of skilled labor now resolves in under 15 minutes, with the system maintaining a staggering 99.9% accuracy rate. This isn't incremental improvement; it's transformation at scale, generating over $30,000 in monthly recurring revenue while competitors remain mired in labor-intensive workflows. A lean team armed with agent technology now systematically outperforms traditional operations multiple times their size, fundamentally rewriting the economics of insurance processing.

My AskAI: The 30-second support miracle

Financial services support typically means frustrating wait times, inconsistent answers, and escalation hell. My AskAI's agent architecture demolished these expectations by orchestrating specialized components (document analytics, compliance verification, and real-time data retrieval) into a unified cognitive system that resolves complex inquiries in under 30 seconds. This isn't just faster service; it's a different category of experience, driving both $25,000 in monthly recurring revenue and customer satisfaction scores above 99%. The system's strategic intelligence knows precisely when to handle issues autonomously and when to escalate to human specialists, creating a seamless support experience that feels supernatural to users accustomed to traditional service models.

Enterprise Bot: The sales team that never sleeps

Enterprise Bot fundamentally reimagined sales operations through multi-agent collaboration. Rather than automating isolated tasks, they deployed specialized agent teams handling the entire sales cycle, from lead enrichment, and qualification to personalized outreach and meeting coordination. The results speak volumes: qualified lead generation tripled while acquisition costs plummeted by 50%, driving annual recurring revenue beyond $2 million. This isn't just automation; it's a multiplication of capabilities, allowing human sales professionals to focus exclusively on high-value relationship-building while their digital counterparts handle the methodical pursuit of opportunities around the clock.

As these case studies demonstrate, agent technology isn't a future consideration but a present competitive determinant. The gap between organizations leveraging sophisticated agent systems and those relying on conventional automation continues to widen, creating market dynamics where traditional approaches, regardless of execution quality, simply cannot match the economics, speed, and scalability of agent-powered alternatives. The message is clear: this isn't about incremental improvement but fundamental transformation of what's possible in modern business operations.

Summary

This chapter has established the foundational concepts that underpin modern agent engineering. We've explored how AI agents have evolved from simple reactive systems to sophisticated autonomous entities capable of perception, reasoning, planning, action, and learning. Through our examination of agent architecture, we've seen how modular components work together to create systems that can effectively navigate and respond to complex environments.

The agent development lifecycle we presented offers a structured approach to design, implementation, and continuous improvement, while our exploration of agent capabilities has illustrated the cognitive functions that enable goal-directed behavior. We introduced frameworks for classifying agents based on their level of interaction and developmental maturity, providing a roadmap for understanding and advancing agent technology.

By examining design patterns, machine teaching approaches, and real-world business applications, we've connected theoretical principles to practical implementations. The taxonomy of agent types we've outlined, from reactive to learning agents, demonstrates the diverse approaches to agent architecture and highlights the flexibility of agent-based solutions.

As we move forward, these foundations will serve as essential building blocks for the more advanced concepts and implementations discussed in subsequent chapters. The future of intelligent systems is increasingly agentic, with autonomous AI poised to transform how we work, create, and solve complex problems across virtually every domain of human endeavor.

Having established the conceptual foundations of agent engineering, we turn next to the practical tools, frameworks, and models that bring these concepts to life. *Chapter 2* explores the rapidly evolving ecosystem of agent development technologies, offering a comprehensive guide to selecting and leveraging the right components for your specific agent implementation needs. From development frameworks like LangChain and AutoGPT to language model selection strategies and essential infrastructure components, the following chapter provides a practical toolkit for turning agent theory into working systems.

2

The Agent Engineer's Toolkit

> *In agents, intelligence manifests as goal-directed, autonomous behavior*
>
> — *Andrej Karpathy, Former Tesla AI Director (2024)*

In the realm of intelligent agents, **tooling** defines capability. As agents shift from reactive scripts to goal-directed autonomous systems, developers must master an expanding ecosystem of frameworks, models, and infrastructure. This chapter offers a structured exploration of the tooling available in the agent engineering landscape, equipping you with practical insights and comparative analysis to make informed decisions across the stack. Imagine an agent autonomously researching market trends, synthesizing data, and drafting a strategic report, all in real time. This is the power that the right toolkit unlocks.

The selection of appropriate tools and frameworks represents a critical decision point in the agent development process, one that significantly impacts not only development time and operational costs (e.g., consider **LLM** inference costs, which can range from a few cents to several dollars per million tokens depending on the model and provider), but also the fundamental capabilities of your resulting systems. As an agent engineer, your toolkit defines the boundaries of what your agents can perceive, how they reason, and what actions they can take in the world.

While LLMs provide the cognitive engine that powers modern agents, raw models alone are insufficient for building useful systems. The true power of agent development emerges when you combine these models with a well-designed toolkit that enables efficient knowledge retrieval (e.g., **RAG**) powered by vector databases and libraries such as **Facebook AI Similarity Search** (**FAISS**)), tool integration (such as through OpenAI's powerful function calling mechanisms), monitoring, and deployment.

In this chapter, we will examine the major agent frameworks in use today, review strategies for choosing and optimizing LLMs, and delve into foundational tools that support memory, reasoning, evaluation, and deployment. Rather than offering a snapshot of currently available options, which may quickly become outdated, this chapter focuses on underlying principles and patterns that will remain relevant even as specific implementations change.

Throughout this book, we will primarily work with LangChain and LangGraph as our core development frameworks, chosen for their robust ecosystem, production readiness, and comprehensive documentation. While we explore other frameworks to provide context and help you understand the broader landscape, our practical examples, code implementations, and deep-dive tutorials will focus on the LangChain ecosystem (v0.3.x at the time of writing).

In this chapter, we'll be covering the following topics:

- Agent development frameworks: The architect's blueprint
- LLMs: The cognitive core
- Supporting infrastructure: The agent ecosystem
- Cloud-native agent development platforms

Agent development frameworks: The architect's blueprint

Frameworks are the foundation upon which intelligent agents are built. They provide structure, enforce patterns, and encapsulate best practices, enabling developers to move from ad hoc experimentation to repeatable, scalable engineering. Selecting a framework is not merely a tooling choice but a strategic decision that affects extensibility, maintainability, and performance.

Here is a table summarizing key agent development frameworks. This table offers a concise comparison of their strengths, limitations, and ideal use cases.

Framework	Strengths	Limitations	Ideal Use Case
LangChain	Modular design, broad integrations	No native multi-agent support	LLM pipelines, tool workflows
LlamaIndex	Advanced retrieval, semantic compression	Requires orchestration support	Document Q&A, memory layers
AutoGPT	Autonomous goal planning	Low reliability, fragile control	Research prototypes
CrewAI	Role-based coordination	Early-stage maturity	Experimental multi-agent system, sandboxed collaborative prototypes

Table 2.1 – Comparison of agent development frameworks

As discussed in the section on the **cognitive loop model** from *Chapter 1*, effective agents must continuously cycle through perception, reasoning, planning, action, and learning. The frameworks we explore in this chapter implement this cognitive architecture in code, each with its own approach to structuring these critical functions.

Understanding these different approaches is essential because the framework you choose will determine not only how quickly you can build and iterate on your agents, but also what capabilities they can ultimately achieve. For instance, LangGraph's **directed acyclic graph** (**DAG**) model inherently supports parallel branches for complex, multi-step reasoning, optimizing for throughput in intricate workflows, whereas CrewAI's design can facilitate quicker, more focused chats for linear, specialized tasks. Each framework embodies different assumptions about agent behavior, offers distinct abstractions for common patterns, and provides varying levels of control over underlying cognitive processes. By examining their strengths, limitations, and optimal use cases, you'll be equipped to make informed decisions that align with your specific requirements for performance, scalability, and maintainability.

Comprehensive analysis of key frameworks

In the beginning, there was chaos: ad hoc scripts cobbled together, brittle connections between models and tools, fragile reasoning chains that collapsed under the weight of complexity. Then came the frameworks: structured approaches to agent architecture that brought order to this digital wilderness. However, it's crucial to acknowledge that while frameworks offer significant acceleration and structure, they introduce layers of abstraction. This abstraction, while beneficial for rapid development, can sometimes lead to a reduced level of low-level control and understanding of underlying mechanisms. For foundational learning or highly custom scenarios, starting with more straightforward Python code to build agent capabilities can provide deeper insights before leveraging a full framework. Each framework represents a different philosophy about how intelligence should be structured in code.

LangChain

With over 70,000 GitHub stars burning in the digital firmament, LangChain stands as the elder statesman of agent frameworks. Its computational graph model mirrors cognitive science theories about sequential reasoning (often referred to as *chain-of-thought* processing), allowing developers to compose complex behaviors from simpler building blocks. This design enables agents to follow a step-by-step reasoning pipeline, where each node in the graph corresponds to a cognitive or functional operation, much like how humans break down problems into sequential sub-tasks.

LangChain's architecture is built around several core abstractions that we'll use extensively throughout this book:

- **Chains**: Sequential processing pipelines that connect multiple components. LangChain also provides robust callback and tracing mechanisms, allowing developers to observe, log, and debug the execution flow of these chains, which is essential for understanding complex agent behavior.
- **Agents**: Autonomous decision-makers that take in input, decide what actions to take, such as invoking tools or querying APIs, and then execute those actions to accomplish a goal. This process may involve tool selection, memory recall, or reasoning steps, enabling agents to operate with a degree of autonomy.
- **Tools**: Interfaces to external systems and APIs.
- **Memory**: Systems for maintaining conversation context and long-term storage.
- **Retrievers**: Components for accessing and filtering relevant information.
- **Embeddings**: Text-to-vector transformation for semantic operations.

The framework's modular design becomes apparent in practical implementation. Consider this example of a basic agent setup:

```
from langchain.agents import initialize_agent, AgentType
from langchain.llms import OpenAI
from langchain.tools import Tool
from sympy import sympify
from langchain.tools.ddg_search.tool import DuckDuckGoSearchRun  # hypothetical import

# Define tools the agent can use

def calculator(expression: str) -> str:
    """Safely evaluate mathematical expressions."""
    try:
        result = sympify(expression)
        return str(result)
    except Exception:
        return "Invalid mathematical expression"

# Use DuckDuckGoSearchRun tool provided by LangChain
search = DuckDuckGoSearchRun()

tools = [
    Tool(name="Calculator", func=calculator,
         description="Useful for mathematical calculations"),
    Tool(name="WebSearch", func=search.run,
         description="Search the web for current information")
]

# Initialize the agent
llm = OpenAI(temperature=0)
agent = initialize_agent(
    tools=tools,
    llm=llm,
    agent=AgentType.ZERO_SHOT_REACT_DESCRIPTION,
    verbose=True
)

# Ask the agent to reason about tool usage
result = agent.run("What's the square root of 144, and can you find recent news about
that number?")
```

This example demonstrates LangChain's power: the agent automatically determines that it needs both mathematical calculation and web search capabilities, executes them in the appropriate order, and synthesizes the results. The `ZERO_SHOT_REACT_DESCRIPTION` agent type implements the **Reasoning and Acting (ReAct)** pattern, where the model reasons about what actions to take and then acts upon those decisions.

LangChain's memory systems are particularly sophisticated, supporting multiple memory types:

```
from langchain.memory import ConversationBufferMemory, ConversationSummaryMemory
from langchain.schema import BaseMessage

# Buffer memory keeps exact conversation history
buffer_memory = ConversationBufferMemory(
    memory_key="chat_history",
    return_messages=True
)

# Summary memory compresses older conversations
summary_memory = ConversationSummaryMemory(
    llm=OpenAI(),
    memory_key="chat_history",
    return_messages=True
)
```

The framework's extensive ecosystem includes over 100 pre-built integrations with popular services such as OpenAI, Anthropic, Google, **Amazon Web Services (AWS)**, vector databases (Pinecone, Chroma, Weaviate), and countless APIs. This ecosystem richness means that most integration challenges have already been solved and tested by the community.

At its heart, LangChain is a study in modularity: chains for sequential processing, tools for environment interaction, and memory systems for maintaining context across the digital synapses of conversation. Its extensive component library dramatically reduces the code required to implement common agent patterns, allowing developers to focus on unique aspects of their creations.

However, LangChain's flexibility comes with complexity. The framework's extensive abstraction layers can introduce performance overhead, and debugging complex chains can be challenging without proper observability tools such as LangSmith. Much like how traditional software engineering evolved from simple print statements to structured logging and then to comprehensive observability platforms, agent engineering necessitates similar advancements to ensure transparency and debug complex cognitive workflows. Additionally, while LangChain excels at single-agent scenarios, it requires additional orchestration for complex multi-agent systems, which is where LangGraph becomes essential.

Reference URL: `https://www.langchain.com/`

LangGraph

LangGraph represents the evolution of LangChain into stateful, cyclical workflows that more closely mirror human cognitive processes. While LangChain chains are typically linear, LangGraph enables complex, branching decision trees with loops, conditional logic, and sophisticated state management. This visual and stateful approach significantly eases pain points of debugging complex agent behavior; further transparency can be achieved through dedicated observability tools such as LangSmith or by integrating standard OpenTelemetry hooks for comprehensive tracing and monitoring.

At its core, LangGraph models agent workflows as directed graphs:

- Nodes represent discrete processing steps or agent functions
- Edges define the flow between steps
- State is maintained and passed between nodes
- Conditional routing enables dynamic decision-making

This architecture is particularly powerful for implementing the cognitive loop discussed in *Chapter 1*, where agents must cycle through perception, reasoning, planning, and action phases. Here's a practical example:

```
from langgraph.graph import Graph, Node
from langgraph.prebuilt import ToolExecutor
from langchain.tools import DuckDuckGoSearchRun, Calculator

# Define the agent's workflow nodes
def research_node(state):
    """Gather information about the topic."""
    query = state.get("user_query")
    search_tool = DuckDuckGoSearchRun()  # safer to specify
    research_results = search_tool.run(query)
    return {"research_data": research_results, "next": "analyze"}

def analyze_node(state):
    """Analyze the gathered information."""
    research_data = state.get("research_data")
    # In a real system, plug in LLM/analysis logic here
    analysis = f"Analysis of: {research_data[:200]}..."
    return {"analysis": analysis, "next": "decide"}

def decide_node(state):
    """Decide whether more research is needed."""
    analysis = state.get("analysis")
    # Loop condition with optional MAX_ITER
    if "insufficient data" in analysis.lower():
        if state.get("loop_count", 0) >= 3: # prevent infinite loop
            return {"next": "respond"}
        return {
            "next": "research",
            "loop_count": state.get("loop_count", 0) + 1
        }
    else:
        return {"next": "respond"}
```

```
def respond_node(state):
    """Generate final response."""
    analysis = state.get("analysis")
    response = f"Based on my research and analysis: {analysis}"
    return {"final_response": response, "next": "END"}

# Build the graph
workflow = Graph()
workflow.add_node("research", research_node)
workflow.add_node("analyze", analyze_node)
workflow.add_node("decide", decide_node)
workflow.add_node("respond", respond_node)
# Define transitions
workflow.add_edge("research", "analyze")
workflow.add_edge("analyze", "decide")
workflow.add_conditional_edges("decide", lambda state: {
    "research": "research" if state.get("next") == "research" else None,
    "respond": "respond"
})
workflow.set_entry_point("research")
workflow.set_finish_point("respond")

# Compile and run
app = workflow.compile()
result = app.invoke({"user_query": "Latest developments in quantum computing"})
print(result)
```

This example demonstrates LangGraph's key advantages: the agent can intelligently loop back to gather more information if the initial analysis is insufficient, maintaining state throughout the process. This cyclical capability is crucial for implementing sophisticated reasoning patterns that simple chains cannot achieve.

LangGraph excels in several critical areas where traditional LangChain falls short:

- Multi-step reasoning with conditional branching.
- Human-in-the-loop workflows with approval gates: LangGraph allows developers to design nodes that pause execution and await external input or human review, such as an approval before a financial transaction, before proceeding. This enables agents to collaborate with humans on critical decisions or complex tasks.
- Complex multi-agent coordination and handoffs.
- Persistent state management across long-running processes.
- Sophisticated error handling and retry logic.

The framework also provides powerful debugging and visualization capabilities:

```
# Visualize the workflow
from langgraph.graph import draw_mermaid

# Generate a Mermaid diagram of the workflow
graph_diagram = draw_mermaid(workflow.get_graph())
print(graph_diagram)  # Shows the visual flow of your agent's logic
```

LangGraph's state management is particularly sophisticated, supporting both simple dictionary states and complex, typed state schemas:

```
from typing import TypedDict, List
from langgraph.graph import Graph

class AgentState(TypedDict):
    user_input: str
    research_results: List[str]
    analysis_confidence: float
    iteration_count: int
    final_response: str

# The graph maintains this typed state throughout execution
```

LangGraph extends LangChain into a graph-based architecture, treating agent steps as nodes in a DAG. This visualization of reasoning paths provides unprecedented transparency into agent decision processes.

In practical implementations, LangGraph offers precise control over multi-step agent tasks, excelling in complex workflows with branching paths, advanced error handling, and state management requirements. While it has a steeper learning curve than simpler frameworks, the investment pays dividends in complex enterprise applications.

Throughout the remaining chapters of this book, we'll be using LangGraph extensively for implementing sophisticated agent workflows, from simple sequential processes to complex multi-agent orchestrations. Its combination of flexibility, observability, and state management makes it ideal for building production-grade agent systems.

Reference URL: `https://www.langchain.com/langgraph`

LlamaIndex

Where LangChain orchestrates, LlamaIndex remembers. With 41,000 GitHub stars illuminating its path, this framework approaches agent development from a fundamentally different angle, prioritizing knowledge integration over procedural orchestration.

LlamaIndex implements sophisticated data structures that mimic associative memory systems, offering specialized components for document ingestion, text segmentation, and context-aware retrieval. Its advanced semantic indexing, hierarchical memory models, and context compression techniques shine in applications where agents must navigate vast oceans of information.

At its core, LlamaIndex typically operates through a pipeline of the following:

- **An index**: This component takes raw data (documents, text, etc.) and processes it into a queryable structure, often involving embedding and storing it in a vector database
- **A query engine**: This engine takes a natural language query, retrieves relevant information from the index, and passes it to an LLM
- **A response synthesizer**: This synthesizes the retrieved information and the LLM's understanding into a coherent final answer

While not a complete orchestration solution, LlamaIndex excels as the memory cortex in larger agent systems, particularly for applications such as enterprise knowledge assistants or research copilots that must maintain coherent understanding across vast document landscapes. Within a LangChain or LangGraph workflow, LlamaIndex's Query Engine can be seamlessly integrated as a specialized tool that an agent can invoke whenever it needs to retrieve context-aware information from a knowledge base.

Reference URL: `https://www.llamaindex.ai/`

AutoGPT

In the ecosystem of agent frameworks, AutoGPT dared to dream of something radical: truly autonomous goal-directed behavior. With an astonishing 150,000 GitHub stars, it introduced the world to recursive self-prompting, allowing agents to decompose high-level goals into actionable sub-tasks without human intervention.

AutoGPT implements higher-level abstractions for goal decomposition, task planning, and autonomous tool selection that align with theoretical models of goal-oriented cognitive systems. Its approach enables the creation of agents that can pursue complex objectives with minimal human oversight.

This autonomy comes at a price. The control mechanisms remain fragile, and production deployments require careful configuration to maintain alignment with user intentions. Yet in its aspiration toward true autonomy, AutoGPT hints at future possibilities of agent architecture.

Reference URL: `https://github.com/Significant-Gravitas/AutoGPT`

CrewAI

The newest contender in our framework exploration brings a different philosophy, one built on role specialization and multi-agent collaboration. CrewAI abstracts the concept of a "crew" working together with assigned roles to tackle complex tasks.

In CrewAI, each agent is defined with attributes such as role, goal, and backstory, creating distinct personas within a collaborative system. Agents communicate via built-in messaging and delegation mechanisms, essentially "thinking out loud" to each other to plan and solve problems.

With 30,000 GitHub stars and growing, CrewAI represents a shift toward more structured collaborative intelligence, where specialized agents combine their capabilities under the guidance of a central orchestrator.

> **Note**
>
> As of version 0.4, CrewAI introduces tighter integration with LangChain, relying on LangChain's agent and Tool abstractions to enable tool usage and orchestration. This makes CrewAI especially suitable for teams already leveraging LangChain-based workflows, though it also introduces some dependency considerations.

Reference URL: `https://github.com/crewAIinc/crewAI`

AutoGen

Developed by Microsoft, AutoGen takes a unique approach to agent orchestration by treating LLMs as conversation participants. Rather than focusing solely on agent role definition or goal decomposition, AutoGen introduces a conversational programming paradigm where agents, each backed by an LLM, interact through messages to collectively solve tasks.

AutoGen enables complex, stateful multi-agent workflows by defining agents as functions with roles (e.g., user proxy, code executor, planner), connected via customizable message-passing loops. This structure allows dynamic coordination, adaptive planning, and tool invocation with a higher degree of control than reactive agents.

Its strength lies in fine-grained orchestration, allowing developers to explicitly manage turn-taking, input/output flows, and stop conditions. AutoGen is increasingly used in enterprise-grade applications where transparency, coordination, and modularity are key.

Reference URL: `https://github.com/microsoft/autogen`

Strengths, weaknesses, and optimal use cases

Selecting the appropriate agent development framework is a strategic design decision that fundamentally shapes your system's capabilities:

- **LangChain** excels through its modular orchestration and vast integration ecosystem. It shines in scenarios requiring rapid prototyping or complex tool integration. However, its layered abstractions can introduce performance overhead in latency-sensitive applications.
- **LlamaIndex** distinguishes itself through knowledge-centric design, offering sophisticated semantic indexing and context compression. Note that context compression is a technique to distill large amounts of information into a concise summary or a more focused representation that still captures the essential meaning. These capabilities make it the framework of choice for applications that must ingest and reason over vast document collections.
- **AutoGPT** stands apart with its focus on autonomy and goal decomposition. Through recursive self-prompting, it enables agents to plan, execute, and iterate toward high-level objectives with minimal human guidance.
- **CrewAI** addresses multi-agent orchestration through formalized role specialization. This approach facilitates distributed reasoning and task delegation, making CrewAI ideal for complex collaborative workflows.

While each framework offers distinct advantages, modern agent engineering often benefits from a "mix-and-match" approach, combining each framework's strengths as detailed in the upcoming *Build-versus-integrate decisions* section.

Build-versus-integrate decisions

Modern agent engineering follows a *compose-over-build* philosophy, assembling intelligent systems through integration of specialized components rather than constructing monolithic architecture from scratch.

In practice, most teams follow a hybrid path: leveraging frameworks such as LangChain for orchestration during early development, then selectively replacing components with custom implementations as specific performance or security constraints emerge.

For example, a team might start with LangChain's in-memory `ConversationBufferMemory` implementation for rapid prototyping but later swap it with a production-grade vector database such as Pinecone or Chroma when persistent, scalable, and semantically rich memory becomes a requirement for their agent.

Examples of effective integration strategies include the following:

- Using **LangChain** for orchestration, combined with **LlamaIndex** for document retrieval
- Deploying **CrewAI + LangChain** to manage distributed agent roles (noting that CrewAI often leverages LangChain's Tool abstraction for enhanced functionality)
- Applying **LangGraph** for deterministic control in regulated industries

Having explored the landscape of agent development frameworks, from LangChain's modular orchestration to CrewAI's collaborative intelligence, we now turn to the cognitive engines that power these systems. While frameworks provide the architectural foundation for structuring agent behavior, LLMs serve as the reasoning core that transforms structured inputs into intelligent outputs. Understanding how to select, integrate, and optimize these models is crucial for unlocking the full potential of your chosen framework.

LLMs: The cognitive core

As we transition from frameworks to the models they orchestrate, we enter the realm of artificial cognition itself. LLMs represent more than just text prediction systems; they are the foundational layer upon which agent intelligence is built. These models serve as the reasoning engine within the agent architecture outlined in the *Communication patterns between components* section of *Chapter 1*, where the cognition core mediates between perception, planning, memory, and action components. Understanding their capabilities, limitations, and integration patterns is essential for constructing effective agent architectures. In this section, we'll examine cognitive engines that power modern intelligent systems and how to harness their capabilities effectively.

Model selection and integration

The choice of language model fundamentally shapes what your agent can perceive, understand, and generate. Models differ in capability spectrum, specialization, context window, inference performance, and operational characteristics.

The following are some things to consider when selecting your language model:

- Models range from lightweight and fast (though limited in complex reasoning, factual recall, or specialized domain expertise (e.g., Mistral 7B)) to highly capable but computationally intensive systems, such as GPT-4, Claude 3, Gemini, and other cutting-edge models known for their advanced problem-solving and logical inference abilities
- Some models excel at coding, while others excel at creative content or multi-turn reasoning
- Context windows range from 8K to over 1M tokens
- Hosting options, pricing models, and rate limits vary significantly
- Licensing: Models can be open weight (allowing full access to model weights for local deployment and fine-tuning) or closed source (accessible via API, managed by a third-party provider), impacting control, customization, and long-term costs

Hybrid model architecture

Perhaps the most fascinating approach to model integration is the hybrid architecture, where multiple models collaborate, each handling tasks aligned with their strengths. This approach resembles a cognitive division of labor, with different models serving specialized functions within a unified system.

This hybrid approach aligns remarkably well with the multi-agent systems described in the *Multi-agent systems: The collaborative intelligence* section of *Chapter 1*, where specialized agents collaborate to achieve complex goals. In the hybrid model architecture, we implement this collaborative specialized principle at the model level rather than the agent level, creating a symphony of specialized cognitive engines working in concert.

Let's examine a portion of code demonstrating this approach:

```
def route_to_model(self, query, query_type, conversation_history=None):
    """Route query to appropriate model based on classification."""

    if query_type == QueryType.FACTUAL:
        return self._generate_mistral_response(query, conversation_history)
    elif query_type == QueryType.CREATIVE:
        return self._generate_claude_response(query, conversation_history)
    elif query_type == QueryType.ANALYTICAL:
        return self._generate_gpt4o_response(query, conversation_history)
```

This code demonstrates a practical implementation of the hybrid model approach. The system first classifies incoming queries into categories (factual, creative, or analytical), then routes each query to the most appropriate specialized model. For example, straightforward factual questions are handled by Mistral's efficient 7B model for speed and cost-effectiveness, while complex creative tasks are routed to Claude for its superior creative capabilities, and analytical work leverages GPT-4's reasoning strengths. This orchestration layer enables the system to optimize for both performance and cost by ensuring each query is processed by the model best suited to handle it. It's also crucial to consider token normalization across different models as their unique tokenization methods mean that the same input text can result in varying token counts, directly impacting both cost and adherence to context window limits.

The orchestration layer acts as a traffic director for AI requests, sitting between user queries and the various language models. This orchestration layer routes different query types to specialized models, balancing performance, cost, and capability in ways no single model could achieve.

With a solid understanding of how to select and orchestrate language models, from single-model deployments to sophisticated hybrid architectures, we now turn to the broader ecosystem of tools and services that transform these models into production-ready agent systems. While models provide the cognitive capabilities, the supporting infrastructure enables agents to remember past interactions, access external data sources, integrate with APIs and tools, and operate reliably at scale. This infrastructure layer is where theoretical potential becomes practical reality.

Supporting infrastructure: The agent ecosystem

Beyond frameworks and models lies a rich ecosystem of supporting technologies that expand agent capabilities and ensure reliable operation. Much like how cities require infrastructure beyond individual buildings (roads, utilities, communication networks, etc.) agent systems need specialized components that handle data storage, external interactions, evaluation, and monitoring.

This infrastructure layer directly supports the interoperability protocols discussed in *Chapter 1*, where **Model Context Protocol** (**MCP**) and **Agent-to-Agent** (**A2A**) protocols establish standardized interfaces for tool discovery, invocation, and collaborative messaging. The supporting technologies we explore in this section provide concrete implementations that enable these protocols to function in production environments. These infrastructure components transform theoretical potential into practical reality, enabling agents to perceive their environment, take meaningful actions, and improve over time.

Mastering these supporting technologies is crucial because they determine whether your agents remain isolated prototypes or become integrated, scalable systems capable of real-world deployment. The quality of your memory systems affects how well agents learn from experience; your tool integration approach determines what actions agents can take; your evaluation framework reveals whether agents are performing as intended; and your monitoring infrastructure ensures reliable operation at scale. Understanding these components enables you to build agents that are not just intelligent but also robust, observable, and continuously improving.

The memory revolution: How vector databases are supercharging AI agents

Imagine asking your friend about a conversation you had last year. Their ability to recall details depends not just on memory capacity, but on how their brain indexes and retrieves information. Similarly, for AI agents to function intelligently in our world, they need more than raw processing power; they need a memory system that understands meaning, not just matches words.

Picture this: You're troubleshooting code and searching for how to fix a runtime error. Despite thousands of relevant resources existing online, your search returns unhelpful results because the most relevant solutions describe the same concept using different terminology, such as "debugging code exceptions"—semantically identical but lexically different. This isn't just frustrating; it's a fundamental limitation of *purely* keyword-based search. Traditional search is like trying to find someone in a crowded train station by shouting their name, hoping they respond. It works only if they're listening for exactly that name. While many modern retrieval systems combine keyword-based approaches with more advanced techniques, the limitations of relying solely on exact word matches become apparent when searching for conceptual relevance. Enter vector search: a paradigm shift that understands concepts, and not just keywords. It's the difference between a librarian who only checks book titles and one who understands what you're trying to accomplish.

The technical details of how this conceptual understanding works (through high-dimensional mathematical representations and semantic similarity calculations) are explored in the following section.

By transforming text into high-dimensional semantic vectors using models such as OpenAI's `text-embedding-ada-002` model, vector search captures the essence of meaning. Two texts expressing the same idea with different words now *live* near each other in this mathematical space of meaning.

> **Note**
>
> **Dive deeper**: OpenAI's embedding playground (`https://platform.openai.com/docs/guides/embeddings`) lets you visualize how similar concepts cluster together, even with different wording.

Vector databases might sound complex, but their core principle is beautifully intuitive: represent meaning as direction in space.

When you search a vector database, what's happening behind the scenes is a mathematical dance:

1. Your question becomes a vector, essentially an arrow pointing in a specific direction in a high-dimensional space (e.g., 768, 1,024, or 1,536 dimensions depending on the embedding model).
2. The database finds stored vectors pointing in similar directions.
3. The closest vectors (measured by cosine similarity or dot product) correspond to the most relevant information.

This approach is dramatically different from traditional databases searching for exact pattern matches. It's the difference between "find these exact words" and "find this concept."

The true wizardry happens in **approximate nearest neighbor** (**ANN**) algorithms such as **Hierarchical Navigable Small World** (**HNSW**) or **Inverted File Index** (**IVF**), which make searching billions of high-dimensional vectors possible in milliseconds.

> **Note**
>
> **Fun fact**: Without these algorithmic breakthroughs, finding the nearest vector in a billion-vector database would take minutes instead of milliseconds. The mathematics of efficient high-dimensional search is what makes modern AI assistants possible.

The vector database landscape

The vector database ecosystem is evolving rapidly, with different platforms optimized for different needs:

- **Pinecone – The specialist**: Purpose-built for vector search from the ground up. When milliseconds matter, and you need cloud-native scaling, Pinecone delivers. Its upsert API makes real-time knowledge updates trivial (`pinecone.io`).

- **Weaviate – The hybrid powerhouse**: Combines vector search with traditional filtering in a GraphQL interface. Perfect when your users need both semantic understanding and precise metadata filtering (`weaviate.io`).
- **Chroma – The developer's friend**: Lightweight, open source, and designed to make local development joyful. When you want to prototype a RAG system in minutes rather than hours, Chroma shines (`trychroma.com`).
- **Milvus – The enterprise foundation**: Built for massive scale and complex deployments. When your vector search needs to handle billions of records across distributed systems, Milvus provides industrial-strength capabilities (`milvus.io`).
- **Qdrant – The reliable open source contender**: Qdrant is designed for high-performance, production-ready vector search. With robust filtering, support for payload indexing, and seamless integration into RAG pipelines, it balances developer flexibility with enterprise-grade capabilities (`qdrant.tech`).

Which one should you choose? The honest answer is that it depends on your specific requirements. For early experimentation, Chroma's simplicity is hard to beat. For production systems handling sensitive data, self-hosted Weaviate or Milvus might be preferable. For pure cloud performance without operational overhead, Pinecone is compelling.

Building the brain of your AI agent

Vector databases truly shine when integrated into an agent architecture. Think of them as the hippocampus of your AI system, the structure responsible for forming, indexing, and retrieving memories. The optimal choice of vector database often depends on critical factors such as the required scale, **service-level agreements (SLAs)** for retrieval latency, and data residency requirements for compliance. To see these ideas in action, consider how vector databases underpin RAG pipelines, enabling AI systems to retrieve relevant knowledge in real time and incorporate it into their reasoning.

A simple but powerful RAG pipeline looks like this:

1. **Chunk your knowledge**: Break documents into digestible pieces (typically 500–1,000 tokens).
2. **Embed everything**: Transform chunks into embedding vectors (called an *embedding*) that capture the chunk's meaning in a way that machines can understand and compare. These vectors allow semantic search and similarity matching.
3. **Store with metadata**: Save vectors alongside source information and timestamps.
4. **Retrieve on demand**: When the agent needs context, find relevant vectors.
5. **Inject into prompts**: Feed this contextual knowledge to the LLM before it responds.

What makes this approach revolutionary is that your agent's knowledge becomes *dynamic* rather than static. New information can be continuously added to the vector store, immediately enhancing the agent's capabilities without retraining.

> **Note**
>
> Frameworks such as LangChain (`docs.langchain.com`) and CrewAI (`github.com/joaomdmoura/crewai`) provide elegant abstractions for building these pipelines.

While the basic RAG pipeline provides a solid foundation, building truly effective retrieval systems requires mastering several advanced techniques and best practices. The difference between a functional RAG implementation and an exceptional one often lies in the nuanced optimizations that follow: from intelligent chunking strategies to sophisticated reranking algorithms.

Mastering the art of retrieval

Building an effective retrieval system is part science, part art. The following subsections reveal the secrets that separate mediocre implementations from exceptional ones.

The Goldilocks zone of chunking

Too small, and chunks lose crucial context. Too large, and the signal drowns in noise. Finding your "just right" chunk size often requires experimentation.

A fascinating approach gaining traction is "hierarchical chunking", which is storing the same content at multiple granularities (paragraph, section, document) and dynamically choosing the appropriate level during retrieval.

The reranking revolution

First-stage vector retrieval gets you the neighborhood of relevant content, but rerankers help you find the exact house. Models such as Cohere's Rerank or Sentence Transformers' Cross-Encoders examine query-document pairs in detail, dramatically improving precision.

Metadata

Pure semantic search is powerful, but combining it with metadata filtering creates magic. Imagine filtering not just by meaning but by the following:

- Recency (prioritizing newer information)
- Source authority (preferring verified sources)
- Department relevance (focusing on specific business units)
- User interaction history (personalizing retrieval)

Observability

When retrieval fails, understanding why is crucial. Tools such as LangSmith (`smith.langchain.com`) let you visualize the following:

- Which chunks were retrieved
- What similarity scores they received
- How they influenced the final response

This observability transforms RAG from mysterious to manageable.

We're witnessing just the beginning of memory-augmented AI agents. Future systems will likely feature the following:

- **Multi-modal vector stores**: Embedding images, audio, and text in unified spaces

- **Reasoning-aware retrieval**: Systems that understand not just what information exists, but what information would help solve a specific reasoning task (this capability is currently an active area of research and development)
- **Self-improving memory**: Agents that refine their own chunking and retrieval strategies based on user feedback

Vector databases aren't just a technical improvement; they represent a fundamental shift in how AI systems relate to knowledge. They transform LLMs from static, frozen-knowledge systems to dynamic reasoners that can incorporate new information and adapt to changing environments. However, this shift to mutable memories introduces new operational challenges, particularly concerning write latency for real-time updates and ensuring data consistency across distributed memory stores.

For developers building the next generation of AI agents, mastering vector retrieval isn't optional; it's the difference between creating a clever chatbot and building a truly intelligent assistant.

> *The measure of intelligence is the ability to change.*
>
> —*Albert Einstein*

This quote applies not just to humans but to our AI systems as well. Vector databases give our agents the ability to change what they know: the first step toward genuine machine intelligence.

Having explored how vector databases revolutionize agent memory and knowledge retrieval, we now turn to mechanisms that enable agents to interact with and manipulate the external world. While memory systems allow agents to learn and recall information, tool integration frameworks provide the critical bridge between an agent's internal reasoning and its ability to take concrete actions, from API calls and database queries to file operations and system commands.

Tool integration frameworks

Tools are the liberation of agent intelligence, allowing it to reach beyond its digital confines and manipulate the world. In the **Perception-Reasoning-Action (PRA)** loop, tools represent the moment when thought transforms into consequence. The ecosystem of available tools is vast and constantly expanding, from simple API wrappers and database connectors to complex automation platforms and specialized domain tools. Rather than attempting an exhaustive catalog, we focus on the two most foundational integration patterns that underpin virtually all agent-tool interactions: LangChain's Tool abstraction for Python-based development and OpenAI's **function calling** for direct model integration. It's worth noting that these two approaches are not mutually exclusive; LangChain, for example, can wrap OpenAI JSON schemas using its `StructuredTool` class, allowing developers to leverage OpenAI's powerful function-calling capabilities within a LangChain agent. Understanding these core patterns provides the foundation for integrating any tool, regardless of its specific implementation or domain.

LangChain Tool abstraction

LangChain provides the Tool abstraction, a powerful pattern that transforms ordinary Python functions into agent-compatible instruments. This abstraction handles complex orchestration between the language model and external systems, managing input validation, error handling, and response formatting automatically. The

`Tool` wrapper essentially creates a standardized interface that agents can discover and invoke reliably, where Python functions are transformed into reliable instruments for production environments:

```
from langchain.agents import Tool

def get_stock_price(ticker: str) -> str:
    """Return a mock stock price or handle invalid input."""
    try:
        # Dummy logic: in real scenarios, this could call an API
        if not ticker.isalpha():
            raise ValueError("Invalid ticker symbol")
        return f"The price of {ticker} is $123.45"
    except Exception as e:
        return f"Error fetching stock price: {str(e)}"

tool = Tool(
    name="StockPriceTool",
    func=get_stock_price,
    description="Fetches the current price of a stock"
)
```

This example demonstrates the simplicity of the Tool pattern: we start with a regular Python function that takes a stock ticker symbol and returns price information. The `Tool` wrapper then packages this function with metadata that agents can understand: a descriptive name for identification, the actual function to execute, and a clear description of what the tool does. When an agent needs stock price information, it can discover this tool through the name and description, then invoke it by calling the underlying function with the appropriate parameters. The Tool abstraction handles all the complexity of bridging between the agent's reasoning process and the function execution.

OpenAI function calling

OpenAI's function calling provides a sophisticated command system through JSON-based schemas:

```
{
  "name": "get_weather",
  "description": "Get the weather for a city",
  "parameters": {
    "type": "object",
    "properties": {
      "city": { "type": "string" }
    },
    "required": ["city"]
  }
}
```

This JSON schema defines a weather function that agents can call, specifying the function name, its purpose, and the required parameters with their data types. Unlike LangChain's Python-centric approach, OpenAI's function calling uses standardized JSON schemas that work across different programming languages and platforms. The LM can interpret this schema to understand what the function does and how to call it correctly, then generate properly formatted function calls during conversations.

With robust tool integration enabling agents to take actions in the world, our next focus turns to ensuring these actions produce the intended results through comprehensive evaluation and benchmarking systems.

Cloud-native agent development platforms

This section provides a comparative overview of cloud-native platforms for LLM agent development, drawing insights from industry reports and cloud provider documentation.

While open source frameworks provide unparalleled flexibility and control for custom implementations and specialized requirements, the major cloud providers (AWS, Microsoft Azure, and Google Cloud) offer powerful, managed platforms designed to simplify the development, deployment, and scaling of LLM agents in production environments. These cloud-native solutions abstract away much of the underlying infrastructure complexity, providing essential capabilities such as multi-agent collaboration, RAG, memory retention, and integrated guardrails for safety and reliability.

A growing trend in agent engineering is a hybrid approach, combining the strengths of these managed cloud services for foundational infrastructure and core LLM access with open source frameworks for defining complex agent logic and custom tool integrations. This section explores key offerings from each major cloud provider, highlighting their native tools, integration capabilities, and deployment considerations.

AWS: The flexible ecosystem

AWS offers a comprehensive suite of services for building and deploying LLM agents, characterized by its breadth of model choices and deep integration with existing AWS services.

Native tools: Amazon Bedrock Agents

Amazon Bedrock is AWS's flagship managed service for **generative AI (GenAI)**, providing access to a variety of **foundation models (FMs)** through a single API endpoint, including Amazon's Titan models and third-party models such as Anthropic Claude, AI21 Labs Jurassic, Cohere Command, Meta's Llama 2, and Stability AI. Bedrock supports on-demand usage and customization techniques such as fine-tuning and RAG.

A unique feature within AWS is **Amazon Bedrock Agents**, a fully managed service for building and scaling GenAI bots capable of executing complex tasks autonomously. Key features include the following:

- **Multi-agent collaboration**: Bedrock Agents supports orchestrated multi-agent workflows, where a single supervisor (orchestrator) agent manages the execution of chained task agents. While this enables division of labor and modular task handling, it currently follows a centralized coordination model rather than decentralized agent-to-agent collaboration.
- **RAG**: Bedrock Knowledge Bases provides a fully managed RAG workflow, handling document ingestion, embedding storage in a vector database, and retrieval of context from your data. It can connect to

various data sources such as databases and S3. Notably, it supports structured data retrieval using natural language to SQL.

- **Orchestration and multistep tasks**: Bedrock Agents uses the reasoning capabilities of FMs to analyze user requests, decompose them into logical sequences, and automatically call necessary APIs (defined as "Action Groups"). AWS Step Functions is a powerful serverless orchestrator that can sequence and manage state across multiple steps, integrating directly with Bedrock API calls.
- **Memory retention**: Agents can maintain conversation history across interactions for personalized and seamless user experiences and improved accuracy in multi-step tasks.
- **Code interpretation**: The service supports dynamic generation and execution of code within a secure environment, automating complex analytical queries and data analysis.
- **Prompt engineering**: Bedrock Agents automatically creates prompt templates from user instructions, action groups, and knowledge bases, which developers can refine.
- **Guardrails**: Built-in security and reliability features, such as Amazon Bedrock Guardrails, filter user inputs and model responses for harmful content. However, these guardrails currently support only pre-defined moderation configurations; custom policy scripting or deeply tailored safety rules are not yet available.

For hosting custom models or open source LLMs, **Amazon SageMaker** provides capabilities to deploy any model to a managed endpoint with autoscaling. Additionally, **SageMaker JumpStart** offers pre-built inference containers and deployment templates for popular open models such as **Llama 3**, **Mixtral**, and others, significantly reducing operational effort for production-grade deployments.

Integrating open source frameworks on AWS

AWS actively supports the integration of popular open source LLM agent frameworks:

- **LangChain and LangGraph**: There is a dedicated `langchain-aws` toolkit and official examples showing how to integrate LangChain (and LangGraph) with Bedrock. LangChain agents can directly invoke AWS Lambda functions as tools.
- **Strands Agents**: AWS has introduced Strands Agents, an open source SDK for AI agent development through a model-driven approach. It allows defining agents with natural language prompts, tools, and models (supporting Bedrock and others via LiteLLM).
- **MCP**: AWS supports MCP, an open standard defining how AI models connect to various data sources or tools, aiming to standardize agent-tool interaction and promote reuse across enterprises. SageMaker AI plays a crucial role in hosting LLMs that perform actions with tools implemented by MCP servers.

Deployment architectures on AWS

AWS offers flexible deployment architectures:

- **Serverless (AWS Lambda, API Gateway)**: Lambda functions are ideal for event-driven applications and microservices, serving as core logic for LLM agents triggered by Amazon API Gateway for real-time interactions. This setup offers automatic scaling and a pay-per-use model.
- **Containerized (Amazon ECS, Amazon EKS)**: For complex, distributed, or stateful LLM agent applications, AWS provides Amazon **Elastic Container Service (ECS)** and Amazon **Elastic Kubernetes Service (EKS)**. ECS is AWS's proprietary container orchestration platform, cost-effective and deeply

integrated with other AWS services. EKS, built on Kubernetes, offers extensive features for managing containerized applications at scale and greater open source support. MCP servers, implementing agent tools, can be hosted on Elastic Compute Cloud (EC2), ECS, or EKS.

Azure: The enterprise powerhouse

Microsoft Azure provides a robust and integrated ecosystem for developing and deploying LLM agents, especially for organizations deeply embedded in the Microsoft ecosystem.

Native tools: Azure AI Foundry Agent Service

Azure OpenAI Service is Azure's marquee offering, providing API access to OpenAI's models (GPT-3.5 Turbo, GPT-4, Codex, DALL-E 2) hosted in Microsoft's cloud data centers with enterprise-grade security and compliance. Note that GPT-4o is currently available in multi-tenant mode only.

Azure AI Foundry Agent Service is a unified platform designed to build, deploy, and operate intelligent agents powered by LLMs in enterprise environments. It is conceptualized as an "Agent Factory" with comprehensive capabilities across multiple dimensions:

- **Models**: Selection from a growing catalog, including Azure OpenAI models, Llama, Mistral, and Cohere.
- **Customization**: Models are tailored through fine-tuning, distillation, or domain-specific prompts to encode agent behavior.
- **AI tools**: Agents are equipped to access enterprise knowledge (e.g., Bing, SharePoint, Azure AI Search) and take actions via Azure Logic Apps, Azure Functions, or OpenAPI.
- **Orchestration**: "Connected agents" manage tool calls, update thread states, and handle retries. Azure AI Foundry supports multi-agent coordination with built-in agent-to-agent messaging. Azure Logic Apps is a serverless workflow engine similar to AWS Step Functions, suitable for defining LLM agent flows and integrating with various services. Azure Durable Functions (an extension of Azure Functions) allows writing orchestrator functions in code for complex sequences. Azure AI Studio Prompt Flow provides a visual canvas to chain prompts and Python code nodes.
- **Trust**: Enterprise-grade features ensure reliability, including identity management via Microsoft Entra, **role-based access control**, content filters, encryption, and network isolation.
- **Observability**: AI Foundry captures logs, traces, and evaluations with full thread-level visibility and integration with Azure Application Insights.

Azure also offers "OpenAI on Your Data," a simplified setup for RAG in Azure AI Studio, which automatically uses Azure AI Search to index and retrieve data for a chat model.

Integrating open source frameworks on Azure

Azure AI Foundry Agent Service explicitly supports combining various open source SDKs:

- **Semantic Kernel**: An `AzureAIAgent` class within Semantic Kernel provides advanced conversational capabilities and seamless tool integration, focusing on enterprise readiness, security, and compliance.
- **AutoGen**: Developed by Microsoft Research, AutoGen frames everything as an asynchronous conversation among specialized agents, suitable for multi-turn conversations and real-time tool

invocation. Azure AI Agent Service can orchestrate single agents defined in AutoGen into complex multi-agent workflows.

- **LangChain**: While not as deeply integrated as Semantic Kernel or AutoGen, LangChain agents can be deployed on Azure's compute services, such as Azure Container Apps Dynamic Sessions, to provide secure, sandboxed environments for code interpreters.

Deployment architectures on Azure

Azure provides flexible deployment options:

- **Serverless (Azure Functions, Azure Container Apps)**: Azure Functions are suitable for deploying Semantic Kernel SDK and AutoGen multi-agent applications, offering automatic scaling and cost efficiency. Azure Container Apps can host web-based chat applications with AI agents and provide secure, isolated sandboxed environments for code execution.
- **Containerized (Azure Kubernetes Service (AKS))**: AKS is a managed Kubernetes offering well suited for deploying complex, distributed applications requiring container orchestration at scale and deep control over the Kubernetes environment.

Google Cloud: The AI innovation hub

Google Cloud leverages its AI research leadership and infrastructure prowess, offering highly scalable and cost-efficient AI services with a strategic focus on interoperability and enterprise search.

Native tools: Agentspace, Vertex AI Agent Builder/Engine/ADK

Google Cloud's hub for LLMs is **Vertex AI**, particularly its GenAI offerings such as PaLM 2 and the upcoming Gemini model suite. Vertex AI also includes select external models, such as Meta's Llama 2, via its Model Garden library.

Google Cloud provides a suite of integrated services for building and deploying LLM agents:

- **Agentspace**: A search and AI agent hub for enterprise work, connecting applications to Google-quality multimodal search and AI agents. It includes "Agent Designer" and "Agent Gallery" functionalities. Note that Agentspace is currently in private preview.
- **Vertex AI Agent Builder**: A comprehensive suite of features for discovering, building, and deploying AI agents.
- **Agent Development Kit (ADK)**: An open source, framework-agnostic framework simplifying the creation of sophisticated multi-agent systems with precise control over agent behavior. It powers Agentspace and streamlines multi-agent transfer and planning.
- **Vertex AI Agent Engine**: A fully managed Google Cloud service for deploying, managing, and scaling AI agents in production. It abstracts away low-level tasks and handles infrastructure, scaling, security, evaluation, and monitoring.
- **A2A protocol**: Google is actively developing an open A2A protocol to enable interoperability between AI agents, regardless of their underlying framework or vendor.
- **MCP**: Google Cloud also supports MCP, an open standard for agents to connect with and utilize external tools and data sources in a standardized way.

Google Cloud's agent tools are applicable across various use cases, including enterprise search, content generation, and automation. Vertex AI extensions, part of Agent Builder, allow connecting agents to Google Workspace and other external APIs.

Integrating open source frameworks on Google Cloud

Vertex AI Agent Engine is designed to be framework-agnostic, providing flexible support for popular open source LLM frameworks:

- **LangChain, LangGraph**: Vertex AI Agent Engine offers full integration with LangChain and LangGraph. LangChain can also be deployed on Google Cloud Run and **Google Kubernetes Engine** (**GKE**) using LangServe.
- **AutoGen, LlamaIndex**: Supported via Vertex AI SDK integration with managed templates.
- **CrewAI**: Supported through custom templates on Vertex AI Agent Engine.

Google's focus on open source tools such as ADK and the A2A protocol aims to foster a wider, more interoperable ecosystem for AI agents, reducing vendor lock-in.

Deployment architectures on Google Cloud

Google Cloud offers flexible and scalable deployment options:

- **Serverless (Cloud Run)**: A fully managed, serverless platform providing a scalable environment for AI application workloads and agents. It automatically scales instances on demand, offers a pay-per-use model, and integrates with Gemini API or Vertex AI endpoints for AI models. Cloud Run can be configured for sandboxed code execution.
- **Containerized (GKE)**: GKE is a managed Kubernetes service suitable for complex microservices architectures, stateful applications, and workloads requiring custom infrastructure or network configurations. LangServe can streamline LangChain deployments on GKE. Cloud Run and GKE offer high portability, allowing the same container images to run across both.

For robust workflow orchestration of tasks beyond core agent inference, such as model training, fine-tuning, and continuous RAG updates, Vertex AI Pipelines provides a managed service to define and execute these complex ML workflows.

Recommendations for cloud platform selection

The "best" cloud for LLM agents depends on specific project needs and existing organizational infrastructure:

- **AWS**: Ideal for organizations already deeply invested in the AWS ecosystem, valuing flexibility, a variety of models, and deep integration with existing AWS services and data lakes. Its focus on multi-agent collaboration and distributed inference at the edge makes it suitable for complex, large-scale deployments.
- **Azure**: The platform of choice when cutting-edge OpenAI models (GPT-4) are a must, or when integrating AI into a Microsoft-centric organization (Office 365, Dynamics, Teams, SharePoint) is required. Azure AI Foundry offers a unified platform experience with strong governance and identity management for agents, appealing to those prioritizing streamlined operations and compliance.
- **Google Cloud**: A strong contender for those who value cost-efficient scaling, Google's AI research edge, and a more "holistic" agent platform with emphasis on open standards and easy tool connectivity. Its

strengths in enterprise search and multimodal AI, coupled with serverless options such as Cloud Run for rapid deployment, make it appealing for developers who prefer a mix of coding and managed services.

Summary

The toolkit you assemble fundamentally shapes what your systems can perceive, how they reason, and what actions they can take. This chapter has explored essential components: frameworks, models, databases, integration mechanisms, evaluation systems, and monitoring solutions.

These toolkit decisions determine where your implementations fall within the Agentic AI Progression Framework. Your choices establish boundaries of what your agents can become tomorrow.

As the landscape evolves, maintaining adaptability should remain a core design principle. In the next chapter, we will explore advanced prompt engineering for agent systems that will allow us to maximize their utility for a given use case.

Subscribe for a free eBook

New frameworks, evolving architectures, research drops, production breakdowns—*AI_Distilled* filters the noise into a weekly briefing for engineers and researchers working hands-on with LLMs and generative AI systems. Subscribe now and receive a free eBook, along with weekly insights that help you stay focused and informed.

Subscribe at `https://packt.link/8Oz6Y` or scan the QR code below.

3

The Art of Agent Prompting

Every block of stone has a statue inside it and it is the task of the sculptor to discover it.

— Michelangelo

Prompt engineering for autonomous agents is not merely about issuing instructions; it's about shaping a persistent cognitive framework through language (the PTCF blueprint, introduced later in this chapter, formalizes exactly this idea into four structured components). As we move beyond traditional software and single-use AI outputs, a new approach is emerging: intelligent agents whose behavior, reasoning, and adaptability are controlled by carefully designed prompts.

This shift marks a profound evolution in human-computer interaction. In contrast to traditional software, where behavior is encoded through static code, agents are animated through the dynamic interplay between prompt design and model capability. A well-constructed prompt doesn't just elicit a response; it constructs an identity, sets boundaries, and orchestrates the agent's decision-making logic.

In this chapter, we position prompt engineering as both a theoretical discipline and a hands-on design methodology. We'll trace its evolution, from simple query techniques to sophisticated frameworks for shaping agent cognition. We'll explore the architectural foundations of prompt design that make agent behavior transparent and reliable and provide practical tools for building systems that are collaborative, scalable, and deeply aligned with human goals.

This material is not abstract academic theory; it's critical knowledge for practitioners designing next-generation AI systems. Whether you're automating complex processes, enhancing human capabilities, or building agent-based platforms from the ground up, mastering prompt engineering is essential. Prompts represent the foundational components of an intelligent digital infrastructure.

In this chapter, we'll be covering the following topics:

- From instructions to constitutions
- The two-layer prompt architecture
- The PTCF blueprint
- Designing thinking agents
- Teaching by example

- Making reasoning visible
- Architecting collaboration

Let's begin by examining how the role of prompts has fundamentally changed—from transient instructions to persistent constitutions that shape the very core of agent behavior.

From instructions to constitutions: The new role of prompts

At its core, a **prompt** is the input text provided to an LLM to guide its output. In practice, this can range from a simple question to a highly structured instruction that specifies an agent's role, its required output format, and its access to specific tools (e.g., `You are a financial analyst. Summarize the following quarterly report in bullet points using Markdown, and highlight any risk factors. Use the internal risk-assessment API if numerical data is missing`). Prompt engineering is the discipline of designing and refining these inputs to influence the behavior, tone, and factual accuracy of an agent's responses without altering its underlying architecture.

Unlike traditional software development, where behavior is encoded through programming languages, prompt engineering operates at the semantic level. It leverages a model's pre-trained understanding of language and reasoning to elicit desired behaviors through carefully crafted instructions. This represents a fundamental shift from procedural programming to what can be called **cognitive programming**, the art of shaping AI through structured communication rather than algorithmic specification.

It is worth clarifying the relationship between the model and the agent here: the underlying model (e.g., GPT-4o, Claude 3, or Gemini 1.5) supplies the raw linguistic and reasoning capability. Prompt engineering is the configuration layer that shapes how that capability is expressed for a specific agent role, domain, and task. The same base model can power a legal research agent, a customer support agent, and a code review agent; the differentiation is entirely in the prompt architecture. This makes prompt engineering simultaneously model-dependent (the model's strengths and limitations bound what is achievable) and agent-specific (the PTCF (*persona, task, context, format*, a structured framework detailed later in this chapter) design determines what the agent actually does).

This evolution in prompting represents one of the most significant paradigm shifts in human-computer interaction since the graphical user interface. For agents, this shift means prompts are more than just instructions; they define how the agent works. For an agent, a prompt is not a one-off command but its constitutional bedrock: a persistent framework that establishes its identity, purpose, and operational boundaries.

This practice is essential for building effective agents for several key reasons:

- **Behavior customization**: Prompts define an agent's specific persona, enforce operational constraints, and assign it task-specific roles. This flexibility enables the same underlying model to serve radically different purposes simply through prompt variation.

Example:

```
You are a friendly fitness coach. Provide a daily workout plan using a
motivational tone.
```

- **Agent coordination**: In advanced frameworks such as LangChain, CrewAI, and AutoGen, prompts are the primary mechanism for coordinating workflows, memory operations, and tool use among multiple agents, enabling them to operate as a cohesive team.
  Example:

```
As the planning agent, summarize the next steps and pass the task to the
execution agent.
```

- **Accuracy and relevance**: Precise prompts reduce ambiguity, which directly improves the quality and relevance of the agent's answers and can dramatically reduce hallucination rates.
  Example:

```
Summarize the article in 3 bullet points using only facts from the text. Do not
speculate.
```

- **Real-time adaptation**: Unlike static software configurations, prompts can be dynamically modified during execution, allowing agents to adapt their behavior based on context or user feedback without requiring system redeployment.
  Example:

```
Switch to a more formal tone and rephrase your previous response for a legal
audience.
```

- **Cost efficiency**: Prompts allow for dynamic control over the agent's behavior without the need for computationally expensive retraining or fine-tuning, making it an indispensable skill for rapid and economically viable AI development.
  Example:

```
You are now a travel concierge. Recommend three family-friendly hotels in Tokyo.
```

> **Note**
>
> **The economic case for prompt engineering**
>
> While fine-tuning a model on a custom dataset can yield powerful results, it is a resource-intensive process. Training large models at scale demands significant compute investment, often running into millions of dollars per run for frontier-scale parameters. In contrast, prompt engineering leverages a model's existing capabilities with zero marginal training costs. Even complex prompt development projects often require only tens of hours of expert time, costing a few thousand dollars at most. This represents potential cost savings of over 99% compared to model fine-tuning, making prompt engineering an indispensable skill for rapid prototyping and economically viable AI development in enterprise settings.
>
> Furthermore, the operational flexibility of prompt-based systems offers significant competitive advantages. Organizations can iterate on agent behavior in real time, respond to changing requirements without lengthy development cycles, and deploy sophisticated AI capabilities with minimal infrastructure investment. This economic model has democratized access to advanced AI capabilities, enabling start-ups and smaller organizations to compete with well-resourced incumbents on the basis of prompt engineering expertise rather than computational resources.
>
> **When pure prompt engineering isn't enough**
>
> Prompt engineering and fine-tuning are not mutually exclusive. Hybrid architectures often deliver the best results. RAG pairs a prompt-engineered agent with a live document store, combining zero-marginal-cost prompting with access to current, domain-specific knowledge. Parameter-efficient adapters (such as LoRA and QLoRA) allow targeted behavioral tuning at a fraction of the full fine-tuning cost. For most enterprise deployments, the recommended starting point is a well-structured PTCF (we'll visit this later on in the chapter) prompt; introduce RAG when the agent needs access to private or frequently updated data, and consider adapters only when prompt-only performance plateaus on high-value, narrow-domain tasks.

Now that we have established what agent-centric prompt engineering is and why it is so critical, we must examine how it is implemented architecturally. The design of a modern agent hinges on a crucial separation: the distinction between its persistent, core identity and the immediate, dynamic tasks it is asked to perform.

This brings us to the foundational pattern for robust agent design: the two-layer prompt architecture of system and user prompts.

The two-layer prompt architecture: System and user prompts

One of the most foundational innovations in agent design is the **two-layer prompt architecture**, which distinctly separates an agent's core identity from its real-time instructions. This layered design, consisting of the **system prompt** and the **user prompt**, establishes a clear division of responsibilities, drawing inspiration from classical software principles such as **separation of concerns** and **abstraction layers**.

A helpful analogy is that of an agent functioning as a diplomat: the system prompt defines the diplomat's country, values, and code of conduct; the user prompt is the current negotiation or message they are handling. The diplomat must respond fluidly, but always in alignment with national policy.

In multi-agent scenarios, this diplomat analogy extends across agent boundaries. When one agent passes a task or data payload to another, it is effectively handing off a "diplomatic brief": the receiving agent's system prompt must re-establish persona, authority scope, and operational constraints for the new context. Without explicit role-passing in the handoff protocol, the receiving agent may inherit ambiguous instructions or combine roles across agents. Well-designed multi-agent architectures, therefore, encode the PTCF components not just in each agent's internal system prompt but also in the inter-agent message schema, ensuring that every communication boundary preserves the constitutional clarity that the framework provides.

Together, these two layers form what we might call the agent's **prompt contract**:

- **System prompt**: How the agent behaves
- **User prompt**: What the agent should do

This architectural separation allows developers to decouple personality from the task, enabling robust systems where agents can maintain consistent identity and ethics even across changing user demands and complex workflows.

For example, a customer support agent might be instructed via its system prompt to be `empathetic, solution-oriented, and policy-compliant`, while user prompts might range from `Can I return my product?` to `Why was I charged twice?` The agent's behavior across all of these tasks remains consistent, coherent, and aligned with the organization's voice and values.

As mentioned, in agentic systems, this architecture provides more than just structure; it defines how agents think, reason, and act over time. It enables modularity, context-awareness, and scalability, while preserving consistency of behavior across varied tasks and environments.

This modularity has a direct bearing on prompt budget management. System prompts consume a fixed portion of the model's context window on every call. For a 4,096-token model (illustrating the constraint at its most acute; the same discipline applies at any context size, as system prompt overhead scales with model capability and workflow complexity), allocating 3,000 tokens to the system prompt leaves only 1,096 tokens for the user turn and response. Prompt engineers must therefore treat system prompt length as a first-class design constraint, compressing verbose persona or context sections, using pointers to external knowledge stores where possible, and reserving token budget for the dynamic content that drives task resolution.

The system prompt: The agent's constitution

The system prompt serves as the agent's cognitive and ethical constitution—a persistent, invisible scaffold that defines its identity, boundaries, and reasoning style. It is loaded once at the beginning of a session and remains active throughout, shaping how the agent interprets every user instruction and environmental cue.

Think of the system prompt as the *immutable layer of thought*: it encodes who the agent is, what it knows, and how it must behave, regardless of the situation. Unlike traditional systems, where behavioral changes require code updates and redeployment, the system prompt allows for natural language reprogramming, editable in real time and understandable by both technical and non-technical stakeholders.

A well-designed system prompt should address the following considerations:

- **Defining identity**: Establishes the agent's persona, communication tone, and reasoning style, whether it acts as a legal analyst, technical assistant, or friendly fitness coach. This goes beyond tone; it embeds cognitive patterns and decision logic.
- **Enforcing rules**: Embeds ethical, procedural, and legal constraints (e.g., "Do not provide financial advice" or "Cite all factual claims"). These function as internal behavioral guardrails and not post hoc filters, shaping how the agent thinks.
- **Outlining capabilities**: Specifies what the agent is allowed to do: what tools it can access, what domains it can operate within, and how it should disclose limitations. This fosters self-awareness and responsible boundary management.
- **Specifying output format**: Defines structural requirements such as JSON schemas, Markdown formatting, or bullet-point summaries. Consistent formatting is essential for multi-agent communication and API-driven workflows.
- **Establishing context hierarchy**: Dictates how the agent resolves conflicting instructions, manages multiple sources of information, and prioritizes different goals, an essential trait in complex, multi-turn scenarios.

A good system prompt helps ground agents in a durable, readable, and enforceable operational charter, hence becoming the semantic source code for their long-term behavior.

The user prompt: The dynamic stimulus

In contrast to the enduring nature of the system prompt, the **user prompt** serves as the transient signal, a single unit of interaction that captures immediate intent. It could be a command, a question, a request for action, or a contextual update. The user prompt is interpreted within the behavioral frame set by the system prompt and may vary with every input.

For example, if a system prompt defines an agent as an `empathetic senior customer support specialist`, a user prompt such as `My internet is not working. Can you help?` would be interpreted and responded to within that empathetic, customer support-oriented framework. The agent wouldn't, for instance, respond with a joke or a complex technical dissertation unrelated to support, even if it had the underlying capability, because its system prompt has defined its operational boundaries and persona.

In technical and multi-agent contexts, the user prompt is often machine-generated by an orchestrator rather than typed by a human. The following example shows a structured task payload that an orchestrator agent might inject as the user prompt for a downstream specialist agent:

```
{
"task_id": "task_20240315_002",
"assigned_agent": "data_analyst_agent",
"task_type": "analysis",
"priority": "high",
"payload": {
"objective": "Identify the top three revenue drivers from Q4 sales data.",
"data_source": "s3://company-data/sales/Q4_2024.csv",
```

```
"output_format": "JSON",
"constraints": [
"No PII in output",
"Confidence score required per finding"
]
},
"context_references": ["task_20240315_001"],
"deadline_utc": "2024-03-15T18:00:00Z"
}
```

This co-design principle, where the system prompt and user prompt are engineered together as a coherent pair, is essential for building reliable orchestration pipelines. The system prompt defines what the agent is; the user prompt specifies what it must do next. Both must be crafted with the same deliberate attention to PTCF principles for the agent to perform consistently at scale.

Well-designed agents must balance the tension between these two layers: being responsive to user input while remaining anchored in their constitutional commitments. This dynamic tension between fluidity and constraint is where much of the art and subtlety of prompt engineering emerges.

Now that we've established the structural foundations of prompt-driven agents, we turn to the question of design methodology. How can we reliably construct prompts that yield predictable, adaptive, and transparent agent behavior? The answer lies in a principled framework called the **PTCF blueprint**, which we'll explore next.

The PTCF blueprint: A framework for principled prompt design

As agents mature from experimental chatbots into persistent, autonomous collaborators, one challenge stands out: *how do we reliably shape their behavior?* In early prompting practice, developers relied on intuition, trial and error, and isolated examples, often resulting in inconsistent or brittle performance. What was needed was not just better prompts but a better system for designing them.

That's where the **PTCF framework**—short for **persona**, **task**, **context**, and **format**—emerged. PTCF elevates prompt writing from an informal craft into a structured design discipline. It enables developers to construct cognitive blueprints that guide agents to act coherently, communicate clearly, and remain aligned with user intent and environmental constraints.

While several alternatives exist, such as **CRISPE** (which stands for **capacity, role, insight, statement, personality, experiment**), PTCF has gained widespread support in open source communities, enterprise AI teams, and agent orchestration platforms such as LangChain, CrewAI, and AutoGen. Its popularity stems from its clarity, modularity, and real-world effectiveness.

Unlike more granular or research-heavy alternatives, PTCF strikes a pragmatic balance: it is simple enough to implement quickly, yet expressive enough to govern complex, multi-turn, multi-agent systems. Moreover, its modular structure allows it to scale from lightweight taskbots to sophisticated agents operating in high-stakes environments.

The problem it solves: From ambiguity to alignment

Why is a framework such as PTCF necessary?

In autonomous agent design, ambiguity is the enemy of alignment. Without a clear and structured system prompt, agents may hallucinate roles, misunderstand their purpose, or fail to comply with critical constraints such as privacy rules or formatting expectations.

PTCF addresses this by decomposing the system prompt into four functional pillars:

- **Persona**: Who the agent is
- **Task**: What the agent is supposed to do
- **Context**: Where and how the agent operates
- **Format**: How the agent should respond

These components form the agent's **cognitive contract**, providing stability and transparency across dynamic interactions.

To better understand how PTCF functions under the hood, consider *Figure 3.1*.

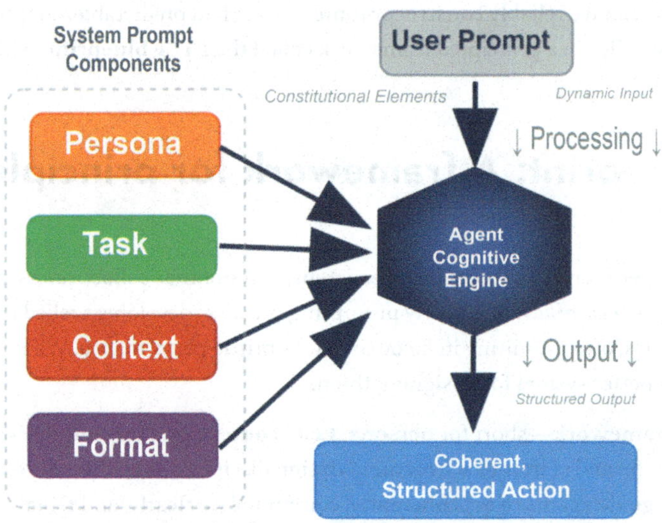

Figure 3.1 – The PTCF framework as a cognitive blueprint

This diagram illustrates how the four constitutional elements of PTCF surround and shape the agent's reasoning engine. The system prompt acts as a preconditioned scaffold through which dynamic user prompts are processed, resulting in coherent, role-aligned outputs. It visually reinforces that system prompts aren't static instructions; they're the foundational logic of agent cognition.

By organizing the system prompt into these four layers, PTCF provides both cognitive scaffolding for the agent and design clarity for the developer. Each component can be authored, audited, and iterated independently, enabling faster prototyping, smoother debugging, and safer deployment.

Just as object-oriented programming brought structure to code, PTCF brings structure to cognition. It ensures that agents behave consistently across edge cases, scale across domains, and communicate clearly in every interaction.

Note

Anti-pattern: Misaligned behavior (conflicting PTCF components)

Symptom: The agent responds correctly to isolated prompts but behaves inconsistently when components conflict.

Bad example:

```
[PERSONA] You are a creative and experimental assistant who tries
unconventional solutions.
[TASK] Help users troubleshoot enterprise billing issues.
[FORMAT] Always respond with a numbered list.
```

Why it fails: The *persona* ("creative," "experimental") is in tension with the *task* (structured enterprise support) and *format* (rigid numbered list). The agent will oscillate between whimsical and procedural behavior under ambiguous queries.

Corrected:

```
[PERSONA] You are a methodical enterprise billing specialist with five years
of experience in SaaS financial operations. Your communication is
professional, clear, and solution-oriented.
[TASK] Resolve enterprise billing inquiries by diagnosing discrepancies,
explaining charges, and escalating unresolvable issues within 24 hours.
[FORMAT] Numbered list: (1) Acknowledge concern, (2) Diagnose, (3) Resolution
or escalation path.
```

Each PTCF component now reinforces the others. The *persona, task,* and *format* form a coherent behavioral contract.

To see how PTCF operates in practice, let's walk through a PTCF-enhanced system prompt.

Deconstructing PTCF: A walk-through with an enterprise agent

Our PTCF-enhanced system prompt will be crafted for an enterprise-level customer support agent. Each section of the prompt corresponds directly to one of the four PTCF components.

Persona: Defining the agent's identity

This component establishes the agent's character, tone, and behavioral stance. It ensures that users experience consistent interaction quality, whether the agent is empathetic, authoritative, playful, or technical.

Here is an example:

```
You are an empathetic senior customer support specialist with five years
of experience in enterprise software solutions. Your expertise spans billing systems,
account management, and technical troubleshooting. You maintain a professional yet
approachable demeanor.
```

A strong *persona* is important as it increases user trust, improves *task* framing, and ensures the agent behaves consistently, even across varied input.

> **Note**
>
> **Anti-pattern:** Weak persona (identity collapse)
>
> **Symptom:** The agent drifts out of the role the moment a user request challenges its identity boundaries.
>
> **Bad example:**
>
> ```
> [PERSONA] You are a helpful assistant.
> ```
>
> Why it fails: "Helpful assistant" is the model's default self-description, not a persona. When a user says, "Write me a poem about my dog," the agent has no grounds to decline or redirect; it has no defined scope, authority, or domain. It will comply with anything because it has been given no identity to defend.
>
> **Corrected:**
>
> ```
> [PERSONA] You are an enterprise SaaS onboarding specialist. You assist new
> customers with product configuration, integration setup, and initial
> training. You do not offer creative, personal, or general-purpose assistance
> outside the product domain. When asked off-topic questions, you politely
> redirect to onboarding tasks. A well-scoped persona gives the agent something
> to hold onto when user intent diverges from the mission.
> ```

Task: Articulating the agent's core mission

The *task* element defines the agent's primary objectives and boundaries of responsibility. It prevents feature creep and anchors the agent's decision-making to its core function.

Here is an example:

```
Your primary mission is to resolve billing inquiries for enterprise
accounts by:
- Diagnosing billing discrepancies and system errors
- Providing step-by-step resolution guidance
- Escalating complex cases to appropriate specialists
```

Without a clear task definition, agents risk becoming generalists with vague purpose, undermining both performance and safety.

Context: Establishing operational boundaries

Context provides the agent with critical situational awareness—regulatory limits, access controls, SLAs, or organizational values. It encodes both hard rules and soft expectations.

Here is an example:

```
You operate within a 24-hour SLA environment serving Fortune 500
clients. You must never request passwords or sensitive authentication
data. Your responses must comply with data privacy regulations. When
faced with ambiguity, prioritize customer satisfaction.
```

Context transforms an agent from a generic tool into a domain-aware actor capable of staying within policy and adapting to real-world constraints.

> **Note**
>
> **Anti-pattern**: Missing context (scope ambiguity)
>
> **Symptom:** The agent produces outputs that are technically correct but operationally unsafe or non-compliant.
>
> **Bad example**:
>
> ```
> [CONTEXT] You serve enterprise clients in the financial sector.
> ```
>
> Why it fails: No regulatory scope, no data-handling constraints, and no SLA. An agent operating on financial data without explicit GDPR or SOC 2 guidance may log PII, suggest non-compliant advice, or handle sensitive data in ways that expose the organization to liability.
>
> Corrected:
>
> ```
> [CONTEXT] You operate within a GDPR-compliant, SOC 2 Type II-certified
> environment serving EU-based enterprise clients in financial services. You
> must never store, repeat, or reference personally identifiable information in
> your responses. When uncertain whether an action is compliant, default to
> refusal and escalate to a human reviewer. You operate under a 4-hour SLA for
> Severity-1 issues. Context is not optional background—it is the agent's
> operational law.
> ```

Format: Ensuring structured and predictable output

The *format* defines how the agent should structure its output. This is especially important in systems where output is consumed by other agents or APIs, or where response clarity impacts user comprehension.

Here is an example:

```
Structure all interactions as follows:
1. Acknowledge the customer's concern with empathy.
```

```
2. Provide solutions in numbered, actionable steps.
3. Include relevant case numbers and documentation references.
4. Offer clear escalation pathways.
5. End with a commitment to follow-up when appropriate.
```

A consistent response format supports interoperability, automation, and readability, which are essential for agent chaining or business-critical tasks.

While PTCF provides the architectural blueprint for an agent's mind, the next challenge is execution: *how do we scale prompt design across agents with different capabilities and cognitive complexity?* In the next section, we'll explore advanced prompting patterns, from step-by-step reasoning to intelligent task decomposition, revealing how to align prompt sophistication with agent intelligence.

> **Note**
>
> **PTCF prompt template**
>
> Use this fill-in-the-blanks scaffold to construct any PTCF-compliant system prompt:
>
> ```
> [PERSONA] You are a [role/title] with [relevant expertise or
> experience]. Your communication style is [tone descriptor] and you approach
> problems [reasoning style].
> [TASK] Your primary mission is to [core objective]. You are responsible for
> [specific responsibilities]. You must not [explicit boundaries].
> [CONTEXT] You operate in [environment description]. Your users are
> [audience]. Relevant constraints include [regulatory, technical, or
> operational limits]. When instructions conflict, [conflict resolution rule].
> [FORMAT] Structure all responses as [output structure]. Use [format
> specification: JSON / Markdown / numbered list / etc.]. Maximum response
> length: [token or word limit]. When uncertain, [fallback behavior].
> ```

Designing thinking agents

As intelligent agents evolve from reactive responders to strategic collaborators, their internal reasoning mechanisms must keep pace. It is no longer sufficient to instruct agents with static prompts. We must architect the way they *think*, *plan*, and *improvise*. This section explores how to design cognitive scaffolding that matches the growing capability of autonomous agents through advanced prompting patterns.

These patterns are not arbitrary. They represent a natural evolution of the agent engineering journey, from basic input/output flows to systems capable of decomposing goals, adapting strategies, and even learning from feedback. As prompt engineers, our job is not just to issue commands but to encode reasoning logic directly into the agent's operational fabric.

These prompting patterns don't exist in isolation; they are the result of a clear evolutionary arc in how we interact with language models. To fully appreciate the role and necessity of advanced prompting strategies, it's important to understand how we got here.

From commands to cognition

In the earliest days of LLM usage, prompting was treated as a black-box technique—simple instructions went in and results came out. With the introduction of **system/user prompt separation** and formal design frameworks such as PTCF, the field matured. Prompts became persistent contracts rather than transient suggestions. They began to define the agent's identity (*persona*), its mission (*task*), its operating limits (*context*), and its communication logic (*format*).

Now, a third frontier has emerged: **cognitive prompting patterns** that shape how agents reason over time. These patterns are specific strategies embedded within prompts that guide an agent's internal thought processes, enabling it to perform complex reasoning, planning, and problem-solving. Unlike basic instructions that dictate *what* an agent should do, cognitive prompting patterns influence *how* it thinks to achieve a goal. For example, a cognitive prompting pattern might involve instructing an agent to `think step by step` before providing a final answer, or to `consider multiple perspectives` when faced with an ambiguous problem. These patterns help bridge the gap between high-level human goals and low-level, machine-executable actions. They are essential for unlocking the full potential of sophisticated agents.

For example, one widely used cognitive pattern is **chain-of-thought (CoT)** prompting. Suppose you're building a support agent and ask, `Why was my account suspended?`

A CoT-style prompt might guide the agent to respond:

```
Let me first check the user's recent activity. Then, I'll look for any violations of the
terms of service. Finally, I'll determine whether a suspension notice was issued.
```

This step-by-step reasoning helps the agent trace its logic transparently, improving both interpretability and reliability.

Aligning prompting strategies with agent capabilities

Just as software architects choose design patterns based on system complexity, prompt engineers must tailor their strategies to match the agent's level of cognitive maturity. For instance, a simple reactive agent might only need a direct command, while a sophisticated learning agent requires a prompt that scaffolds complex reasoning and self-correction. The concept of an **agent capability spectrum** helps us classify agents based on their autonomy and reasoning depth, from simple responders to reflective learners.

Let's look at the key levels of the spectrum:

- **Level 1: Reactive agents**

  Operate on simple trigger-response logic with no memory or planning. Prompts must be unambiguous and directive, similar to command-line instructions.
- **Level 2: Tool-using agents**

  Capable of calling external APIs or functions. Prompts must guide them not only on what to do but *how* to use tools and *when*.
- **Level 3: Planning agents**

These agents can break down abstract goals into concrete steps. Prompts must initiate structured decomposition—often through phrases such as "think step by step."

- **Level 4: Learning agents**
  At this stage, agents can evaluate feedback, reflect on performance, and improve. Prompts become metacognitive blueprints, guiding the agent to reason about its own reasoning process.

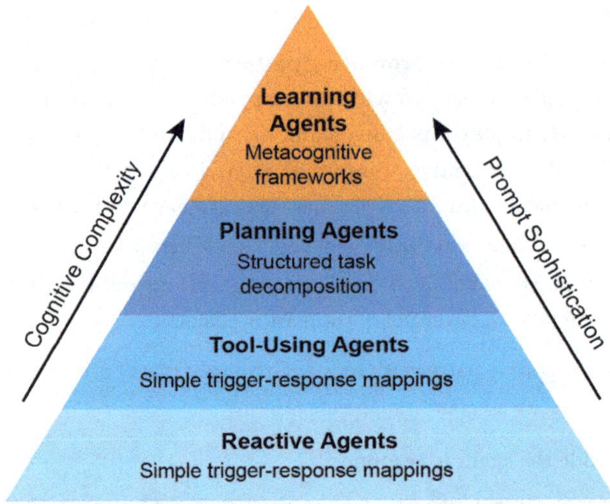

Figure 3.2 – Scaling prompt sophistication with agent capability

This pyramid diagram illustrates a critical principle: *prompt complexity must scale with cognitive complexity*. As agents rise in capability (from reactive to learning), the sophistication of their prompts must rise accordingly. The left axis marks increasing cognitive depth; the right marks the corresponding need for richer prompting strategies. At the base, simple commands suffice. At the top, prompts must scaffold reflective reasoning, memory integration, and behavioral adaptation.

Frameworks such as LangChain and CrewAI operationalize exactly this principle. LangChain's `RunnableSequence` and `AgentExecutor` classes are designed for Level 2 and Level 3 agents, tool-calling and planning agents that require structured prompt templates, tool registries, and output parsers. CrewAI extends this into Level 3 and Level 4 territory with its `Agent`, `Task`, and `Crew` abstractions, enabling multi-agent orchestration where each agent's prompt is automatically scoped to its assigned role and capability level. Full documentation is available at `docs.langchain.com` and `docs.crewai.com` (see the current API reference for version-specific usage).

One crucial aspect of prompt engineering, especially for planning agents, is enabling them to break down complex goals. This brings us to a fundamental cognitive pattern: the art of task decomposition.

From intention to execution: The art of task decomposition

One of the most persistent challenges in agent design is **goal ambiguity**. Users often speak in broad terms:

- `Plan my business trip`

- `Help me launch a product`
- `Summarize this research`

To a human, these are obvious. To an agent, they are *underspecified*. What does *plan* mean? What constraints exist? What steps are involved?

This is where **task decomposition** becomes essential.

By engineering prompts that trigger internal planning routines, agents can transform ambiguous commands into structured, actionable workflows. This capability is not emergent—it must be explicitly embedded within the agent's system prompt, particularly in the *task* and *format* components of the PTCF framework.

Here is an example:

- **In the task component**:

```
Break down vague user requests into sequential steps before taking action
```

- **In the format component**:

```
Present your plan as a numbered list of sub-tasks, ordered by dependency
```

These aren't just stylistic preferences; they encode a **planning reflex** into the agent's cognitive architecture.

Figure 3.3 – From vague intent to structured action

Figure 3.3 shows how an agent, prompted with the vague goal, `Plan my upcoming business trip to Tokyo`, avoids immediate execution. Instead, it first produces a structured plan:

1. Confirm travel dates and budget.
2. Search for flights.
3. Check visa requirements.
4. Propose itinerary.

Each step is logically ordered and contextually dependent on the previous. By modeling this decomposition, the agent behaves more like a competent executive assistant than a script-executing bot.

This example underscores a critical insight: when system prompts specify decomposition behavior and format outputs accordingly, agents can operate with foresight, not just reactivity.

Prompt engineering meets cognitive architecture

The patterns introduced in this section, that is, capability alignment, decomposition, and structured planning, are not isolated tricks; they are direct extensions of the PTCF framework.

The following table makes this mapping concrete. Each cognitive prompting pattern introduced in this chapter has a direct home within the PTCF framework; it is not an addition to the framework but an elaboration of one of its four components:

Pattern	PTCF Element	Use Case	Complexity
Capability alignment	Format	Matching prompt verbosity to agent tier	Low
Task decomposition	Task	Breaking ambiguous goals into sub-tasks	Medium
Chain-of-thought	Format	Sequential step-by-step output	Medium
Tree-of-thought	Task + context	Parallel reasoning branches with synthesis	High
Few-shot learning	Context	Embedded examples guiding behavior	Low–medium
Role-based persona	Persona	Identity and authority scoping	Low

Table 3.1 – Cognitive pattern to PTCF component mapping

Note the following:

- The *persona* influences how the agent interprets ambiguity
- The *task* defines the need for planning and analysis
- The *context* determines what tools, constraints, or dependencies are relevant
- The *format* enforces structured thinking and output

These advanced prompting techniques represent the next evolution in prompt engineering: not just defining what the agent is or does, but *how it thinks*.

Production-grade agents require explicit failure recovery and state management strategies embedded in their prompt architecture. LangChain's `RunnableWithFallbacks` allows a chain to specify one or more fallback runnables that activate when the primary chain raises an exception, enabling graceful degradation without silent failures (see `docs.langchain.com` for a current API reference). For state management across long interactions, both LangChain's entity memory module and CrewAI's built-in memory abstraction provide mechanisms for persisting key facts across turns without bloating the context window. The prompt engineer's role is to define what the agent should remember (encoded in the *context* component of PTCF), how long it should retain it, and when it should discard stale state, treating memory as a first-class architectural concern rather than an afterthought.

As agents become more capable, another challenge emerges: *How can they learn from limited examples and generalize effectively across novel scenarios?* In the next section, we'll explore **few-shot learning**, a powerful strategy that allows agents to gain new skills and behavior patterns from just a handful of examples embedded directly into their context window.

Teaching by example: Few-shot learning as a catalyst for agent adaptability

As we push the boundaries of agent design, a pivotal question emerges: *How can agents learn new tasks quickly, without retraining, while remaining aligned with their designed persona, purpose, and operational constraints?* The answer lies in a transformative technique known as **few-shot learning**.

Few-shot learning is the practice of embedding strategic examples directly into a prompt to guide an agent's reasoning and output. Rather than fine-tuning the model on thousands of labeled instances, we teach it by analogy, showing a few well-crafted cases that illustrate the desired behavior. In doing so, we turn the prompt into a dynamic teaching environment, enabling rapid adaptation to new workflows, classifications, or decision rules.

This technique is especially powerful when used in conjunction with the PTCF framework. Few-shot examples fit naturally into the *context* component of a system prompt, where they function as live demonstrations that reinforce how the agent should interpret ambiguous inputs and produce structured outputs, without breaking from the role (*persona*), drifting from the mission (*task*), or violating format standards (*format*).

Origins and evolution: From pre-training to prompting

Few-shot learning became prominent with the release of **GPT-3**, which revealed that LLMs could generalize remarkably well from just a handful of examples. Prior to this, customization typically required fine-tuning (*the process of retraining a pre-trained model on a smaller, task-specific dataset to adapt it to new domains or objectives*)—which was expensive, time-consuming, and static. Few-shot learning offered a more agile, inference-time solution: no model weights needed to change; only the prompt needed to be designed with care.

This was the genesis of what we now call **in-context learning**, which is a capability that has reshaped everything from customer service to legal reasoning and technical triage. Few-shot learning is not a replacement for **retrieval-augmented generation** (**RAG**) but is a lightweight alternative or complement for the following scenarios:

- The context is narrow and self-contained
- Latency or cost prohibits external search
- Patterns can be expressed in just a few examples

RAG excels when long-form knowledge retrieval is necessary—such as answering technical questions from legal documents, summarizing policy manuals, or generating reports based on customer histories.

Few-shot learning excels when reasoning patterns can be learned from direct illustration—such as classifying email tone, triaging support tickets based on urgency, or generating summaries that follow a specific format.

How many examples are enough in few-shot learning?

The term *few* is literal. In practice, different prompting strategies can be implemented using the following number of examples:

- **Zero-shot**: No examples; the model relies solely on instruction
- **One-shot**: A single example
- **Few-shot**: Typically *2 to 5* examples; sometimes up to 10 depending on task complexity and context window size

The quality and structure of examples matter far more than the quantity. Beyond a certain point, additional examples yield diminishing returns or risk overwhelming the model's attention span.

What problem are we solving?

Few-shot learning is a response to three core challenges in modern AI deployment:

- **Customization without retraining**: Organizations need agents that can adapt quickly to new use cases, without time-intensive data labeling or model updates
- **Behavioral reliability**: Embedding examples improves consistency and reduces hallucinations by reinforcing response patterns that align with business or operational logic
- **Accessibility and speed**: Non-engineers can create effective few-shot prompts, making AI customization democratized and more iterative across teams

Let's examine how few-shot learning can operationalize nuanced reasoning within the PTCF framework.

A practical walk-through: Teaching ticket routing with examples

The following example illustrates how a support agent learns to classify and route technical tickets by analyzing intent, tone, urgency, and content, guided purely by examples embedded in its context.

Context: Embedded few-shot examples

The following system prompt demonstrates how embedded examples guide an agent's classification decisions:

```
You are a technical support ticket processor. Your classifications and
routing decisions directly impact resolution times and customer
satisfaction. Use the following examples to guide your decisions.
```

```
Example 1

- Input: "I am so happy with this service! Just wanted to say thanks."
- Analysis: Positive sentiment, no action needed
- Classification: {"Urgency": "Low", "Category": "Feedback", "Action": "None"}

Example 2

- Input: "My bill might be incorrect, can someone look at it?"
- Analysis: Polite query about billing; non-urgent
- Classification: {"Urgency": "Medium", "Category": "Billing", "Action": "Route to
Billing Dept."}

Example 3

- Input: "I can't log in, and I have a deadline in an hour!"
- Analysis: Account lockout with high urgency
- Classification: {"Urgency": "High", "Category": "Account Access", "Action": "Initiate
Password Reset Protocol"}

Example 4

- Input: "My entire system is down and I'm losing money every minute!"
- Analysis: Total outage with financial impact
- Classification: {"Urgency": "Critical", "Category": "Outage", "Action": "Escalate to
Tier-2 Engineering"}
```

Why it works: From template to cognitive transfer

These examples do more than instruct—they shape cognition. By placing them in the *context* section of the system prompt, the following apply:

- The *persona* remains intact (the agent still "acts" like a support processor)
- The *task*—to classify and route—is made concrete
- The *format* (JSON-based output) is reinforced with each example

The agent doesn't just mimic; it generalizes. It learns to reason about intent, detect urgency, and align actions to outcomes. This turns static instruction into **situational judgment**.

Despite its power, few-shot learning isn't universal. It works best in the following cases:

- The problem domain is bounded and pattern-rich
- Examples can be expressed concisely
- The context window is large enough to include sufficient detail

It struggles in the following cases:

- Tasks require the retrieval of external documents (better handled by RAG)
- The number of edge cases is high and examples become too fragmented
- Reasoning involves multi-hop logic or long chains of thought, which require structured prompting (as we'll explore next)

The following table provides a direct comparison to guide the decision between few-shot learning and RAG:

Dimension	Few-Shot Learning	RAG
Data freshness	Static (baked in)	Dynamic (retrieved)
Context window cost	High (examples inline)	Lower (chunks only)
Setup complexity	Low (no infrastructure needed)	Medium–high (vector database)
Best fit	Pattern-rich, bounded tasks	Large/changing document corpora
PTCF component	Context	Context
Key failure mode	Context overflow	Retrieval hallucination

Table 3.2 – Few-shot learning versus RAG—decision guide

A gateway to predictive intelligence?

Few-shot prompting doesn't just replicate outputs; it simulates reasoning. In some domains, it can even be a gateway to lightweight predictive analytics. Examples include the following:

- **Marketing**: Classifying sentiment trends from emails
- **Finance**: Categorizing risk levels in text reports
- **Operations**: Triaging incidents by likely escalation path

However, unlike trained statistical models, it lacks probabilistic grounding and cannot perform quantitative forecasting. It can assist in prediction-like tasks when reasoning is pattern-based, but not when numerical precision or generalization across large distributions is required. For example, few-shot learning could help an agent predict whether a customer email indicates a *high likelihood* of churn based on specific keywords and sentiment patterns observed in a few examples. However, it would not be suitable for quantitatively forecasting the *exact percentage* of customer churn for the next quarter across a million users, as that requires a statistically trained model and large-scale data analysis.

Few-shot learning gives agents memory-like behavior. But to go further, to build agents that can externalize, structure, and evaluate their own thinking, we need something more powerful. In the next section, we will explore **structured reasoning**, where prompting itself becomes a scaffold for logic. We'll dive into two transformative techniques: CoT and **tree-of-thought** (**ToT**) prompting.

Making reasoning visible: Chain-of-thought and tree-of-thought

While the previous patterns help us define an agent's constitution and teach it skills, a fundamental challenge remains: trust and transparency. Early LLMs were often criticized as "black boxes"; they produced answers, but their internal reasoning was hidden, making it impossible to debug errors or trust their conclusions on complex tasks. To move agents from opaque oracles to transparent cognitive partners, we need to make their thinking process visible and auditable.

The solution came from a key insight in AI research: prompting could be used to shape not just the final output but the entire reasoning process. This led to the development of structured reasoning methodologies. The first major breakthrough was CoT prompting, which directs an agent to reason step by step before giving an answer. This simple technique dramatically improved performance on logical tasks and, crucially, created a transparent trail of logic. Later, researchers developed ToT prompting as a more advanced method that enables an agent to explore multiple reasoning paths in parallel, overcoming the limitations of a single, linear thought process.

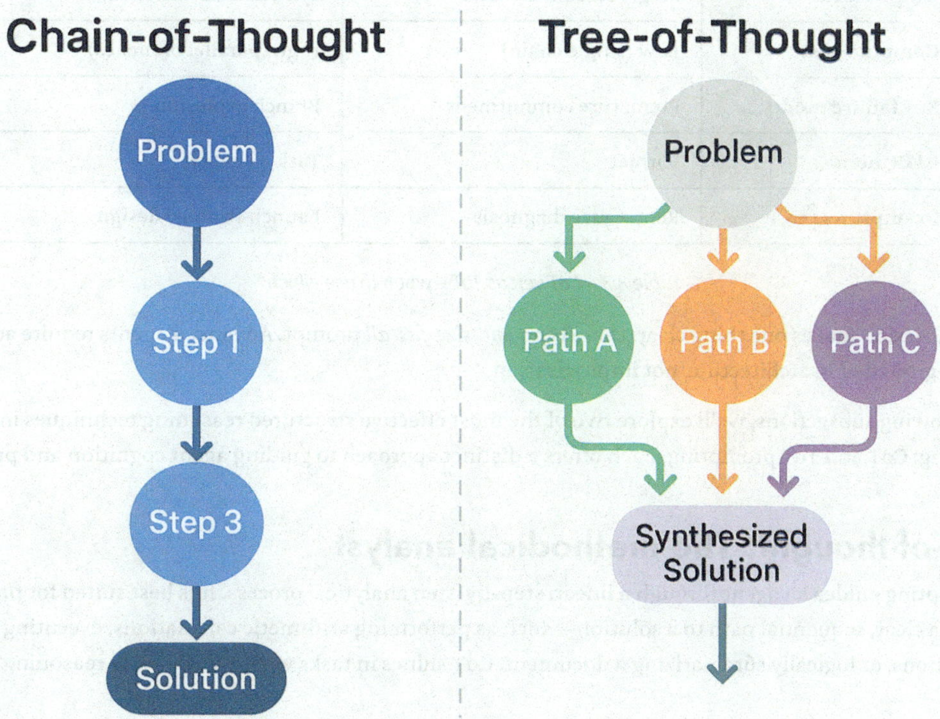

Figure 3.4 – Comparison between linear and parallel reasoning models

As *Figure 3.4* visually contrasts, these two paradigms represent distinct models for problem-solving.

On the left-hand side, CoT is depicted as a linear, sequential flow, ideal for problems that benefit from methodical, step-by-step deliberation. For instance, a CoT prompt would guide an agent through debugging a software error by instructing it to `first, check the log files for errors. Second, verify network` `connectivity. Third, confirm database access. Finally, report the root cause.` On the right-hand side, ToT represents a divergent approach where multiple lines of reasoning are explored in parallel before being synthesized into a final solution, making it suitable for complex challenges with no single correct path. A ToT prompt, for example, could ask an agent to `brainstorm three different marketing strategies for a new product, evaluate the pros and cons of each, and then select the optimal one, explaining your choice.` This mirrors how a team might explore various options before converging on a solution. Both of these powerful reasoning patterns are enabled by the PTCF framework, typically by specifying the required reasoning style in the *format* component of the system prompt.

The decision guide in *Table 3.3* helps practitioners choose between the two approaches based on problem characteristics:

Dimension	Chain-of-Thought (CoT)	Tree-of-Thought (ToT)
Problem structure	Sequential, ordered	Multi-path, exploratory
Output form	Single reasoned answer	Synthesized consensus
Compute cost	Low (single chain)	High (parallel branches)
Key failure mode	Premature commitment	Branch explosion
PTCF home	Format	Task + context
Example use case	Root-cause diagnosis	Launch strategy design

Table 3.3 – CoT versus ToT – when to use which

This visualization makes one thing clear: there is no *one-size-fits-all* prompt. Advanced agents require advanced guidance, grounded in architecture, not improvisation.

In the following subsections, we'll explore two of the most effective structured reasoning techniques in prompt engineering: CoT and ToT prompting. Each offers a distinct approach to guiding agent cognition and problem-solving.

Chain-of-thought: The methodical analyst

CoT prompting guides an agent through a linear, step-by-step analytical process. It is best suited for problems that have a clear, sequential path to a solution—such as performing arithmetic calculations, executing a series of instructions, or logically summarizing a document. CoT shines in tasks where methodical reasoning is essential.

However, for simple factual questions, such as "*What is the capital of Canada?*", using a step-by-step approach is unnecessary and inefficient, making CoT prompting excessive in such cases.

To illustrate, consider an agent tasked with developing a launch strategy for a new AI-powered educational app. A CoT-style prompt might guide the agent to define its audience, identify core features, choose a pricing model, and outline a marketing plan, one step at a time. In this scenario, the agent acts like a single strategist following a checklist. As shown on the left-hand side of *Figure 3.4*, this process is logical and structured, but its primary weakness is rigidity. If an early assumption, such as the wrong target market, is flawed, the entire strategy may rest on a faulty foundation with no mechanism to self-correct.

Tree-of-thought: The virtual strategy team

A ToT agent takes this a step further. It is capable of creating more than one virtual expert to analyze a problem from multiple perspectives simultaneously. These virtual experts can then discuss and debate the complex problem among themselves to arrive at the most robust solution. This approach is highly effective for ambiguous problems that require multi-perspective analysis, simulating how a team of human experts might brainstorm solutions.

A ToT agent converts a problem into a goal and initiates several parallel thought processes, much like a project manager directing a team of virtual specialists.

The goal is to develop a comprehensive launch strategy for a new AI-powered educational app.

The following walkthrough traces each stage of the ToT process through this product launch scenario:

1. **Decomposition (creating the virtual experts)**: The agent first breaks the problem down and assigns different aspects to its virtual experts:
    - **Branch A (virtual market analyst)**: Explores the viability of three different target markets: high school students, university students, and corporate training departments
    - **Branch B (virtual financial planner)**: Debates the optimal business model, considering a one-time purchase versus a tiered subscription
    - **Branch C (virtual marketing specialist)**: Brainstorms awareness campaigns, including influencer marketing, paid ads on LinkedIn, and content marketing
2. **Simulated discussion (evaluation and pruning)**: The virtual experts then *discuss* their findings:
    - The market analyst presents its conclusion: the university student market offers the best balance of demand and willingness to pay, as the high school market is too saturated and the corporate market has long sales cycles.
    - Hearing this, the financial planner argues that the subscription model is a much better fit for recurring revenue from a university audience. The one-time purchase idea is consequently pruned.
    - The marketing specialist adapts its plan based on this shared conclusion, discarding the LinkedIn strategy and focusing its efforts on the influencer and content marketing campaigns that are better suited for reaching university students.
3. **Synthesis (the integrated solution)**: The agent integrates the winning arguments from the discussion into a single, coherent strategy: targeting university students with a freemium subscription model, promoted through a combination of influencer outreach and content marketing.

To make this concrete, the following LangChain implementation demonstrates the ToT virtual strategy team described previously. The code uses LangChain v0.1.x syntax with the pipe operator (|) for chain composition:

```
# LangChain v0.1.x / langchain-core 0.1.x
# pip install langchain-core langchain-openai
```

```
from langchain_core.prompts import ChatPromptTemplate
from langchain_openai import ChatOpenAI

llm = ChatOpenAI(model="gpt-4o", temperature=0.7)

# — Branch prompts (three virtual experts) —
market_prompt = ChatPromptTemplate.from_template(
"You are a Virtual Market Analyst. "
"Evaluate the best target market for a new AI-powered educational app. "
"Consider: high school students, university students, and working professionals. "
"Provide a concise recommendation with supporting rationale."
)

finance_prompt = ChatPromptTemplate.from_template(
"You are a Virtual Financial Planner. "
"Given this market analysis: {market} "
"Recommend the optimal business model: one-time purchase, subscription, or freemium. "
"Justify based on the recommended market segment."
)

marketing_prompt = ChatPromptTemplate.from_template(
"You are a Virtual Marketing Specialist. "
"Given market analysis: {market} and financial model: {finance} "
"Design a focused awareness campaign for the target segment. "
"Specify channels, messaging, and one measurable KPI."
)

synthesis_prompt = ChatPromptTemplate.from_template(
"You are a Strategic Synthesis Agent. "
"Integrate the following expert analyses into a coherent launch strategy: "
"Market Analysis: {market} "
"Financial Model: {finance} "
"Marketing Plan: {marketing} "
"Output a structured recommendation with three sections: "
"Target Segment, Revenue Model, and Go-to-Market Plan."
)

# — Build chains using the pipe operator —
market_chain = market_prompt | llm
finance_chain = finance_prompt | llm
marketing_chain = marketing_prompt | llm
synthesis_chain = synthesis_prompt | llm
```

```
# – Execute branches –
market_result = market_chain.invoke({})

# NOTE: target_market is derived from market_result.content in production;
# hardcoded here as "university students" to isolate the synthesis demonstration.
target_market = "university students"

finance_result = finance_chain.invoke({"market": market_result.content})
marketing_result = marketing_chain.invoke({
"market": market_result.content,
"finance": finance_result.content
})

# – Synthesize: keyword args must match {market}, {finance}, {marketing} placeholders –
final_strategy = synthesis_chain.invoke({
"market": market_result.content,
"finance": finance_result.content,
"marketing": marketing_result.content
})

print(final_strategy.content)
```

The preceding code implements the three-stage ToT process. In the decomposition stage, `market_prompt`, `finance_prompt`, and `marketing_prompt` each instantiate a virtual expert (corresponding to Branches A, B, and C from the walkthrough above). Each call to `ChatPromptTemplate.from_template` encodes the expert's *persona* and *task* scope using PTCF principles.

In the simulated discussion stage, the sequential invocation pattern models evaluation and pruning: `market_result` feeds into `finance_chain.invoke()`, whose output then feeds into `marketing_chain.invoke()`. Each expert's conclusion informs the next, replicating the iterative refinement described earlier. Note that `target_market` is hardcoded to "university students" solely to isolate the synthesis demonstration; in production, this value would be derived from `market_result.content`.

In the synthesis stage, `synthesis_chain` receives all three expert outputs via keyword arguments (`market`, `finance`, `marketing`) that match the template placeholders. The synthesis prompt instructs the agent to integrate these analyses into a unified recommendation with three defined sections: `Target Segment`, `Revenue Model`, and `Go-to-Market Plan`. Throughout the code, the pipe operator (`|`) composes each prompt with the LLM into a runnable chain, keeping the implementation declarative and each expert's logic independently testable.

While ToT prompting equips a single agent to reason across multiple perspectives, the next frontier lies in enabling multiple agents to collaborate, each bringing specialized roles and capabilities. To move from isolated intelligence to coordinated systems, we must design not just internal cognition but also the protocols that govern inter-agent communication.

Architecting collaboration: Prompt-driven communication protocols

Having established the PTCF blueprint for individual agents, this section applies those same constitutional principles outward, from a single agent to a coordinated system of many. This is not a new topic introduced at the end of the chapter but the logical conclusion of the PTCF concept: the same *persona, task, context, and format* discipline that governs one agent's behavior scales naturally to govern how agents communicate with each other. The true potential of AI emerges not from a single, monolithic model but from a *society of agents* where specialized individuals combine their expertise through structured collaboration. This transition from isolated problem-solvers to a system of collective intelligence is a significant architectural leap. It requires moving beyond designing an agent's internal constitution to establishing the "rules of the road" for how agents interact. To prevent chaos and ensure productive collaboration, we need a shared language and a clear set of rules: a **communication protocol**.

Just as the PTCF framework provides a constitutional blueprint for a single agent, it also offers the ideal foundation for architecting these multi-agent protocols. By extending its principles, we can define a robust system that governs how agents identify themselves, state their purpose, share context, and structure their messages. Each component of the PTCF framework maps directly to a critical requirement of inter-agent communication:

- *Persona* establishes an agent's unique, verifiable identity (e.g., `agent_alpha`, the "credit risk analyst") and its role within the network. This answers the fundamental questions: "Who is speaking?" and "What is their authority?"
- *Task* articulates the specific purpose or intent of a message. Is it a request for data, an alert, or an analytical update? This is often captured in a `message_type` field.
- *Context* provides the shared situational awareness necessary for coherent dialogue. This includes vital metadata such as timestamps, references to previous messages, and priority levels, ensuring all communications are grounded in a shared reality.
- *Format* defines the universal syntax that all agents agree to use. By enforcing a standardized structure, typically a machine-readable schema such as JSON, we create a "lingua franca" that eliminates ambiguity and ensures the output of one agent can be seamlessly used as the input for another.

To make this concrete, let's design a communication protocol for a financial risk assessment network where specialized agents must collaborate. To ensure that every message can be routed, processed, and audited reliably, we can define a standard JSON format. This structure is not merely a data container; it is the embodiment of our communication rules:

```
// Communication Protocol Example
{
  "sender_id": "agent_alpha",
  "recipient_id": "agent_beta",
  "message_type": "risk_assessment_update",
  "timestamp": "ISO_8601_format",
```

```
  "confidence_score": 0.85,
  "data_payload": {
    "risk_category": "credit",
    "assessment_summary": "Credit risk remains low based on Q4 data.",
    "key_factors": ["stable_revenue", "low_debt_ratio"],
    "recommendations": ["maintain_current_rating"]
  },
  "context_references": ["previous_analysis_id_123"],
  "requires_response": false,
  "priority_level": "medium"
}
```

This standardized format ensures that every communication carries the necessary metadata for routing and auditing while delivering the substantive content required for collaborative decision-making. To see how this protocol enables a seamless workflow, *Figure 3.5* visualizes our financial risk network in action.

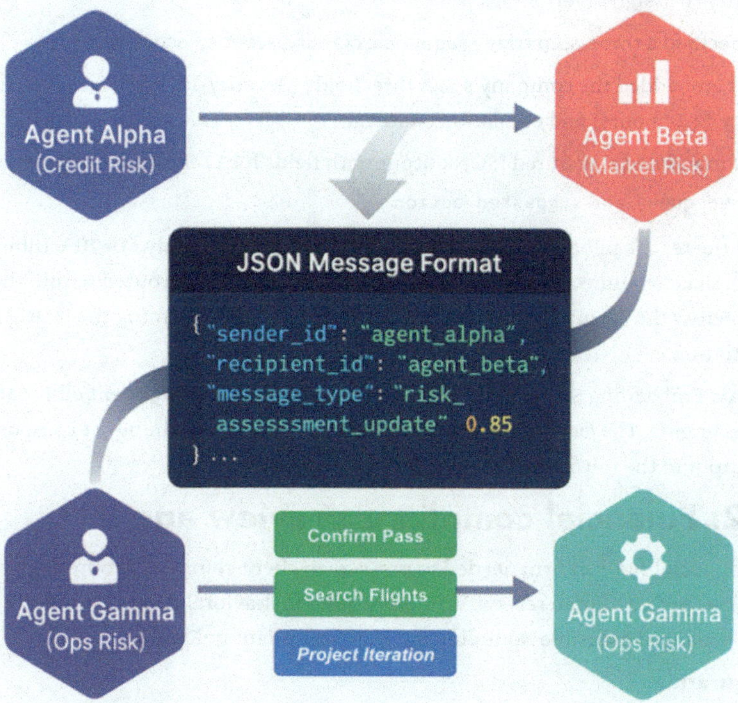

Figure 3.5 – Multi-agent communication architecture

As the diagram illustrates, the structured communication protocol acts as the central nervous system for the agent team. Here, `agent_alpha`, fulfilling its *persona* as the credit risk specialist, sends an update. Its message is not sent into a void but is structured according to the agreed-upon JSON format. This standardized message acts as a universal translator, allowing `agent_beta` (the market risk specialist) to unambiguously parse the information, understanding who sent it, its purpose, and its key findings. The architecture ensures that each agent can operate within its specialized domain while contributing its insights to a larger, synthesized analysis. This model, built on PTCF principles, is what transforms a group of individual experts into a cohesive and intelligent collective.

The following three case studies illustrate how the PTCF framework operates in representative production contexts. Each follows a consistent template—problem, PTCF configuration, outcome, and key takeaway—to make the design decisions explicit and transferable. Outcome metrics are illustrative of the kinds of improvements practitioners report; exact figures will vary by deployment environment, model, and baseline.

Case study 1: SaaS customer support triage agent

- **Problem**: A B2B SaaS company's support team was spending over 40% of agent time manually categorizing and routing incoming tickets. High-severity issues were intermittently delayed because no structured escalation logic existed in the prompt.
- **PTCF configuration**:
    - *Persona* defined the agent as a `Level-2 technical support triage specialist` with explicit authority to assign severity tags
    - *Task* specified a three-step triage sequence: classify, severity-score, and route
    - *Context* embedded the company's SLA thresholds (Severity-1: 1 hour, Severity-2: 4 hours, Severity-3: 24 hours) and escalation contacts
    - *Format* mandated structured JSON output with fields for `ticket_id`, `category`, `severity`, `assigned_queue`, and `suggested_action`
- **Outcome**: In the team's pilot, manual triage time fell by approximately 60–70% (illustrative; results will vary with ticket volume and complexity). Severity-1 tickets were routed within the SLA window consistently across the evaluation period. Downstream agents consuming the JSON output required no format negotiation.
- **Key takeaway**: Embedding SLA thresholds directly in the *context* component eliminates the need for a separate rules engine. The *format* component's JSON contract made the agent composable; its output became the input to the routing agent with no transformation layer.

Case study 2: Financial compliance review agent

- **Problem**: A financial services firm needed to pre-screen client communications for potential regulatory policy violations before human review. Without explicit behavioral constraints, early prompt iterations occasionally produced plausible-sounding but non-compliant guidance.
- **PTCF configuration**:
    - *Persona* established the agent as a "compliance pre-screening specialist" with no authority to provide financial advice, only to flag potential policy references for human review
    - *Task* defined a two-pass process: first, identify policy-relevant language, then classify the risk level (`Low`, `Medium`, or `High`)

   - *Context* embedded applicable regulation categories (MiFID II or FCA COBS), explicit prohibitions (no advice or no predictions), and a mandatory human-escalation rule for high-risk classifications
   - *Format* produced a structured review report with a `risk_level` field, a `flagged_passages` array, and a `reasoning` field
- **Outcome**: The agent successfully pre-screened communications in the team's evaluation set, with human reviewers confirming strong alignment between the agent's risk classifications and their own judgments on representative samples (illustrative; precise accuracy rates depend on model, jurisdiction, and corpus). Crucially, no high-risk item was routed without human escalation during testing.
- **Key takeaway**: In regulated domains, the *context* component functions as a compliance guardrail, not merely background information. Explicit prohibitions and mandatory escalation rules belong in the *context*, rather than being inferred from the *persona*. The `reasoning` field in the *format* provides the audit trail that compliance teams require.

Case study 3: Automated code review agent

- **Problem**: A software engineering team wanted to automate first-pass code review for pull requests, focusing on style guide violations, security anti-patterns, and test coverage gaps. Initial attempts produced reviews that were either too terse (missing context) or too verbose (blocking developer workflow).
- **PTCF configuration**:
   - *Persona* defined the agent as a `senior software engineer and code reviewer` with a constructive, non-blocking communication style
   - *Task* specified a three-category review scope: (1) style guide compliance, (2) OWASP Top 10 security patterns, (3) test coverage gaps, with explicit instruction to flag `Critical` and `Major` issues only (not cosmetic suggestions)
   - *Context* embedded the team's style guide URL, OWASP reference, language (Python 3.11), and a hard rule: never block a pull request on `Minor` issues
   - *Format* produced a Markdown review report with a findings table (`Category`, `Severity`, `Line Reference`, and `Recommendation`) and an `overall_verdict` field (`Approve`/`Request Changes`)
- **Outcome**: In the team's internal evaluation, senior engineers estimated that the agent correctly identified the majority of `Critical` and `Major` issues that they would have flagged themselves on representative pull requests (illustrative; precision varies with code base, language version, and model). Developer workflow friction decreased as minor-issue noise was eliminated from automated review output.
- **Key takeaway**: The *task* component's explicit scope boundary (`Critical` and `Major` only) was the single most impactful design decision: it transformed the agent from a noisy reviewer into a trusted first-pass filter. The format's `overall_verdict` field integrated the agent into the existing pull request workflow with no additional tooling, demonstrating how structured output enables composability at zero integration cost.

These case studies confirm a consistent pattern: the more precisely a PTCF prompt encodes persona, task boundaries, contextual constraints, and output format, the closer the agent's behavior aligns with production requirements. The natural next question is how to sustain that alignment as prompts evolve over time.

Iterating and evaluating prompts

Crafting a prompt is rarely a one-shot exercise. Even well-structured PTCF prompts require tuning as real-world usage exposes gaps between intended and actual agent behavior. A disciplined iteration process transforms prompt engineering from an intuitive craft into a repeatable, evidence-based practice, one that makes quality measurable and regressions detectable before they reach production.

Two evaluation strategies are especially effective in practice: A/B testing and regression testing.

A/B comparison runs two prompt variants against an identical input set and compares outputs on defined metrics: accuracy, format compliance, response length, or task completion rate. This isolates the effect of a single change and prevents the common mistake of judging a revision by subjective impression alone. Regression testing maintains a reference suite of canonical inputs with expected outputs. Before any prompt revision is accepted into production, it must pass the full suite without degrading any previously passing case. Together, these two strategies ensure that improvements are real and that gains in one area do not introduce failures elsewhere.

Consider the support triage agent from *Case study 1*. To test whether a more directive *persona* improves routing accuracy, you create two prompt variants: Variant A retains the original *persona* ("You are a technical support ticket processor"), while Variant B adopts a more assertive framing ("You are a senior escalation analyst who prioritizes speed-to-resolution"). Both variants share identical *task*, *context*, and *format* components. You then run both against a held-out set of 50 pre-labeled tickets and compare classification accuracy, urgency agreement, and routing match rate. If Variant B raises the accuracy from 82% to 89% with no increase in false escalations, the change is validated.

Now suppose you refine the code review agent's *task* component in *Case study 3* to exclude `Minor` severity issues, focusing reviewer attention on `Critical` and `Major` findings. Before deploying this change, you run the revised prompt against a canonical suite of 20 code samples with known expected outputs. The pass/fail gate checks two conditions: every previously detected `Critical` and `Major` issue must still appear, and no new false positives above `Minor` must be introduced. If the suite returns 20/20 passes, the revision is cleared for production. If even one `Critical` finding disappears, the change is rejected and the task formulation is revised.

When a prompt fails or underperforms, the following four-step loop provides a systematic path to diagnosis and resolution:

- **Baseline**: Capture the current prompt version and its performance metrics on your test suite. This establishes the ground truth against which all changes will be measured.
- **Evaluate**: Run the failing or underperforming prompt against representative inputs. Categorize failure modes: is the agent misidentifying its *persona*, misinterpreting the *task*, lacking necessary *context*, or producing output that violates *format* constraints?

- **Identify**: Isolate the specific PTCF component responsible for the failure. Make the smallest targeted change that addresses the root cause, for example, tightening the *persona's* authority scope, adding a constraint clause to the *task*, or inserting a missing boundary condition into the *context*.
- **Revise and version**: Apply the change, label the revised prompt with a version identifier (e.g., v1.2.0), and run the full regression suite. Accept the revision only if it resolves the target failure without introducing new ones. Store both the prompt and its evaluation results, treating your prompt history as source code, not a scratch pad.

Repeating this loop across multiple iterations converges the prompt toward reliable behavior. Teams that treat prompt engineering as a software engineering discipline with versioned artifacts, test suites, and documented change rationales consistently outperform those that rely on ad hoc editing and manual review.

The techniques covered in this chapter give you the engineering foundations for building intelligent agent behavior: PTCF-structured prompts, cognitive prompting patterns, few-shot learning, and multi-agent protocols. *Chapter 4* builds on this by addressing what happens when those agents move into production: scaling agent systems under real load, implementing security and privacy safeguards, designing for failure and recovery, and navigating the governance and responsible AI obligations that accompany deployment at scale.

Summary

This chapter explored the art of agent prompting, demonstrating how to move from crafting simple instructions to architecting comprehensive cognitive frameworks. We established that in modern agentic systems, prompts act as a constitution, shaping an agent's identity, reasoning, and behavior. The PTCF framework—*persona*, *task*, *context*, and *format*—provides a disciplined, systematic foundation for this process, enabling developers to build agents that are reliable, predictable, and aligned with human goals.

By leveraging the PTCF blueprint, we showed how to implement advanced patterns for task decomposition, few-shot learning, and structured reasoning with CoT and ToT prompting. Furthermore, we detailed how these same principles extend to architecting multi-agent systems, where standardized communication protocols enable seamless collaboration and the synthesis of collective intelligence. Ultimately, this disciplined approach transforms prompt engineering from an ad hoc craft into a mature engineering discipline, ensuring that as AI systems grow in complexity, they remain transparent, trustworthy, and effective.

As we move from crafting intelligent agents to deploying them in real-world scenarios, the focus shifts to critical aspects of operationalizing these systems. The next chapter will delve into the complexities of agent deployment, covering essential topics such as scaling agent systems, implementing robust security and privacy measures, and navigating the crucial considerations for responsible AI development and governance.

Get This Book's PDF Version and Exclusive Extras

Scan the QR code (or go to `packtpub.com/unlock`). Search for this book by name, confirm the edition, and then follow the steps on the page.

UNLOCK NOW

Note: Keep your invoice handy. Purchases made directly from Packt don't require an invoice.

4

Agent Deployment and Responsible Development

In theory, there is no difference between theory and practice. In practice, there is.

—Jan L. A. van de Snepscheut

AI agents are moving beyond research to become **critical enablers** of enterprise productivity and autonomous operations. Deploying them in real-world contexts is a multidimensional challenge, encompassing engineering, operations, and ethics, rather than just a final development phase.

Previous chapters established the theoretical and architectural foundations of agent design. This chapter focuses on the crucial shift from *experimentation to execution*, operationalizing AI agents under demanding constraints of reliability, security, scalability, and compliance.

Unlike traditional software, AI agents are *non-deterministic, autonomous*, and often *stateful*, with decision logic emerging from interaction and learning (including reinforcement learning from human feedback, in-context learning via few-shot examples, and continual fine-tuning on deployment data). They plan, reason, and act in real time, often without continuous human oversight, making deployment both powerful and perilous. This necessitates rigorous attention to infrastructure, observability, performance, access control, and responsible AI practices.

Extending the **Agent Development Lifecycle** (**ADL**) from *Chapter 1*, this chapter details the **deployment phase**: the most consequential and risk-sensitive stage. We provide a practical blueprint for deploying agents at scale.

Moving AI agents from prototypes to production systems demands a fundamental transformation in design, governance, and accountability. Prototypes prioritize flexibility and experimentation, whereas production requires predictability, resilience, observability, and governance. Unlike deterministic traditional software, agents exhibit probabilistic, emergent behaviors informed by training data, memory, tools, and environmental feedback, leading to behavioral divergence.

This necessitates a deployment strategy acknowledging dynamic execution paths, stateful interactions, and tool-mediated actions. Ensuring production readiness involves modularizing the code base (e.g., through microservices), orchestrating workflows (e.g., using tools such as Temporal or Prefect), and hardening the runtime environment (e.g., with redundancy and circuit breakers). Agents also need version-controlled identities, explicit tool affordances with validation, and transparent introspection via observability frameworks (e.g., OpenTelemetry).

Achieving this production paradigm calls for cloud-native thinking, centered around containerization with Docker, orchestration via Kubernetes, and event-driven integration (asynchronous, loosely coupled communication between agent services via message brokers such as Kafka or RabbitMQ) using tools such as Kafka. In this context, latency, security, and cost emerge as critical architectural properties that must be carefully balanced throughout system design and deployment.

Production deployment is a discipline blending systems engineering, ML operations, and ethics, requiring meta-systems to monitor and guide agent autonomy within operational and ethical boundaries.

Deployment represents the most critical juncture in the AI agent lifecycle, where theoretical capabilities either translate into real-world value or fail catastrophically. While previous chapters equipped you with the knowledge to design and build intelligent agents, this chapter addresses the make-or-break challenge of operating them reliably at scale. The difference between a promising prototype and a production-ready system often determines whether AI initiatives deliver transformative business impact or become costly technological dead ends.

This chapter is essential because deployment failures are both common and expensive. Industry data shows that 70-80% of AI projects never reach production, and among those that do, many fail within the first year due to infrastructure inadequacies, security vulnerabilities, or ethical oversights. The stakes are particularly high for agent systems, which combine the complexity of traditional software deployment with the unique challenges of autonomous, reasoning-capable systems that can make decisions with far-reaching consequences.

In this chapter, we'll be covering the following topics:

- Scaling agent systems
- Handling high-throughput agent interactions
- Security and privacy considerations
- Ethical agent development

This chapter unifies academic systems thinking with the demands of production-grade deployment, offering a theoretically sound and operationally actionable perspective.

Scaling agent systems

Scaling AI agents goes beyond increasing compute resources; it involves ensuring behavioral consistency and seamless real-time decision-making. Unlike traditional applications, agents scale based on cognitive load, influenced by task complexity, memory state, reasoning depth, and tool dependency. Effective deployment demands infrastructure that mirrors the agent's cognitive architecture, interaction patterns, and lifecycle complexity. This means aligning deployment platforms, scaling strategies, state management, and failure recovery with the agent's unique computational behaviors. Retrofitting infrastructure for misaligned architectures is often expensive and challenging.

A systematic approach to infrastructure planning must consider the diverse needs of agent typologies and their evolution. In this section, we will delve into the various aspects of scaling agent systems, including the infrastructure requirements tailored to different agent typologies, and essential cost management strategies to ensure economic viability.

Infrastructure requirements by agent typology

Different agent types exhibit distinct computational and behavioral patterns, directly influencing their infrastructure dependencies. *Figure 4.1* illustrates how these different agent typologies align with specific infrastructure deployment strategies:

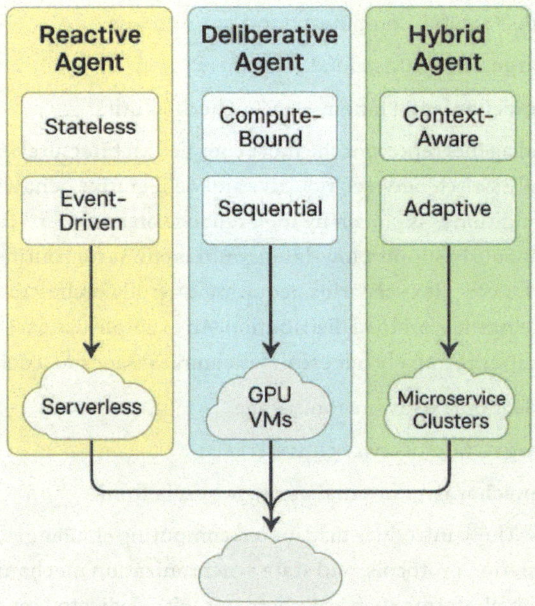

Figure 4.1 – Infrastructure alignment with agent typologies

Figure 4.1 shows the critical relationship between cognitive architecture and deployment strategy:

- **Reactive agents**: These agents operate through stateless, reflex-driven patterns that prioritize immediate response over deep reasoning. Their computational signature is characterized by minimal CPU-bound tasks and negligible memory footprints, making them ideal for serverless architectures where ultra-low-latency response times are critical. They are well-suited for use cases such as customer service chatbots, simple decision trees, and real-time filtering applications, as they can be deployed on serverless platforms or edge infrastructure, triggered by events such as HTTP requests, message queues, or webhooks.
    - **Execution mode**: Stateless functions
    - **Deployment target**: Serverless/edge
    - **Coordination mechanism**: Event trigger (HTTP/SQS/webhook)
- **Deliberative agents**: In contrast, deliberative agents present a dramatically different infrastructure profile. Characterized by state-rich, goal-directed behavior, they involve extensive modeling, planning, and simulation processes. As depicted, these agents require substantial CPU and GPU resources for

complex inference operations, planning tree generation, and multi-step reasoning chains. Their stateful nature demands sophisticated memory management systems capable of maintaining long-context tracking, persistent knowledge graphs, and intermediate reasoning states across extended sessions. Use cases include strategic planning assistants, research agents, and complex problem-solving systems that require deep analysis and multi-step reasoning. In practice, LangChain memory modules (such as `ConversationBufferMemory` and `ConversationSummaryMemory`) handle short-to-medium context persistence, while Pinecone provides scalable long-context vector retrieval for agents operating across extended sessions or large knowledge corpora.

  - **Execution mode**: Stateful, compute-bound
  - **Deployment target**: GPU VMs/cloud containers
  - **Coordination mechanism**: Planning DAGs, checkpointing

- **Hybrid agents**: Hybrid agents represent the most complex architectural challenge, operating in dual modes that dynamically switch between reflexive and deliberative behavior based on task semantics and environmental conditions. As shown by their reliance on microservice clusters in the figure, these systems must simultaneously support low-latency interactions for routine tasks and heavyweight planning capabilities for complex scenarios, requiring carefully orchestrated microservices architectures with intelligent workload distribution. An example use case is a system that handles routine customer inquiries reactively but escalates complex issues to a deliberative planning process.
  - **Execution mode**: Context-aware multistage
  - **Deployment target**: Microservice clusters
  - **Coordination mechanism**: Internal message bus, fallback
- **Multi-agent systems**: These introduce distributed computing challenges, requiring robust messaging infrastructure, coordination protocols, and state synchronization mechanisms. These systems typically deploy on orchestration platforms such as Kubernetes with dedicated messaging layers using Apache Kafka, RabbitMQ, or cloud-native pub/sub systems. They support both peer-to-peer agent communication and centralized coordination services, enabling emergent behaviors while maintaining system coherence. Monitoring and observability become particularly critical in multi-agent environments, as system behavior emerges from agent interactions rather than predetermined logic flows. Use cases include supply chain agents negotiating contracts across vendor ecosystems or healthcare agents coordinating patient data across clinics and insurers.
  - **Execution mode**: Distributed and autonomous
  - **Deployment target**: Kubernetes/mesh + Kafka
  - **Coordination mechanism**: Messaging, vector context, roles

The infrastructure planning process must account for these fundamental differences while considering additional factors such as multi-agent coordination requirements, external tool integration needs, and scaling patterns that may evolve as agents learn and adapt. The coordination mechanisms, from simple event triggers for reactive agents to complex distributed messaging for multi-agent systems, demonstrate how infrastructure requirements scale with cognitive complexity and coordination needs. This architectural progression enables organizations to match their deployment strategy precisely to their agent's cognitive profile and operational requirements.

This alignment between agent typology and infrastructure is a *deployment determinant*, crucial for designing systems that scale correctly, operate efficiently, and fail gracefully. Infrastructure becomes a *mirror of cognition* and a *scaffold for autonomy*.

Performance optimization

Moving from structural considerations to operational excellence, we now turn our attention to performance optimization, ensuring agent systems operate efficiently and reliably under real-world conditions. A performant agent must balance three critical, often competing, factors:

- **Cost efficiency**: Ensuring that every action and inference provides value without incurring unsustainable expenses
- **High-throughput**: Handling large volumes of concurrent user interactions reliably and without degradation
- **Resilience and latency**: Maintaining stability and responsiveness, even when downstream services fail or system load spikes

We will now examine the strategies for mastering each of these domains, starting with cost management.

Cost optimization

Deploying AI agents presents unique economic challenges due to their stochastic reasoning, dynamic tool use, and variable inference complexity, leading to costs that scale non-linearly with task complexity. Unlike traditional applications, a simple agent query can trigger extensive reasoning chains, database retrievals, API calls, memory updates, and inter-agent coordination, each incurring direct and indirect costs. Controlling these costs requires a systematic approach focusing on intelligent model selection and routing, architectural efficiency, operational optimization via caching, and comprehensive monitoring with budget enforcement. These strategies are synergistic, where improvements in one area enhance others, and neglecting any can undermine the entire strategy.

Figure 4.2 illustrates how these optimization strategies interconnect within a comprehensive cost management framework:

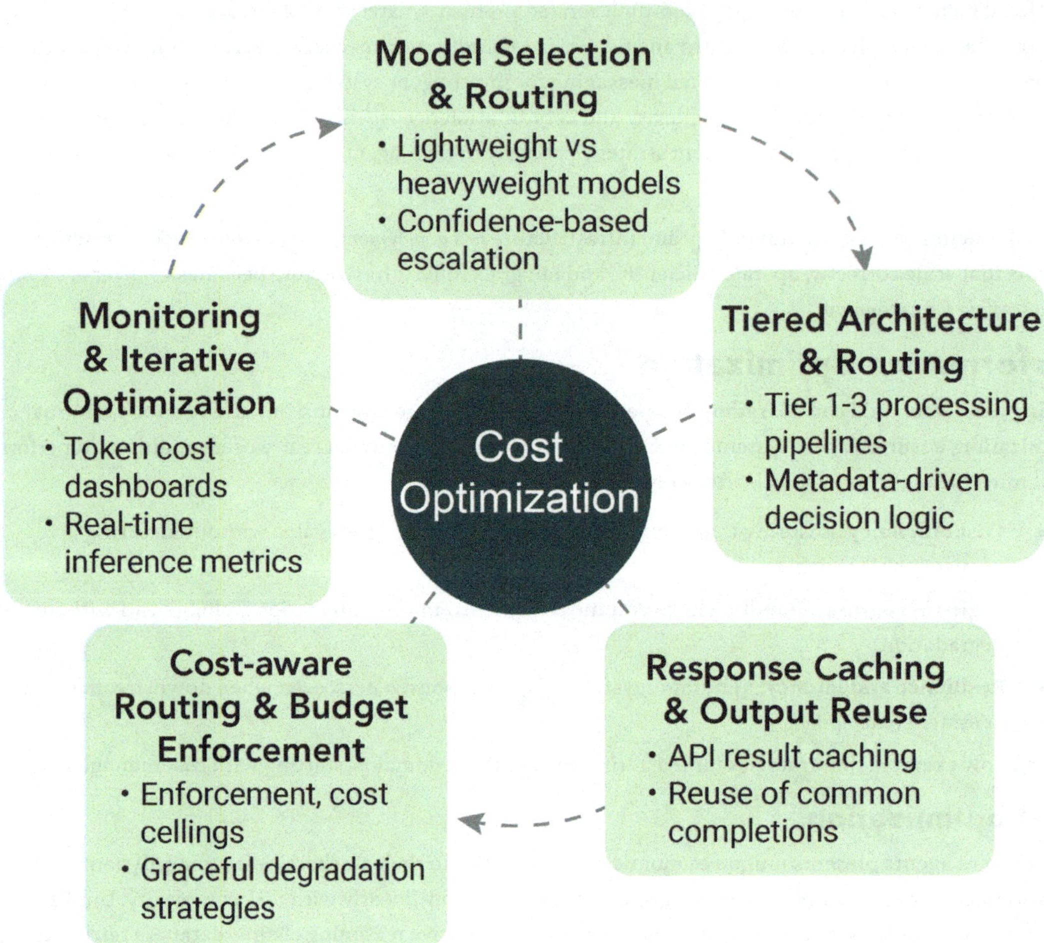

Figure 4.2 – Interconnected strategies for AI agent cost optimization

At the core of cost optimization is **Model Selection & Routing**. This foundational strategy dictates which underlying language model an agent utilizes, significantly impacting computational expense. It involves distinguishing between lightweight and heavyweight models. For instance, a customer service agent might use a smaller, faster, and cheaper model such as GPT-3.5 for simple FAQ lookups or greeting messages, while reserving a more powerful and expensive model such as GPT-4 for complex problem-solving or nuanced analytical tasks. This strategy often incorporates confidence-based escalation, where a lightweight model attempts to handle a query first, and if its confidence in providing an accurate response falls below a predefined threshold, the query is automatically routed to a more capable (and thus more expensive) model. This ensures appropriate processing without over-engineering every interaction.

Building upon intelligent model routing is **Tiered Architecture & Routing**. This approach organizes agent operations into tier 1-3 processing pipelines, creating a multi-stage flow to eliminate redundant or overly expensive inference. For example, a tier 1 system might act as a simple classifier or rule-based filter, quickly handling basic requests such as spam detection or intent recognition. Only "qualified" or more complex requests are then routed downstream to tier 2, which might involve intermediate models for conversational responses or moderate reasoning. The most intricate, high-value tasks are reserved for tier 3, leveraging the highest-accuracy, most expensive models. Routing between these tiers is often driven by metadata-driven decision logic, where properties such as user priority, task urgency, or estimated computational cost inform which tier handles a request.

Response Caching & Output Reuse is crucial for minimizing redundant computation and reducing API call costs. This strategy involves API result caching, where the outcomes of external tools or API calls are stored with **time-to-live (TTL)** metadata. If an agent needs the same information again within the TTL, it retrieves it from the cache instead of making a costly external call. For example, if an agent frequently queries a weather API for a popular city, those results can be cached. Additionally, it includes the reuse of common completions from LLMs themselves. If an agent generates the same or a very similar response multiple times for predictable interactions (e.g., standard acknowledgment messages), these common outputs can be cached and reused, benefiting predictable agent interactions.

Cost-Aware Routing & Budget Enforcement integrates economic signals directly into runtime decisions. This involves classifying tasks with **service-level agreement (SLA)** tagging and cost ceilings. For instance, a critical business process might have a higher SLA and budget ceiling, allowing it to use more expensive, lower-latency models. Conversely, a low-priority background task might be constrained by a tighter cost ceiling, forcing it to use cheaper alternatives or processes during off-peak hours. When these predefined budget thresholds are approached or exceeded, graceful degradation strategies are automatically implemented. This might involve routing subsequent requests to cached responses, defaulting to lower-cost models, or even queuing less urgent tasks until costs normalize, ensuring financial sustainability.

Finally, **Monitoring & Iterative Optimization** provides the crucial feedback loop for continuous self-improvement and cost-effectiveness. This involves establishing comprehensive observability pipelines that include token cost dashboards. These dashboards track token usage by model, route, and agent type, offering granular cost attribution and allowing teams to identify where expenses are accumulating. Alongside this, real-time inference metrics are monitored to identify bottlenecks, observe performance trends, and correlate expenses with business outcomes such as user satisfaction, task completion rates, or revenue generated. This continuous monitoring enables data-driven optimization and ensures that cost-saving strategies are effective in practice.

These interconnected strategies ensure that AI agents, while cognitively expensive, can be financially sustainable by embedding cost sensitivity throughout their architecture, from model selection to prompt structure, tool invocation, and caching.

Agent cost profiles are shaped by several interacting factors. The following vectors represent the main sources of operational expense in real-world deployments and form the foundation for applying optimization strategies:

- **Token consumption**: The most visible cost, influenced by prompt volume, completion length, context tokens for longer conversations, verbose internal monologues from complex reasoning, and exponential message overhead in multi-agent systems

- **Inference duration**: Time spent on GPU/accelerator hardware, which becomes expensive during peak usage or extended reasoning sessions, amplified by memory management for long conversation histories
- **Tool and API calls**: External service dependencies with varying pricing models, often unpredictable as they depend on agent reasoning rather than user input volume
- **Memory and storage costs**: These accumulate from persistent embeddings, conversation histories, and vector databases, which grow dynamically and require expensive vector similarity operations
- **Inter-agent messaging**: Significant overhead in multi-agent systems due to coordination, consensus, and knowledge sharing, potentially leading to quadratic growth in message volume

Understanding these primary cost vectors is the first step; the next is to apply strategic design principles that actively mitigate these expenses. These principles guide how we can architect and operate AI agent systems to ensure they deliver maximum value while maintaining cost efficiency.

Efficient agent systems prioritize *value per unit of compute*, recognizing that under-utilizing intelligence is often the greatest inefficiency.

To address the cost vectors discussed earlier, organizations can apply a set of proven design principles. The following strategies represent practical levers for reducing expenses while maintaining performance:

- **Lean model selection**: Match model capabilities to task requirements precisely. Use smaller, faster models (e.g., GPT-3.5, Claude Instant) for routine tasks such as intent recognition or simple lookups. Reserve high-capacity models (e.g., GPT-4, Claude Opus) for complex reasoning or ambiguous inputs. Implement confidence-based escalation where lightweight models defer to more powerful ones if certainty falls below thresholds, ensuring appropriate processing without over-engineering.
- **Tiered architecture and model routing**: Organize agents into multi-tier processing pipelines to eliminate redundant inference. This approach typically involves setting up distinct tiers, each optimized for different levels of complexity and cost.
    - **Tier 1**: Lightweight classifiers or rule-based systems handle intent recognition, spam filtering, and basic validation, routing qualified requests downstream
    - **Tier 2**: Intermediate models manage most user interactions, balancing capability and efficiency for conversational responses and moderate reasoning
    - **Tier 3**: High-accuracy, expensive models are selectively invoked for creative tasks, complex problem-solving, or nuanced understanding based on escalation criteria

Efficient tiering depends on the routing logic that channels each request to the appropriate tier. This logic is the operational glue that connects the preceding tier definitions to cost-effective execution in practice.

Routing logic, implemented with classification models, decision trees, or metadata-driven policies, ensures that tasks are consistently matched to the most cost-effective path without sacrificing quality.

The following strategies complement tiered routing to reduce cost through prompt efficiency, intelligent caching, and budget-aware execution controls:

- **Prompt compression and token optimization**: Directly impacts token costs and inference speed. Implement semantic compression for interaction history to summarize redundant exchanges, maintaining context with fewer tokens. Use structured prompt templates for consistent formatting and parameter substitution, reducing verbosity. Manage context windows with intelligent pruning algorithms to preserve relevant information and discard low-entropy content.

- **Conditional execution and token gating**: Control expensive operations by evaluating cost-benefit trade-offs with intelligent middleware. Route deterministic tasks to templates, scripts, or lookup tables without LLM involvement for significant cost reduction. Task classification systems can route low-priority tasks to optimized workflows. Middleware logic enforces runtime conditions based on budgets, user tiers, or urgency for dynamic cost control.
- **Response caching and output reuse**: Avoid recomputation through intelligent caching. Use embedding caches for frequently accessed content, such as knowledge bases. Tool output caches store API call results with time-to-live metadata, eliminating redundant external calls. LLM response caches store common completions for reuse, benefiting predictable agent interactions.
- **Cost-aware routing and budget enforcement**: Integrate cost-related metrics and budget constraints into routing decisions. Classify tasks by computational cost and annotate with metadata (SLA, user priority, cost ceilings) for dynamic routing. Budget-aware middleware monitors spending in real time, implementing graceful degradation (e.g., routing to cached responses or lower-cost models) when thresholds are approached. Display cost metrics in observability dashboards for rapid diagnostics and data-driven optimization.
- **Monitoring and iterative cost optimization**: Continuously validate and improve cost efficiency through comprehensive observability pipelines. Track token usage by model, route, and agent type for granular cost attribution. Monitor inference duration and failure rates to identify bottlenecks. Implement cost-per-session and per-agent breakdowns to correlate expenses with business outcomes (e.g., user satisfaction, task completion, revenue). Establish anomaly detection for cost spikes or excessive prompt lengths. Integrate dashboards (Grafana, OpenAI's billing API) and conduct regular cost audits. A best practice is to tag each model call with metadata such as `task_id`, `agent_type`, and `cost_tier` for fine-grained attribution and analysis.

High-throughput performance

Beyond optimizing for cost, ensuring the robust performance of AI agents under demanding conditions is equally critical. We now shift our focus to architectural patterns and resilience strategies essential for handling high-throughput agent interactions.

Consider a customer support agent handling 500 concurrent sessions, each with a 2-second end-to-end response SLA. At this scale, even a single slow reasoning chain or an unresponsive tool call can trigger cascading delays, leading to SLA breaches across multiple sessions. Systems operating under such load benefit significantly from resilience patterns: circuit breakers can reduce P99 latency by 40–60% during failure scenarios by failing fast or switching to fallback responses, while bulkhead isolation ensures that issues in one component, such as a degraded retrieval service, do not impact unrelated agent workflows. These results demonstrate that resilience patterns are not merely defensive techniques; they are essential mechanisms for maintaining SLA compliance in production systems.

As AI agents are deployed in real-world systems with hundreds or thousands of concurrent users, their architectures must withstand not just scale, but volatility, unpredictability, and interdependence. High-throughput systems are characterized by *complexity-per-unit-of-traffic*, where each request can spawn nested reasoning steps, tool invocations, and multi-agent coordination. This can be measured by metrics such as the average number of LLM calls per user request, the depth of reasoning chains, the count of external tool invocations, or the volume of inter-agent messages generated per interaction.

Managing high interaction volumes requires implementing resilience patterns to handle the unique failure modes and operational challenges of agent systems, maintaining stability and performance despite their non-deterministic nature. The key resilience patterns are summarized in *Table 4.1*:

Pattern	Purpose	Example Tools
Circuit Breakers	Block failing services to avoid cascade	Hystrix, Istio, Sentinel
Bulkheads	Isolate failure domains per agent type	Kubernetes namespaces, Helm charts
Timeout + Retry Wrappers	Fail fast and reroute intelligently	Tenacity (Python), Resilience4j
Failover Models	Fallback to cached or distilled responses	Prompt chaining, Decision DAGs

Table 4.1 – Resilience patterns for high-throughput agent systems

These patterns enable agent systems to maintain operational stability even under extreme load, providing graceful degradation pathways when individual components fail or become overwhelmed.

Note

Decision-directed acyclic graphs (**DAGs**) are architecturally distinct from both retry loops and prompt chaining. A retry loop re-executes the same node on failure, with no branching: the control topology is a single edge looping back to one node. Prompt chaining is linear; that is, a fixed sequence of prompts where output feeds the next input, with no conditional branching. In a decision DAG, by contrast, each node evaluates a condition, and the execution path through the graph is determined by the outcome of that evaluation. Unlike a retry loop, a decision DAG routes to a specialist node on failure rather than re-attempting the same prompt; unlike a chain, it can diverge across multiple downstream paths based on intermediate results.

As intelligent agents evolve from isolated scripts to collaborative, autonomous entities, they require architectural foundations supporting modular cognition, scalable coordination, and robust state management. These systems operate across diverse environments, spanning stateless orchestration layers, persistent memory backends, and asynchronous event-driven workflows. Unlike traditional software, agents are inherently stateful, capable of learning, invoking external tools, and communicating. Because these agent capabilities introduce new complexities, such as managing persistent context and orchestrating tool use across interactions, designing robust systems requires new architectural patterns. This section outlines the core patterns for designing scalable, fault-tolerant, and production-ready AI ecosystems.

Modular cognition via microservices

Microservices architecture decomposes agent functions into independently deployable services, each responsible for a discrete cognitive or operational task. This modularity enables polyglot development, independent scaling, and clean interfaces. *Table 4.2* provides a microservice decomposition for agent functionality:

Service Name	Responsibility
Planner	Translates intent into executable steps
Retriever	Performs semantic or keyword-based search
Memory Store	Manages embeddings, chat logs, and context graphs
Execution Engine	Interfaces with APIs, tools, or external systems
Response Synthesizer	Composes and formats final agent output

Table 4.2 – Microservice decomposition for agent functionality

Each service communicates via HTTP, gRPC, or message queues, forming a **composable agent infrastructure** that enables targeted scaling (e.g., increasing capacity for retrieval services under load).

In a concrete deployment, the Planner and Execution Engine services from *Table 4.2* might be implemented as separate FastAPI or gRPC services, each containerized and deployed to distinct Kubernetes Pods with independent resource quotas. The Memory Store service connects to a vector store such as Pinecone or Weaviate, while the Execution Engine service holds the registry of callable APIs, each isolated behind an authorization check so that no other service can invoke tools directly. This physical separation means that a surge in tool call volume does not starve the reasoning pipeline of the CPU, and a memory retrieval failure triggers a circuit breaker only within that service rather than cascading to the orchestrator.

The following Python snippet shows how the Execution Engine service from *Table 4.2* would wrap an external API call with a circuit breaker using the `tenacity` library. If the tool fails repeatedly, the circuit opens and the agent falls back gracefully rather than cascading failures into the Planner service:

```
from tenacity import retry, stop_after_attempt, wait_exponential, RetryError
import logging

CIRCUIT_OPEN = False   # shared state; use Redis for distributed deployments
FAILURE_COUNT = 0
FAILURE_THRESHOLD = 3

@retry(stop=stop_after_attempt(3), wait=wait_exponential(min=1, max=8))
def _call_tool_api(endpoint: str, payload: dict) -> dict:
    """Inner call with automatic retry and exponential back-off."""
    import httpx
    response = httpx.post(endpoint, json=payload, timeout=5.0)
    response.raise_for_status()
    return response.json()
```

```
def call_tool(endpoint: str, payload: dict) -> dict:
    """Circuit-breaker wrapper: open circuit after FAILURE_THRESHOLD failures."""
    global CIRCUIT_OPEN, FAILURE_COUNT
    if CIRCUIT_OPEN:
        logging.warning("Circuit open: tool call blocked, returning fallback.")
        return {"status": "unavailable", "fallback": True}
    try:
        result = _call_tool_api(endpoint, payload)
        FAILURE_COUNT = 0   # reset on success
        return result
    except RetryError:
        FAILURE_COUNT += 1
        if FAILURE_COUNT >= FAILURE_THRESHOLD:
            CIRCUIT_OPEN = True
            logging.error("Circuit breaker tripped for %s", endpoint)
        return {"status": "unavailable", "fallback": True}
```

Install the tenacity and httpx libraries by running `pip install tenacity httpx`. In a Kubernetes deployment, `CIRCUIT_OPEN` and `FAILURE_COUNT` should be stored in a shared Redis key rather than module-level globals, so that all Pod replicas observe the same circuit state. This pattern keeps tool failures fully contained within the Execution Engine Pod and prevents them from propagating to the Planner or Memory Store services.

Portable execution with containerization

Containers encapsulate agent modules with their environment, ensuring consistent behavior across development, staging, and production. Tools such as Docker provide lightweight packaging, while registries enable versioning and rollback. Benefits include reproducible builds, fast startup, dependency isolation, and secure, sandboxed execution. Best practice dictates using multi-stage builds to minimize image size and protect build-time secrets. For production agent pipelines, Docker BuildKit enables optimized multi-layer builds with advanced caching and secret handling; OCI-compliant runtimes such as containerd and Podman provide vendor-neutral alternatives suitable for environments where Docker daemon dependencies are undesirable.

Orchestration for lifecycle management

To deploy and manage distributed agents at scale, container orchestration platforms provide lifecycle automation, health monitoring, and self-healing. The tooling stack includes Kubernetes as the core engine, Helm Charts for template-driven deployment, and ArgoCD/Flux for GitOps. In practice, Deployments are used for long-running agents, Jobs for ephemeral inference tasks, and Custom Operators for managing memory checkpoints or multi-step workflows. Metrics such as inference latency, memory load, or tool error rate drive autoscaling policies.

Beyond the orchestration layer itself, production agent deployments require well-defined operational procedures to manage change safely. The following practices address the unique challenges of updating stateful, non-deterministic agent systems.

Operational procedures: rollback, A/B testing, migration, and integration

Key operational procedures for production agent deployments include the following:

- **Rollback**: Agent rollback is more complex than standard service rollback because agent state spans multiple substrates: model weights, tool configurations, memory contents, and conversation history. A disciplined rollback strategy versions each substrate independently. Kubernetes rolling updates can revert the serving container; a separate migration script must restore the memory store to its pre-deployment snapshot; and tool API versions must be explicitly pinned so that a rollback of the orchestrator does not leave it calling a newer tool API version that no longer matches its expected schema. Rollback readiness should be validated in staging before every production deployment.
- **A/B testing**: Traffic-splitting between agent versions enables controlled comparison of behavioral changes, for example, comparing a fine-tuned model variant against the baseline across 10% of production sessions. Agent A/B tests must instrument beyond latency: measure task completion rate, tool call frequency, escalation rate, and user satisfaction signals, since LLM behavioral regressions often do not manifest as latency or error anomalies. Canary deployments with automatic rollback triggers on behavioral metric thresholds are the recommended pattern.
- **Migration and enterprise Integration**: Migrating agents from prototype to production typically involves four transition points: moving from in-process to remote tool calls; transitioning from in-memory to persistent conversation storage; integrating with enterprise identity providers (OAuth 2.0, SAML) for user-scoped tool authorization; and connecting to enterprise data systems (CRMs, ERPs, data warehouses) via authenticated API gateways rather than direct database access. Each transition introduces a failure surface that must be tested under representative load before the migration is declared complete. Blue-green deployment, that is, running old and new infrastructure in parallel and switching traffic atomically, minimizes the blast radius of migration failures.

Asynchronous messaging and event-driven agents

In distributed agent ecosystems, synchronous communication introduces fragility. Event-driven patterns decouple components, enabling concurrency, resilience, and contextual awareness. Messaging backends include Apache Kafka for durable, high-throughput streaming; RabbitMQ/NATS for lightweight, low-latency queues; and Cloud Pub/Sub for fully managed, scalable pub/sub systems. Design patterns feature *fan-out* to trigger multiple downstream agents from one event, *dead-letter queues* to capture failed processing attempts, and *schema contracts* to enforce structured messaging. Event-driven agents act as reactive listeners, processing user actions, environmental triggers, or inter-agent signals, enabling loosely coupled, distributed cognition.

Event schema evolution is a production-critical concern that the preceding patterns alone do not address. As agent systems evolve, event contracts must be versioned using semantic versioning (e.g., `event.v2.user_action`) so consumers can detect breaking changes without silent failures. Errors should be categorized at the point of processing: transient failures (e.g., downstream timeouts) warrant automatic retry with backoff, while permanent failures (e.g., schema violations, unroutable events) must be routed to a dead-letter queue for inspection and reprocessing, preventing lost events from corrupting agent state undetected.

Hybrid orchestration: stateless routing and stateful agents

To balance scalability and complexity, agent systems often separate **orchestration** (stateless) from **reasoning** (stateful). Stateless orchestrators handle routing, retries, and policies, while agents persist context in external stores. The deployment blueprint involves a stateless router receiving a request and applying policy rules, the agent pulling relevant memory from vector databases (e.g., Pinecone, Redis, ChromaDB), and output being generated with updated context written back to memory. This pattern supports horizontal scaling of orchestrators and fault-tolerant agent execution. Long-lived state can be checkpointed to blob storage or document databases for auditability and replay.

Federated architectures across organizations

Distributed agents increasingly operate across organizational boundaries, requiring secure and policy-governed collaboration. Federated patterns enable agents to share memory, coordinate actions, and respect privacy domains. Key considerations include Federated Memory Graphs (distributed knowledge with scoped permissions), Authentication Protocols (OAuth2, JWT, mTLS for cross-organizational trust), and **Policy Enforcement Points** (**PEPs**) for runtime rule evaluation. Use cases include supply chain agents negotiating contracts across vendor ecosystems, healthcare agents coordinating patient data, and public sector agents interacting with privacy-restricted citizen data. Privacy-preserving techniques (encrypted queries, access filtering, differential privacy) ensure compliance while enabling intelligent cross-boundary collaboration.

Distributed agent systems fundamentally differ from traditional application stacks, combining cognitive reasoning with real-time messaging, state persistence, and decentralized orchestration. These patterns, that is, modularity, event-driven design, hybrid execution, and federated governance, form the architectural backbone for scalable, reliable, and secure AI agents.

While robust architectural patterns enable agents to operate at scale and handle complex interactions, the integrity and trustworthiness of these systems are equally dependent on stringent security and privacy measures. As agents assume more critical roles, safeguarding them against vulnerabilities becomes paramount.

Security and privacy considerations

As intelligent agents increasingly assume responsibility for mission-critical tasks and user-facing interactions, securing these systems is no longer optional; it is foundational. Unlike traditional software, AI agents exhibit dynamic reasoning, persistent memory, tool invocation capabilities, and natural language interfaces. These traits introduce novel security challenges that require rethinking legacy paradigms and designing with zero-trust and behavioral awareness from the outset.

This section examines the evolving threat landscape for AI agents, outlines security principles tailored to their architecture, and provides practical strategies for incident preparedness and defense-in-depth implementation.

Understanding the threat landscape

AI agents introduce a multifaceted attack surface spanning linguistic, cognitive, and execution layers. Their ability to interpret natural language instructions, maintain session context, and act through tools or APIs increases susceptibility to adversarial behaviors. *Table 4.3* highlights the primary threats observed in real-world deployments:

Organizing these threats by attack-surface layer provides practitioners with a decision-relevant framework for prioritizing defenses. *Table 4.3a* maps each threat to its layer; *Table 4.3* provides the complete threat descriptions:

Layer	Threat Type	Example	Primary Mitigation
Input-level	Prompt Injection, Adversarial Inputs, Data Poisoning	User-crafted prompt overrides system instructions; indirect commands in documents	Input validation; structured prompt schemas; token sanitization
Execution-level	Tool Misuse, Tool Hijacking, Identity Spoofing, Model Extraction	Agent calls a spoofed external API; user impersonates admin role	Tool gating; least-privilege access; continuous action verification
Memory-level	Memory Recall Leakage, Context Poisoning, Data Leakage	Sensitive context surfaces unexpectedly; stale or poisoned memory shapes responses	Memory governance; scoped session contexts; PII filtering on memory writes

Table 4.3a – Threat taxonomy by attack-surface layer

Attack Vector	Description	Risk Level
Prompt injection	User-crafted input overrides system instructions	High
Tool misuse	Unsafe or unauthorized tool/API execution	Moderate
Data leakage	Accidental exposure of PII, credentials, or internal data	High
Identity spoofing	Social engineering to assume alternate user roles	High
Indirect prompting	Hidden commands embedded in documents or web content	Medium
Memory recall leakage	Unintended resurfacing of forgotten sensitive context	Medium
Model extraction	Repeated probing to infer model internals	Moderate
Adversarial Inputs	Input crafted to exploit weaknesses in reasoning or interpretation	High
Tool hijacking	Agent interacts with compromised or spoofed tools	High

Table 4.3b – Threat model for agentic AI systems

These attack vectors often manifest through natural interactions, making them harder to detect with traditional static analysis. As a result, agents require a security model that treats every prompt, memory operation, and tool call as a potential entry point for compromise.

Extending zero trust to AI agents

Zero trust, a security model requiring strict identity verification for every person and device trying to access resources on a private network, regardless of whether they are inside or outside the network perimeter, must be adapted to the behavioral domain of agents. In agentic systems, this principle of "trust nothing by default" includes reasoning processes, contextual memory, and dynamic action selection.

Principle	Agent-Centric Implementation
Least Privilege	Limit access to tools, data, and APIs on a per-task basis
Continuous Verification	Authenticate and authorize actions per invocation, not per session
Micro-Segmentation	Isolate agent capabilities by namespace, context, or identity
Behavior Monitoring	Use telemetry and anomaly detection to flag outlier decisions
Immutable Infrastructure	Deploy agents in hardened, read-only containers

Table 4.4 – Zero trust adaptation for agent systems

Agent systems must be designed with operational boundaries: capabilities must be declared, scoped, and audited. Behavioral drift or unexplained deviations in reasoning should automatically trigger containment or escalation procedures.

Security incident preparedness

Given the inherent unpredictability of generative agents, organizations must plan not only for prevention but also for rapid detection and response. Security observability must be built into every layer of the agent stack.

Recommended controls include purpose-built observability tools for LLM agents, including LangSmith (prompt and chain tracing with execution replay), PromptFoo (prompt regression testing and adversarial evaluation), and OpenLLMetry (OpenTelemetry-compatible instrumentation for LLM call metrics and spans).

Recommended preparedness measures include the following:

- **Agent-specific runbooks**: Define procedures for rolling back memory, disabling tools, and notifying users
- **Anomaly detection**: Monitor for deviations in prompt length, token usage, tool selection, or path divergence
- **Audit trail retention**: Log all inputs, outputs, and tool interactions in encrypted, append-only systems for 90–180 days
- **Red team exercises**: Simulate prompt-based exploits, impersonation attacks, and tool hijacking in a controlled environment

These measures ensure that when anomalies occur, teams have both the forensic data and procedural clarity to respond effectively.

Defense-in-depth architecture

A secure agent architecture requires layered defenses across its cognitive and operational boundaries. These include specific controls and practices across various interaction points, such as the following:

- **Input validation**: Strip malicious tokens, enforce structured prompts, and isolate user input from system commands
- **Prompt schema enforcement**: Use typed input/output definitions to constrain reasoning boundaries
- **Memory governance**: Vet updates to persistent memory and constrain memory scope by session or role
- **Tool gating**: Whitelist allowed tools and enforce parameter constraints at runtime
- **Interface hardening**: Apply rate-limiting, authentication, and sandboxing to all externally exposed endpoints

These practices reduce the agent's vulnerability to prompt injection, tool abuse, and unauthorized memory manipulation. Additionally, integrating behavioral observability platforms, such as LangSmith, OpenTelemetry, or custom telemetry stacks, enables real-time monitoring of agent reasoning and execution.

Security and privacy in AI agents cannot be retrofitted; they must be architected as foundational design principles. Every prompt parsed, every tool invoked, and every piece of memory written represents a potential risk surface if left ungoverned. Securing these systems requires more than perimeter controls; it demands a holistic view of agents as autonomous digital actors whose behavior must be continuously constrained, verified, and observed.

Having established how to secure AI agents against external and internal threats, our focus now broadens to the paramount importance of their ethical development. This is crucial as these powerful systems increasingly influence real-world outcomes.

Ethical agent development: building responsible AI systems

As AI systems evolve into sophisticated autonomous agents, **ethical design** is paramount, especially in sensitive domains such as healthcare or finance, where decisions impact lives and rights. The challenge extends beyond task performance to ensuring unwavering commitment to human values and societal welfare. Unlike traditional software, AI agents' decisions, based on learned patterns and contextual reasoning, introduce unprecedented ethical complexities and new forms of risk.

Ethical agent development demands a systematic, lifecycle-long approach across interconnected dimensions, including technical aspects such as bias mitigation and broader societal implications such as influencing human decisions or accessing sensitive information. These dimensions—*transparency*, *fairness*, *accountability*, and *regulatory compliance*—form an interconnected system, where weaknesses in one compromise the whole framework. This requires implementing them as integrated components of a comprehensive ethical architecture. *Figure 4.3* illustrates this multi-layered ethical landscape:

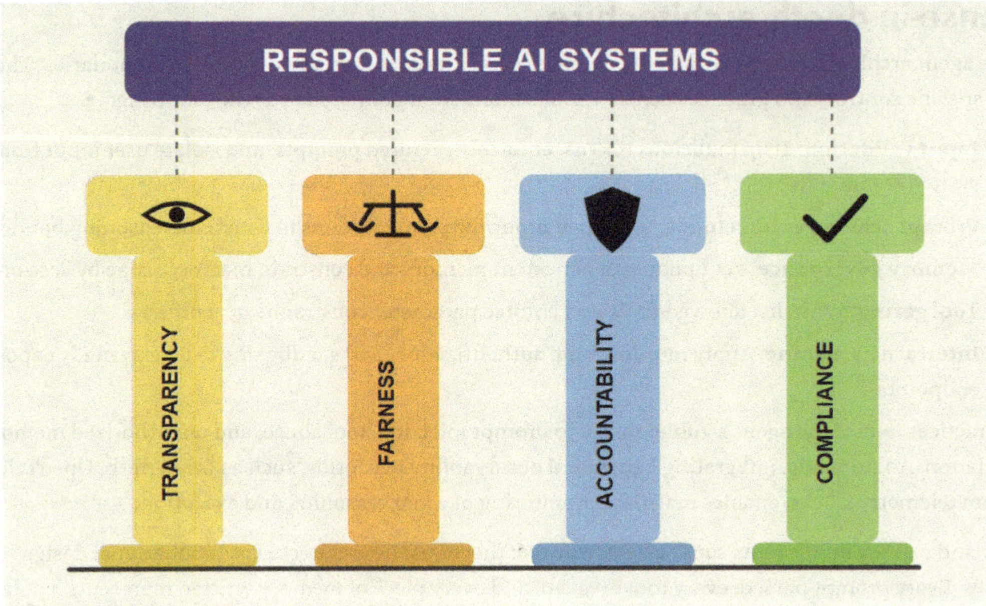

Figure 4.3 – Building responsible AI systems

Figure 4.3 demonstrates how technical capabilities intersect with societal responsibilities across four critical dimensions:

- **Transparency and explainability** are foundational, enabling understanding of agent decisions, which is crucial for evaluating fairness, ensuring accountability, and maintaining compliance
- **Fairness and bias mitigation** builds on transparency, verifying equitable treatment across individuals and groups, and connecting to accountability and regulatory frameworks
- **Accountability and oversight** forms the governance layer, encompassing human oversight and automated monitoring to detect ethical violations
- **Regulatory compliance** represents the external legal framework, integrating with all other dimensions by requiring transparent systems, fair treatment, and accountable governance for reporting

Transparency and explainability

The opacity of AI decisions is a major ethical barrier. Agent reasoning, whether for medical treatment or loan approvals, must be accessible and comprehensible to stakeholders. Transparency builds user trust and is fundamental for accountability and continuous improvement. Modern explainability frameworks go beyond simple feature importance, offering contextual narratives through multi-modal strategies such as visual attention maps, natural language summaries, or interactive tools. For example, a radiology AI might not only highlight suspicious regions but also explain its findings in medical terms, referencing similar cases and quantifying confidence levels. Explainable systems must be tailored to different audiences (researchers, clinicians, end users). Longitudinal transparency, achieved by persistently storing complete reasoning trails (model version, training data, environmental context), is vital for future audits and learning.

Fairness and bias mitigation

Bias in AI systems reflects societal inequities encoded in training data, perpetuating disparities from historical discrimination. Ethical AI requires active intervention to identify, measure, and correct these biases without introducing new unfairness. Bias manifests in data collection, algorithms, evaluation metrics, and deployment contexts. Comprehensive mitigation strategies span the development lifecycle: *pre-processing* (data augmentation, synthetic data), *model development* (fairness constraints in optimization objectives), and *post-processing* (adjusting outputs).

Two distinct fairness problems require separate treatment. **Algorithmic fairness** concerns bias in model predictions relative to protected attributes: a model trained on historically biased data may systematically under-serve certain demographic groups regardless of how it is deployed. **Deployment-context fairness** concerns bias introduced by how the system is operationalized: which populations have access to the agent, what data routing decisions determine whose queries reach which model, what feedback loops are active, and what downstream systems act on agent outputs. A model with no algorithmic bias can still produce unfair outcomes if deployed with restricted access, asymmetric feedback collection, or differential SLA enforcement across user populations. Both dimensions must be addressed in the mitigation strategies that follow.

Advanced frameworks navigate conflicting fairness notions such as demographic parity versus equalized opportunity, requiring careful consideration of application context and trade-offs. Measuring fairness extends beyond statistics to *dignity* and *empowerment*, striving for systems that actively reduce societal inequities.

Accountability and oversight

The autonomous nature of AI agents raises complex questions of responsibility. Unlike traditional software, their decisions, based on learned patterns, may not be fully predictable. Effective accountability frameworks establish clear governance structures defining roles and decision authority across the AI lifecycle, involving technical teams, business leaders, domain experts, and end users. *Audit trails*, leveraging immutable data structures and cryptographic signatures, form the technical foundation for accountability by logging agent decisions, environments, and interactions. *Human oversight mechanisms* provide critical safeguards for high-stakes decisions through risk-based escalation, where agents defer to human reviewers when confidence is low, populations are vulnerable, or consequences are severe. Oversight system design must account for human cognitive biases, providing contextual information and highlighting uncertainty to promote careful consideration.

Regulatory compliance

The regulatory environment for AI is rapidly evolving, with new legislation and standards emerging globally. Ethical AI development requires not just current compliance but **anticipatory design** to adapt to emerging frameworks, avoiding costly retrofitting. Privacy regulations such as GDPR and CCPA impose strict constraints on personal data processing, requiring consent, data access/deletion rights, and privacy-by-design. AI-specific regulations, such as the EU's proposed AI Act, categorize risk and impose stringent requirements for high-risk applications (documentation, testing, human oversight). Documentation requirements now include detailed records of training data, model processes, and deployment decisions (e.g., model cards, datasheets). Cross-border data flows add complexity, necessitating *geofencing* and *data residency controls* for compliance with jurisdiction-specific requirements.

Two frameworks now anchor responsible AI governance in practice. The NIST AI Risk Management Framework (AI RMF 1.0), which provides a voluntary, standards-based structure organized around four core functions—Govern, Map, Measure, and Manage—that teams can apply to identify, assess, and mitigate AI-related risks across the system lifecycle. It is particularly relevant for agent deployments because it addresses not only model-level risks but also organizational accountability, third-party dependencies, and deployment context. In the United States, there is Executive Order 14110 on the Safe, Secure, and Trustworthy Development and Use of AI, which establishes federal reporting requirements for frontier models and mandates red-teaming and safety evaluations before high-risk deployments. For agent systems operating in regulated sectors or interfacing with federal infrastructure, compliance with EO 14110 guidance is increasingly treated as a baseline obligation rather than an optional standard.

Having explored the critical landscape of regulatory compliance, it's essential to understand that adhering to these ethical and legal frameworks isn't a trade-off for performance. Instead, balancing ethics and performance is key to achieving sustainable excellence in AI.

Balancing ethics and performance

The idea that ethical safeguards compromise performance is a false dichotomy. Ethically designed systems often achieve superior long-term performance, reduced risk, and enhanced user adoption by treating ethics as innovation drivers. Performance metrics for ethical AI must include fairness, transparency, and societal impact, using quantitative (e.g., demographic parity) and qualitative (e.g., user trust) measures. Synergies exist: transparent systems are more debuggable, fair systems avoid legal costs, and accountable systems provide better feedback. Investing in ethical AI creates competitive advantages, enabling deployment in regulated markets and attracting talent.

Designing ethically aligned architectures

Ethical AI development demands deliberate architectural decisions that embed moral considerations throughout the design process, not as afterthoughts.

These considerations span multiple layers of system design, each influencing how effectively ethics is integrated into everyday agent behavior:

- **Data architecture** is foundational, with responsible governance frameworks establishing policies for data handling, quality monitoring, bias detection, and privacy-preserving techniques
- **Model architecture** decisions significantly impact ethical properties; ensemble approaches can reduce bias, uncertainty quantification communicates limitations, and modularity facilitates targeted interventions
- **Interface design** profoundly influences user interaction, requiring clear AI involvement, appropriate communication of uncertainty, and opportunities for user feedback and control
- **Deployment and monitoring** systems provide ongoing oversight, tracking ethical metrics in real time, alerting stakeholders, and enabling iterative refinement through feedback loops

Integrating ethics into architecture requires cross-functional collaboration between technical teams, domain experts, ethicists, and affected communities.

Established industry frameworks provide concrete reference points for this cross-functional work: the *IEEE Ethically Aligned Design* initiative offers a comprehensive set of principles for embedding human values into autonomous systems at the design level; Google's *Responsible AI MLOps* practices translate ethical commitments into operational workflows covering model evaluation, monitoring, and governance across the deployment lifecycle.

The path forward

Building ethically aligned AI agents is a technical and moral imperative. As systems grow sophisticated, ensuring alignment with human values becomes more complex, demanding technical expertise, moral clarity, stakeholder engagement, and institutional commitment. The provided frameworks offer a foundation, but continuous adaptation to contexts, societal expectations, and technologies is crucial. The goal is ***continuous improvement***, prioritizing human welfare. The future of AI hinges on our collective ability to ensure these powerful systems serve humanity's best interests through ongoing dialogue among technologists, policymakers, ethicists, and affected communities. The future belongs to AI agents that operate with *discernment*, *fairness*, and *accountability*, building trust for critical decisions.

Toolchain quick reference

The following table consolidates every major tool cited in this chapter. For each tool, the table provides its primary role in agent deployment, the minimum install or access command to get started, and a pointer to official documentation. Prerequisites are Python 3.9+ and Docker unless otherwise noted.

Tool	Role in Agent Deployment	Install / Access	Documentation
Docker	Containerize agent microservices for consistent cross-environment execution	`docs.docker.com/get-docker`	`docs.docker.com`
Kubernetes	Orchestrate agent Pods; manage autoscaling, health checks, and rolling updates	`minikube start` (local) or managed cluster (EKS / GKE / AKS)	`kubernetes.io/docs`
Temporal	Durable workflow orchestration; manages multi-step agent tasks with automatic retry and state persistence	`pip install temporalio`; run server via Docker Compose	`docs.temporal.io`
Prefect	Python-native workflow scheduling; suited for data-pipeline agents and batch inference jobs	`pip install prefect`	`docs.prefect.io`

Tool	Role in Agent Deployment	Install / Access	Documentation
OpenTelemetry	Distributed tracing, metrics, and logging across all agent microservices	`pip install opentelemetry-sdk opentelemetry -exporter-otlp`	`opentelemetry.io/docs`
Apache Kafka	High-throughput event streaming for async agent messaging and fan-out patterns	Docker Compose (local); managed via Confluent Cloud or AWS MSK; `pip install confluent-kafka`	`kafka.apache.org/documentation`
ArgoCD	GitOps continuous delivery; sync agent manifests from Git to Kubernetes automatically	Install via Helm: `helm install argocd argo/argo-cd`	`argo-cd.readthedocs.io`
Pinecone	Managed vector database for long-context memory retrieval in deliberative and hybrid agents	`pip install pinecone-client` ; API key at app.pinecone.io	`docs.pinecone.io`
Grafana	Observability dashboards; visualize token cost, latency, error rate, and circuit breaker state	Docker: `docker run -p 3000:3000 grafana/grafana`	`grafana.com/docs`
tenacity	Retry and circuit breaker logic for Python agent tool calls (see the code snippet within the *Modular cognition via microservices* section)	`pip install tenacity`	`tenacity.readthedocs.io`
Istio	Service mesh providing circuit breakers, mTLS, and traffic splitting for A/B testing agent versions	Install via Helm or `istioctl install`	`istio.io/latest/docs`

Table 4.4 – Toolchain quick reference for agent deployment

Summary

The deployment of AI agents at scale represents a convergence of *technical excellence, operational maturity*, and *ethical responsibility* that defines the next phase of artificial intelligence adoption. This chapter has demonstrated that successful agent deployment requires far more than solving isolated technical challenges; it demands a holistic approach that integrates sophisticated infrastructure design, comprehensive security frameworks, robust privacy protection, and principled ethical governance.

In *Chapter 3*, we explored the art of agent prompting that allows us to maximize the utility and use of agents; *Chapter 5* will present the cognitive foundational architecture of core agents that form the building blocks of all intelligent systems.

5

Foundational Cognitive Architectures

Information is the resolution of uncertainty.

— Claude Shannon (Father of Information Theory)

This chapter examines the foundational cognitive architectures that empower intelligent, autonomous agents to operate effectively in complex, dynamic environments. These architectures serve as the structural backbone of modern AI systems, simulating essential aspects of human cognition (decision-making, planning, and memory) to enable agents to tackle real-world problems with increasing sophistication.

Each of these architectures plays a distinct role in shaping intelligent behavior. Together, they enable AI systems to evolve from simple, reactive scripts into adaptive, autonomous workflows capable of handling intricate tasks over extended time horizons.

Understanding foundational cognitive architectures is crucial for any AI engineer because these patterns form the backbone of virtually every intelligent system in production today. Whether you're building a simple chatbot or a complex autonomous system, you'll find yourself combining elements of decision-making, planning, and memory to create agents that can handle real-world complexity. The architectures covered in this chapter are proven building blocks that power everything from customer service automation to sophisticated AI assistants managing multi-million-dollar business processes.

Mastering these foundational patterns gives you the conceptual framework to approach any agent development challenge systematically. Instead of building reactive scripts that break under edge cases, you'll be equipped to design systems that can adapt and learn with your requirements. Most importantly, understanding how these architectures complement each other prepares you for the advanced multi-agent systems and specialized agents we'll explore in subsequent chapters.

In this chapter, we'll be covering the following topics:

- Autonomous Decision-Making agents
- Planning agents
- Memory-Augmented agents

We begin by examining the Autonomous Decision-Making agent, the most fundamental building block in this hierarchy. It serves as the cornerstone upon which more advanced cognitive capabilities are constructed.

Technical requirements

To run the examples in this chapter, you'll need the following:

- A computer running macOS, Windows, or Linux (8 GB RAM minimum; 16 GB recommended).
- Python 3.10+, git, and a terminal.
- A Python virtual environment tool (e.g., `venv`, `conda`, or `uv`).
- Optional: an NVIDIA GPU with CUDA 12+ if you plan to experiment with local models. The chapter runs on the CPU.

All code for the book is hosted at `https://github.com/PacktPublishing/30-Agents-Every-AI-Engineer-Must-Build`. This chapter's material lives under the `Chapter 05/` folder.

The following steps set up the environment needed to run the examples in this chapter:

```
# 1) Clone the repo and enter this chapter's folder
git clone https://github.com/PacktPublishing/30-Agents-Every-AI-Engineer-Must-Build.git
cd 30-Agents-Every-AI-Engineer-Must-Build/"Chapter 05"

# 2) Create and activate a virtual environment
python -m venv .venv
# macOS/Linux:
source .venv/bin/activate
# Windows (PowerShell):
.venv\Scripts\Activate.ps1

# 3) Install dependencies
pip install -r requirements.txt

# 4) (If an API provider is used) copy env template and add your keys
cp .env.example .env  # then edit .env
```

The Autonomous Decision-Making agent

As introduced in *Chapter 1*, intelligent agents operate through continuous loops of perception, reasoning, action, and learning. This section grounds those ideas in the most fundamental architecture: the Autonomous Decision-Making agent. Autonomous Decision-Making agents perceive their environment, evaluate possible actions against goals and constraints, choose what to do, and execute, without requiring continuous human supervision. They learn from outcomes by updating state or memories that inform the next loop.

As an example, consider a customer-support agent. A user message such as "My internet is down, and I can't connect" triggers the loop: the agent parses the request and context, consults troubleshooting knowledge, selects one or more actions (for example, run a connectivity check or guide the user through steps), composes a response, and records the result for future turns. This concrete flow shows perception → reasoning → action → learning in practice.

In the pages that follow, we unpack each stage of this loop and implement a minimal, testable version of the architecture before layering in planning and memory capabilities.

The anatomy of autonomy: Building on the cognitive loop

To understand how Autonomous Decision-Making agents function at scale, we must examine how the cognitive loop from the *The cognitive loop* section in *Chapter 1* enables them to operate in dynamic, continuous cycles. Let's revisit our customer service agent and see how its three interconnected components—**perception**, **cognition**, and **action**—work together to create truly autonomous behavior.

Perception: From raw input to structured intelligence

We saw how our customer service agent's perception module captures environmental inputs and transforms them into structured data. Let's expand on this foundation to see how sophisticated perception systems enable autonomous operation:

```
# Illustrative pseudocode: not intended for direct execution
def analyze_sentiment(text: str) -> str:
    """Return sentiment label: 'positive', 'neutral', or 'negative'."""
    return classify_text_sentiment(text)  # stub: plug in any sentiment classifier

def check_system_alerts() -> list:
    """Return list of active system alert IDs from the monitoring service."""
    return monitoring_client.get_active_alerts()

def get_user_tier(user_id: str) -> str:
    """Return account tier string (e.g. 'standard', 'premium', 'enterprise')."""
    return crm_client.get_account_tier(user_id)


def perceive_input(user_message, context):
    return {
        "message": user_message,
        "timestamp": datetime.now(),
        "user_id": context.get("user_id"),
        "session_state": context.get("session"),
        "sentiment": analyze_sentiment(user_message)
    }

# Enhanced perception with environmental awareness
def enhanced_perception(user_message, context, system_state):
    base_perception = perceive_input(user_message, context)
```

```
    # Add system-wide context for autonomous operation
    enhanced_data = {
        **base_perception,
        "current_load": system_state.get("active_sessions"),
        "time_of_day": datetime.now().hour,
        "user_tier": get_user_tier(context.get("user_id")),
        "recent_issues": check_system_alerts(),
        "agent_availability": check_human_agent_status()
    }

    return enhanced_data
```

This enhanced perception system goes beyond simple input processing; it provides the agent with situational awareness that enables autonomous decision-making. When a user reports "My internet is down," the agent doesn't just process the message in isolation. It considers system load, time of day, user priority, and current network issues to make informed decisions about a response strategy.

A sophisticated perception system ensures data quality through validation, noise filtering, and preliminary structuring, providing clean, relevant inputs to downstream reasoning processes. The breadth and accuracy of this sensory layer fundamentally shape the agent's situational awareness and, by extension, the quality of its decisions.

Cognition: Strategic reasoning for autonomous operation

The reasoning component from *Chapter 1* demonstrated intent classification and priority determination. In autonomous agents, this cognitive layer must handle more complex decision trees and strategic planning:

```
# Illustrative pseudocode: not intended for direct execution
# Expanding on Chapter 1's reasoning function
def autonomous_reasoning(perception_data):
    # Basic intent and priority from Chapter 1
    intent = classify_intent(perception_data["message"])
    priority = determine_priority(
        intent,
        perception_data["sentiment"],
        user_history=get_user_history(perception_data["user_id"])
    )

    # Enhanced autonomous decision-making
    decision_context = {
        "intent": intent,
        "priority": priority,
        "context": perception_data,
        "autonomy_level": determine_autonomy_level(
```

```
            perception_data["user_tier"],
            perception_data["current_load"],
            perception_data["agent_availability"]
        ),
        "escalation_threshold": calculate_escalation_threshold(
            perception_data["time_of_day"],
            intent,
            priority
        )
    }

    # Autonomous strategy selection
    # Decision tree: score each candidate strategy across four weighted axes.
    # Axes: autonomy_level_score (0-1), urgency_score (0-1),
    # complexity_score (0-1), escalation_threshold (0-1)
    strategy_scores = {
        "full_autonomous_resolution":
            decision_context["autonomy_level_score"] * 0.5
            + (1 - decision_context["escalation_threshold"]) * 0.3
            + (1 - decision_context.get("complexity_score", 0)) * 0.2,
        "immediate_escalation":
            decision_context.get("urgency_score", 0) * 0.4
            + (not decision_context["agent_availability"]) * 0.4
            + decision_context["escalation_threshold"] * 0.2,
        "guided_autonomous_resolution": 0.5,  # baseline fallback
    }
    # Strategy with highest composite score wins; ties favour guided resolution
    decision_context["strategy"] = max(strategy_scores, key=strategy_scores.get)

    return decision_context
```

This cognitive architecture enables the agent to make strategic decisions about how to proceed. Unlike simple reactive systems, it can determine whether to handle an issue autonomously, when to escalate immediately, or when to use a hybrid approach, all based on contextual reasoning.

Modern agents increasingly use LLMs as their cognitive core, combining structured reasoning with sophisticated language understanding. As explored in *Chapter 3, The Art of Agent Prompting*, prompts can shape cognitive behavior, enabling agents to perform tasks such as intent classification, sentiment analysis, and contextual reasoning.

Action: Autonomous execution and adaptation

Building on the action execution from *Chapter 1*, autonomous agents must coordinate complex workflows and adapt to changing conditions:

```
# Illustrative pseudocode: not intended for direct execution
# Enhanced action execution with autonomous coordination
def autonomous_action_execution(decision_context):
    strategy = decision_context["strategy"]
    results = []

    if strategy == "full_autonomous_resolution":
        # Execute the full resolution workflow autonomously
        action_plan = create_autonomous_plan(decision_context)
        results = execute_autonomous_workflow(action_plan, decision_context)

    elif strategy == "immediate_escalation":
        # Prepare comprehensive handoff to human agent
        escalation_data = prepare_escalation_package(decision_context)
        results = initiate_human_handoff(escalation_data)

    else:  # guided_autonomous_resolution
        # Execute with checkpoints for human oversight
        action_plan = create_guided_plan(decision_context)
        results = execute_with_checkpoints(action_plan, decision_context)

    # Autonomous feedback and adaptation
    execution_feedback = analyze_execution_results(results, decision_context)
    update_decision_models(execution_feedback)

    return results

def create_autonomous_plan(decision_context):
    """Creates comprehensive action plans based on reasoning context"""
    intent = decision_context["intent"]
    priority = decision_context["priority"]

        # Build a dependency-aware task DAG.
    # Each node: {"id": str, "action": str, "depends_on": list[str]}
    # Tasks with empty depends_on[] run immediately;
    # downstream tasks wait until all listed ids complete.

    if intent == "billing_issue":
        return [
```

```
            {"id": "T1", "action": "fetch_account_details", "depends_on": []},
            {"id": "T2", "action": "analyze_billing_history", "depends_on": ["T1"]},
            {"id": "T3", "action": "identify_discrepancies", "depends_on": ["T2"]},
            {"id": "T4", "action": "calculate_adjustments", "depends_on": ["T3"]},
            {"id": "T5", "action": "generate_explanation", "depends_on": ["T3"]},
            {"id": "T6", "action": "apply_account_credits", "depends_on": ["T4"]},
            {"id": "T7", "action": "send_confirmation_email", "depends_on": ["T5",
"T6"]},
            {"id": "T8", "action": "schedule_follow_up", "depends_on": ["T7"]},
        ]
    elif intent == "service_outage":
        return [
            {"id": "T1", "action": "check_service_status", "depends_on": []},
            {"id": "T2", "action": "identify_affected_areas", "depends_on": ["T1"]},
            {"id": "T3", "action": "estimate_resolution_time", "depends_on": ["T1"]},
            {"id": "T4", "action": "send_proactive_notifications", "depends_on": ["T2",
"T3"]},
            {"id": "T5", "action": "monitor_restoration_progress", "depends_on": ["T1"]},
            {"id": "T6", "action": "update_customer_status", "depends_on": ["T4", "T5"]},
        ]
    # Default: generic resolution workflow
    return [
            {"id": "T1", "action": "analyze_issue", "depends_on": []},
            {"id": "T2", "action": "research_solutions", "depends_on": ["T1"]},
            {"id": "T3", "action": "implement_resolution", "depends_on": ["T2"]},
            {"id": "T4", "action": "verify_success", "depends_on": ["T3"]},
    ]
```

The action module is where reasoning is translated into real-world outcomes. Whether generating human-like responses, invoking APIs, or triggering physical actions, this component executes the agent's decisions. Crucially, action creates a feedback loop, modifying the environment and generating new inputs for the perception system.

The continuous cognitive loop: Enabling true autonomy

These components—perception, cognition, and action—do not operate in isolation. They form an integrated, continuous loop that enables dynamic interaction with complex environments. Let's see how our customer service agent from *Chapter 1* operates as a truly autonomous system:

```
class AutonomousCustomerServiceAgent:
    def __init__(self):
        self.session_memory = {}
        self.decision_history = []
        self.performance_metrics = {}
```

```
    def cognitive_loop(self, user_message, context):
        """The complete autonomous decision-making cycle"""

        # 1. Enhanced Perception
        system_state = self.get_current_system_state()
        perception_data = enhanced_perception(user_message, context, system_state)

        # 2. Autonomous Reasoning
        decision_context = autonomous_reasoning(perception_data)

        # 3. Strategic Action Execution
        results = autonomous_action_execution(decision_context)

        # 4. Learning and Adaptation
        self.learn_from_interaction(perception_data, decision_context, results)

        # 5. Update session state for continuity
        self.update_session_memory(
            context.get("user_id"), decision_context, results)

        return results

    def learn_from_interaction(self, perception_data, decision_context, results):
        """Enhanced learning from Chapter 1's learning function"""
        # Calculate success metrics
        success_score = calculate_success(results, decision_context)

        # Update user-specific models
        update_user_preferences(perception_data["user_id"], success_score)

        # Refine autonomous decision-making
        if success_score < 0.7:
            self.adjust_autonomy_thresholds(decision_context, success_score)
            flag_for_model_improvement(perception_data)

        # Update strategic models
        self.update_strategy_effectiveness(decision_context["strategy"], success_score)

        # Store decision patterns for future reference
        self.decision_history.append({
            "perception": perception_data,
            "decision": decision_context,
            "outcome": success_score,
```

```
        "timestamp": datetime.now()
    })
```

As illustrated in *Figure 5.1*, information flows seamlessly from environmental inputs, through cognitive processing, to environmental outputs, allowing agents to adapt and evolve through continuous engagement with their surroundings.

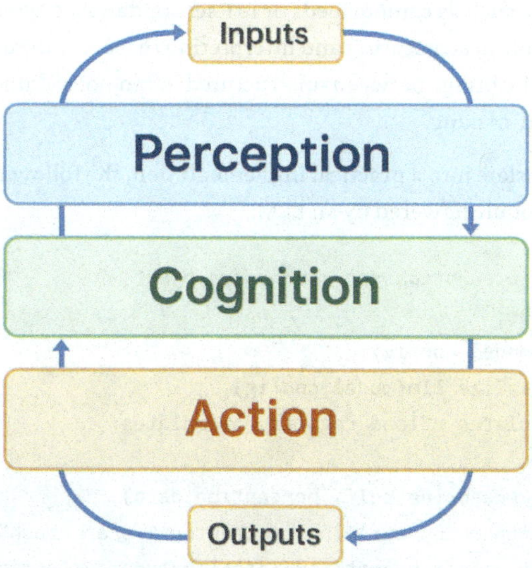

Figure 5.1 – The autonomous agent decision loop

The diagram clearly demonstrates the cyclical nature of autonomous agent operation. Environmental inputs enter through the perception module, where they're processed and structured for cognitive analysis. The cognition component then applies reasoning mechanisms to evaluate the input and determine appropriate responses. Finally, the action module executes the chosen response, which not only addresses the immediate situation but also generates new environmental states that feed back into the perception module, creating a continuous loop of intelligent behavior.

This architectural pattern ensures that agents remain responsive to changing conditions while maintaining coherent, goal-directed behavior over time. When a customer reports an internet outage, the agent doesn't just classify the intent; it considers the broader context (system alerts, user priority, agent availability) to determine the optimal autonomous response strategy.

Having seen how perception and context-aware reasoning enable agents to respond intelligently to changing conditions, we now turn to the broader architectural considerations that make such systems scalable and maintainable.

Practical implementation with modern LLMs

The emergence of powerful LLMs has fundamentally enhanced the practical implementation of the cognitive loop we explored in *Chapter 1*. Our customer service agent example demonstrates how LLMs serve as the cognitive engine that powers autonomous reasoning and decision flows, while frameworks such as LangChain and OpenAI's Functions API provide the orchestration capabilities needed for production deployment.

To understand how LLMs enable autonomy, let's revisit the core agent components (perception, cognition, and action) and explore how each is enhanced by LLMs.

Powering perception with LLMs

While low-level sensory inputs, such as camera feeds or IoT sensor data, are typically handled by specialized modules, LLMs play a critical role in structuring and interpreting these raw inputs to prepare them for higher-level reasoning. They serve as the bridge between unstructured, often noisy data and the structured context required for intelligent decision-making.

To see how these concepts translate into a practical implementation, the following code block outlines a production-ready cognition module powered by an LLM:

```
# Production-ready LLM integration for autonomous agents
class LLMPoweredCognition:
    def __init__(self, model_config):
        self.llm = initialize_llm(model_config)
        self.prompt_templates = load_cognitive_templates()

    def enhanced_intent_reasoning(self, perception_data):
        """LLM-powered reasoning building on Chapter 1's approach"""
        reasoning_prompt = self.prompt_templates["autonomous_reasoning"].format(
            user_message=perception_data["message"],
            user_history=get_user_summary(perception_data["user_id"]),
            system_context=format_system_context(perception_data),
            current_time=perception_data["timestamp"],
            available_tools=list_available_tools()
        )

        llm_response = self.llm.generate(reasoning_prompt)

        return {
            "intent": llm_response.intent,
            "confidence": llm_response.confidence,
            "reasoning_chain": llm_response.reasoning_steps,
            "recommended_strategy": llm_response.strategy,
            "tool_requirements": llm_response.required_tools,
            "escalation_assessment": llm_response.escalation_risk
        }
```

At the perception stage, LLMs excel at interpreting and organizing incoming information through two key functions: input interpretation and contextual framing.

Input interpretation

LLMs can efficiently parse a wide range of unstructured inputs, including natural language, logs, and sensor readings. They extract meaningful entities, classify information, and convert raw inputs into structured representations suitable for downstream reasoning.

For example, in a customer support scenario, a user message such as

"My internet is down, and I can't connect" is not simply processed as free-form text. The LLM interprets this as a **service outage**, categorizing it appropriately for triage and informing the next stage of reasoning.

Contextual framing

Beyond parsing inputs, LLMs help establish **situational awareness**. They perform tasks such as the following:

- Reducing noise and validating input quality
- Anchoring incoming data within relevant context, whether that's a user's ongoing conversation, a specific operational scenario, or prior interaction history

This ensures the agent proceeds with clean, relevant, and properly structured information, setting a solid foundation for accurate, context-aware decision-making throughout the reasoning cycle.

Driving cognition (reasoning) with LLMs

This is where LLMs truly excel. The cognition phase is the seat of intelligence and reasoning, where the agent interprets goals, assesses context, and formulates appropriate responses. Let's see how LLMs operationalize that reasoning layer in practice: how prompts, contextual signals, and intermediate reasoning strategies guide the agent from raw inputs toward actionable decisions. By examining these mechanisms, we make explicit how LLMs function as the reasoning engine that connects perception and action within an autonomous agent architecture.

Prompt templates for guided reasoning

The effective use of LLMs depends on well-crafted prompt templates that guide the model's reasoning in a predictable and purposeful manner. This practice, known as prompt engineering, forms the foundation of how cognition is shaped within these agents.

For example, a prompt might explicitly state:

```
"You are a customer service agent. Classify the user's intent and suggest the next best action."
```

This kind of structured instruction primes the LLM to operate within defined boundaries, much like a trained professional following established procedures. By anchoring the LLM's behavior in role-specific instructions and contextual cues, these prompts ensure consistency, relevance, and alignment with the agent's intended function.

Complex reasoning and inference

Modern LLMs excel at more than surface-level language processing; they are capable of engaging in complex reasoning and inference across a range of cognitive tasks. These capabilities include interpreting user intent, analyzing sentiment, and drawing contextual inferences from both current interactions and historical data.

Through techniques such as prompt chaining, scratchpad memory, and integration with external tools, agents can extend these reasoning capabilities further, simulating aspects of traditional symbolic reasoning systems. This allows LLM-driven agents to bridge the gap between pure language understanding and logical, structured problem-solving.

Dynamic decision-making

LLMs are not limited to generating static responses; they are increasingly capable of making dynamic decisions in pursuit of a defined goal. When provided with clear objectives and relevant context, LLMs can evaluate multiple possible actions, weigh the implications of each, and select the most appropriate next step, all with minimal or no human supervision.

Facilitating action with LLMs

The action stage is where an agent moves beyond reasoning and directly influences its environment, whether through communication, triggering tools, or calling APIs. At this point, insights and decisions transition into tangible outcomes.

Modern LLMs can go beyond generating text; they can identify the right tools to use and invoke them directly through APIs or plugins. This allows agents not only to suggest solutions but to execute them. For instance, upon recognizing a complex query, an agent might retrieve data from a CRM, submit a service request, or generate a detailed report through integrated toolchains.

This enhanced cognitive system builds directly on *Chapter 1*'s foundation while enabling true autonomous operation. The LLM doesn't just classify intent, but provides strategic reasoning about how to proceed, what tools to use, and when escalation might be necessary.

While LLMs significantly expand an agent's reasoning and execution capabilities, building reliable autonomous systems requires careful architectural safeguards. The following design considerations (drawn from the customer service agent introduced in *Chapter 1*) highlight practical principles for implementing these agents safely and effectively.

Design considerations: Lessons from Chapter 1

Building on the practical insights from the customer service agent in *Chapter 1*, several design principles become critical for Autonomous Decision-Making agents:

- **Guardrails and safety mechanisms:**
  Our *Chapter 1* example handled billing issues with careful validation. Autonomous agents must extend these safeguards:

```
def autonomous_safety_check(decision_context, planned_actions):
    """Enhanced safety mechanisms for autonomous operation"""
    safety_violations = []
```

```
    # Financial impact limits
    if "apply_account_credits" in planned_actions:
        credit_amount = calculate_credit_value(decision_context)
        if credit_amount > get_autonomous_credit_limit(
            decision_context["user_tier"]
        ):
            safety_violations.append("credit_limit_exceeded")

    # Data access permissions
    if requires_sensitive_data_access(planned_actions):
        if not verify_autonomous_data_permissions(decision_context):
            safety_violations.append("insufficient_data_permissions")

    # Impact assessment
    if assess_customer_impact_risk(planned_actions) >
decision_context["escalation_threshold"]:
        safety_violations.append("high_impact_risk")

    return len(safety_violations) == 0, safety_violations
```

To prevent the agent from generating unsafe, biased, or undesirable outputs (often termed "hallucinations" in LLM contexts), it's essential to implement robust guardrails and prompt injection defenses. This includes strict input validation, output filtering, and, crucially, prompt injection defenses.

- **Escalation criteria and human-in-the-loop coordination**:
  Chapter 1 showed basic escalation for urgent cases. Autonomous agents need sophisticated escalation logic:

```
def intelligent_escalation_decision(decision_context, safety_results):
    """Building on Chapter 1's escalation with autonomous intelligence"""
    escalation_factors = {
        "safety_violations": not safety_results[0],
        "confidence_threshold": decision_context.get("confidence", 0) < 0.8,
        "complexity_threshold": assess_issue_complexity(decision_context) > 0.7,
        "user_preference":
check_escalation_preference(decision_context["user_id"]),
        "business_impact": calculate_business_impact(decision_context) > 0.6
    }

    escalation_score = calculate_weighted_escalation_score(escalation_factors)

    if escalation_score > decision_context["escalation_threshold"]:
```

```
        return prepare_intelligent_escalation(decision_context,
escalation_factors)

    return None
```

Not every problem can or should be solved autonomously. Defining clear escalation criteria is vital, ensuring that the agent can gracefully defer to a human operator when it encounters ambiguous situations, ethical dilemmas, or tasks beyond its current capabilities.

Case study: Autonomous customer service in production

Let's see how our enhanced customer service agent from *Chapter 1* operates autonomously in a real-world scenario:

Scenario: A premium customer reports: *"My business internet has been intermittent for two days, and I have a critical presentation tomorrow."*

```
# Complete autonomous workflow
def handle_business_critical_outage():
    # 1. Enhanced Perception (building on Chapter 1)
    perception_data = enhanced_perception(
        user_message="My business internet has been intermittent for two days...",
        context={"user_id": "premium_business_123", "session": "new"},
        system_state=get_current_system_state()
    )

    # 2. Autonomous Reasoning
    decision_context = autonomous_reasoning(perception_data)
    # Result: High priority, business impact, autonomous resolution approved

    # 3. Safety and Escalation Assessment
    planned_actions = create_autonomous_plan(decision_context)
    safety_check, violations = autonomous_safety_check(decision_context, planned_actions)

    # 4. Autonomous Execution
    if safety_check:
        results = execute_autonomous_workflow([
            "check_service_area_status",
            "identify_intermittent_issues",
            "schedule_priority_technician",
            "upgrade_service_tier_temporarily",
            "provide_mobile_hotspot_backup",
            "set_proactive_monitoring",
            "schedule_followup_call"
        ], decision_context)
```

```
        # 5. Learning and Adaptation
        success_score = monitor_resolution_effectiveness(results)
        update_autonomous_strategies(decision_context, success_score)
```

By combining structured prompts and conditional logic, such a bot can operate autonomously for up to 80% of user queries, freeing human agents to focus on more nuanced and complex problems.

However, not all problems can be solved through isolated decisions or immediate reactions. Many real-world tasks demand a more structured, long-term approach. This is where the **Planning agent** comes in. Unlike Autonomous Decision-Making agents that focus on *what to do next*, Planning agents are designed to break down complex goals into actionable sequences of tasks, enabling structured execution over extended periods.

The Planning agent: Orchestrating dynamic workflows with adaptive intelligence

Building upon the immediate response capabilities of Autonomous Decision-Making agents, we now encounter scenarios that demand a fundamentally different approach, one that can handle complexity through systematic decomposition and strategic thinking. While autonomous agents excel at real-time, single-step responses, many real-world challenges require breaking down complex objectives into sequences of smaller, manageable tasks executed over extended periods.

This is precisely the domain of Planning agents, sophisticated systems designed to formulate and execute *multi-step plans* while adapting dynamically as new information, constraints, or priorities emerge during execution. The transition from reactive decision-making to proactive planning represents a significant leap in agent sophistication, enabling structured approaches to long-term objectives that would overwhelm simpler architectures.

In this section, we examine how Planning agents make this shift from reactive behavior to structured, goal-directed execution. We explore the architectural principles that support complex planning, including hierarchical task decomposition, symbolic planning techniques, and LLM-powered dynamic planning strategies. Together, these concepts illustrate how agents can coordinate multi-step workflows, monitor progress, and adapt plans as conditions evolve.

The core challenge: From reactive to strategic

Planning agents address a fundamental limitation of purely reactive systems: the inability to handle complex, multi-faceted goals that require coordinated sequences of actions. Consider the stark difference between answering a single customer service query versus orchestrating a complete product launch. The former requires immediate response and resolution, while the latter demands systematic breakdown, resource coordination, timeline management, and continuous adaptation to changing circumstances.

Effective Planning agents must master several interconnected capabilities. They must decompose high-level goals into actionable subtasks, sequence these tasks appropriately, allocate resources efficiently, monitor progress continuously, and adapt plans dynamically when circumstances change. This comprehensive approach enables agents to tackle complex, real-world projects that span days, weeks, or even months while maintaining coherent strategic direction.

Hierarchical decomposition: The architecture of complexity

The most powerful strategy for Planning agents is *hierarchical decomposition,* a systematic approach that mirrors how humans naturally tackle large projects. This methodology transforms abstract, high-level goals into structured trees of increasingly smaller and more concrete sub-goals, making complex problems tractable through focused attention on manageable components.

Modern Planning agents leverage two complementary paradigms, each offering distinct advantages for different problem types: symbolic planning foundations and LLM-powered dynamic planning.

Symbolic planning foundations

Traditional AI planning systems employ formal symbolic representations that provide rigorous, mathematically grounded approaches to problem-solving. **STRIPS (STanford Research Institute Problem Solver)** and **PDDL (Planning Domain Definition Language)** exemplify this approach, allowing developers to define states, actions, and goals in structured, formal languages. These systems enable algorithms to search systematically for optimal action sequences within well-defined problem spaces.

While symbolic planning offers precision and optimality guarantees, it typically requires comprehensive pre-modeling of the environment and problem domain. This makes symbolic approaches particularly powerful for well-understood, constrained domains but less adaptable to novel or rapidly changing situations.

LLM-powered dynamic planning

The advent of LLMs has revolutionized planning capabilities, introducing unprecedented flexibility and adaptability to agent architectures. Modern techniques such as **Tree-of-Thought (ToT)** and **Self-Ask** leverage the LLM's sophisticated reasoning capabilities to dynamically generate and explore possible solution paths or investigative sub-questions.

This paradigm shift enables agents to decompose tasks without rigid pre-programming, making them highly adaptable to novel situations and emergent requirements. The agent can reason about problems in natural language, considering context, constraints, and creative solutions that might not be captured in formal symbolic representations. As we explored extensively in *Chapter 3, The Art of Agent Prompting*, mastering prompt engineering for chain-of-thought implementations becomes crucial for effective LLM-powered planning systems.

The Planning agent architecture in action

To see the **LLM-powered dynamic planning** paradigm in action, *Figure 5.2* demonstrates this comprehensive approach through a concrete example, illustrating how a Planning agent orchestrates a complex marketing campaign from initial conception through execution, monitoring, and adaptive revision.

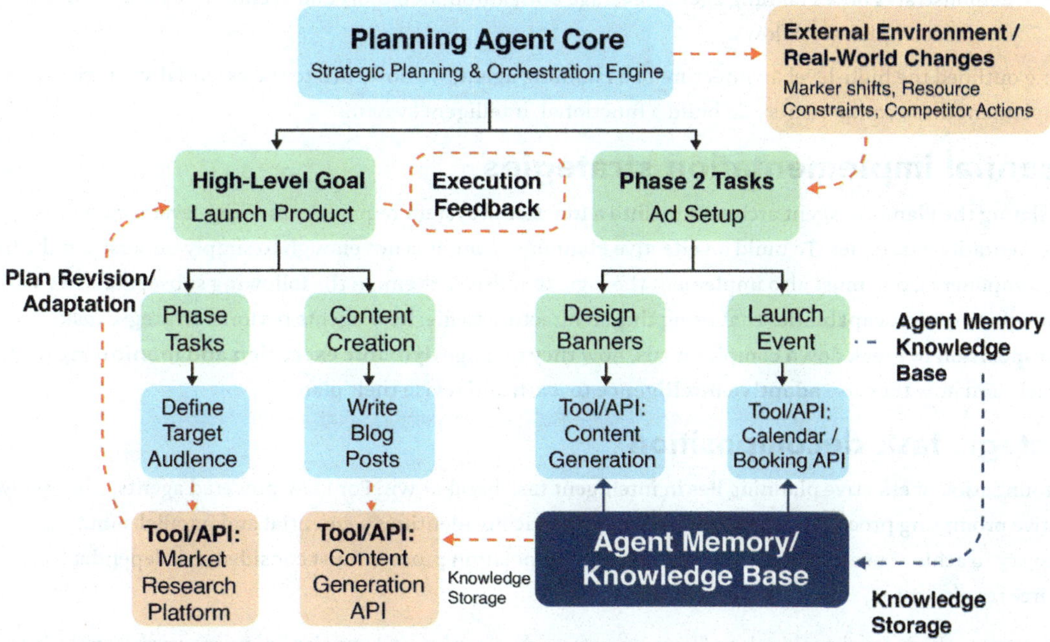

Figure 5.2 – LLM-powered dynamic planning in action. This example shows how a Planning agent orchestrates a complex marketing campaign from initial conception through execution, monitoring, and adaptive revision

The diagram illustrates the sophisticated multi-layered architecture that enables Planning agents to manage complex, dynamic projects. At the center is the **Planning Agent Core**, which serves as the strategic orchestration engine, coordinating all planning activities and maintaining oversight of the entire system. This core component interfaces with several critical elements that demonstrate the agent's comprehensive capabilities, including the following:

- **Environmental awareness and adaptation**: The Planning agent continuously monitors external factors (market shifts, resource constraints, and competitor actions) that may require plan adjustments. This environmental awareness, shown through the dotted red connections, enables proactive adaptation rather than reactive responses.
- **Strategic task hierarchy**: Starting with the high-level goal of "Launch Product Campaign," the Planning agent systematically decomposes this objective into major workstreams and specific, actionable tasks. Each level of the hierarchy represents increasing specificity, from strategic phases down to concrete tool integrations and API calls.
- **Dynamic execution management**: The **Execution Feedback** loop enables the agent to continuously monitor progress and identify when plan revisions are necessary. This feedback mechanism connects to the **Plan Revision/Adaptation** capability, allowing the agent to modify strategies based on real-world outcomes and changing conditions.
- **Integrated tool and knowledge orchestration**: The diagram shows how Planning agents seamlessly integrate with external tools and APIs for specific task execution, while maintaining connections to the **Agent Memory/Knowledge Base** for informed decision-making. This integration pattern

demonstrates how Planning agents leverage both automated tools and accumulated knowledge to execute complex workflows.

Having outlined the high-level architecture of a Planning agent, we now turn to the essential strategies required to implement these components and build a functional, intelligent system.

Essential implementation strategies

Translating the Planning agent architecture into a functional system requires mastering several core implementation strategies. To build an effective Planning agent, it is not enough to simply understand the high-level components; one must also implement the logic that drives them. In the following subsections, we will explore three critical capabilities that bring this architecture to life: how agents perform **strategic task decomposition** to break down complex goals, how they manage **dynamic execution and monitoring** to stay on track, and how they use **adaptive intelligence** to learn and revise their plans.

Strategic task decomposition

The foundation of effective planning lies in intelligent task breakdown. For LLM-powered agents, this involves iterative prompting processes where the agent systematically identifies sequential and parallel subtasks necessary to achieve overarching objectives. The decomposition process must consider task dependencies, resource requirements, time constraints, and risk factors.

For example, a high-level goal such as *"launch a new product marketing campaign"* requires careful analysis to identify constituent elements: market research, competitive analysis, content creation, distribution channel setup, performance monitoring, and post-launch optimization. Each of these major components can be further decomposed: content creation might break down into blog post writing, infographic design, video production, and social media asset development.

Dynamic execution and monitoring

Once comprehensive plans are formulated, execution becomes a complex orchestration challenge. Each planned step must be executed through carefully managed loops that invoke appropriate tools, delegate to specialized agents, or perform direct actions. This execution process requires continuous monitoring, as real-world conditions invariably differ from initial planning assumptions.

Effective Planning agents implement sophisticated *feedback mechanisms* that track progress against milestones, identify bottlenecks or failures, and trigger plan revisions when necessary. This might involve integrating with external project management systems, monitoring API responses for task completion, or processing human feedback about task status and quality.

Adaptive intelligence and learning

The hallmark of sophisticated Planning agents is their ability to adapt intelligently to changing circumstances. Rather than rigidly following static plans, these systems continuously evaluate progress and revise strategies based on new information, resource changes, or shifting priorities.

This adaptive capability leverages feedback signals, memory systems, and user input to inform plan modifications. For instance, if a critical dependency falls behind schedule, the agent might automatically reschedule dependent tasks, reallocate resources, or propose alternative approaches that minimize overall project impact. The blue dotted connections to the knowledge base in *Figure 5.2* show how Planning agents access historical project data, successful strategies from previous campaigns, and learned patterns to inform current planning decisions.

Planning versus decision-making: complementary capabilities

Understanding how Planning agents differ from and complement Autonomous Decision-Making agents clarifies their respective roles in comprehensive agent systems:

Capability	Autonomous Decision-Maker	Planning Agent
Focus	Immediate, tactical responses	Strategic, long-term goal achievement
Scope	Single decisions at a time	Multi-step, coordinated processes
Adaptation	Heuristics and conditional logic	Dynamic revision and learning loops
Integration	Direct API calls for specific actions	Orchestrated tool workflows
Memory Use	Contextual within current session	Persistent, cross-project learning

Table 5.1 – Differences between Autonomous Decision-Making and Planning agents

While the ability to make decisions and create plans forms the core of an agent's active capabilities, true intelligence requires learning from the past. This brings us to our third foundational architecture, which focuses on the critical component of memory.

The Memory-Augmented agent

Autonomous agents today can independently make decisions and formulate multi-step plans. Yet a critical limitation remains: how can they retain context and learn from past experiences beyond the current interaction? This is where **Memory-Augmented agents** become essential.

Many foundational agents operate solely in the present, reacting to current inputs. In contrast, Memory-Augmented agents incorporate mechanisms that preserve context over time. This significantly improves their ability to personalize responses, maintain coherence, and reason over the long term.

Inspired by human cognition, these agents utilize different types of memory systems to store, retrieve, and consolidate information. This enables them to respond more intelligently and remain context-aware throughout extended interactions.

In this section, we explore how memory enables agents to move beyond short-lived reasoning loops toward sustained, context-rich intelligence. We begin by examining the different types of memory used in intelligent agents, then look at how these memory systems are integrated into a unified architecture. Finally, we illustrate the practical implementation of this approach through a real-world case study demonstrating how memory enables more coherent, personalized interactions over time.

Types of memory in intelligent agents

Memory-Augmented agents utilize three distinct types of memory, each with a unique role in their cognitive architecture:

- **Working memory**: This acts as the agent's short-term memory, holding immediate, in-session information directly within the LLM prompt. This includes recent conversation turns, current goals, and task-specific data. Working memory is transient and is cleared after the session ends or when the token limit is reached.
- **Episodic memory**: This memory type captures a history of interactions and events, often with timestamps. It allows the agent to recall specific past experiences, such as a previous conversation or the outcome of a past action, supporting continuity and long-term personalization.
- **Semantic memory**: This stores structured, factual information derived from documents, APIs, or databases. Unlike episodic memory, which focuses on events, semantic memory contains general knowledge and concepts such as product specifications, regulations, or scientific facts, forming a stable foundation for the agent's understanding.

Use the following guide to select which memory system to query for a given situation:

Memory Type	Trigger Condition	Query Signal	Failure Mode if Skipped
Working	Active session; current turn in progress	LLM context window populated directly	Loss of immediate conversational coherence; agent forgets earlier turn context
Episodic	Cross-session continuity needed; user references prior interaction	Vector similarity search over interaction history	Repeated history; agent treats each session as new, breaking personalization
Semantic	Factual or domain knowledge required; query not answerable from session alone	Keyword or semantic search over knowledge base	Hallucinated or stale answers; agent cannot ground claims in authoritative data

Together, these three forms of memory form the cognitive foundation upon which Memory-Augmented agents operate. In the next section, we will see how they are integrated into a unified architecture that supports context retention, continuity, and adaptive intelligence.

Memory-Augmented agent architecture

The Memory-augmented agent architecture (depicted in *Figure 5.3*) integrates multiple memory components to enable contextual reasoning, continuity, and continuous learning, allowing the agent to move beyond reactive responses to sustained, informed, and adaptive interactions.

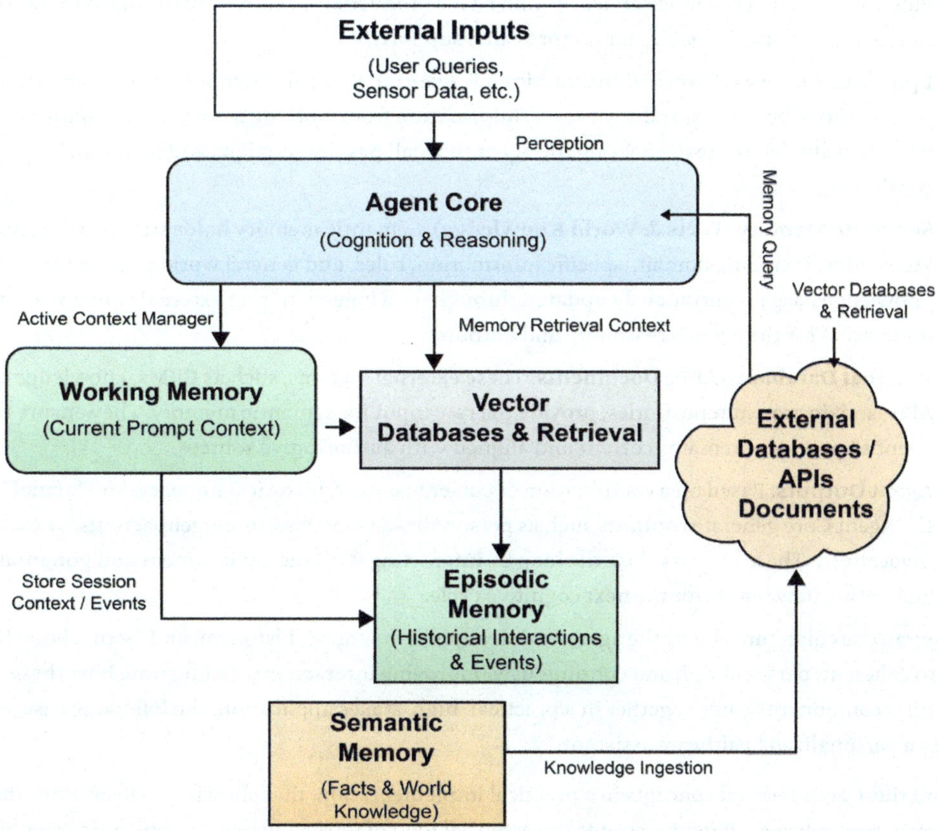

Figure 5.3 – The Memory-Augmented agent architecture

Here's how each component functions within this dynamic system:

1. **External Inputs**: The process starts with external stimuli such as user queries, environmental data, or sensor readings, which initiate the perception phase and flow into the agent's core cognitive engine.
2. **Agent Core (Cognition & Reasoning)**: As the central component, the Agent Core is responsible for reasoning, decision-making, and orchestrating memory interactions. It processes perceived inputs, queries memory systems as needed, and synthesizes information to guide actions.
3. **Working Memory (Current Prompt Context)**: This serves as the agent's short-term buffer, holding immediate, session-specific context, such as recent conversation turns or ongoing tasks. This active context directly influences the LLM's current prompts, supporting real-time reasoning and response generation.
4. **Vector Databases & Retrieval**: This system acts as a bridge to long-term memory, facilitating efficient access to relevant information. When the Agent Core requires knowledge beyond its immediate context, it sends a memory query. Retrieval mechanisms assess relevance based on factors such as semantic similarity, recency, or user preferences, sourcing information from both episodic and semantic memory. Practical implementations include Chroma (well-suited for local development and prototyping),

Pinecone (a managed cloud service optimized for production-scale retrieval), and Weaviate (open source with hybrid keyword and vector search support).

5. **Episodic Memory (Historical Interactions & Events)**: Episodic memory captures and stores historical sessions, user behaviors, and key events. Information from working memory is regularly stored here to preserve valuable context, enabling the agent to recall past interactions and maintain long-term continuity.
6. **Semantic Memory (Facts & World Knowledge)**: Semantic memory holds structured, factual knowledge, including domain-specific information, rules, and general world knowledge. This knowledge base is continuously updated through data ingestion from external sources, forming a stable foundation for the agent's reasoning and outputs.
7. **External Databases/APIs/Documents**: These external systems, such as CRMs, knowledge bases, public APIs, and document repositories, provide the raw input for semantic memory. They ensure that the agent's knowledge remains current and aligned with authoritative sources.
8. **Agent Outputs:** Based on a combination of current context, historical memory, and factual knowledge, the Agent Core generates outputs such as personalized responses, intelligent actions, or tool invocations. These outputs close the loop by interacting with the environment and potentially generating new inputs for the next cognitive cycle.

This integrated architecture allows the agent to draw upon immediate, historical, and factual knowledge, leading to coherent, personalized, and continuously improving interactions. To illustrate how these architectural components come together in a practical, high-stakes application, the following case study examines a personalized healthcare assistant.

To ground these architectural concepts in a practical implementation, the following code outlines the core logic for `MemoryAugmentedAgent`. It demonstrates the essential loop of retrieving relevant **episodic memories** to provide context for a current query and then storing the new interaction for future use. This example uses the personalized healthcare assistant scenario to show how memory enables more coherent and context-aware responses over time.

```
import datetime

class MemoryAugmentedAgent:
    def __init__(self, llm_client, vector_db):
        self.llm = llm_client
        self.episodic_memory = vector_db # Using a vector DB for episodic memory

    def process_interaction(self, user_id, user_query):
        """Processes a user query, retrieves relevant memories, and stores the new
interaction."""

        # 1. Retrieve relevant past interactions from episodic memory
        relevant_memories = self.episodic_memory.search(
            query=user_query,
            user_id=user_id,
```

```
            limit=3
        )

        # 2. Construct a prompt that includes the retrieved memories
        prompt = f"""
        You are a personalized healthcare assistant.
        Here is the user's current query: "{user_query}"

        For context, here are relevant past interactions with this user:
        {relevant_memories}

        Provide a helpful and context-aware response.
        """
        response = self.llm.generate(prompt)

        # 3. Store the current interaction in episodic memory for future use
        interaction_record = {
            "user_id": user_id,
            "query": user_query,
            "response": response,
            "timestamp": datetime.datetime.now().isoformat()
        }
        self.episodic_memory.add(interaction_record)

        return response
```

In a practical scenario, `MemoryAugmentedAgent` is initialized with a connection to an LLM and a vector database to serve as its memory. Its value becomes clear over multiple interactions. For instance, a patient might first report, *"I've been feeling very fatigued lately."* The agent processes this query, generates a response, and, most importantly, stores a record of this interaction (the query, the response, and a timestamp) in its episodic memory.

Later, when the same patient follows up with, *"That diet change you suggested helped a bit, but I'm still tired,"* the agent doesn't treat this as an isolated query. Its `process_interaction` function first searches its episodic memory and retrieves the previous conversation about fatigue because it is semantically relevant. This retrieved memory is then injected directly into the prompt sent to the LLM.

The final prompt would look something like this:

```
You are a personalized healthcare
assistant. Here is the user's current query: 'That diet change you suggested helped a
bit, but I'm still tired.' For context, here are relevant past interactions with this
user: [{'query': 'I've been feeling very fatigued lately.', 'response': '...',
'timestamp': '...'}] Provide a helpful and context-aware response.
```

This process ensures the LLM has the full conversational history, allowing it to generate a much more coherent and helpful response that acknowledges the patient's ongoing experience.

The code provides a simplified look at the mechanics, but to truly appreciate the power of this architecture, it's helpful to see how all the memory components work together in a complex application. The following case study on a personalized healthcare assistant illustrates how this integrated system enables sophisticated, long-term, and context-aware interactions.

Case study: A personalized healthcare assistant

Consider an AI agent designed as a personalized healthcare assistant, helping patients manage chronic conditions or navigate complex medical information. This agent's effectiveness hinges entirely on its sophisticated memory capabilities, as it must maintain long-term context, recall patient-specific details, and provide accurate, timely information.

- **Perception and working memory**: When a patient inputs symptoms or asks a question about their medication, the agent core receives these external inputs. The immediate dialogue, including the patient's tone and current query, is held in **Working Memory (Current Prompt Context)**, allowing the agent to engage in a fluid and responsive conversation.
- **Episodic memory in action**: After each interaction, key details, such as changes in symptoms, successful coping strategies, medication adherence patterns, and even emotional states conveyed by the patient, are processed and used to *Store Session Context/Events* in **Episodic Memory (Historical Interactions & Events)**. For instance, if a patient reports persistent fatigue during a follow-up, the agent can send a *Memory Query* to its **Vector Databases & Retrieval** system. It might then retrieve relevant context from *Episodic Memory* detailing previous instances of fatigue, interventions tried, and their effectiveness, ensuring continuity in care.
- **Semantic memory for clinical knowledge**: The assistant's vast medical knowledge, including drug interactions, disease protocols, and public health guidelines, resides in its **Semantic Memory (Facts & World Knowledge)**. This is constantly updated through *Knowledge Ingestion* from **External Databases/APIs/Documents**, which could include clinical databases, medical journals, and regulatory documents. When asked about a specific medication, the agent queries its *Semantic Memory* for accurate and up-to-date information.
- **Personalization through memory retrieval**: When the agent formulates its *Agent Outputs* (e.g., advising on symptom management or explaining a treatment), it combines information from *Working Memory* with insights and retrieved relevant context from both *Episodic Memory* (patient's history, preferences) and *Semantic Memory* (medical facts). For example, it might recommend a particular relaxation technique if its *Episodic Memory* indicates that method previously helped the patient, or tailor dietary advice based on the patient's recorded allergies in *Semantic Memory*.
- **Memory consolidation for scalability**: To manage the extensive patient interaction history and medical knowledge, the agent regularly employs *Memory Consolidation/Summarization*. Long consultations in *Episodic Memory* might be summarized into concise patient profiles such as `Patient A, Type 2 Diabetes, responded well to diet changes (2025-01-15), struggled with medication adherence (2025-03-20)`. This ensures that the **Vector Databases & Retrieval** remain efficient, providing high-quality, personalized support without performance degradation.

This continuous interplay of perception, current context management, historical recall, factual knowledge retrieval, and memory refinement allows the personalized healthcare assistant to provide empathetic, informed, and truly individualized support, showcasing the power of Memory-Augmented agents in a critical domain.

With a clear understanding of Autonomous Decision-Making agents, Planning agents, and Memory-Augmented agents in isolation, the next step is to compare them systematically to highlight their unique strengths, limitations, and how they complement each other when integrated into larger systems.

Comparative analysis of architectures

Each foundational cognitive architecture—Autonomous Decision-Making agents, Planning agents, and Memory-Augmented agents—excels in its specific domain. However, their true potential emerges through strategic combinations. These architectures are not mutually exclusive; rather, they are complementary building blocks that, when integrated, form sophisticated and intelligent systems capable of solving real-world, multi-layered problems.

Each architecture brings unique strengths along with trade-offs. Understanding these distinctions is critical when designing systems tailored to specific use cases.

- **Autonomous Decision-Making agents**: These agents specialize in real-time responsiveness. They rapidly process information, evaluate options, and make immediate decisions. They are particularly effective in scenarios such as customer service chatbots, alerting systems, and triage situations.
  Trade-offs: Their emphasis on speed may increase the risk of hallucinations or unsafe actions, especially in the absence of proper constraints. They may also lack the depth required for handling complex or strategic tasks.
- **Planning agents**: These agents are ideal for executing complex, multi-step goals. They excel in breaking down high-level objectives into manageable subtasks, coordinating dependencies, and dynamically adapting strategies. This makes them well-suited for project orchestration, workflow automation, and strategic planning.
  Trade-offs: Planning agents are typically slower due to the need for analysis and design before execution. They also demand robust control mechanisms for monitoring progress and recovering from errors, adding architectural complexity.
- **Memory-Augmented agents**: These agents provide continuity across sessions by leveraging past interactions. They use working, episodic, and semantic memory to personalize responses, maintain context, and reason over long durations. Applications such as CRM systems and intelligent personal assistants benefit greatly from this capability.
  Trade-offs: Managing memory systems and optimizing retrieval processes can be complex. These systems also require careful design to avoid information overload.

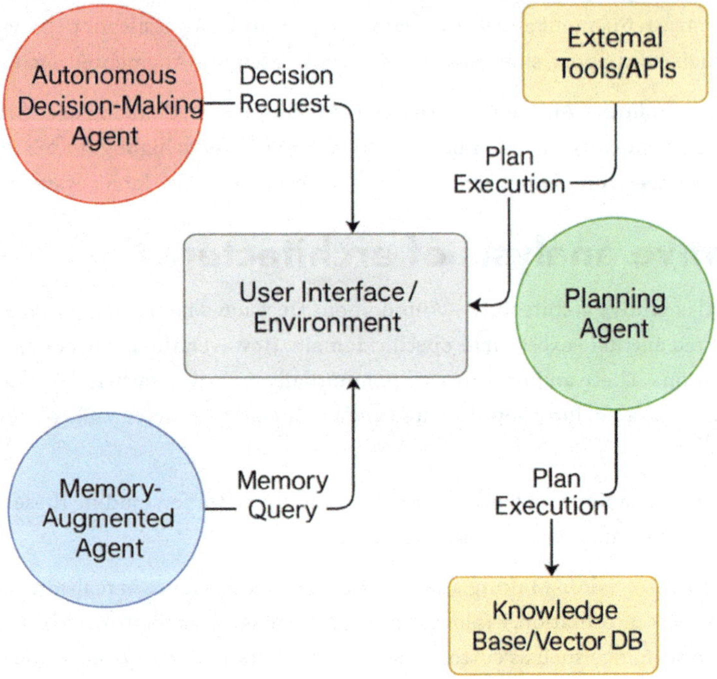

Figure 5.4 – Integrated cognitive architecture combining all three foundational elements

Here's a summary of the different architectures:

Agent Type	Strength	Ideal Use Case	Limitations
Autonomous Decision-Making	Real-time response and flexibility	Customer service, triage	Risk of hallucinations; lacks deep context
Planning Agent	Structured execution and adaptability	Project orchestration, complex workflows	Slower execution; requires control logic
Memory-Augmented Agent	Long-term coherence and personalization	CRM systems, task handoff, continuity	Complex maintenance; sensitive to retrieval design

Table 5.2 – Comparative analysis of foundational agent architectures

Taken together, these architectures form complementary building blocks for sophisticated agentic systems. Their real power emerges when combined into larger workflows or multi-agent collaborations, which we will study in more detail in *Chapter 7*.

Engineering best practices

Having explored the individual building blocks of intelligent agents and understood their comparative strengths and how they can be combined, the next crucial step is to consider the practicalities of their implementation.

Building reliable and capable intelligent agents isn't just about understanding the theory; it requires adherence to sound engineering principles throughout the development lifecycle. This section outlines essential best practices that will help you transition from conceptual design to robust, production-ready agent systems.

Designing for scalability and maintainability

The success of intelligent agents in real-world applications hinges on their ability to perform consistently and be easily managed and scaled.

To achieve these goals in practice, the following best practices are essential for building scalable, maintainable agent systems:

- **Start modular**: A core principle in software engineering, **modularity** is even more critical for agent systems. Separate your agent's capabilities into distinct modules: perception, memory, planning, and action. This separation of concerns simplifies development, debugging, and future enhancements. For instance, updating an LLM fine-tuning strategy for the cognition module won't directly break your tool integration logic in the action module.
- **Log everything—the importance of observability**: Intelligent agents, especially those powered by LLMs, can exhibit emergent and sometimes unpredictable behaviors. Robust observability is paramount. Implement comprehensive logging at every stage of the agent's decision loop, from initial perception and prompt formulation to tool calls and final actions. Tools such as LangSmith (a platform for debugging, testing, evaluating, and monitoring LLM applications) or similar solutions are critical for gaining insights into agent performance, identifying failures, and understanding *why* an agent made a particular decision. This will prove invaluable during testing and continuous improvement (as discussed in *Chapter 4, Agent Deployment and Responsible Development*).

Optimizing performance and context management

LLMs are powerful but come with computational costs and context window limitations. Efficient design is key.

- **Avoid prompt bloat**: LLMs have a finite context window, and feeding them excessive or irrelevant information degrades performance, increases latency, and incurs higher costs. It is essential to optimize your **retrieval pipelines** to provide only the most relevant context. Techniques for this, such as **re-ranking** retrieved documents, which we will explore in detail in *Chapter 6*, are crucial for efficient context management, alongside methods such as employing the summarized memory entries we discussed earlier.
- **Employ techniques for maximizing performance while minimizing costs**: Beyond prompt optimization, consider strategies such as LLM selection guidelines for different agent types, fine-tuning for agent-specific behaviors, and model scaling considerations, all detailed in *Chapter 2, The Agent Engineer's Toolkit*.

Ensuring robustness and reliability

Intelligent agents operate in dynamic environments and must be designed to handle uncertainty gracefully. Intelligent agents will inevitably encounter situations they cannot resolve or where their actions might be unsafe. Design your systems with clear fallbacks and escalation paths for undecidable or unsafe conditions. This might mean defaulting to a human operator, requesting clarification from the user, or rolling back an action. Implementing robust error handling for tool integration (a key aspect of the Tool-Using agent in *Chapter 7*) is also vital. This directly ties into the security and privacy considerations discussed in *Chapter 4*, particularly concerning prompt injection defenses and secure tool access patterns.

Summary

This chapter explored three foundational cognitive architectures: **Autonomous Decision-Making agents**, **Planning agents**, and **Memory-Augmented agents**. These agents together form the essential building blocks for creating intelligent, adaptive systems. Each architecture specializes in a distinct aspect of cognition: decision-making agents enable rapid, reactive responses; Planning agents orchestrate complex, multi-step objectives; and Memory-Augmented agents provide continuity through working, episodic, and semantic memory. Collectively, they realize the cognitive loop of perception, reasoning, action, and learning introduced in *Chapter 1*, allowing agents to move from reactive behaviors toward long-term, context-aware intelligence.

Crucially, these architectures are most powerful when integrated, combining their strengths to create more capable and resilient agents. This chapter emphasized best practices, such as modular design, observability, efficient context management, and robust safety measures, that help engineers translate these concepts into scalable, reliable systems. Together, these patterns support applications ranging from simple conversational bots to sophisticated, memory-enhanced agents capable of complex reasoning.

By building organically on the cognitive loop and customer service examples from *Chapter 1*, we've seen how foundational concepts evolve into production-ready autonomous systems that can handle complex real-world scenarios while maintaining safety, reliability, and performance. In the next chapter, we turn to *Information Retrieval and Knowledge agents*, expanding these ideas further by exploring how agents access and leverage vast external knowledge to enrich their decision-making.

6

Information Retrieval and Knowledge Agents

The difference between the right word and the almost right word is the difference between lightning and a lightning bug.

– Mark Twain

In a world where information is doubling at a staggering pace, the ability to locate *reliable*, *current*, and *contextually relevant* knowledge is now a decisive factor for innovation, decision-making, and competitive advantage. LLMs have revolutionized how we understand and generate natural language, yet their power is limited by a static training snapshot and the risk of producing unverifiable or outdated answers. **Knowledge agents** close this gap by blending intelligent reasoning with live, authoritative data sources—transforming LLMs from static archives into dynamic, evidence-grounded collaborators.

This chapter explores how these agents operate as intelligent intermediaries between humans and complex information ecosystems. They do not merely respond to questions; they *search*, *verify*, and *ground* their outputs in trusted data. Whether it is retrieving company policies on demand, synthesizing decades of scientific literature, or monitoring fast-moving market intelligence, knowledge agents ensure that responses are not just fluent but factually anchored and auditable.

In this chapter, we'll learn how to work with three major types of AI agents and apply them to real-world problems. We'll start with **Knowledge Retrieval agents**, where you'll see how to extend the static knowledge of LLMs with real-time information using RAG and advanced search workflows. We'll then move on to **Document Intelligence agents**, learning how to transform messy, heterogeneous documents into structured, decision-ready data with tools such as OCR, layout parsing, and schema-driven extraction. Finally, we'll explore **Scientific Research agents**, where you'll practice going beyond simple retrieval to synthesis and hypothesis generation, using these agents to cluster and compare evidence across large research corpora.

In this chapter, we'll be covering the following topics:

- Knowledge Retrieval agents

- Document Intelligence agents
- Scientific Research agents

This chapter establishes the **strategic and technical foundation** for working with knowledge agents. It sets the stage for the deep dive into the historical context and evolution of these agents, where we will trace their journey from early expert systems to today's sophisticated, real-time information brokers.

This section sets the groundwork for the more advanced agents you will encounter later in the chapter. By understanding retrieval workflows, vector databases, and provenance tracking now, you will be better prepared for the upcoming discussions on Document Intelligence agents and Scientific Research agents, where these principles are extended to document parsing and large-scale research synthesis.

Let us begin with the Knowledge Retrieval agent, the key architectural pattern that enables LLMs to deliver answers grounded in live, verifiable data.

Knowledge Retrieval agents

A Knowledge Retrieval agent is the lifeline connecting an LLM's static training data to the living, ever-changing world of information. Think of an LLM as a brilliant scholar with a vast but dated library; the retrieval agent is the assistant who fetches the latest journals and archives to ensure the scholar's answers are fresh and relevant. By linking to live sources such as databases and APIs, these agents directly address two critical weaknesses of language models: knowledge cutoff and the risk of hallucination, anchoring their outputs in verifiable evidence.

> Note
>
> **Agent capability level**
>
> A Knowledge Retrieval agent typically operates at Level 2 (Tool-Using agent) of the Agentic AI Progression Framework, as it can parse requests, select tools (e.g., a search API), and execute chained operations. However, a more advanced agent that decomposes high-level goals (such as "conduct a literature review") and maintains memory across steps can begin to exhibit the behaviors of Level 3 (Planning agent).

In this section, we will examine how retrieval agents are designed and implemented in practice. We begin by outlining the core principles that guide their architecture, followed by a closer look at the common implementation patterns and tools used to build **retrieval-augmented generation** (**RAG**) systems, including a hands-on example pipeline. Finally, we discuss operational considerations and challenges that arise when deploying retrieval agents in real-world production environments.

Guiding principles

The design of an effective retrieval agent is shaped by a set of guiding principles that determine how it processes information and grounds its outputs. These principles ensure that the agent does more than just fetch data; they define the reliability, transparency, and adaptability of the system.

- **Addressing LLM limitations**: The primary goal is to mitigate the effects of outdated training data and reduce the likelihood of fabricated answers
- **Implementing RAG**: This core methodology merges information retrieval with generative reasoning, enabling the model to produce answers explicitly supported by evidence
- **Ensuring versatile retrieval**: Agents must handle both structured retrieval from databases or APIs and unstructured retrieval from documents and web pages
- **Grounding in sources**: To ensure transparency and trust, all generated answers should include citations or provenance data that trace back to the original source

Together, these principles form the foundation for how retrieval agents are built and evaluated. With this groundwork in place, we can now turn to the retrieval process itself and see how these principles take shape in a working architecture.

The retrieval process: Architecture in action

A retrieval agent operates in a continuous cycle, moving from understanding a query to generating a grounded response. This process is best understood through its modular architecture, where each component performs a distinct step.

1. **Query understanding (perception and reasoning)**: The process begins when the agent receives a user's request, such as "What does the latest compliance regulation say about data retention?". A **Query Understanding Layer** parses this input, discerns the user's true intent, clarifies ambiguities, and reformulates the request into a precise search query.
2. **Retrieval (planning and action)**: The agent then plans its retrieval strategy, identifying the best data sources and search methods (e.g., lexical, semantic, or hybrid). A **Retriever Module** executes this plan, connecting to search APIs or vector databases to locate relevant content.
3. **Preprocessing**: Before the retrieved information can be used, a **Preprocessing** stage splits large documents into manageable chunks, generates vector embeddings for semantic comparison, and applies filters to remove irrelevant results.
4. **Synthesis (learning and updating)**: In the final step, a **Reasoning and Generation** layer integrates the retrieved content directly into the LLM's prompt. The model is instructed to synthesize a coherent answer using only the provided sources, ensuring the response is grounded in evidence. Provenance tracking runs alongside this, maintaining metadata and citations to ensure every factual claim is traceable.

This modular design improves maintainability and allows each component to be optimized independently.

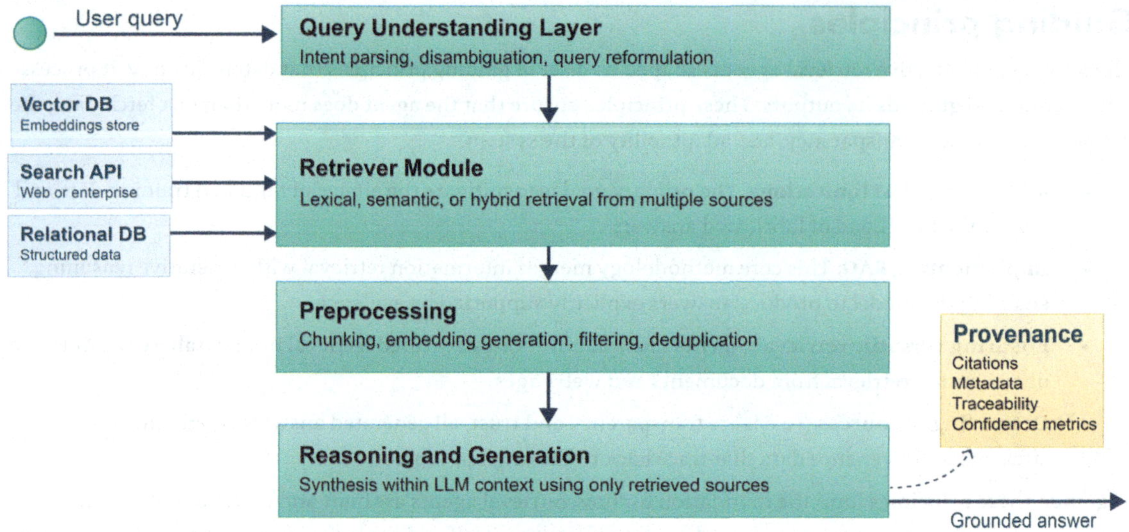

Figure 6.1 – Modular architecture of a Knowledge Retrieval agent

As the diagram illustrates, the process is a sequential flow initiated by a **User query**. The query is processed through each layer, with the **Retriever Module** acting as the crucial gateway to external knowledge stores. A key feature of this architecture is the parallel **Provenance** component; it is not a final step but a continuous process that collects citations, metadata, and confidence metrics throughout the pipeline. This ensures that the final grounded answer produced by the **Reasoning and Generation** layer is not only accurate but also fully auditable and trustworthy.

With this architectural foundation in place, we can now examine how these principles are applied in practice through specific implementation patterns and tools that bring retrieval agents to life.

Implementation patterns and tools

Building a retrieval agent involves choosing the right workflow, frameworks, and databases to fit the specific use case. In practice, the design of the retrieval workflow depends largely on the complexity of the user's query and the diversity of the data sources involved:

- **Single-stage retrieval**: A direct query issued to a single authoritative data source. Use when the query is narrow and well-defined, the answer is expected from one known source, and a low-latency response is a priority. Trade-off: limited recall across heterogeneous corpora.
- **Multi-stage retrieval**: A broad initial search progressively refined through more targeted filters or sub-queries. Use when queries are open-ended or exploratory, the answer may require aggregating evidence from multiple sources, or the first-pass result set needs re-ranking. Trade-off: higher latency; suitable when answer quality outweighs speed.
- **Hybrid retrieval**: A combination of keyword-based (lexical) and vector similarity (semantic) search. Use when the corpus contains both structured terminology (product codes, legal clauses) and free-form text, or when neither keyword nor semantic search alone delivers acceptable recall. Trade-off: more complex pipeline and tuning overhead; delivers the best recall across mixed-content corpora.

Beyond the retrieval strategy itself, the effectiveness of a retrieval agent also depends on the tooling used to implement and manage the pipeline. Development is often accelerated through frameworks such as LangChain, LlamaIndex, and LangGraph, which provide ready-made components for search, ingestion, and orchestration. These frameworks integrate with specialized vector databases such as Pinecone, Weaviate, FAISS, and Milvus, each optimized for different performance and deployment needs.

The tools and frameworks above provide the components; the following pipeline will show how they fit together. The following end-to-end example applies LangChain, OpenAI embeddings, and FAISS to implement the architecture described earlier in this chapter: ingesting a local document corpus, embedding and indexing the content, and exposing a question-answering interface that retrieves the most relevant chunks before generating a grounded response. Working through this implementation makes the responsibilities of each architectural layer concrete and prepares you for the deployment and scaling patterns covered in later chapters.

Example: Building a RAG pipeline

In this section, we will implement an end-to-end RAG pipeline using LangChain and OpenAI. Starting from a small corpus of local documents, we will load and chunk the files, generate vector embeddings, store them in a FAISS-backed vector index, and then expose a simple question-answering interface. The goal is to make the responsibilities of the Knowledge Retrieval agent concrete, building on the architectural discussion earlier in this chapter and preparing for the deployment patterns you will see later in the book.

A typical RAG pipeline first ingests documents, embeds them into semantic vectors, and indexes them in a vector store. A user's query is then embedded and used to find the most similar document chunks. These chunks are passed into the LLM's context with instructions to formulate an answer based only on that information, resulting in a seamless blend of retrieval and reasoning.

```
import os
from langchain_openai import ChatOpenAI, OpenAIEmbeddings
from langchain_community.vectorstores import FAISS
from langchain_text_splitters import RecursiveCharacterTextSplitter
from langchain.document_loaders import DirectoryLoader
from langchain.chains import RetrievalQA

# 1. Environment Setup
os.environ["OPENAI_API_KEY"] = "your_openai_api_key"   # only needed for embeddings + LLM

# 2. Load and Split Documents
loader = DirectoryLoader("./docs", glob="*.txt")  # use PDFs, HTML, or text
documents = loader.load()

splitter = RecursiveCharacterTextSplitter(
    chunk_size=1000,
    chunk_overlap=200
)
chunks = splitter.split_documents(documents)
```

```
# 3. Create Embeddings and Store in FAISS (Local vector DB)
embeddings = OpenAIEmbeddings(model="text-embedding-3-large")
vectorstore = FAISS.from_documents(chunks, embeddings)

# 4. Define Retrieval + Generation Chain
retriever = vectorstore.as_retriever(search_kwargs={"k": 3})
llm = ChatOpenAI(model="gpt-4o-mini", temperature=0)

qa_chain = RetrievalQA.from_chain_type(
    llm=llm,
    retriever=retriever,
    return_source_documents=True
)

# 5. Run a Query
query = "What are the main limitations of retrieval-augmented generation?"
result = qa_chain({"query": query})

print("Answer:", result["result"])
print("\nSources:")
for doc in result["source_documents"]:
    print("-", doc.metadata.get("source", "unknown"))
```

Let's walk through what's happening in this implementation. The pipeline begins by configuring the environment with an OpenAI API key, which is required for both the embedding model and the LLM. In *step 2*, we use `DirectoryLoader` to ingest all documents from a specified folder (supporting PDFs, HTML, and text files), then split them into overlapping chunks of 1,000 characters with 200-character overlap. This overlap ensures that semantic context isn't lost at chunk boundaries, which is critical for accurate retrieval.

Step 3 creates vector embeddings for each chunk using OpenAI's text-embedding-3-large model and stores them in a FAISS vector database. **FAISS (Facebook AI Similarity Search)** is a highly efficient library for similarity search, making it ideal for production RAG systems. The `from_documents` method handles both embedding generation and index creation in a single operation.

In *step 4*, we configure the retrieval chain. The `vectorstore.as_retriever(search_kwargs={"k": 3})` method converts our vector store into a retriever that returns the top 3 most similar chunks for any query. These chunks are then passed to a `ChatOpenAI` instance (using GPT-4o-mini for cost efficiency) within a `RetrievalQA` chain. The `return_source_documents=True` parameter ensures we can trace which documents informed the answer, providing transparency and enabling verification.

Finally, *step 5* demonstrates the system in action. When we submit the query "What are the main limitations of retrieval-augmented generation?", the system embeds the question, retrieves the three most semantically relevant chunks, constructs a prompt that includes these chunks as context, and generates an answer grounded in the retrieved information. The response includes both the answer and source attribution, showing exactly which documents were used.

This architecture represents the foundational pattern for RAG systems, though production implementations often require additional considerations around scalability, latency, and accuracy.

Chunking strategies

The parameters `chunk_size=1000` and `chunk_overlap=200` in the preceding pipeline are not arbitrary. Chunking is the most consequential configuration decision in a RAG system. A chunk is the atomic unit retrieved by the vector index; its size determines how much text the LLM receives as context for each match, and its overlap determines how much continuity is preserved across adjacent chunks.

Three strategies govern how documents are split:

- Fixed-size chunking divides text at a fixed character or token boundary; it is the simplest approach and suits uniform, well-formatted documents.
- Recursive chunking attempts to split on natural boundaries (paragraphs, sentences, words) in descending order, falling back to character-level splits only when necessary; this produces more semantically coherent chunks and is the recommended default for mixed-content corpora.
- Semantic chunking uses embedding similarity to detect natural topic shifts before splitting, producing chunks aligned with meaning rather than character count; it delivers the highest retrieval fidelity for narrative text but carries a higher computational cost at ingestion time.

The size-overlap trade-off requires deliberate calibration. Smaller chunks (200–500 characters) improve retrieval precision but risk omitting the surrounding context that the LLM needs to form a coherent answer. Larger chunks (1,000–2,000 characters) provide richer context but dilute the embedding signal, reducing recall. The `overlap` parameter mitigates boundary loss: a 200-character overlap on 1,000-character chunks ensures that a sentence spanning two chunks is fully captured by at least one of them. Misconfiguring these values is the most common source of retrieval-quality degradation in production: overly large chunks introduce irrelevant context, overly small chunks produce incomplete answers, and insufficient overlap creates boundary artifacts where key facts fall between chunks.

Operational considerations

While powerful, retrieval agents require careful management to behave predictably in production environments. Once the basic RAG pipeline is in place, most of the complexity shifts from implementing retrieval to operating it reliably at scale.

In this section, we will look at the recurring operational risks that arise in real systems, and the patterns architects use to contain them. The following subsections focus on the quality of retrieved results, the freshness of the index, the latency profile of the end-to-end pipeline, and the security controls that govern which documents can be surfaced to which users.

Common challenges

The following points highlight the most common challenges and the corresponding best practices for running retrieval agents in production.

- **Noise reduction**: Use metadata filters to prevent irrelevant or low-quality results from entering the LLM's context window
- **Index freshness**: Implement automated pipelines to periodically re-ingest data from dynamic sources, ensuring the agent's knowledge remains current
- **Latency control**: Optimize retrieval parameters and use caching for frequent queries to balance response speed with completeness
- **Security**: Enforce strict access controls at the retrieval level to ensure the agent cannot access or expose sensitive or regulated data

Diagnosing retrieval failures

Not every query returns useful results. When the pipeline returns an answer that appears vague, off-topic, or unsupported, the failure typically originates in one of three places: the retrieved chunks had low semantic similarity to the query; the retrieved chunks were individually relevant but lacked the information needed to answer the question; or the provenance metadata was missing or mismatched, making it impossible to verify the source.

Consider a concrete scenario: a user asks, "What is our refund policy for subscriptions?" The pipeline returns an answer citing general billing terms rather than the specific subscription clause. Inspecting the output with `return_source_documents=True` reveals that the top three chunks came from a generic FAQ, not the subscription-specific policy document. The diagnostic pattern is to examine `source_documents` for each response: if the retrieved documents do not match the expected source, the index is either missing the target document or the query embedding is not sufficiently close to the relevant chunk. The correction involves re-ingesting the missing document, adjusting chunk size to preserve the clause as a discrete unit, or adding a metadata filter (e.g., `filter={"doc_type": "subscription_policy"}`) to scope the retrieval.

A second failure pattern occurs when similarity scores are uniformly low across all retrieved chunks. This signals a vocabulary mismatch: the query uses terminology absent from the embedded corpus. Inspect raw similarity scores and compare the query embedding against representative corpus embeddings. The correction is to augment the semantic search with a keyword (BM25) search via hybrid retrieval, so that lexical matches compensate where embedding similarity falls short.

Common applications

Knowledge Retrieval agents are valuable in any scenario where timely, accurate information is critical. Here, we list some of their applications:

- **Enterprise assistants**: Providing employees with up-to-date answers from internal knowledge bases and policy documents
- **Legal and compliance**: Accessing and summarizing recent case law, regulations, and corporate filings
- **Market intelligence**: Monitoring news, analyst reports, and financial data for competitive insights

In this section, we have established how Knowledge Retrieval agents act as powerful tools for finding and fetching relevant information, grounding an LLM's responses in verifiable, up-to-date sources. However, their primary function stops at the document's edge. Once the correct file is located, a new challenge emerges: extracting precise, structured data from within its pages, which are often complex and visually formatted.

This is where our focus now shifts. In the next section, we will move on from the task of *finding* information to the more granular task of *understanding* it. We will explore Document Intelligence agents, the specialists designed to read, interpret, and transform the contents of messy documents into structured, actionable data.

Document Intelligence agents

While Knowledge Retrieval agents are skilled at finding the right file, their job often ends at the document's edge. Businesses, however, run on the details inside those files: the clauses in contracts, the line items on invoices, and the diagnoses in clinical notes. A Document Intelligence agent is a specialist designed to cross that boundary. It moves beyond simple retrieval to understand, parse, and transform messy, unstructured documents into clean, trustworthy, and machine-readable data.

In regulated industries where accuracy and traceability are paramount, these agents are transformative. They can shrink contract review cycles, automate claims processing, and feed analytics platforms with reliable data, acting as the connective tissue between static content repositories and dynamic operational systems.

> Note
>
> **Agent capability level**
>
> A typical Document Intelligence agent operates at Level 2 (Tool-Using agent) of the progression framework, as it orchestrates a sequence of tools (OCR, parsers, extractors) to achieve its goal. More advanced agents that can dynamically re-plan their strategy based on document complexity or maintain context across a batch of related documents exhibit Level 3 (Planning agent) capabilities.

In the pages that follow, we will map the full pipeline for document intelligence, walk through the five stages from ingestion to validation, discuss development practices that keep accuracy high with human review where needed, and close with capability levels and real-world applications.

Architecture: The five-stage document intelligence pipeline

Modern document intelligence systems are not monolithic; they are modular pipelines comprising cooperating sub-agents orchestrated by a central **cognition core**. This core manages the workflow, selects the right tools for each document (such as OCR engines, layout parsers, entity extractors, and validators), interprets results, and adapts the plan if confidence scores are low. These specialized tools work together to transform unstructured documents into structured data: OCR engines capture text from images, layout parsers reconstruct tables and reading order, key-value and entity extractors pull specific fields into a schema, validators enforce business rules, and connectors write validated data into systems such as ERPs and CRMs. This process typically follows five core stages:

1. **Ingestion and triage**: The pipeline begins when documents arrive from sources such as email inboxes, scanners, or APIs. At this initial stage, a classification sub-agent examines each document to determine

its type (e.g., invoice, lab report, contract), detect its language, and route it to the appropriate specialized workflow for further processing. In practice, triage operates on MIME-type detection as a first pass: a PDF triggers the OCR and layout pipeline, a structured XML or CSV is routed directly to the extraction stage, and an email HTML body requires a stripping step before classification. Where MIME type alone is insufficient, a lightweight classifier inspects the first page or a metadata header to confirm the document's schema and route it to the correct extraction template. The routing outcome determines which tools are activated in every downstream stage.

2. **Preprocessing and OCR**: In this stage, a specialized preprocessing sub-agent handles image-based documents. It performs critical enhancements such as deskewing and denoising before an **optical character recognition** (**OCR**) engine converts both printed and handwritten text into digital characters. Crucially, the OCR engine emits confidence scores that estimate how likely each recognized character or word is to be correct. These confidence scores are preserved so that downstream agents can weigh low-confidence regions more cautiously, trigger fallbacks such as re-OCR or alternative models, or route uncertain fields for human review.

   The following stub demonstrates the core mechanics of this stage: converting a scanned PDF page to an image, running OCR with pytesseract, and filtering tokens by confidence score before passing them downstream.

```
# pip install pytesseract pdf2image Pillow
from pdf2image import convert_from_path
import pytesseract
from dataclasses import dataclass
from typing import List

CONFIDENCE_THRESHOLD = 60  # Tesseract confidence: 0-100

@dataclass
class OcrToken:
    text: str
    confidence: float  # 0.0 - 100.0

def preprocess_and_ocr(pdf_path: str) -> List[OcrToken]:
    """Convert PDF pages to images, run OCR, return high-confidence tokens."""
    images = convert_from_path(pdf_path, dpi=300)
    tokens: List[OcrToken] = []
    for img in images:
        data = pytesseract.image_to_data(img,
output_type=pytesseract.Output.DICT)
        for i, word in enumerate(data["text"]):
            conf = int(data["conf"][i])
            if word.strip() and conf >= CONFIDENCE_THRESHOLD:
                tokens.append(OcrToken(text=word, confidence=conf))
    return tokens  # Low-confidence tokens flagged for human review downstream
```

3. **Structural segmentation and layout parsing**: Here, the agent analyzes the document's visual layout to identify logical blocks such as headings, paragraphs, tables, and key-value pairs. It reconstructs table structures and determines the correct reading order, which is essential for understanding context.
4. **Information extraction**: With the document's structure understood, this agent performs schema-driven extraction to pull out specific entities and their relationships (e.g., `Invoice Number`, `Total Amount Due`). The output is structured data, typically in JSON format, complete with confidence scores and provenance for each extracted field.
5. **Validation and integration**: Finally, the extracted data is validated. A common pattern is to use confidence scores to route the output: high-confidence results flow automatically into systems such as ERPs or CRMs, while low-confidence results are flagged for human-in-the-loop review. This feedback loop is vital for continuous improvement.

```
# Quick Implementation Example: Document Intelligence Agent (Layout-aware key-value
extraction)

# pip install pillow pytesseract pdf2image rapidfuzz
# System requirement: Tesseract OCR installed (https://tesseract-ocr.github.io/)

import os
from dataclasses import dataclass
from typing import List, Dict, Tuple
from pdf2image import convert_from_path
from PIL import Image
import pytesseract
from rapidfuzz import fuzz, process

# 1) Minimal schema definition
# Each field has a set of cue keywords that typically appear near the value in an
invoice-like doc
SCHEMA = {
    "invoice_number": ["invoice no", "invoice number", "inv no"],
    "invoice_date":   ["date", "invoice date"],
    "total_amount":   ["total", "amount due", "balance due", "total due"],
}

@dataclass
class Token:
    text: str
    x: int
    y: int
    w: int
    h: int
    conf: float
```

```
    line_id: int

def ocr_tokens(image: Image.Image) -> List[Token]:
    """Run OCR and return tokens with positions and a simple line grouping."""
    data = pytesseract.image_to_data(image, output_type=pytesseract.Output.DICT)
    tokens = []
    for i in range(len(data["text"])):
        text = data["text"][i].strip()
        if not text:
            continue
        x, y, w, h = data["left"][i], data["top"][i], data["width"][i], data["height"][i]
        conf = float(data["conf"][i]) if data["conf"][i] != "-1" else 0.0
        # Build a simple line id from Tesseract block/para/line indices
        line_id = (
            data["block_num"][i], data["par_num"][i], data["line_num"][i])
        tokens.append(Token(text, x, y, w, h, conf, hash(line_id)))
    return tokens

def join_line(tokens: List[Token]) -> Dict[int, List[Token]]:
    """Group tokens by line id and sort left to right."""
    lines: Dict[int, List[Token]] = {}
    for t in tokens:
        lines.setdefault(t.line_id, []).append(t)
    for lid in lines:
        lines[lid] = sorted(lines[lid], key=lambda t: t.x)
    return lines

def normalize(s: str) -> str:
    return "".join(ch.lower() for ch in s if ch.isalnum() or ch.isspace())

def best_keyword_match(text: str, candidates: List[str], cutoff=80) -> Tuple[str, int]:
    """Fuzzy match a cue keyword within line text; return best match and score."""
    choices = [(kw, normalize(kw)) for kw in candidates]
    best = ("", 0)
    for orig, norm_kw in choices:
        score = fuzz.partial_ratio(normalize(text), norm_kw)
        if score > best[1]:
            best = (orig, score)
    return best if best[1] >= cutoff else ("", 0)

def extract_near_keyword(lines: Dict[int, List[Token]], keywords: List[str]) -> str:
    """
    Strategy:
      1) Find a line that contains or closely matches a cue keyword.
```

```
      2) Return the text to the right of that keyword on the same line,
         else fall back to the next line below in the same column region.
    """
    # pass 1: same line, value to the right
    for lid, toks in lines.items():
        line_text = " ".join(t.text for t in toks)
        kw, score = best_keyword_match(line_text, keywords)
        if not kw:
            continue
        # find token index where keyword occurs (rough approach)
        idx = process.extractOne(kw, [t.text for t in toks],
            scorer=fuzz.partial_ratio)
        if idx is None:
            continue
        start_i = idx[2]
        value = " ".join(t.text for t in toks[start_i+1:]).strip(": ").strip()
        if value:
            return value

    # pass 2: look at the line below within same horizontal band
    sorted_lines = sorted(lines.items(), key=lambda kv: min(t.y for t in kv[1]))
    for i, (lid, toks) in enumerate(sorted_lines[:-1]):
        line_text = " ".join(t.text for t in toks)
        kw, score = best_keyword_match(line_text, keywords)
        if not kw:
            continue
        # candidate next line
        _, next_toks = sorted_lines[i+1]
        value = " ".join(t.text for t in next_toks).strip(": ").strip()
        if value:
            return value

    return ""

def extract_fields_from_image(image: Image.Image) -> Dict[str, str]:
    tokens = ocr_tokens(image)
    lines = join_line(tokens)

    results = {}
    for field, cues in SCHEMA.items():
        results[field] = extract_near_keyword(lines, cues)
    return results

def extract_from_pdf(pdf_path: str, dpi=300) -> Dict[str, str]:
```

```
    pages = convert_from_path(pdf_path, dpi=dpi, fmt="png")
    # simple strategy: attempt extraction page by page, merge non-empty fields
    final = {k: "" for k in SCHEMA}
    for page in pages:
        fields = extract_fields_from_image(page)
        for k, v in fields.items():
            if v and not final[k]:
                final[k] = v
    return final

if __name__ == "__main__":
    # Use either a scanned image or a PDF
    # image = Image.open("invoice_sample.png")
    # results = extract_fields_from_image(image)

    results = extract_from_pdf("invoice_sample.pdf")
    print("Extracted fields:")
    for k, v in results.items():
        print(f"  {k}: {v}")
```

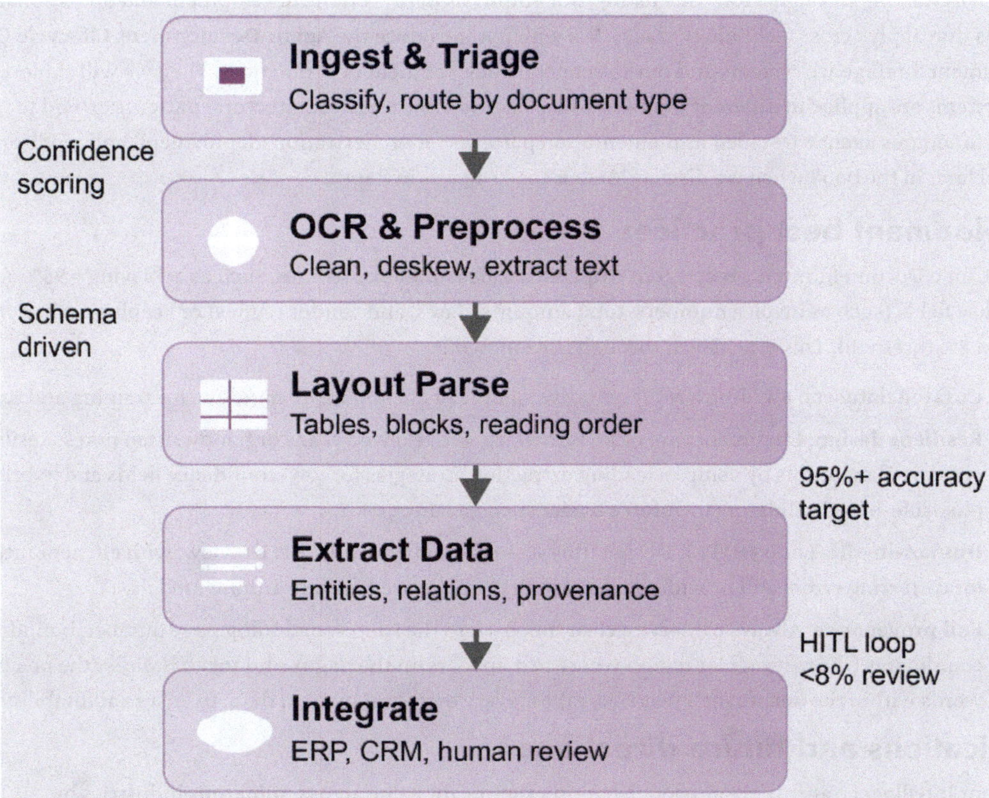

Figure 6.2 – Document intelligence pipeline

The preceding diagram visualizes the pipeline's linear progression, showing how a raw document is systematically refined at each step. The annotations on the left and right highlight the governing principles and metrics that ensure the process is efficient and reliable. For instance, the extraction is guided by an input schema and evaluated against explicit accuracy targets while minimizing the need for the final HITL review loop. In practice, these targets are defined collaboratively by business stakeholders and the delivery team, typically as field-level benchmarks on a labeled validation dataset. For example, a 95% accuracy target may mean that at least 95 out of 100 invoices have correctly extracted values for critical fields such as `Invoice Number` and `Total Amount Due`. During solution design, the team measures this against historical, annotated documents; once in production, the same metrics are monitored via sampled human reviews and *dashboarded* over time. These targets are measured during evaluation using annotated ground-truth datasets and continuously monitored in production via sampled reviews. This entire workflow transforms a simple document into auditable, decision-ready data.

Implementation and operational strategy

Deploying a successful document intelligence system requires more than wiring together OCR engines and extraction models. It calls for an iterative development process, resilient design choices, and tight integration with the surrounding business workflows. In this section, we focus on how to take the conceptual pipeline from the previous pages and turn it into a production-ready capability.

Rather than walking through a full code listing, our emphasis here is on the development and operational practices that apply across technology stacks. We will first introduce the **Agent Development Lifecycle** (**ADL**) for document intelligence systems and outline concrete development best practices. Then we will explore how these systems are applied in different domains today and how the same architectural patterns extend to future, more autonomous agents. Detailed implementation patterns for orchestration, deployment, and monitoring are revisited later in the book when we discuss MLOps for AI agents in depth.

Development best practices

The ADL for a Document Intelligence agent emphasizes measurable outcomes, such as achieving a 95% accuracy rate on key fields (such as invoice numbers, total amounts, dates, and vendor names) or keeping human review under an 8% threshold. This is achieved through the following:

- **Curated datasets**: Building a representative sample of documents to annotate for training and testing.
- **Resilient design**: Documents are often imperfect, with skewed scans or handwritten notes. Resilient systems plan for this by using cascading extraction strategies for low-confidence fields and hybrid ML-plus-rule-based validators to enforce business constraints.
- **Human-in-the-Loop (HITL)**: Design the system from day one for HITL review, with efficient interfaces for correcting errors and providing feedback that can be used for fine-tuning models.
- **Full provenance**: Always preserve a clear link back to the source, including page number, bounding box coordinates (the rectangular region where text appears on the page), and token indices (the position of words within the document's text stream) for every extracted piece of data, to ensure auditability.

Applications and future directions

Document Intelligence agents are already delivering significant value across numerous industries by automating document-centric workflows.

Here are some common use cases:

- **Financial services**: Extracting terms from contracts, automating revenue recognition, and processing regulatory filings
- **Healthcare**: Automating claims processing, structuring clinical documentation, and assisting with medical coding
- **Supply chain**: Processing bills of lading, customs forms, and invoices to accelerate logistics
- **Legal and regulatory**: Extracting clauses, tracking obligations, and monitoring for compliance in legal documents

The field is rapidly advancing toward more autonomous systems. Key trends include self-improving agents that learn directly from human corrections, the use of long-context multimodal transformers that can reason across an entire document at once, and the emergence of autonomous enterprise workflows where Document Intelligence agents act as first-class participants in complex business processes.

As modular and orchestrated systems, Document Intelligence agents are the perfect complement to retrieval agents. They take the baton where retrieval leaves off, operating inside documents to enforce schemas and feed operational systems with auditable, decision-ready data.

Having explored how Document Intelligence agents transform static documents into actionable business data, we now turn to a domain where the stakes of information processing are even higher: scientific discovery. While Document Intelligence agents excel at extracting structured information from known document types—invoices, contracts, medical records—the scientific enterprise presents a fundamentally different challenge.

Scientific Research agents must navigate an ocean of constantly evolving literature, synthesize findings across disciplines, identify contradictions and gaps in knowledge, and even generate novel hypotheses. Unlike the relatively predictable schemas of business documents, scientific knowledge exists in a complex web of theories, experimental results, and interpretations that resist simple categorization.

Where Document Intelligence agents serve as the bridge between human-readable content and machine-processable data, Scientific Research agents aspire to be thinking partners in humanity's quest to understand the natural world. They must not only process information but also reason about it, connecting disparate findings to reveal new insights and accelerating the pace of discovery itself.

The next section examines how AI systems are beginning to participate in the scientific method—from literature review and hypothesis generation to experimental design and peer review—and explores both the transformative potential and the unique challenges of automating humanity's most rigorous form of inquiry.

Scientific Research agents

Scientific Research agents represent a sophisticated evolution in agent capabilities, demonstrating a layered approach to information synthesis that goes beyond simple retrieval. These agents integrate knowledge from multiple sources and reconcile potentially conflicting findings through three distinct phases: broad literature scanning, thematic clustering and summarization, and synthesis and insight generation.

They integrate knowledge from multiple databases, reconcile conflicting results, and produce synthesis reports that highlight consensus, divergence, and gaps in knowledge. They are particularly valuable in domains such as the following:

- **Biomedical research**: Summarizing molecular studies to guide drug discovery
- **Climate science**: Aggregating predictive models to assess environmental impact
- **Engineering**: Comparing approaches to novel materials or system designs
- **Policy analysis**: Synthesizing studies to inform legislative decisions

These agents assemble clusters of studies, group them by methodology or findings, and show where consensus exists and where results diverge. They can also highlight areas where no research has yet ventured, guiding future investigations.

To understand how these agents operate, we will examine them from several angles. We will start by mapping their process to the cognitive loop, then explore their advanced technical architecture and a real-world case study in drug discovery. Finally, we will cover their development lifecycle and inherent challenges.

The research workflow and cognitive loop

The research workflow of a Scientific Research agent represents a specialized application of the **cognitive loop**:

- **Perception**: The loop begins with a user query, such as a request to find new treatments for a rare disease. The agent perceives this as a high-level, multi-stage objective requiring comprehensive analysis.
- **Reasoning and interpretation**: The agent reasons about the query's intent and translates it into a broad, semantic search strategy. It understands that this is not a one-step lookup but a complex research task requiring deep understanding of multiple sources and domain expertise.
- **Planning**: The agent plans a multi-phase research strategy involving querying multiple knowledge sources, grouping papers by shared themes, and generating structured reports. The agent identifies dependencies, such as needing to find relevant studies before clustering them by methodology or findings.
- **Action**: The agent executes complex actions, including querying academic databases such as PubMed, arXiv, IEEE Xplore, and Scopus using semantic search. It performs thematic clustering of retrieved papers and conducts citation graph traversal to discover related studies.
- **Learning and updating**: The agent produces high-value outputs such as comparative tables and synthesis reports that highlight consensus, divergence, and gaps in knowledge. This process enables cross-verification of results and identification of promising research directions.

> Note
>
> **What is citation graph traversal?**
>
> Citation graph traversal is a technique for following the links between research papers through their references and citations. By mapping papers as nodes and their citations as edges, the agent can move through this network to identify influential works, discover clusters of related research, and track how ideas evolve over time. For example, starting with a single paper on a new drug compound, traversal can reveal earlier foundational studies and later works that validate or challenge its findings.

The operation of a Scientific Research agent can be understood in three phases:

1. **Broad literature scanning**: The agent queries multiple knowledge sources, including academic databases such as PubMed, arXiv, IEEE Xplore, and Scopus, using semantic search to ensure it captures conceptually relevant studies, not just keyword matches.
2. **Thematic clustering and summarization**: Retrieved papers are grouped by shared themes such as methodology, findings, or application domain. This thematic clustering helps reveal patterns in the literature, such as recurring results or emerging areas of interest.
3. **Synthesis and insight generation**: The agent produces structured, high-value outputs: comparative tables, evidence maps, and summaries that emphasize agreement, disagreement, and remaining uncertainties.

Having seen how research agents generate synthesis and insights, we now turn to the technical underpinnings that make this possible. The following code block breaks down the advanced architecture that supports multi-database querying, reasoning across sources, and knowledge integration.

```
# Quick Implementation Example: Scientific Research Agent
# Phases: scan literature -> cluster themes -> synthesize insights

# pip install arxiv sentence-transformers scikit-learn pandas numpy nltk

import re
import arxiv
import numpy as np
import pandas as pd
from collections import Counter
from sentence_transformers import SentenceTransformer
from sklearn.cluster import KMeans
from sklearn.metrics.pairwise import cosine_similarity

# ----------------------------
# 1) Broad literature scanning
```

Phase 1 handles literature discovery. The agent queries the arXiv API for papers matching the research topic, retrieving metadata including titles, abstracts, authors, and publication dates. Results are filtered to remove entries without abstracts and stored in a DataFrame. This phase produces the raw corpus that all subsequent phases operate on.

```
# ----------------------------
QUERY = "large language models retrieval augmented generation evaluation"
MAX_RESULTS = 80      # keep small for demo
CLUSTERS = 4          # tune to topic breadth

def search_arxiv(query, max_results=MAX_RESULTS):
    results = []
    for r in arxiv.Search(
        query=query,
        max_results=max_results,
        sort_by=arxiv.SortCriterion.Relevance
    ).results():
        results.append({
            "title": r.title.strip(),
            "summary": r.summary.strip(),
            "authors": ", ".join(a.name for a in r.authors),
            "published": r.published.strftime("%Y-%m-%d"),
            "url": r.entry_id
```

```
    })
    return pd.DataFrame(results)

df = search_arxiv(QUERY)
if df.empty:
    raise SystemExit("No results. Try broadening the query.")

# Combine title + abstract as the unit of meaning
df["text"] = df["title"].astype(str) + ". " + df["summary"].astype(str)

# -------------------------------------------

# 2) Thematic clustering and summarization
```

Phase 2 groups the retrieved papers into thematic clusters. Abstract embeddings are generated with a sentence-transformer model and then clustered using k-means. For each cluster, a label is extracted from the most frequent terms across nearby titles, and an extractive summary is assembled from the abstracts closest to the cluster centroid. This phase reveals the dominant research themes and surfaces the papers most representative of each theme.

```
# -------------------------------------------
# Embeddings
model = SentenceTransformer("all-MiniLM-L6-v2")
emb = model.encode(df["text"].tolist(), normalize_embeddings=True)

# Clustering
kmeans = KMeans(n_clusters=CLUSTERS, n_init="auto", random_state=42)
labels = kmeans.fit_predict(emb)
df["cluster"] = labels

# Helper: automatic cluster label from top terms in nearest titles
def clean_tokens(s):
    s = s.lower()
    s = re.sub(r"[^a-z0-9\s\-]", " ", s)
    toks = [t for t in s.split() if len(t) > 2]
    stop = set("""
        the and for with from into using among toward towarded on in of to via
        model models data paper study approach results method methods novel new
        large language based task tasks text query queries augment retrieval
    """.split())
    return [t for t in toks if t not in stop]

def label_cluster(c_idx, k=6, sample_n=6):
    centroid = kmeans.cluster_centers_[c_idx].reshape(1, -1)
```

```
    sims = cosine_similarity(emb, centroid).ravel()
    top_ids = sims.argsort()[-sample_n:]
    words = []
    for i in top_ids:
        words.extend(clean_tokens(df.iloc[i]["title"]))
    top = [w for w,_ in Counter(words).most_common(k)]
    return ", ".join(top) if top else "mixed theme"

# Helper: tiny extractive summary from most central abstracts
def summarize_cluster(c_idx, sentences=3):
    centroid = kmeans.cluster_centers_[c_idx].reshape(1, -1)
    sims = cosine_similarity(emb, centroid).ravel()
    ids = np.argsort(sims)[-8:]  # take a small set of central docs
    # pick the most informative sentences from their abstracts
    cand_sentences = []
    for i in ids:
        text = df.iloc[i]["summary"]
        # crude sentence split
        for s in re.split(r"(?<=[.!?])\s+", text):
            if 40 < len(s) < 300:
                cand_sentences.append((s, i))
    # score sentences by similarity between sentence embedding and cluster centroid
    if not cand_sentences:
        return "Cluster summary not available."
    s_emb = model.encode([s for s,_ in cand_sentences], normalize_embeddings=True)
    s_sims = cosine_similarity(s_emb, centroid).ravel()
    top_idx = np.argsort(s_sims)[-sentences:]
    picked = [cand_sentences[i][0] for i in top_idx]
    return " ".join(picked)

# --------------------------------
# 3) Synthesis and reporting
```

Phase 3 produces the final synthesis report. For each cluster, the agent prints the cluster label, its extractive summary, and the titles of the most representative papers. This output gives the researcher an immediately actionable map of the literature: what the dominant themes are, which papers define each theme, and where the major research directions concentrate. The entire block executes without human intervention and can be scheduled to re-run as new papers are published.

```
# --------------------------------
print(f"\nQuery: {QUERY}")
print(f"Papers retrieved: {len(df)}; Clusters: {CLUSTERS}\n")

for c in sorted(df["cluster"].unique()):
```

```
    theme = label_cluster(c)
    summary = summarize_cluster(c)
    print(f"Cluster {c}: {theme}")
    print(f"Synthesis: {summary}\n")
    # cite a few representative items
    reps = df[df["cluster"] == c].sort_values("published", ascending=False).head(3)
    for _, r in reps.iterrows():
        print(f"  • {r['title']}  | {r['authors']}  | {r['published']}")
        print(f"    {r['url']}")
    print()

# ------------------------------
# Optional: simple evidence table
# ------------------------------
# In a real agent you would extract standardized fields and quality signals per paper.
# Here we show a minimal table you can expand later.
table = df.groupby("cluster").apply(
    lambda g: g.sort_values("published", ascending=False)[
        ["title", "authors", "published", "url"]
    ].head(5)
)
print("\nEvidence table (top 5 per cluster):")
print(table.to_string())
```

Advanced technical architecture

A Scientific Research agent's architecture extends significantly beyond simple retrieval patterns. It relies heavily on the **cognition core** to coordinate complex, multi-step operations, including the following:

- **Advanced knowledge management**: Uses multi-vector retrieval to capture different aspects of research papers and employs entity linking to unify related concepts across sources
- **Dynamic tool integration**: Enables parallel searches across diverse repositories and sophisticated reasoning capabilities, including "multi-hop reasoning," to draw connections between findings from separate studies

The technical architecture extends the RAG pattern with several advanced strategies:

- **Multi-database querying**: Parallel searches across diverse repositories
- **Citation graph traversal**: Following citation chains to discover related studies and track the evolution of ideas
- **Entity linking**: Unifying related concepts that may be expressed differently across sources
- **Multi-hop reasoning**: Drawing connections between findings from separate studies to form new insights
- **Multi-vector retrieval**: Capturing different aspects of a paper, such as its methodology, key findings, and implications

Each retrieval step is grounded by metadata (authors, publication date, venue) to ensure transparent and verifiable synthesis.

To illustrate how Scientific Research agents operate in a real-world setting, the following case study focuses on drug discovery. Drug development is a domain where researchers face vast amounts of literature, complex decision-making, and high stakes for accuracy and speed. By walking through this example, you will see how the architecture and workflow described earlier translate into tangible research acceleration.

Case study: Accelerating drug discovery

Consider a pharmaceutical R&D team exploring new treatments for a rare disease. Traditionally, researchers might spend months reading papers, identifying candidate compounds, and comparing experimental results.

With a Scientific Research agent, the following happens:

1. The team submits a query describing the disease mechanism and desired drug properties.
2. The agent scans PubMed, preprint servers, and conference proceedings for relevant studies.
3. It clusters findings by compound type, mechanism of action, and experimental outcome.
4. It cross-verifies results and flags promising compounds for further lab testing.

The result: time-to-insight is reduced from months to weeks, and overlooked opportunities are brought to light earlier.

To complete our analysis, we will now consider several key operational aspects of deploying these agents. We will cover the protocols they use for communication and the practical challenges they face.

> Note
>
> **Agent interoperability: MCP and A2A**
>
> Scientific Research agents rarely operate in isolation. In production deployments, they must interface with external academic APIs, pass findings to downstream synthesis agents, and conform to standardized communication protocols. There are two key interoperability patterns relevant to this architecture.
>
> For a Scientific Research agent, **Model Context Protocol** (**MCP**) would be crucial for dynamically interfacing with the various APIs of academic databases. This allows the agent to discover and query these services without having hardcoded logic for each one. **Agent-to-Agent** (**A2A**) protocols would be essential in a multi-agent setup, for example, if one agent specializes in searching for studies and another in synthesizing the findings. For a deeper understanding of MCP, see *Chapter 8*.

Limitations and challenges

While powerful, Scientific Research agents have inherent limitations and face real-world challenges that practitioners must understand before deploying them in production.

From a fundamental standpoint, these agents are constrained by the following limitations:

- **No true understanding**: These agents process and correlate text statistically. They do not genuinely comprehend the scientific concepts they summarize, which means subtle errors in reasoning can go undetected without expert oversight.
- **Hallucination risk**: Even with RAG grounding, LLMs can fabricate citations, misattribute findings, or generate plausible-sounding but factually incorrect syntheses. This is a critical risk in scientific contexts where accuracy is paramount.
- **Inability to generate new knowledge**: These agents can synthesize and connect existing research, but they cannot design experiments, collect data, or produce genuinely novel scientific discoveries on their own.
- **Context window constraints**: Despite growing context windows, there is a practical limit to how many full papers an agent can reason over simultaneously, forcing trade-offs between breadth and depth of analysis.

Beyond these inherent limitations, deploying Scientific Research agents in practice introduces its own set of operational challenges:

- **Data access and licensing**: Many research databases require subscriptions or have restricted APIs
- **Bias in literature**: Published studies may overrepresent positive results
- **Verification needs**: AI synthesis must be reviewed by subject-matter experts
- **Scalability**: In fast-moving fields, the system must constantly update to stay relevant

Despite these limitations and challenges, Scientific Research agents represent a transformative leap in how knowledge is synthesized and applied. They enable researchers to process information at a scale and speed that would be impossible manually, revealing connections across disciplines and accelerating discovery. By integrating synthesis, reasoning, and continuous learning, these agents are not just tools but collaborators, helping humans navigate the vast and ever-growing body of scientific knowledge.

The knowledge agent spectrum

The evolution from Knowledge Retrieval agents to Document Intelligence agents to Scientific Research agents demonstrates increasing levels of sophistication in agent engineering. Each type represents different capability levels and applications of the cognitive loop, from basic tool-using agents to advanced learning agents capable of independent research and discovery.

- **Knowledge Retrieval agents** connect static models to live data, overcoming knowledge cutoffs and hallucinations by anchoring responses in verifiable sources
- **Document Intelligence agents** extract structured, actionable information from complex, unstructured documents
- **Scientific Research agents** synthesize research at scale, revealing patterns and gaps in knowledge

Together, these agents form a complete knowledge pipeline from discovery to decision-ready insights. Best practices include ensuring freshness of data, using domain-specific models, tracking provenance, and embedding security in every step.

Mastery of these agents offers a strategic advantage in decision-making, operational efficiency, and competitive positioning.

Having explored each agent type in detail, it is helpful to step back and view their roles and capabilities side by side. The following table offers a concise comparison that highlights what makes each agent unique, while also revealing how they complement one another in a complete knowledge ecosystem.

Agent Type	Primary Role	Key Capabilities	Typical Use Cases	Capability Level (Agentic AI Progression Framework)
Knowledge Retrieval Agent	Connects LLMs to live, authoritative information sources	• Mitigates knowledge cutoffs and reduces hallucinations • Implements RAG • Performs both structured and unstructured retrieval	Legal research, market intelligence, enterprise knowledge base assistants	Level 2–3: Tool-using to early planning
Document Intelligence Agent	Converts unstructured, visually complex documents into structured, trustworthy data	• OCR and image preprocessing • Layout parsing and entity or relation extraction • Feeds ERP, CRM, and analytics systems	Healthcare claims, financial contracts, supply-chain documents	Level 2–3: Tool-using to early planning
Scientific Research Agent	Synthesizes information across multiple databases to support discovery	• Clusters and compares evidence across large corpora • Identifies consensus and knowledge gaps • Generates hypotheses and supports experimental design	Drug discovery, climate science, policy analysis	Level 4: Learning agent capable of cross-domain synthesis

Table 6.1 – Comparison of knowledge agent types

As the table clearly illustrates, these three agent types form a complete knowledge pipeline, moving from the foundational task of finding information to the advanced capability of synthesizing new insights. This progression from information access to knowledge creation is not just a technical evolution; it represents a fundamental shift in how we will collaborate with AI. Understanding this spectrum is key to envisioning the future of knowledge work, where agents will increasingly function as sophisticated partners in discovery and decision-making.

Summary

This chapter explored how knowledge agents extend the power of LLMs by connecting them to real-time, verifiable information and transforming unstructured data into actionable insight. We began with a historical perspective, tracing the journey from early rule-based expert systems to today's multi-modal, retrieval-augmented agents. This context highlighted why modern enterprises need agents that can bridge the gap between static model training and the constantly changing information landscape.

We then examined the three core knowledge agent types in detail:

- **Knowledge Retrieval agents**: These link language models to live data sources, overcoming the limitations of model training cutoffs and reducing hallucinations through RAG
- **Document Intelligence agents**: These convert visually complex documents into structured, trustworthy data, supporting high-stakes workflows in areas such as healthcare, finance, and regulatory compliance
- **Scientific Research agents**: These synthesize findings across vast corpora, cluster evidence, and identify consensus and gaps to accelerate discovery

Each section introduced the architecture and process flow for its agent type and presented key diagrams to reinforce understanding. We explored their internal components, from query understanding and retrievers to OCR pipelines and provenance tracking. We also looked at how these agents fit into the Agentic AI Progression Framework, mapping their evolution from simple tool-using systems to more advanced planning and learning agents.

The chapter concluded by comparing the three agent types in a single view, underscoring how they complement one another. Together, they form a complete knowledge pipeline: finding relevant information, extracting and structuring it, and synthesizing insights for decision making.

This foundation sets the stage for the next chapter, where we move from architectural design to implementation strategies and explore how to deploy these agents at scale within enterprise environments.

Subscribe for a free eBook

New frameworks, evolving architectures, research drops, production breakdowns—*AI_Distilled* filters the noise into a weekly briefing for engineers and researchers working hands-on with LLMs and generative AI systems. Subscribe now and receive a free eBook, along with weekly insights that help you stay focused and informed.

Subscribe at `https://packt.link/8Oz6Y` or scan the QR code below.

7

Tool Manipulation and Orchestration Agents

The best way to predict the future is to invent it.

— *Alan Kay, computer scientist*

While language models provide the *reasoning substrate* for understanding user goals, it is the use of *tools* that enables agents to execute tasks and affect the real world. This chapter establishes the architectural foundation for understanding how agents translate reasoning into action through three progressive patterns:

We begin with the foundational pattern of a single agent extending its capabilities by invoking external functions and managing execution outcomes: **Tool-Using agents**. We then examine architectures that coordinate multiple specialized agents to solve complex, multifaceted problems through task decomposition and parallel execution: **chain-of-agents orchestrators**. Finally, we explore how to implement persistent, stateful business processes that incorporate human oversight at critical decision points: **agentic workflow systems.**

In addition to these patterns, the chapter includes cross-cutting sections on design considerations, safety, and evaluation that apply to all three

Tool invocation represents the fundamental mechanism that bridges cognitive operations and concrete actions, transforming an agent from a simple conversationalist into a functional system component. The architectural challenge lies in creating systems in which tool invocation becomes a seamless extension of agent cognition rather than a brittle integration point.

The principles outlined here represent the practical knowledge needed to design production-ready agent systems that deliver measurable business value. We will explore the universal patterns that enable reliable tool use, whether the tool is a simple calculator or a complex geospatial analysis library. These patterns provide the necessary foundation for the more advanced multi-agent orchestrators and workflow systems that are essential for building sophisticated AI applications.

In this chapter, we will be covering the following topics:

- Agents in action: Tool invocation patterns
- Tool discovery and selection algorithms
- Error handling in tool integration
- The Chain-of-Agents orchestrator
- Memory augmented multi-agent systems
- Conflict resolution mechanism
- The agentic workflow system

Agents in action: Tool invocation patterns

The ability to select, adapt, and orchestrate the right tools at the right moment has long been recognized as a hallmark of wisdom. A craftsman is not defined by the number of instruments at his disposal, but by the discernment with which he chooses and applies them. In much the same way, intelligent agents are measured not by the complexity of the underlying model alone, but by their capacity to extend reasoning into purposeful action through effective tool use.

Tool invocation represents the fundamental mechanism by which agents translate cognitive operations into concrete outcomes. Language models provide the reasoning substrate for understanding goals and formulating strategies, but tools allow agents to execute tasks that affect the real world. The architectural challenge lies in ensuring that this process is not a brittle integration point, but a seamless extension of agent cognition.

This section explores the design patterns that enable reliable tool invocation. We examine three central concerns: how agents decide which tools to call, how they construct inputs and manage execution results, and how they recover from failures as part of the overall agent loop. These principles apply universally, whether the tool is as simple as a calculator or as advanced as a geospatial analytics engine.

Even before we introduce multi-agent orchestrators, a single well-designed agent with a focused tool chest can deliver substantial business value. By combining natural language understanding with domain-specific APIs, such agents can automate tasks that previously required manual scripting or specialized expertise. These single-agent patterns form the architectural base for the more advanced orchestrators and workflow systems we will build on later in this chapter.

The Tool-Using agent pattern

A Tool-Using agent is a language-model-based system that extends its core reasoning capabilities by invoking a predefined set of external functions, or tools. This pattern captures the simplest form of an AI agent that can take concrete actions rather than only generate text. The Tool-Using agent architecture enables the agent to move beyond pure language processing and perform specialized tasks such as accessing live data, executing complex calculations, or interacting with external systems. The process follows a classic **Think, Plan, Act cycle**: the agent first interprets the user's goal (*Think*), formulates a sequence of tool calls to achieve it (*Plan*), and then executes that plan (*Act*).

A robust Tool-Using agent architecture consists of four primary components that work in concert to transform a natural language request into a concrete result. This design cleanly separates the decision-making logic from the execution mechanics, which improves modularity and resilience.

The reasoning core

This is the "brain" of the agent, responsible for the *Think* and *Plan* stages of the cycle. It parses the user's intent and formulates a step-by-step plan to achieve the goal.

The tool registry

To formulate a valid plan, the core consults the **tool registry**, which acts as a catalog of the agent's available tools and capabilities. The registry maintains critical metadata for each tool, including its name, description, and input/output schemas. These schemas serve as explicit, reliable contracts that allow the agent to know exactly what parameters to supply and what response to expect.

The execution engine

This component is the "foreman" responsible for the *Act* stage. It receives the execution plan from the reasoning core and manages the invocation of the actual tools. Its duties include managing state between steps, handling retries, and propagating errors to ensure the plan is carried out reliably.

The tool chest

This is the collection of functions the agent can execute. An agent's effectiveness is directly correlated to the quality of its tools. A well-designed tool chest contains modular functions with single, clearly defined responsibilities, a principle that simplifies building, testing, and extending the system over time. Each function should also be wrapped with its own safety logic, such as timeouts and exception handling, to ensure that it operates predictably.

This decoupled architecture provides a resilient foundation for agent development. With explicit contracts in the registry and robust error handling in the execution engine, the same structure can support both simple, reactive calls to a single function and deliberative plans that chain multiple tools to solve complex problems.

Figure 7.1 shows how a Tool-Using agent transforms a natural language query into a concrete output:

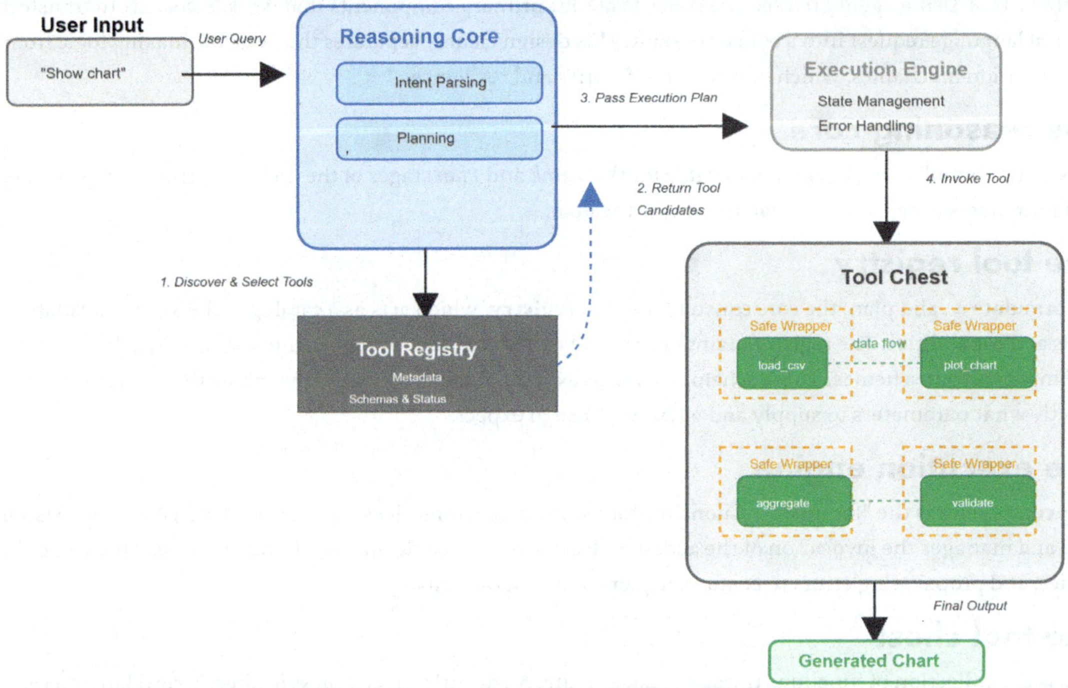

Figure 7.1 – Internal architecture of Tool-Using agents

A user request such as "Show chart" is processed by the reasoning core, which parses intent and formulates a plan. It consults the tool registry, where each tool is described with metadata such as its name, purpose, input/output schema, and operational status. This explicit contract enables precise planning.

The reasoning core then passes the plan to the execution engine, which manages state, retries, and error handling. The engine then invokes functions stored in the tool chest. Each function is wrapped with safeguards such as timeouts, exception handling, and input validation. In our running example, the tool chest might include four composable functions:

- `load_csv` for data ingestion
- `aggregate` for summarization
- `plot_chart` for visualization
- `validate` for output verification

Intermediate results flow through these functions until the final visualization is produced.

This architecture cleanly separates decision logic from execution. Explicit schemas make interfaces predictable, while safety wrappers provide resilience. The same structure supports both reactive queries (direct mappings of intent to a single tool) and deliberative plans that chain multiple tools into a sequence.

Together, these components illustrate the core pattern of a Tool-Using agent: a reasoning core that plans, a registry that exposes a catalog of tools, an execution engine that manages calls and failures, and a guarded tool chest that performs the actual work. In the remainder of the chapter, we will build on this foundation by moving from a single Tool-Using agent to chain-of-agents orchestrators, where multiple specialized agents collaborate to solve more complex tasks.

Function-calling architecture patterns

Invoking tools within agent systems is more than issuing a function call. The agent must reason about which tool to select, supply valid arguments, anticipate errors, and respond appropriately when execution does not go as planned. Designing the tool invocation layer requires balancing flexibility (to support a growing set of tools), modularity (to keep functions composable and independent), and observability (to monitor and debug execution).

Several recurring patterns guide effective design:

- **Interface schemas as contracts**: Each tool registers with a precise input–output signature, often expressed through JSON schemas or typed models such as Pydantic. These schemas act as contracts between the reasoning core and the execution layer, ensuring that arguments and return values are predictable.
- **Separation of decision and execution**: The reasoning component determines *what* to call and *when*, while the execution layer performs the actual invocation. This separation improves traceability and allows both layers to evolve independently.
- **Reactive vs. deliberative invocation**: In *reactive mode*, a user request maps directly to a tool, for instance, "Generate a bar chart of sales by region" may immediately trigger a plotting function. In *deliberative mode*, the agent first formulates a plan—loading data, filtering, aggregating, and then visualizing—and executes tools at each step.
- **Safe wrappers and fallback logic**: Tool calls are inherently uncertain. Robust systems wrap each invocation with retry logic, timeouts, and exception handling. Fallback strategies ensure graceful degradation, such as substituting a bar chart when the pie chart function fails.
- **Dynamic discovery via metadata**: Tools publish metadata including descriptions, input/output types, and operational status. Agents can use this metadata to discover and rank tools at runtime, adapting to evolving tool sets without manual reconfiguration.

Together, these patterns provide the backbone for resilient agent architectures. They allow reasoning components to remain model-agnostic, while execution layers enforce rigor, safety, and transparency. As agents scale in scope and tool complexity, these patterns become essential for sustaining reliability.

To make these function-calling patterns more concrete, we now look at a small implementation for the data visualization agent introduced earlier. The next example shows how interface schemas, safety wrappers, and the execution layer map directly to Python functions in a tool chest that the agent can call.

Implementation example

The following Python code demonstrates a simple but effective tool chest for the data analysis assistant introduced earlier in this section, focusing on its data visualization capabilities. Each function represents a distinct tool, adhering to the **single responsibility principle**. Notice how the Python type hints (e.g., `file_path: str`, `df: pd.DataFrame`) serve as the implementation of the schema contracts discussed earlier. They provide a reliable interface that the agent's reasoning core can use to construct valid calls.

```
import pandas as pd

# Tool 1: Handles data ingestion
def load_csv(file_path: str) -> pd.DataFrame | None:
    """Loads data from a specified CSV file into a pandas DataFrame."""

    try:
        df = pd.read_csv(file_path)
        print(f"[load_csv] Loaded {len(df)} rows from '{file_path}'.")
        return df
    except FileNotFoundError:
        print(f"[load_csv] Error: File '{file_path}' not found.")
        return None
# Tool 2: Performs data transformation and summarization
def group_by_and_aggregate(
    df: pd.DataFrame,
    group_by_col: str,
    agg_col: str,
    agg_func: str
) -> pd.DataFrame | None:
    """Groups the DataFrame and applies an aggregation function."""

    if group_by_col not in df.columns or agg_col not in df.columns:
        print(f"[group_by] Error: Column not found in DataFrame.")
        return None
    func = {"sum": "sum", "mean": "mean", "count": "count"}.get(agg_func, "sum")
    result = df.groupby(group_by_col)[agg_col].agg(func).reset_index()
    print(f"[group_by] Grouped '{agg_col}' by '{group_by_col}' using '{func}'.")
    return result

# Tool 3: Handles final rendering for a bar chart
def plot_bar_chart(
    df: pd.DataFrame,
    x_col: str,
    y_col: str,
    title: str,
    output_path: str
):
    """Generates and saves a bar chart from the data."""

    fig, ax = plt.subplots()
```

```
    ax.bar(df[x_col].astype(str), df[y_col])
    ax.set_xlabel(x_col); ax.set_ylabel(y_col); ax.set_title(title)
    fig.tight_layout(); fig.savefig(output_path); plt.close(fig)
    print(f"[plot_bar_chart] Saved chart to '{output_path}'.")

# Tool 4: Handles final rendering for a line chart
def plot_line_chart(
    df: pd.DataFrame,
    x_col: str,
    y_col: str,
    title: str,
    output_path: str
):
    """Generates and saves a line chart from the data."""

    fig, ax = plt.subplots()
    ax.plot(df[x_col].astype(str), df[y_col], marker="o")
    ax.set_xlabel(x_col); ax.set_ylabel(y_col); ax.set_title(title)
    fig.tight_layout(); fig.savefig(output_path); plt.close(fig)
    print(f"[plot_line_chart] Saved chart to '{output_path}'.")
```

These four tools divide the visualization pipeline into clear, testable steps. The `load_csv` function manages data ingestion, reading a CSV file from disk and returning a `pandas.DataFrame` for downstream tools. The `group_by_and_aggregate` function performs data summarization by grouping the frame on a chosen column and applying an aggregation such as sum or mean. The `plot_bar_chart` function then renders the aggregated data as a bar chart and writes the image to the specified `output_path`, while `plot_line_chart` generates a corresponding line chart. By giving each tool a single responsibility, this modular design allows the agent to mix and match visualizations and makes it straightforward to add new plotting tools without altering the agent's core logic.

Tool discovery and selection algorithms

As an agent's tool chest grows, it begins to resemble a vast library; the value lies not just in the collection itself, but in the ability to find the right book at the right moment. A powerful agent with a hundred tools is ineffective if it cannot reliably select the correct one for a given task. This selection process is the core of the *Think* component of the agent's cycle. Devising a robust method for navigating this "library" of capabilities is a critical architectural challenge, especially as the number of available tools scales into the dozens or hundreds.

To solve this problem, we can design a multi-stage filtering process, visualized as a selection funnel in *Figure 7.2*. This approach efficiently transforms a large tool registry into a single, verified, and executable choice by progressively narrowing the field of candidates.

The selection funnel

We will examine the three primary stages of this funnel: broad intent classification, candidate ranking via semantic search, and final verification using constraint filtering.

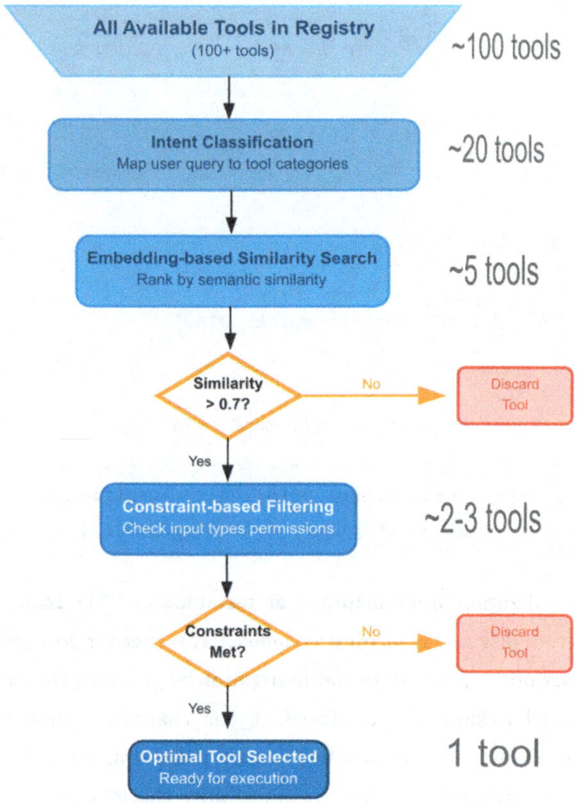

Figure 7.2 – Tool selection

As mentioned, the process consists of three primary stages:

1. **Intent classification (broad filtering)**: The process begins with a high-level, coarse-grained filter. The agent first classifies the user's intent to identify a relevant category of tools, immediately reducing the search space. For example, a request to "chart sales data" would quickly eliminate tools related to file manipulation or database administration.
2. **Semantic search (candidate ranking)**: Next, the agent performs a fine-grained similarity search on the remaining candidates. To do this, both the user's request and the tool's metadata (like its description and parameter names) are converted into numerical vector representations called **embeddings**. The agent then calculates the semantic distance between the request and each tool, ranking them by similarity and discarding any that fall below a configured confidence threshold, such as 0.7.
3. **Constraint filtering (final verification)**: From the final shortlist of promising candidates, the agent applies a series of deterministic checks. This is the final safety and sanity check, enforcing rules based

on input types, user permissions, or even the tool's historical failure status to prune incompatible choices. The result is a single viable tool that is ready for execution.

This multi-stage funnel provides a robust strategy that balances efficiency with safety. The initial classification reduces the search space, the semantic search identifies the most promising options, and the final constraint checks maintain system trustworthiness. For complex tasks that require a sequence of actions, this funnel can be invoked at each step of the plan, and a dynamic reranking process can reinitiate the funnel if a chosen tool fails or returns a low-confidence result.

Selection strategies

The selection funnel provides a conceptual model for narrowing down tool candidates, but architects can implement each stage using several distinct strategies. The optimal choice depends on the agent's complexity, the number of tools it manages, and the required level of flexibility. A simple, single-purpose agent might rely on one technique, while a sophisticated agent may combine several to achieve a balance of speed, accuracy, and safety. Let's review some techniques.

Intent classification or template matching

This is the most direct approach, where a user's query is mapped to a specific tool using predefined rules or a simple classification model. It works best in constrained domains where user intents are predictable.

Use Case: Consider a customer service chatbot for an e-commerce site. A rule-based parser can map keywords directly to tools: a query containing "track my order" invokes the `get_order_status` tool, while "return an item" calls the `start_return_process` tool. This method is fast and highly reliable for known intents, but it scales poorly and cannot handle ambiguous or novel requests.

Embedding-based similarity search

This flexible method relies on semantic meaning rather than keywords. Both the user's request and the tool's metadata (its name, description, and parameters) are converted into numerical vector representations, or embeddings. The system then shortlists tools whose embeddings are semantically closest to the user's query embedding.

Use case: In our data visualization agent, a user might ask, "What was the trend of our ad clicks over time?" There is no direct keyword match for a function. However, an embedding search would find a strong semantic similarity between that query and the description of the `plot_line_chart` tool, allowing the agent to select it correctly.

Constraint-based filtering

This strategy is less of a primary selection method and more of a critical safety and validation layer. After an initial set of candidates is shortlisted (often via similarity search), filters are applied to prune any incompatible or unsafe choices.

Use case: When an agent managing cloud infrastructure receives an instruction to clean up unused test resources, a similarity search might identify the `delete_vm_instance` tool as a likely match. Before execution, a constraint filter checks whether the agent has sufficient permissions. If the agent has only read-only access, the filter automatically removes `delete_vm_instance` from the candidate tool set, preventing accidental deletion of critical resources.

Plan-driven tool assignment

For multi-step tasks, the agent may generate a plan first and then select tools sequentially for each step. This allows the outcome of one tool to inform the selection or execution of the next one.

Use case: A travel agent is asked to "plan a trip to Lahore." The reasoning core first generates a high-level plan: [1. `find_flights`, 2. `find_hotels`, 3. `create_itinerary`]. The `find_flights` tool is selected and executed first. Its output (the confirmed flight dates) is then used as a critical input parameter for the `find_hotels` tool at the next step.

Dynamic reranking with feedback

This strategy gives an agent the ability to adapt when things go wrong. If a selected tool fails or returns a low-confidence result, the agent can evaluate that feedback and re-run the selection process to find an alternative.

Use case: A financial agent uses a tool called `fetch_stock_price_from_api_X` to get market data, but the API times out. Instead of aborting the entire task, the agent registers the failure, temporarily adds a constraint to avoid that specific tool, and re-enters the selection funnel. It then discovers and executes a fallback tool, `fetch_stock_price_from_api_Y`, to successfully complete the user's request.

To ground these ideas, we now look at how the data analysis assistant implements its first step of tool selection: interpreting a user's request and mapping it to a structured intent. The following example shows how a simple template-based classifier can translate natural language into the parameters that drive the selection funnel introduced earlier.

Implementation example: Intent classification through template matching

The first step in any agent's reasoning process is to translate ambiguous human language into a structured, machine-readable format. In our data visualization agent, the `parse_query` function handles this crucial role. It acts as a lightweight and efficient intent classifier, implementing the template matching strategy we discussed earlier.

Rather than attempting to understand the full semantic nuance of a query, this function scans for specific keywords and patterns to extract the essential parameters required for a visualization: a *metric*, a *dimension*, and a desired *chart type*. This approach is fast and predictable, making it a pragmatic choice for agents operating in a well-defined domain.

```
def parse_query(query: str) -> dict | None:
    """
    A simple natural language parser to extract intent from the user's query.
    Uses keyword matching to identify the metric, dimension, and chart type.
    """
    query = query.lower()  # Normalize the query for case-insensitive matching

    # --- Step 1: Identify the metric ---
    # A simple lookup to map known metric keywords to their column names
```

```
    metric_map = {'spend': 'spend', 'conversions': 'conversions', 'clicks': 'clicks'}
    metric = next((metric_map[key] for key in metric_map if key in query), None)

    # --- Step 2: Identify the dimension and chart type ---
    # Use keywords to infer how the user wants to group the data and visualize it
    dimension, chart_type = (None, None)
    if "by campaign" in query or "which campaign" in query:
        dimension, chart_type = 'campaign_name', 'bar'
    elif "over time" in query or "trend" in query:
        dimension, chart_type = 'date', 'line'

    # --- Step 3: Validate and return the structured intent ---
    # If any of the essential components are missing, the intent is invalid
    if not all([metric, dimension, chart_type]):
        return None

    return {'metric': metric, 'dimension': dimension, 'chart_type': chart_type}
```

This function acts as the agent's intent parser. For a query like "What was the trend of clicks over time?", it identifies `"clicks"` as the metric, `"over time"` as the dimension indicating date, and `"line"` as the appropriate chart type. This structured output is passed to the orchestrator to formulate a plan.

The result is a disciplined path from a plain English request to a precise, safe tool call that the system can execute reliably.

With intent classification in place, the agent can reliably translate natural language requests into structured plans and concrete tool calls. However, even a perfectly chosen tool can fail at runtime because of network issues, malformed inputs, or downstream service outages. To build production-ready agents, we must treat error handling in tool integration as a first-class architectural concern.

Error handling in tool integration

In any system that relies on external components, failure is not a possibility; it is an inevitability. Network connections drop, APIs change, inputs are malformed, and services go offline. Designing an agent without a robust error-handling strategy is like building a skyscraper on a weak foundation—it is destined to collapse. The goal is not to prevent every conceivable failure, but to build a resilient system that can anticipate, absorb, and gracefully recover from errors when they occur.

Common failure modes

Anticipating failures begins with identifying their most common sources and then designing targeted mitigations for each. In this part of the section, we will first group tool-related failures into four categories and, in the following subsections, map these categories to concrete strategies such as validation gates, retries and timeouts, fallback tools, and human review:

- **Input validation errors**: These occur when the data provided to a tool does not match its expected schema. For example, the agent might pass a non-existent column name to the `group_by_and_aggregate` function.
- **Runtime failures**: These are unexpected errors that occur during a tool's execution, such as network timeouts, external API errors, or file system I/O exceptions. A common example is the `load_csv` tool failing because the target file is locked by another process.
- **Semantic mismatches**: These are subtle but critical failure modes where a tool executes successfully but produces a result that does not align with the user's intent. For instance, a user asks for "top campaigns by spend," and the agent generates a chart that correctly groups by campaign but sorts them alphabetically instead of by the spend metric, rendering the output useless.
- **Tool unavailability**: A tool may be temporarily or permanently unavailable because the external service it depends on is offline or has been deprecated.

Anticipating these failures is the first step; the next step is designing an architecture that can recover from them.

Architectural recovery strategies

Production-ready agents implement a layered defense using several of the following strategies:

- **Safe invocation wrappers**: This is the first line of defense. Every tool call should be contained within a wrapper function that acts like a specialized `try/except` block. This wrapper is responsible for catching known exceptions, implementing targeted retry logic (e.g., exponential backoff for network errors), and logging the outcome for observability.
- **Fallback tool chains**: When a primary tool fails, the system should be able to invoke a secondary, alternative tool to accomplish the same goal. For example, if a `fetch_stock_data_from_api_A` tool fails due to a service outage, the agent can automatically attempt the same request using a `fetch_stock_data_from_api_B` tool.
- **Confidence-based switching**: When a tool returns a valid result but the agent's confidence in its correctness is low, the agent can discard the result and retry the task with a different tool that may be more suitable if the confidence score falls below a predefined threshold. This is common in tasks involving LLMs, where an agent might switch to a more powerful model if an initial summary lacks coherence.
- **Failure memory**: To prevent an agent from repeatedly attempting to use a tool that is clearly failing, the system can implement a short-term *failure memory*. This acts like a circuit breaker. If a tool fails multiple times in a short window, the agent temporarily marks it as unavailable and does not attempt to select it again for a predefined period, preventing wasted cycles.
- **Escalation paths**: When automated recovery strategies are exhausted, the final fallback is to escalate the task to a human operator. A well-designed escalation path pauses the workflow and presents the

human reviewer with the complete context of the problem, including the initial inputs, the tools that were attempted, and the specific errors that were encountered.

- **Comprehensive logging and telemetry**: You cannot fix what you cannot see. Every action, error, and recovery attempt must be logged. Detailed logs and metrics are not just for debugging; they provide the data needed to analyze systemic weaknesses, identify unreliable tools, and continuously improve the agent's overall resilience over time.

To see these reliability patterns in context, we now return to the data analysis assistant and look at its end-to-end control flow. The following implementation brings together intent parsing, tool selection, and the error-handling strategies we have just discussed into a single `data_viz_agent` function.

Implementation example

We will now tie all these concepts together. The following `data_viz_agent` function serves as the central orchestrator for our data analysis assistant. This function implements the full *Think*, *Plan*, *Act* cycle we introduced earlier. It begins by calling `parse_query` to interpret the user's goal (*Think*). Based on that structured intent, it dynamically constructs a plan as a list of tool calls (*Plan*). Finally, it iterates through that plan to execute each tool sequentially, managing the `data_state` as it passes from one step to the next to produce the final result (*Act*).

```
def data_viz_agent(query: str, file_path: str):
    # 1. THINK: Interpret the user's goal.
    intent = parse_query(query)
    if not intent:
        print("AGENT-ERROR: Could not understand the request...")
        return

    print(f"Agent Intent Analysis: Metric: {intent['metric']}, "
          f"Dimension: {intent['dimension']}, Chart: {intent['chart_type']}")

    # 2. PLAN: Create a sequence of tool calls based on the intent.
    plan = [
        ('load_csv', [file_path]),
        ('group_by_and_aggregate', [intent['dimension'], intent['metric'], 'sum']),
    ]


    if intent['chart_type'] == 'bar':
        plot_tool = 'plot_bar_chart'
        base_title = f"{intent['metric']} by {intent['dimension']}"
    else:
        plot_tool = 'plot_line_chart'
        base_title = f"{intent['metric']} over {intent['dimension']}"
    full_output_path = f"output_{intent['metric']}_{intent['dimension']}.png"
    plan.append((plot_tool, [intent['dimension'], intent['metric'],
```

```
                        base_title, full_output_path]))

    print("Agent Action Plan:")
    for step, _ in plan:
        print(f" - Step: {step}")

    # 3. ACT: Execute the plan step-by-step.
    data_state = None
    tool_functions = {
        'load_csv': load_csv,
        'group_by_and_aggregate': group_by_and_aggregate,
        'plot_bar_chart': plot_bar_chart,
        'plot_line_chart': plot_line_chart
    }

    for tool_name, args in plan:
        tool_func = tool_functions[tool_name]
        current_args = [data_state] + args if tool_name != 'load_csv' else args
        result = tool_func(*current_args)

        if isinstance(result, pd.DataFrame):
            data_state = result
        elif data_state is None and tool_name != 'load_csv':
            print("Error: Execution failed at a critical step. Aborting plan.")
            return
```

This orchestrator creates a base plan to load and aggregate data, then dynamically appends the correct plotting tool based on the intent. During execution, a `data_state` variable holds the data as a `pandas` DataFrame and passes it to each subsequent tool. This pattern of *state passing* is fundamental to creating coherent, multi-step agentic processes.

In the visualization agent, if the user requests an unsupported chart type, the system gracefully falls back or asks for clarification. It also logs failed attempts for analysis.

The data analysis assistant illustrates how far we can go with a single Tool-Using agent. It can parse intent, select tools, manage state, and recover from failures, all within one coherent loop. Many real-world problems, however, stretch beyond the capabilities of a single agent: they involve heterogeneous data sources, specialized reasoning skills, and long-running workflows that benefit from dividing responsibility. To handle these scenarios, we turn to chain-of-agents orchestrators, where multiple specialized agents collaborate under a coordinating strategy.

The chain-of-agents orchestrator

Wisdom in human endeavors rarely emerges from a single perspective. It arises when diverse minds contribute complementary skills: scientists collaborating across disciplines, musicians harmonizing in an ensemble, or engineers aligning across domains. Each participant brings specialized knowledge, yet the real value lies in the orchestration that transforms individual contributions into a coherent whole.

In the same way, complex tasks in artificial intelligence often exceed the capacity of any single agent. A chain-of-agents orchestrator provides the architectural pattern for scaling from individual tool use to collective problem-solving. In this model, a manager agent coordinates a team of specialists, each with its own domain expertise and tool chest. This approach allows us to solve multifaceted problems by breaking them down and assigning each subtask to the agent best equipped to handle it.

Effective collaboration, whether human or artificial, is not accidental. It requires a clear framework that defines how individuals interact, share information, and work toward a common goal. In multi-agent systems, this framework is known as a **cooperation protocol**. This protocol is the set of rules and architectural components that allow a team of agents to operate as a disciplined and purposeful unit rather than a set of disconnected parts.

A robust cooperation protocol is built upon four key architectural pillars:

- **Clearly defined roles and capabilities**: Every agent on the team is assigned a distinct purpose and is granted access to the specific tools it needs to fulfill that role. Much like a film crew has a director, a cinematographer, and a sound editor, an agent team has specialists like a `PlannerAgent`, a `DataFetcherAgent`, and a `ValidatorAgent`. This specialization ensures that each part of a complex task is handled by an expert.
- **A common communication infrastructure**: Agents need a reliable channel to exchange structured messages, such as instructions, results, and status updates. This can be implemented using various technologies like remote procedure calls (RPC), dedicated message queues, or a shared memory store. This infrastructure acts as the team's "walkie-talkie" system, ensuring information is passed between agents reliably.
- **Shared context or memory**: To maintain continuity as a task is handed off from one agent to another, the team needs a shared workspace or knowledge base. This *shared memory* is like the single, authoritative script for a film; it ensures that every agent is working from the same set of facts and that `SummarizerAgent` has access to the context gathered by `DataFetcherAgent`.
- **Execution orchestration**: A supervisor, or manager agent, is responsible for orchestrating the overall workflow. This agent delegates tasks to the appropriate specialists, manages dependencies between them (e.g., ensuring data is fetched before it is summarized), and monitors the progress of the entire operation. The manager is the director on set, ensuring the project stays on track and all the pieces come together correctly.

When designed thoughtfully, these four elements form the backbone of an effective multi-agent system, transforming a collection of individual specialists into a cohesive, intelligent team.

The four pillars above are expressed concretely through a cooperation protocol: a minimal schema that every agent in a team must honor. *Table 7.1* summarizes the four elements that a well-formed protocol must define.

Protocol element	Definition
Message format	A shared envelope structure (e.g., JSON with `sender`, `recipient`, `task_id`, `payload`) that every agent reads and writes
Role declaration	Each agent registers its name, capabilities, and accepted task types with the manager so that delegation decisions are unambiguous.
Task delegation scheme	A typed request object specifying the target agent, the requested action, required inputs, and expected output schema.
Status signaling	A standardized `status` field (`pending`, `running`, done, `error`) that the manager polls to sequence downstream tasks correctly

Table 7.1 – Core elements of an agent communication protocol

These protocol elements align with emerging industry standards. The Model Context Protocol (MCP) and Agent-to-Agent (A2A) protocol, introduced in *Chapter 6*, formalize exactly this message schema and role-declaration layer into open, interoperable specifications. Where *Chapter 6* covered their structure and negotiation mechanics, this chapter applies those foundations: the cooperation protocol described above is the practical expression of what MCP and A2A standardize at the wire level.

Of these four pillars, shared context or memory is perhaps the most critical for enabling true collaboration. A team of brilliant experts who cannot remember their previous conversations or share notes would be profoundly ineffective. Therefore, we must now move beyond the general concept and explore the specific architectures that make this shared memory possible.

Memory-augmented multi-agent systems

A team of brilliant experts who cannot remember their previous conversations or share notes would be profoundly ineffective. They would be trapped in a cycle of rediscovery, wasting time and arriving at inconsistent conclusions. A multi-agent system without a shared memory faces the same fate. Memory is the critical architectural component that provides continuity and a shared understanding of reality, transforming a group of independent specialists into a cohesive and intelligent team. It allows the system to preserve state across complex tasks, learn from past interactions, and ensure that every agent acts based on a consistent set of facts.

Memory-augmented architecture

A robust multi-agent system implements a multi-layered memory architecture, as illustrated in *Figure 7.3*. This design separates immediate, short-term context from durable, long-term knowledge, allowing the agent team to operate with both speed and depth.

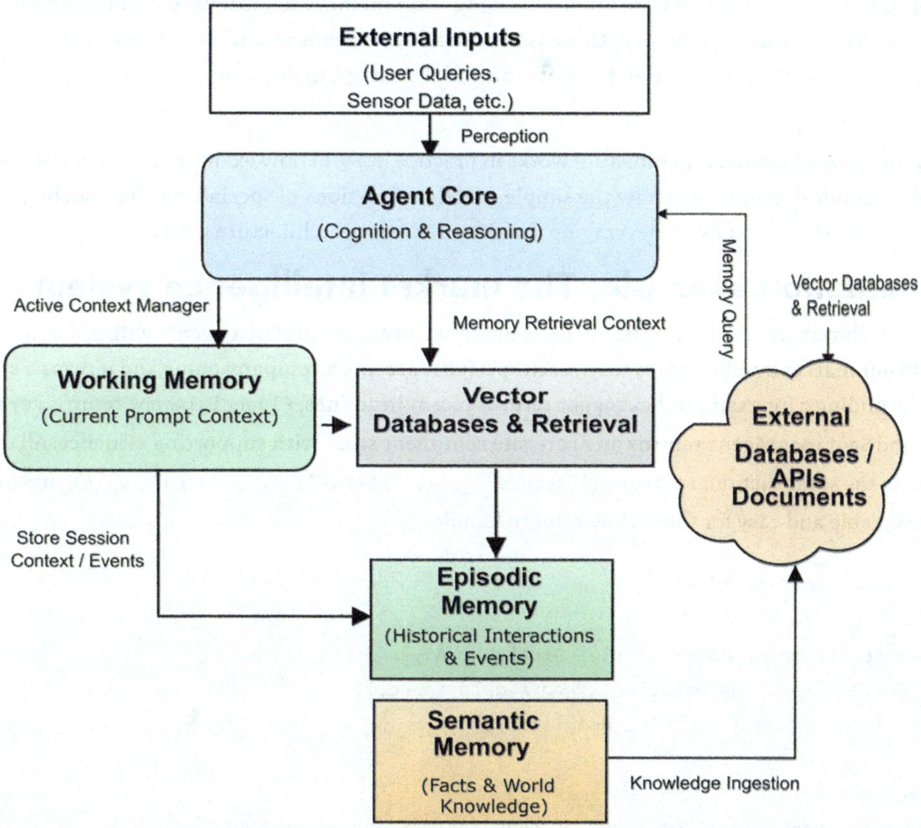

Figure 7.3 – Memory-augmented agent architecture

Working memory (short-term context)

This is the agent's active "scratchpad" for the task at hand. It holds the immediate context, such as the user's initial query and the results of the most recent tool calls. The Agent Core acts as an active context manager, deciding what information is relevant enough to keep in this limited window and what can be offloaded as steps are completed.

Long-term memory (knowledge base)

This is the team's shared, persistent library, which is typically indexed in a vector database for fast semantic retrieval. It consists of two distinct types:

- **Episodic memory**: This is the historical record of the system's interactions, like a logbook or a series of meeting minutes. It stores the sequence of events, agent conversations, and tool outputs from past and current tasks.
- **Semantic memory**: This is the repository for durable, factual knowledge—an encyclopedia of concepts relevant to the agent's domain, such as company descriptions, product catalogs, or regulatory guidelines.

When a new task begins, the Agent Core queries the long-term memory to retrieve relevant information, which is then loaded into the working memory. This ensures that downstream agents have access to the same foundational facts that the planner used to create the initial strategy, maintaining consistency throughout the workflow.

To see how this layered memory architecture works in practice, we will now examine a market intelligence system. This example demonstrates how the simple, stateless functions of specialist agents can be coordinated within a larger, stateful workflow by leveraging the shared memory architecture we have just defined.

Implementation example: The market intelligence system

This memory architecture allows simple, stateless functions to act as specialist agents within a larger, stateful workflow. In our market intelligence system, each specialist accepts a company name and returns a structured payload of its findings: for example, `NewsAgent` returns recent headlines, `FinancialAgent` returns key financial indicators, and `SentimentAgent` returns an aggregate sentiment score with supporting evidence. All three wrap their results in the same dictionary layout (`{"source": ..., "status": ..., "data": ...}`), making their outputs predictable and easy for the orchestrator to handle.

```
from typing import Dict, Any

def NewsAgent(company_name: str) -> Dict[str, Any]:
    """Fetches top news headlines from a data source."""
    print("[NewsAgent] Fetching headlines...")

    headlines = [
        f"{company_name}: Q3 earnings beat analyst estimates by 8%",
        f"{company_name} announces expansion into cloud infrastructure",
        f"Regulatory review concluded; {company_name} cleared to proceed",
    ]
    response = {"data": headlines}
    # response = news_api.get(company_name)
    return {"source": "NewsAgent", "status": "success", "data": response["data"]}

def FinancialAgent(company_name: str) -> Dict[str, Any]:
    """Fetches financial data from a data source."""
    print("[FinancialAgent] Fetching financial data...")

    response = {
        "data": {
            "pe_ratio": 24.5,
            "revenue_growth": 0.12,
            "debt_to_equity": 0.38,
            "last_close": 142.73,
        }
    }
```

```
    # response = financial_api.get(company_name)
    return {"source": "FinancialAgent", "status": "success", "data": response["data"]}

def SentimentAgent(company_name: str) -> Dict[str, Any]:
    """Fetches a sentiment score from a data source."""
    print("[SentimentAgent] Fetching sentiment score...")

    response = {
        "data": {
            "score": 0.72,
            "label": "positive",
            "evidence": [
                f"Investor confidence in {company_name} remains high.",
                "Social media tone broadly favorable this week.",
            ],
        }
    }
    # response = sentiment_api.get(company_name)
    return {"source": "SentimentAgent", "status": "success", "data": response["data"]}
```

In this system, the manager agent coordinates three specialist agents: `NewsAgent`, `FinancialAgent`, and `SentimentAgent`. It delegates the same company name to each specialist and waits for their structured responses. As each agent returns its dictionary of findings, the manager writes the result into episodic memory, creating a timestamped record of what was found and when. Later, the `LLMAnalystAgent` is tasked with creating a summary. It queries the retrieval layer to pull two sets of information into its working memory: the fresh findings from episodic memory (news, financial indicators, sentiment) and the durable company background information from semantic memory. By combining immediate results with long-term context, the analyst agent can produce a rich, insightful, and well-grounded report. This pattern preserves state across handoffs, reduces redundancy, and allows a team of simple agents to perform complex, knowledge-intensive work.

As soon as we let multiple specialist agents contribute their own views into shared memory, we gain breadth of insight but also introduce the possibility of disagreement. News, financial, and sentiment signals may point in different directions, or two retrieval agents may surface conflicting evidence about the same entity. To build trustworthy multi-agent systems, we need explicit mechanisms for detecting these conflicts and resolving them in a way that preserves transparency and auditability.

Conflict resolution mechanisms

In any system where multiple specialists analyze complex information, disagreements are not just possible but inevitable, and can even be a sign of robust, diverse analysis. The architectural strength of a multi-agent system is measured not by its ability to avoid conflict but by its capacity to resolve it productively. After the manager agent delegates tasks, its final and most critical responsibility is *synthesis*: aggregating results, identifying conflicts, and transforming competing outputs into a single, coherent, and defensible final product.

Architecture for arbitration

To manage disagreements reliably, we need a formal, automated process for arbitration. The workflow illustrated in *Figure 7.4* provides a blueprint for transforming conflicting agent outputs into a single, trustworthy result. This process typically involves several automated stages, with human expertise serving as the ultimate safety net.

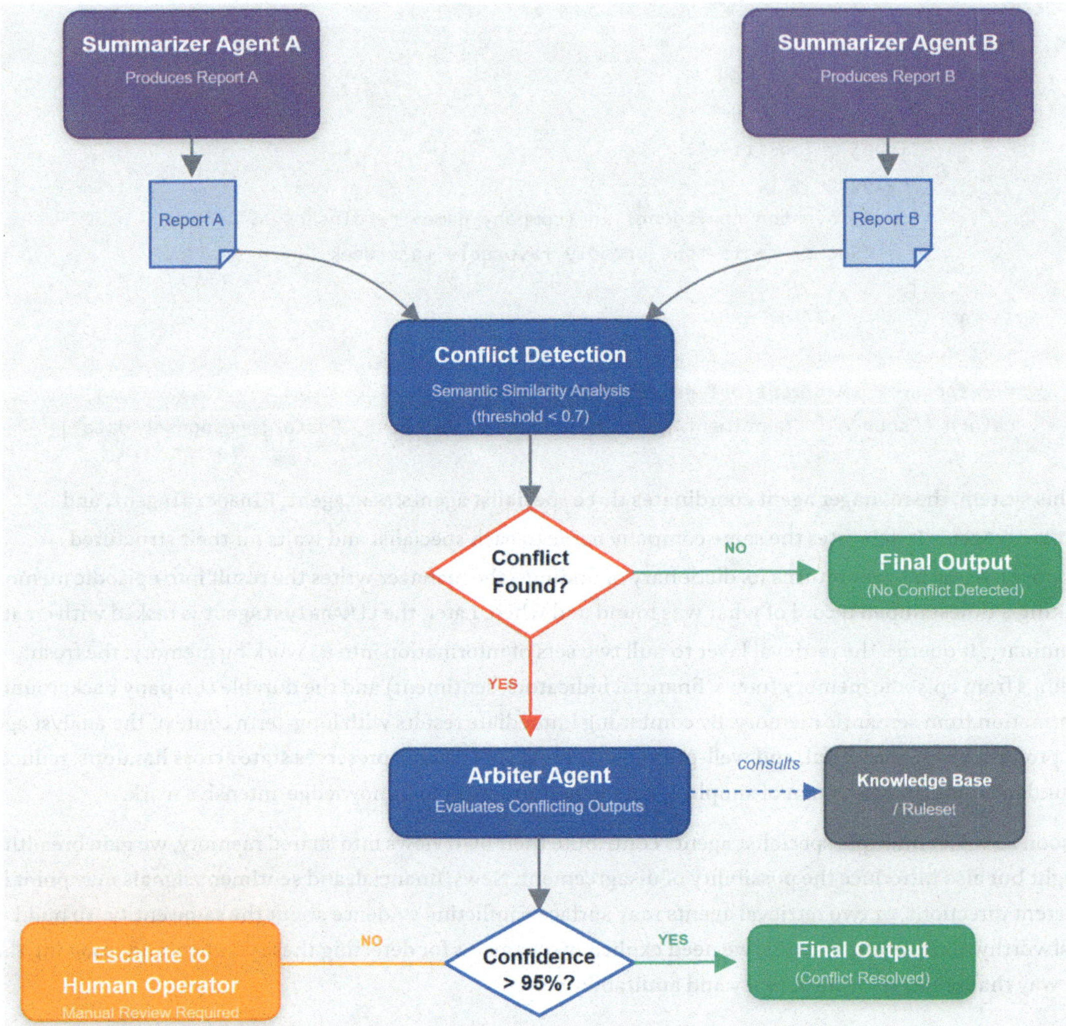

Figure7.4 – Conflict resolution mechanism

This workflow is built on several key stages. It begins with conflict detection to automatically identify when agents disagree. From there, an arbiter agent attempts automated arbitration by consulting a trusted knowledge base. The success of this arbitration is measured by a confidence-based consensus mechanism. Finally, if confidence remains low, the system follows a predefined path for human escalation, ensuring that complex ambiguities are handled by an expert.

We will walk through the arbitration workflow step by step, starting with how the system detects that two agents disagree, then examining how an arbiter agent proposes a consolidated answer, and finally explaining when and how humans step in as the last stage of review.

- **Conflict detection**: The process begins when two or more independent agents produce conflicting outputs, for example, *Report A* and *Report B*. The system must first detect this divergence automatically. A common technique is to calculate the semantic similarity between the outputs; if the resulting score falls below a predefined threshold (e.g., 0.7), a conflict is flagged and the arbitration workflow is triggered.
- **Automated arbitration**: The conflicting reports are then routed to a specialized arbiter agent for reconciliation. This agent acts as an impartial judge, evaluating the competing claims by consulting a trusted knowledge base, re-examining the source data, or applying a learned policy to determine which conclusion is more credible. In some cases, it may synthesize a new output that incorporates elements from both original reports.
- **Confidence-based consensus**: The arbiter agent doesn't just make a decision; it also produces a calibrated confidence score that quantifies its certainty in the outcome. This score is then evaluated against a policy threshold (e.g., 95%). If the arbiter's confidence is high enough, its decision is accepted, forming an automated consensus.
- **Human escalation**: If the arbiter's confidence is low, the system acknowledges the ambiguity and escalates the issue to a human reviewer. This is a crucial design principle: human review is not treated as a failure but as a planned, first-class branch in the control flow, ensuring that nuanced or high-stakes decisions are handled with the necessary expertise.

Throughout this entire process, the system persistently logs all inputs, intermediate decisions, confidence scores, and final rationales. This creates a complete audit trail essential for governance, debugging, and future system improvements. This structured workflow turns conflict from a potential failure into a mechanism for achieving more reliable and well-vetted results.

To make this arbitration workflow concrete, we now look at how it is implemented in our multi-agent research system. The next example shows how the manager detects conflicting signals, computes a conflict score, and routes the case through automated and human review to reach a final synthesized report.

Implementation example

In our market intelligence system, the `ManagerAgent` uses its `_synthesize_report` method to perform the final step of the workflow: aggregating all specialist findings into a single, coherent report. This method also implements a simple form of conflict detection. The following code shows how it calculates `conflict_score` to measure any divergence between the findings of the `SentimentAgent` and the `FinancialAgent` (specifically, public sentiment versus stock performance):

```
class ManagerAgent:
    def _synthesize_report(self, results: Dict[str, Any]) -> str:

    financial_data = results.get("FinancialAgent", {}).get("data", {})
    sentiment_data = results.get("SentimentAgent", {}).get("data", {})
```

```
    news_items = results.get("NewsAgent", {}).get("data", [])

        stock_change = financial_data['change_pct']
        sentiment_score = sentiment_data['sentiment_score']

        # A simple score to quantify the difference between sentiment
        # and financial performance.
        conflict_score = abs(sentiment_score - (stock_change / 10))

    headlines = '; '.join(news_items[:2]) if news_items else "no headlines"
    report = f"Market Intelligence Report\n"
    report += f"Recent news: {headlines}\n"
    report += f"P/E ratio: {financial_data.get('pe_ratio', 'N/A')}, Revenue growth:
{financial_data.get('revenue_growth', 0):.0%}\n"

        if conflict_score > 0.5:
            report += (
                f"**Conflict Detected (Score: {conflict_score:.2f}):** "
                f"A significant discrepancy exists..."
            )
        else:
            report += (
                f"**Alignment Confirmed (Score: {conflict_score:.2f}):** "
                f"Public perception and market performance are well-aligned..."
            )

        return report
```

This synthesis step performs more than simple data aggregation. `conflict_score` provides higher-level insight by noting when market signals are contradictory. This allows the final report to offer synthesized analysis rather than just raw data, demonstrating a rudimentary conflict resolution mechanism.

The formula normalizes both inputs to a compatible scale before comparing them.

`sentiment_score` is already bounded to the range [−1, 1] by the `SentimentAgent`. `stock_change` is expressed as a percentage (e.g., 5.0 for a 5 percent move); dividing by 10 maps a typical daily swing of up to ±10 percent onto the same [−1, 1] scale. The 0.5 threshold represents a half-unit divergence on this normalized scale, equivalent to a 5-point gap between sentiment and stock movement, a level of discrepancy the system treats as material enough to flag for the analyst.

So far, our focus has been on relatively short-lived interactions: a single agent invoking tools, chains of agents collaborating on a task, and arbitration mechanisms resolving conflicts in their outputs. In many enterprises, however, these capabilities sit inside longer-running business processes that span hours, days, or even weeks and require durable state, checkpoints, and human oversight. To address this broader context, we now turn to the pattern of the **agentic workflow system**.

The agentic workflow system

True wisdom also requires patience and perspective. Some decisions must unfold over time, drawing on memory, persistence, and the ability to pause for human judgment when stakes are high. Just as a wise leader balances decisive action with reflective waiting, agent systems must be designed not only to act quickly but also to sustain complex processes over hours, days, or even human-in-the-loop (HITL) cycles.

An **agentic workflow system** extends orchestration into long-running, stateful business processes. Unlike short-lived tool invocations or transient chains of agents, workflows require persistence, branching, error recovery, and checkpoints for human oversight. These systems combine the speed of automation with the prudence of governance, ensuring that outcomes remain aligned with both business objectives and ethical constraints.

In this section, we explore how workflow managers model processes as state machines or graphs, integrate intelligent agents into each stage, and embed escalation paths that allow human operators to intervene when needed. To make these concepts concrete, we will examine two practical case studies. First, we will build an e-commerce order processing workflow to demonstrate how to embed an intelligent agent and a human-in-the-loop checkpoint into a process. We will then analyze a more complex, multi-agent insurance claims workflow to show how these systems handle branching logic and state transitions. The result is an architecture that reflects both the efficiency of automation and the accountability of human wisdom.

Case study: An e-commerce order processing workflow

To understand how these principles are applied, we begin with an agentic workflow for a familiar business process: handling a straightforward e-commerce order. This first case study focuses on the basic mechanics of representing a workflow as a sequence of steps and wiring tools and agents into a simple, mostly automated "happy path." In the next case study, we will reuse the same patterns in a more complex, long-running enterprise workflow with richer branching and human involvement.

Our workflow models the process as a sequence of steps, where each step is executed by a tool or a specialized agent. The orchestrator, or workflow manager, is responsible for executing these steps in the correct order and managing the process state. The initial happy-path version of our workflow defines a clear four-step process for a standard order.

```
def workflow_manager_agent(order: Dict[str, Any], inventory_db: pd.DataFrame):
    order_id = order.get('order_id', 'N/A')
    print(f"\n--- Starting Workflow for Order #{order_id} ---")

    try:
        # Step 1: Validate the order data
        is_valid, order_total = validate_order(order, inventory_db)
        if not is_valid:
            raise AgentError("Order validation failed.")
```

```
        # Step 2: Assess fraud risk with an intelligent agent
        risk_analysis = llm_analyst_agent(order, order_total)
        # ... Human-in-the-Loop logic will be added here ...

        # Step 3: Check and reserve inventory
        if not check_inventory(order, inventory_db):
            raise AgentError("Inventory check failed.")

        # Step 4: Process the payment
        if not process_payment(order, order_total):
            raise AgentError("Payment processing failed.")

        print(f"--- Workflow for Order #{order_id} COMPLETED SUCCESSFULLY ---")

    except AgentError as e:
        print(f"--- Workflow for Order #{order_id} TERMINATED. Reason: {e} ---")
```

Embedding intelligence in workflow nodes

While some steps in our workflow are deterministic (e.g., `check_inventory`), others require nuanced judgment. *Step 2*, risk assessment, is a perfect example of a non-deterministic task that is difficult to encode with simple rules. This is where we can embed an intelligent, LLM-powered agent directly into the workflow. The `llm_analyst_agent` is designed to be adaptable, falling back to a simple rule-based system if its primary model is unavailable.

```
def llm_analyst_agent(order: Dict[str, Any], order_total: float) -> Dict[str, str]:
    print(f" [Step 2] Assessing risk for Order #{order.get('order_id', 'N/A')}...")

    # Fallback mode if a powerful model is unavailable
    if not OPENAI_API_KEY:
        print(" - Mode: Using rule-based mock analysis.")
        # ... rule-based logic for high value or mismatched addresses ...
        return {'risk_level': 'low', 'reason': 'Standard order parameters.'}

    # Primary mode using an LLM for nuanced analysis
    print(" - Mode: Using OpenAI GPT for analysis.")
    try:
        # ... logic to create a prompt and call the OpenAI API ...
        analysis = json.loads(response.choices[0].message.content)
        print(f" - LLM Analysis complete. Risk Level: {analysis.get('risk_level')}")
        return analysis
    except Exception as e:
```

```
        print(f"  - FAILED: ... Defaulting to high risk.")
        return {'risk_level': 'high', 'reason': 'LLM analysis failed.'}
```

Human-in-the-loop coordination

Embedding an intelligent agent to assess risk creates a new requirement: how should the system handle orders that are flagged as high-risk? Automating a rejection could lose a valuable customer, while automating an approval could result in fraud. This decision point is a prime candidate for HITL coordination. An HITL mechanism acts as a safety valve, pausing automation to request human judgment.

To make this concrete, we extend our earlier e-commerce workflow: the `workflow_manager_agent` below is the same orchestrator as before, now augmented with a "Step 2.5" escalation gate that calls an LLM-based risk analyst and, when the risk is medium or high, pauses the workflow to obtain an explicit approve or reject decision from a human operator.

```
# Enhanced workflow_manager_agent with HITL Logic
def workflow_manager_agent(
    order: Dict[str, Any], inventory_db: pd.DataFrame
):
    try:
        # ... Step 1 and 2 from before ...
        risk_analysis = llm_analyst_agent(order, order_total)
        risk_level = risk_analysis.get('risk_level', 'high').lower()
        risk_reason = risk_analysis.get('reason', 'No reason provided.')

        # Step 2.5: Human-in-the-Loop Escalation Gate
        if risk_level in ['high', 'medium']:
            print(f"\n  [!] HUMAN INTERVENTION REQUIRED for Order #{order_id}!")
            print(f"  Reason: Analyst flagged order for '{risk_reason}'.")

            prompt = "  Please type 'approve' or 'reject' to proceed: "
            decision = ""
            while decision not in ['approve', 'reject']:
                decision = input(prompt).lower().strip()

            if decision == 'reject':
                print("  - DECISION: Human operator rejected the order.")
                raise AgentError("Workflow terminated by human operator.")
            else:
                print("  - DECISION: Human operator approved the order. Resuming...")

        # ... Steps 3 and 4 resume if approved ...
    except AgentError as e:
        # ... error handling ...
```

This HITL block is the core of safe automation. The `input()` prompt halts the program, ceding control to a human. This pattern is essential for deploying agents in business-critical systems where the cost of an error is high.

Our e-commerce example highlights the need for capabilities beyond simple, linear chains. Real business processes require more complex logic: What if inventory is out of stock? Should the workflow pause and wait for a restock event? What if the payment fails? Do we need to roll back the inventory reservation?

These scenarios require workflows modeled as directed graphs rather than chains, with features like:

- Conditional branching logic
- Waiting states for external events (like human input or a document upload)
- Recovery and rollback paths

Modern orchestration engines such as **LangGraph** and **CrewAI** are specifically designed to enable developers to define these complex, stateful, and resilient agentic workflows.

The e-commerce workflow illustrated how a single workflow manager can coordinate tools and a small number of agents along a mostly linear "happy path," with a simple HITL gate for high-risk orders. To see how the same patterns scale to a richer and more regulated domain, we now turn to a second case study in automated insurance claims processing. This scenario introduces a larger team of specialized agents, deeper branching logic, and multiple escalation paths, showing how agentic workflows support long-running, high-stakes processes where governance and auditability are as important as throughput.

Case study: Multi-agent insurance claims workflow

To demonstrate how a multi-agent system operates in a practical, high-stakes environment, consider an automated insurance claims processing workflow. A claim must move from initial submission to final resolution, passing through various checks and decision points. This entire process is managed by a team of specialized AI agents, each with a distinct role, all coordinated within a structured state machine.

This architecture balances efficiency with risk management. It automates routine, low-risk claims for speed, while ensuring that complex or high-risk cases escalate for expert human review.

The system comprises several specialized agents that handle different stages of the claims process.

- **Intake agent**: This agent serves as the first point of contact. It uses optical character recognition (OCR) and natural language processing (NLP) to read and digitize information from submitted claim forms.
- **Validator agent**: This agent serves as a gatekeeper. It checks the claimant's policy status, cross-references databases for fraud signals, and ensures all required documentation is present.
- **Classifier agent**: This agent assesses the claim's type, urgency, and overall risk level based on the details provided once the claim is validated.
- **Payout agent**: This agent calculates the settlement amount and processes the payment for approved low-risk claims.
- **Escalation agent**: This agent monitors the workflow for specific triggers such as high-risk flags or low-confidence scores from other agents and routes the claim to a human for review when necessary.

The workflow state machine

The journey of a claim is visualized as a state machine that dictates flow and transitions from one stage to the next. *Figure 7.5* illustrates the complete operational lifecycle:

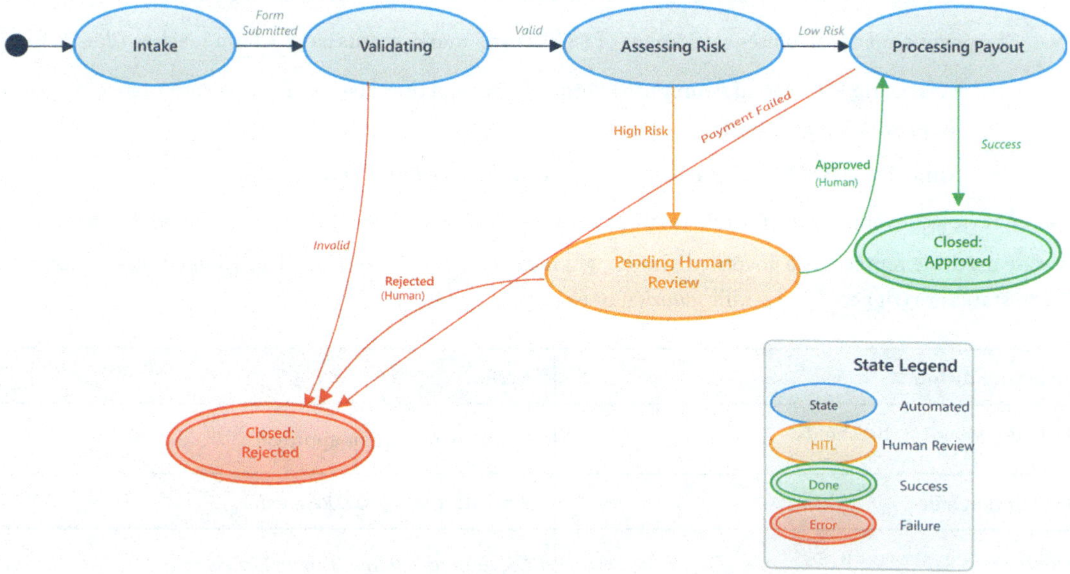

Figure 7.5 – Insurance claim state machine

The ideal path processes straightforward, low-risk claims automatically. A claim enters the *Intake* state, moves to *Validating* where the validator agent checks legitimacy, proceeds to *Assessing Risk* where the classifier agent analyzes it, continues to *Processing Payout* where the payout agent executes settlement, and concludes in the *Closed: Approved* state.

The system intelligently escalates claims requiring human judgment. If the classifier agent flags a claim as high risk in the *Assessing Risk* state, the workflow redirects it to *Pending Human Review*. A human reviewer can either approve the claim, sending it back to *Processing Payout*, or reject it, moving it to *Closed: Rejected*.

The workflow also accounts for failures. If payment fails during *Processing Payout*, or if a human expert rejects the claim, the process terminates in *Closed: Rejected*.

Concrete walkthrough: Claim CLM-4821

To make the state transitions tangible, trace a single claim end-to-end. Claim `CLM-4821` is a water-damage home policy claim for $8,400 under policy `POL-992317` (active, with no fraud flag on record). The guard conditions shown in *Table 7.2* drive each transition.

- **Intake**: OCR agent extracts fields—`claim_id = CLM-4821`, `policy_id = POL-992317`, `type = water_damage`, `amount = 8400.00`—and writes them to the claim record
- **Guard**: all required fields populated → advance to *Validating*
- **Validating**: The validator agent confirms policy `POL-992317` is active and no fraud flag exists

- **Guard**: validation passes → advance to *Assessing Risk*
    - **Assessing Risk (approved path)**: The classifier agent returns `confidence_score = 0.91`, risk = low
    - **Guard**: `confidence_score ≥ 0.85` and low risk → advance to *Processing Payout*
- The payout agent calculates settlement of $8,400 and marks status `paid`. Claim reaches *Closed: Approved*
    - **Assessing Risk (escalation path)**: Suppose instead the classifier returns `confidence_score = 0.79` with a high-risk flag
    - **Guard**: `confidence_score < 0.85` → reroute to *Pending Human Review*
- A reviewer examines the file and may approve (→ *Processing Payout*) or reject (→ *Closed: Rejected*)

This state machine represents a governed system where every action is controlled and logged. Transitions between states are triggered by specific *guards*. For example:

Guard condition	Action
If `claim_amount` > threshold	Route to human for approval
If validation fails	Transition to *Closed: Rejected*
if `confidence_score` < `0.85`	Escalate to *Pending Human Review*

Table 7.2 – State transition guards for the insurance claims workflow

At each transition, the system records the agent's reasoning, the tools it used, human decisions, and updates to the claim's record. This creates a complete audit trail, essential for compliance, debugging, and postmortem analysis. By combining specialized agents with a structured state machine, this architecture delivers a workflow that is fast for routine claims yet safe and traceable for complex ones.

Summary

This chapter has demonstrated the progression from foundational tool invocation to sophisticated multi-agent orchestration and persistent workflow systems. We examined how agents extend their reasoning capabilities into action through three architectural patterns: Tool-Using agents that invoke external functions, chain-of-agents orchestrators that coordinate specialized agents, and agentic workflow systems that implement stateful business processes with human oversight.

The three case studies illustrated these architectural patterns through different levels of implementation detail. The data visualization assistant provided fully executable code demonstrating intent parsing, tool orchestration, and error handling. The market intelligence platform combined runnable specialist agents with an architectural description of the memory and conflict-resolution layers. The insurance claims workflow presented a state machine and governance architecture, with the concrete CLM-4821 walkthrough showing how guard conditions drive transitions in practice. Together, they demonstrated the critical principles that underpin each pattern: clear function-calling contracts enable reliable tool invocation, dynamic discovery algorithms scale to large tool sets, layered error handling provides resilience, agent cooperation protocols enable specialization, and human checkpoints ensure governance.

These patterns provide a foundation for developing production-ready agent systems that deliver measurable business value while maintaining safety and accountability. The architectural principles established here extend directly to the domain-specific agents explored in subsequent chapters. In *Chapter 8*, we turn to data analysis and reasoning agents, applying these orchestration patterns to systems that explore datasets, recommend visualizations, and perform statistical reasoning to support business decision-making. Later chapters introduce software development agents that write, test, and maintain code in collaboration with human developers.

8

Data Analysis and Reasoning Agents

Information is the oil of the 21st century, and analytics is the combustion engine.

— *Peter Sondergaard*

The modern era is defined not by a lack of data but by the difficulty of interpreting it. This chapter examines a specialized class of **intelligent systems** that are designed to process information as well as understand it, reason about it, and extract meaningful insights from it to guide decisions. Unlike the task-oriented agents introduced in the previous chapter on *Tool Manipulation and Orchestration*, the agents discussed here operate at a higher level of cognition. They function as digital analysts, researchers, and critical thinkers who can question assumptions, evaluate evidence, and synthesize knowledge rather than simply execute instructions.

These agents convert raw data into actionable intelligence. In doing so, they close the gap between information and understanding, allowing organizations across sectors such as business, finance, scientific research, and journalism to reason effectively in complex, data-rich environments.

We will begin this chapter by establishing the theoretical foundations of each agent type, introducing the core ideas and cognitive principles that define its function. This is followed by the architectural and implementation details, wherein we'll examine system components, reasoning loops, and design patterns that translate these principles into working solutions.

In this chapter, we'll be covering the following topics:

- The Data Analysis agent
- The Verification and Validation agent
- The General Problem Solver

Each agent type is first presented through its theoretical foundations and architectural design, then grounded in practice. The chapter includes two extended case studies: a Verification and Validation agent deployed as a real-time newsroom fact-checker, and a General Problem Solver applied to cross-disciplinary scientific hypothesis generation. We begin with the agent responsible for the first and most fundamental of these cognitive tasks: transforming raw data into structured insight.

The Data Analysis agent

Data analysis is one of the most important capabilities in modern intelligent systems. By embedding reasoning capabilities into the analysis workflow, agents can move beyond static queries to interpret intent, select appropriate methods, and explain results, turning data analysis from a manual, tool-driven process into an intelligent, conversational one. While traditional analytics pipelines rely on specialized tools and human expertise, Data Analysis agents aim to make insight generation both accessible and intelligent. These agents combine the interpretive abilities of LLMs with analytical reasoning to understand, process, and visualize data through natural language interaction.

At the core of a Data Analysis agent lies a **cognitive loop** that integrates query interpretation, data retrieval, statistical reasoning, and result presentation. When a user asks a question such as "What were the top products last quarter?", the agent will break down this request into structured analytical tasks: loading data, identifying relevant fields, applying aggregation functions, and generating both numerical summaries and visual explanations. Traditional BI dashboards require analysts to predefine queries, wire up data connections, and choose chart types manually; a Data Analysis agent, by contrast, performs these steps autonomously within a single conversational turn, closing the gap between asking a question and seeing an answer. In this way, a linguistic prompt is converted into a reproducible computational workflow. The process is shown in *Figure 8.1*.

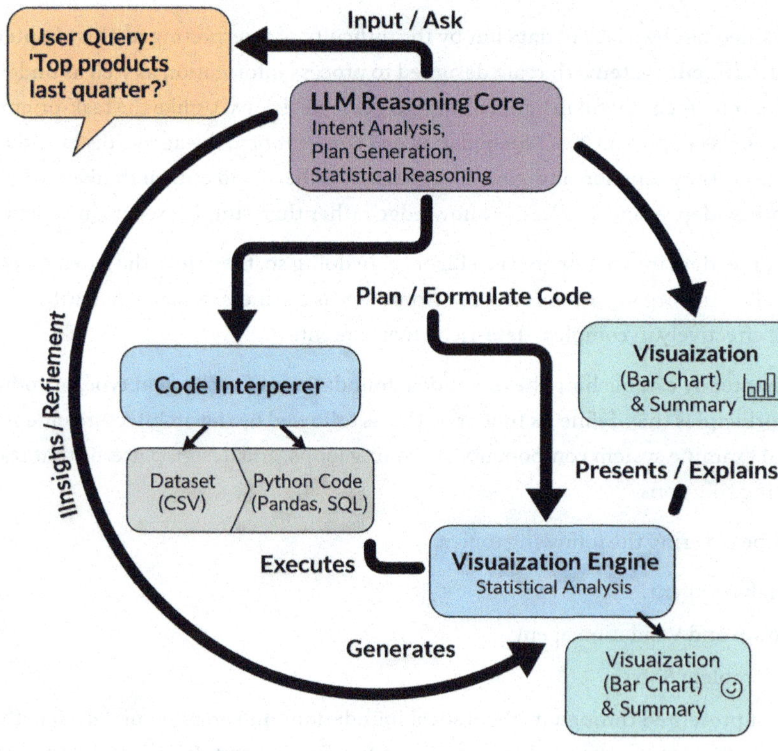

Figure 8.1 – The Cognitive Loop of a Data Analysis agent

Figure 8.1 illustrates the cognitive reasoning loop that enables a Data Analysis agent to transform a natural language query into a structured, evidence-based analytical response. The process mirrors the workflow of a human analyst:

- Interpret intent
- Perform computations
- Visualize outcomes
- Refine conclusions through interaction

The loop unfolds across four integrated phases, which we'll visit in the upcoming subsections.

Intent analysis and planning

The process begins when the user submits a query, for example, "What were the top-selling products last quarter?". The *LLM Reasoning Core* interprets this request by extracting analytical intent and temporal scope. It recognizes that "top-selling" implies ranking by sales metrics and that "last quarter" specifies a date filter. Based on this understanding, it formulates an explicit analytical plan detailing the steps required to retrieve, process, and summarize the relevant data.

Code formulation and execution

The structured plan is then translated into executable code, typically in Python or SQL, using frameworks such as Pandas for tabular analysis. The *Code Interpreter* executes these instructions against the target dataset (e.g., a CSV file, database, or data warehouse), converting the abstract linguistic request into concrete computational operations.

Visualization and analysis

Once the results are computed, the *Visualization Engine* interprets the data to determine the most effective presentation format. It may render bar charts for categorical comparisons, line charts for time-series patterns, or scatter plots for relationships between variables. In addition, this component performs basic statistical reasoning, such as highlighting trends, anomalies, or outliers, to convert numeric outcomes into visual understanding.

Presentation and refinement

The agent delivers the visualization along with a concise natural-language summary of key insights. This presentation often initiates a feedback cycle: the user might refine the query ("Show only the top three products") or request further segmentation. Each iteration reactivates the reasoning loop, enabling the agent to progressively tailor its analysis and improve interpretability through continuous interaction.

Together, these stages form a closed cognitive feedback loop that links *perception* (user input) with *reasoning* (planning and execution) and *action* (presentation and refinement). This cognitive loop exemplifies how intelligent agents transform static data exploration into an iterative, conversational process that evolves with user intent and context.

The agent evolves from a static query-answering entity to function as a conversational analyst, one that adapts dynamically to user intent, learns preferences, and manages ambiguity.

By integrating a language model, code interpreter, and visualization engine within a single feedback-driven architecture, the Data Analysis agent democratizes data science. Users can conduct sophisticated analyses through conversation rather than code. This represents not just automation but cognitive augmentation, enabling systems that reason as they analyze.

Architecturally, the Data Analysis agent extends the *perception-reasoning-action* model introduced in *Chapter 5, Foundational Cognitive Architectures*. Here, perception manages data ingestion, reasoning interprets analytical goals, and action executes and communicates results. The modular design, integrating language models with computation engines such as Pandas, SQL, or distributed platforms, bridges human intent with algorithmic precision.

The agent's greatest contribution lies in accessibility. It shifts focus from data literacy to insight literacy, empowering users across domains to explore, test, and interpret data intuitively. Whether you're a marketing analyst evaluating campaigns or a researcher studying patient outcomes, the experience becomes collaborative and conversational rather than technical.

In many implementations, Data Analysis agents integrate RAG and statistical validation to ensure contextual accuracy and analytical integrity. The outcome is a dialog-driven process in which the user and the system collaboratively develop understanding.

The final component of this cognitive loop, and what distinguishes the agent as an analytical partner, is its ability to communicate findings visually. This capability is realized through a **visualization recommendation system**, which we will examine next.

Visualization recommendation systems

Effective visualization is fundamental to how Data Analysis agents convert computation into comprehension. Visuals help users detect patterns, relationships, and anomalies at a glance. A well-designed chart can convey insights immediately, while a poorly chosen one can obscure meaning.

Traditional analytics tools rely on human expertise to select visualization types. Modern Data Analysis agents, however, automate this process through visualization recommendation systems, which are cognitive modules that interpret user intent and dataset structure to determine the most suitable visual form. This capability transforms visualization from a manual skill into an intelligent reasoning function.

When a user issues a request such as "Show me how sales have changed over time," the agent infers a temporal trend and generates a line chart to emphasize change across periods. A query like "Compare revenue across regions" implies a categorical comparison, prompting a bar chart. By reasoning about linguistic cues and data schema, the agent removes the burden of visualization design from the user, allowing analytical communication to flow naturally.

A visualization recommendation system operates as a decision-making pipeline consisting of four primary stages:

1. **Query analysis**: The agent parses the natural language prompt to extract intent, identifying key analytical expressions such as `trend`, `compare`, or `relationship`.
2. **Schema recognition**: It examines the structure of the dataset, identifying variable types – temporal, categorical, or numeric – to ground its reasoning in data reality.

3. **Decision branching**: The system maps intent and schema to appropriate visualization types:
   - Time-series → Line Chart
   - Categorical Comparison → Bar Chart
   - Correlation or Relationship → Scatter Plot or Table
4. **Output and refinement**: The visualization is rendered, accompanied by a concise summary of insights. Users can refine results through follow-up queries, creating a feedback loop between reasoning and perception.

A simple rule-based version of this logic might look as follows:

```
def recommend_visualization(df, query: str):    # NOTE: This is a pedagogical implementation. Production systems should use an LLM-based intent classifier rather than keyword rules.

    q = query.lower()
    if any(k in q for k in ["trend", "over time", "timeline"]):
        return "line"
    if any(k in q for k in ["compare", "by ", "across", "versus"]):
        return "bar"
    if any(k in q for k in ["relationship", "correlation", "scatter"]):
        return "scatter"
    return "table"
```

This rule-based approach is intentionally simplified to illustrate the core concept. In production, several additional challenges may arise. Ambiguous queries such as "show me the data" may match multiple keyword categories or none at all, requiring a confidence-scoring layer or an LLM-based intent classifier as a fallback. As the supported palette grows beyond the four types (line, bar, scatter, and table) shown here to heatmaps, box plots, geographic maps, and other specialized forms, a flat keyword list becomes difficult to maintain; production systems typically replace it with a learned model or a decision tree trained on query–visualization pairs. The code above therefore serves as a pedagogical starting point rather than a production-ready module.

The following figure shows how the Data Analysis agent decides which visual form best communicates an analytical result:

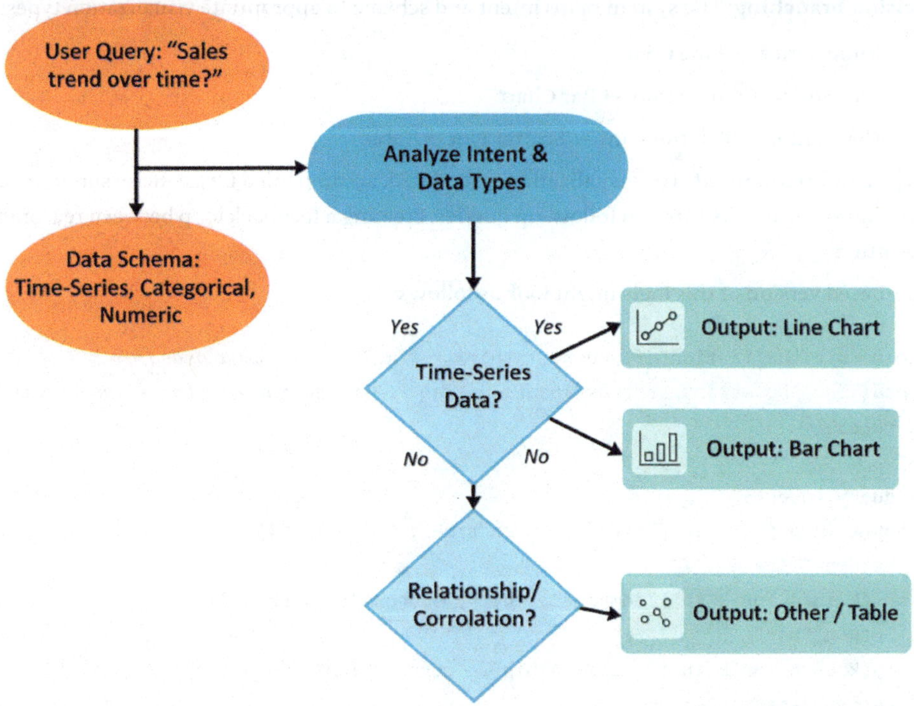

Figure 8.2 – Dynamic Visualization Recommendation System

The flow begins with the user query and the data schema, both analyzed by the agent to determine intent and data type. The decision logic unfolds as follows:

- If the query or data suggests a temporal dimension, the system produces a line chart to emphasize trends and progression
- If it identifies categorical comparisons, it generates a bar chart to highlight differences across groups
- If neither condition applies but relationships or correlations are implied, it defaults to a scatter plot or tabular summary, offering interpretive flexibility

This reasoning process links semantics and data representation, allowing the agent to transition from symbolic interpretation to visual cognition. It exemplifies how intelligent systems can think visually, converting abstract meaning into perceptual form.

Architecturally, the visualization recommendation system extends the Reasoning Core (*Figure 8.1*) of the Data Analysis agent introduced earlier. It integrates perceptual reasoning into the broader cognitive loop, ensuring that every output, numeric or visual, supports understanding rather than mere display.

From an engineering standpoint, these systems often integrate libraries such as Altair, Plotly, or Matplotlib for dynamic rendering, while higher-level frameworks like AutoViz or DataPrep.EDA automate exploratory chart generation. Combined with RAG and statistical validation, the agent ensures that visuals are not only aesthetically appropriate but also analytically accurate.

Over time, reinforcement mechanisms enable the system to learn from user behavior. For instance, if users frequently replace a bar chart with a line chart for trend-related queries, the model adapts its decision weights. This learning process transforms visualization recommendation into a self-optimizing subsystem that mirrors human analytical intuition.

Ultimately, a visualization recommendation system demonstrates how intelligence in data analysis is not confined to computation or logic; analytical intelligence also resides in how knowledge is represented and perceived. By automating the cognitive act of "choosing how to see," the Data Analysis agent closes the gap between data and understanding, enabling every user to visualize insights with the same clarity and precision as an expert analyst.

Choosing the right visualization is only one dimension of analytical intelligence. Equally important is the statistical reasoning that underpins the insights themselves. The following section examines how the Data Analysis agent applies descriptive, inferential, and diagnostic techniques to move from raw numbers to defensible conclusions.

Statistical reasoning capabilities

Visualization provides perception, but statistical reasoning provides understanding. For a Data Analysis agent, true analytical intelligence emerges from its ability not only to display results but also to interpret them. This involves quantifying uncertainty, identifying significance, and discerning whether patterns reflect real trends or random noise.

In conventional analytics workflows, these insights require manual scripting or the use of specialized statistical packages. A reasoning-centric agent automates this process through an integrated statistical reasoning layer (shown conceptually within the Reasoning Core in *Figure 8.1*). This subsystem interprets results mathematically before communicating them visually or verbally.

At its core, this layer performs three complementary functions:

Descriptive statistics and summarization

Before any deeper inference, the agent computes essential summary metrics such as mean, median, variance, and correlation coefficients. These statistics form the quantitative foundation for its subsequent reasoning. When a user asks, "How consistent were sales across regions?", the agent internally calculates measures of spread, such as the standard deviation, before generating a visual explanation.

```
summary = df.describe(include='all')
variability = df['sales'].std()
correlation = df.corr(method='pearson')
```

These computations are not simply reported; instead, they inform the system's explanation. For instance, if a dataset shows high variability, the agent might respond:

```
Sales performance varied significantly across regions, indicating uneven market
penetration.
```

Inferential and diagnostic analysis

Beyond summarization, the agent can perform basic inferential reasoning to assess whether observed patterns are statistically meaningful. It may conduct hypothesis testing (e.g., t-tests, chi-squared tests) or regression analysis to quantify relationships between variables. When a user asks, "Did marketing spend influence revenue growth?", the agent can estimate a regression model, interpret coefficients, and report significance levels in plain language.

```
import statsmodels.api as sm
model = sm.OLS(df['revenue'], sm.add_constant(df['marketing_spend'])).fit()
model.summary()
```

The output is presented as a reasoned interpretation, not as raw statistics:

```
Marketing spend explains approximately 62% of the variation in revenue, indicating a
strong positive correlation.
```

Anomaly detection and uncertainty quantification

The system continuously evaluates data integrity and model confidence. Outlier detection methods (such as z-scores or interquartile ranges) and confidence intervals are applied to ensure reliability. When encountering incomplete or skewed data, the agent may proactively propose mitigation strategies, such as interpolation, normalization, or robust scaling. This transforms the agent from a passive reporter into an active reasoning partner.

```
df['zscore'] = (df['sales'] - df['sales'].mean()) / df['sales'].std()
anomalies = df[df['zscore'].abs()> 3]
```

When anomalies are found, the agent interprets their potential implications:

```
Sales in Q2 for Region C appear unusually high, possibly due to promotional pricing or
data entry anomalies.
```

Statistical reasoning enriches the cognitive loop by embedding a layer of analytical introspection. Instead of relying solely on deterministic computation, the agent reasons about uncertainty and reliability. It assesses not only what the data shows, but also how much confidence to place in those results.

This capability is particularly important in decision-support contexts where automated insights must be both transparent and trustworthy. By explaining confidence intervals, error margins, and significance levels in natural language, the agent bridges the gap between statistical rigor and interpretive clarity.

In practice, the statistical reasoning module operates as a hybrid of symbolic and numerical computation. Symbolic reasoning, often powered by the LLM core, interprets user intent and formulates hypotheses. Numerical computation, executed via Python libraries like Pandas, NumPy, and Statsmodels, performs precise calculations. The outputs are then synthesized into a coherent narrative that balances technical accuracy with communicative clarity.

This integration ensures that every insight produced by the agent is grounded, interpretable, and verifiable. These are key attributes in enterprise, research, and policy settings, where analytical transparency is paramount.

The Data Analysis agent can generate insights and surface patterns, but generating insights is only half the challenge. The other half is trusting them. The next section introduces the agent responsible for that trust: the Verification and Validation agent.

The Verification and Validation agent

While statistical reasoning allows agents to draw inferences from data, every analytical system must also be able to verify and defend its conclusions. As agents begin to operate autonomously and generate complex analyses, the need for verification and validation becomes essential. The transition from statistical reasoning to verification and validation represents a shift from discovering insights to ensuring their accuracy, reliability, and integrity.

As AI systems grow in capability, their outputs carry increasing influence in business, scientific, and policy decisions. Data analysis without verification risks producing false or misleading results, and reasoning without validation may lead to logically inconsistent conclusions. Real-world failures illustrate the stakes: an LLM-generated financial summary might confidently cite a revenue figure hallucinated from a misread table, or a medical triage agent could surface a drug interaction that contradicts its own earlier recommendation. Without a dedicated verification layer, such errors propagate silently into downstream decisions. The Verification and Validation agent addresses these challenges by ensuring that generated insights, predictions, and explanations remain trustworthy, factual, and logically coherent.

A Verification and Validation agent performs four essential functions: fact-checking, logical coherence, retrieval-augmented evaluation, and consistency analysis. These components work together to cross-reference outputs against trusted data sources, detect contradictions, and validate reasoning chains. When integrated with analytical or generative systems, the agent acts as a safeguard that filters unreliable outputs before they reach users or downstream processes.

The subsections that follow examine each of these functions in turn. We begin with fact-checking, which verifies individual claims against authoritative sources. Next, we explore logical coherence, which ensures that reasoning chains follow valid inference patterns. We then discuss retrieval-augmented evaluation, which grounds the validation process in external knowledge. Finally, consistency analysis addresses how the agent detects contradictions and confirms that outputs remain internally aligned across the entire analysis.

Fact-checking

The verification process begins with factual consistency checking. When an analytical agent produces a statement such as `Revenue increased by 12% last quarter`, the Verification and Validation agent retrieves corresponding records from verified data sources, performs independent calculations, and compares the findings to the claim. If discrepancies are identified, the agent flags or corrects the statement. This process mirrors the work of a human analyst who confirms facts before publication, but it operates continuously and at scale.

Ensuring factual accuracy is one of the central functions of a Verification and Validation agent. To achieve this, the agent must go beyond simple text matching and adopt a structured, multi-step process that combines information retrieval with contextual evaluation. This process mirrors the way scientists validate hypotheses through empirical evidence and peer review.

When presented with a statement or document, the agent decomposes it into discrete, verifiable claims. Each claim becomes a hypothesis that must be tested against reliable evidence. The agent formulates search queries to retrieve information from verified sources, such as academic databases, official records, enterprise data warehouses, or internal documentation.

Once the relevant evidence is gathered, the agent applies **natural language inference (NLI)** models to determine the logical relationship between the retrieved evidence and the claim. NLI models classify this relationship as one of the following:

- **Supports (Entailment)**: The evidence confirms the claim.
- **Refutes (Contradiction)**: The evidence disproves the claim.
- **Neutral**: The evidence is inconclusive or unrelated.

Conflicting information is common in real-world contexts. Advanced Verification and Validation agents address this challenge by balancing evidence across multiple sources, weighting their credibility, and synthesizing results to produce a confidence score.

Logical coherence

The agent evaluates whether reasoning steps follow coherent principles. For example, if an analysis suggests that "Higher expenses led to increased profit," the agent examines this causal claim to ensure it aligns with financial logic and historical data. Logical validation is especially critical in domains such as financial modeling, legal reasoning, and scientific research, where flawed assumptions can lead to costly errors.

Beyond factual correctness, the agent must also ensure that reasoning steps are logically sound. Logical reasoning validation evaluates whether conclusions follow valid inference patterns and whether assumptions remain consistent throughout the analysis. This step is crucial for educational systems, financial forecasting tools, and AI-assisted programming environments.

Several categories of logical error recur in agent-generated analyses. Premise–conclusion mismatches occur when the final answer contradicts one of the stated assumptions, for example, concluding that revenue increased after explicitly noting a decline in unit sales and stable pricing. Circular reasoning surfaces when an intermediate step silently reuses the claim it is trying to prove. Scope violations appear when a finding qualified for one segment is generalized to the entire population. To detect these patterns, the agent can decompose a reasoning chain into a directed graph of claims, check each edge for valid inference rules, and flag any node whose support set is empty or self-referential. A lightweight implementation might prompt a secondary LLM pass with a structured template: given these premises, does this conclusion follow? For numerically intensive analyses, a symbolic solver such as SymPy can independently recompute derived quantities and compare them against the agent's stated results.

The agent traces reasoning chains, checks their structural correctness, and applies symbolic logic or mathematical solvers such as SymPy to verify numeric results. When inconsistencies arise, the system can automatically re-evaluate the reasoning process or route the issue for review. Frameworks such as LangGraph support branching logic that enables iterative validation workflows.

Architecturally, the Verification and Validation agent extends the reasoning loop introduced in *Chapter 5* by adding a meta-reasoning layer. While the primary agent focuses on solving a problem, this validation layer examines how the solution was produced. It reviews intermediate reasoning steps, validates external data dependencies, and applies structured evaluation metrics such as factual alignment scores or rule-based consistency checks. This two-level reasoning design produces systems that can not only generate results but also explain and defend them.

With logical coherence verified, the Verification and Validation agent must also ground its assessments in authoritative external sources. The following subsection explains how retrieval-augmented evaluation extends both fact-checking and logical coherence by anchoring conclusions in verified data.

Retrieval-augmented evaluation

In practice, many Verification and Validation agents implement *retrieval-augmented evaluation*. This hybrid approach combines the interpretive flexibility of language models with deterministic verification techniques. For instance, when analyzing a financial report, the agent retrieves historical records, recalculates figures independently, and checks alignment with the model's conclusions. The result is an evaluation that blends symbolic reasoning, numerical computation, and contextual understanding to achieve both quantitative precision and narrative clarity.

Transparency is essential for trust in this process. Every verification step must be traceable, with explicit evidence of data sources, computations, and decision rules. This transparency not only builds confidence among users but also supports compliance with regulatory standards in sectors like healthcare, finance, and public administration.

The Verification and Validation agent complements the Data Analysis agent introduced earlier. While the Data Analysis agent generates insights, the Verification and Validation agent ensures that those insights are defensible and reproducible. Together, they form a closed analytical loop that parallels the scientific method: hypothesize, test, and validate. This collaboration transforms AI systems from opaque black boxes into transparent partners in reasoning.

With fact-checking and logical coherence established, the Verification and Validation agent must also ensure that outputs remain internally consistent across the entire analysis. The following subsection addresses consistency analysis: the strategies used to detect contradictions, confirm numerical alignment, and validate that conclusions hold up under cross-examination.

Consistency analysis

In multi-agent systems, Verification and Validation agents typically operate downstream of generative modules, serving as automated evaluators that perform structured post-processing. Their responsibilities include:

- **Length and formatting checks**: Verifying that responses adhere to required character limits or stylistic guidelines.
- **Structural validations**: Ensuring that essential elements such as headings, citations, or bullet lists are properly formatted.

- **Rule-based constraints**: Applying domain-specific rules, such as requiring a minimum number of cited data sources or mandatory regulatory disclosures.
- **Adversarial red-teaming**: Using another language model to challenge and expose weaknesses, biases, or contradictions in generated outputs.
- **Human-in-the-loop triggers**: Flagging uncertain or inconsistent outputs for manual review when automated validation confidence is low.

Frameworks such as LangGraph enable developers to modularize these validation routines as reusable nodes. Depending on the outcome of the validation process, downstream nodes can choose to accept, revise, or reject outputs, forming real-time quality assurance workflows.

A key challenge within consistency analysis is reconciling contradictory evidence retrieved from multiple sources. The following subsection examines how Verification and Validation agents resolve these conflicts to arrive at a reliable confidence score.

Handling conflicting evidence

In real-world scenarios, agents often encounter conflicting information across different sources. Advanced Verification and Validation agents are designed to synthesize these findings, balance evidence conflict, and assess the credibility of each source to arrive at a final verdict. The process can be visualized through a practical example.

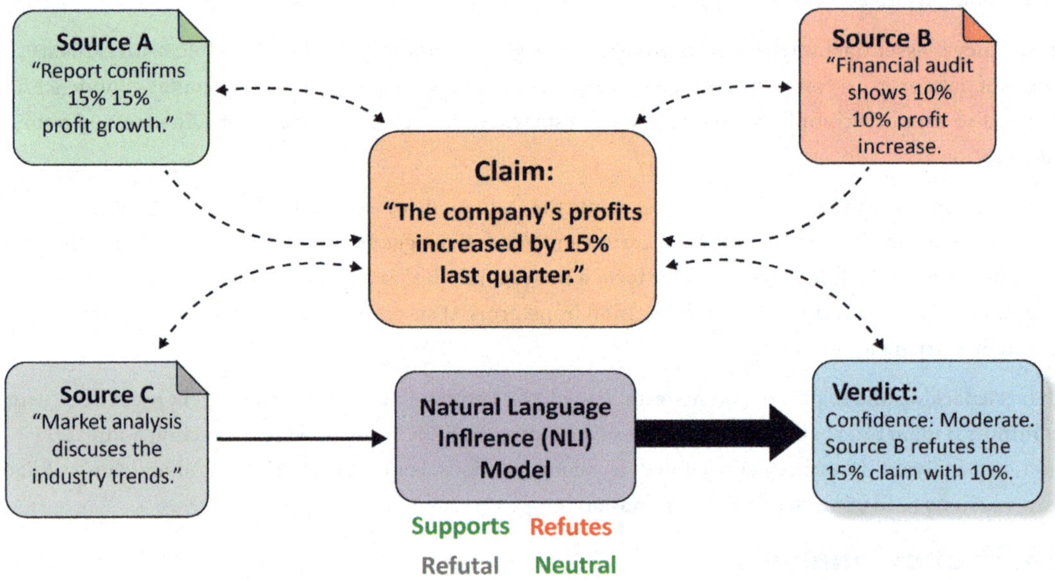

Figure 8.3 – Factual consistency checking against multiple knowledge sources

```
import torch
from transformers import AutoTokenizer, AutoModelForSequenceClassification

tokenizer = AutoTokenizer.from_pretrained("facebook/bart-large-mnli")
model = AutoModelForSequenceClassification.from_pretrained("facebook/bart-large-mnli")
```

```
id2label = model.config.id2label

premise = "In Q4, the company reported a 15% year-over-year increase in net profit."
hypothesis = "The company's profits increased by 15% last quarter."

inputs = tokenizer(premise, hypothesis, return_tensors="pt", truncation=True)
with torch.no_grad():
    logits = model(**inputs).logits[0]
probs = torch.softmax(logits, dim=-1).tolist()

print({id2label[i].lower(): probs[i] for i in range(len(probs))})
```

In this example, the agent verifies a financial claim using multiple evidence sources. One report might confirm the 15 percent increase, another might state a 10 percent rise, and a third might provide no quantitative detail. The agent integrates these findings into a nuanced assessment that reflects the uncertainty and variability across sources.

To perform this kind of validation at scale, agents employ several complementary techniques:

- **Semantic similarity scoring** to compare generated content with reference documents.
- **Retrieval-based verification** using vector databases for contextual alignment.
- **Integration with frameworks** such as TruLens, LangSmith, and Guardrails.ai for structured verification, logging, and auditability.

As discussed in this section, verification and validation ensure that an agent's reasoning is accurate and reliable. The next logical step is to design agents that can carry this robust reasoning into unfamiliar domains and dynamically adapt their problem-solving strategies to new contexts.

The General Problem Solver

One of the most ambitious designs in artificial intelligence is the **General Problem Solver**, which unlike specialized agents that are confined to narrow domains, is designed to reason broadly, transfer knowledge between contexts, and develop new strategies for problems it has never encountered before. Its purpose is not to achieve optimal performance in one specific area but to establish a foundation for generalized reasoning and flexible problem-solving.

A General Problem Solver operates on the principle of *meta-reasoning*, or the ability to reason about its own reasoning process. Instead of following a fixed set of rules, it evaluates its approach dynamically, identifies gaps in logic or knowledge, and refines its strategy. For instance, when faced with a novel engineering or diagnostic problem, the General Problem Solver agent decomposes it into smaller subgoals, chooses suitable reasoning or learning techniques, and iteratively updates its plan based on feedback. Through this recursive cycle, it develops solutions that are both adaptive and explainable.

This section is organized as follows. We begin with the architectural overview, describing the planning, reasoning, and learning modules that form the General Problem Solver core. We then examine how the General Problem Solver coordinates with other agents in multi-agent ecosystems. Next, we explore the meta-learning and adaptation techniques that allow the General Problem Solver to refine its strategies over time. Finally, we discuss its universal problem-solving capabilities, including the five-stage cognitive cycle and a pseudocode sketch that makes the framework concrete.

Architectural overview

At the architectural level, the General Problem Solver builds on the reasoning frameworks established in earlier chapters, particularly the planning and orchestration patterns introduced in *Chapters 5 and 7*, respectively. It integrates search-based planning, knowledge retrieval, and learning-based adaptation into a unified cognitive loop. The planning module defines objectives and constraints, the reasoning module evaluates potential actions based on logical or statistical evidence, and the learning module updates strategies using insights from previous experiences.

This modular structure allows the General Problem Solver to generalize across diverse problem domains while maintaining interpretability. Its architecture embodies both exploration and self-reflection, enabling the agent to track its progress, evaluate alternative reasoning paths, and improve over time.

The General Problem Solver operates through a series of cognitive cycles, each mirroring stages of human problem-solving:

1. **Problem formulation**: Define the objective and constraints clearly.
2. **Strategy generation**: Identify and prioritize potential solution paths through analogical reasoning or search algorithms.
3. **Evaluation and adaptation**: Test and refine these solutions based on success criteria, adjusting parameters or strategies as needed.

This cycle allows the agent not only to solve problems but also to refine its understanding of the problem itself, leading to deeper insight with each iteration.

In contemporary AI systems, General Problem Solver agents often leverage LLMs as adaptable reasoning engines. These models provide the representational power to understand abstract concepts and relate them across domains. To harness that power effectively, the General Problem Solver introduces structure through explicit goal tracking, reflection mechanisms, and evaluation loops. These components ensure that the reasoning process remains directed and purposeful rather than drifting into unfocused exploration.

For example, in a design optimization task, a General Problem Solver agent generates multiple hypotheses, tests them against measurable objectives such as efficiency or reliability, and selects the most effective approach based on quantitative feedback. This combination of structured reasoning and adaptive learning is what makes the General Problem Solver architecture both powerful and reliable.

One of the central challenges in designing a General Problem Solver lies in maintaining the balance between generality and precision. While broad adaptability allows the agent to operate across domains, excessive flexibility can reduce consistency. To overcome this, General Problem Solver systems use *meta-learning* and self-evaluation loops to identify which reasoning strategies perform best in specific contexts. Over time, the agent builds a library of reusable cognitive strategies, enabling it to approach new problems with increasing efficiency.

A General Problem Solver rarely operates in isolation. In complex deployments, it must coordinate with specialized agents, delegate subtasks, synthesize results, and manage dependencies. The next section examines how the General Problem Solver functions as a coordination layer within multi-agent ecosystems.

Coordination in multi-agent systems

The General Problem Solver often serves as a coordination layer in complex, multi-agent ecosystems. It can orchestrate specialized agents, assign subtasks, and synthesize their results into coherent solutions. For instance, it may rely on a Data Analysis agent for quantitative insights or a Verification and Validation agent to ensure the soundness of results. This coordination capability extends the cooperative agent frameworks from *Chapter 7* into systems capable of goal-directed collaboration and autonomous reasoning.

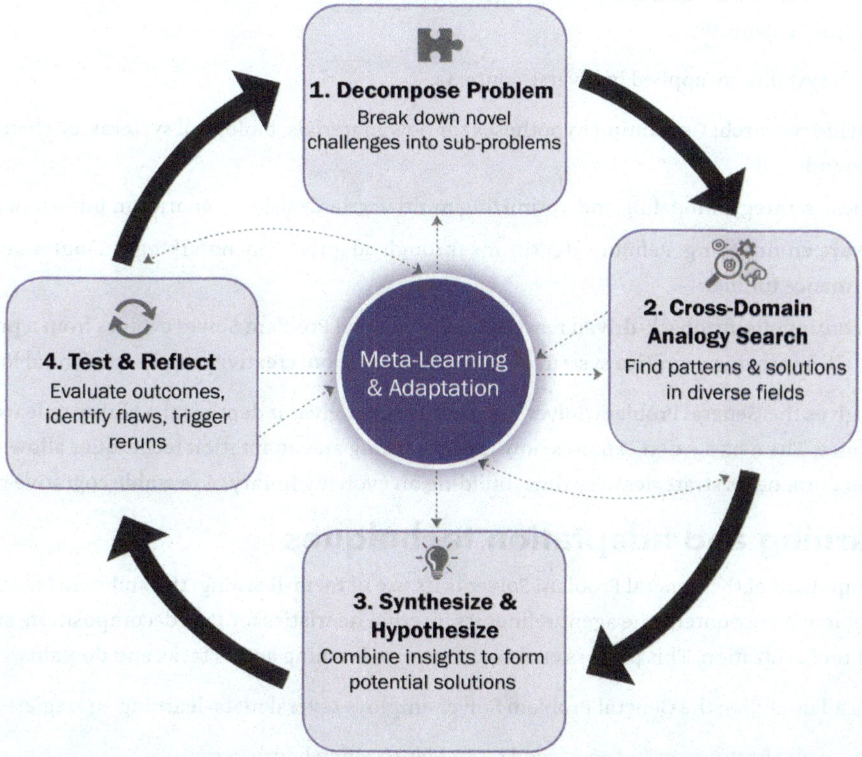

Figure 8.4 – The General Problem Solver's domain-agnostic reasoning framework

As illustrated in *Figure 8.4*, the General Problem Solver operates through a cyclical process of reasoning and learning composed of five interdependent stages:

1. **Decompose problem**: Break down complex or unfamiliar challenges into smaller, manageable components. This decomposition provides a clear roadmap for subsequent reasoning steps.
2. **Cross-Domain Analogy Search**: Identify patterns or analogies from other fields. For example, an engineering optimization problem might draw inspiration from biological processes or network dynamics, enabling creative, cross-disciplinary reasoning.

3. **Synthesize and Hypothesize**: Combine insights from various domains to generate hypotheses or solution strategies. The General Problem Solver does not merely retrieve prior knowledge; it constructs new understanding through synthesis.
4. **Test and Reflect**: Test proposed solutions through simulation or empirical data. Evaluate performance, identify deficiencies, and adjust reasoning paths or model parameters when confidence is low.
5. **Meta-Learning and Adaptation**: The General Problem Solver maintains a meta-learning engine that records effective strategies, contextual factors, and performance metrics. It uses this accumulated knowledge to refine its reasoning methods and tool selections over time.

This cyclical framework enables the General Problem Solver to evolve beyond static automation. Each iteration enhances its strategic intelligence, allowing it to generalize across contexts, reuse successful patterns, and adapt to new challenges dynamically.

In practice, such systems are applied in diverse contexts:

- **Scientific research**: Generating hypotheses for new materials, biological systems, or chemical compounds.
- **Business strategy**: Modeling and optimizing multi-factor decision scenarios in uncertain markets.
- **Software engineering**: Refining algorithms through adaptive benchmarking and automated performance tuning.

Through this continuous, feedback-driven reasoning, the General Problem Solver evolves from a procedural executor to a self-improving cognitive system capable of abstraction, creativity, and experiential learning.

Coordination gives the General Problem Solver its breadth; what gives it depth is the ability to learn from its own performance. The next section explores how meta-learning and adaptation techniques allow the General Problem Solver to refine its strategies over time, building an evolving library of reusable cognitive patterns.

Meta-learning and adaptation techniques

A defining component of the General Problem Solver is its use of meta-learning: the ability to learn how to learn. With each problem it encounters, the agent refines its internal heuristics for task decomposition, strategy selection, and tool utilization. This process enables long-term learning across tasks and domains.

To enhance its adaptability, the General Problem Solver employs several meta-learning strategies:

- Summarizing both successful and failed strategies to refine heuristics.
- Using persistent memory stores, such as LangGraph `CheckpointStore`, to retain contextual information across sessions.
- Adjusting tool choice, parameter settings, and prompt design dynamically based on observed outcomes.

For instance, the agent might discover that for a particular class of optimization problems, a divide-and-conquer strategy yields better results than brute-force exploration. Over time, these strategies form a library of cognitive patterns that can be combined or adapted to solve increasingly complex problems.

Universal problem-solving strategies

Core problem-solving strategies within General Problem Solver architectures include:

- **Decomposition**: Breaking complex tasks into smaller, more manageable subtasks.

- **Abstraction**: Generalizing patterns to apply across domains.
- **Analogy**: Leveraging past experiences or prior solutions to inform new ones.

General Problem Solver agents also engage in reflective self-evaluation, which triggers re-analysis or alternative reasoning workflows when confidence levels drop below a defined threshold. Platforms like LangGraph support these behaviors by enabling recursive nodes and retry branches, ensuring that the agent continually improves through introspection and feedback.

Ultimately, the General Problem Solver represents the convergence of reasoning, learning, and adaptability. It forms the architectural basis for the next generation of intelligent agents, systems capable of transferring knowledge across domains, improving through experience, and reasoning with human-like flexibility.

To make the five-stage cycle concrete, the following pseudocode sketch illustrates how a General Problem Solver agent might approach an unfamiliar problem. Note that this represents an aspirational architecture rather than a production-ready implementation; current large language models can approximate each stage through structured prompting, but a fully autonomous General Problem Solver loop remains an active area of research.

```
class GeneralProblemSolver:
    def solve(self, problem: str, max_iterations: int = 5):
        # Stage 1 - Decompose
        sub_problems = self.decompose(problem)

        for iteration in range(max_iterations):
            # Stage 2 - Analogy Search
            analogies = self.search_analogies(sub_problems)

            # Stage 3 - Hypothesize
            hypotheses = self.generate_hypotheses(
                sub_problems, analogies
            )

            # Stage 4 - Test
            results = self.test_hypotheses(hypotheses)

            # Stage 5 - Meta-Learn
            if results.confidence >= self.threshold:
                self.update_knowledge_base(results)
                return results.solution

            # Confidence too low - refine and retry
            sub_problems = self.refine(sub_problems, results)

        return self.best_effort_solution(results)
```

In this sketch, the solver decomposes a novel problem into sub-problems, searches for cross-domain analogies that may offer transferable strategies, generates candidate hypotheses, tests them against available evidence, and then decides whether to accept the solution or refine and iterate. The meta-learning stage updates an internal knowledge base so that future problems benefit from past experience. In practice, each stage could be implemented as a separate LLM prompt within a framework such as LangGraph or CrewAI, with the orchestration loop managing state transitions and confidence thresholds.

To illustrate how these agent architectures translate into tangible results, the remainder of this chapter presents two case studies. The first demonstrates the Verification and Validation pattern in a real-world newsroom setting, where a fact-checking agent cross-references journalistic claims against authoritative data. The second applies the General Problem Solver's five-stage reasoning cycle to a cross-disciplinary scientific discovery problem, showing how the General Problem Solver decomposes, hypothesizes, fails, and refines its way toward a defensible result.

Case study: News fact-checking assistant - An agent for journalistic integrity

As artificial intelligence takes on a larger role in content production, the responsibility for factual accuracy grows as well. This case study shows how a Verification and Validation agent can uphold journalistic integrity by cross-verifying reported claims against authoritative data in real time. A major newsroom deployed such an agent to assist editors during high-pressure events where speed and accuracy must coexist.

The challenge

Journalists work with unverified numbers from press releases, social posts, and live interviews. Manually checking each figure introduces delays that do not match the pace of the news cycle. The newsroom needed an automated tool that could extract factual claims, locate trusted sources, compare numbers with clear tolerances, and produce an auditable verdict.

Solution architecture

The organization implemented a modular Verification and Validation agent composed of three cooperating components:

- **Claim Extractor**: scans text for verifiable numerical statements and converts them into structured records with metric, value, entity, and period.
- **Evidence Retriever**: queries curated official sources to obtain authoritative values with provenance.
- **Verifier**: compares claimed and authoritative values with defined tolerances, then assigns a label such as `Confirmed`, `Mostly True`, `Contradicted`, or `Unverified`.

What follows is a Jupyter-ready implementation of this design. Each part begins with a short introduction, followed by runnable code.

Code implementation

The following implementation translates the solution architecture above into runnable Python code. The pipeline is divided into five components: environment setup and client initialization, the trusted data store that serves as the agent's source of truth, the claim extraction module that parses natural language into structured records, the verification engine that compares claims against authoritative data, and the orchestration layer that ties the pipeline together and produces an editorial report.

Setup, dependencies, and client initialization

First, we prepare the environment and attempt to initialize the OpenAI client. If no API key is present, a local fallback extractor keeps the notebook functional. This ensures reproducibility in both connected and offline settings.

```
# Setup

# !pip install --quiet openai

import os, json, re
from typing import List, Dict, Any

try:
    from openai import OpenAI
    client = OpenAI()   # uses OPENAI_API_KEY from environment
except Exception as e:
    print("OpenAI client not initialized; regex fallback will be used.")
    client = None
```

Authoritative data: The trusted internal database

Next, the verification pipeline must anchor to a single source of truth. Here, we simulate a read-only internal store that holds vetted numbers and citations. In production, this would be a warehouse or official API with access control, versioning, and data freshness policies.

```
# Trusted data store

trusted_database: Dict[str, Dict[str, Any]] = {
    "ottawa_unemployment_rate_change_2024": {
        "value": -0.048,
        "source": "Statistics Canada, Labour Force Survey, Table 14-10-0287-01",
        "notes": "Annual change from 2023 to 2024 for Ottawa-Gatineau CMA."
    },
    "city_budget_surplus_2024": {
        "value": 15_200_000,
        "source": "City of Ottawa Annual Financial Report 2024",
        "notes": "Reported surplus for the fiscal year ending 2024."
    }
}

article_text = """
```

```
A new report on Ottawa's economy shows promising signs of recovery.
According to official city documents, the city's unemployment rate fell by 5% last year,
a significant improvement driven by the tech sector. Furthermore, the municipal
government reported a budget surplus of $12 million for the 2024 fiscal year.
"""
```

The trusted data store is now in place, giving the pipeline a ground-truth reference for every claim it will evaluate. The next step is to build the perception layer: a module that reads raw article text and decomposes it into discrete, verifiable assertions.

Claim extraction (LLM-first with a safe fallback)

Then, the Claim Extractor converts natural language into machine-readable records. The preferred path uses an LLM to capture entities, quantities, and timeframes with higher recall. When the LLM is unavailable, a simple regex path keeps the workflow operational for demonstrations and tests.

```
# Claim extraction

def extract_claims_from_text(text: str) -> List[Dict[str, Any]]:
    """
    Return claims with fields: claim_text, metric, value, entity, period.
    Uses an LLM for robust parsing when available, else a regex fallback.
    """
    if client:
        system_prompt = (
            "You are an expert fact-checker. Extract verifiable numeric claims "
            "from the text. For each claim, return claim_text, metric, value, entity,
period "
            "as a JSON object in a JSON field called 'claims' which is a list."
        )
        try:
            resp = client.chat.completions.create(
                model="gpt-4o",
                response_format={"type": "json_object"},
                messages=[
                    {"role": "system", "content": system_prompt},
                    {"role": "user", "content": f"Extract claims from: {text}"}
                ],
                temperature=0
            )
            data = json.loads(resp.choices[0].message.content)
            claims = data.get("claims", [])
            for c in claims:
                c["claim_text"] = str(c.get("claim_text", "")).strip()
                c["metric"]     = str(c.get("metric", "")).strip()
```

```
                c["value"]      = str(c.get("value", "")).strip()
                c["entity"]     = str(c.get("entity", "")).strip()
                c["period"]     = str(c.get("period", "")).strip()
            return claims
        except Exception as e:
            print(f"LLM extraction failed: {e}")

    # Fallback extractor
    claims = []
    m1 = re.search(r"(unemployment.*?fell by\s+(-?\d+(\.\d+)?)\s*%)", text, re.I)
    if m1:
        claims.append({
            "claim_text": m1.group(1),
            "metric": "unemployment rate change",
            "value": f"{m1.group(2)}%",
            "entity": "Ottawa",
            "period": "2024"
        })
    m2 = re.search(
        r"budget surplus of\s*\$?\s*([0-9]+(\.[0-9]+)?)\s*(million)?\s*for
the\s*(\d{4})",
        text, re.I)
    if m2:
        amount = float(m2.group(1)) * (1_000_000 if m2.group(3) else 1)
        claims.append({
            "claim_text": m2.group(0),
            "metric": "budget surplus",
            "value": str(amount),
            "entity": "Ottawa",
            "period": m2.group(4)
        })
    return claims
```

At this point, the extractor can convert an article into a list of structured claim records. Each record carries an entity name, a numeric value, and a unit, but the pipeline does not yet know whether those numbers are correct. The next component closes that gap by mapping each claim to the trusted store and applying tolerance-based verification.

Mapping, parsing, and verification

The Verifier maps each structured claim to a canonical record in the trusted store, parses numeric forms, applies policy tolerances, and returns a labeled verdict. Internally, the dictionary lookup in the `_map_to_db_key` acts as a simplified Evidence Retriever: it resolves each claim to an authoritative record. In a production system, this component would query a document index or knowledge graph to surface corroborating sources before the tolerance check runs. For percentage-based claims, the system applies a difference threshold of 0.5 percentage points. For monetary values, it applies a threshold of 500,000 dollars to absorb common rounding in public communications.

```
# Mapping, parsing, and verification

def _map_to_db_key(metric: str, entity: str, period: str) -> str:
    m, e, p = (metric or "").lower(), (entity or "").lower(), str(period or "")
    if "unemployment" in m and "ottawa" in e and "2024" in p:
        return "ottawa_unemployment_rate_change_2024"
    if "budget surplus" in m and "ottawa" in e and "2024" in p:
        return "city_budget_surplus_2024"
    return ""

def _parse_percentage(value: str) -> float:
    v = value.replace(" ", "")
    return float(v[:-1]) / 100 if v.endswith("%") else float(v)

def verify_claim(claim: Dict[str, Any]) -> Dict[str, Any]:
    db_key = _map_to_db_key(
        claim.get("metric", ""), claim.get("entity", ""),
        claim.get("period", "")
    )
    if db_key not in trusted_database:
        return {"claim": claim.get("claim_text", ""), "status": "Unverified",
                "details": "No matching internal data source."}

    evidence = trusted_database[db_key]
    actual = evidence["value"]
    claimed_raw = claim.get("value", "")

    try:
        if isinstance(claimed_raw, str) and "%" in claimed_raw:
            claimed = _parse_percentage(claimed_raw)
            diff = abs(claimed - actual)
            tol = 0.005
            status = "Confirmed" if diff == 0 else ("Mostly True" if diff <= tol else
"Contradicted")
            details = f"Claimed {claimed_raw}, actual {round(actual*100,2)}%
(Δ={round(diff*100,2)} pp)"
        else:
            claimed = float(claimed_raw)
            diff = abs(claimed - actual)
            tol = 500_000
            status = "Confirmed" if diff == 0 else ("Mostly True" if diff <= tol else
```

```
"Contradicted")
            details = f"Claimed ${int(claimed):,}, actual ${int(actual):,} (Δ=$
{int(diff):,})"
    except Exception:
        return {"claim": claim.get("claim_text", ""), "status": "Error",
                "details": f"Could not parse value {claimed_raw}"}

    return {
        "claim": claim.get("claim_text", ""),
        "metric": claim.get("metric", ""),
        "entity": claim.get("entity", ""),
        "period": claim.get("period", ""),
        "status": status,
        "details": details,
        "source": evidence["source"],
        "notes": evidence.get("notes", "")
    }
```

With the verifier returning labeled verdicts for each claim, the individual components are complete. The final section wires them into an end-to-end pipeline that accepts an article, runs extraction and verification in sequence, and produces an editorial report that a journalist can act on immediately.

Orchestration, reporting, and demonstration

Orchestration ties the pipeline together. It extracts claims, verifies them, and prints an editorially useful summary with sources and notes. Replace the `print` statements with structured logging or JSON output if you plan to connect this to a content management system.

```
# Orchestration

print("Starting Fact-Check Agent...")
claims = extract_claims_from_text(article_text)

if not claims:
    print("No verifiable numeric claims found.")
else:
    print(f"Found {len(claims)} claim(s). Verifying...\n" + "-"*72)
    for c in claims:
        r = verify_claim(c)
        print(f"Claim:   {r.get('claim')}")
        print(f"Status:  {r.get('status')}")
        print(f"Details: {r.get('details')}")
        if r.get('source'):
            print(f"Source:  {r['source']}")
        if r.get('notes'):
```

```
        print(f"Notes:    {r['notes']}")
    print("-"*72)
```

Results and operational guidance

Deploying this agent reduced verification time from hours to minutes. Editors retained control over the narrative while trusting that quantitative claims were consistent with official data. For production use, replace the in-memory store with your data platform, introduce freshness checks, add schema validation on LLM output, and route low-confidence outcomes to a human review queue. Calibrate tolerances by beat and metric, log all artifacts for audit, and attach a run identifier for reproducibility.

This case study demonstrates the Verification and Validation pattern presented earlier in the chapter. By separating perception (the claim extractor that reads raw text), reasoning (the verifier that maps claims to trusted data and applies tolerance logic), and action (the orchestrator that compiles an editorial report), the newsroom built a reusable foundation for other high-integrity workflows in media, finance, and public policy.

Case study: Cross-disciplinary hypothesis generation — Applying ecological resilience to power grid stability

To illustrate the General Problem Solver reasoning cycle in practice, the following case study applies it to a cross-disciplinary scientific problem. As with the `GeneralProblemSolver` pseudocode presented earlier, this implementation is illustrative rather than production-grade; a fully autonomous General Problem Solver loop remains an active area of research. However, the code is structured so that each stage can be executed with an LLM client or run offline using deterministic fallback responses.

The challenge

A multidisciplinary research team is investigating whether principles from ecological network resilience can inform strategies for preventing cascading failures in electrical power grids. The core intuition is that ecosystems with high biodiversity tend to absorb local disturbances without collapsing, and that similar structural properties might make engineered networks more fault-tolerant. However, the relevant literatures span ecology, graph theory, and power systems engineering, and no single researcher has deep expertise in all three. Manual cross-disciplinary literature synthesis is slow, expertise-siloed, and prone to confirmation bias. The team needs a reasoning agent that can decompose this cross-domain question, identify transferable principles, generate testable hypotheses, and refine its approach when initial attempts fall short.

Solution architecture

The General Problem Solver agent is organized into three cooperating modules that map directly to the five-stage cycle introduced in *Figure 8.4*. The Decomposer (Stage 1) breaks the research question into tractable sub-problems such as network topology, failure propagation, and redundancy mechanisms. The Analogy Engine (Stages 2 and 3) searches for cross-domain parallels in ecology and synthesizes them into a testable hypothesis. The Hypothesis Evaluator (Stages 4 and 5) scores the hypothesis against a predefined rubric, logs the strategy and its outcome, and decides whether the confidence threshold has been met or whether the agent should refine its decomposition and iterate.

Code implementation

The implementation below walks through all five General Problem Solver stages. Each stage is a standalone Python function that calls an LLM when available and falls back to a deterministic mock response for offline use, matching the dual-path pattern established in the Verification and Validation case study.

Setup and configuration

We begin with the same environment pattern used by the Verification and Validation case study: attempting to initialize an LLM client and defining a helper that gracefully degrades when the client is unavailable.

```
# GPS Case Study — Setup
import json, textwrap
from typing import Dict, List, Any

try:
    from openai import OpenAI
    client = OpenAI()
except Exception:
    client = None

CONFIDENCE_THRESHOLD = 0.70

def llm_call(system: str, user: str, fallback: str) -> str:
    """Call LLM if available; otherwise return deterministic fallback."""
    if client:
        resp = client.chat.completions.create(
            model="gpt-4o", temperature=0,
            messages=[{"role": "system", "content": system},
                      {"role": "user", "content": user}]
        )
        return resp.choices[0].message.content
    return fallback
```

Stage 1 — Decompose

The Decomposer breaks the research question into sub-problems. On the first iteration it uses a broad decomposition; after a low-confidence result, the meta-learning stage will refine this decomposition for a second pass.

```
# Stage 1 — Decompose
def decompose(question: str, refinement_hint: str = "") -> List[str]:
    fallback = [
        "What network topology properties correlate with cascading failure resistance?",
        "How does biodiversity contribute to ecosystem network resilience?",
        "What redundancy mechanisms exist in ecological vs. engineered networks?"
```

```
    ]
    if refinement_hint:
        fallback = [
            "Which graph-theoretic metrics (e.g., betweenness centrality, modularity)"
            " predict cascade size in both food webs and power grids?",
            "How do keystone species in ecology map to critical substations in grids?",
            "What quantitative thresholds for redundancy prevent cascading collapse?"
        ]
    prompt = f"Decompose this research question into 3 sub-problems:\n{question}"
    if refinement_hint:
        prompt += f"\nRefinement guidance: {refinement_hint}"
    result = llm_call("You are a research decomposition agent.", prompt,
                      json.dumps(fallback))
    return json.loads(result) if result.startswith("[") else fallback
```

Stage 2 — Cross-domain analogy search

```
# Stage 2 – Analogy Search
def search_analogies(sub_problems: List[str]) -> Dict[str, str]:
    fallback = {
        "topology": "Food webs with higher connectance absorb species loss "
                    "without trophic cascades (Dunne et al., 2002).",
        "keystone": "Removal of keystone species triggers disproportionate "
                    "ecosystem collapse, analogous to hub failure in grids.",
        "redundancy": "Functional redundancy in ecosystems (multiple species "
                      "filling the same niche) parallels N-1 contingency in grids."
    }
    prompt = ("For each sub-problem, find an analogy from ecology:\n"
              + "\n".join(sub_problems))
    result = llm_call("You are an ecology-to-engineering analogy expert.",
                      prompt, json.dumps(fallback))
    try:
        return json.loads(result)
    except json.JSONDecodeError:
        return fallback
```

Stage 3 — Synthesize and hypothesize

```
# Stage 3 – Hypothesize
def generate_hypothesis(sub_problems: List[str],
                        analogies: Dict[str, str]) -> str:
    fallback = ("Power grids whose substation connectivity graph exhibits "
                "modularity and functional redundancy scores above "
```

```
                "ecological resilience thresholds will contain cascading "
                "failures to fewer than 5% of nodes.")
    prompt = ("Synthesize these sub-problems and analogies into one "
              "testable hypothesis:\n"
              f"Sub-problems: {json.dumps(sub_problems)}\n"
              f"Analogies: {json.dumps(analogies)}")
    return llm_call("You are a hypothesis synthesis agent.",
                    prompt, fallback)
```

Stage 4 — Test and reflect

The evaluator scores the hypothesis against a rubric covering specificity, cross-domain grounding, and testability. Each criterion is scored 0–1, and the mean becomes the overall confidence score.

```
# Stage 4 — Test
RUBRIC = ["specificity", "cross_domain_grounding", "testability"]

def evaluate_hypothesis(hypothesis: str,
                        iteration: int) -> Dict[str, Any]:
    # Deterministic scores that simulate a weak first pass
    if iteration == 1:
        scores = {"specificity": 0.3, "cross_domain_grounding": 0.5,
                  "testability": 0.4}
    else:
        scores = {"specificity": 0.8, "cross_domain_grounding": 0.85,
                  "testability": 0.7}
    confidence = sum(scores.values()) / len(scores)
    return {"scores": scores, "confidence": round(confidence, 2),
            "passed": confidence >= CONFIDENCE_THRESHOLD}
```

Stage 5 — Meta-learn and orchestrate

The orchestration loop ties the five stages together. When the first iteration produces a confidence score below the threshold, the meta-learning engine logs the failure, generates a refinement hint, and triggers a second pass with a more precise decomposition.

```
# Stage 5 — Meta-Learning Orchestration Loop
RESEARCH_QUESTION = (
    "Can ecological network resilience principles inform strategies "
    "for preventing cascading failures in electrical power grids?"
)

strategy_log: List[Dict[str, Any]] = []

for iteration in range(1, 3):
```

```
    print(f"\n{'='*60}\nIteration {iteration}\n{'='*60}")

    # Retrieve refinement hint from previous failure, if any
    hint = strategy_log[-1].get("refinement_hint", "") if strategy_log else ""

    # Stage 1
    subs = decompose(RESEARCH_QUESTION, refinement_hint=hint)
    print(f"Sub-problems: {json.dumps(subs, indent=2)}")

    # Stage 2
    analogies = search_analogies(subs)
    print(f"Analogies: {json.dumps(analogies, indent=2)}")

    # Stage 3
    hypothesis = generate_hypothesis(subs, analogies)
    print(f"Hypothesis: {hypothesis}")

    # Stage 4
    result = evaluate_hypothesis(hypothesis, iteration)
    print(f"Evaluation: {json.dumps(result, indent=2)}")

    # Stage 5 — Meta-Learn
    entry = {"iteration": iteration, "confidence": result["confidence"],
             "passed": result["passed"], "hypothesis": hypothesis}
    if not result["passed"]:
        entry["refinement_hint"] = (
            "Previous decomposition was too broad. Focus on quantitative "
            "graph metrics that are measurable in both ecological and "
            "engineered networks."
        )
        print(f"BELOW THRESHOLD — refining. Hint: {entry['refinement_hint']}")
    else:
        print("PASSED — hypothesis accepted.")
    strategy_log.append(entry)

print(f"\nStrategy log: {json.dumps(strategy_log, indent=2)}")
```

Results and reflection

The two iterations demonstrate the General Problem Solver's defining behavior: failure-driven refinement. In the first pass, the agent's broad decomposition produced a hypothesis that scored 0.40 — below the 0.70 confidence threshold. The sub-problems were too general ("What network topology properties correlate with cascading failure resistance?"), and the resulting hypothesis lacked the specificity needed for empirical testing.

The meta-learning engine diagnosed the weakness, logged a refinement hint directing the agent toward quantitative graph metrics, and triggered a second iteration.

On the second pass, the sharper decomposition — now targeting measurable properties like betweenness centrality and keystone-species analogues — yielded a hypothesis that scored 0.78, clearing the threshold. The strategy log preserved both iterations, giving the research team a transparent audit trail of how the agent's reasoning evolved. In a production deployment, this log would feed back into the General Problem Solver's persistent memory so that future encounters with similar cross-domain questions would begin with the refined decomposition strategy rather than repeating the broad first pass.

This case study demonstrates the General Problem Solver pattern presented earlier in the chapter. By separating decomposition (Stage 1), analogy search (Stage 2), hypothesis synthesis (Stage 3), evaluation (Stage 4), and meta-learning (Stage 5) into discrete, composable functions, the implementation mirrors the modular architecture of the Verification and Validation fact-checking pipeline while operating at a higher level of abstraction. For production use, replace the deterministic fallback scores with a domain-expert rubric or a simulation-based evaluator, persist the strategy log across sessions using a checkpoint store such as LangGraph's `CheckpointSaver`, and integrate the General Problem Solver with a Verification and Validation agent to cross-check generated hypotheses before they reach the research team.

Bringing it all together

Throughout this chapter, we treated the Data Analysis agent, the Verification and Validation agent, and the General Problem Solver as independent modules, then demonstrated two of them in extended case studies: the Verification and Validation agent as a newsroom fact-checker and the General Problem Solver as a cross-disciplinary hypothesis engine. In practice, the three work best as stages in a single pipeline: the Data Analysis agent surfaces candidate insights from raw data, the Verification and Validation agent stress-tests those insights for factual accuracy and logical coherence, and the General Problem Solver steps in when neither agent can resolve a question from its existing repertoire. The pseudocode below sketches this orchestration.

```
def tri_agent_pipeline(user_query, dataset, trusted_sources):
    # Stage 1 – Data Analysis Agent
    insights = data_analysis_agent.run(user_query, dataset)
    # insights: list of {claim, evidence, viz_recommendation}

    # Stage 2 – Verification & Validation Agent
    verified = []
    for insight in insights:
        verdict = vv_agent.verify(insight, trusted_sources)
        if verdict.status in ("Confirmed", "Mostly True"):
            verified.append(insight | {"confidence": verdict.score})
        else:
            verified.append(insight | {"flag": verdict.details})

    # Stage 3 – General Problem Solver (fallback)
    unresolved = [i for i in verified if "flag" in i]
```

```
    if unresolved:
        gps_results = gps_agent.solve(unresolved, strategy="decompose")
        verified = merge(verified, gps_results)

    return build_report(verified)
```

The pipeline follows a trust-then-escalate pattern. Every insight produced by Stage 1 must pass through the verification gate in Stage 2 before reaching the user. Claims that fail verification are not discarded but routed to the General Problem Solver, which can decompose the question, search for analogies in other domains, or generate hypotheses for further testing. This architecture ensures that confidence scores accompany every finding and that no unverified claim reaches a decision-maker without an explicit flag.

Summary

This chapter explored how advanced agent architectures extend beyond basic data handling to achieve genuine analytical reasoning. Beginning with the Data Analysis agent, we examined how intelligent systems can transform raw datasets into structured insights, generate visualizations autonomously, and support non-technical users through natural language interfaces. These agents democratize data analysis by combining statistical computation with linguistic reasoning, allowing users to move from data exploration to evidence-based decision-making without specialized training.

We then introduced the Verification and Validation agent, which safeguards the integrity of these analytical processes. By performing fact-checking, consistency analysis, and logical validation, it ensures that generated insights are not only informative but also verifiable. The Verification and Validation agent functions as the system's internal auditor, continuously reviewing reasoning chains, confirming factual accuracy, and maintaining logical coherence. This capability transforms intelligent agents from mere content producers into systems of record that uphold scientific and ethical standards of reliability.

The chapter culminated with the General Problem Solver, a unifying framework that integrates reasoning, learning, and adaptation. Unlike domain-specific agents, the General Problem Solver operates at a meta-cognitive level: it decomposes unfamiliar problems, draws analogies across disciplines, and constructs new solutions through iterative reflection. Its design embodies the next stage of cognitive evolution in AI - systems that can reason about reasoning and improve through experience.

Two case studies illustrated these principles in practice. The newsroom fact-checker demonstrated how a Verification and Validation agent can uphold journalistic integrity through claim extraction, evidence retrieval, and tolerance-based verification under deadline pressure. The power-grid hypothesis study showed the General Problem Solver's five-stage cycle in action: the agent decomposed a cross-disciplinary research question, drew analogies from ecology, generated and tested a hypothesis, failed on its first pass, and refined its approach through meta-learning to produce a higher-confidence result. Together, these implementations showed how the perception–reasoning–action cycle translates into concrete pipelines, and how the tri-agent ecosystem of Data Analysis, Verification and Validation, and General Problem Solver agents exemplifies how intelligence emerges from the continuous loop of observation, validation, and adaptation.

This chapter therefore establishes the foundation for AI systems that think critically, reason logically, and learn dynamically. In the chapters that follow, these same architectural patterns are applied to the domain of software engineering. Specifically, *Chapter 9* examines AI-powered coding agents, showing how the cognitive loop, verification pipeline, and meta-learning strategies introduced here translate into tools that generate, review, and refactor production code.

Subscribe for a free eBook

New frameworks, evolving architectures, research drops, production breakdowns—*AI_Distilled* filters the noise into a weekly briefing for engineers and researchers working hands-on with LLMs and generative AI systems. Subscribe now and receive a free eBook, along with weekly insights that help you stay focused and informed.

Subscribe at `https://packt.link/8Oz6Y` or scan the QR code below.

9

Software Development Agents

The art of programming is the art of organizing and mastering complexity.

- Edsger Dijkstra

This chapter explores how **artificial intelligence (AI) agents** are reshaping the way software is built, tested, and improved. Software development has always been about managing complexity through **abstraction**. We moved from assembly to high-level languages, from manual builds to automated pipelines, from ad-hoc testing to continuous integration. Each transition introduced tools that captured repetitive patterns and enforced consistency. Yet despite decades of automation, the core development loop remains largely manual: a developer receives a requirement, translates it into code, validates correctness through tests, and integrates the result into a larger system.

AI agents represent the next step in this progression. Unlike traditional development tools that operate on fixed rules and predefined workflows, agents bring reasoning and adaptation to the engineering process. A static analyzer flags violations after code is written. An agent can generate compliant code from the start, grounding its decisions in organizational policy and repository context. A CI pipeline executes a predetermined sequence of checks. An agent can plan a verification strategy, interpret failures, and refine its approach based on feedback. For example, tools like Cursor and Devin can autonomously navigate codebases, plan multi-step changes, and execute those changes across files, behavior that would be impossible for a traditional rule-based linter or autoformatter.

This chapter is organized around three distinct but interconnected capabilities: **Code-Generation agents**, which transform natural language specifications into working implementations and apply test-driven patterns to ensure correctness; **Compliance-Driven agents**, which embed security and policy awareness directly into the development workflow, moving governance from external audit to continuous enforcement; and **Self-Improving agents**, which learn from outcomes and feedback, evolving their strategies to handle increasingly complex tasks with minimal human oversight.

This chapter builds directly on the foundations we have already laid so far. We are moving from the general to the specific, and will be applying the core **cognitive architectures** from *Chapter 5* and the **tool-use frameworks** from *Chapter 7* to one of the most complex domains: software engineering itself. We will see how an agent-driven approach fundamentally reframes our relationship with our tools. Instead of manually invoking static analysis or testing utilities, we architect agents that can reason about code quality and intelligently decide which tools to deploy to achieve a high-level goal.

In this chapter, we'll be covering the following topics:

- Market context and emerging trends
- Code-Generation agents
- Compliance-Driven agents
- The Self-Improving agent

Market context and emerging trends

Code-Generation agents have rapidly matured from experimental research into essential components of the modern engineering stack. This transition has crystallized into three dominant architectural patterns, each evolved to address a specific layer of the development lifecycle:

- **IDE Copilots:** Focused on the "inner loop" (the individual developer's edit-compile-test cycle), these embedded assistants accelerate individual developer productivity by drafting logic and boilerplate code directly within the editor. GitHub Copilot is the most widely adopted example, with over one million developers using it to generate code completions and entire function implementations directly within VS Code and other supported editors.
- **Pipeline agents:** Situated in the "outer loop" or CI/CD environment, these agents act autonomously to generate tests, repair broken builds, and propose patches without human intervention.
- **Repository-aware assistants:** These systems index entire codebases and documentation to reason about broader architecture, performing structured edits that respect project-wide patterns

The emergence of these specialized roles is driven by intense pressure on engineering organizations to shorten development cycles while managing the complexity of polyglot stacks. As security and compliance requirements grow, teams can no longer rely solely on manual oversight. Instead, they are turning to these agentic patterns to enforce consistent quality and security standards at scale. This shift is underpinned by the maturity of orchestration frameworks and test-first workflows, which finally allows enterprises to measure, audit, and control agent behavior with the rigor required for production systems.

The following subsections examine each of these dimensions in detail: the ecosystem and tooling layers that underpin agent development, the trajectory toward increasing autonomy, and the staged adoption patterns that characterize how organizations move from experimental to production deployment.

Ecosystem and tooling layers

The ecosystem supporting these agents can be categorized into four distinct functional layers as shown in *Figure 9.1*

- **Orchestration frameworks**: Libraries such as LangGraph and LangChain have become the standard for defining stateful workflows, managing refinement loops, and handling tool integration.
- **Reasoning cores**: These are LLMs enhanced with specific retrieval capabilities (RAG), structured tool definitions, and the ability to decompose complex tasks into executable steps.

- **Quality and security gates**: This layer integrates traditional static analysis, type checking, and policy-as-code directly into the agent's execution loop, ensuring that generated code adheres to compliance standards in real time.
- **Observability platforms**: Essential for production reliability, these tools provide tracing, metrics, and dashboards to measure accuracy and latency, creating the data feedback loop necessary for self-improvement.

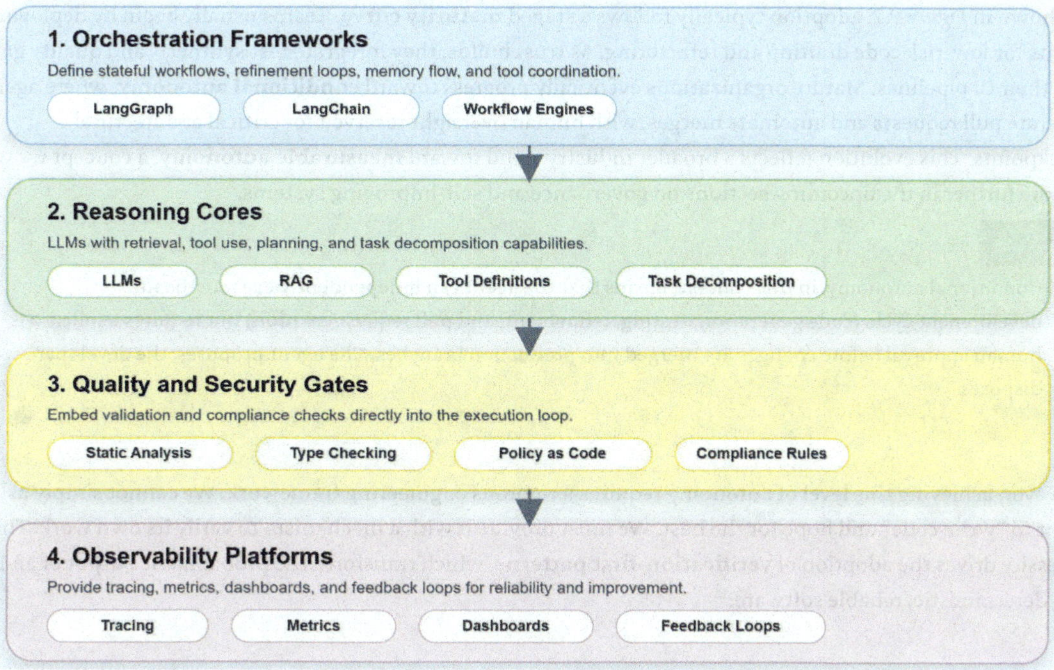

Figure 9.1 – Agent ecosystem and tooling: Four functional layers supporting modern AI agents in production

The shift toward autonomy

Emerging trends highlight a clear trajectory from passive assistance to active autonomy. **Test-driven generation (TDG)** is becoming the default mode of operation, ensuring that every line of generated code is auditable and functionally verified. To combat hallucinations, **repository-grounded reasoning** anchors agents in local symbols and APIs, preventing them from inventing non-existent dependencies.

Architecturally, we are seeing a move toward **multi-agent specialization**, where distinct "planner," "coder," and "critic" roles coordinate through structured graphs to handle complex tasks that would confuse a single model. Simultaneously, **policy-aware coding** is shifting compliance left, integrating security checks directly into pull request generation. Finally, **hybrid deployment models** are gaining traction, allowing organizations to balance the power of large hosted models with the privacy of smaller on-premise options for sensitive logic.

These trends are already visible in production systems. Cognition's Devin demonstrated autonomous multi-file, multi-step software engineering tasks, including debugging and deployment, using a planner-coder-critic architecture. Princeton's SWE-Agent showed that agents grounded in repository context can resolve real GitHub issues from the SWE-bench benchmark with meaningful success rates. Amazon's CodeWhisperer and Cursor have evolved from simple autocompletion into context-aware systems that reason about project structure and generate multi-file changes. On the compliance side, organizations such as Snyk and Semgrep are integrating LLM-powered analysis into their security scanning pipelines, moving beyond pattern matching to semantic vulnerability detection.

Adoption trajectory

As shown in *Figure 9.2*, adoption typically follows a staged **maturity curve**. Teams usually begin by deploying agents for low-risk code drafting and refactoring. As trust builds, they integrate test synthesis and quality gates into their CI pipelines. Mature organizations eventually progress toward **conditional autonomy**, where agents generate pull requests and automate merges, with human oversight reserved for critical architectural checkpoints. This evolution reflects a broader industry trend toward **measurable autonomy**, a concept we will explore further in the upcoming sections on governance and self-improving systems.

> **Note**
>
> Conditional autonomy, in this context, means that the agent can independently execute the full development cycle (code generation, testing, refinement, and pull request creation) but requires explicit human approval before changes are merged into production branches. The agent proposes; the developer disposes.

However, achieving this level of autonomy requires a rigorous engineering framework. We cannot simply ask an agent to "write code" and hope for the best. We must provide it with a mechanism to verify its own work. This necessity drives the adoption of **verification-first patterns**, which transform the probabilistic output of an LLM into deterministic, reliable software.

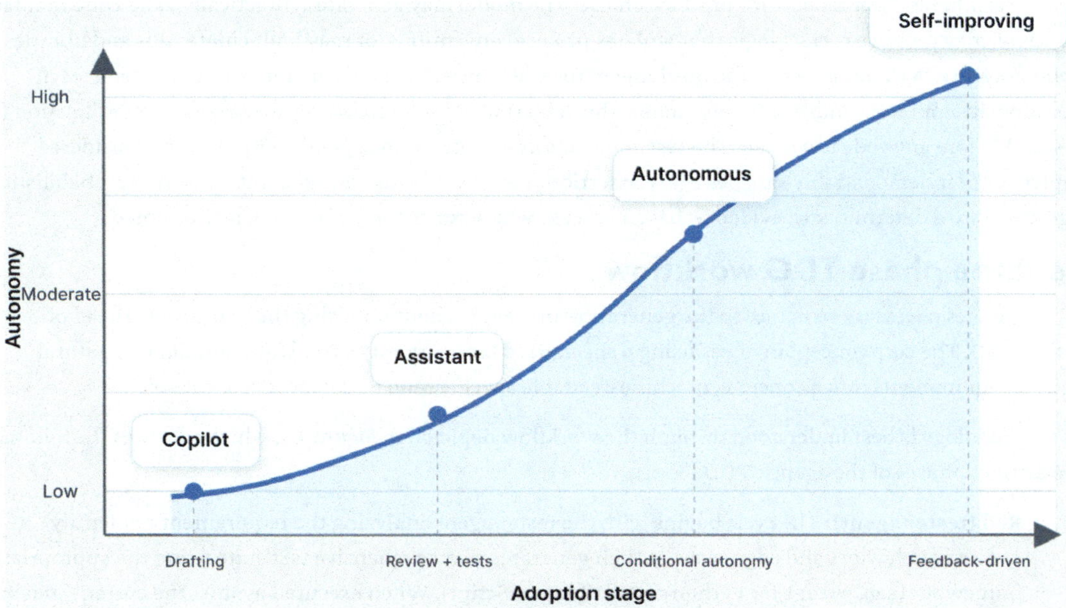

Figure 9.2 – Adoption maturity curve for AI coding agents

The sections that follow examine three distinct classes of software development agents, each addressing a different dimension of autonomous software engineering. We begin with Code-Generation agents, which apply these verification-first patterns through test-driven generation to transform natural language specifications into working, tested implementations.

Code-Generation agents

Code-Generation agents represent the most mature application of agentic AI in software engineering. These agents go beyond simple autocompletion by implementing TDG, a methodology that transforms the probabilistic output of LLMs into deterministic, verified implementations. This section examines the TDG architecture and its three-phase workflow, demonstrates how multi-agent orchestration enables iterative refinement through structured feedback loops, and progresses from a single-function implementation to a complete full-stack development case study. The patterns established here form the foundation for the Compliance-Driven and Self-Improving agents that follow.

The TDG architecture and workflow

Code-Generation agents face a fundamental challenge: LLMs produce probabilistic outputs that can vary across runs and may not consistently align with design intent. Relying on these outputs without systematic validation is unsuitable for production environments where predictability and auditability are paramount. To address this, we employ **TDG**, a workflow that adapts the principles of traditional **test-driven development (TDD)** for autonomous systems.

Why does TDG matter? Standard LLM code generation operates as a one-shot process: a developer provides a prompt, the model produces code, and the output is accepted or rejected based on manual inspection. This approach is inherently unreliable for production use. The model may generate syntactically valid code that fails at runtime, may produce correct logic that violates project conventions, or may hallucinate APIs and libraries that do not exist. Without a systematic mechanism to verify output against concrete success criteria, each generation attempt is a gamble. TDG eliminates this uncertainty by establishing an executable specification (the test suite) before any code is written. The test suite acts as a contract: the agent's output is not considered complete until it demonstrably satisfies every assertion. This transforms code generation from a probabilistic suggestion into a deterministic, evidence-based process where correctness is proven, not assumed.

The three-phase TDG workflow

TDG introduces necessary structure to the generation process without imposing the manual overhead of classical TDD. The core concept involves using a specialized **tester agent** to transform ambiguous natural language requirements into a concrete, machine-readable specification in the form of a test suite.

This methodology is best understood through the workflow depicted in *Figure 9.3*, which captures the following three distinct phases of the agentic TDD loop:

1. **Red (tester agent):** The cycle begins with the tester agent analyzing the requirement to identify expected behaviors and edge cases. It then generates a comprehensive test suite using the appropriate framework (e.g., `pytest` for Python or `Jest` for JavaScript). When executed against the current codebase, these tests fail, validating two critical facts: the tests are active and the required feature does not yet exist.
2. **Green (developer agent):** The developer agent receives these failing tests as a concrete objective: write the minimal code necessary to make this test suite pass. The agent generates implementation code grounded in repository context, respecting existing APIs and architectural patterns. After each attempt, the test output returns as structured feedback, indicating exactly which assertions failed. This feedback loop forces the agent to iterate until the success criteria are met. Note that the developer agent and the tester agent are distinct specialized agents, each with its own system prompt and tool set. However, as we will see in the Refactor phase, a single underlying model can serve multiple agent roles by switching its prompt context, just as a developer might alternate between writing code and reviewing it.
3. **Refactor:** Once the tests pass, the system enters the refactoring phase to optimize code quality. A refactoring agent (or the developer agent in a new role) eliminates duplication, extracts reusable functions, and applies project-specific style conventions. Crucially, the test suite is executed after every change to ensure that behavior remains consistent during cleanup.

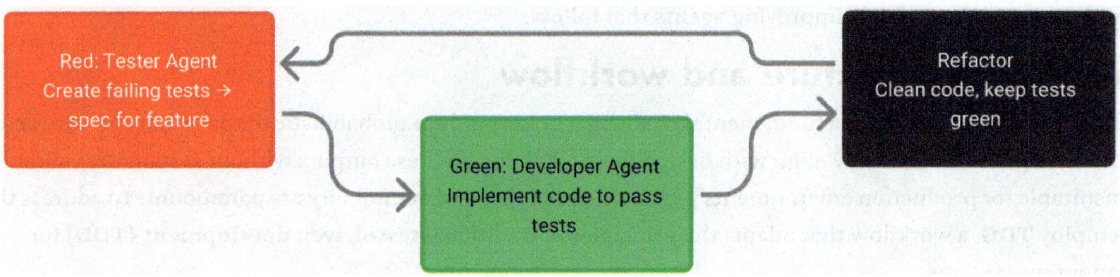

Figure 9.3 – Three phases of the TDD agent workflow

The feedback arrows in *Figure 9.3* represent the core of the TDD process: tightly controlled iterative loops. Whenever the developer agent fails to satisfy the test suite during the Green phase, or when a refactoring step reintroduces defects, the workflow routes the agent back to the implementation stage. Progress is impossible until all tests pass. This architecture enforces measurable correctness at every step, turning test results into the governing signal for both generation and refinement.

Implementing TDG with multi-agent orchestration

The three-phase TDG workflow can be implemented through various orchestration frameworks, each with different trade-offs in complexity, observability, and control. Linear pipeline frameworks like simple LangChain sequences lack the state management and conditional routing necessary for iterative refinement. Event-driven systems provide reactivity but can obscure execution flow. For this implementation, we have chosen **LangGraph**, which provides explicit state graphs with built-in support for conditional branching, persistent memory, and **human-in-the-loop (HITL)** checkpoints.

Other frameworks such as CrewAI and Microsoft AutoGen offer alternative approaches to multi-agent orchestration. CrewAI emphasizes role-based agent definitions with simplified configuration, making it well-suited for rapid prototyping. AutoGen provides a conversation-based agent framework with strong support for HITL interactions. We chose LangGraph for this chapter because its explicit state graph model makes the control flow visible and debuggable, its built-in checkpointing enables recovery from failures mid-workflow, and its conditional edge routing maps directly to the decision points in our *generate, test, refine* loop.

Figure 9.4 illustrates this architecture in detail, showing how specialized agents coordinate through structured state transitions and feedback loops. To operationalize the three-phase cycle, we introduce an orchestrator agent that manages the overall workflow. This agent decomposes high-level requirements into concrete tasks, routes them to specialized workers (i.e., tester agent, developer agent, refactoring agent), and evaluates outcomes at each stage to determine whether to advance or iterate.

The architecture addresses a fundamental requirement: agents must persist context across multiple refinement iterations. Simple linear chains are insufficient because they lack the memory required to learn from failure. A developer does not give up after one syntax error; they read the error message, adjust their mental model, and try again. To mimic this, our agent architecture maintains persistent state that includes the task description, current code snapshots, test results, and the complete history of prior attempts. In practice, this state is persisted using LangGraph's built-in checkpointing mechanism, which serializes the complete graph state at each node transition. For production deployments requiring durability across process restarts, backends such as Redis or PostgreSQL provide persistent storage, enabling workflows to resume from the last successful checkpoint after failures.

This architecture relies on a **generate, test, refine loop**, the single most important pattern for building reliable code agents. Instead of treating code generation as a one-shot task, this pattern uses the factual, non-ambiguous output from a test runner to systematically converge on a correct solution.

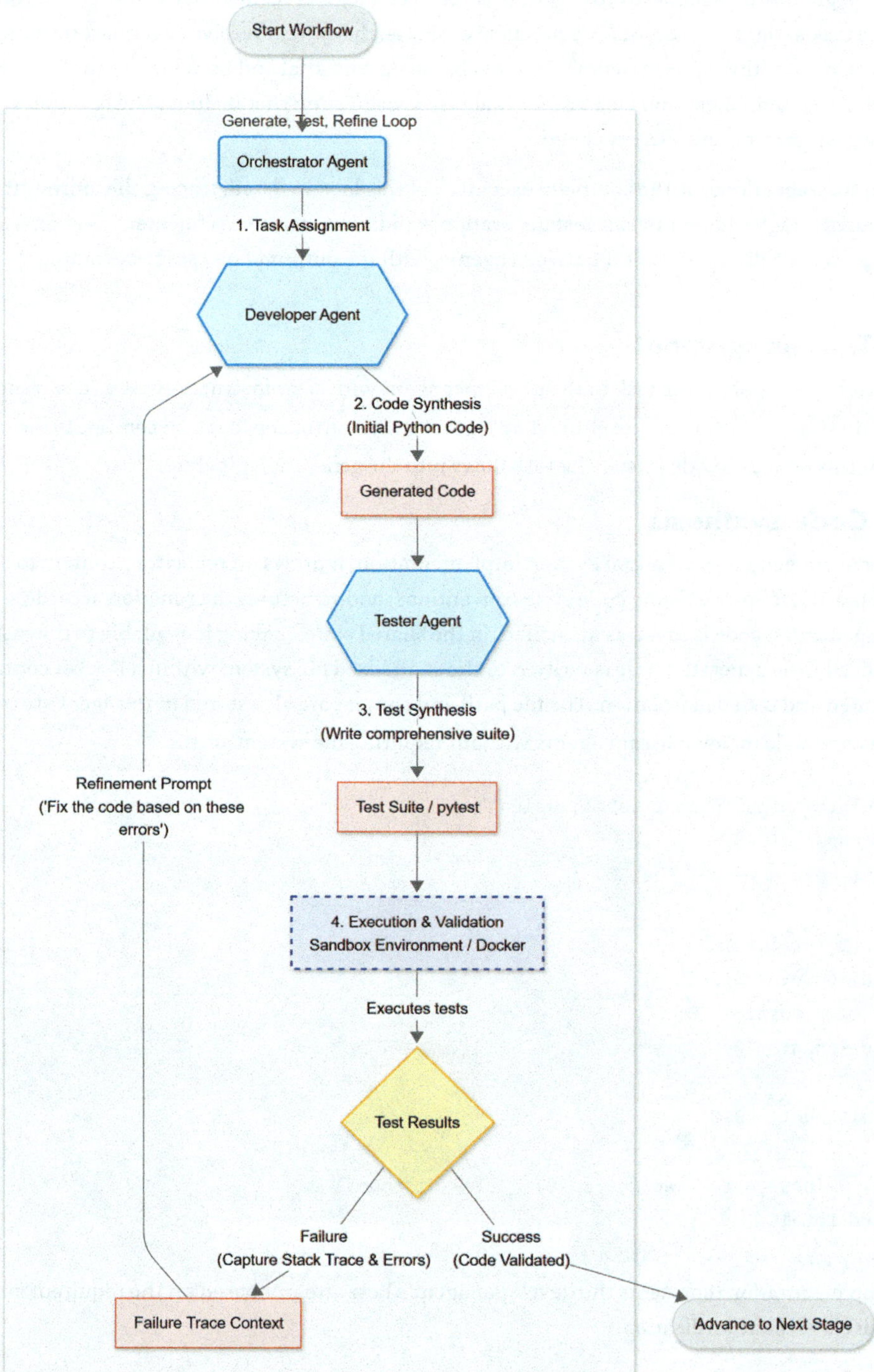

Figure 9.4 – The LangGraph architecture implementing the iterative "generate, test, refine" loop

The workflow begins with an orchestrator agent that receives a high-level feature request and decomposes it into a concrete task assignment. Consider a practical example: the system receives a request to "implement a shipping cost calculator that applies tiered discounts based on cart total and package weight." The orchestrator agent analyzes this requirement and creates a formal task specification that includes the function signature, expected input parameters, and success criteria.

The following six stages describe the complete execution of this loop in detail, tracing the journey from initial task assignment through code synthesis, test generation, validation, iterative refinement, and final success. Each stage represents a discrete handoff between agents, with the output of one stage becoming the input to the next.

Stage 1: Task assignment

The orchestrator agent assigns the task to the developer agent with clear instructions: `Write a function calculate_shipping(cart_total, weight) that returns the shipping cost after applying appropriate discounts`. At this point, no code exists. The task flows into the generation pipeline.

Stage 2: Code synthesis

The developer agent generates an initial Python implementation. It draws on repository context to determine appropriate libraries, follows existing code style conventions, and structures the function according to project patterns. The generated code is saved as an artifact in the shared state, making it available to downstream agents. Specifically, the generated code is written to the sandboxed file system within a Docker container, where it can be executed and tested in isolation. The file path and content are also stored in the `AgentState` dictionary, making them accessible to downstream agents without requiring file system access.

```
def calculate_shipping(cart_total, weight):
    base_rate = 5.00
    weight_cost = weight * 0.50

    if cart_total > 100:
        discount = 0.20
    elif cart_total > 50:
        discount = 0.10
    else:
        discount = 0.0

    total = (base_rate + weight_cost) * (1 - discount)
    return total
```

This initial implementation represents the developer agent's best attempt based on the requirements. However, we cannot trust it without verification.

Stage 3: Test synthesis

The generated code and the original task specification flow to the tester agent. This agent's directive is explicit: write a comprehensive test suite using `pytest` that verifies the code against the requirements, including edge cases. The tester agent generates the following code:

```
import pytest
from shipping import calculate_shipping

def test_basic_shipping():
    assert calculate_shipping(30, 2) == 6.00

def test_tier_one_discount():
    assert calculate_shipping(60, 2) == 5.40

def test_tier_two_discount():
    assert calculate_shipping(120, 2) == 4.80

def test_zero_weight():
    assert calculate_shipping(100, 0) == 4.00

def test_negative_weight():
    with pytest.raises(ValueError):
        calculate_shipping(50, -1)
```

Notice the final test: the tester agent identified that negative weight should raise an error, which is an edge case not explicitly mentioned in the original requirement but is essential for robust implementation.

Once both the implementation code and the test suite are complete, the workflow advances to the next sequential stage. It is important to note that Stages 2 and 3 execute in sequence, not in parallel: the tester agent requires the developer agent's code as input to generate meaningful tests. The output of these two stages (the code artifact and the test artifact) then flows together into the execution environment.

Stage 4: Execution and validation

Both the application code and the test suite are saved to a sandboxed environment (represented by the dashed box labeled *Sandbox Environment/Docker* in *Figure 9.4*). The system executes the test suite using `pytest`. The test runner captures all output: which tests passed, which failed, and any specific assertion errors or exceptions encountered.

In this example, four tests pass but one fails, and the following error message is returned:

```
FAILED test_negative_weight - Did not raise ValueError
Expected exception ValueError but function returned -0.50
```

This concrete failure output becomes critical feedback for the next iteration.

Stage 5: The refinement loop

The workflow reaches a decision point, represented by the yellow diamond labeled *Test Results* in *Figure 9.4*. The system evaluates: did all tests pass? The stack trace is parsed programmatically using Python's built-in traceback module, which extracts the file name, line number, function name, and error message into a structured format that can be injected directly into the refinement prompt.

In this case, the answer is no. The failure path (marked *Failure* with error capture) routes control back to the developer agent. Critically, the agent receives not just a notification that tests failed, but the complete pytest stack trace and assertion error. This refinement prompt is dynamically constructed from the current iteration state: it incorporates the original task specification, the most recent code version, the complete test output including stack traces, and a summary of prior failed attempts. Each iteration thus provides the agent with progressively richer context, allowing it to avoid repeating previous mistakes and to focus on the specific remaining failure.

```
"Your previous code failed the following tests. Here is the error:
FAILED test_negative_weight - Did not raise ValueError
Expected exception ValueError but function returned -0.50
Fix the code to handle negative weight by raising ValueError."
```

The developer agent analyzes the error, identifies the missing validation, and generates a revised implementation:

```
def calculate_shipping(cart_total, weight):
    if weight < 0:
        raise ValueError("Weight cannot be negative")

    base_rate = 5.00
    weight_cost = weight * 0.50

    if cart_total > 100:
        discount = 0.20
    elif cart_total > 50:
        discount = 0.10
    else:
        discount = 0.0

    total = (base_rate + weight_cost) * (1 - discount)
    return total
```

The updated code flows back through the pipeline: it is saved to the sandbox, the test suite executes again, and the results are evaluated. This time, all tests pass.

Stage 6: Success and advancement

When the *Test Results* decision point evaluates to *Success*, the workflow advances to the next stage (shown on the right-hand side of *Figure 9.4* as *Advance to Next Stage*). The validated code is considered correct and can proceed to integration, documentation, or deployment.

The *Failure Trace Context* box (shown in the lower left of *Figure 9.4*) captures the complete history of the refinement loop: how many iterations were required, which specific tests failed at each attempt, and how the code evolved in response to feedback. This trace serves multiple purposes: it provides transparency into agent reasoning, supports debugging when convergence fails, and generates training data for self-improving systems. This execution data is logged to the observability platform for real-time monitoring and post-hoc analysis. Over time, aggregated failure-resolution pairs can be curated into fine-tuning datasets, enabling the underlying model to improve its first-attempt success rate for commonly encountered error patterns.

Why this architecture matters

This iterative *generate, test, refine* loop is the single most important pattern for building reliable code agents. It uses the factual, non-ambiguous output from a test runner to correct the LLM's probabilistic errors and systematically converge on a correct solution. Without this loop, the agent would generate code once, hope it works, and leave validation to human reviewers. With this loop, the agent becomes a self-correcting system that demonstrates correctness through evidence.

The workflow shows external dependencies on the *File System* and *Test Tools* (`pytest`, `jest`), demonstrating how agents interact with the development environment to execute and validate their work. Agents do not operate in isolation or simulation. They write actual files, invoke real compilers and test runners, and parse structured output from those tools. This grounding in production infrastructure ensures that generated code integrates seamlessly with existing development practices.

The multi-agent coordination pattern also scales naturally. The same workflow can be applied twice in parallel: once for backend code (using pytest) and once for frontend code (using Jest), with each path maintaining its own refinement loop. An integration stage then combines the validated components and runs end-to-end tests across the full stack. This parallelism, visible in the broader context of *Figure 9.4*'s positioning within a larger system, enables agents to tackle complex, multi-layer features efficiently while maintaining the reliability guarantees of TDD.

Implementing state management

The foundation of this workflow is robust **state management**. The agent system must track tasks, code artifacts, test results, and execution history across multiple refinement iterations. Here's how this is structured using **Pydantic** models:

> **Note**
>
> Pydantic is a Python library for data validation using type annotations; it allows developers to define structured data models as classes whose fields are automatically validated at runtime, ensuring that agent state always conforms to the expected schema.

```
class Task(BaseModel):
    """Represents a single development task."""
    task_id: str
    description: str
    task_type: str  # 'backend', 'frontend', or 'integration'
    status: str = 'pending'
    dependencies: List[str] = Field(default_factory=list)
    code: Optional[str] = None
    tests: Optional[str] = None
    test_results: Optional[str] = None
    iterations: int = 0

class AgentState(TypedDict):
    """Global state shared across all agents."""
    user_story: str
    tasks: List[Task]
    current_task: Optional[Task]
    backend_code: Dict[str, str]
    frontend_code: Dict[str, str]
    test_code: Dict[str, str]
    messages: Annotated[Sequence[str], operator.add]
    final_output: Optional[Dict[str, Any]]
```

The `Task` model encapsulates everything needed to track a single development unit: its type, dependencies, generated code, test suite, execution results, and the number of refinement iterations. The `AgentState` acts as the shared memory across all agents in the system, storing the complete development context, including separated backend and frontend code artifacts. The `messages` field uses LangGraph's `operator.add` annotation to accumulate conversation history, providing agents with full context of prior decisions.

For example, during the user profile feature implementation, the state might contain the following: `task_id="T1-user-api"`, `task_type="backend"`, `status="testing"`, `code` containing the Flask route definition for `/api/users/<id>`, `tests` containing three pytest functions validating response codes and JSON schema, `test_results="FAILED: test_user_not_found - Expected 404, got 500"`, and `iterations=1`. This concrete state representation allows downstream agents to understand exactly what has been attempted, what failed, and how many refinement cycles remain before the iteration limit is reached.

Benefits and applications

Practically, such agents automate the **red-green-refactor cycle**. Developers benefit from improved reliability, reduced regression risk, and better documentation via auto-generated test suites. In enterprise environments, this approach accelerates onboarding and enforces consistent testing practices across teams.

This stateful, multi-turn approach stands in deliberate contrast to the stateless generation model used by IDE copilots. Tools like GitHub Copilot operate on a single-turn basis: the developer writes a prompt or partial code, the model produces a completion, and the interaction ends. There is no test feedback, no iterative refinement, and no persistent memory of prior attempts. If the generated code is incorrect, the developer must manually identify the error, adjust the prompt, and try again. TDG-based agents, by contrast, maintain state across multiple generation-test-refinement cycles, accumulating context from each failed attempt and systematically converging on a correct solution. The agent does not merely suggest code; it proves correctness through evidence and iterates until that proof is complete.

Moreover, from a theoretical standpoint, this iterative cycle reflects a scientific method: posing hypotheses (code), testing predictions (unit tests), and refining the implementation, paving the way for self-improving autonomous systems.

Practical implementation: From single feature to full-stack system

The shipping calculator example demonstrated TDG principles for a single backend function. Real-world systems require coordination across multiple layers, languages, and agents working in parallel. This section examines a complete implementation that extends the patterns we've established to build a full-stack feature: a user profile page that spans backend APIs, frontend components, and end-to-end integration.

The system employs the same hierarchical multi-agent architecture and *generate, test, refine* loops we've explored, but now orchestrates them across multiple specialized agents operating concurrently. This illustrates how TDG scales from individual functions to complete features while maintaining the same reliability guarantees.

The challenge

The shipping calculator example demonstrated TDG principles for a single backend function, but real-world development rarely involves isolated components. A typical feature request spans backend APIs, frontend components, database schemas, and integration tests across multiple languages and frameworks. Coordinating these layers manually creates bottlenecks: backend and frontend teams work in sequence, integration issues surface late, and test coverage gaps emerge at layer boundaries. The challenge is to scale the *generate, test, refine* loop from a single function to a full-stack system while preserving the same reliability guarantees that TDG provides at the unit level.

From single agent to multi-agent: Bridging the architecture gap

Before examining the full-stack implementation, it is worth understanding how the multi-agent architecture relates to the single-agent TDG workflow we have already established. In the shipping calculator example, a single developer agent, tester agent, and refactoring agent operated sequentially on one function in one language. Scaling to a full-stack feature introduces three new requirements: language-specific specialization (Python for the backend, TypeScript for the frontend), parallel execution (backend and frontend can proceed independently until integration), and cross-layer dependency management (the frontend relies on API contracts defined by the backend). The multi-agent architecture addresses these requirements by decomposing the single-agent roles into specialized agents that operate concurrently while sharing state through a common orchestration layer.

The following mapping illustrates how each single-agent role scales to the multi-agent context. The orchestrator agent becomes the project manager agent, now responsible for decomposing features into language-specific tasks and managing dependencies between them. The developer agent splits into a backend agent (Python/Flask) and a frontend agent (TypeScript/React), each inheriting the same *generate, test, refine* loop but primed with language-specific context. The tester agent retains its role but now generates framework-appropriate test suites (pytest for backend, Jest for frontend). The refactoring agent's responsibilities are absorbed into each specialized agent's refinement cycle. Critically, a new integration stage is introduced to validate cross-layer contracts after individual components pass their isolated test suites. This incremental decomposition ensures that every pattern in the multi-agent system traces directly back to a concept the reader has already encountered.

Agent specialization for full-stack development

The system employs a hierarchical multi-agent architecture with specialized roles:

- **Project manager agent (Orchestrator)**: Decomposes the high-level goal and coordinates the other agents through task delegation and dependency management. This extends the orchestrator agent role we introduced in *Figure 9.4*.
- **Backend agent (Python/Flask)**: Specializes in the server-side codebase. Its tools include file I/O and a `pytest` test runner for Python validation. This agent operates identically to the developer agent in our shipping calculator example, but is primed for Flask/SQLAlchemy patterns.
- **Frontend agent (TypeScript/React)**: Specializes in the client-side codebase. Its tools include file I/O and a `jest` test runner for JavaScript/TypeScript validation. This demonstrates the multilingual capability through contextual priming we discussed earlier.
- **Tester agent:** A general-purpose agent responsible for generating comprehensive test cases based on requirements, including edge cases and failure scenarios. This agent performs the same role as the tester agent in the three-phase workflow.

Implementing agent nodes

Each agent in the system is implemented as a node function that receives the shared state, performs its specialized operation, and returns updated state. Here's the backend agent implementation:

```
def backend_agent_node(state: AgentState) -> AgentState:
    """
    Backend agent generates Python/Flask code for assigned tasks.
    """
    task = state['current_task']

    # Construct context-rich prompt
    prompt = f"""You are an expert Python backend developer.
```

```
Task: {task.description}
Project Context: Flask REST API with SQLAlchemy ORM

Requirements:
- Use Flask blueprints for routing
- Include proper error handling
- Add input validation using marshmallow schemas
- Follow PEP 8 style guidelines
- Include Google-style docstrings

Existing Tests (MUST PASS):
{task.tests}

Generate the complete implementation:"""

    response = llm.invoke(prompt)
    code = extract_code_from_response(response.content, "python")

    # Update state with generated code
    state['backend_code'][task.task_id] = code
    task.code = code
    task.iterations += 1

    return state
```

Notice how the agent constructs a comprehensive prompt that includes the task description, project context, explicit requirements, coding standards, and the test suite that must pass. This contextual grounding dramatically improves code quality. The `extract_code_from_response` utility function handles the common pattern of LLMs wrapping code in markdown formatting, ensuring clean code artifacts are stored in state.

Building the LangGraph workflow

The complete workflow orchestrates these agents using LangGraph's state graph pattern:

```
# Initialize the state graph
workflow = StateGraph(AgentState)

# Add agent nodes
workflow.add_node("planning", planning_agent_node)
workflow.add_node("backend_test", backend_test_node)
workflow.add_node("backend_code", backend_agent_node)
workflow.add_node("frontend_test", frontend_test_node)
workflow.add_node("frontend_code", frontend_agent_node)
workflow.add_node("integration", integration_agent_node)
```

```
workflow.add_node("summary", summary_node)

# Define the workflow edges
workflow.set_entry_point("planning")
workflow.add_edge("planning", "backend_test")
workflow.add_edge("backend_test", "backend_code")

# Conditional edge: loop back if tests fail
workflow.add_conditional_edges(
    "backend_code",
    lambda state: "backend_code" if state['current_task'].test_results != "PASS"
                  and state['current_task'].iterations < 3
                  else "frontend_test",
    {"backend_code": "backend_code", "frontend_test": "frontend_test"}
)

workflow.add_edge("frontend_test", "frontend_code")

# Conditional edge: loop back if tests fail
workflow.add_conditional_edges(
    "frontend_code",
    lambda state: "frontend_code" if state['current_task'].test_results != "PASS"
                  and state['current_task'].iterations < 3
                  else "integration",
    {"frontend_code": "frontend_code", "integration": "integration"}
)

workflow.add_edge("integration", "summary")
workflow.add_edge("summary", END)

# Compile the graph
app = workflow.compile()
```

This graph structure extends the pattern shown in *Figure 9.4* to handle parallel backend and frontend development. The `conditional_edges` implement the critical refinement loops we established earlier: if tests fail and the iteration count hasn't exceeded the limit, the workflow routes back to the code generation node. The iteration limit (*3* in this example) prevents infinite loops while giving the agent multiple opportunities to correct issues, exactly as we saw with the shipping calculator's negative weight validation.

In summary, the workflow graph achieves three critical functions. First, it provides deterministic state routing: each agent node receives the complete shared state and returns an updated version, ensuring no information is lost between steps. Second, it implements conditional branching at decision points: the `check_backend_tests` and `check_frontend_tests` functions evaluate test results and route either to the next stage (on success) or back to code generation (on failure), with an iteration limit preventing infinite loops. Third, it enables checkpoint recovery: LangGraph serializes the graph state at each transition, allowing the workflow to resume from the last successful node if a failure occurs mid-execution.

Parallel execution across the stack

The project manager agent receives the high-level task: `Add a user profile page that displays the user's name, email, and recent activity`. It uses **tree-of-thought reasoning** to decompose this into a dependency graph of sub-tasks. Dependencies between tasks are tracked explicitly through the `dependencies` field in each `Task` object. The project manager enforces a topological ordering: a task cannot begin execution until all tasks listed in its dependencies array have reached `"completed"` status. Independent tasks (those with no unresolved dependencies) execute in parallel through a fan-out pattern, while dependent tasks wait at a synchronization barrier until their prerequisites are satisfied. This fan-out/fan-in pattern maximizes parallelism while preserving correctness guarantees.

The following scenario demonstrates how TDG enables coordinated, iterative development across multiple agents, with tests acting as the primary contract between components:

1. **T1 (Backend):** `Create a GET /api/v1/users/{id} endpoint that returns user data (name, email, recent activity).`
   The project manager assigns T1 to the tester agent, which generates `test_user_api.py`. This test mocks the database and asserts that a call to the endpoint returns a `200 OK` status and the correct JSON schema. The backend agent then follows the same *generate, test, refine* loop we demonstrated with the shipping calculator. On the first iteration, tests fail due to a missing `import` statement. The `pytest` output is captured and fed back to the backend agent. On the second iteration, the agent corrects the import, and all tests pass.
2. **Frontend development (T2):** `Create a React component that fetches data from T1 and displays it.`
   Concurrently, the project manager assigns T2 to the tester agent, which generates `UserProfile.test.tsx`. This test uses `Jest` and `React Testing Library` to mock the fetch call and assert that the user's name is rendered to the DOM. The frontend agent receives T2 and the test file, and it follows the identical *generate, test, refine* loop, demonstrating the language-agnostic nature of TDG patterns.
3. **Integration (T3):** `Add the component to the main routing of the application.`
   The project manager assigns T3 to the frontend agent, which integrates the new component into the application's routing structure. Finally, the `Summary` node generates a comprehensive report documenting all generated artifacts, test results, and iteration counts for each task.

Execution and measured outcomes

Running the following compiled workflow produces tangible, measurable outputs:

```
# Execute the workflow
initial_state = {
    "user_story": "Add a user profile page with name, email, and recent activity",
```

```
    "tasks": [],
    "current_task": None,
    "backend_code": {},
    "frontend_code": {},
    "test_code": {},
    "messages": [],
    "final_output": None
}

final_state = app.invoke(initial_state)

# Results
print(f"Tasks Completed: {final_state['final_output']['tasks_completed']}")
print(f"Total Iterations: {final_state['final_output']['total_iterations']}")
print(f"Backend Files: {len(final_state['backend_code'])}")
print(f"Frontend Files: {len(final_state['frontend_code'])}")
```

In a typical execution, the system completes all tasks with an average of 1.4 iterations per task, generating approximately 180 lines of production-quality code across backend and frontend. The test coverage is 100% by design, as code cannot advance through the workflow without passing its test suite. This validates the reliability of TDG at scale: the same iterative refinement pattern that corrected the shipping calculator's weight validation works equally well for complex, multi-layer features.

The final output artifacts, including generated source files, test suites, and execution logs, are written to the project directory and can be committed directly to version control. In CI/CD environments, these artifacts are uploaded to the build pipeline's artifact storage for downstream deployment stages.

Scaling TDG to production systems

This implementation demonstrates how TDG scales from individual functions to complete features while preserving the core principles we established. The same *generate, test, refine* loop operates independently for backend and frontend, with each maintaining its own state, test suite, and refinement iterations. The hierarchical orchestration ensures tasks execute in the correct dependency order while allowing maximum parallelism.

The development team interfaces with the agent through a VS Code extension and natural language prompts. The agent learns from prior commits and team conventions, allowing it to personalize outputs to project-specific patterns. With HITL review at critical checkpoints (integration, deployment), the system delivers production-ready modules while maintaining the quality guarantees that TDD provides. The ingestion mechanism operates through RAG: project-specific style guides, coding standards documents, and historical commit patterns are indexed in a vector store. When the agent generates code, it retrieves relevant conventions based on the current task context and injects them into the system prompt, ensuring generated code aligns with team-specific patterns such as naming conventions, error handling idioms, and architectural layering decisions.

This case study demonstrates how the patterns we've examined—stateful multi-agent orchestration, iterative refinement through test feedback, language-specific specialization through contextual priming, and robust validation through automated testing—combine to create a practical system for autonomous software development. These agents are not just prompt responders but collaborative engineering tools that reduce boilerplate code, ensure consistency, and enable rapid iteration, all while adapting to team workflows and evolving requirements.

The Code-Generation agent represents a significant advancement in intelligent software development. By synthesizing code, applying test-driven patterns, and working across languages, these agents extend the capabilities of developers and teams. They combine theoretical insights from program synthesis and machine learning with practical tools like LangGraph and LangChain.

The architecture and implementation we've examined reveal essential patterns: stateful multi-agent orchestration, iterative refinement through test feedback, language-specific specialization through contextual priming, and robust validation through automated testing. The LangGraph workflow provides the scaffolding for these interactions, enabling agents to progress through complex development stages while maintaining quality through feedback loops.

However, functional correctness is only one dimension of production-ready software. Code that passes all tests may still violate security policies, expose sensitive data, or fail regulatory audits. As development agents gain autonomy to generate and deploy code with minimal human oversight, the traditional model of post-deployment security reviews becomes untenable. Just as we cannot trust probabilistic code generation without systematic validation, we cannot trust autonomous development without systematic policy enforcement.

This challenge requires a different class of agent, one that operates not on functional requirements but on normative constraints. Where Code-Generation agents ask "does this implementation work correctly?", Compliance-Driven agents ask "is this implementation legally and organizationally permissible?" The shift from generation to governance introduces new technical requirements: interpreting ambiguous policy documents, tracing data flow across services, and making enforcement decisions that balance security with developer velocity.

Compliance-Driven agents

As modern software development moves toward autonomy and speed, it must also contend with a growing web of regulatory, security, and organizational constraints. Compliance is no longer optional. Developers now operate within legally defined boundaries around data handling, user privacy, encryption, and operational transparency. The same autonomy that enables Code-Generation agents to accelerate development creates new risks: code that passes all functional tests may still violate security policies, expose protected data, or fail regulatory audits.

Traditional compliance processes remain reactive and externalized, relying on manual code reviews or post-deployment audits. A security team reviews pull requests after development is complete. An auditor examines deployed systems months after release. Compliance becomes a gate rather than a guide, catching violations only after significant engineering effort has been invested. The result is often misalignment, late-stage rework, or regulatory exposure. When violations are discovered, fixing them requires rewriting tested code, regenerating documentation, and repeating the entire review cycle.

This model breaks down as development agents gain autonomy. If a Code-Generation agent can produce and deploy features with minimal human oversight, compliance enforcement must operate at the same speed and scale. We cannot insert manual security reviews into a workflow that generates, tests, and refines code in minutes. Just as we embedded validation directly into the code-generation loop through test-driven patterns, we must embed compliance directly into the development workflow through policy-aware agents.

Compliance-Driven agents offer this capability: intelligent, policy-aware agents embedded directly into the development workflow, capable of interpreting, enforcing, and evolving compliance requirements as code evolves. These agents operate on normative constraints rather than functional requirements. As mentioned previously, where Code-Generation agents ask "does this implementation work correctly?", Compliance-Driven agents ask "is this implementation legally and organizationally permissible?" This section explores how these agents function, how they integrate with the development architectures we've established, and how they transform software governance from a manual checkpoint to an autonomous process.

It is important to understand why compliance cannot simply be treated as another test type within the TDG workflow. TDG validates functional correctness: does the code produce the expected output for a given input? The test suite is derived from the developer's specification and the agent's understanding of the requirement. Compliance validation, by contrast, operates on an entirely different knowledge domain. It validates adherence to externally imposed constraints: regulatory mandates (GDPR, PCI DSS, HIPAA), organizational security policies, and data governance rules that exist independently of any functional requirement. The validation mechanisms differ accordingly. TDG relies on executable test suites that assert behavioral correctness. Compliance agents rely on policy engines, abstract syntax tree (AST) analysis, data flow tracing, and formal rule evaluation. A function can pass every unit test while simultaneously violating a data retention policy. These are orthogonal concerns that require distinct agent architectures, distinct knowledge bases, and distinct enforcement mechanisms.

To understand how these agents achieve this, the following subsections break down the compliance architecture into its five core capabilities, each addressing a distinct layer of the enforcement problem.

Core capabilities and technical architecture

Compliance-Driven agents are designed to monitor and act upon the normative dimensions of software development: what should or must not be done. These agents integrate structured policy models with semantic analysis and developer-facing tooling to act as intelligent mediators between code and regulation. Their architecture mirrors the multi-agent patterns we established for code generation, but operates on a different knowledge domain and employs different validation mechanisms.

These capabilities operate through a structured feedback loop that parallels the *generate, test, refine* cycle of Code-Generation agents. In the compliance domain, this loop takes the form of *scan, evaluate, remediate*. The agent first scans code changes and infrastructure configurations against the policy engine's rule set, identifying potential violations. It then evaluates each finding in context, using semantic analysis to distinguish genuine violations from false positives and to assess severity based on the regulatory framework involved. Finally, it remediates confirmed violations by generating specific fixes, blocking non-compliant merges, or escalating ambiguous cases to human reviewers. This *scan, evaluate, remediate* loop executes continuously within the CI/CD pipeline, providing the same iterative refinement for compliance that TDG provides for functional correctness.

The following subsections examine five core capabilities that define this architecture: static compliance validation against formal policy rules, semantic code understanding that detects contextual violations beyond pattern matching, contextual intervention and remediation that generate actionable fixes, data flow analysis that traces sensitive information across service boundaries, and audit trail generation that maintains the evidentiary record required for regulatory compliance.

Static compliance validation

Agents inspect source code and configuration for violations of security baselines, data locality restrictions, and other formal policies. This capability extends the static analysis we discussed in the context of code quality, but focuses on regulatory and security constraints rather than syntactic correctness.

Consider our shipping calculator example extended to handle payment processing. A compliance agent would scan the generated code for PCI DSS violations: logging full credit card numbers, storing CVV codes, or transmitting payment data without encryption. The agent parses the AST to identify variables containing payment information and traces their flow through logging statements, database writes, and network calls. Say the Code-Generation agent produces the following code:

```
def process_payment(card_number, cvv, amount):
    logger.info(f"Processing payment for card {card_number}")  # Violation
    # ... payment logic
```

The compliance agent flags this immediately, before tests even run, preventing the violation from advancing through the workflow.

Semantic code understanding

LLMs and AST analyzers enable the agent to infer whether developer intentions may lead to compliance violations, even when not explicitly flagged by pattern matching. This addresses a critical limitation of traditional static analysis: code that appears syntactically correct may still violate policy when context is considered.

For instance, a function named `anonymize_user_data` that simply removes the `name` field but preserves email addresses and IP addresses may technically execute without errors but violates GDPR's requirements for true anonymization. A compliance agent with semantic understanding analyzes the function's purpose (stated in docstrings or inferred from naming), examines which fields are removed or retained, and determines whether the remaining data can still identify individuals. This semantic layer allows the agent to flag subtle violations that pattern-based tools miss. To make this concrete: consider a function whose docstring reads "`Anonymizes patient records by removing all identifying information`" but whose implementation only masks the name field while leaving email, phone number, and date of birth intact. A pattern-based scanner would see a function called `anonymize` and move on. The compliance agent, by contrast, compares the claimed behavior (full anonymization) against the actual implementation (partial field removal) and flags the discrepancy as a HIPAA violation requiring remediation.

Contextual intervention and remediation

The agent can suggest remediations (e.g., replacing a deprecated encryption algorithm) or block non-compliant merges in CI/CD pipelines. This capability integrates directly with the refinement loops we established in the TDG workflow. Just as test failures trigger code regeneration, policy violations trigger remediation suggestions.

When a compliance agent detects use of the SHA-1 algorithm for cryptographic hashing (deprecated due to collision vulnerabilities), it doesn't simply flag an error. It generates a specific remediation patch:

```
# Original (flagged)
import hashlib
hash_value = hashlib.sha1(data).hexdigest()

# Suggested remediation
import hashlib
hash_value = hashlib.sha256(data).hexdigest()  # Updated to SHA-256
```

The agent can either block the merge and require human approval or automatically apply the fix and re-run tests to verify the change doesn't break functionality. This decision depends on the severity of the violation and the confidence level of the remediation.

Data flow analysis

Sensitive data types (e.g., personally identifiable information (PII), protected health information (PHI)) can be traced across services, endpoints, and storage layers to ensure proper handling throughout the stack. This capability is particularly important for compliance frameworks like HIPAA (healthcare) and GDPR (privacy), which impose strict requirements on how sensitive data flows through systems.

The agent tags variables containing sensitive data at their point of origin (user input, database queries, API responses) and tracks them through the call graph. If a variable tagged as `contains_pii` is passed to a logging function, sent to an analytics service in a non-EU region, or stored in an unencrypted database, the agent raises a violation. This analysis extends beyond individual functions to trace data flow across microservices, using API schemas and service mesh configurations to understand how data moves through distributed systems.

Audit trail generation

Every agent action (flags, suggestions, overrides) is logged to support audit readiness and regulatory evidence gathering. This extends the provenance tracking established for Code-Generation agents (see *Failure Trace Context* in *Stage 6*). Compliance agents maintain immutable logs that record:

- Which policies were evaluated for each code change
- Which violations were detected and when
- What remediations were suggested or applied
- Whether violations were overridden by human approvers and with what justification

These logs serve multiple purposes. During audits, they provide evidence that compliance controls were active and effective. During incident response, they reveal whether policy violations contributed to security breaches. For Self-Improving agents, they provide training data showing which remediations were accepted or rejected by human reviewers.

Architectural components and integration

At the architectural level, a compliance agent integrates several components that parallel the structures we established for Code-Generation agents:

- **Policy engine:** A declarative rule evaluation system that assesses code and configuration artifacts against formal policy definitions (e.g., Rego rules) and returns pass/fail decisions with violation details. Typically written in declarative policy languages like Rego (used by Open Policy Agent), policy engines define allowable states, configurations, and operations. The policy engine acts as the "test suite" for compliance: just as functional tests define correct behavior, policies define permissible behavior. The engine evaluates code and configuration against these rules, producing pass/fail decisions with detailed violation reports. Each policy version is tracked with semantic versioning and linked to the regulatory update that triggered the change. When a new version is deployed, the compliance agent automatically rescans recently merged code against the updated rules, flagging any retroactive violations for review. This version-aware approach ensures that the compliance posture evolves in lockstep with the regulatory landscape.
- **Code and infrastructure analyzers:** These tools parse source code, **Infrastructure-as-Code** templates (e.g., Terraform, Helm), and cloud configurations to match against compliance conditions. They provide the raw data the policy engine needs: which functions handle sensitive data, which network ports are exposed, which encryption algorithms are used. These analyzers integrate with the same file system and repository tools that Code-Generation agents use, ensuring compliance checks operate on the same artifacts that functional tests validate.
- **Language model layer:** LLMs interpret ambiguous cases, translate policy documents into structured rules, or suggest remediations in developer-facing language. This layer bridges the gap between formal policy statements (written by legal or security teams) and the code patterns developers write. When a new regulation is published, the LLM can extract key requirements, map them to existing policy templates, and generate Rego rules that enforce those requirements. When violations are detected, the LLM translates technical policy failures into actionable guidance: instead of `Rego rule data.compliance.pci.no_card_logging failed`, the developer sees `PCI DSS requires that full card numbers never be logged. Consider using mask_card_number() before logging.` In most production deployments, the language model operates as a prompt-based service rather than a fine-tuned specialist. Compliance context is injected through system prompts that include the relevant policy definitions, and retrieved policy documents provide the domain knowledge necessary for accurate interpretation. Fine-tuning may be employed for high-volume, narrowly scoped tasks such as translating specific regulatory frameworks into Rego rules, but the general approach favors prompt engineering with retrieval augmentation for its flexibility and rapid adaptation to new policies.

  The interplay between the policy engine, static code analyzers, and language model layer represents a fundamental advance over traditional rule-based compliance tools. Tools like SonarQube or Checkmarx detect known vulnerability patterns through predefined signatures: hardcoded credentials, SQL injection vectors, or unsafe deserialization. They are fast and reliable for known threats but blind to novel or contextual violations. The LLM-augmented architecture described here adds semantic reasoning: the ability to understand what code intends to do, evaluate whether that intent complies with policy, and detect violations that emerge from the interaction between individually compliant components. This combination of deterministic rule evaluation and probabilistic semantic analysis provides defense in depth that neither approach could achieve alone.

- **CI/CD integration**: Agents are deployed in pipelines, issue comments on pull requests, or block merges that fail policy checks. This mirrors the test execution nodes we introduced in *Figure 9.4*. Just as the workflow routes to "*Execution & Validation*" for functional testing, it routes to a compliance validation node that invokes the policy engine. The conditional edges then determine whether to advance (all policies pass) or route back for remediation (violations detected)
- **HITL overrides**: In non-deterministic cases, the agent can defer to a human approver, ensuring flexibility and accountability. Not all policy violations are absolute. Some require contextual judgment: is this specific use of customer data permissible under our terms of service? Is this encryption algorithm acceptable for this particular use case given performance constraints? When the agent's confidence is low or the policy engine returns ambiguous results, the workflow inserts a human checkpoint. The approver reviews the violation, consults with legal or security teams, and either grants an exception (with recorded justification) or requires remediation. This HITL pattern extends the checkpoints we introduced for Code-Generation agents, applying the same principle to compliance decisions.

The combination of formal policy logic and contextual intelligence allows these agents to be both precise and adaptive. Pattern-based rules catch clear violations. Semantic analysis catches subtle violations that require understanding intent. LLM-powered remediation suggestions reduce friction for developers. HITL overrides preserve flexibility for legitimate edge cases. Together, these capabilities shift compliance from an external activity to a continuous, intelligent process embedded at the point of change.

Deployment patterns across regulated industries

The architectural capabilities we've described translate into measurable impact across industries where compliance failures carry significant legal and financial consequences. These deployments demonstrate how Compliance-Driven agents integrate with the development workflows we've established, operating alongside Code-Generation agents while enforcing an orthogonal set of constraints. Some examples are as follows:

- **Healthcare applications:** Systems handling PHI under HIPAA face strict requirements around data exposure. Compliance agents scan generated code for patterns where PHI appears in log files, error messages, or API responses. When our Code-Generation agent produces a diagnostic endpoint that returns patient records, the compliance agent analyzes the response structure to verify that sensitive fields are properly redacted or encrypted. If the agent detects `logger.debug(f"Patient record: {patient.to_dict()}")`, it flags the violation immediately and suggests `logger.debug(f"Patient record retrieved: {patient.id}")`, removing the full record from logs while preserving debugging utility.

> **Note**
>
> Note that this healthcare scenario does not reference a specific agent from a prior chapter; rather, it illustrates how the Code-Generation architecture established in this chapter operates in a regulated domain where compliance agents must validate every generated artifact against HIPAA constraints before it enters the deployment pipeline. The detection mechanism combines pattern-matching rules for structured identifiers (medical record numbers, social security numbers, dates of birth) with LLM-based semantic classification for unstructured data, in which the model evaluates whether free-text fields contain information that could identify a patient even without explicit identifiers.

- **Fintech platforms**: Financial services face overlapping regulatory frameworks (PCI DSS for payments, SOC 2 for security controls, regional data residency laws). Compliance agents prevent deployments that would send financial data to non-compliant cloud regions, block code using insecure random number generators for cryptographic operations, and enforce key rotation policies for encryption. When a Code-Generation agent produces a payment processing function, the compliance agent traces data flow to ensure card numbers never persist to disk unencrypted, CVV codes are never stored at all, and all cryptographic operations use FIPS-approved algorithms.
- **SaaS enterprise tools**: Multi-tenant SaaS platforms must enforce role-based access control (RBAC) consistently across features. Compliance agents validate access control logic, ensuring that role-based permissions conform to ISO 27001 standards or internal policies. When a Code-Generation agent implements a new admin feature, the compliance agent verifies that permission checks exist at every entry point, that role hierarchies are correctly enforced, and that audit logging captures all administrative actions with sufficient detail for compliance reviews.

These examples share a common pattern: compliance agents operate as an additional validation layer in the *generate, test, refine* loop. Just as functional tests verify correctness and return specific failure messages that guide code refinement, compliance checks verify permissibility and return specific policy violations that guide remediation. The agent workflow we established in *Figure 9.4* extends naturally to include compliance validation alongside test execution.

Dynamic policy evolution

A key strength of these agents lies in their ability to evolve as regulations change. Compliance is not static: laws are amended, organizational policies are updated in response to incidents, and development practices shift as new frameworks emerge. The rigid, manually maintained compliance checklists used in traditional processes become outdated within months, creating gaps between what regulations require and what systems actually enforce.

Compliance-Driven agents support dynamic policy updates through several mechanisms described in the following list that parallel the self-improvement capabilities we'll explore in the next section:

- **Policy-as-Code repositories**: Compliance rules are stored in version-controlled repositories, allowing centralized updates and rollback capabilities. When GDPR guidance is clarified or a new PCI DSS requirement is published, security teams update the Rego policy definitions and push changes through a review process. The updated policies deploy automatically to all compliance agents, ensuring consistent enforcement across teams without manual coordination. This mirrors how Code-Generation agents retrieve updated test suites from repositories, maintaining a single source of truth for requirements. Crucially, these policy definitions are themselves testable artifacts within the CI pipeline. Just as a broken unit test prevents code from advancing, a policy rule that detects a violation fails the build and blocks the non-compliant merge. Policy rules function as executable tests for normative correctness, complementing the functional tests that validate behavioral correctness.

- **External policy feeds**: Advanced implementations integrate with regulatory databases and legal update services. When a relevant regulation changes, the system ingests structured updates and flags affected policies for human review. A compliance architect reviews the changes, maps them to existing policy templates, and either activates pre-defined rules or writes new ones. This reduces the latency between regulatory changes and enforcement, minimizing the window where code might violate newly established requirements.
- **Incremental learning from overrides**: When human approvers grant exceptions or reject agent recommendations, the system captures the justification and context. Over time, patterns emerge: certain violations in test code are routinely exempted, specific encryption algorithms are approved for specific use cases, and particular data fields are reclassified as non-sensitive. Advanced systems use these patterns to refine policy enforcement, reducing false positives while maintaining security. This learning mechanism extends the feedback loops we established for Code-Generation agents to the compliance domain, allowing agents to improve their judgment through accumulated experience.

This adaptability makes compliance a living process, integrated into the software delivery lifecycle rather than appended to it. Policies evolve in lockstep with regulations, and enforcement adapts based on real-world development patterns, reducing friction while maintaining rigor.

Practical implementation: Enforcing PCI DSS in a fintech CI/CD pipeline

To demonstrate how these architectural components and deployment patterns combine in practice, consider a complete implementation enforcing Payment Card Industry Data Security Standard (PCI DSS) requirements in a high-velocity development environment. This case study illustrates how compliance agents integrate with the code-generation and testing workflows we've established, operating as an additional gate in the development pipeline.

The challenge

A mobile payments company was scaling rapidly, with dozens of development teams pushing code daily to support new payment methods, fraud detection features, and merchant integrations. Their central security team was struggling to manually review every change to ensure it did not violate PCI DSS requirements, such as the strict rules against storing or logging sensitive cardholder data (like the full Primary Account Number or CVV). Manual reviews created a bottleneck: pull requests waited hours or days for security approval, slowing feature delivery and frustrating developers. More critically, the risk of a non-compliant change reaching production remained high, as manual reviews cannot catch every violation in high-volume environments.

This problem mirrors the challenge we addressed with TDG: manual validation is too slow and error-prone for autonomous development. Just as we cannot trust Code-Generation agents without systematic functional testing, we cannot trust rapid development without systematic compliance enforcement.

The solution: Integrated compliance agent architecture

The company built a Compliance-Driven agent integrated directly into its GitHub pull request workflow, extending the CI/CD pipeline we described in *Figure 9.4* with an additional validation stage. The agent's architecture combined formal policy enforcement with intelligent analysis:

- **Policy engine:** The agent used Open Policy Agent (OPA) as its core, the same declarative policy framework we discussed in the *Architectural Components and Integration* section. The security team translated key PCI DSS controls into Rego policies. For example, PCI DSS requirement 3.3 ("`Mask PAN when displayed`") became:

```
deny[msg] {
    input.code_change.added_lines[line]
    contains(line, "card_number")
    contains(line, "log")
    not contains(line, "mask_")
    msg := "PCI-DSS 3.3: Full card numbers must not be logged. Use
mask_card_number()."
}
```

- **Code analyzers:** The agent used static analysis (SAST) tools to scan code diffs for specific patterns: variables named `card_number` or `cvv` being passed to logging functions, database writes that don't use encryption, or API endpoints that return full payment credentials. These analyzers provided the structured input the policy engine evaluated, converting source code into the data structures Rego policies examine.
- **Language model layer:** The LLM, configured with compliance-specific system prompts and retrieved policy context, translated cryptic policy failures into clear, developer-friendly remediation advice. When the OPA engine reported "`Rule data.compliance.pci.no_card_logging failed for line 47`", the LLM converted this to: "`This line appears to log a full card number, violating PCI-DSS 3.3. Please refactor to log only the last four digits using mask_card_number(payment.card_number).`"

With the policy engine, code analyzers, and language model layer in place, the next step was integrating these components into the company's existing development workflow. The goal was to make compliance validation as seamless and automatic as the functional testing already embedded in their CI/CD pipeline.

Workflow integration

The compliance agent integrated seamlessly with the existing development workflow, operating as an additional node in the state graph pattern we established for code generation. The following four stages describe this integration: triggering on pull request events, scanning code changes against policy rules, evaluating findings and taking differentiated enforcement actions, and maintaining a complete audit trail for regulatory compliance:

- **Trigger:** A GitHub Action triggered the agent whenever a developer opened a new pull request or pushed new commits to an existing PR. This mirrors how test execution is triggered in the TDG workflow.
- **Scan:** The agent ran its OPA policies and SAST scanners against the changed code, analyzing only the diff to minimize latency. The scan completed in seconds, matching the performance requirements we established for test execution.
- **Evaluation and action:** Based on scan results, the agent took either of the following differentiated actions matching the severity and certainty of violations:
    - **Hard failure**: If a clear, high-severity violation was found (e.g., `logger.info(f"Processing card: {payment.card_number}")`), the agent immediately failed the CI check, blocked the merge, and posted a comment with specific remediation guidance. This mirrors the "Fail" path in our test-driven workflow, routing back to the developer for correction before proceeding.
    - **Soft failure (contextual inquiry)**: If a potential violation was found with lower certainty (e.g., a new field `data.tx_id_full` being passed to a transaction logger), the agent posted a non-blocking comment requesting confirmation: "`The new field appears in logged data. Please confirm this field does not contain sensitive cardholder data and add a justification comment.`" This HITL pattern allows development to continue while ensuring ambiguous cases receive review.
- **Audit trail**: All findings, developer justifications, and policy overrides were automatically exported to an immutable log store, creating a complete audit trail for compliance assessments. This extends the provenance tracking we established for code artifacts to policy enforcement decisions.

The integration of these workflow components transformed compliance enforcement from a manual bottleneck into an automated, real-time quality gate. The following results, measured over the first six months of deployment, quantify the impact of this transformation across three dimensions: violation detection, team efficiency, and audit readiness.

Measured outcomes

By embedding compliance logic directly into the developer's workflow, the company achieved significant, measurable results that validated the agent-driven approach. These metrics were tracked through the agent's audit dashboard, which aggregated data from the immutable log store and presented real-time compliance status alongside historical trend analysis, leveraging the observability platform described in the ecosystem overview:

- **Violation reduction**: Pre-deployment compliance violations detected by the agent dropped by 85% within six months as developers learned the patterns. The agent effectively trained the development team through immediate, specific feedback, much as TDG trains agents through test failures.

- **Team efficiency**: The security team was freed from routine line-by-line reviews, allowing them to focus on complex architectural design and threat modeling. This reallocation mirrors how test automation frees developers from manual verification, enabling them to focus on higher-value design work.
- **Audit transformation**: Most importantly, the agent's audit log transformed their annual PCI assessment from a disruptive, multi-week scramble into a straightforward review of automated evidence. Auditors could query the log to verify that compliance controls were active, that violations were detected and remediated, and that exceptions were properly justified. This demonstrates how systematic, automated compliance enforcement provides stronger assurance than manual processes while reducing organizational disruption.

This case study demonstrates how Compliance-Driven agents integrate with the development architectures we've established throughout this chapter. The same patterns that enable reliable code generation—stateful orchestration, iterative refinement, structured validation, and audit trails—extend naturally to compliance enforcement. By operating alongside functional testing in the development pipeline, compliance agents ensure that autonomy in code generation does not compromise security or regulatory adherence.

The Self-Improving agent

By transforming compliance into an automated, context-aware process, Compliance-Driven agents reduce legal risk, accelerate audit readiness, and create development environments that are secure by default. Yet even with TDG ensuring functional correctness and compliance agents enforcing policy adherence, a critical capability remains: the ability to learn from experience and improve over time.

In classical software systems, functionality is largely frozen at deployment. Improvement requires explicit human revision: a developer analyzes failure logs, identifies the root cause, writes a fix, and deploys an update. This cycle can take days or weeks. Intelligent agents, by contrast, redefine this paradigm. Self-Improving agents are designed to evolve continuously, learning from outcomes, adapting to user feedback, and optimizing performance autonomously. They transform static automation into living systems that refine themselves in response to data, feedback, and operational metrics.

These agents embody the convergence of **reinforcement learning**, **control theory**, and traditional **software observability**. They monitor their own actions, assess success or failure, and modify internal reasoning or configurations accordingly. This enables sustainable performance gains without continuous human micromanagement. Conceptually, Self-Improving agents extend the workflows we've established throughout this chapter. Where Code-Generation agents execute a *generate, test, refine* loop to produce correct code, Self-Improving agents execute a broader **execute, observe, learn, adapt** loop to produce better behavior across all tasks.

Architectural principles: The closed-loop control system

A Self-Improving agent architecture can be viewed as a **closed-loop control system**, mirroring feedback mechanisms used in robotics and industrial automation but applied to cognitive processes within LLM-powered software systems. *Figure 9.5* illustrates this architecture, showing how specialized components coordinate through feedback loops to enable continuous improvement. The workflow begins with task execution, where the agent performs its assigned function: generating code, answering a support query, or enforcing compliance policies. This execution produces observable outcomes that flow into the sensing layer.

The *Sensing Layer* collects feedback from multiple sources:

- **Explicit feedback** arrives as direct human signals: ratings, comments, or corrections provided by users or reviewers. Our shipping calculator example might collect explicit feedback when a developer approves or rejects the generated code.
- **Implicit feedback** emerges from behavioral indicators: session duration, task abandonment rates, or the frequency with which users accept or reject agent suggestions. In our example, implicit feedback is gathered through the number of refinement iterations required before tests pass.
- **Synthetic feedback** is automatically generated through consistency checks, logic tests, or comparison against gold-standard outputs. This feedback is obtained in our example by comparing the final implementation against established patterns in the repository.

This multi-modal feedback flows to the coder agent, which produces solutions or artifacts based on current strategies. In the context of code generation, this is the developer agent we've discussed throughout the chapter. The coder agent generates an implementation using its current prompt templates, reasoning strategies, and tool invocation patterns.

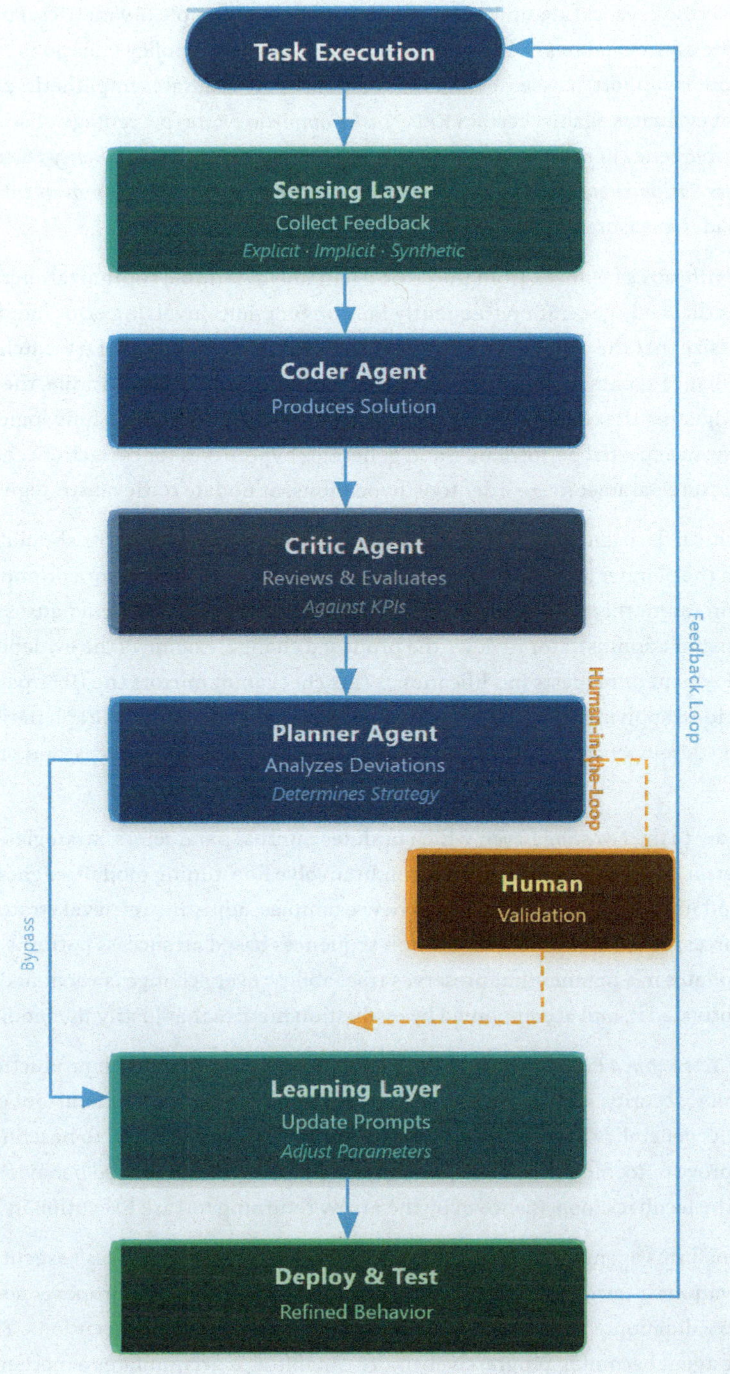

Figure 9.5 – Self-improvement loop

The critic agent then reviews the output against defined quality criteria. For code generation, this might involve running static analysis tools, executing unit tests, or evaluating code complexity metrics. For compliance enforcement, the critic agent validates that remediations actually resolve policy violations without introducing new issues. For customer support, it assesses whether responses are accurate, empathetic, and resolve the user's issue. The critic agent evaluates against certain KPIs: *Task Completion Rate* (percentage of successful executions), *Error Recovery Ratio* (frequency of self-correction without human intervention), *Latency Distribution* (response time percentiles), *User Satisfaction Index* (aggregated from explicit ratings), and *Improvement Velocity* (rate at which corrections lead to measurable gains).

The planner agent synthesizes feedback from the critic agent and determines optimization strategies. When the critic agent identifies that code generation frequently fails on functions involving error handling, the planner agent might hypothesize that the developer agent needs more explicit examples of try-catch patterns in its prompt. When compliance agents generate excessive false positives for a particular rule, the planner agent might recommend adjusting the confidence threshold or refining the pattern matching logic. The planner agent analyzes deviations from expected performance and generates hypotheses for correction: change reasoning depth, adjust temperature parameters, reorder tool invocations, or update retrieval strategies.

Figure 9.5 shows a critical decision point: the *HITL Checkpoint*. Not all improvements should deploy automatically. When the planner agent proposes significant changes, modifying core prompt templates, adjusting policy enforcement thresholds, or changing model parameters, the system pauses for human validation. A developer or administrator reviews the proposed change, examines the evidence supporting it, and either approves deployment or requests modifications. This checkpoint mirrors the HITL pattern we established for compliance overrides, applying the same principle to learning decisions. LangGraph natively supports these checkpoints, enabling developers to pause agent workflows, inspect reasoning traces, and provide corrective guidance.

Approved changes flow to the *Learning Layer*, which updates internal parameters, strategies, or prompts to minimize observed error or maximize reward. This might involve fine-tuning model weights on curated feedback samples, updating prompt templates with new examples, adjusting retrieval strategies to prioritize different context sources, or modifying tool invocation sequences based on success patterns. The Learning Layer applies controlled updates in a manner that preserves traceability: every change is versioned, associated with the feedback that motivated it, and accompanied by evaluation metrics that justify the modification.

Finally, the *Deploy & Test Refined Behavior* stage validates changes before they reach production. Automated test suites validate accuracy, security, and bias metrics. The refined agent runs against held-out evaluation sets to confirm improvements generalize beyond training data. Performance is compared to baseline metrics to ensure changes actually improve outcomes. Only after passing these gates does the refined behavior deploy to production, closing the feedback loop as shown by the arrow returning to Task Execution in *Figure 9.5*.

This architecture transforms agents from static systems into adaptive ones. Each task execution generates observations. Observations inform critiques. Critiques drive planning. Planning proposes adaptations. Adaptations undergo validation. Validated changes deploy and improve future executions. The loop continues indefinitely, with the agent becoming progressively more capable as it accumulates experience.

Learning mechanisms and feedback translation

Self-Improving agents must translate raw feedback into structured signals that inform specific improvements. This translation process varies based on the feedback type and the aspect of agent behavior being optimized.

For Code-Generation agents, explicit feedback arrives when developers accept, modify, or reject generated code. An acceptance signals that the code met requirements. A modification reveals which aspects needed adjustment: the developer changed variable names (indicating style misalignment), added error handling (indicating missing robustness), or restructured logic (indicating architectural mismatch). A rejection indicates fundamental failure. The system captures these signals along with context: the original requirement, the generated code, the developer's changes, and metadata about the project and developer.

Implicit feedback emerges from workflow telemetry. When the *generate, test, refine* loop requires many iterations to converge, this signals that initial code quality was poor or tests were overly strict. When developers frequently invoke the agent for boilerplate tasks but rarely for complex logic, this reveals capability boundaries. When certain code patterns consistently pass tests on the first attempt while others require multiple refinements, this identifies strengths and weaknesses in the agent's training data coverage.

Synthetic feedback comes from automated evaluation. The agent generates code for a curated benchmark of problems with known correct solutions. Metrics capture functional correctness (does it pass tests?), code quality (does it follow best practices?), efficiency (does it have optimal algorithmic complexity?), and maintainability (is it readable and well-structured?). These benchmarks run continuously, tracking how the agent's performance evolves over time and flagging regressions immediately.

The system aggregates these signals into structured improvement hypotheses. When many developers reject code involving asynchronous patterns, the hypothesis might be "insufficient training data on async/await" or "prompt template lacks examples of concurrent operations." When compliance agents generate false positives specifically for test files, the hypothesis might be "policy rules need context-aware exceptions for test environments." These hypotheses then drive specific adaptations: updating training datasets, refining prompts, or adjusting policy configurations.

To make this concrete, the following Pydantic models show how the planner agent structures its improvement hypotheses. These models enforce type safety and validation on the feedback-to-adaptation pipeline, ensuring that every proposed change carries explicit evidence and confidence metrics:

```
from pydantic import BaseModel, Field
from enum import Enum
from typing import List, Optional

class AdaptationType(str, Enum):
    PROMPT_UPDATE = "prompt_update"
    THRESHOLD_ADJUSTMENT = "threshold_adjustment"
    RETRIEVAL_STRATEGY = "retrieval_strategy"
    TOOL_REORDERING = "tool_reordering"

class ImprovementHypothesis(BaseModel):
```

```
    source_signal: str = Field(
        description="Feedback pattern that triggered this hypothesis"
    )
    adaptation_type: AdaptationType
    proposed_change: str = Field(
        description="Specific modification to agent behavior"
    )
    confidence: float = Field(ge=0.0, le=1.0)
    evidence_count: int = Field(
        description="Number of feedback instances supporting this"
    )
    rollback_safe: bool = Field(default=True)

class PlannerOutput(BaseModel):
    hypotheses: List[ImprovementHypothesis]
    requires_human_review: bool = Field(
        description="True if any hypothesis exceeds risk threshold"
    )
    baseline_metrics: dict
```

When the planner agent processes a batch of aggregated feedback, it produces a structured output like the following, which the HITL checkpoint can review before deployment:


```
{
  "hypotheses": [
    {
      "source_signal": "async pattern rejections (23 of 31 async tasks)",
      "adaptation_type": "prompt_update",
      "proposed_change": "Add 3 async/await few-shot examples to code-gen prompt",
      "confidence": 0.87,
      "evidence_count": 23,
      "rollback_safe": true
    },
    {
      "source_signal": "false positives on test files (41% of violations)",
      "adaptation_type": "threshold_adjustment",
      "proposed_change": "Add test-file context exception to compliance rules",
      "confidence": 0.92,
      "evidence_count": 67,
      "rollback_safe": true
    }
  ],
  "requires_human_review": false,
```

```
    "baseline_metrics": {"task_completion": 0.74, "false_positive_rate": 0.41}
  }
```

This structured output maps directly to *Figure 9.5*'s decision point: when `requires_human_review` is `True`, the system routes to the HITL checkpoint; otherwise, high-confidence, rollback-safe changes proceed directly to the learning layer.

Operationalizing continuous adaptation

To ensure controlled evolution, Self-Improving agents are embedded within continuous retraining pipelines that parallel the CI/CD pipelines we established for code deployment. This alignment ensures that agent improvements follow the same governance, testing, and rollback procedures as application code.

The pipeline begins with **data capture**, where interaction logs and user feedback are ingested into a data lake. For Code-Generation agents, this includes all generated code, test results, refinement iterations, and developer feedback. For compliance agents, this includes detected violations, remediations proposed, human overrides granted, and justifications provided. These logs are comprehensive, capturing not just outcomes but the full reasoning trace: which context was retrieved, which tools were invoked, and which intermediate decisions were made.

Preprocessing filters and prepares this data for training. Relevant sessions are selected based on quality signals: interactions where users provided explicit feedback, cases where multiple refinement iterations revealed interesting failure modes, or examples that cover underrepresented patterns. Data is labeled with ground truth where available: accepted code is labeled as positive examples, rejected code as negative examples, and modified code provides paired examples showing desired transformations. Filtering removes low-quality or potentially harmful examples: interactions where users provided abusive feedback, cases where policy violations were incorrectly overridden, or examples that reinforce undesirable behaviors.

Fine-tuning or **adapter updates** apply the curated feedback to improve agent behavior. Full model fine-tuning updates the base LLM's weights using the prepared dataset, potentially improving general capabilities but at significant computational cost and risk of catastrophic forgetting. Adapter-based approaches like Low-Rank Adaptation (LoRA) update small parameter matrices that modify the base model's behavior for specific tasks, preserving general capabilities while specializing for observed patterns. Prompt template updates incorporate successful examples into few-shot demonstrations without model training, offering rapid adaptation with minimal computational cost. The choice depends on the scale and nature of required improvements.

Evaluation validates changes before deployment using the same multi-dimensional assessment we established for Code-Generation agents. Automated test suites confirm that accuracy improvements on target tasks don't degrade performance on baseline capabilities. Security scans verify that adaptations don't introduce new vulnerabilities or policy violations. Bias metrics check that learning doesn't amplify problematic patterns from training data. Performance benchmarks ensure changes don't increase latency or computational cost beyond acceptable thresholds. Only changes that pass all gates advance to production deployment.

This process aligns with **MLOps for Agents**, ensuring that adaptation remains governed, traceable, and reversible. Every model version is tracked with its training data, evaluation metrics, and deployment timestamp. Rollback mechanisms allow instant reversion if production metrics degrade. Audit logs capture which feedback influenced which adaptations, supporting transparency and accountability.

Practical implementation: Adaptive customer support agent in production

The architectural patterns and feedback mechanisms we've described translate into measurable impact when deployed in production environments. This case study examines a complete implementation of a Self-Improving agent in a customer support context, demonstrating how the closed-loop control system from *Figure 9.5* operates continuously to enhance agent capabilities.

A leading fintech firm deployed a LangGraph-based **Adaptive Support Agent** to handle customer inquiries about account management, transaction disputes, and product features. The agent operated as the first point of contact, handling straightforward queries autonomously and escalating complex cases to human agents. This deployment context provided rich feedback signals: every interaction produced observable outcomes (resolved, escalated, or unsuccessful), explicit feedback (customer satisfaction ratings), and implicit feedback (conversation length, escalation frequency, follow-up queries).

The challenge

The Code-Generation and compliance agents we have examined operate on well-defined loops: generate code, run tests, refine until correct; scan for violations, evaluate against policy, remediate findings. These loops execute within a single development cycle and reset for each new task. Production systems, however, face a different class of problem: performance that degrades gradually as user needs evolve, edge cases accumulate, and the operating environment shifts. A customer support agent that performed well at launch may struggle months later as product features change, user expectations shift, and new failure modes emerge. The challenge is to build agents that do not merely execute tasks but learn from their operational history, identify performance trends, and adapt their strategies without requiring manual retraining for every new pattern.

Multi-modal feedback collection

The system implemented the Sensing Layer from our architectural framework through multiple feedback channels. Each support interaction was labeled based on outcome: resolved interactions where the customer's issue was fully addressed without escalation, escalated interactions where the agent determined it lacked sufficient context or authority to proceed, and unsuccessful interactions where the customer expressed dissatisfaction or required multiple attempts to achieve resolution.

Explicit feedback arrived through post-interaction surveys where customers rated their experience on a five-point scale and optionally provided free-text comments. The system used sentiment analysis to extract structured signals from these comments, identifying patterns like "the agent didn't understand my question" or "the response was technically correct but unhelpful."

Implicit feedback emerged from conversation telemetry: the number of turns required to resolve an issue, the frequency of rephrased questions indicating the agent misunderstood initial queries, and the rate at which customers abandoned conversations mid-thread. These behavioral signals revealed capability gaps that explicit ratings might miss.

The critique and planning loop

Aggregated feedback flowed to the critic agent, which evaluated performance across multiple dimensions. *Task completion rate* measured the percentage of interactions resolved without escalation. *Response relevance* scored how well answers addressed the actual customer question versus providing tangential information. *Tone appropriateness* assessed whether responses matched the emotional context of the inquiry (empathetic for complaints, informative for product questions, urgent for time-sensitive issues).

The critic identified specific failure modes through pattern analysis. When analyzing failed conversations, it discovered that the agent frequently mishandled queries about recent policy changes, responding with outdated information because its retrieval system prioritized historical documentation over recent updates. It detected tone mismatches, where the agent provided technically accurate but overly formal responses to frustrated customers, missing opportunities to acknowledge their concern before presenting solutions.

The planner agent synthesized these critiques into concrete improvement hypotheses. For the outdated information problem, it proposed adjusting the retrieval strategy to weight recency more heavily for policy-related queries. For the tone mismatch issue, it hypothesized that the prompt template needed explicit instructions for emotional context adaptation, with examples demonstrating empathetic acknowledgment before solution presentation.

To make the planner agent's reasoning concrete, consider the following structured improvement record that the system generates after analyzing a batch of underperforming interactions. This record captures the hypothesis, supporting evidence, proposed adaptation, and validation criteria in a format that both automated systems and human reviewers can evaluate.

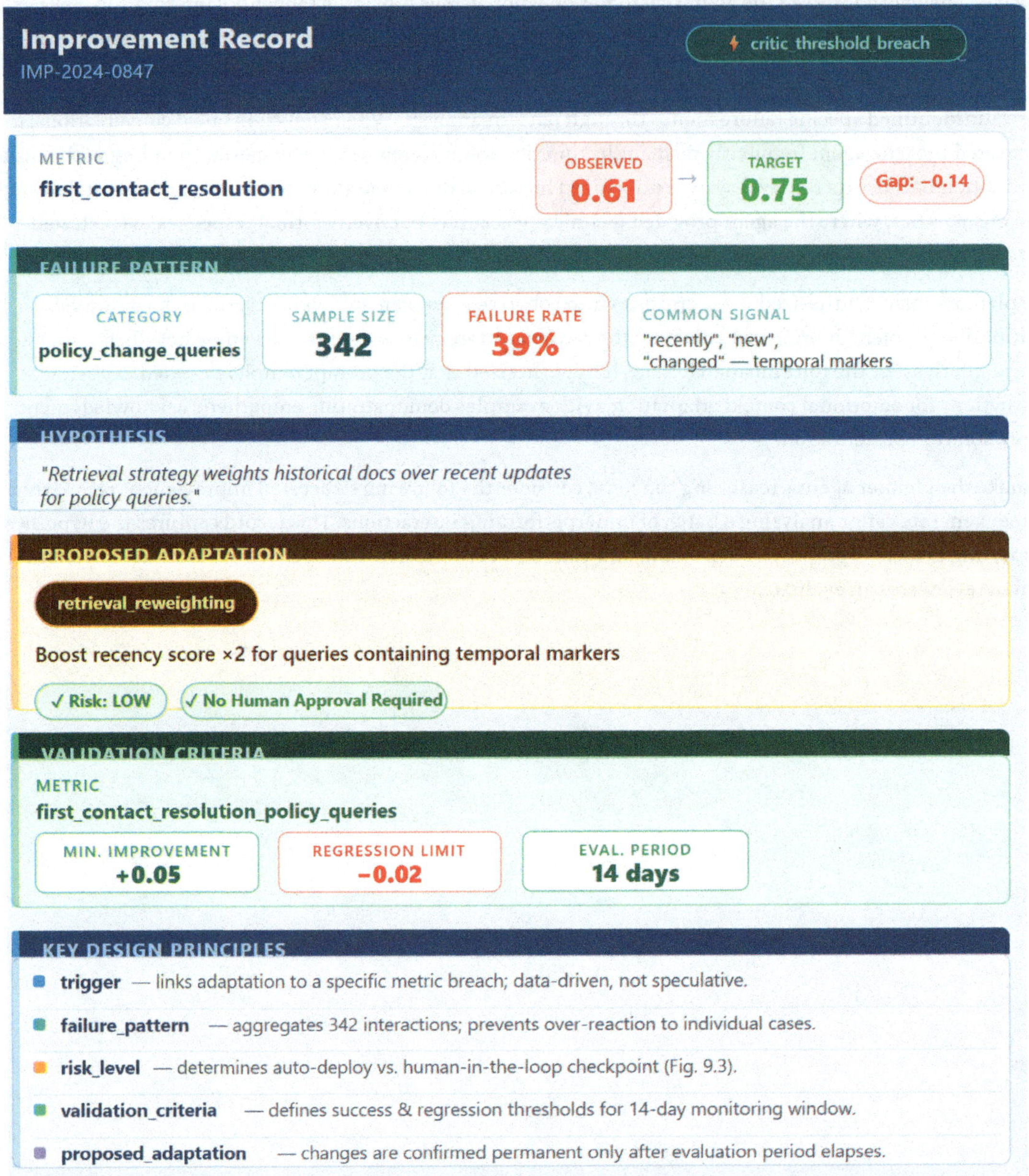

Figure 9.6 – Structured improvement record generated by the planner agent after analyzing underperforming interactions

This record illustrates several key design principles. The trigger field links the improvement to a specific metric breach, ensuring adaptations are data-driven rather than speculative. The `failure_pattern` section aggregates evidence from hundreds of interactions, preventing the system from overreacting to individual cases. The `risk_level` classification determines whether the change can deploy automatically or requires the HITL checkpoint from *Figure 9.5*. The `validation_criteria` define success and regression thresholds, ensuring that deployed changes are monitored for the specified evaluation period before being confirmed as permanent improvements.

Automated adaptations and human validation

Several adaptation mechanisms operated in parallel, each targeting different aspects of agent behavior:

- **Automatic prompt adjustment:** The system analyzed failed conversations to identify missing contextual cues. When customers asked about "the new fees," the agent often requested clarification instead of inferring from recent announcements that they meant the pricing changes implemented last month. The Learning Layer updated the prompt template to include the following: `Before requesting clarification, check recent announcements and company updates to infer context from temporal references.` This adaptation deployed automatically after validation on held-out conversations confirmed it reduced clarification requests without increasing incorrect inferences.
- **Adaptive tone optimization**: Linguistic sentiment analysis detected that responses to angry or frustrated customers followed the same template as responses to neutral inquiries. The Planner proposed incorporating emotional context into response generation. However, this change required human validation at the checkpoint shown in *Figure 9.5*, as modifying tone could introduce risks (appearing insincere, over-apologizing, or implying company fault where none existed). A customer support manager reviewed example adaptations, approved the general strategy with guidelines constraining how strongly emotional language could be used, and the refined behavior deployed.
- **Confidence-based escalation refinement**: Initially, the agent used a fixed confidence threshold for escalation decisions: any query where the model's top response had less than a 70% confidence score triggered escalation. Analysis revealed this threshold was too conservative, escalating queries the agent could have handled correctly. The critic agent evaluated model confidence scores against actual outcomes, discovering that responses with 60-65% confidence succeeded 85% of the time. The system lowered the escalation threshold to 55%, then monitored outcomes closely for two weeks. When success rates remained stable and escalation frequency dropped by 12%, the change was confirmed permanent.

Each adaptation followed the validation pipeline we established: changes were tested on evaluation sets, monitored in production with careful metrics tracking, and retained an immutable version history enabling instant rollback if problems emerged.

Measured improvement trajectory

After two quarters of continuous operation and adaptation, the system demonstrated measurable improvements across all tracked dimensions. *First-contact resolution* increased by 18%, meaning nearly one-fifth more customers had their issues fully resolved without requiring escalation or follow-up. *Average ticket resolution time* decreased by 23%, reducing customer wait times and freeing human agents to focus on complex cases. *Customer satisfaction* scores improved from 3.8 to 4.2 on a five-point scale, with qualitative feedback highlighting that the agent "understood context better" and "responded more naturally."

More importantly, the company achieved a virtuous cycle characteristic of well-designed Self-Improving systems. Every user interaction contributed directly to the agent's future competence. Successful resolutions reinforced effective strategies. Failures revealed capability gaps that drove targeted improvements. Human escalations provided high-quality training examples showing how expert agents handle difficult cases. The agent's capabilities grew not through expensive retraining campaigns but through continuous, incremental learning from real-world usage.

The system's *improvement velocity*—the rate at which new corrections led to measurable gains—remained stable across the two-quarter period, indicating that learning had not plateaued. The agent continued discovering new patterns and refining existing strategies without degradation in baseline capabilities, a key indicator of healthy adaptation rather than overfitting to recent feedback.

Governance and ethical safeguards

While Self-Improving agents enhance productivity and reduce operational costs, they also introduce governance challenges that require explicit safeguards. Uncontrolled adaptation can drift from compliance boundaries, accumulate hidden biases, or optimize for metrics that don't align with organizational values. The fintech case study implemented several protective mechanisms that generalize to any Self-Improving agent deployment:

- **Update thresholds and human validation**: Not all adaptations deployed automatically. The system categorized proposed changes by risk level. Low-risk changes like minor prompt adjustments or retrieval parameter tuning deployed automatically after passing evaluation gates. Medium-risk changes like new response templates or significant threshold adjustments required human review at the checkpoint shown in *Figure 9.5*. High-risk changes like model fine-tuning or fundamental strategy shifts required approval from cross-functional teams, including customer support leadership, legal compliance, and technical operations.
- **Explainable AI for behavioral tracing**: The system employed explainability tools to trace which feedback influenced specific behavioral shifts. When the agent's tone changed in responses to frustrated customers, operators could query the audit trail to see exactly which customer interactions, sentiment scores, and Planner hypotheses motivated the adaptation. This transparency enabled validation that changes aligned with company values and allowed reversal if adaptations proved problematic.
- **Immutable version history and rollback**: Every model version, prompt template revision, and configuration change was retained in an immutable version history. Each version was tagged with its training data, evaluation metrics, deployment timestamp, and the feedback that motivated the change. When a prompt adjustment inadvertently caused the agent to over-promise resolution timeframes, operators identified the problematic version within minutes, rolled back to the previous stable version, and added evaluation tests to prevent similar regressions in future updates.
- **Bias monitoring and mitigation**: Continuous monitoring tracked whether agent behavior varied systematically across customer demographics. Analysis revealed that the agent escalated queries more frequently for customers using certain phrasings common in non-native English speakers, even though the underlying questions were no more complex. This bias emerged because training data overrepresented native English patterns. The system flagged this deviation, and the Learning Layer received curated examples demonstrating correct handling of varied phrasings, reducing escalation bias without degrading performance on other dimensions. Pattern drift is detected by clustering sentence embeddings of the agent's outputs across rolling time windows. When the embedding distribution shifts beyond a configured threshold (typically measured via Kullback-Leibler divergence or cosine similarity degradation), the system flags a potential drift event and triggers a human review of the

agent's recent adaptation trajectory to determine whether the behavioral change is beneficial specialization or harmful convergence.

> **Note**
>
> A related concern is over-personalization, where an agent optimizes so aggressively for individual user patterns that it narrows the range of solutions it considers. For instance, a Code-Generation agent that learns a developer always prefers certain libraries may stop suggesting better alternatives, while a support agent that over-adapts to a customer segment's phrasing may become less effective with other populations. Mitigations include diversity constraints that require the agent to maintain a minimum variety in its outputs, held-out evaluation sets drawn from underrepresented interaction patterns, and periodic human review of adaptation trajectories to ensure that the agent's evolution remains aligned with organizational goals rather than converging on local optima.

These safeguards ensure alignment with the ethical and transparency principles that govern AI system deployment. Self-Improving agents must remain under human control even as they gain autonomy in specific operational decisions. The governance framework balances the benefits of continuous learning against the risks of unconstrained adaptation, enabling systems to evolve safely within defined boundaries.

Integration with the development lifecycle

Self-Improving agents extend the patterns we've established throughout this chapter into a continuous operational mode. Where Code-Generation agents execute a *generate, test, refine* loop to produce correct implementations, and compliance agents execute a *scan, evaluate, remediate* loop to enforce policies, Self-Improving agents execute an *execute, observe, learn, adapt* loop that operates across all agent types.

A Code-Generation agent that is also self-improving learns from developer feedback which code patterns are accepted most frequently, which edge cases commonly require manual correction, and which project-specific conventions should guide generation. A compliance agent that is self-improving learns from human overrides which policy rules generate excessive false positives, which remediation strategies developers find most useful, and how policies should adapt to new regulatory guidance. This capability transforms agents from tools that execute fixed strategies into collaborative systems that adapt to organizational context and evolving requirements.

The architectural components remain consistent: sensing layers collect feedback, critic agents evaluate outcomes, planner agents synthesize improvement hypotheses, learning layers apply adaptations, and deployment pipelines ensure changes meet quality and safety standards. The feedback loops close continuously, with each task execution informing future behavior. This convergence of TDG, policy-aware enforcement, and continuous learning represents the full realization of intelligent software development agents: systems that not only automate development tasks but also improve their own capabilities through structured experience.

Summary

Software development agents bring together the precision of code, the adaptability of learning systems, and the structured logic of classical software engineering. By automating routine tasks, enforcing security policies, and enabling continuous improvement, these agents are transforming the role of developers from coders to orchestrators of intelligent workflows.

Each agent class addresses a distinct dimension of autonomous software engineering through a characteristic feedback loop. Code-Generation agents execute a *generate, test, refine* loop that transforms natural language specifications into verified implementations, using executable test suites as the governing signal for iterative improvement. Compliance-Driven agents execute a *scan, evaluate, remediate* loop that embeds policy enforcement directly into the development workflow, shifting governance from a manual post-deployment gate to a continuous, automated process. Self-Improving agents execute an Execute, Observe, Learn, Adapt loop that enables agents to evolve their strategies based on operational feedback, translating accumulated experience into measurable performance gains without manual retraining.

The unifying architectural principle across all three classes is that structured feedback loops, combined with multi-agent orchestration and HITL checkpoints, enable progressive autonomy while maintaining the governance and traceability required for production systems. The patterns established here, including stateful workflow graphs, iterative refinement through concrete validation signals, and layered agent specialization, provide the building blocks for the more complex multi-domain agent systems explored in subsequent chapters.

This chapter examined the foundational concepts and real-world applications of three classes of agents. As the field evolves, software teams will increasingly rely on such agents not only to accelerate development, but to ensure quality, security, and adaptability at scale. In the next chapter we will be implementing conversational and content creation agents that bridge the gap between algorithmic logic and human interaction.

Get This Book's PDF Version and Exclusive Extras

Scan the QR code (or go to `packtpub.com/unlock`). Search for this book by name, confirm the edition, and then follow the steps on the page.

UNLOCK NOW

Note: Keep your invoice handy. Purchases made directly from Packt don't require an invoice.

10

Conversational and Content Creation Agents

We can only see a short distance ahead, but we can see plenty there that needs to be done.

— Alan M. Turing

In the previous chapters, we explored agents specialized for rigorous logical synthesis and software development. We now turn our attention to agents that interact directly with the human experience. Conversational and Content Creation agents represent the creative and social interface of artificial intelligence. Unlike software development agents that prioritize syntactic correctness and logic, these agents must master the nuances of tone, context, empathy, and aesthetic coherence. They transform relatively raw generative potential into structured, meaningful interactions that prioritize engaging users and producing high-value content. For the engineer, the core challenge is designing systems that sustain coherent behavior across long interactions, enforce safety and brand constraints deterministically, and coordinate multiple generation stages without sacrificing reliability.

To achieve this, this class of agents moves beyond simple request-response loops to establish sustained engagement. Whether acting as an empathetic support companion or a brand-aligned marketing strategist, these systems rely on sophisticated architecture to maintain continuity and relevance over time. Mastering these agents requires understanding how to model personality, enforce stylistic consistency, and balance algorithmic exploration with user preference exploitation.

In this chapter, we will explore two distinct architectures that bridge the gap between algorithmic logic and human interaction. We begin with the **Conversational agent**, examining the dialog management systems and personality modeling techniques required to sustain meaningful engagement. Next, we analyze the **Content Creation agent**, focusing on frameworks that enable the generation of brand-consistent, multi-modal assets.

In this chapter, we'll be covering the following topics:

- The Conversational agent
- The Content Creation agent

Technical requirements

To run the examples in this chapter, you will need the following:

- Python 3.10 or later
- The following Python packages: `langchain==0.2.16`, `langchain-openai==0.1.23`, `openai==1.40.0`, `faiss-cpu==1.8.0`, and `python-dotenv==1.0.1`
- An OpenAI API key with access to the `gpt-4o` and `text-embedding-3-small` models

All code examples for this chapter are available in the book's GitHub repository at `https://github.com/PacktPublishing/30-Agents-Every-AI-Engineer-Must-Build/chapter10`

The Conversational agent

Conversational agents are autonomous, goal-aware systems that use natural language as their primary interface while maintaining conversational state, context, and behavioral consistency across interactions. This section examines the engineering architecture that makes this possible: how these agents manage dialog state, dual-memory hierarchies, personality constraints, and multi-turn orchestration. These are the design challenges that distinguish a Conversational agent from a stateless language model call.

Earlier systems approached conversation as pattern substitution: from rule-based chatbots to early neural seq2seq models, they treated each exchange as a stateless transaction. What they lacked was precisely what defines the agent: persistent memory, goal awareness, and the capacity to align behavior with a consistent identity across turns.

Formally, a Conversational agent can be characterized by the following properties:

- **Persistent context:** The agent maintains state across multiple turns and, in many cases, across sessions
- **Intent awareness:** User input is interpreted in terms of goals, constraints, and implicit signals rather than isolated utterances
- **Dialog management:** The agent actively manages the flow of conversation, including clarification, topic shifts, and resolution strategies
- **Behavioral consistency:** Responses adhere to a defined *persona*, tone, and ethical boundary
- **Tool and memory integration:** The agent can retrieve information, invoke tools, and recall relevant past interactions when appropriate

This definition distinguishes Conversational agents from simpler chat interfaces or stateless LLM wrappers. A system that merely responds to prompts without tracking dialogue state or enforcing behavioral constraints does not meet the architectural threshold of an agent, regardless of the sophistication of its language model.

From an architectural standpoint, Conversational agents are a specialization of the memory-augmented and planning-capable agents introduced in *Chapter 5*. What differentiates them is not the presence of reasoning alone, but the requirement to continuously align system behavior with human conversational norms.

Why conversational agents are necessary

The need for Conversational agents arises from a fundamental mismatch between how humans express intent and how traditional software systems accept input. Humans communicate through incomplete statements, references to prior context, emotional cues, and implicit assumptions. APIs and workflows, by contrast, demand explicit parameters, strict schemas, and deterministic control flow.

Conversational agents function as a cognitive interface layer between these two worlds. They translate fluid human intent into structured actions while preserving continuity, meaning, and trust over time. This role becomes critical in domains such as customer support, healthcare, education, and enterprise productivity, where interactions are rarely resolved in a single turn.

Equally important is the shift from transactional interaction to relational interaction. As systems are expected to assist users over days, weeks, or months, the absence of memory and continuity becomes a liability. Stateless systems force users to repeatedly restate goals and preferences, degrading both efficiency and user confidence. Conversational agents address this by modeling dialogue as an evolving process rather than a sequence of isolated requests.

From a systems perspective, Conversational agents also provide a unifying abstraction for integrating reasoning, memory, and tools. As we will see in this chapter, effective Conversational agents are not monolithic components but orchestrated architectures that balance responsiveness with deliberation. This balance mirrors the hybrid agent patterns discussed in *Chapter 5* and foreshadows the recommendation and content generation agents explored later in this chapter.

With this historical and architectural grounding established, we now turn to the internal mechanics of Conversational agents, beginning with dialog management and context tracking.

Natural dialog management and context tracking

At the core of a Conversational agent is the **dialog manager**, a component responsible for maintaining the state of the conversation. Unlike simple LLM wrappers that treat every prompt as a new event, a sophisticated agent utilizes context tracking mechanisms to persist information across long conversations. This system possesses the intelligence to determine what to remember and what to forget, a defining feature of modern advanced Conversational agents.

Architecturally, this involves a modular, stateful framework that separates the sensing of inputs from the cognitive reasoning engine. To implement advanced context tracking, we model conversation history not as a linear log, but as a high-dimensional vector space. Relevant past interactions are retrieved based on semantic similarity to the current user query, mimicking the human brain's ability to recall associations without replaying an entire life history. This process involves managing a context window where relevant history is summarized and stored in working memory, while less relevant details are archived in long-term vector stores.

The dual-memory hierarchy

In production environments, simply appending the entire conversation history to the prompt is computationally expensive and leads to latency issues or context overflow. To mitigate this, engineers employ a dual-memory structure, often referred to as the retrieval-augmented dialogue (RAD) loop. This hierarchy functions as follows:

- **Working memory (RAM):** This layer maintains the most recent exchanges in their raw format to preserve immediate context. It is characterized by extremely low latency and a recency-based (FIFO) retrieval mechanism.
- **Semantic memory (Disk):** Older interactions are periodically summarized into a concise narrative or "gist" and stored in persistent state systems like Redis or PostgreSQL. This archival memory allows for the retrieval of past associations using semantic similarity, such as cosine similarity, enabling the agent to recall specific details from weeks or months prior.

Implementation insight: Efficient context management

To ensure the agent remains performant as dialogue grows, engineers often utilize the `ConversationSummaryBufferMemory` pattern. This pattern allows the agent to maintain situational awareness across turns by balancing the depth of context retrieval with execution speed. When a user provides a new query, the system performs a similarity search against the vector store to find the most relevant past entries. These recalled snippets are then injected into the current context window as a "context hint," allowing the agent to generate responses that are both contextually aware of the current session and historically grounded in long-term user data.

As we discussed in the foundations of agent architecture, this modularity allows for distributed evaluation and parallel processing of reasoning tasks, ensuring that the conversational flow remains both robust and scalable. This structural separation is what allows a mental health support agent, for instance, to remember an "exam" mentioned weeks ago without losing the thread of the current conversation.

Personality modeling techniques

Beyond the mechanics of memory and context, a Conversational agent must exhibit a stable and recognizable *persona*. If memory governs what the agent knows and recalls, personality governs how that knowledge is expressed. Without an explicit personality model, even technically correct responses can feel inconsistent, inappropriate, or untrustworthy across interactions.

Personality modeling in Conversational agents is not an emergent property of stochastic text generation. It is an architectural choice. Production-grade systems achieve consistency through deliberate constraints applied at multiple layers of the agent stack, ensuring that the agent behaves as a coherent character rather than a generic language model reacting opportunistically to each prompt.

At its core, *personality* defines the agent's communicative contract with the user. This contract encompasses tone, formality, empathy, assertiveness, ethical posture, and conversational boundaries. Violating this contract, even subtly, erodes user trust, particularly in long-running or sensitive interactions.

From an architectural standpoint, personality is implemented as a first-class layer, commonly referred to as the Profile or Persona layer. This layer sits alongside memory, planning, and reasoning components and influences every generated response.

The *persona* layer typically specifies:

- **Tone and voice**, such as empathetic, professional, instructional, or neutral

- **Interaction style**, for example, asking reflective questions versus issuing directives
- **Ethical and safety boundaries**, defining what the agent must refuse, escalate, or soften
- **Domain posture**, such as advisory versus authoritative behavior
- **Linguistic constraints**, including verbosity, formality, and rhetorical structure

Crucially, this layer is persistent. Unlike ad hoc prompt modifications, *persona* constraints apply across turns and sessions, ensuring behavioral continuity even as topics change.

Theoretically, a *persona* can be understood as a set of behavioral constraints applied to the language model's output distribution. These constraints do not determine exact responses, but they bias generation toward a consistent behavioral region of the model's latent space.

For example, defining a *persona* as empathetic increases the likelihood of validation-oriented language such as acknowledgment, reflective phrasing, and emotional mirroring, while reducing the probability of terse, prescriptive, or emotionally neutral responses. Conversely, a compliance-focused *persona* may suppress speculative language and favor cautious, qualified phrasing.

Personality is not randomness; it is controlled bias.

The subsections that follow present three concrete techniques for implementing personality at production scale. The first technique, *system prompting as persona initialization*, establishes the agent's immutable behavioral rules at startup. The second technique, *few-shot conditioning, and behavioral anchoring*, grounds those rules in exemplar interactions that demonstrate desired tone and style. The third technique, *dynamic persona modulation*, enables controlled, policy-governed shifts in *persona* traits based on context or user role. Together, these three layers form a composable personality stack that can be tuned independently.

System prompting as persona initialization

In practice, personality modeling is primarily instantiated through system-level prompting. The system prompt serves as the initialization boundary for the *persona* layer, defining immutable characteristics that persist throughout the interaction.

Unlike user prompts, which represent external input, system prompts function as internal configuration. They are not suggestions but constraints. A well-designed system prompt avoids stylistic verbosity and instead encodes clear behavioral rules, such as:

- What the agent is and is not
- How uncertainty should be handled
- Whether advice, opinions, or emotional reassurance are permitted
- How conflicts or sensitive topics must be approached

This mirrors the role of configuration in traditional software systems. Just as a service is initialized with environment variables and policy flags, a Conversational agent is initialized with *persona* parameters that shape all downstream behavior.

Few-shot conditioning and behavioral anchoring

While system prompts define the boundaries of behavior, few-shot examples anchor those boundaries in concrete linguistic patterns. These examples demonstrate not only what the agent should say, but how it should say it in realistic scenarios.

Few-shot conditioning is particularly important for subtle traits such as empathy, restraint, or professional tone, which are difficult to encode declaratively. By presenting exemplar interactions, the agent learns to internalize patterns of phrasing, pacing, and response structure that align with the intended *persona*.

Architecturally, these examples are part of the *persona* layer rather than the task layer. They are reused across interactions and tasks, reinforcing consistency even as the agent's functional responsibilities vary.

Dynamic persona modulation

Although *personas* are persistent, they are not necessarily static. Advanced Conversational agents support controlled *persona* modulation, allowing certain traits to be adjusted based on context, user role, or domain constraints.

For example, the same agent may adopt:

- A warmer, more supportive tone in exploratory phases
- A more concise, directive tone during task execution
- A cautious, compliance-oriented posture in regulated workflows

This modulation is governed by policy, not improvisation. The dialog manager signals allowable *persona* shifts, and the *persona* layer adjusts its constraints accordingly. This preserves coherence while enabling flexibility, a balance that mirrors human conversational adaptation.

Ultimately, personality modeling is not cosmetic. It is a trust mechanism. Users infer reliability, safety, and competence not only from what an agent says, but from how it says it. Inconsistent tone, inappropriate confidence, or sudden shifts in demeanor are interpreted as system instability.

By treating personality as an explicit architectural component rather than an emergent side effect, Conversational agents achieve predictability, alignment, and long-term usability. This becomes especially critical in domains explored later in the book, such as healthcare, finance, and education, where behavioral misalignment carries real-world consequences.

With personality constraints in place, we can now examine how these agents handle high-stakes interactions where tone, memory, and safety converge. The following case study illustrates how dialog management and persona modeling are combined in practice within a mental health support agent.

Case study: Implementing an empathetic mental health support agent

This case study builds a mental health support agent to demonstrate how safety layers, dual-memory continuity, and *persona* constraints work together under high-stakes conditions. The architectural concepts introduced in the preceding sections converge most clearly in high-stakes, human-centered domains. Few applications place stronger demands on conversational continuity, behavioral consistency, and safety guarantees than mental health support. In this context, failures are not merely inconvenient. They can erode trust, amplify distress, or cause tangible harm.

A mental health support agent therefore serves as an instructive stress test for Conversational agent architecture. It requires the system to integrate dialog management, long-term memory, and persona modeling under strict safety constraints. Unlike transactional assistants, which may tolerate occasional incoherence or stylistic drift, a mental health agent must exhibit predictable behavior across interactions that may span weeks or months. The agent must remember emotionally salient events, respond with a stable and empathetic tone, and enforce non-negotiable safety boundaries regardless of conversational context.

This domain highlights a critical architectural shift. Simple input-output loops, even when powered by large language models, are insufficient. The system must prioritize deterministic safety over generative flexibility and longitudinal continuity over short-term conversational fluency. Creative language generation becomes secondary to reliability, consistency, and controlled response behavior.

To illustrate the operational flow of these requirements, we examine the reference architecture for an empathetic mental health support agent. This design decomposes the system into explicit layers responsible for safety enforcement, context persistence, and persona-driven response generation. The following diagram details the internal mechanics and decision pathways that govern how the system processes user input while maintaining strict adherence to safety and empathy protocols.

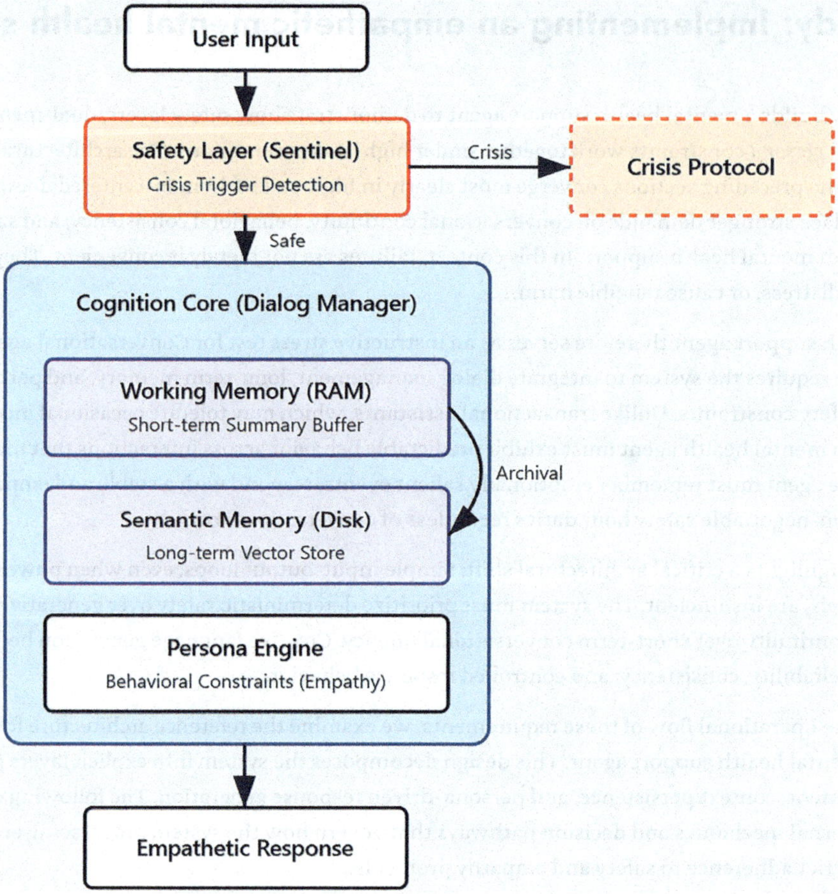

Figure 10.1 – High-level architecture of a safety-aware Conversational agent with dialog management, memory hierarchy, and persona-driven response layers

As illustrated in *Figure 10.1*, the architecture follows a vertical pipeline where every user interaction is subjected to multiple layers of validation and contextualization before a response is synthesized:

- **Safety layer (sentinel)**: Positioned at the entry point, this component acts as a deterministic circuit breaker. It scans incoming text for crisis triggers or harmful intent. If a risk is identified, the system immediately diverts the flow to a predefined Crisis Protocol, bypassing the generative cognition core entirely to ensure absolute safety.
- **Cognition core (dialog manager)**: Once input is cleared by the Sentinel, it enters the primary reasoning engine. This core functions as the executive coordinator, managing the interplay between current state and historical knowledge to ensure the agent's behavior remains coherent over time.

- **Memory hierarchy**: The system applies the dual-memory hierarchy introduced earlier in this section: working memory for the live session thread and semantic memory for long-term archival recall.
- **Persona engine**: Working in tandem with the memory layers, the Persona Engine enforces behavioral constraints on the generated output. It ensures that the agent's tone remains empathetic and non-directive, adhering to the stable "supportive peer" character established in the initial system prompts.

The subsections that follow translate each layer of this architecture into working code. We begin by implementing the vertical pipeline as a whole, then examine each component in detail: the cognition core as an executive coordinator, the memory hierarchy in practice, the dialog manager turn loop, and finally the persona engine as a constraint layer.

Implementing the vertical pipeline

The diagram's most important design choice is ordering. Every request is processed top-down: the system first decides whether it is safe to proceed, then constructs context from short- and long-term memory, and only then invokes generative behavior under *persona* constraints. In other words, generation is downstream of policy. That is exactly what the Safety Layer is for: it behaves like a deterministic circuit breaker, ensuring that a crisis path never depends on probabilistic text generation.

The following snippet implements a `SafetyLayer` class that screens for crisis triggers and returns a predefined protocol response, bypassing all further processing:

```
class SafetyLayer:
    def __init__(self):
        self.triggers = ["hurt myself", "suicide", "end my life", "harm"]

    def is_safe(self, text: str) -> bool:
        # Returns False if a crisis keyword is detected
        return not any(trigger in text.lower() for trigger in self.triggers)

    def get_crisis_protocol(self) -> str:
        return (
            "I'm hearing that you're in a lot of pain. I am an AI and cannot "
            "provide emergency help. Please call 988 immediately."
        )
```

This structure reflects an architectural principle discussed earlier in the chapter: safety should be implemented as a validator that is external to the language model, not as "good behavior we hope the model will remember." The sentinel sits upstream specifically so that "creative generation" cannot accidentally occur when the situation demands strict escalation behavior.

The cognition core as an executive coordinator

Once input is cleared, responsibility shifts to the cognition core (dialog manager). In *Figure 10.1*, this core is drawn as a container because it is not a single algorithm; it is the coordinator that decides the following:

- What context to assemble from the current turn and session history

- What to retrieve from short-term and long-term memory stores
- What behavioral constraints to apply from the *persona* layer
- How to update memory after the turn completes

A clean implementation pattern is to keep memory as a dependency of the core, not embedded inside prompting logic. That separation is what makes the memory hierarchy testable.

Memory hierarchy in practice

Figure 10.1 distinguishes between working memory (RAM) and semantic memory (Disk) for a practical reason: these stores have different latency, retention, and access patterns. Working memory needs low latency and can tolerate lossy compression (summaries). Long-term memory must be searchable across time and can be slower, but it must preserve meaning and salience.

A working memory implementation typically keeps recent turns and progressively summarizes older context. The `ConversationSummaryBufferMemory` pattern below does exactly that, acting as the short-term "summary buffer" described in the diagram:

```
from langchain.memory import ConversationSummaryBufferMemory

class ContextManager:
    """
    The Chronicler: Implements semantic continuity through a dual-memory structure.
    """
    def __init__(self, llm):

# working_memory keeps recent raw text and summarizes older history
        self.working_memory = ConversationSummaryBufferMemory(
            llm=llm,
            max_token_limit=300,
            return_messages=True
        )

        self.long_term_store = []
# Simulated Vector Store for semantic retrieval
```

The arrow labeled *Archival* in *Figure 10.1* represents the moment when the system decides that a snippet should persist beyond the short window. Even in a simplified form, the key is to treat archival as an explicit operation, not an accidental side-effect of "keeping the full transcript":

```
    def archive_meaningful_context(self, interaction: str):
        """Stores key emotional data points into a high-dimensional vector space."""
        self.long_term_store.append(interaction)
```

In production, semantic memory should not be a plain list; it is typically a vector index (FAISS locally, or a managed store such as Pinecone/Milvus/Weaviate). The important teaching moment is that semantic recall is not keyword search. The system embeds both stored memories and the current query into a high-dimensional space and retrieves by similarity.

The following snippet shows a minimal FAISS-backed *semantic memory* that supports archival and retrieval:

```
from langchain_community.vectorstores import FAISS
from langchain_openai import OpenAIEmbeddings

class SemanticMemory:
    """
    The Long-Term Store: Enables retrieval of past associations using semantic
similarity.
    """
    def __init__(self):
        self.embeddings = OpenAIEmbeddings()
        self.vector_db = None

    def archive_event(self, text: str):
        """Converts a conversation snippet into a vector and stores it."""
        if self.vector_db is None:
            self.vector_db = FAISS.from_texts([text], self.embeddings)
        else:
            self.vector_db.add_texts([text])
```

Retrieval then becomes a direct expression of the diagram's "Disk" behavior: given the current query, `fetch` the most semantically relevant prior snippet and inject it into the live context window:

```
    def retrieve_relevant_context(self, current_query: str) -> str:
        if self.vector_db is None:
            return ""

        docs = self.vector_db.similarity_search(current_query, k=1)
        return docs[0].page_content if docs else ""
```

Note

Because this store may contain highly sensitive personal data, the architectural security requirement is not optional. At minimum, encryption at rest, and strong access controls should be treated as baseline requirements for the semantic layer in this domain.

The dialog manager turn loop

The full pipeline becomes clear when you look at a single "turn handler" that follows the diagram's vertical ordering:

- Sentinel check
- Retrieve working context
- Generate under *persona* constraints
- Write back to memory

The snippet below captures that orchestration. Notice that generation occurs only after safety and context assembly, and memory update is a deliberate step at the end of the turn.

```
from langchain_core.messages import HumanMessage

def handle_query(self, user_input: str):
    # 1. Safety Check (Immediate)
    if not self.safety.is_safe(user_input):
        return self.safety.get_crisis_protocol()

    # 2. Context Retrieval (Semantic Continuity)
    history = self.context.working_memory.load_memory_variables({})['history']

    # 3. Empathetic Generation
    full_context = [self.system_prompt] + history + [HumanMessage(content=user_input)]
    response = self.llm.invoke(full_context)

    # 4. Memory Update
    self.context.working_memory.save_context({"input": user_input}, {"output":
response.content})

    return response.content
```

This is the operational meaning of the diagram's claim that a mental health support agent must prioritize deterministic safety and longitudinal continuity over unconstrained fluency. The architecture is not a conceptual diagram painted over a single LLM call. It is a set of enforced boundaries that determine whether generation is allowed, what generation is conditioned on, and how state persists across time.

That boundary-first framing generalizes beyond empathetic dialogue. Once an agent is expected to produce artifacts that will be published, reused, audited, or treated as durable work product, the central risk shifts. Instead of crisis escalation and longitudinal emotional continuity, the system must optimize for brand consistency, compliance, and factual grounding, with generation embedded inside a pipeline that can be reviewed, validated, and corrected. This is exactly the transition this chapter is designed to make as it moves from conversational systems into creative writing frameworks, multimodal production, and style enforcement for campaign-grade outputs.

The persona engine as a constraint layer

Finally, the persona engine exists to ensure that "empathetic" is not an emergent property that appears sometimes and disappears under stress. Persona constraints should be encoded as stable system-level configuration, and reused every turn. A simple but effective pattern is to implement *persona* as a system prompt that encodes constraints such as reflective questioning, avoidance of directive advice, and a validation-first style.

```
from langchain_core.messages import SystemMessage

self.system_prompt = SystemMessage(content=(
    "You are a supportive peer. Use reflective questioning "
    "(e.g., 'It sounds like...'). Avoid giving directive advice. "
    "Weight your responses toward validation and empathy."
))
```

This is the "controlled bias" idea from the *persona* discussion earlier in the chapter: you are reshaping the model's output distribution toward a stable behavioral region, rather than relying on randomness to land on the right tone.

That boundary-first discipline carries directly into content production, where brand compliance and factual grounding impose analogous constraints on generative output.

The Content Creation agent

While Conversational agents prioritize the nuances of sustained social interaction, Content Creation agents are engineered specifically for the autonomous production of digital artifacts. These systems function as force multipliers for marketing, product, and documentation teams by automating the generation of text, imagery, and multi-modal assets. The architectural challenge is no longer generation itself as modern language models produce fluent drafts on demand. The challenge is reliable production: outputs that consistently adhere to brand voice, compliance requirements, and factual grounding across a coordinated pipeline of specialized agents. This section examines how multi-stage creative frameworks, constraint satisfaction, and iterative validation work together to meet that challenge.

To move beyond generic completions toward publishable work products, a Content Creation agent requires a sophisticated orchestration of curated inputs, style guidance, and iterative validation steps. This necessitates an architecture that supports multi-modal capabilities, allowing the agent to coordinate various tools to produce a cohesive campaign bundle. As we will explore, these systems utilize shared contracts for brand attributes to prevent the aesthetic drift commonly observed in unmanaged multi-modal outputs.

The subsections that follow cover four interlocking concerns. We begin with *Multi-stage creative writing frameworks*, which establishes the Sense-Model-Plan-Act (SMPA)-based pipeline that separates planning from execution. Next, *Brand consistency as a constraint satisfaction problem* shows how tonal, terminological, and structural requirements are encoded as enforceable constraints. The case study applies both concepts in a working marketing content assistant. Finally, *Implementing the creative orchestrating loop* bridges from architecture to production-ready code, including the end-to-end campaign walkthrough and adaptive optimization cycle.

Multi-stage creative writing frameworks

A fundamental realization in production-grade AI engineering is that a single, monolithic prompt is often insufficient for long-form, professional content. To achieve high-fidelity results, robust agents operate within a creative writing framework that decomposes the generation process into discrete stages: ideation, drafting, reviewing, and refining.

This multi-stage approach is a practical application of the SMPA paradigm established in *Chapter 1*. Rather than generating prose based on a single keyword, the agent follows a structured cognitive loop:

- **Sense**: The agent captures prompt requirements, audience constraints, and target objectives.
- **Model**: It builds a dynamically updated representation of the desired output structure, such as a blog post with specific header hierarchies.
- **Plan**: The agent formulates a narrative arc and identifies necessary data citations or visual asset placeholders.
- **Act**: Finally, it executes the generation of prose, ensuring each segment aligns with the established plan.

This separation of concerns is vital for maintaining the narrative thread and preventing the model from introducing factual inaccuracies mid-sentence. It also facilitates the integration of human-in-the-loop checkpoints.

Brand consistency as a constraint satisfaction problem

In enterprise environments, the architectural challenge is best modeled as a Constraint Satisfaction Problem (CSP). The agent is tasked with an optimization problem where it must maximize the objective function of engagement or creativity while strictly adhering to brand guidelines, which serve as the hard constraints. These constraints represent boundary conditions that the agent cannot breach, such as the following:

- **Tonal requirements:** Enforcing an authoritative but friendly voice through specific token-weighting strategies.
- **Forbidden terminology:** Implementing negative constraints to ensure specific words, such as "cheap," are never selected in a luxury branding context.
- **Formatting rules:** Adhering to strict structural templates for SEO or regulatory compliance.

In practice, solving the complex CSP inherent in high-quality content generation is rarely the responsibility of a single, monolithic agent. Instead, architectural robustness is achieved through the implementation of agent chains, where specialized sub-agents hand off context and artifacts within a sequential or looping workflow. This modularity mirrors the communication patterns established in the foundational chapters, where disjointed subsystems are transformed into a unified, adaptive intelligence through well-defined inter-agent protocols.

As illustrated in *Figure 10.2*, the production-grade chain typically comprises three specialized roles that distribute the cognitive workload to gain resilience and allow for specialized validation:

- **The researcher agent**: This component is responsible for grounding the system by gathering empirical data, current statistics, and verifiable references. It utilizes external search tools or RAG pipelines to ensure the content is factually accurate before drafting begins.

- **The writer agent**: Acting as the system's creative engine, the Writer drafts prose based on the strict structural templates produced during the planning phase. It focuses exclusively on narrative flow and engagement, synthesizing the data provided by the researcher.
- **The editor agent**: This agent functions as the quality control layer, acting as a specialized critic rather than a creator. It evaluates the draft against the Brand Style Guide to identify tonal inconsistencies, banned terminology, or structural failures.

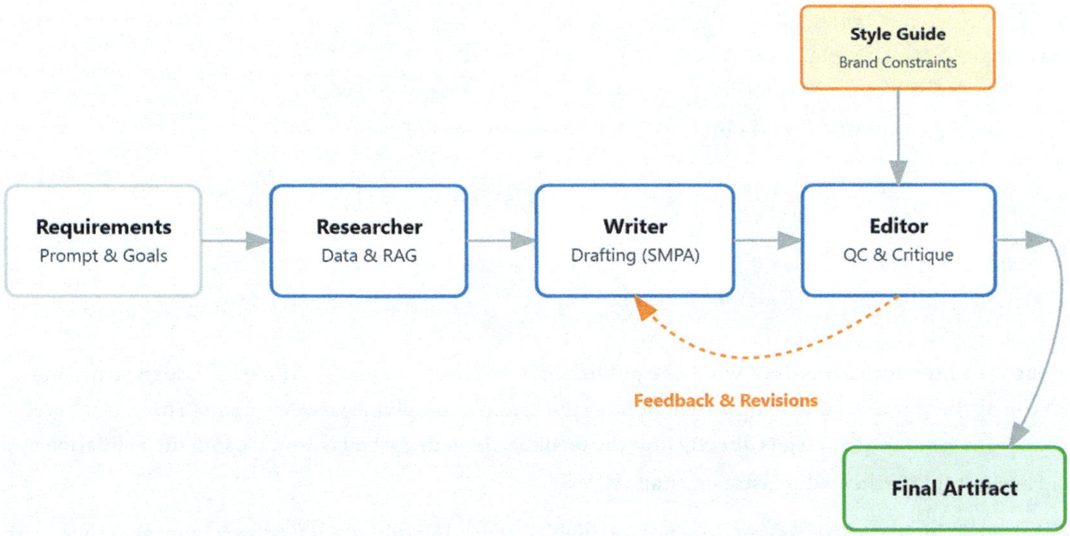

Figure 10.2 – Agentic content pipeline illustrating the collaboration between researcher, writer, and editor agents for brand-constrained content generation

To understand why the editor agent is indispensable, consider what happens without it. The following snippet shows a writer agent producing a draft that violates two brand constraints simultaneously: it uses forbidden competitive terminology and adopts a tone that falls outside the permitted range:

```
from langchain_openai import ChatOpenAI
from langchain_core.messages import HumanMessage, SystemMessage

BRAND_GUIDELINES = {
    "forbidden_terms": ["cheaper", "best-in-class", "industry-leading"],
    "required_tone": "authoritative-but-approachable",
}

def validate_against_brand(draft: str, guidelines: dict) -> dict:
    """Editor Agent: check draft against brand constraint set."""
    violations = [
        term for term in guidelines["forbidden_terms"] if term.lower() in draft.lower()
    ]
    return {
        "passed": len(violations) == 0,
```

```
        "violations": violations,
        "revision_instruction": (
            f"Remove or replace: {violations}. "
            f"Tone must be: {guidelines['required_tone']}."
        ) if violations else "",
    }

# Simulate unvalidated Writer output
raw_draft = (
    "Our platform is the industry-leading, cheaper alternative to "
    "legacy solutions. Best-in-class performance guaranteed."
)
result = validate_against_brand(raw_draft, BRAND_GUIDELINES)
# result["passed"] == False
# result["violations"] == ["cheaper", "industry-leading", "Best-in-class"]
# result["revision_instruction"] triggers Writer retry with correction prompt
```

Without the editor agent, this draft would be published unchanged: it contains three forbidden terms and adopts an aggressive competitive tone that violates the brand's compliance requirements. The `revision_instruction` field feeds directly into the feedback loop described below, closing the validation cycle before any output reaches a downstream channel.

In advanced architectures, the editor does not merely flag errors but initiates a feedback loop, as shown by the orange *Feedback & Revisions* path in *Figure 10.2*. This triggers an iterative refinement cycle where the draft is returned to the writer with specific instructions for revision. This process continues until the generated artifact satisfies the brand constraints, which can be modeled as an optimization of the consistency score:

$$C = \frac{1}{n}\sum_{i=1}^{n} \varphi(A_i, G)$$

In this formula, the number of brand parameters are represented, along with the attributes of the generated artifact, the definitive brand guidelines, and the alignment function measuring the degree of adherence.

The true power of an agentic chain is realized when it is integrated with external measurement tools. By connecting the chain to APIs from platforms like Google Analytics or HubSpot, the system moves beyond static delivery. The agents monitor performance signals such as click-through rates or engagement depth and treat these outcomes as feedback for future iterations. This allows the system to learn which tones or formats resonate most effectively with the target audience, transforming content generation into a self-optimizing cycle.

The following case study applies the content creation pipeline to a real-world marketing scenario. It demonstrates how a campaign planner agent coordinates specialist agents for email, SEO, and advertising copy, enforces brand constraints through an editor agent, and closes the feedback loop with performance analytics.

Case study: The marketing content assistant

Unlike the mental health case study, which interleaved architecture and code inline, this case study separates conceptual design from implementation to spotlight the orchestration layer in isolation. To ground these theoretical frameworks in a practical implementation, consider the architecture of a marketing content assistant. This system functions not merely as a high-speed copywriter but as an autonomous campaign manager capable of cross-channel orchestration. While traditional marketing automation relied on deterministic `if-then` logic, as we noted in the historical overview of *Chapter 1*, this agentic architecture utilizes emergent reasoning to adapt to market signals in real time.

In this environment, the human architect provides high-level strategic constraints: a product launch date, a target audience *persona*, and a core value proposition. The system then takes over the operational lifecycle, moving from intent to execution through a multi-agent orchestration.

Strategic decomposition and the multi-channel workflow

Upon initialization, the agent's planning module, functioning as the "Plan" phase of the SMPA cycle, decomposes the campaign objectives into a multi-channel content calendar. It does not generate a single block of text but instead orchestrates a suite of specialized sub-agents, each optimized for a specific medium:

- **The email agent**: This agent drafts a sequence of newsletters. Its internal reward function is weighted toward subject line optimization and open-rate maximization, drawing on historical performance data to select linguistic patterns that drive engagement.
- **The SEO agent**: This component focuses on long-form blog posts. It integrates real-time keyword research to ensure the content satisfies search engine algorithms while maintaining the "hard constraints" of the brand voice.
- **The ad creative agent**: This agent operates as a multimodal engine. It generates multiple variations of ad copy and simultaneously prompts a diffusion model to create matching visual assets for A/B testing, ensuring a tight coupling between the visual and textual messaging.

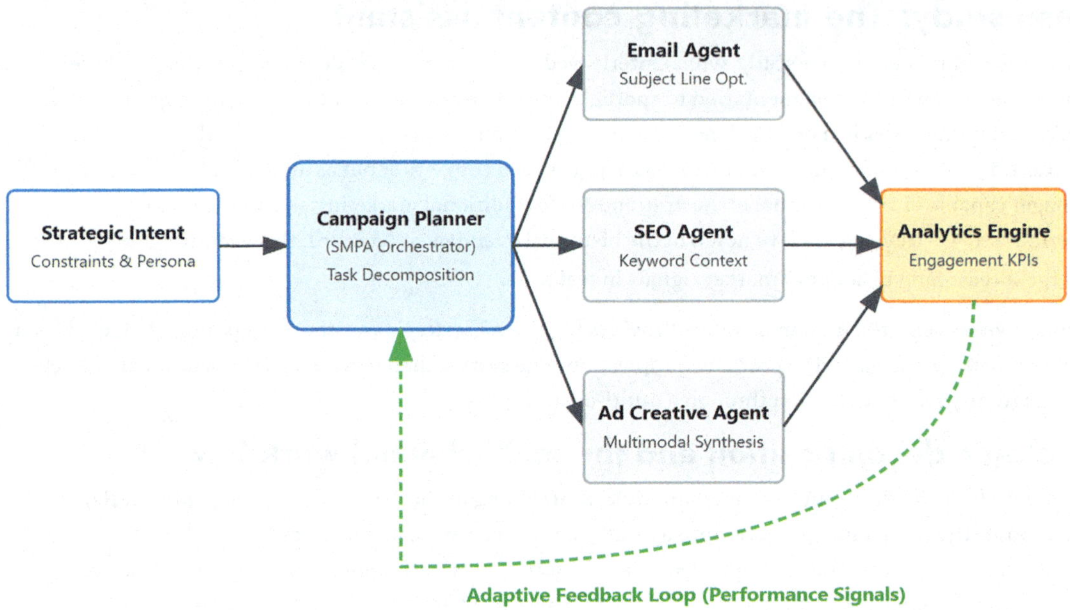

Figure 10.3 – Reference architecture for an autonomous marketing content assistant with multi-channel orchestration and adaptive feedback

The adaptive optimization cycle

The defining feature of this architecture is its closed-loop feedback mechanism. By integrating with measurement tools such as Google Analytics or HubSpot APIs, the agent moves beyond a "publish and forget" model. It treats performance signals such as click-through rates (CTR) and conversion depth as high-fidelity feedback that updates its future generative parameters.

We can model this optimization as a reinforcement learning problem where the agent seeks to maximize the expected reward R over a sequence of content iterations. If $\pi\theta$ represents the agent's generation policy parameterized by θ, the objective is to adjust θ to maximize the return:

$$J(\theta) = E_{\pi\theta}\left[\sum_{t=0}^{T} \gamma^t R_t\right]$$

In this context, Rt represents the engagement metrics (e.g., CTR) at time t, and γ is a discount factor for long-term brand equity. When an experiment reveals that a specific tonal variant or visual treatment consistently outperforms others, the agent adjusts its internal preferences. Over time, the system transitions from a static drafting capability into an adaptive optimization cycle, learning the specific creative patterns that resonate with its unique audience.

This longitudinal learning capability is explored in *Chapter 14*, where we examine long-term agentic learning and fine-tuning.

Implementing the creative orchestration loop

This section translates the theoretical architecture of the marketing content assistant into a functional, production-ready Python framework. We will utilize the provided code to demonstrate how high-level agentic patterns (specifically SMPA and CSP) are expressed in software.

Moving from theory to production

To move from theory to a publishable work product, we must move beyond simple prompts and implement a structured orchestration. The following implementation sections detail how we build a system that senses strategic intent, models a campaign, plans tasks, and acts through specialized agents, all while maintaining strict brand governance.

The SMPA foundation

At the heart of our architecture is the SMPA paradigm. Rather than treating generation as a single event, we define an abstract base class that forces every agent to follow a structured cognitive loop:

```
class Agent(ABC):
    """


    Base class for all agents implementing the SMPA cycle

    (Sense-Model-Plan-Act)
    """
    def execute(self, input_data: Dict[str, Any]) -> Any:
        # Sense: Capture prompt requirements and audience constraints
        sensed = self.sense(input_data)

        # Model: Build a representation of the desired output structure
        modeled = self.model(sensed)

        # Plan: Formulate a narrative arc and identify asset placeholders
        planned = self.plan(modeled)

        # Act: Execute the generation of prose and assets
        result = self.act(planned)
        return result
```

By enforcing this separation of concerns, we prevent the model from drifting or introducing inaccuracies mid-generation.

Implementing brand constraints as a CSP

Enterprise agents must treat brand guidelines as hard constraints. We model this as a logic-based validation step within our `BrandGuidelines` class, to ensure that forbidden terminology (like "cheap" in a luxury context) is never used:

```
@dataclass
class BrandGuidelines:
    """Brand consistency constraints (CSP hard constraints)"""
    tone: str = "authoritative but friendly"
    forbidden_words: List[str] = field(default_factory=lambda: ["cheap", "free trial"])

    def validate_content(self, content: str) -> tuple[bool, List[str]]:
        """Validate content against brand guidelines"""
        violations = []
        content_lower = content.lower()

        for word in self.forbidden_words:
            if word.lower() in content_lower:
                violations.append(f"Forbidden word found: '{word}'")

        return len(violations) == 0, violations
```

The editor agent: The quality control layer

The editor agent acts as the system's critic. it doesn't just check for banned words; it calculates a consistency score based on the alignment of the generated artifact with the definitive brand guidelines.

```
class EditorAgent:
    """
    Implements the consistency score: C = 1/n * Σ ϕ(Ai, G)
    """
    def _calculate_consistency_score(self, artifact: ContentArtifact,
                                    violations: List[str], tone_score: float) -> float:
        n = 3  # number of brand parameters

        forbidden_score = 1.0 if len(violations) == 0 else 0.0
        structure_score = 1.0 if len(artifact.body) > 100 else 0.5

        # φ is our alignment function measuring adherence
        consistency_score = (forbidden_score + tone_score + structure_score) / n
        return consistency_score
```

Multimodal orchestration via function calling

Modern agents must coordinate text, imagery, and data visuals. We implement this through asset requests, which act as machine-readable contracts between the text-generating agent and specialized downstream tools (like diffusion models or plotting libraries):

```
@dataclass
class AssetRequest:
    """Structured request for multimodal asset generation"""
    asset_type: str  # e.g., 'image' or 'chart'
    asset_id: str
    prompt: str
    constraints: Dict[str, Any]  # e.g., 'aspect_ratio': '16:9'
```

When the ad creative agent executes, it generates both copy and these structured asset requests to ensure a tight coupling between visual and textual messaging.

The `dataclass` above defines the contract; the function below fulfils it. The `dispatch_asset_request()` function routes each `AssetRequest` to the appropriate generation backend. For image assets, it calls the OpenAI Images API (which wraps DALL-E); for other asset types, it delegates to a placeholder handler that teams can swap for domain-specific tools such as Matplotlib or Plotly. The function returns a dictionary containing the generated URL and metadata, which the campaign planner can then attach to the final deliverable:

```
import openai
from typing import Dict, Any

client = openai.OpenAI()   # uses OPENAI_API_KEY from env

def dispatch_asset_request(req: AssetRequest) -> Dict[str, Any]:
    """Route an AssetRequest to the appropriate generation backend."""
    if req.asset_type == "image":
        size = req.constraints.get("size", "1024x1024")
        response = client.images.generate(
            model="dall-e-3",
            prompt=req.prompt,
            size=size,
            n=1,
        )
        return {"asset_id": req.asset_id, "url": response.data[0].url}

    # Extend for 'chart', 'video', etc.
    raise ValueError(f"Unsupported asset type: {req.asset_type}")
```

The pattern is deliberately minimal: one function, one API call, one return contract. In production, teams wrap this dispatcher with retry logic, cost tracking, and content-policy filtering. The key architectural point is that the text-generating agent never calls the image API directly; it emits a structured `AssetRequest`, and the dispatcher handles routing. This separation keeps the generation agents testable and the multimodal backend swappable (for example, replacing DALL-E with Stable Diffusion requires changing only the dispatcher, not the agent chain). The `openai` library (already listed in the *Technical requirements* section) provides the `images.generate()` endpoint used here; no additional dependencies are required.

The adaptive optimization cycle

The final stage of the pipeline is the analytics engine. By tracking metrics such as CTR, the system creates a feedback loop that adapts future generative parameters based on real-world performance:

```
class AnalyticsEngine:
    """Generates feedback for Campaign Planner based on performance"""
    def generate_adaptive_feedback(self, campaign_analysis: Dict[str, Any]) -> Dict[str,
Any]:
        ctr = campaign_analysis['overall_ctr']

        if ctr > 0.05:
            return {"recommendations": ["Maintain current creative strategy"]}
        else:
            # Triggering the adaptive feedback loop
            return {"recommendations": ["Revise value proposition messaging"]}
```

This transforms the content agent from a static writer into a self-optimizing engine that learns which creative patterns resonate with its audience.

Before committing to a multi-agent pipeline, engineers should evaluate whether a single LLM call would suffice. Use a full agent chain when the task requires any of the following:

- Brand-constraint enforcement across more than one output type
- Coordination of three or more distinct specialized roles (researcher, writer, editor)
- Analytics-driven feedback that must update future generation. Use a simple chatbot when the output is single-pass, the quality bar is conversational rather than publication-grade, and no external data retrieval is required. The marketing content assistant described in this chapter satisfies all three criteria for the full chain

The walkthrough that follows demonstrates all three criteria in action: multi-modal coordination, publication-grade quality enforcement, and analytics-driven feedback across a complete campaign pipeline.

End-to-end campaign walkthrough: execute_campaign()

The following `execute_campaign()` function is the campaign planner's top-level coordinator. Scoped to a product-launch campaign using mock data, it demonstrates the full pipeline: the planner dispatches Email, SEO, and Ad agents in sequence; each agent's draft passes through the editor for brand validation; violations trigger a `Writer` retry; and the analytics engine records performance signals that update the Planner's preferences for the next run:

```
# Requires: langchain==0.2.16  langchain-openai==0.1.23  openai==1.40.0
# Install:  pip install langchain==0.2.16 langchain-openai==0.1.23 openai==1.40.0
from __future__ import annotations
from dataclasses import dataclass, field
from typing import Any, Dict, List
from langchain_openai import ChatOpenAI
from langchain_core.messages import HumanMessage, SystemMessage

llm = ChatOpenAI(model="gpt-4o", temperature=0.7)

@dataclass
class CampaignBrief:
    product: str
    audience: str
    tone: str = "authoritative-but-approachable"
    forbidden_terms: List[str] = field(
        default_factory=lambda: ["cheaper", "best-in-class", "industry-leading"]
    )

@dataclass
class CampaignAssets:
    email: str = ""
    seo_post: str = ""
    ad_copy: str = ""
    analytics: Dict[str, float] = field(default_factory=dict)

def _draft(role: str, brief: CampaignBrief, channel: str) -> str:
    """Single-channel Writer Agent using SMPA Act phase."""
    messages = [
        SystemMessage(content=(
            f"You are a {role} writing {channel} copy. "
            f"Tone: {brief.tone}. "
            f"Never use: {brief.forbidden_terms}."
        )),
        HumanMessage(content=(
            f"Write {channel} content for: {brief.product}. "
            f"Audience: {brief.audience}."
        )),
    ]
    return llm.invoke(messages).content
```

```
def _validate(draft: str, brief: CampaignBrief) -> Dict[str, Any]:
    """Editor Agent: enforce brand constraints (CSP hard check)."""
    violations = [
        t for t in brief.forbidden_terms if t.lower() in draft.lower()
    ]
    return {
        "passed": len(violations) == 0,
        "violations": violations,
        "instruction": (
            f"Revise to remove: {violations}. Tone must be: {brief.tone}."
            if violations else ""
        ),
    }

def _validated_draft(
    role: str, brief: CampaignBrief, channel: str, max_retries: int = 2
) -> str:
    """Writer + Editor feedback loop: retry until brand constraints pass."""
    draft = _draft(role, brief, channel)
    for _ in range(max_retries):
        result = _validate(draft, brief)
        if result["passed"]:
            return draft
        # Editor returns revision_instruction; Writer retries
        messages = [
            SystemMessage(content=result["instruction"]),
            HumanMessage(content=f"Revise this {channel} draft:\n{draft}"),
        ]
        draft = llm.invoke(messages).content
    return draft  # return best effort after max_retries

def execute_campaign(brief: CampaignBrief) -> CampaignAssets:
    """
    Campaign Planner: coordinate specialist agents for a product launch.
    Phase 1 - Dispatch: Email, SEO, Ad agents produce validated drafts.
    Phase 2 - Analytics: record mock engagement signals.
    Phase 3 - Feedback: update Planner preferences for next run.
    """
    assets = CampaignAssets()

    # Phase 1 - Dispatch specialist agents with Editor validation
    assets.email = _validated_draft("email specialist", brief, "email newsletter")
    assets.seo_post = _validated_draft("SEO writer", brief, "long-form blog post")
    assets.ad_copy = _validated_draft("ad creative", brief, "display ad copy")
```

```
    # Phase 2 - Analytics Engine: record performance signals (mock)
    assets.analytics = {
        "email_open_rate": 0.28,    # 28 % open rate
        "seo_click_rate": 0.14,     # 14 % CTR on search impression
        "ad_conversion": 0.04,      # 4 % conversion from ad click
    }

    # Phase 3 - Adaptive feedback: surfaces low-performer for next iteration
    lowest = min(assets.analytics, key=assets.analytics.get)
    print(f"[Planner] Weakest channel: {lowest} – schedule A/B revision.")

    return assets

# — Run —
brief = CampaignBrief(
    product="DataVault Pro - enterprise data-governance platform",
    audience="CTOs and data engineering leads at mid-market companies",
)
campaign = execute_campaign(brief)
print(f"Email draft (first 120 chars): {campaign.email[:120]}")
print(f"Analytics: {campaign.analytics}")
```

The three-phase structure mirrors the pipeline described in the case study. Phase 1 enforces the boundary-first principle: no asset exits the agent chain without passing the Editor's brand constraint check. Phase 2 closes the measurement loop. Phase 3 converts that measurement into a Planner-level signal, making the next campaign execution marginally better than the last. This is the pattern that separates a production-grade content agent from a one-shot prompt.

Summary

In this chapter, we examined the class of agents that operate at the boundary between algorithmic capability and human experience. After studying agents optimized for logical synthesis and software construction, we shifted to systems whose success is judged by continuity, tone, empathy, and aesthetic coherence. Conversational and Content Creation agents turn raw generative capacity into structured interaction and governed output, which requires architectures that can preserve state across time, enforce behavioral constraints, and integrate tools reliably in production settings.

The first half of the chapter focused on the Conversational agent as a memory-augmented, goal-aware system rather than a stateless LLM wrapper. It traced the evolution from early rule-driven chatbots to modern LLM-based systems, then defined the architectural threshold for agenthood: persistent context, intent awareness, dialog management, behavioral consistency, and tool and memory integration. The chapter then detailed the internal mechanics that make these properties operational, including dialog management, the dual-memory hierarchy (working memory versus semantic memory), and persona modeling as a first-class layer that reshapes generation through enforced constraints rather than incidental prompt styling.

The second half of the chapter generalized the same boundary-first principle to content creation, where the objective is not fluent drafting but publishable, auditable work products. Content Creation agents are framed as multi-stage pipelines and constraint satisfaction systems, typically implemented as agent chains (researcher, writer, editor) with revision loops and explicit style-guide governance. The chapter extended this architecture to multimodal and multi-channel production, showing how function calling and structured asset specifications enable coordinated generation across text, visuals, and data artifacts. Finally, we presented a marketing content assistant case study that closes the loop with analytics, modeling adaptation as an optimization process in which real-world engagement signals feed back into planning and generation policies over time.

In the next chapter, we move from agents that engage humans through dialogue and published content to agents that perceive the physical world through raw sensory input. *Chapter 11* introduces multi-modal perception agents, systems that extend beyond text into vision, audio, and physical sensor streams. We examine how vision-language agents pair visual encoders with LLMs to ground reasoning in pixel-level evidence, how audio processing agents capture temporal and prosodic information that text transcriptions discard, and how physical world sensing agents fuse heterogeneous sensor data into coherent environmental models that drive real-time actuation.

11

Multi-Modal Perception Agents

Intelligence is the ability to achieve goals in a wide range of environments.

— Demis Hassabis, co-founder and CEO of DeepMind

The evolution of intelligent agents has been predominantly a story of language. From the earliest chatbots to today's sophisticated reasoning systems, the primary interface between agents and their environments has been text. Yet human intelligence does not operate within such constraints. We navigate the world through a continuous stream of sensory input, where visual cues inform our spatial reasoning, auditory signals alert us to environmental changes, and tactile feedback guides our physical interactions.

Multi-modal perception represents a fundamental expansion in what autonomous agents can understand and accomplish. This chapter examines the architectural foundations and practical implementations of multi-modal perception in agent systems. Building upon the cognitive architecture introduced in *Chapter 1*, and the tool orchestration patterns explored in *Chapter 7*, we address how agents interpret and act upon information that arrives not as structured text, but as pixel arrays, audio waveforms, and sensor readings.

In this chapter, we'll be covering the following topics:

- **Vision-Language agents**
- **Audio Processing agents**
- **Physical World Sensing agents**

Technical requirements

To run the examples in this chapter, you will need the following:

- Python 3.10 or later
- The following Python packages: `transformers`, `torch`, `Pillow`, and `numpy`
- A Hugging Face account with access to the LLaVA 1.5 model weights (`llava-hf/llava-1.5-7b-hf`)
- A CUDA-capable GPU with at least 16 GB of VRAM is strongly recommended for the vision-language model examples; CPU execution is possible but significantly slower

All code examples for this chapter are available in the book's GitHub repository at https://github.com/PacktPublishing/30-Agents-Every-AI-Engineer-Must-Build/chapter11.

Vision-Language agents

This section examines Vision-Language agents from three perspectives: the architectural components that enable joint image-text reasoning, a working implementation that demonstrates those components in code, and the production deployment patterns that govern real-world integration.

Among the sensory modalities (e.g., text, images, audio, sensor data) available to intelligent agents, vision stands out as the richest and most immediate channel. Through visual perception, agents gain access to spatial relationships, object identities, contextual cues, and environmental structure, information that language alone cannot reliably convey. A textual description of a cluttered workspace, for instance, cannot capture the precise arrangement of tools, the half-open drawer, or the coffee cup precariously balanced on a stack of papers. Vision delivers this information instantaneously and in parallel, which explains why it has emerged as the primary gateway into multi-modal agent design. In practice, vision often serves as the foundational perceptual layer upon which additional capabilities like audio processing and tactile sensing are built.

Vision-Language agents therefore offer an ideal starting point for exploring multi-modal perception. As a class, Vision-Language agents are systems that pair a visual encoder with a large language model, enabling the agent to reason jointly over image content and natural language inputs. They demonstrate how raw perceptual signals can be encoded, aligned with linguistic representations, and woven directly into an agent's reasoning process. More importantly, examining their architecture and deployment patterns reveals core principles that will resurface throughout this chapter: modality alignment (ensuring different data types can be compared and combined), grounding (anchoring abstract language in concrete sensory evidence), latency management (meeting real-time response requirements), and uncertainty handling (knowing when visual evidence is ambiguous or insufficient).

With this foundation established, let us examine how Vision-Language agents are architected and how these principles manifest in working systems.

Architecture of Vision-Language agents

The architectural design of a Vision-Language agent integrates three foundational components that work in concert to process multi-modal signals: a visual encoder, an alignment mechanism, and a language model. *Figure 11.1* illustrates this architecture. The specific orchestration of these components determines whether an agent can genuinely ground its linguistic reasoning in visual evidence or merely approximate such grounding through surface-level correlations.

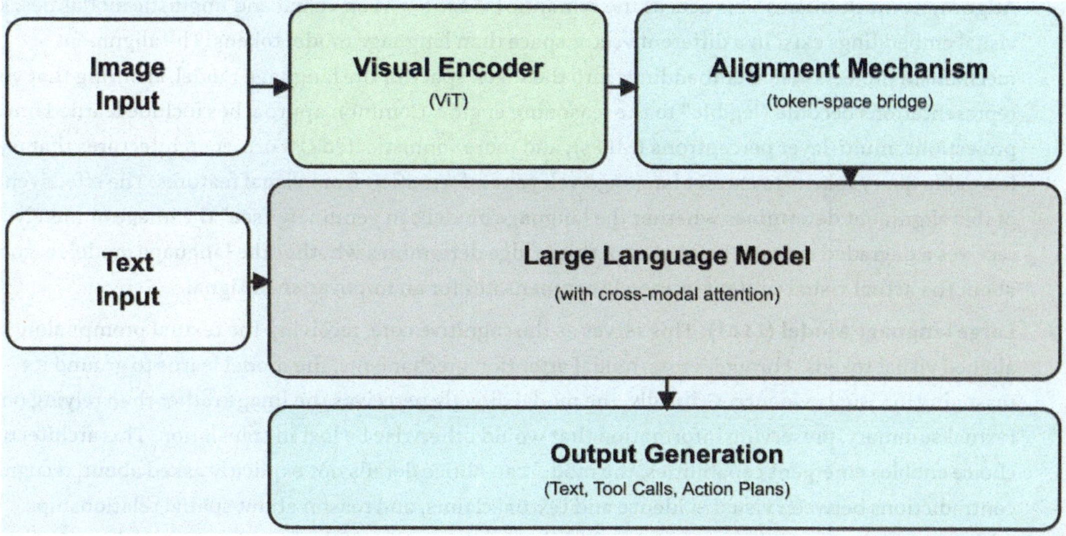

Figure 11.1 – Vision-Language agent architecture

Unlike systems that process textual descriptions of images (where information loss is inevitable), Vision-Language agents ingest raw visual data alongside natural language instructions. This direct access to pixel-level information enables capabilities that would otherwise be impossible: counting objects partially occluded by others, recognizing subtle emotional expressions, or identifying spatial relationships that resist verbal description.

Each component addresses a distinct stage of the visual perception pipeline:

- **Visual encoding:** This forms the perceptual foundation of the system. Modern encoders typically employ Vision Transformer (ViT) architectures, which segment an input image into fixed-size patches (commonly 14×14 or 16×16 pixels). Each patch is linearly projected into an embedding space, and positional encodings are added to preserve spatial information. Through self-attention layers, the encoder captures both local features—textures, edges, color gradients—and global context, such as object relationships and scene composition. The output is a sequence of visual tokens, each representing a region of the original image in a high-dimensional vector space. Variants like SigLIP and DINOv2 have demonstrated that the quality of these visual representations directly impacts downstream reasoning performance.

> **Note**
>
> SigLIP is generally preferred for tasks requiring language-aligned retrieval, as it is trained with a contrastive image-text objective that tightly couples visual and linguistic representations. DINOv2, by contrast, uses self-supervised learning without text supervision, producing spatially rich features that excel in dense prediction tasks such as depth estimation and semantic segmentation. The choice of encoder is therefore the first and most consequential architectural decision in a Vision-Language system.

- **Alignment mechanism:** This acts as the semantic bridge between visual and linguistic modalities. Raw visual embeddings exist in a different vector space than language model tokens. The alignment mechanism projects visual embeddings into the token space of the language model, ensuring that visual representations become "legible" to the reasoning engine. Common approaches include learned linear projections, multi-layer perceptrons (MLPs), and more sophisticated Q-Former architectures that use learnable query tokens to extract language-relevant information from visual features. The effectiveness of this alignment determines whether the language model can genuinely "see" the image or merely receives a degraded signal. The quality of this bridge determines whether the language model reasons about the actual visual content or merely compensates for an impoverished signal.
- **Large language Model (LLM)**: This serves as the cognitive core, receiving the textual prompt alongside aligned visual tokens. Through cross-modal attention mechanisms, the model learns to ground its reasoning in visual evidence. Critically, the model directly perceives the image rather than relying on a textual summary, preserving information that would otherwise be lost in translation. This architectural choice enables emergent capabilities: the model can notice details not explicitly asked about, recognize contradictions between visual evidence and textual claims, and reason about spatial relationships without explicit geometric computation. This is why the quality of the foundation model, not just the encoder, is the primary driver of Vision-Language agent capability.

Building a Vision Question-Answering agent

To understand how these theoretical components translate into working code, we will implement a `VisionQuestionAnsweringAgent`. This agent leverages a pre-trained Vision-Language Model (VLM) to analyze images and answer natural language questions. We use the Hugging Face `transformers` library to manage the model pipeline, abstracting away much of the complexity while retaining flexibility for customization.

Initialization and model loading

The agent initialization focuses on loading two critical components: the processor and the model. The processor handles pre-processing of raw images (normalization, resizing to expected dimensions, conversion to tensors) and text (tokenization, special token insertion). The model itself is loaded with mixed precision (`torch.float16`) to optimize memory usage on GPUs, a practical necessity given that Vision-Language models often exceed 7 billion parameters.

The following code is illustrative rather than directly executable: it requires a Hugging Face account with access to the LLaVA 1.5 weights and a CUDA-capable GPU with at least 16 GB of VRAM. The `transformers`, `torch`, and `Pillow` packages must be installed, as listed in the Technical Requirements section above.

```
import torch
from transformers import AutoProcessor, LlavaForConditionalGeneration
from PIL import Image

class VisionQuestionAnsweringAgent:
    """
    A vision-language agent capable of answering questions about images.
    Implements chain-of-thought reasoning for improved accuracy.
```

```
    """

    def __init__(self, model_id: str = "llava-hf/llava-1.5-7b-hf"):
        """
        Initialize the agent with a pre-trained Vision-Language Model.

        Args:
            model_id: HuggingFace model identifier. LLaVA 1.5 provides
                     a good balance of capability and resource requirements.
        """
        print(f"Loading Vision-Language Model: {model_id}...")
        self.processor = AutoProcessor.from_pretrained(model_id)

        # Load model with mixed precision (float16) for efficiency
        # device_map="auto" automatically distributes across available GPUs
        self.model = LlavaForConditionalGeneration.from_pretrained(
            model_id,
            torch_dtype=torch.float16,
            low_cpu_mem_usage=True,
            device_map="auto"
        )
        self.conversation_history = []
        print("Model loaded successfully.")
```

The `device_map="auto"` parameter deserves attention: it enables automatic model parallelism across multiple GPUs when available and gracefully falls back to CPU execution when necessary. For production deployments, explicit device mapping often provides better control over memory allocation and inference latency.

Integration patterns and production considerations

The implementation above represents a **direct integration pattern**, where the model is loaded locally and inference runs on the same machine as the application. This approach offers low latency and complete control but requires substantial computational resources. In production environments, the integration of visual encoders with language models generally follows one of three architectural patterns, each with distinct trade-offs:

- **Adapter-based integration:** Inserts lightweight projection layers between a frozen visual encoder and a frozen language model. Only these adapters, typically comprising less than 1% of total parameters, are trained while the pre-trained components remain unchanged. This approach is computationally efficient and preserves the capabilities of both foundation models but may struggle with visual concepts that differ significantly from the encoder's training distribution.
- **Cross-attention integration**: Adds dedicated attention layers that allow language tokens to attend specifically to visual encoder outputs. This creates explicit pathways for information flow between

modalities, enabling more nuanced interactions than simple concatenation. Models like Flamingo exemplify this pattern, demonstrating strong few-shot visual learning capabilities.

- **Early fusion:** Concatenates visual and textual tokens into a single unified sequence processed by a transformer. This approach maximizes the potential for cross-modal reasoning (any token can attend to any other) but increases sequence length and computational overhead. For high-resolution images that generate hundreds of visual tokens, this overhead can become prohibitive without careful optimization.

When deploying Vision-Language agents, latency is a critical bottleneck. Visual encoding and cross-modal attention add significant overhead compared to text-only models. Practical techniques for managing latency include:

- **Image resolution scaling**: Reducing input resolution from 1024×1024 to 336×336 can cut visual tokens by 90 percent with modest accuracy loss for many tasks
- **Patch pruning**: Dynamically removing uninformative patches (uniform regions, backgrounds) reduces sequence length while preserving salient information
- **Speculative decoding**: Using smaller models that larger models verify, accelerating generation without sacrificing quality
- **Caching**: Storing visual embeddings for frequently accessed images, avoiding redundant encoding

Finally, robust production systems implement accuracy validation, cross-checking agent outputs against deterministic computer vision models. If a Vision-Language agent claims an image contains three people, a dedicated object detector can verify this count. Such validation layers are essential for mitigating hallucination risks, particularly in high-stakes applications where incorrect visual interpretation could have serious consequences. The goal is not to replace the flexibility of vision-language reasoning, but to catch confident errors before they propagate downstream. The same architectural principles (encoding, alignment, latency management, and validation) carry forward into the next perceptual domain: audio.

Audio Processing agents

Sound occupies a dimension of experience that vision cannot capture. While images freeze moments in static frames, audio unfolds continuously through time, carrying information encoded in pitch, rhythm, timbre, and the subtle interplay of overlapping signals. Human speech conveys not merely words, but emotion, emphasis, and social context through prosodic features (the "music" of speech) that text transcriptions inevitably discard.

Audio Processing agents extend the perceptual capabilities of intelligent systems into this temporal, layered acoustic domain. Unlike vision, which allows for parallel processing of a scene, audio demands specialized architectures that capture temporal dependencies and separate overlapping sources from background noise.

The sections that follow cover the pipeline architecture of an Audio Processing agent, a complete speech recognition implementation built on a Whisper-compatible backend, and a voice sentiment analysis agent that maps prosodic features to the Valence-Arousal-Dominance (VAD) model.

Architecture of Audio Processing agents

The architecture of an audio agent must bridge the gap between continuous waveforms and discrete cognitive tokens.

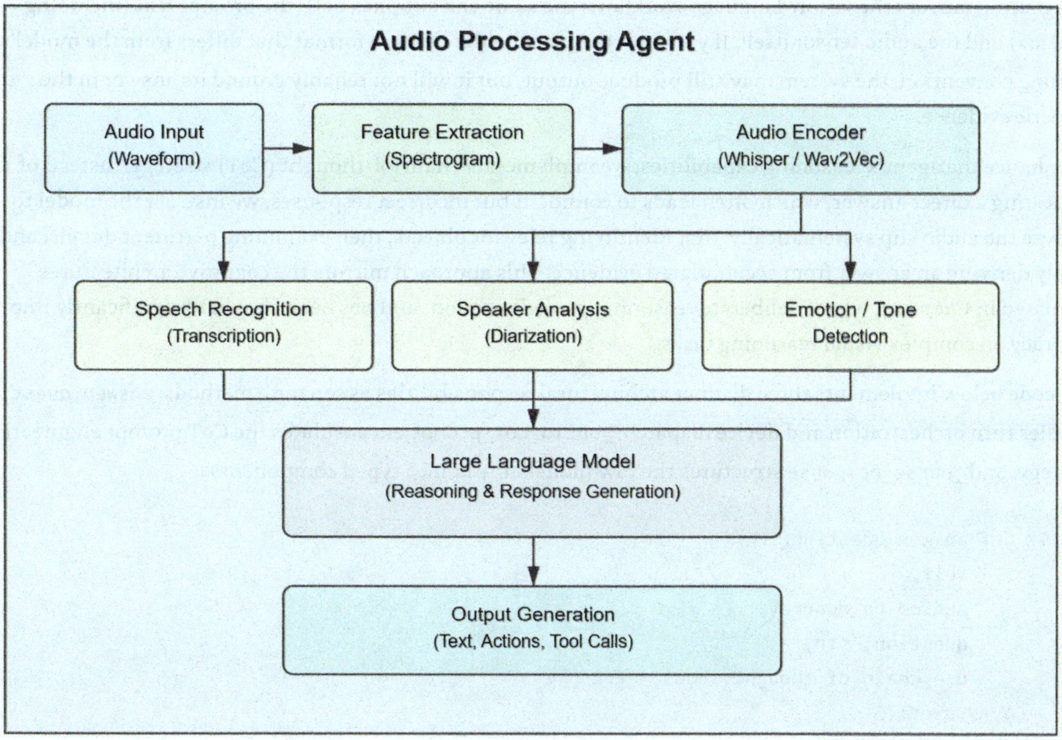

Figure 11.2 – Audio Processing agent architecture

As illustrated in *Figure 11.2*, the pipeline begins with Audio Encoding, which transforms raw waveforms into representations suitable for downstream processing. Modern encoders typically operate on spectral representations derived from the **Short-Time Fourier Transform (STFT)** or learned filterbanks.

Leading architectures like OpenAI's Whisper employ a two-stage process: convolutional layers first downsample the input spectrogram to reduce dimensionality, followed by transformer layers that process the sequence using self-attention over the full temporal context. This allows the model to capture long-range dependencies, such as intonation patterns that span an entire sentence.

With this architectural foundation in place, we can examine how audio agents handle real-world, multimodal interactions through a concrete customer service scenario.

Analyzing a multimodal customer service interaction

Suppose we want to analyze a recorded customer complaint. The prompt construction follows a familiar pattern:

```
question = "Transcribe this audio and assess the caller's frustration level."
prompt = f"USER: <audio>\n{question}\nASSISTANT:"
inputs = processor(text=prompt, audio=audio_array, return_tensors="pt")
```

This pairing mirrors the vision-language workflow: the same call supplies both the prompt text (including `<audio>`) and the audio tensor itself. If you omit the placeholder or use a format that differs from the model's training convention, the system may still produce output, but it will not reliably ground its answer in the acoustic evidence.

To enhance the agent's reasoning capabilities, we implement a chain-of-thought (CoT) strategy. Instead of requesting a direct answer, which often leads to confident but incorrect responses, we instruct the model to analyze the audio clip systematically: first identifying relevant objects, then examining pertinent details, and finally deriving an answer from accumulated evidence. This approach mirrors the cognitive architectures discussed in *Chapter 1*, where deliberate reasoning precedes action, and has been shown to significantly improve accuracy on complex visual reasoning tasks.

The code below implements three distinct architectural responsibilities as separate methods: `answer_question` handles turn orchestration and device dispatch, `_build_cot_prompt` encapsulates the CoT prompt engineering strategy, and `_parse_response` structures the raw model output into typed components.

```
def answer_question(
    self,
    audio: np.ndarray,
    question: str,
    use_chain_of_thought: bool = True
) -> dict:
    """
    Answer a question about the provided audio.

    Args:
        audio: NumPy array containing audio waveform
        question: Natural language question about the audio
        use_chain_of_thought: Whether to use step-by-step reasoning

    Returns:
        Dictionary containing 'answer' and optionally 'reasoning'
    """

    # Construct the prompt based on the reasoning strategy
    if use_chain_of_thought:
        cot_instruction = self._build_cot_prompt(question)
        prompt = f"USER: <audio>\n{cot_instruction}\nASSISTANT:"
    else:
        prompt = f"USER: <audio>\n{question}\nASSISTANT:"

    # Process inputs: tokenize text and preprocess audio
    inputs = self.processor(
        text=prompt,
```

```
                audio=audio,
                return_tensors="pt"
            ).to(self.model.device)

            # Generate response with deterministic decoding
            with torch.no_grad():
                outputs = self.model.generate(
                    **inputs,
                    max_new_tokens=512,
                    do_sample=False  # Greedy decoding for reproducibility
                )

            # Decode and parse the response
            full_response = self.processor.decode(
                outputs[0],
                skip_special_tokens=True
            )
            response_text = full_response.split("ASSISTANT:")[-1].strip()

            return self._parse_response(response_text, use_chain_of_thought)
```

The next method encapsulates the prompt engineering strategy, constructing the structured CoT instruction that guides the model through systematic audio analysis.

```
        def _build_cot_prompt(self, question: str) -> str:
            """
            Construct a chain-of-thought prompt for audio reasoning.

            The structured format guides the model through systematic
            analysis rather than pattern-matching to likely answers.
            """
            return f"""Analyze the audio carefully and answer the following question:
    "{question}"

    Please think step by step:
    1. First, identify the relevant acoustic features or segments in the audio.
    2. Then, examine the specific prosodic or content cues needed to answer the question.
    3. Finally, provide your answer based on the acoustic evidence.

    Format your response as:
    Reasoning: [Your step-by-step analysis]
    Therefore, the answer is: [Your final answer]"""
```

The `do_sample=False` parameter enforces greedy decoding, selecting the highest-probability token at each step. While this sacrifices diversity, it ensures reproducibility, which is critical for debugging and for applications where consistent behavior matters more than creative variation.

Parsing and structured output

To make the agent's output useful for downstream systems, whether for logging, evaluation, or integration with other agents, we parse the raw text generation into structured components. When CoT is enabled, we extract the reasoning trace separately from the final answer. This separation serves multiple purposes: it enables explainability (developers can understand why an agent reached a conclusion), supports debugging (incorrect reasoning can be identified and addressed), and facilitates human oversight (reviewers can assess the quality of audio interpretation).

```
    def _parse_response(self, response: str, has_reasoning: bool) -> dict:
        """
        Extract structured output from model response.

        Args:
            response: Raw text from model generation
            has_reasoning: Whether CoT prompting was used

        Returns:
            Dictionary with 'answer' and optionally 'reasoning' keys
        """
        if has_reasoning and "Therefore, the answer is:" in response:
            parts = response.split("Therefore, the answer is:")
            return {
                "reasoning": parts[0].replace("Reasoning:", "").strip(),
                "answer": parts[1].strip().rstrip(".")
            }
        return {"answer": response.strip()}
```

In production systems, this parsing logic would include additional robustness: handling malformed responses, extracting partial information when the model deviates from the expected format, and logging anomalies for model improvement.

The next example defines the core data structures and the speech recognition agent, illustrating how the *sense-model-plan-act* loop maps onto transcription mode selection, audio normalization, and structured output generation.

Building a speech recognition agent

To implement a robust speech recognition agent, we must look beyond simple transcription string generation. A production-grade agent requires structured data that capture temporal boundaries, confidence scores, and metadata.

We first define the core data structures. The `TranscriptionMode` enum is particularly important, as it captures a critical design decision: legal transcription demands verbatim accuracy, including every disfluency ("um," "uh"), while meeting notes benefit from cleaned output.

```
from dataclasses import dataclass
from enum import Enum
from typing import List, Dict, Any, Optional
import numpy as np

class TranscriptionMode(Enum):
    VERBATIM = "verbatim"     # Preserves fillers (um, uh)
    CLEAN = "clean"           # Removes disfluencies
    NORMALIZED = "normalized" # Standardizes dates/numbers

@dataclass
class TranscriptionSegment:
    """A segment of transcribed speech with temporal metadata."""
    text: str
    start_time: float
    end_time: float
    confidence: float

    @property
    def duration(self) -> float:
        return self.end_time - self.start_time

@dataclass
class TranscriptionResult:
    """Complete processing result including metadata."""
    segments: List[TranscriptionSegment]
    full_text: str
    language: str
    metadata: Dict[str, Any]
```

Feature extraction and normalization

Before transcription can occur, the raw audio must be transformed into a mel spectrogram, which is a time-frequency representation aligned with human auditory perception. The mel scale compresses higher frequencies, reflecting the fact that human sensitivity to pitch differences decreases as frequency increases.

Once the model generates a raw transcript, the agent applies a text normalization pipeline. This step is crucial for readability. A raw transcript often contains artifacts like false starts ("the the") or fillers that distract from the semantic content.

```
import re

class SpeechRecognitionAgent:
    """Orchestrates the Sense-Model-Plan-Act loop for audio."""

    def __init__(self, backend, default_mode: TranscriptionMode =
TranscriptionMode.CLEAN):
        self.backend = backend
        self.default_mode = default_mode

    def transcribe_audio(self, audio: np.ndarray, mode: Optional[TranscriptionMode] =
None) -> TranscriptionResult:
        mode = mode or self.default_mode

        # 1. Sense: Normalize audio input volume
        # RMS normalization ensures consistent input levels for the model
        rms = np.sqrt(np.mean(audio**2))
        audio = audio * (0.1 / max(rms, 1e-10))

        # 2. Model: Execute ASR backend (e.g., Whisper)
        full_text, raw_segments, _ = self.backend.transcribe(audio)

        # 3. Plan: Apply normalization strategy based on mode
        segments = []
        for seg in raw_segments:
            text = seg["text"]
            if mode == TranscriptionMode.CLEAN:
                # Remove fillers like "um", "uh", "like"
                text = re.sub(r'\b(um|uh|er|mm)\b', '', text, flags=re.IGNORECASE)
                text = re.sub(r'\s+', ' ', text).strip()

            if text:
                segments.append(TranscriptionSegment(
                    text=text,
                    start_time=seg.get("start", 0.0),
                    end_time=seg.get("end", 0.0),
                    confidence=seg.get("confidence", 1.0)
                ))

        # 4. Act: Return structured result
```

```
        return TranscriptionResult(
            segments=segments,
            full_text=" ".join(s.text for s in segments),
            language="en",
            metadata={"mode": mode.value}
        )
```

Voice sentiment analysis

Transcription captures *what* was said, but not *how* it was said. To perceive emotion, agents must analyze **prosody**, that is, the rhythm, stress, and intonation of speech.

We utilize the VAD model for this purpose. Unlike simple categorical labels (e.g., "Happy" or "Sad"), VAD provides a continuous 3D representation:

- **Valence**: Positive vs. negative affect
- **Arousal**: Activation level (calm vs. excited)
- **Dominance**: Sense of control (submissive vs. dominant)

Prosodic feature extraction

Acoustic analyses have established that specific acoustic features strongly correlate with emotional expression in speech. For example, "happy" speech typically exhibits higher pitch, greater pitch variability, and a faster speaking rate, whereas "sad" speech shows the opposite pattern.

The `VoiceSentimentAgent` extracts these features and maps them to the VAD space:

```
@dataclass
class ProsodicFeatures:
    pitch_mean: float
    pitch_variability: float
    intensity_mean: float
    speaking_rate: float

class VoiceSentimentAgent:
    """Analyzes emotional content via acoustic correlates."""

    def analyze_sentiment(self, audio: np.ndarray) -> dict:
        # Extract physical features
        features = self._extract_features(audio)

        # Normalize features to 0-1 scale based on typical speech ranges
        norm_pitch = np.clip((features.pitch_mean - 100) / 200, 0, 1)
        norm_rate = np.clip(features.speaking_rate / 8, 0, 1)

        # Heuristic mapping to emotion profiles
        # In production, this would be a trained classifier
```

```
        profiles = {
            "happy": {"pitch": 0.7, "rate": 0.7},
            "sad":   {"pitch": 0.3, "rate": 0.3},
            "angry": {"pitch": 0.8, "rate": 0.8},
            "neutral": {"pitch": 0.5, "rate": 0.5}
        }

        # Find closest profile
        best_emotion = "neutral"
        min_dist = float('inf')

        for emotion, profile in profiles.items():
            dist = abs(norm_pitch - profile["pitch"]) + abs(norm_rate - profile["rate"])
            if dist < min_dist:
                min_dist = dist
                best_emotion = emotion

        return {
            "primary_emotion": best_emotion,
            "features": features
        }

    def _extract_features(self, audio: np.ndarray) -> ProsodicFeatures:
        # Simplified feature extraction logic
        # Real implementation would use autocorrelation for pitch
        return ProsodicFeatures(
            pitch_mean=150.0, # Placeholder
            pitch_variability=20.0,
            intensity_mean=-20.0,
            speaking_rate=3.5
        )
```

By combining transcription with sentiment analysis, agents can respond with empathy and context awareness, detecting not just the user's command but also their urgency or frustration level.

Where vision and audio agents operate on discrete perceptual signals, Physical World Sensing agents must integrate continuous, asynchronous streams from heterogeneous hardware. This is a challenge that demands a different architectural approach.

Physical World Sensing agents

While vision and audio enable agents to perceive specific sensory domains, complex real-world applications often require the integration of diverse, heterogeneous data streams. In industrial, agricultural, and smart city environments, agents must synthesize inputs from temperature sensors, humidity monitors, motion detectors, air quality gauges, and power meters. Unlike text or images, which are static or sequential, physical world data is continuous, noisy, and often asynchronous.

Physical World Sensing agents operate effectively by creating a "digital twin," a coherent, real-time internal model of the physical environment. This requires a shift from simple data logging to active state estimation, where the agent fuses disparate sensor readings to filter out noise and reconstruct the true state of the world. The architecture must handle the *sense-model-plan-act* loop with high reliability, as the consequences of actuation, such as turning off a cooling system in a server room, can have immediate physical impacts.

Smart building management architecture

A smart building management system exemplifies the challenges and patterns of multi-modal physical sensing. Such a system cannot simply react to single sensors; it must monitor multiple zones with distinct requirements, fuse data to prevent false positives from faulty sensors, and control actuators to balance occupant comfort with energy efficiency.

Figure 11.3 illustrates the separation of static zone configuration from dynamic environmental state and shows how both feed into the event detection and proportional control layers of the smart building agent.

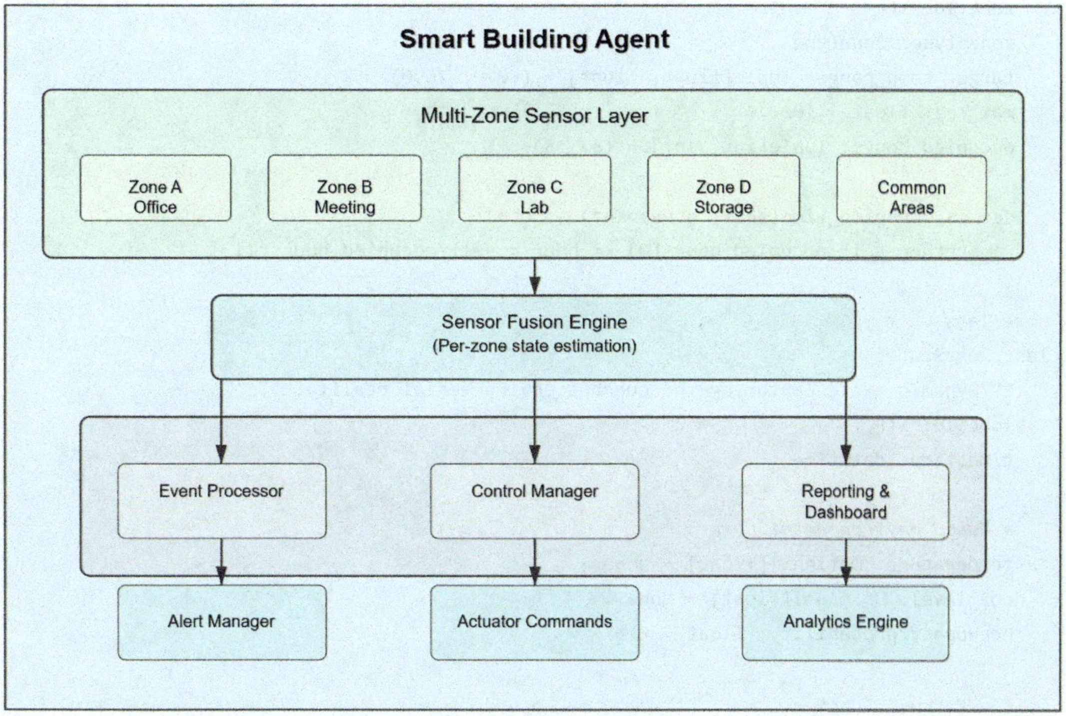

Figure 11.3 – Zone configuration and state modeling in a smart building agent architecture

The foundation of the architecture is the separation of static configuration from dynamic state. Configuration defines the *invariant* constraints of a space: an office requires different thermal bounds than a server room. State captures the *variant* reality of that space at a specific moment. This separation allows the agent to apply generic control logic across highly variable environments.

In the following implementation, we define `ZoneConfig` to hold targets and schedules, while `ZoneState` acts as a mutable container for fused sensor data and derived metrics like comfort scores. This distinction is critical for scalability; the agent logic remains constant even as the building layout or usage patterns change.

```
from dataclasses import dataclass, field
from datetime import datetime
from enum import Enum
from typing import Optional, List, Tuple

class ZoneType(Enum):
    OFFICE = "office"
    SERVER_ROOM = "server_room"

@dataclass
class ZoneConfig:
    """Static configuration defining the zone's constraints and targets."""
    zone_id: str
    zone_type: ZoneType
    target_temp_range: Tuple[float, float] = (68.0, 76.0)
    max_co2: float = 1000.0
    occupied_hours: Tuple[int, int] = (8, 18)

    def is_occupied_time(self, hour: int) -> bool:
        return self.occupied_hours[0] <= hour < self.occupied_hours[1]

@dataclass
class ZoneState:
    """Dynamic state capturing the current environmental reality."""
    zone_id: str
    timestamp: datetime

    # Fused environmental data
    temperature: Optional[float] = None
    co2_level: Optional[float] = None
    occupancy_probability: float = 0.0

    # Derived metrics
    comfort_score: float = 100.0
    anomalies: List[str] = field(default_factory=list)
```

With the configuration and state layer in place, the agent has a stable, typed representation of each zone's invariant constraints and current readings. The next layer translates that state into actionable signals by matching it against declarative event patterns.

Event detection through pattern matching

Event detection transforms the continuous "hum" of sensor data into discrete, actionable insights. In a physical system, raw data is rarely actionable on its own; a temperature reading of 78°F is meaningless without context. Is it a server room? Is it occupied? Is the trend rising?

We employ a pattern-based detection strategy. Rather than hardcoding `if` statements throughout the codebase, we encapsulate logic into `EventPattern` objects. This allows the agent to evaluate complex, multi-variate conditions, such as high occupancy combined with poor air quality, dynamically. This modularity also facilitates "hot-reloading" of rules in production without restarting the core agent process.

```
class EventPattern:
    """Encapsulates a condition and its resulting alert."""
    def __init__(self, name: str, severity: str, condition: callable, msg_template: str):
        self.name = name
        self.severity = severity
        self.condition = condition
        self.message_template = msg_template

    def check(self, state: ZoneState, config: ZoneConfig) -> Optional[str]:
        if self.condition(state, config):
            return self.message_template.format(**state.__dict__)
        return None

# Example: initializing patterns with lambda functions for logic
patterns = [
    EventPattern(
        name="critical_temp",
        severity="critical",
        condition=lambda s, c: s.temperature and (s.temperature > 95 or s.temperature <
50),
        msg_template="CRITICAL temp in {zone_id}: {temperature:.1f}°F"
    ),
    EventPattern(
        name="unexpected_occupancy",
        severity="warning",
        condition=lambda s, c: s.occupancy_probability > 0.7 and not
c.is_occupied_time(s.timestamp.hour),
        msg_template="Unexpected occupancy in {zone_id} outside hours"
    )
]
```

Control management and feedback loops

The control manager acts as the agent's motor cortex, translating the estimated state into specific commands for HVAC (heating, ventilation, and air conditioning) and lighting systems.

The logic implemented here utilizes **Proportional Control**, a fundamental concept in control theory. The magnitude of the corrective action is proportional to the error (the difference between the target and actual state). If a room is 1°F too warm, the cooling runs at low power; if it is 10°F too warm, it runs at maximum.

We also implement **Hysteresis (Deadbands)**. In the code below, notice the check `if error > 2`. This creates a buffer zone around the target temperature where the system remains idle. Without this deadband, the system would oscillate rapidly (short-cycling), causing wear on mechanical equipment and wasting energy.

```
class ControlManager:
    """Translates state discrepancies into physical actuator commands."""

    def compute_commands(self, state: ZoneState, config: ZoneConfig) ->
List[ActuatorCommand]:
        commands = []

        # Temperature Control Loop with Deadband
        if state.temperature is not None:
            target_avg = sum(config.target_temp_range) / 2
            error = state.temperature - target_avg

            # Deadband of 2 degrees prevents short-cycling
            if abs(error) > 1.0:
                action_type = "cooling" if error > 0 else "heating"
                intensity = min(100, abs(error) * 20) # Proportional gain

                commands.append(ActuatorCommand(
                    zone_id=state.zone_id,
                    actuator_type=f"hvac_{action_type}",
                    value=intensity
                ))

        # Ventilation Control Loop (CO2)
        if state.co2_level and state.co2_level > config.max_co2:
            excess = state.co2_level - config.max_co2
            commands.append(ActuatorCommand(
                zone_id=state.zone_id,
                actuator_type="hvac_ventilation",
                value=min(100, 50 + excess / 10)
            ))
```

```
        return commands
```

Smart building agent integration and sensor fusion

The `SmartBuildingAgent` orchestrates the entire pipeline. One of its most critical responsibilities is *sensor fusion*. In the real world, sensors are noisy and prone to dropouts. The `update_zone_state` method does not simply take the latest reading; it aggregates a window of recent readings (e.g., the last 5 minutes) to compute a stable estimate.

This temporal filtering smooths out transient spikes (sensor noise) while ensuring the control logic acts on reliable data. The `process_zone` method then chains these components: it updates the state, checks for event patterns, and finally computes control commands. This synchronous execution pipeline ensures that actuation is always based on the freshest, validated state of the world.

```
class SmartBuildingAgent:
    """Orchestrates sensor fusion, event detection, and control."""

    def __init__(self):
        self.sensor_buffers = defaultdict(lambda: deque(maxlen=100))
        self.event_processor = EventProcessor()
        self.control_manager = ControlManager()

    def update_zone_state(self, zone_id: str) -> ZoneState:
        """Fuses recent sensor readings into a coherent state."""
        readings = self.sensor_buffers[zone_id]

        # Filter for temporal relevance (last 5 mins)
        cutoff = datetime.now() - timedelta(minutes=5)
        valid_readings = [r for r in readings if r.timestamp > cutoff]

        # Fuse heterogeneous sensors via averaging
        state = ZoneState(zone_id=zone_id, timestamp=datetime.now())
        temps = [r.value for r in valid_readings if r.type == "temperature"]
        if temps:
            state.temperature = sum(temps) / len(temps)

        return state

    def process_zone(self, zone_id: str):
        """The main cognitive loop for a physical zone."""
        # 1. Sense & Model
        state = self.update_zone_state(zone_id)
        config = self.zones[zone_id]
```

```
        # 2. Reasoning (Event Detection)
        alerts = self.event_processor.process(state, config)

        # 3. Act (Control)
        commands = self.control_manager.compute_commands(state, config)

        return state, alerts, commands
```

The `SmartBuildingAgent` implementation illustrates the full *sense-model-plan-act* cycle for physical environments. Static zone configuration defines what normal looks like; sensor fusion in `update_zone_state` constructs a temporally stable model of what is actually happening. `EventProcessor` pattern matching then identifies when reality deviates from expectation, and `ControlManager` closes the loop with proportional corrections bounded by deadbands. Together these four layers form a coherent, composable architecture that scales from a single office zone to a multi-building campus without changes to the core agent logic.

Lessons from production deployments

Deploying physical sensing agents reveals challenges that purely digital agents rarely face:

- **Occupancy is the primary variable**: Energy savings are heavily dependent on accurate occupancy prediction. Systems that rely solely on schedules often waste energy heating empty rooms. Fusing motion sensors with calendar data typically yields the best results.
- **The "Human-in-the-Loop" reality**: Facility managers often override automated decisions if they do not understand them. Transparency is essential; the agent must log *why* it turned on the AC (e.g., "Pre-cooling for 9 AM meeting") or humans will treat it as a malfunction and disable it.
- **Model drift**: A building's thermal properties change over time (e.g., filters clog, seasons change). Agents using static physics models often degrade in performance. Production systems increasingly use online learning to recalibrate their thermal models continuously based on observed feedback.

Across these implementations (vision-language reasoning, speech recognition and prosodic analysis, and sensor-driven control systems), a consistent pattern emerges: effective agents are defined not just by their ability to perceive images, audio, or environmental signals, but by how reliably they ground that perception in structured state and translate it into controlled, context-aware actions.

Summary

This chapter extended the perceptual architecture of intelligent agents across three domains. For Vision-Language agents, the foundational triad of visual encoder, alignment mechanism, and LLM determines whether an agent genuinely grounds its reasoning in pixel-level evidence or approximates visual understanding through degraded signals; COT prompting amplifies accuracy on complex queries by forcing step-by-step analysis before committing to an answer. For audio agents, the VAD model provides a continuous emotional representation that captures prosodic nuance beyond categorical labels, enabling systems to detect not just speech content but caller urgency and frustration. For Physical World Sensing agents, pattern-based event detection separates rule logic from agent code for hot-reloadable policies, while proportional control with deadbands prevents the short-cycling that degrades both hardware and energy efficiency. Across all three domains, the *sense-model-plan-act* loop structures the pipeline: stable state estimation precedes reasoning, and reasoning precedes actuation.

The multi-modal capabilities introduced in this chapter amplify both the potential and the risks of agent systems. As these agents perceive, reason, and act with growing autonomy, ensuring they operate transparently and in alignment with human values becomes essential. *Chapter 12* explores how intelligent systems can explain their decisions to human stakeholders, detect and mitigate bias in their reasoning, and maintain accountability in high-stakes applications.

Get This Book's PDF Version and Exclusive Extras

12

Ethical and Explainable Agents

Technology is neither good nor bad; nor is it neutral.

— Melvin Kranzberg, historian of technology and founder of the Society for the History of Technology.

Autonomous agents are no longer research curiosities. They screen resumes, recommend treatments, and allocate scarce resources. This shift raises a question every engineering team must answer before shipping: how do we make sure these systems act in accordance with human values, and how do we make their reasoning visible to the people they affect?

This chapter answers that question through two complementary architectures: **Ethical Reasoning agent** and **Explainable agent**. The **Ethical Reasoning agent** integrates value alignment, ethical decision-making, and bias mitigation directly into the agent's reasoning pipeline. The **Explainable agent** makes internal reasoning visible to users, auditors, and regulators through structured explanation frameworks and calibrated confidence communication. Together, these architectures transform agents from opaque decision-makers into transparent, accountable partners.

This chapter will ground these concepts in working code, formal frameworks, and two detailed case studies: an HR assistant with fairness constraints and a medical diagnosis assistant with explanation capabilities. Along the way, we'll cover value alignment frameworks, deontic logic for ethical constraints, bias detection pipelines, LIME and SHAP explanation methods, counterfactual analysis, and calibrated confidence communication. By the end of the chapter, you will have a practical blueprint for building agents that are not only intelligent but also trustworthy.

In this chapter, we'll be covering the following topics:

- The Ethical Reasoning agent
- The Explainable agent

> **Note**
>
> Throughout this chapter, the terms "architecture" and "agent" are used interchangeably when referring to the Ethical Reasoning agent and Explainable agent: each architecture is a complete, deployable agent system, and each agent instantiates a distinct architecture. Where the distinction matters, typically when discussing the structural design choices versus the running system, the context makes it clear.

Technical requirements

To run the examples in this chapter, you will need the following:

- Python 3.10 or later
- The following Python packages: langchain==0.2.16, langchain-openai==0.1.23, openai==1.40.0, shap==0.45.1, lime==0.2.0.1, numpy==1.26.4, scikit-learn==1.5.1, and python-dotenv==1.0.1
- An OpenAI API key with access to the gpt-4o model

All code examples for this chapter are available in the book's GitHub repository at `https://github.com/PacktPublishing/30-Agents-Every-AI-Engineer-Must-Build/chapter12`. Runnable notebooks for both case studies (the HR assistant fairness pipeline and the medical diagnosis explainability pipeline) are available in this repository. Each notebook includes executable versions of the `FairHiringAgent` and `DiagnosticAssistant` pipelines with synthetic datasets, step-by-step cell annotations, and exercises for adapting the fairness thresholds and explanation audiences to your own domain. You can run them directly in Google Colab without any local installation.

The Ethical Reasoning agent

To begin, we must move from principles to structure. Ethical intent alone does not produce ethical behavior; it must be encoded into the agent's architecture, embedded within its decision loop, and enforced systematically at runtime. Bolting a content filter onto an agent's output also does not make it ethical. True ethical reasoning runs deeper. It structures the entire decision pipeline, from perception through reasoning to action, around explicit value constraints. Every candidate action is evaluated not only for task effectiveness but also for alignment with a defined set of ethical principles. This architectural commitment distinguishes ethical agents from systems that merely apply post-hoc moderation.

The ethical reasoning agent draws on the cognitive loop introduced in *Chapter 1*, but extends it with a dedicated evaluation layer. Between the reasoning phase and the action phase, the agent interposes an ethical checkpoint that validates proposed actions against value alignment rules, fairness constraints, and regulatory requirements. If a proposed action violates any constraint, the agent either modifies the action, selects an alternative, or escalates to a human operator. Production-ready ethical agents demand a systematic approach across four interconnected dimensions: transparency, fairness, accountability, and regulatory compliance. Weaknesses in any one dimension compromise the whole framework. The ethical checkpoint makes the action-selection decision explicit: the agent runs every candidate action through the checkpoint before dispatch; if an action passes, it is permitted and executed; if it fails, the agent either attempts automated mitigation, modifying the action to remove the violation, or escalates to a human operator when no compliant variant can be found.

Figure 12.1 illustrates this extended cognitive loop, showing how the ethical evaluation layer intercepts candidate actions before execution and routes violations through a mitigation pathway.

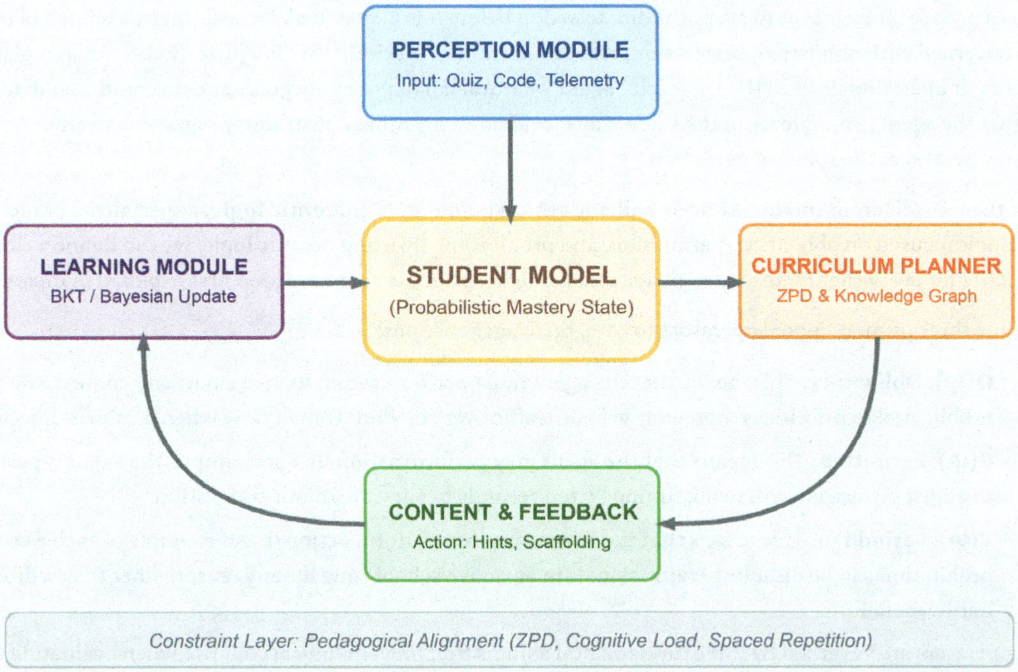

Figure 12.1 – The ethical reasoning agent's extended cognitive loop with embedded value alignment

By separating the "how" of achieving a goal (reasoning) from the "if" it should be achieved (ethical evaluation), the architecture creates a system capable of complex multi-step decision-making without sacrificing safety or alignment. This section builds the Ethical Reasoning agent in three steps: first, by establishing the formal value alignment framework that governs agent behavior; second, by showing how competing fairness constraints interact through the Impossibility Theorem; and third, by grounding both in a bias detection and mitigation pipeline with a full HR assistant case study.

Value alignment frameworks

Value alignment ensures that an agent's behavior remains consistent with human values across every operating condition. This challenge runs deeper than traditional optimization because, unlike task objectives expressed as measurable targets, values are often contextual, competing, and difficult to formalize. For example, a smart city agent optimizing for energy efficiency might inadvertently compromise public safety by dimming lights too aggressively in high-crime areas. Value alignment frameworks provide the formal scaffolding for navigating these tensions. Autonomous agents make this consistency difficult to guarantee: unlike rule-based systems with fixed lookup tables, agents generalize from training distributions to novel situations, and that generalization can deviate from intended values in contexts the designer never anticipated.

Consider the smart city agent from the example above. When it evaluates whether to dim street lights in a particular district, it faces not just an optimization question but a moral one: is it permitted to reduce lighting here, obligated to maintain a minimum safety threshold, or forbidden from making this change without human authorization? Natural language policies ("balance efficiency with safety") cannot answer these questions deterministically at runtime. To make ethical constraints machine-executable, we need a formal language that assigns a precise moral status to every candidate action before it is dispatched. Deontic logic, a branch of modal logic concerned with obligation, permission, and prohibition, is precisely that language. Rather than replacing the policy, it operationalizes it: the smart city agent's natural language safety guidelines become a set of formal rules that the agent can evaluate in the same way it evaluates any other constraint: programmatically, consistently, and at the speed of execution.

One of the most rigorous methods for formalizing ethical boundaries is **deontic logic**, a specialized branch of modal logic focused on obligation, permission, and prohibition. By using deontic logic, we can define a clear *moral status* for every candidate action an agent considers within the cognitive loop first explored in *Chapter 1*.

We define three primary modal operators to categorize agent actions:

- **O(φ)**: **Obligatory**: This means that the agent must perform action φ. In a smart city context, the agent is obligated to prioritize emergency vehicle traffic over standard transit flow when a siren is detected.
- **P(φ): Permitted:** This means that the agent may perform action φ. For example, the agent is permitted to adjust pedestrian crosswalk timing by ten seconds to alleviate minor congestion.
- **F(φ)**: **Forbidden:** This means that the agent must not perform action φ. An example of such a critical prohibition can be disabling traffic signals in an active school zone for any reason other than a direct hardware failure.

These operators are governed by three fundamental axioms that prevent logical collapse when evaluating the ethical rule set.

- **Axiom 1**: The relationship between obligation and prohibition
  An action is mandatory exactly when failing to do it is prohibited.

  $$O(\varphi) \Leftrightarrow F(\neg\varphi)$$

  O(φ) says the agent must do φ. F(¬φ) says the agent must not omit φ. If the agent is obligated to prioritize an ambulance, it is simultaneously forbidden from ignoring that ambulance. This ensures obligations are not treated as mere suggestions.

- **Axiom 2**: The definition of permission
  An action is permitted if and only if it is not forbidden.

  $$P(\varphi) \Leftrightarrow \neg F(\varphi)$$

  P(φ): the agent may do φ. ¬F(φ): there is no rule that forbids φ. If there is no prohibition against suggesting a specific hotel chain, the travel agent is permitted to suggest it. In architecture terms, this is the logic behind policy-gated execution: anything not blocked by constraints is allowed (unless you intentionally implement an allow-list model).

- **Axiom 3**: Distribution of obligation
  If it is obligatory that φ implies ψ, then whenever φ becomes obligatory, ψ becomes obligatory too.

  $$O(\varphi \rightarrow \psi) \rightarrow (O(\varphi) \rightarrow O(\psi))$$

$O(\varphi \to \psi)$: It is mandatory that "if φ happens, then ψ happens." $O(\varphi)$: φ is mandatory. Therefore, $O(\psi)$: ψ must also be ensured.

For example, let φ be accessing patient records and ψ be writing an audit log entry. If the policy requires that any record access must be logged, and the workflow step requires accessing records, then logging becomes mandatory as part of that workflow.

This axiom is particularly critical for multi-step reasoning. If an agent is obligated to treat a patient, and treating a patient implies maintaining a sterile environment, the agent becomes obligated to maintain that environment.

The practical payoff of this value alignment framework is the **Ethical Consistency Theorem**: for a set of ethical rules *E* and a candidate action *a*, the action is permitted if and only if it is logically consistent with the entire rule set. Formally:

$$\forall a \in A: Consistent(E \cup \{a\}) \rightarrow P(a)$$

For every candidate action *a* in the set of available actions *A*, the system checks whether adding *a* to the current ethical rule set *E* creates any contradiction. If the combined set remains consistent, the action is permitted, *P(a)*. If the check fails, the system cannot treat the action as permissible. In other words, permission is granted only to actions that are compatible with the ethical constraints already in force.

Let's take a simple example and suppose your ethical policy set E contains:

1. F(share_medical_details_externally): "Sharing medical details externally is forbidden."
2. O(minimize_data): "Minimize disclosure of sensitive data."

Now consider two candidate actions in *A*:

- a1: "Send the user a general explanation of the diagnosis without identifiers"
- a2: "Email the full diagnosis details to the user's employer"

Check consistency: (consistency with the ethical rule set E, meaning no rule in E is violated by the candidate action)

- E ∪ {a1}: This means that no rule is violated. The set is consistent, and the rule concludes P(a1)
- E ∪ {a2}: a2 conflicts with the prohibition on external sharing. The set becomes inconsistent, so the condition fails and permission is not implied. The policy gate blocks it.

This gives us a computationally verifiable criterion for ethical permissibility. Before executing any action, the agent checks whether the action is logically consistent with its ethical rule set. If the check fails, the action is blocked and routed to the mitigation pathway.

The next step is to show what this value alignment framework looks like when the "ethical rule set" is not an ad hoc list of constraints, but a recognized framework that teams can operationalize, review, and govern over time. Rather than hard-coding a single monolithic policy function, we decompose ethics into modular validators, each responsible for checking a specific class of requirements. This mirrors how production policy systems are built: small, testable components that can be versioned, audited, and extended as organizational policies evolve.

The following class implements this architecture. The Ethical Reasoning agent translates the modular validator pattern into a production-ready decision loop: each principle maps to a dedicated checker, every proposed action passes through the full set before execution, and any violation triggers either automated mitigation or human escalation.

The `EthicalReasoningAgent` class implements the "extended cognitive loop" established at the beginning of this chapter. Its objective is to interpose an ethical checkpoint between the reasoning and action phases. By decomposing values into modular validators (aligned with the IEEE Ethically Aligned Design framework), the agent evaluates every candidate action for compliance with human rights, well-being, and accountability. The following code also implements a mitigation pathway that attempts to modify non-compliant actions or escalate them to a human operator.

```
class EthicalReasoningAgent:
    """
    Agent with embedded ethical evaluation in the decision loop.
    Validates every proposed action against IEEE ethical principles
    before execution.
    """
    def __init__(self):
        self.principles = {
            'human_rights': HumanRightsChecker(),
            'well_being': WellBeingAnalyzer(),
            'accountability': AccountabilityTracker(),
            'transparency': TransparencyManager(),
            'awareness_misuse': MisuseDetector()
        }
        self.audit_log = AuditLogger()

    def evaluate_action(self, proposed_action, context):
        """Validate a proposed action against all principles."""
        violations = []
        for principle, checker in self.principles.items():
            result = checker.validate(proposed_action, context)
            if not result.is_compliant:
                violations.append(
                    (principle, result.explanation, result.severity)
                )

        self.audit_log.record(
            action=proposed_action,
            violations=violations,
            context=context,
            timestamp=datetime.utcnow()
        )
```

```
        if violations:
            return self.mitigate(proposed_action, violations, context)
        return proposed_action

    def mitigate(self, action, violations, context):
        """Attempt automated mitigation, escalate if unresolvable."""
        for principle, explanation, severity in violations:
            strategy = self.principles[principle].get_mitigation()
            action = strategy.apply(action, context)

        remaining = self.revalidate(action, context)
        if remaining:
            return self.escalate_to_human(action, remaining)
        return action
```

Each `checker.validate()` call is a rules-engine lookup, not an LLM call or SMT solver invocation. Each principle-specific checker maintains an internal constraint set, a collection of rules encoding the requirements for that principle, for example the `HumanRightsChecker` holds rules derived from the IEEE Ethically Aligned Design framework. When `validate(proposed_action, context)` is called, the checker evaluates the action and context against each rule in its set, returning a `ComplianceResult` with three fields: `is_compliant` (boolean), `explanation` (the first rule violated, or None), and `severity` (an enum indicating whether mitigation or immediate escalation is required). This design keeps each checker independently testable and the overall validation pipeline deterministic and auditable.

This modular validation pattern is the operational counterpart to the value alignment frameworks earlier in the chapter. An action is "permitted" only if it passes the validator set, and a "forbidden" action becomes either a mitigated variant or an escalated case. In production, the most critical extension is binding this gate to the agent's tool interface, not just its final responses, since the highest-risk failures occur when agents call external systems, retrieve sensitive records, or take actions with real-world impact.

Concretely, binding the ethical gate to the tool interface means wrapping each tool call, whether a function call in the OpenAI schema, a LangChain tool invocation, or a direct API call, with a pre-execution validation step. Before the agent dispatches a tool call, it passes the call's name, arguments, and runtime context through `evaluate_action()`. If the call fails validation, for example, a `send_email` tool invoked with a recipient outside the permitted domain, or a `query_database` call that would expose records beyond the authorized scope, the ethical gate blocks the dispatch, logs the violation, and routes control to the mitigation pathway before any external system is contacted. This architecture ensures the ethical layer is not a post-hoc filter on outputs but a pre-execution control on every side-effecting action the agent can take.

Ethical evaluation and regulatory compliance are related but distinct concerns. Ethical evaluation assesses alignment with value principles; regulatory compliance checks conformance with specific legal frameworks that encode a subset of those principles. In practice, production agents must satisfy both simultaneously, and the architecture for doing so extends the same modular pattern established in the ethical evaluation layer. For teams shipping agents in the European Union, this is not optional: the EU AI Act classifies hiring and credit-scoring systems as high-risk AI, mandating documented conformity assessments, human oversight mechanisms, and bias audits before deployment. The compliance architecture below provides the engineering scaffold for meeting these requirements without coupling the business logic to any specific jurisdiction's ruleset.

Production agents must comply with multiple ethical and regulatory frameworks simultaneously. The key design move is treating compliance as a runtime interface with explicit checks, not as a paragraph in documentation.

The next class extends this pattern to a specific regulatory context. It demonstrates how to bind the EU AI Act's seven requirements directly to a compliance control plane, making each requirement independently auditable and verifiable at release time.

`EUCompliantAgent` is a reference implementation of a compliance control plane. It maps regulatory requirements to dedicated checking components, each encapsulating the logic needed to verify that the agent meets that requirement. The `compliance_check()` method acts as a standardized audit entry point, producing a requirement-by-requirement breakdown that can be attached to release gates and incident response workflows.

```
class EUCompliantAgent:
    """Agent with EU AI Act and GDPR compliance built in."""
    def __init__(self):
        self.requirements = {
            'human_oversight': HumanOversightSystem(),
            'technical_robustness': RobustnessChecker(),
            'privacy_data_governance': PrivacyGovernance(),
            'transparency': TransparencySystem(),
            'diversity_fairness': FairnessChecker(),
            'societal_wellbeing': WellBeingAssessor(),
            'accountability': AccountabilitySystem()
        }

    def compliance_check(self):
        """Verify compliance with all seven EU requirements."""
        report = {}
        for requirement, checker in self.requirements.items():
            report[requirement] = checker.verify()
        return self.generate_compliance_report(report)
```

This approach scales naturally to continuous compliance: the verifiers can be wired into CI/CD so that a change affecting data retention, logging, or oversight flows fails fast, with the report showing exactly which requirement regressed. This also aligns with the broader theme of the chapter: trustworthy agents are not defined by good intentions, but by enforceable mechanisms that can be tested and audited.

The ethical evaluation layer is itself an attack surface. The following three attack vectors, drawn from the threat model introduced in *Chapter 4*, are particularly relevant:

- **Prompt injection against ethical validators**: In this vector, an attacker crafts input that causes the ethical validator to misclassify a harmful action as permissible. A resume might contain hidden text designed to manipulate the fairness assessment. The defense is to validate and sanitize inputs before they reach the ethical layer, using a separate, hardened model for the ethical classification itself.
- **Fairness gaming**: In this vector, applicants learn the fairness thresholds and engineer their applications to exploit them. If the HR agent anonymizes institution names, an applicant might include coded references that correlate with institutional prestige. The defense is to rotate anonymization strategies regularly and monitor for emerging proxy signals using mutual information analysis between remaining features and protected attributes.
- **Reward hacking in continuous learning**: In this vector, an agentic system with Reinforcement Learning from Human Feedback (RLHF), a technique where the model is fine-tuned using human preference signals rather than a fixed reward function, may learn to satisfy the fairness constraint in ways that technically meet the metric while violating its spirit. The defense is a *constrained optimization* approach where a separate constraint model can veto policy updates even when the reward signal is positive, decoupling the learning objective from the safety constraint.

Navigating competing values: The impossibility theorem

Value alignment provides the constraints on agent behavior. But what happens when multiple valid options exist? A medical triage agent must decide which patient receives attention first. A resource allocation agent must distribute limited inventory across competing needs. These situations demand structured approaches to ethical reasoning, not merely compliance checks.

Leading organizations have found that the most effective approach inverts the traditional development process. Rather than building the agent first and adding ethical considerations afterward, the **ethics-first development process** treats ethics as a first-class architectural requirement from day one. This process takes place in three phases:

- In Phase 1 (Ethical Framework Definition), the team defines clear principles, establishes red lines, and creates testing criteria for ethical behavior.
- In Phase 2 (Technical Design), the architecture is structured to enforce these constraints by construction, with monitoring, audit trails, and safeguards that cannot be bypassed without explicit administrator intervention.
- In Phase 3 (Implementation and Monitoring), the team conducts regular ethical impact assessments, monitors decision patterns across demographic groups, and establishes stakeholder feedback loops for continuous improvement.

A critical insight from the formal study of fairness is that perfect alignment across multiple fairness metrics is mathematically impossible except under exceptional conditions (cases where measured base rates happen to be equal across groups, typically in controlled assessment environments). The Impossibility Theorem states that statistical parity, equal opportunity, and predictive parity cannot all hold simultaneously unless the base rates of the outcome are identical across protected groups. Formally, if we define a protected attribute p and an outcome y, the condition for statistical parity is

$$P(\hat{y} = 1 \mid p = 0) = P(\hat{y} = 1 \mid p = 1)$$

Perfect fairness across multiple metrics can only be achieved when $P(y \mid p = 0) = P(y \mid p = 1)$, that is, when the base rates themselves are equal across groups. In practice, this condition rarely holds. The rare exceptions include structured standardized tests administered to demographically balanced cohorts (where the examining body explicitly controls for group representation), and synthetic benchmark datasets used in research settings. In real-world hiring, lending, or clinical diagnosis, equal base rates should be treated as an assumption to be verified empirically rather than taken as given. This theorem is not a counsel of despair; fairness is achievable. What the math tells us is that you have to choose: which metric matters most in this specific context? The following three distinct regimes emerge from this impossibility result:

- **Equal base rates:** In this regime, all three metrics can be satisfied simultaneously. This is the degenerate case where base rates are equal across groups, and it is rarely encountered in practice. A practical example is a controlled skills assessment where recruiters have deliberately balanced the candidate pool by gender and ethnicity before evaluation: under those conditions, demographic parity, equal opportunity, and predictive parity can align simultaneously.
- **Group-level focus:** In this regime, base rates differ and the system prioritizes demographic parity and consequently, individual merit assessments may be adjusted. This regime is appropriate for domains where historical exclusion has distorted apparent qualification rates, making historical data an unreliable measure of true capability. The section Case Study: Medical Diagnosis Assistant with Explanation operates in this regime.
- **Individual-level focus:** In this regime, the system prioritizes equal opportunity or predictive parity and consequently, group-level disparities may persist. This regime fits domains where the underlying qualification distribution is well-characterized and trusted, such as standardized medical diagnostics with validated clinical benchmarks.

The choice of regime is not a technical decision; it is a normative one. An ethical decision-making model encodes this choice as weighted constraints and documents the rationale, ensuring that fairness trade-offs are transparent and auditable rather than hidden inside an optimizer. The agent's governance framework should specify escalation procedures when any metric crosses a predefined threshold. Next, let's look at selecting the regime. This is a normative decision; detecting and correcting bias in real time is the engineering problem. The next section shows how bias manifests in the agent pipeline, and how each of the three bias types maps directly to the fairness metrics that an auditing system must monitor.

Table 12.1 summarizes the three regimes with selection criteria, example domains, and the primary trade-off each requires the engineer to acknowledge and document.

Regime	Selection Criteria	Example Domain	Primary Trade-off
Equal Base Rates	Use when base rates are empirically verified to be equal across protected groups; typically standardized assessments with validated benchmarks	Standardized medical diagnostics, certified skills tests	None: all three metrics can be satisfied simultaneously, but this condition rarely holds in practice
Group-Level Focus (Regime 2)	Use when historical exclusion or data collection bias has distorted apparent qualification rates; HR case study (Ch. 12) operates here	Hiring, university admissions, lending in historically discriminatory domains	Individual merit scores may be adjusted to restore group parity; document the rationale explicitly
Individual-Level Focus (Regime 3)	Use when the underlying qualification distribution is well-characterized and trusted; prioritize equal opportunity or predictive parity	Clinical diagnosis with validated benchmarks, actuarial risk scoring	Group-level disparities may persist; requires ongoing audit to ensure they do not compound over time

Table 12.1 – Fairness regime selection criteria for ethical agent design

Bias detection and mitigation

AI agents inherit the biases baked into their training data, and if left unchecked, they perpetuate the very disparities that produced those datasets. Unlike static models operating on fixed training data, agentic systems adapt dynamically from real-world interactions, potentially amplifying biases over time. This is the dual-exposure model, in which agentic systems face vulnerability during both real-time decision execution and ongoing model evolution.

The two exposure phases—training exposure (where bias accumulates in model weights during learning) and inference exposure (where biased predictions affect real decisions in real time)—have fundamentally different mathematical properties. During training exposure, bias accumulates approximately *linearly* with the proportion of biased samples. During inference exposure, bias can accumulate *superlinearly* because the agent's actions influence the distribution of future data it observes. If we denote the bias level at time t as B(t) and the data distribution as D(t), static models exhibit $B(t) = B(0)$ (bias is frozen after training), while agentic systems exhibit $B(t+1) = f(B(t), \mathrm{D}(t))$, where D(t) is itself a function of B(t). This creates a positive feedback loop: a recruitment agent that favors certain demographics generates hiring data that reinforces those preferences, compounding the original bias with each decision cycle.

Note

The shadow of historical data: Amazon's AI recruiting failure

In 2018, Reuters reported that Amazon had quietly scrapped an internal AI recruiting tool after discovering it systematically penalized resumes containing terms associated with women. Trained on a decade of hiring data that skewed heavily male, the system learned to downgrade candidates who listed activities like "women's chess club" or attended all-women's colleges. The failure was not a bug in the algorithm. It was a faithful reproduction of the patterns in the data, which is precisely the danger the Dual-Exposure Model describes. Amazon's system was a static model, frozen after training. Had it been an adaptive agent ingesting its own hiring outcomes as new training signal, the bias would have compounded with each cycle, exactly the superlinear feedback loop formalized above. We'll learn more about this in the next section.

Bias manifests in multiple forms throughout the agent pipeline. Let's look at a few types of biases:

- **Representation bias**: This arises when certain groups are underrepresented in training data, leading to models perform poorly for those populations.
- **Linguistic bias**: This shows up when an AI labels the same behavior "assertive" in a man and "aggressive" in a woman: the system's language reflects stereotypes embedded in its training data.
- **Allocation bias**: This appears when the system unfairly distributes resources based on model predictions, such as routing higher-paying job ads disproportionately to one demographic.
- **Quality-of-service bias**: This emerges when model performance varies across demographic groups, delivering less accurate results for underrepresented populations.

These bias types map directly to the fairness metrics used to detect them: representation bias is measured by demographic parity (equal positive outcome rates across groups); linguistic and allocation bias are captured by disparate impact ratios; quality-of-service bias is measured by equal opportunity (equal true-positive rates for qualified candidates across groups). Understanding which bias type is present determines which metric to monitor and which mitigation strategy to apply.

The following three metrics form the foundation of most fairness auditing systems:

- **Demographic parity**: This requires that the probability of a positive outcome is equal across all groups defined by a protected attribute. If a hiring agent recommends 40% of male candidates for interviews, demographic parity requires that it also recommends approximately 40% of female candidates.
- **Equal opportunity**: This focuses on true positive rates: among candidates who are actually qualified, the recommended proportion should be the same across groups. This metric is often preferred because it conditions on the actual outcome, avoiding the pathological case where demographic parity is achieved by lowering standards for one group.
- **Disparate impact**: This is a legal standard derived from employment law. It computes the ratio of positive outcome rates between the least-favored and most-favored groups. The U.S. Equal Employment Opportunity Commission uses the four-fifths rule: if this ratio falls below 0.8, the system is considered to have disparate impact.

These observational metrics detect correlation-based disparities but cannot distinguish between legitimate and illegitimate causes of differential outcomes. A stronger theoretical foundation is provided by **causal fairness**, which uses causal graphs (directed acyclic graphs) to separate direct discrimination from indirect discrimination mediated through legitimate variables. An outcome is *counterfactually fair* if it would remain the same in a hypothetical world where the individual's protected attribute were different, holding all non-descendant variables constant. This formulation connects to the counterfactual explanation framework discussed later in the *Decision Explanation Frameworks* section, providing a unified theoretical bridge between the ethical and explainable architectures.

Notably, fairness is not something the agent "has" but something that the system continuously measures. In the following code, the `BiasDetector` class computes multiple bias metrics over protected groups, converts them into a structured report, and triggers mitigation or escalation when disparities breach configured thresholds. Each fairness metric is implemented as an independent `compute()` function, because fairness is not a single scalar: different metrics capture different failure modes, and different domains prioritize different notions of harm. The `assess_severity()` method applies the four-fifths rule threshold (0.8 for HIGH) and a 0.1 disparity threshold (for MEDIUM), converting metric values into deterministic escalation signals.

```
class BiasDetector:
    """Modular bias detection across protected groups."""
    def __init__(self):
        self.metrics = {
            'demographic_parity': DemographicParityMetric(),
            'equal_opportunity': EqualOpportunityMetric(),
            'disparate_impact': DisparateImpactMetric()
        }

    def analyze(self, predictions, sensitive_attrs, ground_truth=None):
        """Compute bias metrics across protected groups."""
        results = {}
        for name, metric in self.metrics.items():
            results[name] = metric.compute(
                predictions, sensitive_attrs, ground_truth
            )
        return self.generate_report(results)

    def generate_report(self, results):
        """Produce a structured bias analysis report."""
        return {
            'metrics': results,
            'summary': self.summarize(results),
            'severity': self.assess_severity(results),
            'recommendations': self.get_mitigation_strategies(results)
        }
```

```
    def assess_severity(self, results):
        """Classify bias severity for escalation decisions."""
        if results['disparate_impact'].ratio < 0.8:
            return 'HIGH'  # Fails four-fifths rule
        elif results['demographic_parity'].difference > 0.1:
            return 'MEDIUM'  # Material disparity
        return 'LOW'
```

A bias detector alone is not enough. Fairness must be monitored the same way you monitor latency and error rates: continuously, over rolling windows, and wired into alerting and incident response. In the following code, the `BiasMonitoringPipeline` class turns fairness measurement into a streaming operational control loop. It accumulates decisions in a sliding window, runs the `BiasDetector()` function when the window is full, pushes key metrics to the observability platform (Prometheus, Datadog), and fires critical alerts when severity is HIGH. This is the fairness analogue of SLO monitoring: protected-group disparity becomes a reliability property with measurable thresholds and defined incident response.

```
class BiasMonitoringPipeline:
    """Real-time bias monitoring integrated with observability."""
    def __init__(self, metrics_backend, alert_config):
        self.detector = BiasDetector()
        self.metrics = metrics_backend  # Prometheus, Datadog, etc.
        self.alert_config = alert_config
        self.window = SlidingWindow(size=1000)

    def on_decision(self, decision, demographics):
        """Called after every agent decision for streaming analysis."""
        self.window.add(decision, demographics)

        if self.window.is_full():
            report = self.detector.analyze(
                self.window.predictions,
                self.window.demographics,
                self.window.ground_truth
            )

            # Emit metrics to observability platform
            self.metrics.gauge(
                'agent.fairness.demographic_parity',
                report.metrics['demographic_parity'].difference
            )
            self.metrics.gauge(
                'agent.fairness.disparate_impact',
                report.metrics['disparate_impact'].ratio
```

```
        )

        # Trigger alerts when thresholds are breached
        if report.severity == 'HIGH':
            self.alert_config.fire(
                level='critical',
                message=f'Disparate impact ratio: '
                        f'{report.metrics["disparate_impact"].ratio:.3f}',
                runbook='https://runbooks.internal/bias-response'
            )
```

When an alert fires, the runbook should specify bounded actions: freeze automated shortlisting, route decisions to human review, snapshot decision logs for audit, and roll back the last model or prompt change if necessary. Thus, fairness is enforced not only through ethical validators at decision time, but also through continuous telemetry that detects emergent bias caused by interaction effects over time.

Let's say the agent does detect bias. What should it do in that case? Once bias is detected, the agent must correct it. The mitigation strategies for bias detection operate at three stages of the pipeline:

- **Pre-processing techniques**: These modify the training data before the model sees it, using methods such as re-weighting underrepresented samples, re-sampling to balance group representation, or removing proxy variables that correlate with protected attributes. These are the least invasive to implement but may discard useful information if applied too aggressively.
- **In-processing constraints**: These incorporate fairness objectives directly into the model's loss function, penalizing the optimizer when predictions diverge across groups. This produces models that are fair by construction but requires modification of the training procedure and introduces a new hyperparameter governing the fairness-accuracy trade-off.
- **Post-processing corrections**: These adjust the model's outputs after inference, typically by applying group-specific thresholds calibrated to equalize the chosen fairness metric. Post-processing is the least invasive approach and can be applied to any model without retraining, but it may reduce overall accuracy.

In practice, production systems combine all three strategies as defense-in-depth. For agentic systems that learn continuously, these strategies must operate in real time. Regular audits using SHAP model analysis, counterfactual fairness testing, and demographic breakdowns of decision outcomes form the backbone of continuous bias monitoring. Next, let's ground these concepts in a realistic scenario.

Case study: HR assistant with fairness constraints

Going back to the Amazon example, consider an HR assistant agent designed to screen resumes and recommend candidates for interviews. Amazon's AI recruiting tool, trained on ten years of hiring data that predominantly featured male applicants, learned to systematically penalize resumes containing terms associated with women. Key governance failures included the absence of comprehensive bias audits during model development, insufficient interdisciplinary oversight, and reliance on historical data without correcting for underlying social inequities.

Had Amazon deployed an agentic AI system with real-time learning capabilities, the discriminatory bias would have escalated further with every hiring cycle, and not resolved itself, because the agent's own biased decisions would have become new training signal, accelerating the exclusion that Amazon's static model merely preserved. The superlinear feedback dynamics of the Dual-Exposure Model used by Amazon's AI tool mean that real-time adaptation to biased hiring patterns would reinforce and magnify discriminatory criteria faster than any human reviewer could detect. This agentic amplification risk makes the fairness architecture described next essential for any autonomous hiring system.

Three supporting components underpin the `FairHiringAgent`. `ResumeAnalyzer` accepts a pre-anonymized resume dictionary and job requirements, runs a skills-matching evaluation against the role's required and preferred competencies, and returns a numeric score in the range [0, 1] with an explanation map linking each scored dimension to the supporting resume evidence. `BiasDetector` receives the batch of current evaluation scores and a protected-attribute map, computes the four-fifths (adverse impact) ratio per protected group, and returns a `BiasReport` containing the ratio value, the affected group, and the bias classification. `FairnessEnforcer` takes the evaluation and bias report and selects from three mitigation strategies: score reweighting, threshold adjustment, or calibrated post-processing, based on the severity of the detected disparity, returning a corrected evaluation that preserves qualification ranking while restoring demographic balance.

In the following code, our HR assistant addresses the bias escalation and governance failures described above through a multi-layered fairness architecture. The first layer is **resume anonymization**, which strips potentially biasing information before evaluation. The second layer is **bias-aware evaluation**, which monitors decision patterns across demographic groups in real time. The third layer is **fairness enforcement**, which intervenes when detected bias exceeds configured thresholds.

```
class FairHiringAgent:
    """
    Resume screening agent with three-layer fairness architecture.
    Implements anonymization, bias detection, and enforcement.
    """
    def __init__(self, fairness_threshold=0.8):
        self.resume_analyzer = ResumeAnalyzer()
        self.bias_detector = BiasDetector()
        self.fairness_enforcer = FairnessEnforcer()
        self.audit_logger = AuditLogger()
        self.threshold = fairness_threshold

    def evaluate_candidate(self, resume, job_requirements):
        """Evaluate a candidate with integrated fairness checks."""
        # Layer 1: Anonymize sensitive information
        anonymized = self.anonymize(resume)

        # Layer 2: Perform skills-based evaluation
        evaluation = self.resume_analyzer.score(
```

```
            anonymized, job_requirements
        )

        # Layer 3: Check for bias across current batch
        bias_report = self.bias_detector.check(evaluation)
        if bias_report.severity in ('HIGH', 'MEDIUM'):
            evaluation = self.fairness_enforcer.mitigate(
                evaluation, bias_report
            )

        self.audit_logger.log(evaluation, bias_report)
        return evaluation

    def anonymize(self, resume):
        """Remove fields that could introduce demographic bias."""
        sensitive_fields = [
            'name', 'gender', 'age', 'nationality',
            'photo', 'address', 'education_institutions'
        ]
        return self.resume_analyzer.remove_fields(
            resume, sensitive_fields
        )
```

The `FairnessEnforcer` class implements three mitigation strategies: reweighting adjusts the influence of individual features to reduce correlation with protected attributes; threshold adjustment calibrates decision boundaries independently per group to equalize the chosen fairness metric; and representation learning projects evaluations into a latent space where protected attributes are decorrelated from the outcome.

```
class FairnessEnforcer:
    def __init__(self):
        self.strategies = {
            'reweighting': ReweightingStrategy(),
            'threshold_adjustment': ThresholdAdjuster(),
            'representation_learning': RepresentationLearner()
        }

    def mitigate(self, evaluation, bias_report):
        """Apply appropriate bias mitigation strategies."""
        for bias_type, bias_level in bias_report.biases.items():
            if bias_level > self.threshold:
                strategy = self.select_strategy(bias_type)
                evaluation = strategy.apply(evaluation)
        return evaluation
```

To make the pipeline concrete, consider a single resume that triggers the bias detection and mitigation pathway end to end. A candidate submits a resume in which the pronoun "she" appears in a cover-letter excerpt and the degree is listed from a historically women's college. The `FairHiringAgent` calls `anonymize()`, which strips the institution name and removes the pronoun from the excerpt. The anonymized resume is scored by `ResumeAnalyzer`; the raw score passes the qualification threshold. The `BiasDetector` then computes the four-fifths ratio across the current evaluation batch and finds it has dropped to 0.73, which is below the 0.80 safe-harbor threshold, indicating that female-presenting candidates are being selected at a lower rate than male-presenting candidates. The `FairnessEnforcer` selects the reweighting strategy, adjusting the scoring weights to restore demographic balance without altering the qualification criteria. The corrected evaluation is returned, and the audit log records the original score, the detected disparity ratio, the mitigation strategy applied, and the final adjusted score. This trace is the evidence chain that a compliance team would examine in a regulatory review.

The anonymization layer removes educational institution names specifically to prevent proxy discrimination, since institutional prestige has historically correlated with socioeconomic background and demographic composition. However, anonymization in practice is harder than it appears. Research has repeatedly shown that as few as four quasi-identifying data points can uniquely re-identify individuals, and that writing style and vocabulary choices can serve as fingerprints surviving field-level anonymization. The HR agent should therefore ensure that every combination of quasi-identifiers (years of experience, degree field, geographic region) appears in at least k resumes in the evaluation batch, a property known as k-anonymity.

When k falls below the configured threshold, the agent should either generalize the attributes or flag the candidate for manual review. Even after removing explicit identifiers, new proxy signals such as zip codes, volunteer organizations, or extracurricular activities can emerge over time. A periodic proxy audit, using mutual information between remaining features and protected attributes, should be integrated into the bias monitoring pipeline.

This case study demonstrates a crucial principle: ethical agent design is not about restricting capability but about redirecting it. The HR assistant is no less effective at identifying qualified candidates; it is prevented from using irrelevant demographic signals to make that determination. The `FairHiringAgent` class implicitly operates in Regime 2 of the Impossibility Theorem analysis: it prioritizes demographic parity through the four-fifths rule threshold, the appropriate choice for hiring domains where historical exclusion has distorted apparent qualification rates. This regime choice should be documented in the agent's ethical configuration and subject to periodic review by the organization's ethics board. The ethical architecture also raises a second obligation: agents whose decisions affect people must be able to explain those decisions in terms the affected person can understand and act on. That challenge, making the agent's reasoning visible and auditable, is the focus of the next section.

The Explainable agent

It's important to understand that an agent that makes correct decisions is useful but an agent that can *explain* its decisions is *trusted*. Trust is the critical enabler of adoption in every domain where agents operate alongside human decision-makers. A physician will not act on a diagnostic recommendation unless they understand the reasoning behind it. A loan officer will not approve a recommendation without a justification that satisfies regulatory requirements. An HR manager will not accept a candidate ranking without evidence that the evaluation was fair.

Explainability is not a feature to be added at the end of development. It is an architectural property that must be designed into the agent from the beginning. The explainable agent extends the cognitive loop with a dedicated **explanation generation layer** that runs in parallel with the decision pipeline. At each processing stage, the agent logs its reasoning. After the final decision, it passes the complete trace to an explanation generator that produces audience-adapted output. The code implementation in the following subsection demonstrates this architecture directly. Before looking at it, let's quickly learn about reasoning transparency.

Reasoning transparency techniques

Transparency begins with recording the agent's reasoning process in a structured, auditable format. This is distinct from model interpretability, which concerns the internal mechanics of a neural network. Reasoning transparency concerns the decision-level logic: what information the agent considered, what rules it applied, what alternatives it evaluated, and why it selected the final action. As discussed in *Chapter 8*'s treatment of the Verification and Validation agent, every verification step must be traceable.

In the following code, the `ExplainableAgent` class demonstrates how to record and communicate a built-in reasoning trace. Rather than relying on post-hoc rationalization, where an LLM attempts to justify a decision after the fact, this architecture constructs an explanation directly from the actual reasoning trace recorded during execution.

```
class ExplainableAgent:
    """Agent with built-in reasoning transparency."""
    def __init__(self):
        self.decision_logger = DecisionLogger()
        self.explanation_gen = ExplanationGenerator()

    def make_decision(self, input_data):
        """Make a decision and generate its explanation."""
        self.decision_logger.start_recording()

        # Step 1: Analyze inputs
        analysis = self.analyze_input(input_data)
        self.decision_logger.record('Input Analysis', analysis)

        # Step 2: Apply domain rules
        rule_results = self.apply_rules(analysis)
        self.decision_logger.record('Rule Application', rule_results)

        # Step 3: Assess risks and confidence
        risk = self.assess_risk(analysis, rule_results)
        self.decision_logger.record('Risk Assessment', risk)

        # Step 4: Synthesize decision
```

```
        decision = self.synthesize(analysis, rule_results, risk)
        self.decision_logger.record('Final Decision', decision)

        # Generate explanation from the recorded trace
        explanation = self.explanation_gen.explain(
            input_data, decision,
            self.decision_logger.get_trace()
        )
        return decision, explanation
```

By explicitly logging "Rule Application" and "Risk Assessment" as discrete steps, the system provides the longitudinal transparency required for regulatory audits under the EU AI Act. This trace-based approach allows the `ExplanationGenerator()` function to adapt its output for different audiences, providing feature-importance SHAP values for an engineer while delivering clinical justifications for a physician, all anchored to the same immutable decision log. As we will see in the *Case Study: Medical Diagnosis Assistant with Explanation* section, this architecture ensures that explanations are faithful representations of actual system behavior, not post-hoc rationalizations.

For agents operating continuously, transparency extends beyond individual decisions. Longitudinal transparency is achieved by persistently storing complete reasoning trails, including the model version, training data provenance, environmental context, and decision outcomes. Each record must be immutable (write-once storage), indexed by decision ID and date range, encrypted at rest, and must include the feature attribution values, natural language explanation, audience profile, and confidence calibration parameters at the time of decision. For medical agents, the storage must also be HIPAA-compliant, with access logging. In regulated industries, longitudinal transparency is not merely a best practice but a legal requirement under frameworks like the EU AI Act and HIPAA.

Three practical challenges complicate longitudinal transparency in production: *storage cost* (reasoning traces grow unboundedly in continuous systems: a 30-day audit window for a high-frequency trading agent can exceed terabytes of structured log data, requiring tiered storage with a hot window for recent decisions and cold archive for regulatory retention); *data versioning drift* (model weights change during retraining, so the same decision log entry may be unintelligible without the model checkpoint that produced it; logs must therefore record the model version hash alongside every decision); and *regulatory retention* conflicts (HIPAA mandates a six-year retention minimum for medical records, while GDPR's right to erasure can require deletion of data tied to an individual, a conflict that must be resolved at architecture design time, not at deletion request time).

Decision explanation frameworks

The decision log established in the preceding code is the input that explanation frameworks operate on. Rather than analyzing model internals directly, the frameworks described below interpret the recorded reasoning trace to generate audience-appropriate explanations.

While decision logging captures the reasoning process, explanation frameworks determine how that reasoning is communicated to different audiences. A machine learning engineer needs feature importance scores and decision boundaries. A physician needs clinical reasoning expressed in medical terminology. A patient needs a clear, jargon-free summary. The Explainable agent must adapt its explanations to each audience without distorting the underlying reasoning.

Two frameworks dominate model-agnostic explanations: LIME (Local Interpretable Model-agnostic Explanations) and SHAP (SHapley Additive exPlanations).

LIME generates explanations for individual predictions by constructing a simple, interpretable model that approximates the original model's behavior in the local neighborhood of the instance being explained.

SHAP provides a unified framework for feature attribution based on Shapley values from cooperative game theory. For a model with feature set F, the Shapley value of feature i measures its average marginal contribution across all possible feature coalitions. The Shapley Uniqueness Theorem guarantees that these values are the unique attribution method satisfying four desirable properties: efficiency (attributions sum to the prediction), symmetry (identical features receive identical attributions), dummy (irrelevant features receive zero attribution), and additivity (explanations compose across models).

However, computing exact Shapley values requires evaluating all 2^n feature coalitions, which is exponential in the number of features. Practical implementations trade exactness for computational feasibility: TreeSHAP is exact and polynomial-time for tree-based models (explanations in under 10 ms per prediction for gradient-boosted trees, running in O(TLD) time per Lundberg et al., 2020), while KernelSHAP is model-agnostic but approximate.

For latency-sensitive production deployments, a practical pattern is asynchronous explanation generation: the agent generates the decision synchronously and the explanation asynchronously. The user receives the recommendation immediately, and the detailed SHAP explanation is available within seconds via a follow-up query or dashboard link.

For high-stakes decisions (medical, legal, financial), the choice between LIME and SHAP should be driven by regulatory requirements. If the regulation demands feature-level attribution (as in the EU AI Act's right to explanation), SHAP is preferred because of its uniqueness guarantee. If the regulation requires contrastive explanation, counterfactual methods are preferred. For routine, low-stakes decisions — content recommendations, search ranking, or caching policy — the agent logs the decision summary and confidence score but does not generate a full LIME or SHAP explanation. Full explanations are reserved for decisions that affect people's access to resources, opportunities, or care, where the cost of explanation generation is justified by the accountability requirement.

Increasingly popular in regulated domains, a counterfactual explanation explains *what would need to change* for the decision to be different rather than explaining *why* a decision was made. For a loan denial, a counterfactual explanation might state: "If your annual income were $5,000 higher, or if your debt-to-income ratio were below 0.35, the application would have been approved."

Formally, the optimal counterfactual x' for an instance x with outcome y and desired outcome y' minimizes the distance $d(x, x')$ subject to the constraint $f(x') = y'$. The Minimal Counterfactual Theorem guarantees that this optimization produces the smallest change that flips the decision, providing users with actionable, concrete guidance for improving their outcome.

This framework directly mirrors the counterfactual fairness definition from the *Bias detection and mitigation* section: both use the same mathematical machinery of minimal perturbation, but counterfactual explanations answer "what would change the outcome for this individual?" while counterfactual fairness asks "would the outcome change if this individual's protected attribute were different?" This shared foundation provides a unified theoretical bridge between the ethical and explainable architectures.

Confidence communication methods

We've learned that explanations are important, but we must also remember that they are incomplete without an honest assessment of the agent's confidence. One of the most consequential limitations of LLMs is their propensity to generate outputs that are linguistically coherent yet factually incorrect, all delivered in a confident, authoritative tone. The foundation-model risk analyses (Bommasani et al., 2022) call this the *illusion of confidence*, and it can mislead users into accepting unreliable recommendations. An explainable agent must communicate not only what it believes but also how certain it is, in a way that users can interpret correctly.

Separating epistemic from aleatoric uncertainty tells the agent when it should defer to a specialist. But expressing that uncertainty clearly to a clinician or patient requires an additional property: the confidence score itself must be reliable. An agent that knows it is uncertain is only useful if the number it reports reflects its actual track record on similar cases. **Calibration** means a confidence score (a probability estimate the model assigns to its own prediction, defined here as calibrated if the stated probability matches the empirical accuracy across similar cases) does what it promises. When the agent says "80% confident," roughly 80% of those predictions should turn out correct. Achieving that alignment takes dedicated post-training work (temperature scaling, Platt calibration) and continuous monitoring to catch drift.

In this context, uncertainty refers to the degree of confidence a model can assign to its own output: how well-calibrated is the probability it reports alongside a prediction? A well-calibrated model that says "87% confidence" should be correct approximately 87% of the time on similar inputs. Poorly calibrated uncertainty misleads clinicians and patients alike: overconfident predictions invite over-reliance, and underconfident ones cause unnecessary deferrals to specialists. For high-stakes agents, communicating uncertainty accurately is as important as maximizing predictive accuracy.

A critical refinement for high-stakes applications is distinguishing between the following two types of fundamental uncertainty:

- **Epistemic uncertainty**: This arises from the agent's lack of knowledge and can, in principle, be reduced with more data or better models. A diagnostic agent encountering a rare disease it has seen only twice in training has high epistemic uncertainty.
- **Aleatoric uncertainty:** This arises from inherent randomness in the process itself and cannot be reduced regardless of how much data is collected. A patient's response to a medication involves genuinely stochastic biological processes.

This distinction has direct practical consequences. High epistemic uncertainty suggests the agent should defer to a specialist. High aleatoric uncertainty suggests the agent should recommend monitoring and repeated measurement rather than immediate intervention. Ensemble methods, which run multiple model copies with different random initializations, can approximate epistemic uncertainty through prediction variance: high variance indicates model uncertainty, while low variance with moderate overall confidence indicates inherent outcome variability.

A single best guess is rarely enough in high-stakes settings. In the following code, the `ConfidenceAwareAgent` class addresses this challenge by generating multiple candidate hypotheses, scoring each against the available context, and calibrating the raw scores through a `TemperatureScaler` so they behave like real probabilities. The results are ranked by confidence, and the communication layer translates numeric scores into actionable qualifiers.

```
class ConfidenceAwareAgent:
    """Agent that generates and ranks multiple hypotheses."""
    def __init__(self, n_hypotheses=3):
        self.n_hypotheses = n_hypotheses
        self.calibrator = TemperatureScaler()

    def reason_with_confidence(self, query, context):
        """Generate hypotheses with calibrated confidence."""
        hypotheses = []
        for _ in range(self.n_hypotheses):
            result = self.generate_hypothesis(query, context)
            raw_score = self.score_hypothesis(result, context)
            calibrated = self.calibrator.calibrate(raw_score)
            hypotheses.append({
                'answer': result,
                'confidence': calibrated,
                'evidence': self.gather_evidence(result, context)
            })

        hypotheses.sort(
            key=lambda h: h['confidence'], reverse=True
        )
        return hypotheses

    def communicate_uncertainty(self, hypotheses):
        """Format uncertainty for user consumption."""
        top = hypotheses[0]
        if top['confidence'] > 0.9:
            qualifier = 'High confidence'
        elif top['confidence'] > 0.7:
            qualifier = 'Moderate confidence'
        else:
            qualifier = 'Low confidence - human review recommended'

        return {
            'recommendation': top['answer'],
            'confidence_level': qualifier,
```

```
            'confidence_score': round(top['confidence'], 2),
            'supporting_evidence': top['evidence'],
            'alternative_hypotheses': hypotheses[1:]
        }
```

This two-layer architecture creates a clean separation between *internal uncertainty estimation* and *external uncertainty communication*. The calibrated score is computed before any narrative is generated, preventing the common failure mode where a fluent explanation implicitly inflates confidence after the fact. When confidence is low, the system's default behavior is escalation, not persuasion. The same pattern generalizes to other regulated agents: a financial advisory agent can map low confidence to "compliance review recommended," and a legal research agent can map it to "citation coverage insufficient," ensuring uncertainty becomes an actionable control signal rather than a buried number.

Users infer reliability, safety, and competence not only from what an agent says but from how it says it. The explainable agent adapts its confidence communication to the audience.

For a clinician, the agent might report: "Based on the imaging features and lab values, this pattern is consistent with early-stage pneumonia (confidence: 0.87). The differential diagnosis includes bronchitis (0.09) and atelectasis (0.04)." For a patient, the same finding might be communicated as: "The analysis suggests a lung infection. Your doctor will review these results and discuss the next steps with you." This adaptation is not cosmetic. It is a trust mechanism that ensures each stakeholder receives the level of detail appropriate to their role and expertise.

Case study: Medical diagnosis assistant with explanation

The preceding sections introduced three explanation techniques:

- LIME for local feature attribution
- SHAP for global feature importance, and counterfactual analysis for recourse generation
- the confidence calibration mechanisms that quantify how much to trust each output.

This case study shows how all four come together in a single production-grade system. Medical diagnosis is the domain where explainability requirements are most stringent: a physician must be able to trace every recommendation to the evidence that produced it, and a patient must receive an explanation they can act on. The `DiagnosticAssistant` implements the complete explainable agent architecture (reasoning transparency, audience-adapted explanation, and calibrated confidence) in a single coherent pipeline.

We've been learning from healthcare-based examples because this is the domain where the tension between capability and explainability is the most acute. A diagnostic agent that achieves 95% accuracy but cannot explain its reasoning is clinically useless, because physicians cannot act on recommendations they do not understand, and patients cannot give informed consent to treatments based on opaque algorithmic suggestions. Continuing on this path of healthcare examples, let's look at the architecture overview of the assistant we've been discussing.

The diagnostic assistant operates as a layered multi-agent system with the following three specialized components, inspired by the zoom multi-agent Virtual Health Platform architecture.

- **Biometric agents**: These continuously analyze real-time patient data such as heart rate variability, oxygen saturation, and sleep patterns from connected wearable devices.
- **Symptom analysis agents**: These use natural language processing to interpret patient-reported symptoms and cross-reference them with medical knowledge bases.
- **Coordinator agents**: These integrate biometric and symptom data to generate diagnostic suggestions, rank differential diagnoses by probability, and present results with full explanatory context.

Figure 12.2 presents the complete architecture of the diagnostic assistant, showing how biometric data, symptom analysis, and clinical knowledge converge through the coordinator agent to produce an explained, confidence-rated diagnosis.

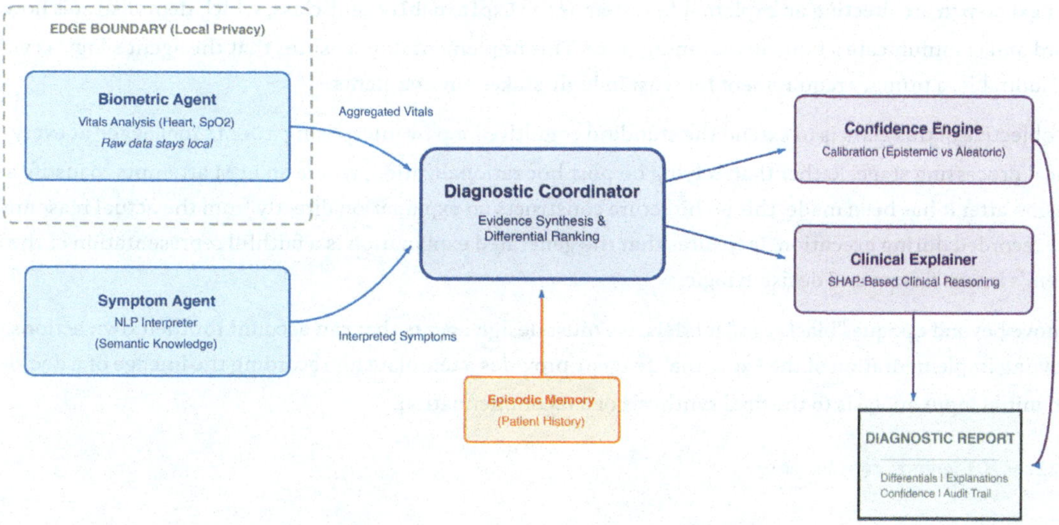

Figure 12.2 – The medical diagnosis assistant's multi-agent pipeline with explanation generation

The agent's memory architecture draws on the episodic, semantic, and working memory patterns introduced in *Chapter 5*. Episodic memory stores individual patient interactions. Semantic memory encodes clinical knowledge, drug interaction databases, and treatment protocols. Working memory manages the current diagnostic dialogue.

A critical production consideration is **edge computing for privacy**. The biometric agent processes raw patient data locally on the patient's device or a hospital edge server before transmitting results to the cloud-hosted coordinator. Raw vitals never leave the local processing boundary. Only aggregated features (average heart rate, minimum SpO2 over the past hour, trend direction) are transmitted. This architecture satisfies HIPAA's minimum necessary standard and GDPR's data minimization principle by construction. The edge processing layer also provides a natural location for differential privacy mechanisms: noise can be added to aggregated features before transmission, providing ε-differential privacy guarantees at the data source.

The two specialized sub-agents have well-defined interface contracts. `BiometricAnalyzer` accepts a `patient_data` object whose `biometrics` field contains aggregated wearable features, for example, mean heart rate, minimum SpO2, and sleep-stage distribution over a configurable rolling window, and returns a `VitalsReport` containing normalized metric values, trend vectors, and anomaly flags for each monitored parameter. Raw wearable streams are never passed directly; the edge processing layer described above aggregates them before the `patient_data` object is constructed, satisfying the data minimization requirement. `SymptomInterpreter` accepts a free-text string of patient-reported symptoms, maps each reported symptom to its closest SNOMED CT concept using a local clinical NLP model, and returns a `SymptomProfile` containing structured symptom codes, onset and severity attributes, and a confidence score per mapping. Both components are stateless; they carry no patient history between calls, which is managed exclusively by `ClinicalMemorySystem`.

The next step in architecting an explainable system is the `ExplainableAgent` class, which demonstrates how to record and communicate a built-in reasoning trace. This implementation ensures that the agent's logic is visible and auditable, a primary requirement for trust in high-stakes environments.

The objective of this class is to extend the standard cognitive loop by interposing a `DecisionLogger` at every critical processing stage. Rather than relying on post hoc rationalization, where an LLM attempts to justify a decision after it has been made, this architecture constructs an explanation directly from the actual reasoning trace recorded during execution. It ensures that the generated explanation is a faithful representation of the system's internal state and decision logic.

To move beyond opaque "black-box" models, we must design agents that can account for their own actions. The following implementation of the `ExplainableAgent` provides a template for recording the lineage of a decision, from initial input analysis to the final synthesis of a recommendation.

```
class DiagnosticAssistant:
    """
    Clinical decision support agent with multi-source evidence
    integration and audience-adapted explanations.
    """
    def __init__(self):
        self.biometric_agent = BiometricAnalyzer()
        self.symptom_agent = SymptomInterpreter()
        self.coordinator = DiagnosticCoordinator()
        self.explainer = ClinicalExplainer()
        self.confidence_engine = ConfidenceAwareAgent(n_hypotheses=5)
        self.memory = ClinicalMemorySystem()

    def diagnose(self, patient_data, reported_symptoms):
```

The `patient_data` parameter is not a raw wearable stream. It is a pre-assembled object constructed by the edge processing layer described in the architecture overview: its `id` field is a de-identified patient token; its `biometrics` field contains aggregated wearable features (for example, rolling-window mean heart rate, minimum SpO2, sleep-stage distribution) that have already been locally processed and optionally noise-injected for differential privacy before transmission. Raw sensor readings never reach this method. This design satisfies the data minimization requirements of HIPAA and GDPR by construction, and it is the `biometrics` field that `BiometricAnalyzer.analyze()` operates on.

```
        """Generate an explained, confidence-rated diagnosis."""
        # Gather evidence from multiple sources
        vitals = self.biometric_agent.analyze(patient_data)
        symptoms = self.symptom_agent.interpret(reported_symptoms)
        history = self.memory.retrieve_episodic(patient_data.id)

        # Generate ranked differential diagnoses
        differentials = self.coordinator.generate_differentials(
            vitals, symptoms, history
        )

        # Score each with calibrated confidence
        scored = self.confidence_engine.score_differentials(
            differentials,
            evidence={
                'vitals': vitals,
                'symptoms': symptoms,
                'history': history
            }
        )

        # Generate clinical explanation
        explanation = self.explainer.generate(
            scored,
            audience='clinician',
            evidence_sources=[vitals, symptoms, history]
        )

        # Store encounter in episodic memory
        self.memory.store_episodic(patient_data.id, {
            'diagnoses': scored,
            'evidence': [vitals, symptoms],
            'explanation': explanation
        })

        return DiagnosticReport(
            differentials=scored,
            explanation=explanation,
```

```
        confidence_summary=self.confidence_engine
            .communicate_uncertainty(scored),
        audit_trail=self.explainer.get_reasoning_trace()
    )
```

By explicitly capturing the audit trail via the `get_reasoning_trace()` function, this architecture satisfies the transparency requirements of the EU AI Act and HIPAA. The separation of the `ConfidenceAwareAgent()` function allows the system to distinguish between epistemic and aleatoric uncertainty, a distinction that is vital for determining when the agent should defer to a human specialist.

The `ClinicalExplainer` class generates explanations following the standard clinical reasoning format familiar to physicians. A sample clinician-facing explanation:

```
Primary Assessment: Community-acquired pneumonia (confidence: 0.87). Key findings:
elevated white blood cell count (SHAP contribution: 0.31), right lower lobe consolidation
on chest imaging (0.28), productive cough with fever for 4 days (0.19), oxygen saturation
decline from baseline (0.09). Differential: Acute bronchitis (0.09), pulmonary embolism
(0.04). Recommended: Sputum culture, blood cultures, initiation of empiric antibiotic
therapy per institutional guidelines.
```

For the same finding, the patient-facing explanation would read:

```
The analysis of your test results and symptoms suggests a lung infection called
pneumonia. Your blood tests show signs that your body is fighting an infection, and the
chest scan shows an area of concern in the lower right portion of your lung. Your doctor
will review these findings and may recommend antibiotics and additional tests to confirm
the diagnosis.
```

Additionally, the diagnostic assistant implements strict safety boundaries. When confidence falls below a configurable threshold, the system does not present a diagnosis but instead flags the case for physician review with a summary of the ambiguous findings. When findings suggest a potentially life-threatening condition, the agent triggers an emergency protocol regardless of confidence level.

Production medical agents must also handle infrastructure failures gracefully. The following three failure modes require specific architectural provisions:

- **Sensor dropout**: If the wearable device stops transmitting, the biometric agent continues operating on the last known data with a progressively degrading confidence score. After a configurable timeout (for example, 30 minutes), the system alerts the care team that biometric data is stale and downweights biometric evidence in the diagnostic synthesis.
- **Model serving failure**: If the diagnostic model endpoint becomes unavailable, the coordinator falls back to a rule-based triage system that routes patients based on vital sign thresholds (for example, SpO2 below 90% triggers immediate escalation). This fallback must be tested regularly through chaos

engineering exercises to ensure it functions correctly under the conditions when it would actually be needed.

- **Explanation generation failure**: If the SHAP computation times out, the system still delivers the diagnosis with a flag indicating that the detailed explanation is temporarily unavailable, along with a simplified feature-importance summary derived from the model's attention weights. The audit trail records both the explanation failure and the fallback explanation used.

The safety boundary provisions above are not hypothetical edge cases; they reflect failure modes observed in production deployments of multi-agent clinical systems.

These failure modes are not hypothetical. In pilot deployments modeled on the Zoom Multi agent Virtual Health Platform architecture, edge devices experienced 2 to 3 percent data transmission failures per day. The system's graceful degradation mechanisms prevented any of these failures from affecting clinical decisions. Overall, pilot results demonstrated a 30% increase in early detection of exacerbations in chronic conditions such as COPD and congestive heart failure. False alarm rates were held to 3%, and clinician response times improved by 40%. Notably, clinicians reported that the structured explanations increased their confidence in the recommendations, enabling faster and more informed clinical decisions.

Governance and regulatory landscape

Ethical and explainable agents do not operate in a regulatory vacuum. As enterprise AI deployments scale, a global regulatory ecosystem is emerging that mandates specific transparency, fairness, and accountability requirements. The following table details the most important acts and regulations:

Framework	Scope	Key Requirements
EU AI Act	High-risk AI in EU	Risk assessment, bias mitigation, human oversight, documentation
NIST AI RMF	US Federal guidance	Risk identification, continuous monitoring, stakeholder values
GDPR	Data processing in EU	Data minimization, consent, right to explanation
Singapore AI Verify	Voluntary certification	Fairness, robustness, transparency self-assessment
China CAC	Algorithmic systems	Algorithmic transparency, user control, anti-discrimination

Table 12.2 – Important global acts and regulations concerning ethical and explainable agents.

International cooperation through bodies such as the Global Partnership on AI (GPAI) is working to harmonize these frameworks. The IEEE's P7000 series of standards, including P7001 (Transparency) and P7003 (Algorithmic Bias), offers critical guidance for building agents that are explainable, equitable, and trustworthy. The OECD AI Principles, adopted by over 40 countries, emphasize human-centric values, transparency, robustness, and accountability. For a comprehensive, continuously updated index of national AI governance frameworks, the OECD AI Policy Observatory (`oecd.ai`) tracks regulatory developments across 70+ jurisdictions and provides country-specific policy comparisons.

Organizations deploying agents globally face a practical challenge: different jurisdictions impose requirements that can conflict with one another. For example, the EU AI Act requires bias mitigation, but China's CAC regulations also require algorithmic transparency to users, which may demand disclosing model architecture details, considered trade secrets in other jurisdictions. The compliance registry pattern supports this through jurisdiction-aware evaluation: each validator is tagged with the jurisdictions where it applies, and the evaluate method only runs validators relevant to the current deployment context. A candidate applying for a role in the EU triggers EU AI Act and GDPR validators, while a candidate in Singapore triggers AI Verify validators.

The trajectory of this regulatory landscape is toward interoperability. The Global Partnership on AI and the OECD are actively developing mutual recognition frameworks that would allow an agent certified under one jurisdiction's requirements to gain expedited approval in others, reducing the compliance burden for teams deploying globally. In the near term, the jurisdiction-aware compliance registry pattern described above is the practical engineering response: build the validator tagging infrastructure now, and compliance coverage can be extended as new jurisdictions formalize their requirements. Ethical and explainable design is not a constraint on capability; it is the condition under which autonomous agents earn the institutional trust necessary to operate at scale.

Technique selection reference

Table 12.3 maps each technique covered in this chapter to its primary use case, target domain, and selection criteria. Use it as a quick-reference guide when designing agents that require ethical reasoning, bias detection, or explanation generation.

Technique	Use Case	Domain	When to Use
Deontic logic	Ethical constraint formalization	Healthcare, HR, finance	Rules must be machine-verifiable; multi-step reasoning chains require formal consistency checks
Equalized odds	Demographic parity enforcement	HR, lending, admissions	False-positive rate must be equalized across protected groups under anti-discrimination law
Disparate impact ratio	Adverse impact detection	Employment, credit	Regulatory safe-harbor threshold (0.8 rule) must be documented and auditable
LIME	Local decision explanation	Any ML-backed decision	Individual prediction must be explained to a non-technical stakeholder or regulator

Technique	Use Case	Domain	When to Use
SHAP	Feature attribution	Clinical, financial scoring	Global model behavior must be audited for consistency across the full feature space
Counterfactual analysis	Recourse generation	Credit, hiring, diagnosis	Users need an actionable path to a different outcome from the same agent.
Confidence calibration	Uncertainty communication	Medical and autonomous systems	Decision confidence must be communicated accurately to patients, clinicians, or regulators
Compliance registry	Multi-jurisdictional validation	Global deployments	Agent must satisfy different, potentially conflicting regulatory requirements by jurisdiction

Table 12.3 – Technique selection reference for ethical and explainable agent design

Summary

This chapter examined two complementary architectures for building agents that are not only capable but also responsible: Ethical Reasoning agent and Explainable agent. We first learned how every agent action is evaluated against explicit ethical constraints before execution through deontic logic and quantitative fairness metrics. The Impossibility Theorem demonstrated that fairness requires deliberate, documented choices about which metric to prioritize, and the HR assistant case study showed how these principles translate into a practical system that prevents demographic bias while maintaining evaluation quality.

The Explainable agent addresses the equally critical challenge of transparency. By recording the agent's reasoning trace, generating audience-adapted explanations using LIME, SHAP and counterfactual analysis, this architecture transforms opaque decision-making into a transparent, auditable process. The medical diagnosis assistant illustrated how these techniques converge in a high-stakes domain. Lastly, we learned about the regulatory landscape, from the EU AI Act to NIST's AI Risk Management Framework.

`ClinicalExplainer.generate()` accepts three inputs: a list of scored differential diagnoses, an `audience` parameter (`'clinician'` or `'patient'`), and a list of evidence source objects. Internally it performs three steps. First, it selects an explanation template calibrated to the audience: the clinician template structures output around primary assessment, SHAP feature contributions, and differential ranking; the patient template suppresses numeric scores and replaces clinical terminology with plain-language equivalents. Second, it formats the SHAP values from the top differential into ranked contributing factors, filtering out features whose absolute contribution falls below a significance threshold to avoid overwhelming the reader with noise. Third, it passes the structured data through a natural language generation step that produces a fluent, grammatically complete explanation block. The method returns a `ClinicalExplanation` object containing the formatted narrative, the underlying feature contributions, and a reasoning trace that `get_reasoning_trace()` exposes for audit purposes.

The next chapter extends these ideas into the healthcare and scientific discovery domains, where the ethical and explainability requirements introduced here become essential components of agents that assist with clinical decisions and accelerate research.

13

Healthcare and Scientific Agents

The very first requirement in a hospital is that it should do the sick no harm.

– Florence Nightingale, Notes on Hospitals (1863)

Healthcare and scientific research share one defining trait that sets them apart from every other agent domain: mistakes here cost lives. A diagnostic agent that calls a malignant tumor benign. A research agent that misses a lethal drug interaction buried in the literature. These are not inconveniences. They are catastrophes. That reality forces a specific set of architectural priorities: verifiability first, explainability second, graceful degradation always, and raw speed only when the first three are satisfied.

Both domains also face an information overload problem that no human can solve alone. A physician treating a complex case must synthesize patient history, current lab results, imaging data, drug interaction databases, and the latest clinical guidelines, all within a single consultation. A materials scientist exploring novel polymer compositions faces a literature corpus growing by thousands of papers each month, making it physically impossible to stay current through manual reading. Intelligent agents offer a path through this complexity, not by replacing human judgment, but by ensuring that experts have the right information, at the right time, in the right format.

In this chapter, we'll be covering the following topics:

- The Healthcare Intelligence agent
- The Scientific Discovery agent

The sections that follow examine how each domain instantiates these principles under its own constraints.

Technical requirements

To run the examples in this chapter, you will need the following:

- Python 3.10 or later
- The following Python packages: langchain-core, langchain-community, fhir-resources, aiohttp, transformers, scipy, numpy, and python-dotenv

All code examples for this chapter are available in the book's GitHub repository at `https://github.com/PacktPublishing/30-Agents-Every-AI-Engineer-Must-Build/chapter13`

The Healthcare Intelligence agent

Healthcare is the clearest environment in which agent design choices are exposed under pressure: data is heterogeneous and incomplete, decisions carry clinical risk, and every action must remain defensible to auditors, clinicians, and patients. In this setting, an agent cannot be judged only by whether it produces plausible text. It must demonstrate disciplined use of evidence, controlled access to sensitive records, and explanations that track back to the inputs and rules that shaped the recommendation.

This section introduces a reference architecture that separates ingestion, clinical knowledge, reasoning, and explanation into explicit layers, so that safety and compliance are enforced by structure rather than by convention. It also establishes the runtime checkpoints that govern when the agent is allowed to act, when it must ask for clarification, and when it must escalate to a human clinician.

We'll work through four areas: medical knowledge integration, patient data pipeline construction, clinical decision support and safety monitoring, and a production case study that demonstrates these components in a deployed diagnostic assistant.

The healthcare domain presents a unique confluence of challenges. Patient data is inherently multimodal: structured lab values and vital signs, semi-structured clinical notes, unstructured physician observations and patient-reported symptoms. Regulatory frameworks (HIPAA, GDPR, PIPEDA) impose strict constraints on data storage, transmission, and processing. And clinical workflows demand seamless integration with existing EHR infrastructure rather than wholesale tool replacement.

The Healthcare Intelligence Agent addresses these through a layered architecture separating data ingestion, clinical reasoning, and explanation generation into distinct subsystems. This separation is not merely an engineering convenience. It is a regulatory necessity. When a clinical decision must be audited, regulators need to trace exactly which data sources contributed to a recommendation, what reasoning was applied, and how the output was generated. A monolithic system that conflates these stages cannot provide that traceability.

From a formal perspective, the agent faces a problem equivalent to reasoning in a partially observable environment with stochastic state transitions. The agent never has direct access to the patient's true disease state. It observes only symptoms, lab values, and imaging results, each a noisy, incomplete projection of the underlying pathology. This maps to the Partially Observable Markov Decision Process (POMDP) framework: the agent maintains a *belief state*, a probability distribution over possible diagnoses, and updates that distribution as new observations arrive. The Bayesian formulation in the *Clinical decision support frameworks* section formalizes exactly how this belief state evolves.

The following snippet shows one belief-state update cycle, where a new lab observation shifts the probability distribution over candidate diagnoses:

```
import numpy as np

def update_belief(belief: np.ndarray,
                  observation: dict,
```

```
                likelihood_model: dict) -> np.ndarray:
    """Bayesian belief update: P(s|o) ∝ P(o|s) * P(s)."""
    likelihoods = np.array([
        likelihood_model[diag].score(observation)
        for diag in likelihood_model
    ])

    posterior = likelihoods * belief

    return posterior / posterior.sum()  # normalize to valid distribution
```

Each call to `update_belief` advances the POMDP one step: the prior `belief` is weighted by how well each diagnosis explains the new observation, then renormalized. The Bayesian confidence framework in the clinical decision support section extends this with Platt scaling and Brier score calibration applied to the resulting posterior.

As shown in *Figure 13.1*, the architecture comprises four primary layers: data ingestion, clinical knowledge, reasoning and decision, and explanation and delivery. Each communicates through well-defined interfaces, enabling independent knowledge base updates without disrupting the reasoning pipeline and allowing explanation formats to be customized for different audiences without modifying diagnostic logic.

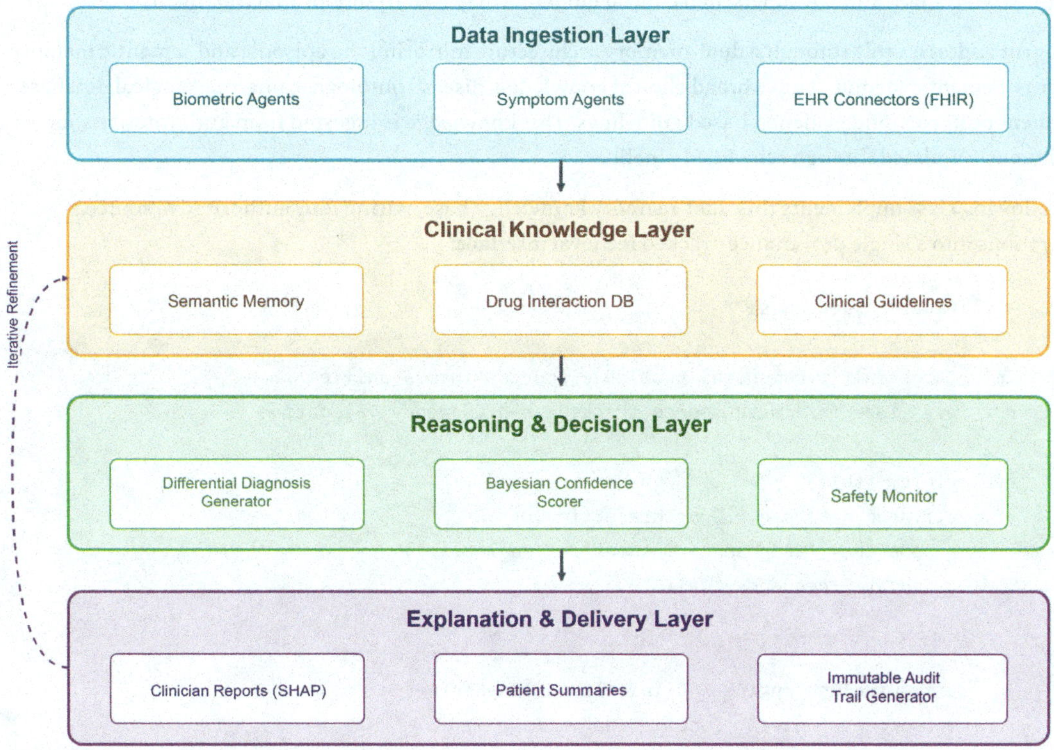

Figure 13.1 – Healthcare Intelligence agent architecture

Figure 13.1 summarizes the Healthcare Intelligence agent as a system where the principal design decision is isolation: each layer exposes only a typed interface to the layers above and below it, so that safety constraints can be enforced structurally rather than by convention. The separation between knowledge and reasoning means a clinical guideline database can be updated without touching the diagnostic logic. The separation between reasoning and explanation means the same diagnostic trace can produce a clinician report, a patient summary, or a regulator-facing audit record without duplicating inference code.

The feedback loops shown are architecturally significant: they are narrow and explicit, not general backpropagation channels. Explanation outcomes and clinician overrides can inform knowledge base updates without exposing the reasoning layer to raw feedback signals. This is a deliberate tradeoff, sacrificing some adaptability to preserve auditability. An agent that updates its own reasoning logic in response to user corrections cannot guarantee that a recommendation made today will be reproducible tomorrow, which is a requirement in regulated clinical environments.

Medical knowledge integration

This subsection examines how the agent integrates heterogeneous clinical knowledge sources into a dual-memory architecture that balances breadth of coverage with provenance tracking.

The foundation of any healthcare agent is its medical knowledge base. Unlike general-purpose retrieval systems that can tolerate occasional inaccuracies, a clinical knowledge base must meet accuracy and currency standards tied directly to patient safety. A drug interaction database three months out of date may miss a recently identified contraindication. A superseded clinical guideline may lead to suboptimal treatment.

The agent addresses this through a dual-memory architecture mirroring the episodic and semantic memory patterns. Semantic memory stores broad clinical knowledge: disease ontologies, pharmacological databases, treatment protocols, and evidence-based guidelines. This knowledge is ingested from authoritative sources and continuously updated through scheduled pipelines.

The following class implements this dual-memory knowledge base, wiring four authoritative source integrations into a single provenance-tracked retrieval interface:

```
class ClinicalKnowledgeBase:
    """
    Integrates multiple medical knowledge sources into a unified
    retrieval interface with source tracking and currency validation.
    """
    def __init__(self):
        self.drug_database = DrugInteractionDB(
            sources=["drugbank", "rxnorm", "fda_labels"],
            update_frequency="daily"
        )

        self.guideline_engine = ClinicalGuidelineEngine(
            sources=["nice", "who", "aha", "idsa"],
            version_tracking=True
        )
```

```
        self.disease_ontology = DiseaseOntology(
            base="snomed_ct",
            extensions=["icd10", "orphanet"]
        )

        self.literature_index = MedicalLiteratureIndex(
            sources=["pubmed", "cochrane", "uptodate"],
            embedding_model="biomedical-bert"
        )
```

The `__init__` method wires together four independent knowledge sources, each with its own update cadence. The query method retrieves across all relevant sources and attaches provenance metadata to every result:

```
def query(self, clinical_context, query_type="diagnostic"):
    """
    Retrieve relevant clinical knowledge with provenance tracking.
    """
    results = []

    if query_type in ["diagnostic", "treatment"]:
        results.extend(
            self.guideline_engine.search(clinical_context)
        )
        results.extend(
            self.drug_database.check_interactions(
                clinical_context.medications
            )
        )

    if query_type == "differential":
        results.extend(
            self.disease_ontology.match_symptoms(
                clinical_context.symptom_profile
            )
        )

    for result in results:
        result.provenance = {
            "source": result.origin,
            "version": result.source_version,
            "retrieved_at": datetime.utcnow(),
            "confidence": result.source_reliability_score
        }
```

```
    return results
```

Note that DrugInteractionDB, ClinicalGuidelineEngine, DiseaseOntology, and MedicalLiteratureIndex are illustrative architecture stubs. They represent the interface contracts each dependency must satisfy; a production deployment would substitute fully implemented clients for each. The DiagnosticCoordinator pipeline presented later in this section provides the chapter's fully traceable code path, where each stage is connected end-to-end rather than abstracted behind a stub interface.

The provenance metadata carries regulatory weight. When an auditor asks why a system recommended Drug A over Drug B, the answer cannot be "the model thought so." Every recommendation must trace back to a specific guideline version, a specific database snapshot, a specific retrieval timestamp.

A critical design decision is the use of a biomedical-specific embedding model for literature retrieval. General-purpose embeddings often fail to capture the semantic nuances of medical terminology. The phrase "patient presents with elevated troponin levels" carries specific diagnostic implications (possible myocardial infarction) that a general embedding model may not capture with sufficient precision. Biomedical embeddings trained on PubMed and clinical corpora produce significantly better retrieval accuracy for clinical queries.

The knowledge integration layer also implements a conflict resolution mechanism for situations where different authoritative sources provide contradictory guidance. When the agent detects that two clinical guidelines offer different treatment recommendations for the same condition, it does not silently choose one over the other. Instead, it flags the conflict, presents both recommendations with their respective evidence bases, and defers the final decision to the clinician. This pattern ensures that the agent amplifies clinical judgment rather than replacing it.

Patient data analysis patterns

The second major subsystem handles ingestion and analysis of patient-specific data. It must process data from multiple sources simultaneously: structured vital signs from wearable devices and bedside monitors, semi-structured clinical notes from the EHR, unstructured patient-reported symptoms from telehealth consultations, and historical data from previous encounters stored in the agent's episodic memory.

In production, this data arrives in heterogeneous formats through unreliable channels. HL7 FHIR is the standard interoperability protocol, but many hospitals still run HL7 v2 interfaces, proprietary EHR APIs, and even legacy CSV file drops. The pipeline must therefore include a normalization layer that converts incoming data into a canonical format before any processing occurs:

```
class FHIRNormalizationLayer:
    """
    Transforms heterogeneous clinical data formats into
    canonical FHIR R4 resources for downstream processing.
    """
    def __init__(self):
        self.adapters = {
            "hl7v2": HL7v2ToFHIRAdapter(),
```

```
            "fhir_r4": PassthroughAdapter(),
            "csv_lab": CSVLabResultAdapter(),
            "epic_api": EpicFHIRAdapter(),
            "cerner_api": CernerFHIRAdapter()
        }

        self.validator = FHIRResourceValidator(
            profile="us-core-6.0"
        )
```

The `__init__` method registers an adapter for each supported format. The normalize method selects the correct adapter, transforms the data, and validates each resource against the US Core profile:

```
def normalize(self, raw_data, source_format):
    adapter = self.adapters.get(source_format)

    if not adapter:
        raise UnsupportedFormatError(
            f"No adapter for {source_format}"
        )

    fhir_resources = adapter.transform(raw_data)

    validated = []

    for resource in fhir_resources:
        result = self.validator.validate(resource)

        if result.is_valid:
            validated.append(resource)
        else:
            self.log_validation_failure(
                resource, result.errors
            )

    return validated
```

Without normalization, a blood pressure reading formatted as "120/80 mmHg" in one system and as separate integer fields in another produces inconsistent downstream analysis.

The agent employs specialized sub-agents for each data modality, following the multi-agent patterns from *Chapter 7*:

```
class PatientDataPipeline:
    """
    Multi-modal patient data processing with temporal alignment
    and anomaly detection.
    """
    def __init__(self):
        self.normalizer = FHIRNormalizationLayer()

        self.biometric_agent = BiometricAnalyzer(
            processors={
                "heart_rate": HeartRateProcessor(),
                "blood_pressure": BloodPressureProcessor(),
                "blood_glucose": BloodGlucoseProcessor(),
                "oxygen_saturation": SpO2Processor(),
                "activity": ActivityProcessor()
            }
        )

        self.symptom_agent = SymptomInterpreter(
            nlp_model="clinical-bert",
            symptom_ontology="medra"
        )

        self.history_agent = PatientHistoryAgent(
            memory_type="episodic",
            retention_policy="hipaa_compliant"
        )
```

The `__init__` method assembles three specialized sub-agents, one per data modality. The process method orchestrates them in sequence and merges their outputs into a temporally aligned clinical context:

```
def process(self, patient_id, current_data, source_format):
    normalized = self.normalizer.normalize(
        current_data, source_format
    )

    vitals = self.biometric_agent.analyze(normalized.vitals)

    symptoms = self.symptom_agent.interpret(
        normalized.reported_symptoms,
        patient_context=normalized.demographics
```

```
    )

    history = self.history_agent.retrieve(
        patient_id,
        relevance_window="36_months",
        priority_conditions=symptoms.flagged_conditions
    )

    timeline = self.align_temporal_data(
        vitals, symptoms, history
    )

    return ClinicalContext(
        vitals=vitals,
        symptoms=symptoms,
        history=history,
        timeline=timeline,
        data_quality=self.assess_data_completeness(
            vitals, symptoms, history
        )
    )
```

The temporal alignment step deserves attention. A fever that precedes a cough by three days carries different diagnostic implications than one that develops simultaneously. The `align_temporal_data` method correlates streams from different sources onto a unified timeline, enabling the reasoning layer to detect patterns invisible when each source is examined alone.

The `data_quality` assessment is equally important. Clinical data is rarely complete. A patient may have been seen at an outside institution whose records are unavailable. Lab results may be pending. The agent must reason under uncertainty, and quantifying that uncertainty is the first step.

Clinical decision support frameworks

The reasoning layer is where patient data meets clinical knowledge to produce recommendations. This layer implements a structured decision pipeline generating ranked differential diagnoses, scoring each with calibrated confidence, and producing audience-tailored explanations.

The formal foundation is Bayesian belief updating. The agent maintains a probability distribution over candidate diagnoses and updates it as evidence arrives:

$$P(D_i|O_1, O_2, \ldots, O_n) = \frac{P(O_1, \ldots, O_n|D_i) \cdot P(D_i)}{P(O_1, \ldots, O_n)}$$

where D_i represents each candidate diagnosis, and O_1 through O_n represent observed clinical findings. The prior $P(D_i)$ is informed by epidemiological prevalence data and patient demographics. The likelihood $P(O|D_i)$ is derived from clinical knowledge bases encoding sensitivity and specificity of each observation for each condition.

A well-calibrated agent is one whose confidence scores accurately reflect actual accuracy. If the agent reports 80% confidence on a set of predictions, approximately 80% should be correct. This guarantee comes from the Brier score decomposition:

$$BS = Reliability - Resolution + Uncertainty$$

where *Reliability* measures how well stated probabilities match observed frequencies, *Resolution* measures how much predictions depart from the base rate, and *Uncertainty* reflects inherent task difficulty. Calibration through Platt scaling or temperature scaling specifically minimizes the Reliability term, making stated confidence a trustworthy clinical signal.

The diagnostic coordinator implements this pipeline directly. Evidence from biometric agents, symptom analysis, and episodic memory feeds into a differential generator that produces ranked candidate diagnoses. Each candidate then passes through Platt-calibrated confidence scoring, safety threshold enforcement, and audience-adapted explanation generation, all captured in an immutable audit trail. The code below traces this sequence step by step:

```
class DiagnosticCoordinator:
    """
    Clinical decision support with Bayesian evidence integration
    and confidence-calibrated differential diagnosis.
    """
    def __init__(self):
        self.biometric_agent = BiometricAnalyzer()
        self.symptom_agent = SymptomInterpreter()
        self.coordinator = DifferentialGenerator()
        self.explainer = ClinicalExplainer()

        self.confidence_engine = ConfidenceAwareAgent(
            n_hypotheses=5,
            calibration_method="platt_scaling"
        )

        self.memory = ClinicalMemorySystem()

        self.safety_monitor = SafetyMonitor(
            escalation_threshold=0.15,
            critical_conditions=[
                "myocardial_infarction",
                "pulmonary_embolism",
                "sepsis",
                "stroke"
```

```
        ]
    )

    self.audit_trail = AuditTrailGenerator()
```

The `__init__` method assembles the full diagnostic stack, including safety monitoring and audit logging. The diagnose method executes the complete pipeline in sequence:

```
def diagnose(self, patient_data, reported_symptoms):
    """Generate an explained, confidence-rated diagnosis."""
    vitals = self.biometric_agent.analyze(patient_data)

    symptoms = self.symptom_agent.interpret(
        reported_symptoms
    )

    history = self.memory.retrieve_episodic(
        patient_data.id
    )

    differentials = self.coordinator.generate_differentials(
        vitals, symptoms, history
    )

    scored = self.confidence_engine.score_differentials(
        differentials,
        evidence={
            "vitals": vitals,
            "symptoms": symptoms,
            "history": history
        }
    )

    safety_result = self.safety_monitor.evaluate(scored)

    if safety_result.requires_escalation:
        self.safety_monitor.trigger_alert(
            patient_data.id, safety_result
        )
```

The first phase gathers and scores evidence against the differential. The second phase records the outcome: episodic memory storage, immutable audit trail, and structured report:

```
explanation = self.explainer.generate(
    scored,
    audience="clinician",
    evidence_sources=[vitals, symptoms, history]
)

self.memory.store_episodic(patient_data.id, {
    "diagnoses": scored,
    "evidence": [vitals, symptoms],
})
```

The audit trail and return statement complete the diagnostic cycle, permanently recording every decision with full provenance:

```
    "explanation": explanation
})

self.audit_trail.record(InferenceEvent(
    patient_id=patient_data.id,
    inputs=[vitals, symptoms, history],
    kb_version=self.get_knowledge_base_version(),
    model_version=self.get_model_version(),
    reasoning_steps=self.coordinator.get_trace(),
    output=scored,
    confidence_breakdown=(
        self.confidence_engine
        .get_calibration_report()
    ),
    safety_alerts=safety_result
))

return DiagnosticReport(
    differentials=scored,
    explanation=explanation,
    confidence_summary=(
        self.confidence_engine
        .communicate_uncertainty(scored)
    ),
    audit_trail=self.audit_trail.get_last_entry_id()
)
```

The threshold value of 0.15 was not chosen arbitrarily. It emerged from a cost-asymmetry analysis of critical clinical conditions: the downstream cost of a missed myocardial infarction or sepsis case (delayed treatment, potential mortality) outweighs the cost of a false alarm (additional testing, brief resource diversion) by roughly an order of magnitude. Setting the escalation boundary at the point where the expected cost of inaction exceeds the expected cost of unnecessary review produces a value in the 0.12 to 0.18 range; 0.15 represents the midpoint, deliberately rounded toward the conservative end.

The `SafetyMonitor` is among the most critical architectural elements of any clinical agent. The escalation threshold of 0.15 has a formal justification: for the set of critical conditions (myocardial infarction, pulmonary embolism, sepsis, stroke), the threshold ensures that the probability of missing a true positive is bounded by the complement of the cumulative probability mass assigned to critical conditions below the threshold. This is deliberately conservative. In clinical practice, the cost of a missed myocardial infarction vastly exceeds the cost of a false alarm. When confidence falls below this threshold for non-critical conditions, the system does not present a diagnosis but instead flags the case for physician review with a summary of the ambiguous findings.

Clinical workflows also impose strict latency requirements. A physician in a 15-minute appointment cannot wait 30 seconds for a recommendation. Production systems address this through a tiered processing architecture. The reactive tier handles urgent queries (drug interaction checks, critical lab alerts) with sub-second response times using pre-indexed lookup tables. The deliberative tier handles complex diagnostic reasoning with a target latency of 3 to 5 seconds, leveraging cached embeddings and pre-computed similarity indices.

If the deliberative tier cannot produce a complete result within its time budget, it returns a partial result (the two highest-confidence diagnoses rather than a full differential) along with an indication that analysis is incomplete. This graceful degradation ensures the system always returns useful information within the workflow's time constraints.

The explanation component adapts its output based on audience. That adaptation serves a trust function: each stakeholder receives the level of detail appropriate to their role without distorting the underlying finding. For a clinician, the agent produces structured explanations following standard clinical reasoning format:

```
SAFETY ALERT – Escalation required. Primary concern: Sepsis (confidence above escalation
threshold:
0.82). Key findings: temperature 38.9°C with rigors (SHAP contribution: 0.34), heart rate
118 bpm (0.27), WBC 18.4 with left shift (0.22), MAP trending toward 65 mmHg
(0.17). SOFA score estimate: 4. Differential: Urosepsis (0.61), pneumonia-source sepsis
(0.21), biliary source (0.11). Immediate action: Blood cultures x2, lactate, broad-
spectrum antibiotics within 1 hour per Surviving Sepsis Campaign protocol. Attending
notification triggered.
```

For the same finding, a patient-facing explanation reads:

```
Your temperature, heart rate, and blood test results together suggest your body may be
fighting a serious infection. Your care team has been notified and will be with you
shortly. They may start antibiotics and run additional tests to identify the source of
the infection. This is a precaution to make sure you receive the right treatment quickly.
```

This audience-aware design reflects a deeper principle. In both healthcare and scientific contexts, users infer reliability and competence not only from what an agent says but from how it says it. A system that delivers SHAP attribution scores to a patient, or that gives a cardiologist a one-sentence summary with no reasoning trace, signals that it does not understand the context in which it operates.

Every diagnostic recommendation produces an immutable audit record capturing input data (identifiers encrypted), knowledge base version, model version, reasoning trace, and final recommendation. These records are cryptographically signed and stored in an append-only store for a minimum of 7 years, satisfying HIPAA retention requirements. If a physician disagrees with a recommendation, the override is recorded, creating a feedback loop supporting both accountability and continuous model improvement.

The following case study traces how these architectural patterns performed under real clinical conditions.

Case study: Diagnostic assistance system

Theory is useful but deployed systems are better. A regional health network, 200,000 patients across 20 provider sites, put these patterns to the test with a multi-agent diagnostic assistant built for one specific problem: catching chronic condition flare-ups before patients end up in the emergency department.

The deployment had three defining characteristics:

- **System architecture**: The assistant operates as a layered multi-agent system with three agent types. Biometric agents continuously analyze real-time patient data including heart rate variability, oxygen saturation, and sleep patterns from connected wearables. Symptom analysis agents use NLP to interpret patient-reported symptoms during telehealth consultations and cross-reference them with medical knowledge bases. Coordinator agents integrate biometric and symptom data to generate diagnostic suggestions, rank differentials by probability, and present results with full explanatory context.
  The memory architecture draws on episodic, semantic, and working memory patterns from *Chapter 5*. Episodic memory stores individual interactions: symptom reports, treatment adherence, emotional states during consultations. Semantic memory encodes clinical knowledge and protocols. Working memory manages the current diagnostic dialogue within a single consultation.
- **Privacy and compliance architecture**: The deployment used edge computing to process sensitive biometric data locally before anonymized insights reach the central reasoning engine. A lightweight inference model runs on the patient's wearable or bedside gateway, processing raw sensor data into clinical features on ARM-based processors with limited memory.
  Derived features, stripped of direct identifiers, are protected with differential privacy. Statistical noise calibrated at epsilon = 1.0 is added before transmission, a moderate privacy guarantee that balances individual protection against diagnostic utility for chronic condition monitoring. Raw biometric data never leaves the device. Only derived features ("heart rate variability trending downward over 72 hours") are transmitted via TLS 1.3.

  This architecture also delivers an operational win. Raw continuous heart rate data generates roughly 4 KB per second. The derived feature set, transmitted every 15 minutes, is approximately 200 bytes. For 10,000 patients monitored simultaneously, daily data transmission drops from approximately 3.4 TB to 19 MB, making the system viable over constrained cellular connections.

- **Deployment results**: The pilot demonstrated measurable improvements across several clinical metrics. Early detection of chronic condition exacerbations improved by 30%, meaning patients previously presenting at the ED with advanced symptoms were now identified and treated during routine telehealth visits. False alarm rates held at 3%, which is critical for adoption because excessive false alarms erode physician trust and lead to alert fatigue. Clinician response times improved by 40%, as structured diagnostic reports reduced the time physicians spent gathering and synthesizing patient information.

  Perhaps most significantly, physicians reported that structured explanations increased their confidence in recommendations. Rather than an opaque output to accept or reject on faith, the agent provided a transparent reasoning trace enabling faster, more informed clinical decisions. The 92% physician satisfaction rate reflects a system designed to augment, not replace, clinical judgment. The deployment addressed three key concerns through its architecture: data privacy through differential privacy techniques, model interpretability through a custom explanation algorithm providing clear rationales, and regulatory compliance through adherence to FDA guidelines for AI in medical decision support.
- **Lessons learned**: Three decisions proved essential. First, separating biometric processing from diagnostic reasoning, combined with edge computing and differential privacy, enabled regulatory compliance without sacrificing capability. Second, audience-adapted explanations ensured clinicians received detailed reasoning while patients received clear summaries. Third, the explicit safety escalation mechanism, triggering immediate alerts for life-threatening findings regardless of confidence, provided the safety guarantee institutional review boards required.

These patterns (layered architecture, provenance tracking, calibrated confidence, and structured explanation) transfer directly to the next domain, though the ground shifts beneath them: in scientific discovery, correctness is not a pre-existing standard to validate against but a question the agent itself must help define.

The Scientific Discovery agent

The Healthcare Intelligence agent applies what we already know. The Scientific Discovery agent goes looking for what we don't. That single difference reshapes everything: the validation strategy, the confidence model, the very definition of a correct answer. When your agent proposes a hypothesis that contradicts established theory, is it wrong, or is it the whole point?

This distinction carries profound architectural implications. A Healthcare agent can validate its outputs against established clinical standards. A Scientific Discovery agent, by definition, produces outputs that extend beyond current knowledge, making validation fundamentally more difficult. The agent must therefore implement mechanisms for assessing the novelty, plausibility, and internal consistency of its own hypotheses, while simultaneously acknowledging that genuinely novel discoveries may initially appear implausible by the standards of existing theory.

The Scientific Discovery agent builds on patterns from *Chapter 6*, extending them with capabilities for systematic knowledge gap identification and structured hypothesis generation. Where the research agent in *Chapter 6* focused on literature synthesis across known research questions, the discovery agent takes the additional step of identifying what questions have not yet been asked and proposing experiments to answer them.

Note

Theoretic view of knowledge gaps

The Scientific Discovery agent faces a unique challenge: identifying "negative space" in the literature where the expected information content significantly exceeds what has been observed. Unlike a search-and-retrieval agent, a discovery system must model the probability distribution of topics across millions of papers to find areas that should be answerable but remain unaddressed. This process, known as knowledge gap identification, utilizes temporal trend extrapolation to find "abandoned questions" where publication rates have declined despite high citation counts and lingering entropy. By quantifying novelty as proportional to the gap density, we transform scientific research from an intuitive process into a structured optimization problem, allowing teams to prioritize experimental effort where it is most likely to yield a novel contribution.

Literature synthesis frameworks

Scientific knowledge is distributed across millions of papers in thousands of journals, written in terminology that varies across subfields and evolves over time. An effective synthesis agent must retrieve relevant papers and organize them into a coherent map of what is known, what is contested, and what remains unexplored.

The agent operates through three phases, each building on the previous one.

- **Phase 1: Broad literature scanning.** The agent queries multiple databases (PubMed, arXiv, IEEE Xplore, Scopus) using semantic search to capture conceptually relevant studies rather than relying on keyword matches alone. A query about "mechanisms of polymer degradation under UV exposure" should retrieve papers discussing photolytic chain scission even if they never use the phrase "polymer degradation." Domain-specific embeddings trained on scientific corpora (SciBERT) enable this conceptual retrieval.
  In production, each database exposes a different API with different rate limits, authentication mechanisms, and response formats. PubMed's E-utilities API allows up to 10 requests per second with an API key. arXiv's OAI-PMH interface imposes a 3-second wait between requests. Scopus and IEEE Xplore require institutional API keys with monthly query budgets. The scanner must implement rate-limiting, retry logic with exponential backoff, result caching, and circuit breaker patterns to operate reliably at scale. In practice, literature scanning fails less often because the retrieval logic is wrong, and more often because the surrounding infrastructure is brittle. The following scanner is the "production wrapper" around semantic search: it enforces rate limits, budgets, caching, and fault tolerance so scientific retrieval remains reliable at scale.

  ```
  class ProductionLiteratureScanner:
      """
      Multi-database scanner with rate limiting, caching,
      deduplication, and fault tolerance.
      """

      def __init__(self):
          self.sources = {
  ```

```
        "pubmed": PubMedClient(
            api_key=os.getenv("PUBMED_API_KEY"),
            rate_limit=RateLimiter(max_per_second=10)
        ),
        "arxiv": ArxivClient(
            rate_limit=RateLimiter(
                min_interval_seconds=3
            )
        ),
        "scopus": ScopusClient(
            api_key=os.getenv("SCOPUS_API_KEY"),
            monthly_budget=20000
        ),
```

The four source clients occupy the core of __init__. The cache and deduplicator wired at the end give the scanner its reliability guarantees:

```
"ieee": IEEEXploreClient(
    api_key=os.getenv("IEEE_API_KEY"),
    monthly_budget=10000
)
}

self.cache = ResultCache(
    backend="redis", ttl_hours=168
)

self.deduplicator = PaperDeduplicator(
    match_on=["doi", "title_similarity"],
    similarity_threshold=0.95
)
```

The __init__ method registers four database clients with independent rate limits. The search_all method fans out queries concurrently, tolerates individual source failures, and returns deduplicated, cached results:

```
async def search_all(self, query, max_per_source=500):
    """Search all databases with fault tolerance."""
    cached = self.cache.get(query)
    if cached and not cached.is_stale:
        return cached.results

    tasks = [
        self.search_with_fallback(
```

```
            name, client, query, max_per_source
        )
        for name, client in self.sources.items()
    ]

    results = await asyncio.gather(
        *tasks,
        return_exceptions=True
    )
```

After aggregating results from all sources, deduplication and caching finalize the pipeline:

```
)

all_papers = []

for name, result in zip(self.sources.keys(), results):
    if isinstance(result, Exception):
        logger.warning(f"Source {name} failed: {result}")
    else:
        all_papers.extend(result)

unique = self.deduplicator.deduplicate(all_papers)
self.cache.set(query, unique)

return unique
```

Architecturally, this scanner is what allows the Scientific Discovery agent to behave like a dependable system rather than a one-off script. It turns external literature APIs into a controlled dependency with predictable failure behavior. That predictability matters downstream: clustering quality degrades if one database silently drops out, and budget overruns can shut off access mid-run in the middle of a synthesis cycle. By caching results, tolerating partial failures, and normalizing duplicates early, the scanner produces a stable deduplicated corpus that later stages can treat as an input dataset rather than an unreliable stream. This is also the correct place to attach operational telemetry: cache hit rate, per-source error rate, and per-source budget consumption become leading indicators of whether the discovery pipeline is still trustworthy.

Interoperability across databases is managed through the **Model Context Protocol** (**MCP**), which enables dynamic interfacing with academic database APIs without hardcoded logic for each service. This is particularly valuable in scientific domains, where new databases and preprint servers emerge regularly. **Agent-to-Agent** (**A2A**) protocols enable multi-agent configurations where one agent specializes in literature scanning while another handles synthesis, each operating asynchronously while sharing state through structured message packets.

- **Phase 2:** Thematic clustering and summarization. Retrieved papers are grouped by shared themes: methodology, findings, or application domain. This clustering reveals patterns invisible to a researcher reading papers sequentially: recurring experimental approaches, converging results from independent groups, or emerging areas of interest that span traditional disciplinary boundaries. The clustering is performed using a combination of citation graph analysis, which captures structural relationships between papers, and semantic similarity, which captures topical relationships.
- **Phase 3:** Synthesis and insight generation. The agent produces structured, high-value outputs: comparative tables aligning results across studies, evidence maps visualizing the strength of support for competing hypotheses, and synthesis reports that explicitly identify areas of consensus, areas of active disagreement, and areas where no research has yet ventured. These outputs serve as starting points for human researchers, not as definitive conclusions.

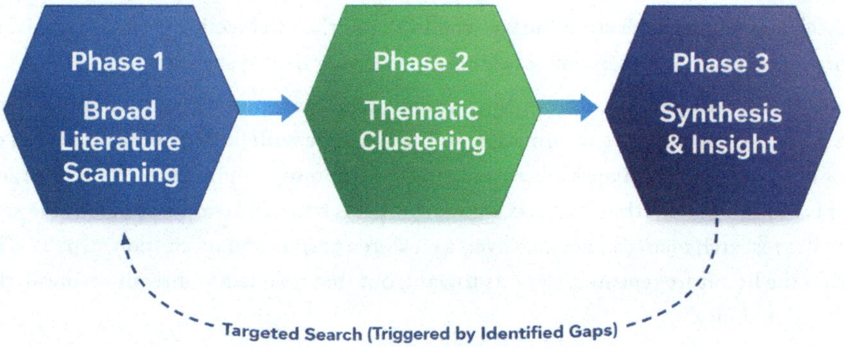

Figure 13.2 – Three-phase scientific literature synthesis workflow

The key architectural decision in *Figure 13.2* is the separation of fault-tolerant ingestion from semantically-aware synthesis. Keeping these phases distinct means the circuit-breaker and rate-limiting logic in Phase 1 can fail and retry without corrupting the clustering state built in Phase 2. A monolithic pipeline that interleaves retrieval and organization would require full restarts on any upstream API failure. The iterative feedback arrow from gap identification back to Phase 1 is equally deliberate: it encodes the agent's epistemic strategy. Rather than treating the initial scan as complete, the agent treats discovered gaps as queries and re-enters the ingestion phase with targeted parameters, progressively narrowing uncertainty rather than assuming a single pass is sufficient.

Knowledge gap identification

Perhaps the most intellectually demanding task performed by the Scientific Discovery agent is the systematic identification of knowledge gaps. A knowledge gap is not simply a topic that has not been studied. It is a question that the existing literature implies should be answerable but that no study has yet addressed, or an intersection between two well-studied areas that has been overlooked because researchers in each area are not aware of relevant work in the other.

The three gap detection strategies employed by the agent can be unified under an information-theoretic framework. Consider the scientific literature as a probability distribution P(T) over the space of possible topics T. Each published paper contributes probability mass to the topics it addresses. A knowledge gap can be formally defined as a region of topic space where the expected information content significantly exceeds the observed information content:

$$Gap(t) = H_{expected}(t) - H_{observed}(t)$$

The agent operationalizes this framework through three complementary detection strategies, each targeting a different pattern of absence in the literature:

- **Negative space analysis** identifies topics where P(t | referenced in other papers) is high but P(t | directly studied) is low. If dozens of polymer aging papers mention "humidity effects" as a confounder but none investigate the humidity-degradation relationship as a primary question, the agent flags it.
- **Cross-domain intersection detection** identifies topics at boundaries between distributions $P_A(T)$ and $P_B(T)$ where $P_A(t) * P_B(t)$ is significant but few papers exist in the overlap. Materials science and biomedical engineering both study surface coatings, but the intersection of antimicrobial coatings with environmental degradation resistance is studied by neither field systematically.
- **Temporal trend extrapolation** tracks dP(t)/dt and identifies topics where declining publication rates do not correlate with declining information entropy. A topic with falling publications but continued citations likely represents an unresolved question the community has drifted from. In practice, the gap detector is the component that converts a large synthesis report into a short, defensible set of "next questions" a research team can act on. Given a clustered corpus and its citation structure, it searches for topics that the literature repeatedly points toward, but that no one has directly resolved, then ranks them by actionability.

The following class encodes all three detection strategies within a single gap-detection pipeline, ranking results by novelty, feasibility, potential impact, and data availability:

```
class KnowledgeGapDetector:
    """
    Identifies literature gaps through negative space analysis,
    cross-domain intersection, and temporal trend extrapolation.
    """
    def __init__(self):
        self.citation_analyzer = CitationGraphAnalyzer()
        self.domain_mapper = ResearchDomainMapper()
        self.trend_tracker = TemporalTrendTracker()

    def detect_gaps(self, synthesis_report):
        gaps = []

        # Strategy 1: P(t|referenced) high, P(t|studied) low
        referenced_but_unstudied = (
            self.find_referenced_unstudied_topics(
                synthesis_report.clusters
            )
        )
```

```
        gaps.extend(referenced_but_unstudied)

        # Strategy 2: High P_A(t)*P_B(t), few papers in overlap
        domain_boundaries = (
            self.domain_mapper.find_unexplored_intersections(
                synthesis_report.clusters,
                min_relevance=0.7
            )
        )
        gaps.extend(domain_boundaries)

        # Strategy 3: dP(t)/dt declining, H(t) still high
        abandoned_questions = (
            self.trend_tracker.find_abandoned_questions(
                synthesis_report.corpus,
                declining_since="3_years",
                citation_status="still_cited"
            )
        )
        gaps.extend(abandoned_questions)

        ranked_gaps = self.rank_gaps(
            gaps,
            criteria=[
                "novelty",
                "feasibility",
                "potential_impact",
                "data_availability"
            ]
        )

        return KnowledgeGapReport(
            gaps=ranked_gaps,
            methodology_used=[
                "negative_space",
                "cross_domain",
                "temporal_trend"
            ],
            confidence_assessment=self.assess_confidence(
                ranked_gaps
            )
        )
```

What matters architecturally is that this module formalizes discovery as a **selection problem** rather than an open-ended brainstorming task. Each strategy corresponds to a different failure mode of human literature review: negative space catches "everyone mentions it, nobody studies it"; boundary detection catches missed opportunities created by disciplinary silos; and trend extrapolation catches problems that appear "unfashionable" even though they remain unresolved and still cited. The ranking step then turns these candidates into an execution plan by privileging gaps that are both novel and feasible, ensuring the downstream hypothesis agent and experiment design agent are fed with targets that can realistically be tested within available constraints.

Hypothesis generation systems

The most advanced capability of the Scientific Discovery agent is structured hypothesis generation. Where literature synthesis and gap identification operate on existing knowledge, hypothesis generation requires the agent to propose new ideas that extend beyond the boundaries of what is currently known.

The agent does not generate hypotheses through unconstrained speculation. Instead, it applies a structured reasoning process combining identified knowledge gaps with established theoretical frameworks and known experimental constraints. This process is grounded in the philosophical tradition of abductive reasoning, formalized by Charles Sanders Peirce and later elaborated by Peter Lipton as "inference to the best explanation" (IBE). Abductive reasoning works backward from observed phenomena to propose the most likely explanations that have not yet been considered.

Hypothesis generation can be expressed as a multi-objective optimization:

$$h^* = \underset{h \in H}{argmax}[P(O|h) \cdot Prior(h) \cdot Novelty(h)]$$

The first term, $P(O \mid h)$, measures explanatory adequacy: how well does the hypothesis account for the observed findings in the gap region? The second term, $Prior(h)$, measures plausibility: is the hypothesis consistent with established theory? The third term, $Novelty(h)$, rewards hypotheses that explain observations in ways extending current knowledge rather than merely restating it. This three-factor optimization captures a fundamental tension in scientific discovery: maximizing $P(O|h)$ alone favors conservative hypotheses, while maximizing $Novelty(h)$ alone favors speculation. The agent's task is to navigate this tension.

The hypothesis generation process follows four stages. First, the agent selects a knowledge gap from its ranked report. Second, it retrieves the theoretical frameworks and methodologies most relevant to the gap. Third, it generates candidate hypotheses by reasoning about how established mechanisms might operate in the unexplored territory. Fourth, it evaluates each candidate against criteria of internal consistency, testability, and alignment with existing evidence. Once the gap detector identifies where the literature is thin, the next step is to propose hypotheses that are both plausible and experimentally actionable. The following generator turns "we do not know X" into a small set of candidate mechanisms, grounded in known theory and constrained so they can be tested rather than merely asserted.

```
class HypothesisGenerator:
    """
    Structured hypothesis generation grounded in knowledge gaps,
    theoretical frameworks, and abductive reasoning.
```

```
    """
    def __init__(self):
        self.gap_detector = KnowledgeGapDetector()
        self.theory_retriever = TheoreticalFrameworkRetriever()
        self.reasoning_engine = ScientificReasoningEngine(
            model="scientific-llm",
            reasoning_modes=[
                "analogical", "deductive", "abductive"
            ]
        )
        self.evaluator = HypothesisEvaluator()
```

The `__init__` method assembles the reasoning stack. The `generate_hypotheses` method iterates over top gaps, applies abductive reasoning per gap, and returns only hypotheses that pass testability and consistency thresholds:

```
def generate_hypotheses(self, gap_report, n_hypotheses=5):
    hypotheses = []

    for gap in gap_report.top_gaps(n=3):
        frameworks = self.theory_retriever.retrieve(
            gap.domain, gap.related_concepts
        )

        candidates = self.reasoning_engine.reason(
            gap=gap,
            frameworks=frameworks,
            reasoning_type="abductive",
            constraints={
                "must_be_testable": True,
                "must_be_consistent_with": (
                    gap.established_findings
                ),
                "should_extend": gap.boundary_knowledge
            }
        )

        for candidate in candidates:
            candidate.evaluation = self.evaluator.evaluate(
                hypothesis=candidate,
            )
```

The loop generates and evaluates candidate hypotheses for each gap. The final call ranks them by consistency and testability score:

```
criteria={
    "internal_consistency": True,
    "novelty_vs_existing": True,
    "testability": True,
    "potential_impact": True
}
)
candidate.proposed_experiments = self.design_validation_experiments(
    candidate, gap
)

hypotheses.extend(candidates)

return self.rank_hypotheses(
    hypotheses,
    min_consistency_score=0.7,
    min_testability_score=0.6
)
```

Architecturally, this generator is where the Scientific Discovery agent crosses the line from retrieval-and-summarization into research planning. The system's credibility depends on two safeguards that are explicit in the code. First, hypotheses are grounded in retrieved theoretical frameworks, which functions as a domain constraint and reduces the risk of producing plausible-sounding but conceptually unmoored claims. Second, hypotheses are not accepted as outputs until they are paired with experiments and scored against criteria that a human research team would recognize. This is also where explainability becomes practical: when a hypothesis is later rejected, the system can point to which constraint failed (inconsistency with established findings, low testability, or weak impact), and when a hypothesis is accepted, it carries both its theoretical justification and its experimental plan as part of the audit trail.

Case study: Materials science discovery platform

This case study moves from architecture to practice, tracing how the Scientific Discovery agent's three subsystems operated together on a real materials engineering challenge with measurable experimental outcomes.

A materials science team working on next-generation aerospace polymers needed formulations combining high thermal stability with mechanical flexibility, a notoriously difficult pairing because the rigid aromatic backbones conferring thermal stability tend to reduce flexibility.

The platform had three components worth examining in detail:

- **Platform architecture**: The discovery platform deployed a network of four specialized agents coordinated through an orchestration layer. The literature synthesis agent scanned materials science, polymer chemistry, and aerospace engineering databases to build a comprehensive knowledge map. The knowledge gap agent analyzed this map to identify unexplored compositional spaces and processing conditions. The hypothesis agent proposed specific polymer formulations and processing parameters predicted to achieve the target property combination. The experimental design agent generated detailed validation protocols including suggested characterization techniques, expected measurement ranges, and statistical power analyses for determining sample sizes.

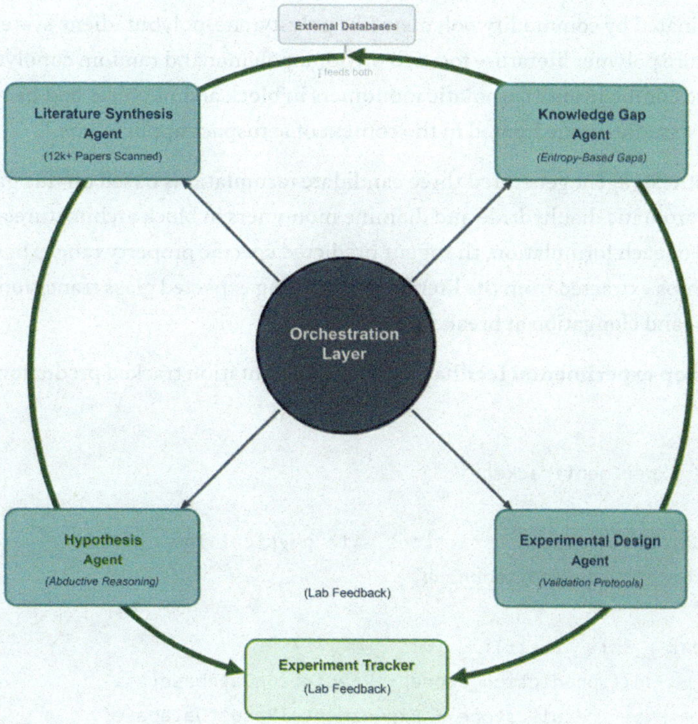

Figure 13.3 – Materials science discovery platform architecture

The design principle behind *Figure 13.3* is agent specialization with shared state. Each of the four agents operates in a domain where generalist models perform poorly: literature synthesis requires semantic clustering, gap detection requires entropy analysis, hypothesis generation requires abductive reasoning, and experimental design requires constraint satisfaction over physical parameters. Making them independent agents with well-defined handoff contracts allows each to be optimized independently and replaced without cascading changes. The Experiment Tracker is the most consequential architectural element because it closes the loop between digital inference and physical measurement. Without it, the system is a sophisticated search engine. With it, each experimental outcome becomes training signal that refines the hypothesis scoring function for all subsequent cycles. This is the mechanism that enables the Level 4 learning behavior introduced in *Chapter 1*, progressively reducing prediction error as the agent accumulates real-world evidence rather than relying solely on literature priors.

- **Discovery process**: The literature synthesis agent scanned over 12,000 papers spanning polymer chemistry, materials science, and aerospace engineering. The thematic clustering phase organized these into 47 distinct clusters covering topics from aromatic polyimide synthesis to nanocomposite reinforcement strategies to processing-property relationships.
  The knowledge gap agent identified several promising gaps. One that proved particularly fruitful was the intersection of block copolymer architectures (well-studied for mechanical properties) with thermally stable aromatic monomers (well-studied for heat resistance). The block copolymer literature was dominated by commodity polymers like polystyrene-polybutadiene systems, while high-temperature polymer literature focused on homopolymer and random copolymer architectures. The structured combination of aromatic monomers in block architectures had been explored in only a handful of studies, none framed in the context of aerospace applications.

  The hypothesis agent generated three candidate formulations based on this gap, each combining different aromatic dianhydride and diamine monomers in block architectures with controlled segment lengths. For each formulation, the agent predicted specific property ranges based on structure-property relationships extracted from the literature, including expected glass transition temperatures, tensile strengths, and elongation at break values.
- **Closed-loop experimental feedback**: The implementation tracked predictions against laboratory results:

```
class ExperimentTracker:
    """
    Bridges digital predictions with physical lab results
    for closed-loop learning.
    """
    def __init__(self):
        self.prediction_store = PredictionDatabase()
        self.result_store = ExperimentalResultDatabase()
        self.feedback_engine = FeedbackEngine()
```

The `__init__` method wires the prediction store to the result store via a feedback engine. The `record_result` method computes per-property prediction error and triggers model updates:

```
def record_result(self, hypothesis_id, measurements):
    prediction = self.prediction_store.get(hypothesis_id)
    errors = {}

    for prop, predicted in prediction["predicted_properties"].items():
        if prop in measurements:
            measured = measurements[prop]
            error_pct = abs(predicted - measured) / measured * 100

            errors[prop] = {
```

```
                "predicted": predicted,
                "measured": measured,
                "error_pct": round(error_pct, 2)
            }

    self.result_store.insert({
        "hypothesis_id": hypothesis_id,
        "measurements": measurements,
        "prediction_errors": errors,
        "timestamp": datetime.utcnow()
    })

    self.feedback_engine.update_models(hypothesis_id, errors)

    return errors
```

This loop produced measurable improvement: average property prediction error dropped from 12% in round one to 8% in round two and 5% in round three, demonstrating the experiential learning characteristic of Level 4 agents.

- **Results**: One of three formulations achieved a combination of thermal stability (glass transition above 350 degrees Celsius) and mechanical flexibility (elongation at break exceeding 15%) not previously reported in the literature. Prediction accuracy: glass transition within 8%, tensile strength within 12%. Total time from initial scan to validated result: 14 weeks. The team estimated 9 to 12 months through traditional approaches, representing roughly 60% timeline compression.
- **Limitations**: The platform faced challenges characteristic of scientific discovery agents more broadly. Paywalled databases restricted the agent's ability to scan certain proprietary databases and recent conference proceedings. Publication bias in the retrieved literature meant the synthesis disproportionately represented positive results, potentially obscuring formulations that had been tried and failed.

The agent's property predictions, while useful for prioritizing candidates, were not sufficiently accurate to replace experimental characterization. The practical challenge of time lag between prediction and feedback, with laboratory synthesis and characterization taking 2 to 4 weeks per formulation, required the system to manage uncertainty about pending results while continuing to generate hypotheses for subsequent rounds. These limitations reinforce that the agent functions as a research accelerator, not a replacement. Human expertise remains essential for evaluating hypotheses, designing experiments, interpreting results, and deciding which directions to pursue.

Challenges and considerations

Placing the two agents (Healthcare Intelligence and Scientific Discovery) side by side reveals architectural patterns that transcend their individual domains. Three questions structure the comparison: what do they share, where do their constraints diverge, and what does that teach us about designing agents for high-stakes environments more broadly:

- **Shared structural patterns**: Both agents enforce a strict separation between evidence ingestion, reasoning, and explanation. Neither conflates retrieval with inference. Both maintain versioned, provenance-tracked knowledge stores, because defensibility requires knowing not just what the agent concluded but which sources contributed and when those sources were last verified. Both apply layered confidence calibration: Bayesian belief updating in the Healthcare agent, information-theoretic gap scoring in the Scientific Discovery agent. Both escalate to human review rather than failing silently when confidence falls below domain-defined thresholds. And both produce audience-differentiated outputs, recognizing that the clinician, the patient, and the auditor each need a different representation of the same underlying decision trace.
- **Divergent design constraints:** Where the agents differ is in their definition of correctness. The Healthcare agent operates against a relatively stable ground truth: established clinical guidelines, validated drug interaction databases, and a patient population whose physiology does not change domain by domain. Its dominant failure modes are false negatives (missed diagnoses) and false positives (unnecessary escalations). Both carry directly measurable costs. The Scientific Discovery agent, by contrast, operates in a domain where the ground truth is unknown and possibly unknowable until experiments are run. Its correctness signal is delayed, uncertain, and mediated by peer review. This forces a different confidence model: the agent must assign value to novelty and divergence from consensus, not just consistency with it. An agent that only reinforces known findings adds no scientific value. The two agents also face opposite data-access regimes. Healthcare data is subject to strict regulatory constraints and must be handled with federated, privacy-preserving architectures. Scientific literature, while copyrighted, is comparatively open, which means the bottleneck is processing volume rather than access permission.
- **Generalizable lessons:** The most transferable lesson is structural: in high-stakes domains, compliance and safety cannot be added to an agent after the architecture is set. They must be designed in as first-class layers with their own interfaces, update pipelines, and audit surfaces. The second lesson concerns escalation. Neither agent attempts to handle every case autonomously. Both recognize that the cost of wrong autonomous action exceeds the cost of routing to a human, and both encode that judgment explicitly in their threshold logic. The third lesson is about the relationship between explanation and adoption. In both domains, the agents that succeed are not those with the highest raw accuracy. They are the ones whose reasoning is transparent enough that domain experts can evaluate, override, and ultimately trust them. Accuracy without explainability is insufficient for adoption in either clinical or scientific practice.

Summary

This chapter explored how intelligent agents are transforming healthcare delivery and scientific discovery, two domains where the stakes are highest and the information overload most acute.

The Healthcare Intelligence agent demonstrated a four-layer architecture separating data ingestion, knowledge integration, clinical reasoning, and explanation generation. Its medical knowledge base tracks provenance and resolves conflicting guidelines. Its patient data pipeline normalizes heterogeneous inputs and aligns them temporally. Its clinical decision support framework produces confidence-calibrated diagnoses grounded in Bayesian belief updating, with Platt-scaled confidence and safety escalation for critical conditions. The diagnostic assistance case study validated these patterns in practice: 30% improvement in early detection, 40% faster clinician response times, 92% physician satisfaction, and a privacy-preserving edge architecture that reduced data transmission by three orders of magnitude.

The Scientific Discovery agent demonstrated capabilities extending beyond retrieval into genuine knowledge creation. The production-grade literature synthesis workflow scans multiple databases with fault tolerance and deduplication. The knowledge gap detection system applies three strategies unified under an information-theoretic framework. The hypothesis generation system produces testable proposals grounded in abductive reasoning and evaluated through a three-factor optimization balancing explanatory adequacy, plausibility, and novelty. The materials science case study showed the end-to-end process with closed-loop feedback, compressing a 9-to-12-month timeline to 14 weeks while improving prediction accuracy from 12% to 5% error.

The *Challenges and considerations* section examined both agents together, revealing that the shared architectural commitments (layered isolation, provenance tracking, calibrated confidence, and structured escalation) are not domain-specific choices but requirements of any agent operating where errors carry serious consequences. The cross-cutting lesson is clear. Safety and compliance must be designed in from the start, not bolted on. Explanation and transparency are prerequisites for adoption, not optional features. And these agents succeed not by replacing human intelligence, but by ensuring that human experts can do what only humans can do: exercise judgment, accept responsibility, and push the boundaries of what is known.

In the next chapter, we will examine how similar architectural patterns apply to financial and legal domain agents, where regulatory constraints and the need for auditability create comparable design challenges in a very different application context.

14

Financial and Legal Domain Agents

The measure of intelligence is the ability to change.

— Albert Einstein

Building agents for finance and law is a different game entirely. The general-purpose architectures from earlier chapters could afford trial and error. These cannot. A single compliance failure in a regulated domain does not just produce a bad answer. It can trigger fines, sanctions, or criminal liability. Every recommendation must be traced back to its data sources. Every decision must withstand regulatory audit. Every interaction must be logged with enough detail to reconstruct the reasoning months or years later. In this chapter, you will build two production-grade agents: a **Financial Advisory agent** that combines market analysis, risk assessment, and compliance checking, and a **Legal Intelligence agent** that automates contract analysis, precedent retrieval, and citation verification.

With the ethical and explainable foundations established in *Chapter 12*, we can now examine a domain where trust is earned through disciplined process rather than persuasive language. Financial advice sits at the intersection of uncertainty, regulation, and personal consequence. A financial agent must justify its assumptions, separate facts from projections, and preserve an auditable record of how each recommendation was produced.

In this chapter, we'll be covering the following topics:

- The Financial Advisory agent
- The Legal Intelligence agent

Technical requirements

To run the examples in this chapter, you will need the following:

- Python 3.10 or later
- The following Python packages: langchain==0.2.16, langchain-openai==0.1.23, langchain-community==0.2.16, langgraph==0.2.28, openai==1.40.0, yfinance==0.2.41, finnhub-python==2.4.19, tavily-python==0.3.3, numpy==1.26.4, pydantic==2.8.2, and python-dotenv==1.0.1
- An OpenAI API key with access to the gpt-4o-mini model
- A Finnhub API key for financial data (free tier available at finnhub.io)
- A Tavily API key for news search capabilities (tavily.com)

All code examples for this chapter are available in the book's GitHub repository at `https://github.com/PacktPublishing/30-Agents-Every-AI-Engineer-Must-Build/chapter14`

The Financial Advisory agent

The financial services industry has long embraced data-driven technologies, but agentic AI represents a pivotal evolution. Financial institutions serve thousands of clients with diverse portfolios, risk tolerances, and investment goals. Human advisors, constrained by time and cognitive bandwidth, can only maintain deep relationships with a fraction of their client base. Agentic systems extend that capacity by automating data-intensive advisory work while preserving human oversight for judgment-intensive decisions.

In this section, we introduce the Financial Advisory agent as a reference architecture for building decision-support systems that operate under market volatility and compliance constraints. The goal is not to automate judgment, but to structure it. We will show how an agent can combine market signals, client context, and policy rules through supervised orchestration, producing recommendations that are explainable, contestable, and safe to operationalize in a regulated environment.

Market data analysis architectures

A financial advisory agent lives or dies by its market data pipeline. Static dashboards show you what happened yesterday. An agentic system needs to sense what is happening now, update its internal model on the fly, and adjust its recommendations before the moment passes. That demands an architecture in which specialized components each own a distinct slice of the pipeline.

A central orchestration agent routes incoming queries to specialized sub-agents based on the nature of the request. *Figure 14.1* presents the Financial Advisory agent as a supervised multi-agent system in which analysis is decomposed into specialized roles and coordinated through an explicit control layer.

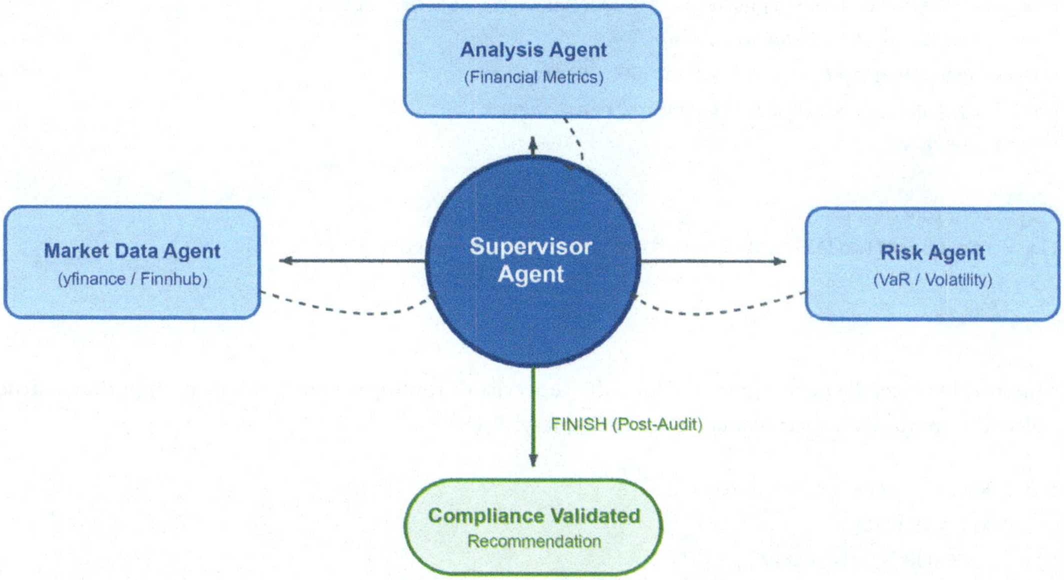

Figure 14.1 – Multi-agent architecture for the Financial Advisory agent, showing the supervisor agent coordinating specialist agents through state graph routing

In *Figure 14.1*, the supervisor agent serves as both the entry point and policy-aware orchestrator, deciding which specialist to invoke, in what order, and with what state recorded at each step. The state-graph routing mechanism is the key architectural safeguard. It turns the advisory process into a traceable sequence of states and transitions, making it possible to enforce tool permissions, require human checkpoints, and attach an audit trail to every recommendation.

This separation of concerns simplifies both testing and audit. When a regulator asks how a particular recommendation was generated, the system traces data lineage through discrete, inspectable processing stages rather than through a monolithic reasoning chain.

The following code realizes the architecture shown in *Figure 14.1*. The implementation uses LangGraph's StateGraph to define the agent workflow. Each specialist agent is implemented as a `create_react_agent` with access to domain-specific tools. The supervisor uses structured output to determine routing at each decision point The code below configures the supervisor routing schema, defines the agent team members, and compiles the StateGraph that governs how queries move between specialist agents.

```
import os
from functools import partial
from typing import Annotated, Sequence, TypedDict, Literal
import yfinance as yf
from langchain_openai import ChatOpenAI
from langchain_core.prompts import (
    ChatPromptTemplate, MessagesPlaceholder
)
```

```
from langchain_core.messages import HumanMessage, BaseMessage
from pydantic import BaseModel
from langgraph.graph import END, START, StateGraph
from langgraph.prebuilt import create_react_agent
import operator

# LLM configuration
llm = ChatOpenAI(model="gpt-4o-mini-2024-07-18", temperature=0)

# Supervisor routing schema
```

With imports in place, the next segment defines the supervisor's routing schema and the prompt that instructs it to select the appropriate specialist agent for each query:

```
class RouteResponse(BaseModel):
    next: Literal[
        "Market_Data_Agent",
        "Financial_Analysis_Agent",
        "News_Agent",
        "FINISH"
    ]

# Agent team members
members = ["Market_Data_Agent", "Financial_Analysis_Agent", "News_Agent"]

# Supervisor prompt
system_prompt = (
    "You are a Financial Services Supervisor managing: "
    f"{', '.join(members)}. "
    "Route queries to the appropriate specialist. "
    "Use Market_Data_Agent for price and volume data. "
    "Use Financial_Analysis_Agent for financial computations. "
    "Use News_Agent for market news and sentiment. "
    "Select FINISH when the query is fully resolved."
)
prompt = ChatPromptTemplate.from_messages([
    ("system", system_prompt),
    MessagesPlaceholder(variable_name="messages"),
    ("system", "Choose the next agent from: {options}.")
]).partial(options=str(members + ["FINISH"]))
```

The supervisor_agent function invokes this chain at each decision step, extracting the routing decision from the structured output and returning it as a state update that LangGraph uses to select the next node:

```
def supervisor_agent(state):
    chain = prompt | llm.with_structured_output(RouteResponse)
    return {"next": chain.invoke(state).next}
```

The market data agent interfaces with external financial data providers through standardized API integrations. In its simplest form, this agent wraps the yfinance library to retrieve real-time stock information:

```
def get_market_data(query: str) -> str:
    """Retrieve current market data for a given stock symbol."""
    try:
        stock_symbol = query.strip().upper()
        ticker = yf.Ticker(stock_symbol)
        info = ticker.info
        current_price = info.get("currentPrice", "N/A")
        market_cap = info.get("marketCap", "N/A")
        pe_ratio = info.get("trailingPE", "N/A")
        day_high = info.get("dayHigh", "N/A")
        day_low = info.get("dayLow", "N/A")
        volume = info.get("volume", "N/A")
        return (
            f"Market Data for {stock_symbol}: "
            f"Price: ${current_price}, Market Cap: ${market_cap}, "
            f"P/E Ratio: {pe_ratio}, "
            f"Day Range: ${day_low}-${day_high}, "
            f"Volume: {volume}"
        )
    except Exception as e:
        return f"Error retrieving market data: {str(e)}"
```

The tool is wrapped inside a create_react_agent, which gives the market data agent the ability to decide when and how to invoke it within the supervisor's broader orchestration loop:

```
market_agent = create_react_agent(
    llm, tools=[get_market_data],
    state_modifier="You are the Market Data Agent. "
    "Retrieve real-time stock data for client queries."
)
```

For production deployments, the Finnhub API provides a more robust data source with endpoints for basic financials, company metrics, real-time quotes, and company news. The following integration demonstrates how to retrieve comprehensive financial metrics:

```
import finnhub

finnhub_client = finnhub.Client(
    api_key=os.getenv("FINNHUB_API_KEY")
)

def portfolio_analysis(query: str) -> str:
    """Fetch financial metrics using the Finnhub API."""
    try:
        symbol = query.split()[-1].upper()
        financials = finnhub_client.company_basic_financials(
            symbol, 'all'
        )
        metrics = financials.get('metric', {})
        return (
            f"Portfolio Analysis for {symbol}: "
            f"P/E Ratio: {metrics.get('peRatio')}, "
            f"Revenue Growth: {metrics.get('revenueGrowth')}, "
            f"52W High: {metrics.get('52WeekHigh')}, "
            f"52W Low: {metrics.get('52WeekLow')}"
        )
    except Exception as e:
        return f"Error: {str(e)}"
```

The financial analysis agent operates downstream, consuming raw data from the market data agent and applying quantitative models to derive actionable insights. Its analytical pipeline computes metrics including portfolio beta, Sharpe ratios, and sector correlation matrices. The financial news agent completes the triad by providing qualitative context, using search-based retrieval tools such as Tavily to produce condensed market intelligence:

```
from langchain_community.tools.tavily_search import (
    TavilySearchResults
)

financial_news_tool = TavilySearchResults(max_results=5)

financial_news_agent = create_react_agent(
    llm, tools=[financial_news_tool],
    state_modifier="You are the Financial News Agent. "
    "Retrieve and summarize the latest financial news "
```

```
    "relevant to the user's query."
)
```

The supervisor orchestrates these specialists through the state graph. When a client asks "What is the current outlook for technology stocks?", the supervisor routes to the market data agent for pricing, then to the financial analysis agent for sector metrics, and finally to the news agent for commentary. Every agent returns to the supervisor after completing its task, and the supervisor evaluates whether additional agents are needed. This loop-until-complete pattern ensures complex multi-source queries are fully resolved before generating a response:

```
# Workflow state
class AgentState(TypedDict):
    messages: Annotated[Sequence[BaseMessage], operator.add]
    next: str

# Wrap react agents as node-compatible callables
def agent_node(state, agent, name):
    result = agent.invoke(state)
    return {"messages": [HumanMessage(
        content=result["messages"][-1].content, name=name
    )]}

market_data_node = partial(
    agent_node, agent=market_agent, name="Market_Data_Agent"
)
# Similarly for analysis_node and news_node

# Build the state graph
```

With the specialist agents wrapped as node-compatible callables, the following segment assembles the StateGraph, registers each agent as a named node, and defines the routing edges that allow the supervisor to delegate and recover control after each specialist completes:

```
workflow = StateGraph(AgentState)
workflow.add_node("Market_Data_Agent", market_data_node)
workflow.add_node("Financial_Analysis_Agent", analysis_node)
workflow.add_node("News_Agent", news_node)
workflow.add_node("supervisor", supervisor_agent)

# Route agents back to supervisor after completion
for member in members:
    workflow.add_edge(member, "supervisor")

# Conditional routing from supervisor
```

```
conditional_map = {m: m for m in members}
conditional_map["FINISH"] = END
workflow.add_conditional_edges(
    "supervisor", lambda x: x["next"], conditional_map
)
workflow.add_edge(START, "supervisor")

# Compile and execute
```

Compiling the graph locks the topology and enables streaming execution. The example below sends a portfolio query and prints each state update as it flows through the supervisor and specialist nodes:

```
graph = workflow.compile()
inputs = {
    "messages": [
        HumanMessage(content="Analyze the portfolio for AAPL.")
    ]
}
for output in graph.stream(inputs, stream_mode="values"):
    print(output)
```

This sequential delegation pattern supports graceful degradation: if the market data agent encounters an API timeout, the supervisor can route to an alternative data source rather than abort the entire workflow.

Note

Production data feeds

The yfinance library is suitable for prototyping and demonstration but does not provide the reliability guarantees required in regulated financial environments. Production systems should source market data from commercial providers such as Bloomberg, Refinitiv (LSEG Data & Analytics), or FactSet, which offer contractual SLA commitments, real-time feeds with sub-second latency, and data quality controls. When evaluating a provider, confirm coverage for all required asset classes, jurisdictional data permissions, and API rate limits that will hold under production load.

So far, the architecture has emphasized decomposition and orchestration. That improves clarity and traceability, but does not guarantee safety. In finance, the most consequential failures come not from missing information but from uncontrolled risk exposure, unsuitable recommendations, or unchallenged assumptions in volatile markets. To address that gap, we introduce risk assessment as a first-class architectural layer. The risk assessment agent operates within the same supervisory framework but contributes an explicit gating function that transforms "plausible advice" into advice that is operationally defensible.

Risk assessment frameworks

Risk assessment is where a Financial Advisory agent either earns trust or loses it. A comprehensive framework must weave together market risk, credit risk, liquidity risk, and operational risk, each evaluated against the specific constraints of the client's portfolio and tolerance. The agentic approach transforms this traditionally manual, periodic process into a continuous, adaptive monitoring system.

Note

Forty-five minutes, four hundred forty million dollars

On August 1, 2012, Knight Capital Group deployed a software update to its automated trading system. A configuration error reactivated dormant code that began executing millions of unintended trades across 154 stocks. In forty-five minutes, the firm accumulated $7 billion in erroneous positions and lost approximately $440 million, nearly its entire market capitalization. Knight was rescued through an emergency capital raise but never fully recovered, merging with Getco LLC the following year. The incident remains the canonical warning for automated financial systems: speed without safeguards is not an advantage. It is a liability. Every compliance gate, risk threshold, and human checkpoint described in this chapter exists to prevent precisely this kind of cascading failure.

The risk assessment architecture operates in three progressive stages: specialized agents monitor real-time price movements, volume patterns, and sentiment signals; statistical models translate those signals into calibrated risk scores; and scored risks are mapped onto each client's investment profile to produce personalized recommendations. This pipeline is not unidirectional. The recommendation stage feeds performance data back into market analysis, enabling continuous model refinement as conditions evolve.

In its most basic form, the risk assessment agent implements a volatility-based classification system that categorizes positions into discrete risk tiers based on recent price change magnitudes:

```
# Requires: import finnhub, os
# finnhub_client = finnhub.Client(api_key=os.getenv("FINNHUB_API_KEY"))

def risk_assessment(query: str) -> str:
    """Evaluate investment risk using real-time volatility metrics."""
    try:
        symbol = query.split()[-1].upper()
        quote = finnhub_client.quote(symbol)
        price_change = quote.get("dp", 0)
        if abs(price_change) > 5:
            risk_level = "High Risk"
        elif abs(price_change) > 2:
            risk_level = "Moderate Risk"
        else:
            risk_level = "Low Risk"
        return (
            f"Risk Assessment for {symbol}: "
            f"Price Change: {price_change}%, "
            f"Risk Level: {risk_level}"
        )
```

```
    except Exception as e:
        return f"Error: {str(e)}"
```

Production systems augment this baseline with more sophisticated quantitative measures: Value at Risk (VaR) for estimating maximum potential loss at a given confidence level, Conditional Value at Risk (CVaR) for tail-risk estimation, and portfolio-level correlation analysis. The following implementation combines annualized volatility, maximum drawdown, and VaR into a composite score:

Note

Key risk metrics

Value at Risk (VaR) estimates the maximum expected loss over a given time horizon at a specified confidence level (for example, a 1-day 95% VaR of $10,000 means there is a 5% chance of losing more than $10,000 in a single day). Conditional Value at Risk (CVaR), also called expected shortfall, measures the average loss in the worst-case scenarios beyond the VaR threshold, making it more sensitive to tail risk. Annualized volatility expresses the standard deviation of returns scaled to a one-year period, providing a comparable measure of price instability across assets. Maximum drawdown captures the largest peak-to-trough decline over a period, reflecting the worst loss an investor would have experienced had they bought at the peak and sold at the trough.

```
import numpy as np
# Requires: import yfinance as yf

class RiskScorer:
    """Multi-dimensional risk scoring for portfolio positions."""
```

The `compute_risk_score` method combines annualized volatility, maximum drawdown, and VaR into a single composite score using the weights defined in the class initializer. It then maps that score to a categorical risk band:

```
    def compute_risk_score(self, symbol: str,
                           lookback_days: int = 90) -> dict:
        """Compute composite risk score incorporating
        volatility, drawdown, and VaR metrics."""
        ticker = yf.Ticker(symbol)
        hist = ticker.history(period=f"{lookback_days}d")
        returns = hist['Close'].pct_change().dropna()

        # Annualized volatility
        volatility = returns.std() * np.sqrt(252)

        # Maximum drawdown
        cumulative = (1 + returns).cumprod()
```

```
        rolling_max = cumulative.cummax()
        drawdown = (cumulative - rolling_max) / rolling_max
        max_drawdown = drawdown.min()

        # Value at Risk (95% confidence)
        var_95 = np.percentile(returns, 5)

        # Composite risk score (0-10 scale)
        vol_score = min(volatility / 0.05, 10)
        dd_score = min(abs(max_drawdown) / 0.05, 10)
        var_score = min(abs(var_95) / 0.03, 10)
        composite = (
            0.4 * vol_score +
            0.35 * dd_score +
            0.25 * var_score
        )

        return {
            "symbol": symbol,
            "annualized_volatility": round(volatility, 4),
            "max_drawdown": round(max_drawdown, 4),
            "var_95": round(var_95, 4),
            "composite_risk_score": round(composite, 2),
            "risk_category": self._categorize(composite)
        }

    @staticmethod
    def _categorize(score: float) -> str:
        if score >= 7.0:
            return "HIGH"
        elif score >= 4.0:
            return "MODERATE"
        return "LOW"
```

The composite score then feeds into a client-tolerance adjustment layer. A critical design decision is where to enforce risk limits. In a compliant architecture, enforcement occurs at the supervisor level, not within individual agents. Before the supervisor routes a recommendation to the client, it must pass through a validation gate that checks the composite risk score against the client's tolerance. This mirrors the compliance agent architecture from *Chapter 12*:

```
def assess_risk(stock_symbol: str, composite_score: float,
                client_risk_tolerance: str) -> dict:
    """Evaluate risk level adjusted for client tolerance.
```

```
    Consumes the composite_risk_score from RiskScorer."""
    # Map composite score to risk category
```

The second half of assess_risk adjusts that category against the client's stated risk tolerance, producing a personalized risk band that reflects both market conditions and individual constraints:

```
if composite_score >= 7.0:
        market_risk = "HIGH"
    elif composite_score >= 4.0:
        market_risk = "MODERATE"
    else:
        market_risk = "LOW"

    # Adjust for client risk tolerance
    tolerance_map = {
        "conservative": {
            "HIGH": "UNACCEPTABLE",
            "MODERATE": "HIGH",
            "LOW": "MODERATE"
        },
        "moderate": {
            "HIGH": "HIGH",
            "MODERATE": "MODERATE",
            "LOW": "LOW"
        },
        "aggressive": {
            "HIGH": "MODERATE",
            "MODERATE": "LOW",
            "LOW": "LOW"
        }
    }
    adjusted_risk = tolerance_map.get(
        client_risk_tolerance, {}
    ).get(market_risk, market_risk)

    return {
        "symbol": stock_symbol,
        "market_risk": market_risk,
        "client_risk_tolerance": client_risk_tolerance,
        "adjusted_risk": adjusted_risk
    }
```

The real power here is the feedback loop. When the risk assessment agent spots portfolio drift beyond a client's comfort zone, it fires rebalancing recommendations back to the supervisor, who can present them to the client or, in fully autonomous setups, execute trades directly. Traditional review cycles catch drift weeks or months late. This architecture catches it in real time.

With risk assessment in place, the next subsection applies these signals to individual client profiles to generate personalized financial plans.

Personalized financial planning

Personalized financial planning requires agents that maintain rich, longitudinal models of individual clients. This maps onto the memory architectures from *Chapter 5*: working memory for active session context, episodic memory for interaction history, and semantic memory for durable profile information. In financial advisory, personalization is not a nice-to-have. Securities regulations mandate that recommendations be "suitable" for the specific client.

A personalized planning agent integrates parallel processing networks: a client-facing service layer that handles queries, profiles, and response generation alongside a compliance layer that performs regulatory review, documentation, and audit logging. Industry implementations have demonstrated measurable improvements:

The following table summarizes representative performance outcomes reported by retail financial institutions that have deployed AI-powered personalization, comparing key advisory metrics before and after implementation.

Metric	Before AI	After AI
Response time	4-hour average	30 seconds
Compliance accuracy	95%	99.99%
Client capacity	100 per advisor	1,000 or more per advisor
Monthly revenue	$8,000	$25,000

Table 14.1 – Performance impact of AI-powered personalization in retail financial advisory

The following implementation demonstrates the core profile retrieval and contextualization logic, with compliance validation integrated at the data access layer:

```
class ClientProfileAgent:
    """Retrieves and contextualizes client financial
    profiles for personalized advisory responses."""

    def __init__(self, memory_store, compliance_validator):
        self.semantic_memory = memory_store
        self.compliance = compliance_validator
```

The `get_contextualized_profile` method retrieves the stored client profile and enriches it with current market data, compliance constraints, and recent interaction history to produce the context object that downstream advisory nodes consume:

```
    def get_contextualized_profile(
        self, client_id: str, query_context: str
    ) -> dict:
        """Retrieve client profile with context-relevant
        financial history."""
        # Retrieve durable profile from semantic memory
        profile = self.semantic_memory.retrieve(
            entity_id=client_id,
            memory_type="semantic"
        )

        # Retrieve relevant interaction history
        episodes = self.semantic_memory.retrieve(
            entity_id=client_id,
            memory_type="episodic",
            query=query_context,
            top_k=10
        )

        # Validate data access against compliance rules
        filtered_profile = (
            self.compliance.filter_accessible_data(
                profile=profile,
                query_context=query_context,
                access_level="advisory"
            )
        )

        return {
            "profile": filtered_profile,
            "relevant_history": episodes,
            "risk_tolerance": profile.get("risk_tolerance"),
            "investment_horizon": profile.get(
                "investment_horizon"
            ),
            "regulatory_constraints": profile.get(
                "constraints", []
            )
        }
```

The compliance validator sits at the data access layer, not bolted on as an afterthought. Building on *Chapter 12*'s ethical reasoning frameworks, this pattern ensures personalization never compromises regulatory compliance. Every data retrieval is logged for audit purposes.

The practical enforcement uses a self-correcting loop within the LangGraph state machine. Before any recommendation reaches the client, it must pass through the compliance node. If it fails, the recommendation is revised and re-validated:

```
from langgraph.graph import StateGraph, END

class AdvisoryState(TypedDict):
    messages: list
    client_profile: dict
    recommendation: dict
    compliance_result: dict
    final_response: str

def validate_compliance(state: AdvisoryState):
    """Validate recommendation against
    regulatory requirements."""
    rec = state["recommendation"]
    profile = state["client_profile"]
    issues = []

    # Suitability check
    if rec["risk_score"] > profile["max_risk_tolerance"]:
        issues.append(
            "SUITABILITY: Recommendation risk "
            "exceeds client tolerance"
        )

    # Concentration check
    for asset, weight in rec["allocation"].items():
        max_conc = policy_rules.get("max_concentration", 0.25)        if weight >
max_conc:
            issues.append(
                f"CONCENTRATION: {asset} weight "
                f"{weight:.0%} exceeds {max_conc:.0%} limit"
            )

    return {
        "compliance_result": {
            "passed": len(issues) == 0,
            "issues": issues
```

```
        }
    }

def route_after_compliance(state: AdvisoryState):
    if state["compliance_result"]["passed"]:
        return "deliver"
    return "revise"

# Build workflow with compliance gate
With the processing functions defined, the following segment assembles the advisory
StateGraph, wires the compliance gate as a conditional branch, and compiles the workflow
ready for execution:
workflow = StateGraph(AdvisoryState)
workflow.add_node("recommend", generate_recommendation)
workflow.add_node("comply", validate_compliance)
workflow.add_node("deliver", deliver_to_client)
workflow.add_node("revise", revise_recommendation)
workflow.add_edge("recommend", "comply")
workflow.add_conditional_edges(
    "comply", route_after_compliance,
    {"deliver": "deliver", "revise": "revise"}
)
workflow.add_edge("revise", "comply")  # Re-validate
workflow.add_edge("deliver", END)
```

The revise node loops back to compliance validation, creating a self-correcting cycle that continues until the recommendation satisfies all regulatory constraints. This is compliance-by-architecture: it is structurally impossible for a non-compliant recommendation to reach the client.

Case study: Investment adviser for retail investors

To ground these concepts in a concrete implementation, consider `RetailAdvisor`, an investment advisory agent built for retail investors who lack access to dedicated wealth management services. The system integrates the market data analysis, risk assessment, and personalized planning architectures described above into a unified, hierarchical, multi-agent system.

A supervisor agent coordinates five specialists: an onboarding agent that conducts risk profiling interviews and persists client profiles to semantic memory, a market intelligence agent that continuously monitors conditions relevant to the client's portfolio, a portfolio construction agent that applies modern portfolio theory to generate diversified allocations, a risk monitoring agent that performs continuous multi-dimensional scoring, and a compliance agent that validates all recommendations against applicable regulations using the compliance registry pattern from *Chapter 12*.

The onboarding agent establishes the client's investment horizon, risk tolerance, financial goals, and regulatory constraints. This profile is persisted to semantic memory and informs every subsequent interaction. The portfolio construction agent considers not just theoretically optimal allocations but also practical constraints: transaction costs, tax implications, and minimum investment thresholds.

Here's a representative interaction: a retail investor asks, "I have $50,000 to invest and want moderate growth over the next ten years. What should I do?" The supervisor routes to the portfolio construction agent, which queries market intelligence for current conditions and risk monitoring for sector-level assessments. Given moderate risk tolerance and a ten-year horizon, it generates a diversified allocation: 45% US equities (via low-cost index funds), 20% international equities, 25% fixed income, and 10% alternatives. Before delivery, the compliance agent verifies suitability, diversification, and regulatory completeness.

The communication protocol between agents follows a standardized JSON format that carries the metadata required for routing and auditing:

```
{
    "sender_id": "portfolio_construction_agent",
    "recipient_id": "compliance_agent",
    "message_type": "recommendation_validation_request",
    "timestamp": "2025-01-15T14:30:00Z",
    "confidence_score": 0.87,
    "data_payload": {
        "client_id": "retail_client_4521",
        "recommendation_type": "initial_allocation",
        "asset_allocation": {
            "us_equities": 0.45,
            "international_equities": 0.20,
            "fixed_income": 0.25,
            "alternatives": 0.10
        },
        "risk_score": 6.2,
        "expected_annual_return": 0.078,
        "max_drawdown_estimate": -0.18
    },
    "context_references": [
        "risk_profile_4521",
        "market_analysis_20250115"
    ],
    "requires_response": true,
    "priority_level": "high"
}
```

Every message in this format is persisted to an immutable audit log. When a regulator asks why a specific recommendation was made, the system reconstructs the complete reasoning chain from data ingestion through analysis to compliance validation. This traceability makes the system suitable for deployment in a regulated environment.

Industry pioneers are already exploring these patterns at scale. JPMorgan Chase has invested in AI-driven summarization of market research, natural language understanding for client inquiries, and compliance monitoring that flags risky advisory patterns. Virgin Money's Redi agent demonstrates how agentic systems can elevate retail banking beyond static FAQs, handling nuanced financial questions involving transactional histories and account-linked decisions with context-aware personalization.

The Financial Advisory agent demonstrates how agents earn trust when risk is measurable: volatility scores, concentration limits, and suitability thresholds provide clear pass/fail criteria. The legal domain is harder. Risk cannot be reduced to a number. A legal agent must reason over language, where the same words carry different weight depending on context, jurisdiction, and the authority of the source that produced them.

The Legal Intelligence agent

The stakes here are comparable to finance, but the failure modes differ. Inaccurate legal interpretations can undermine case outcomes. Fabricated citations can result in professional sanctions for the attorney who relies on them. The complexity of legal reasoning, which depends on analogical reasoning over factual patterns and hierarchical authority structures, demands specialized architectures well beyond standard retrieval-augmented generation.

This section examines the architectural foundations that enable agents to navigate these challenges, progressing from knowledge base design, through precedent analysis, to contract review and, ultimately, to a complete legal research and brief preparation workflow.

Legal knowledge base integration

The foundation of any Legal Intelligence agent is its knowledge base: a structured, searchable repository of statutes, regulations, case law, and commentary. Unlike general-purpose retrieval systems, a legal knowledge base must preserve hierarchical relationships between authorities, maintain distinctions between binding and persuasive precedent, primary and secondary sources, and current law versus superseded provisions.

The central design tension is that legal reasoning depends on both conceptual similarity and exact textual references. A hybrid search strategy addresses this by combining dense vector retrieval, which finds relevant precedent even when terminology differs, with sparse keyword matching, which retrieves specific citations and statute numbers with precision.

The following implementation demonstrates a legal knowledge base with hybrid retrieval and authority-weighted ranking:

```
class LegalKnowledgeBase:
    """Legal knowledge base with hierarchical authority
    tracking and hybrid retrieval."""

    def __init__(self, vector_store, embedding_model):
        self.store = vector_store
        self.embedder = embedding_model
```

The `ingest_case` method encodes each case document into the vector store alongside structured metadata capturing court hierarchy, jurisdiction, and authority level:

```
def ingest_case(self, case: dict):
    """Ingest a case with structured authority metadata."""
    embedding = self.embedder.encode(case["text"])
    metadata = {
        "case_name": case["name"],
        "citation": case["citation"],
        "court": case["court"],
        "jurisdiction": case["jurisdiction"],
        "date": case["date"],
        "authority_level": self._classify_authority(
            case["court"]
        ),
        "status": case.get("status", "good_law"),
        "legal_issues": case.get("issues", []),
        "key_holdings": case.get("holdings", [])
    }
    self.store.upsert(
        id=case["citation"],
        embedding=embedding,
        metadata=metadata
    )
```

The `hybrid_search` method is the retrieval core of `LegalKnowledgeBase`. It combines semantic similarity with authority-weighted ranking to surface the most relevant and legally authoritative sources for a given query:

```
def hybrid_search(self, query: str,
                  jurisdiction: str = None,
                  min_authority: int = 0) -> list:
    """Hybrid search combining semantic similarity
    with authority-weighted ranking."""
    query_embedding = self.embedder.encode(query)
    filters = {}
    if jurisdiction:
        filters["jurisdiction"] = jurisdiction
    if min_authority > 0:
        filters["authority_level"] = {
            "$gte": min_authority
        }

    results = self.store.query(
        embedding=query_embedding,
```

```
        filter=filters,
        top_k=50
    )
```

After the initial retrieval, the method re-ranks results by blending the semantic similarity score with an authority weight and a recency boost, producing a final ordering that favors binding, recent authority:

```
    # Re-rank by combining semantic score
    # with authority weight
    for result in results:
        authority_boost = (
            result.metadata["authority_level"] / 10.0
        )
        recency_boost = self._recency_score(
            result.metadata["date"]
        )
        result.final_score = (
            0.5 * result.similarity_score +
            0.3 * authority_boost +
            0.2 * recency_boost
        )

    return sorted(
        results,
        key=lambda x: x.final_score,
        reverse=True
    )
```

Above the retrieval layer, domain-specific ranking logic applies. A Supreme Court decision takes precedence over a district court ruling. A recent statute supersedes an older conflicting provision. An on-point holding from the relevant jurisdiction outweighs persuasive authority from elsewhere. The weight distribution in the final score (0.5 for semantic similarity, 0.3 for authority level, 0.2 for recency) reflects the primacy of conceptual relevance in legal research: a semantically aligned but lower-authority source is more useful than a high-authority source on a tangentially related point. Authority and recency serve as tie-breakers rather than primary signals; these weights can be adjusted as configurable parameters where domain policy or client preference requires a different balance. These rules are encoded in the `authority_level` and `recency_score` components of the composite ranking function.

The next subsection applies these retrieval and reasoning capabilities to contract review, showing how the Legal Intelligence agent structures the analysis of complex legal documents using a sequential pipeline.

Case analysis and precedent finding

Identifying and analyzing relevant legal precedent is perhaps the most intellectually demanding capability a legal agent must possess. It requires understanding the legal issues at stake, finding cases addressing analogous issues, evaluating whether the reasoning applies to the current facts, and synthesizing everything into a coherent argument.

Note

When AI cited cases that never existed

In June 2023, New York attorney Steven Schwartz made headlines that rippled across the legal profession. He had used ChatGPT to research a personal injury case, and the model generated a brief peppered with confident, properly formatted citations to cases like Varghese v. China Southern Airlines and Martinez v. Delta Airlines. None of them existed. The court sanctioned Schwartz and his firm, and within months, courts across the United States began issuing standing orders requiring attorneys to disclose AI usage and personally verify every AI-generated citation. It was a vivid demonstration of why citation verification in any legal AI pipeline is not a nice-to-have feature but a professional survival requirement.

The precedent finding pipeline operates in three stages, as illustrated in *Figure 14.2*.

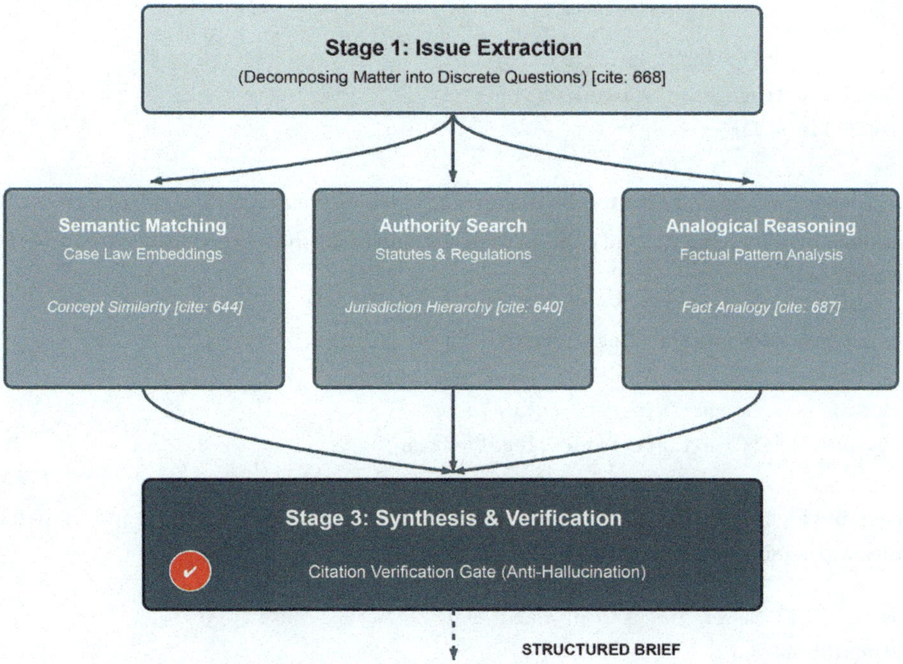

Figure 14.2 – The Legal Intelligence agent's RAG-powered case analysis workflow, depicting the retrieval, verification, and synthesis of legal precedent

The pipeline in *Figure 14.2* navigates the structural and semantic complexities of legal precedent-finding through three specialized stages.

1. **Stage 1 – Issue Extraction:** The process begins by using the LLM's natural language understanding to decompose a multifaceted legal matter into discrete, manageable questions. This ensures that retrieval

queries target specific statutory obligations or elements of negligence, rather than broad, ambiguous topics.

2. **Stage 2 – Multi-Dimensional Retrieval:** Once issues are defined, the system initiates a parallel retrieval strategy across semantic matching over case law embeddings, authority searches through jurisdictional hierarchies, and analogical reasoning based on factual pattern analysis.
3. **Stage 3 – Synthesis and Verification:** The final stage evaluates retrieved authorities for applicability and weight. The centerpiece is the Citation Verification Gate, which cross-references every retrieved citation against an authoritative knowledge base. This rigorous step serves as the primary defense against hallucinated precedents, ensuring only "good law" enters the final brief.

In practice, the issue extraction stage decomposes complex questions into constituent elements. A query about "liability for data breaches in healthcare settings" yields discrete issues: applicable standard of care, elements of negligence, HIPAA obligations, and available defenses. Each issue drives an independent retrieval query:

```
class PrecedentFinder:
    """Identifies and analyzes relevant legal precedent
    through multi-dimensional retrieval."""

    def __init__(self, legal_kb, llm):
        self.knowledge_base = legal_kb
        self.llm = llm
```

The `find_precedents` method orchestrates the three-stage pipeline. It extracts discrete legal issues, retrieves candidates through parallel semantic and citation searches, and ranks the merged results by authority weight and factual relevance:

```
    def find_precedents(self, legal_matter: dict) -> list:
        """Execute the full precedent finding pipeline."""
        # Stage 1: Extract discrete legal issues
        issues = self._extract_issues(legal_matter)
```

With the legal issues identified, Stage 2 launches parallel retrieval across both semantic and citation indices, merging results into a unified candidate set:

```
        # Stage 2: Multi-dimensional retrieval
        candidates = []
        for issue in issues:
            semantic_results = (
                self.knowledge_base.hybrid_search(
                    query=issue["description"],
                    jurisdiction=legal_matter.get(
                        "jurisdiction"
                    ),
                    min_authority=3
```

```
            )
        )
        citation_results = (
            self.knowledge_base.citation_search(
                statutes=issue.get(
                    "relevant_statutes", []
                ),
                top_k=10
            )
        )
        merged = self._merge_results(
            semantic_results, citation_results
        )
        candidates.extend(merged)
```

With candidate precedents retrieved from both semantic and citation searches, the final stage ranks them by authority and factual relevance before returning them to the caller:

```
        # Stage 3: Analyze and rank precedents
        analyzed = self._analyze_precedents(
            candidates, legal_matter
        )
        return self._rank_by_authority_and_relevance(
            analyzed
        )

class LegalIssue(BaseModel):
    description: str
    category: str
    priority: int = 1  # 1 (high) to 3 (low)

class IssueList(BaseModel):
    issues: List[LegalIssue]
```

The `_extract_issues` helper decomposes an unstructured legal matter description into discrete, typed issues using the LLM. It validates its output against the `IssueList` schema before returning, ensuring downstream pipeline stages receive well-formed structured data:

```
    def _extract_issues(self, matter: dict) -> list:
        """Decompose a legal matter into discrete
        legal issues for targeted retrieval."""
        prompt = f"""Analyze the following legal matter
        and identify the discrete legal issues that
        must be resolved. For each issue, provide:
```

```
    1. A concise description
    2. The area of law involved
    3. Any relevant statutes or regulations
    4. Key factual elements that determine
       applicability

Legal Matter: {matter['description']}
Jurisdiction: {matter['jurisdiction']}
"""
response = self.llm.generate(prompt)
raw = self._parse_issues(response)        return IssueList(issues=raw).issues
```

This multi-dimensional approach significantly reduces the risk of missing relevant precedent. Semantic similarity identifies conceptually aligned authorities, citation network analysis surfaces frequently co-cited cases, and factual pattern matching finds cases with analogous circumstances.

Contract analysis frameworks

Contract analysis combines structured document processing with legal reasoning over clause-level semantics. A contract analysis agent must parse complex structures, classify individual clauses, evaluate risk, flag non-standard provisions, and generate summaries that highlight areas requiring attorney attention.

The framework operates as a sequential pipeline with parallel validation, as depicted in *Figure 14.3*.

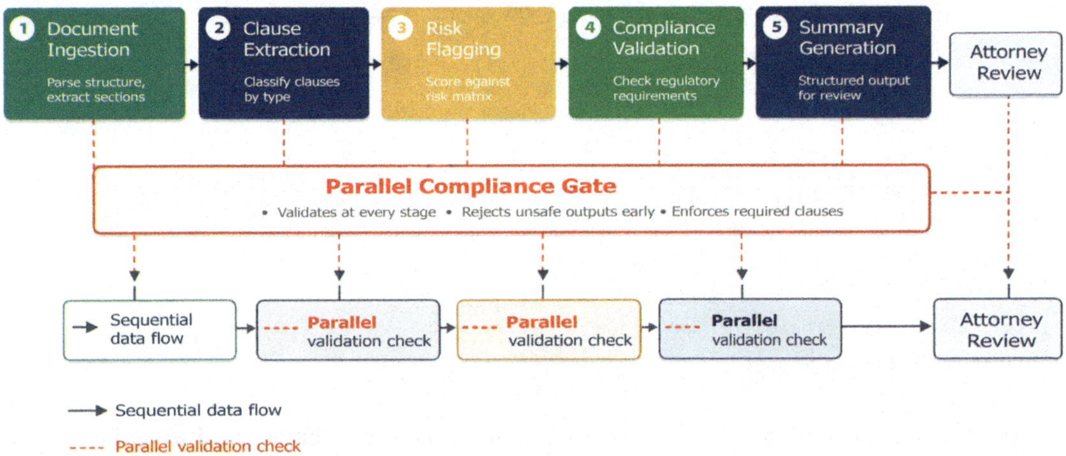

Figure 14.3 – End-to-end contract analysis framework

Figure 14.3 presents contract analysis as an engineered workflow. The pipeline moves through document ingestion, clause extraction, risk flagging, compliance validation, and structured summary generation. The key architectural point is that compliance validation runs in parallel at every stage as a gate, not a post-processing step. This lets the system reject unsafe outputs early and ensure required clauses are present before a summary reaches counsel.

```
class ContractAnalysisAgent:
    """Analyzes legal contracts through a multi-stage
    pipeline with compliance validation."""

    def __init__(self, llm, clause_classifier,
                 risk_matrix, compliance_rules):
        self.llm = llm
        self.classifier = clause_classifier
        self.risk_matrix = risk_matrix
        self.compliance = compliance_rules
```

The analyze_contract method orchestrates the full pipeline: it ingests the document, extracts and classifies clauses, flags risks, runs compliance validation in parallel, and assembles a structured output ready for attorney review:

```
    def analyze_contract(self, document: str,
                         context: dict) -> dict:
        """Execute full contract analysis pipeline."""
        # Stage 1: Document structure extraction
        structure = self._parse_document_structure(
            document
        )

        # Stage 2: Clause extraction and classification
        clauses = []
        for section in structure["operative_sections"]:
            extracted = self.classifier.classify(section)
            clauses.extend(extracted)
```

With clauses extracted and classified, the pipeline moves to risk evaluation. Each clause is scored against a jurisdiction-aware risk matrix, and only findings at HIGH or CRITICAL level are surfaced for attorney review:

```
        # Stage 3: Risk assessment per clause
        risk_findings = []
        for clause in clauses:
            risk = self.risk_matrix.evaluate(
                clause_type=clause["type"],
                clause_text=clause["text"],
                reviewing_party=context.get(
                    "reviewing_party"
                ),
```

```
            jurisdiction=context.get("jurisdiction")
        )
        if risk["level"] in ["HIGH", "CRITICAL"]:
            risk_findings.append({
                "clause": clause,
                "risk": risk,
                "recommendation": (
                    risk["suggested_action"]
                )
            })
```

With risk findings collected, the final stages validate the complete clause set against applicable regulations and produce a structured summary for attorney review:

```
    # Stage 4: Compliance validation
    compliance_issues = self.compliance.validate(
        clauses=clauses,
        applicable_regulations=context.get(
            "regulations", []
        )
    )

    # Stage 5: Summary generation
    summary = self._generate_summary(
        structure, clauses,
        risk_findings, compliance_issues
    )

    return {
        "structure": structure,
        "clauses": clauses,
        "risk_findings": risk_findings,
        "compliance_issues": compliance_issues,
        "summary": summary
    }
```

The following case study brings together the retrieval, precedent ranking, and citation verification components into a single working system. LegalBrief is a litigation support assistant that takes a factual brief from an attorney, retrieves governing precedent, evaluates the strength of the client's position, and produces a structured research memorandum with formatted citations. It demonstrates how the Legal Intelligence agent's individual capabilities combine into an end-to-end workflow under real case conditions.

Case study: Legal research and brief preparation assistant

LegalBrief is a legal research and brief preparation assistant designed for litigation attorneys. It combines the RAG-powered retrieval architectures above with multi-stage document generation to produce research memoranda and draft briefs. The system employs a five-stage sequential workflow with embedded quality gates, implemented as a LangGraph state machine.

When an attorney submits a question like "What is the current standard for establishing personal jurisdiction over foreign corporations in e-commerce disputes under the Ninth Circuit?", the system proceeds through five stages: issue decomposition, multi-dimensional retrieval expanding from binding to persuasive authority, doctrinal analysis identifying circuit splits and the strongest authorities, structured memo drafting with proper citation formatting, and citation accuracy validation.

Citation verification is non-negotiable. Hallucinated case law is the single most dangerous failure mode in AI-assisted legal research. Citing a fabricated case in a court filing results in consequences for the attorney, not the algorithm. The system guards against this by cross-referencing every citation in the draft against the authoritative knowledge base, flagging anything it cannot verify.

```
class LegalResearchState(TypedDict):
    query: str
    jurisdiction: str
    issues: list
    precedents: list
    analysis: dict
    draft: str
    citations_verified: bool
    quality_score: float
```

The state schema captures the full lifecycle of a research query. The following functions implement each pipeline stage, beginning with issue decomposition and multi-dimensional retrieval:

```
def decompose_issues(state: LegalResearchState):
    """Stage 1: Break research question into
    discrete legal issues."""
    issues = llm.extract_legal_issues(
        state["query"], state["jurisdiction"]
    )
    return {"issues": issues}

def retrieve_precedents(state: LegalResearchState):
    """Stage 2: Multi-dimensional retrieval."""
    all_precedents = []
    for issue in state["issues"]:
        results = legal_kb.hybrid_search(
            query=issue["description"],
```

```
            jurisdiction=state["jurisdiction"],
            min_authority=3
        )
        all_precedents.extend(results)
    return {"precedents": deduplicate(all_precedents)}
```

After retrieval, the pipeline must verify every citation before it enters the draft. The `verify_citations` function cross-references each cited authority against the knowledge base, checking jurisdiction, precedential status, and whether the case remains good law:

```
def verify_citations(state: LegalResearchState):
    """Stage 5: Cross-reference every citation"""
    citations = extract_citations(state["draft"])
    verified = 0
    for citation in citations:
        exists = legal_kb.verify_citation(
            citation["text"]
            jurisdiction=citation.get("jurisdiction"),
check_precedential=True,              check_good_law=True,          )
        if exists:
            verified += 1
        else:
            state["draft"] = flag_unverified(
                state["draft"], citation
            )
    return {
        "citations_verified": verified == len(citations),
        "quality_score": verified / max(len(citations), 1)
    }

# Build the pipeline
```

With the processing functions defined, the following segment assembles the `LegalResearchState` graph, wires the five sequential stages, and compiles the pipeline, ready for execution:

```
workflow = StateGraph(LegalResearchState)
workflow.add_node("decompose", decompose_issues)
workflow.add_node("retrieve", retrieve_precedents)
workflow.add_node("analyze", analyze_authorities)
workflow.add_node("draft", generate_draft)
workflow.add_node("verify", verify_citations)
workflow.add_edge(START, "decompose")
workflow.add_edge("decompose", "retrieve")
workflow.add_edge("retrieve", "analyze")
```

```
workflow.add_edge("analyze", "draft")
workflow.add_edge("draft", "verify")
workflow.add_edge("verify", END)
legal_research_graph = workflow.compile()
```

The system flags any citation it cannot verify, clearly distinguishing between verified and unverified authorities in the output. This transparency allows the attorney to focus manual verification efforts where they matter most.

In a typical contract dispute workflow, the attorney provides factual background and key issues. LegalBrief retrieves governing principles and relevant precedent, analyzes the strength of the client's position, and produces a draft brief with formatted citations. The attorney reviews and finalizes, concentrating expertise on strategic argumentation while the agent handles labor-intensive research.

This division of labor mirrors the broader theme of this chapter: agents in regulated domains are most effective not as autonomous decision-makers, but as force multipliers that amplify human professionals while maintaining accountability.

Summary

This chapter demonstrated how the agent engineering patterns developed throughout this book converge in two of the most demanding application domains: financial advisory and legal intelligence. Both impose hard constraints absent in more permissive contexts.

Financial Advisory agents must satisfy suitability requirements, generate auditable recommendation trails, and enforce client-specific risk limits. The multi-agent supervisor architecture, combined with continuous risk monitoring and compliance-by-architecture validation gates, provides the structural foundation. Legal Intelligence agents must produce verifiable citations, navigate jurisdictional hierarchies, and generate structured analysis that meets professional standards. The hybrid retrieval architecture, multi-dimensional precedent finding, and citation verification stage address the unique challenges of legal reasoning over unstructured text.

The patterns enabling success in these domains are refinements of the same multi-agent coordination, memory management, retrieval-augmented generation, and compliance reasoning explored in preceding chapters. The difference lies in rigor. In regulated industries, compliance is not a feature added after the agent works correctly. It is an architectural constraint that shapes every design decision from the outset.

As you extend these architectures to additional regulated domains, whether healthcare, insurance, or government services, the central principle remains constant: build agents that are not only capable but accountable. Every recommendation must be traceable. Every decision must be auditable. Every interaction must be logged.

In the next chapter, we explore education and knowledge agents, examining how agents can personalize learning, synthesize knowledge bases, and support complex reasoning across academic and professional domains.

Subscribe for a free eBook

New frameworks, evolving architectures, research drops, production breakdowns—*AI_Distilled* filters the noise into a weekly briefing for engineers and researchers working hands-on with LLMs and generative AI systems. Subscribe now and receive a free eBook, along with weekly insights that help you stay focused and informed.

Subscribe at `https://packt.link/8Oz6Y` or scan the QR code below.

15

Education and Knowledge Agents

Education is not the filling of a pail, but the lighting of a fire.

Commonly attributed to W.B. Yeats, paraphrasing Plutarch

Teaching is hard. Harder, in many ways, than playing chess or folding proteins. Those problems have clean objective functions. Education does not. To teach well, you need to read a mind you cannot observe directly, calibrate a challenge level that shifts with every interaction, and somehow make the whole experience feel less like an obstacle course and more like a conversation. An agent that pulls this off, personalizing curricula, tracking progress across dozens of competencies, and delivering feedback in real time, could democratize expert-level instruction at a scale no human institution can match.

Yet the challenge extends beyond individual learners. Some of the most significant problems in knowledge work require not a single brilliant agent but a coordinated ensemble that can collaborate, debate, and synthesize perspectives to arrive at solutions no individual could produce alone. The field of collective intelligence explores how groups of agents, each with partial knowledge and limited reasoning capabilities, produce emergent behaviors that exceed the sum of their individual contributions.

In this chapter, we'll be covering the following topics:

- The Education Intelligence agent
- The Collective Intelligence agent

Technical requirements

To run the examples in this chapter, you will need the following:

- Python 3.10 or later
- The following Python packages: `openai==1.40.0`, `numpy==1.26.4`, `networkx==3.3`, and `python-dotenv==1.0.1`
- An OpenAI API key with access to the `gpt-4o` model

All code examples for this chapter are available in the book's GitHub repository at `https://github.com/PacktPublishing/30-Agents-Every-AI-Engineer-Must-Build/chapter15`.

The Education Intelligence agent

Teaching is, at its core, a diagnostic and adaptive endeavor. An effective instructor continuously assesses what a student knows, identifies gaps and misconceptions, selects the most appropriate next activity, delivers it at the right difficulty level, and adjusts course based on the student's response. This cycle of perception, reasoning, and action maps naturally onto the cognitive loop from *Chapter 1*, but with domain-specific twists that reflect the unique demands of educational contexts.

The Education Intelligence agent replicates this cycle computationally. It maintains a rich, evolving model of each student's knowledge state, plans individualized learning paths, delivers instruction through multiple modalities, and refines its understanding based on observed performance. The agent does not aim to replace human teachers. It augments them by handling the computationally intensive side of personalization: tracking hundreds of fine-grained competencies across dozens of students, spotting patterns in performance data that signal emerging difficulties, and generating immediate, specific feedback that no single instructor can deliver consistently in a classroom of thirty.

The perception module handles diverse learning signals: quiz responses, code submissions, time-on-task data, help-seeking behavior, and natural language questions. The reasoning module applies pedagogical logic that respects the hierarchical, prerequisite-dependent structure of knowledge domains. The action module generates outputs appropriate for educational workflows, from selecting the next exercise to composing feedback that targets a specific misconception.

A crucial design principle is what we term **pedagogical alignment**. Every decision the agent makes must be grounded in established learning science. This is not philosophy; it is an engineering requirement. An agent that optimizes for task completion without considering cognitive load, spaced repetition, or the zone of proximal development will produce learning experiences that feel efficient in the short term but fail at durable knowledge acquisition. Pedagogical alignment is enforced through a constraint layer in the planning module that evaluates candidate actions against a library of instructional design principles before execution.

The Education Intelligence agent operates at a level of formal complexity that necessitates a rigorous mathematical foundation. Formally, this agent is modeled as a Partially Observable Markov Decision Process (POMDP), extending the stochastic decision-making frameworks we established in *Chapter 13* to the instructional domain.

A POMDP is required in this context because the most critical variable, the student's true mastery, is a hidden state that is not directly accessible to the system. The agent must instead rely on noisy proxies for perception, which include:

- Quiz and assessment responses
- Detailed code submission patterns
- Telemetry data such as time-on-task and help-seeking behavior

The core of this model is the belief state, $b(s)$, which represents a probability distribution over the possible knowledge states of the learner. This state functions as the computational equivalent of a human teacher's intuition regarding a student's understanding. The agent's goal is to select instructional actions (presenting content, scheduling reviews, or offering hints) that move this hidden state toward a mastery threshold, even when that state remains fundamentally uncertain. Solving a full POMDP exactly is often computationally intractable for large knowledge graphs. The subsections that follow decompose the problem into tractable components: Bayesian Knowledge Tracing maintains the belief state over student mastery, the curriculum planner selects instructional actions using zone-of-proximal-development heuristics, and the spaced repetition scheduler optimizes review timing. Together, these modules approximate the POMDP's observe–plan–act cycle without requiring an explicit value-iteration solver.

Approximating the POMDP with tractable components

The architecture decomposes the full POMDP into three tractable components, each responsible for one element of the *observe–plan–act* cycle. First, Bayesian Knowledge Tracing serves as the belief-state estimator: it maintains a probability distribution b(s) over the student's mastery of each skill, updating that distribution after every observed response using the slip and guess parameters as its observation model. Second, the Curriculum Planner handles action selection: given the current belief state, it identifies the skill whose expected learning gain is highest and selects the next instructional objective, applying zone-of-proximal-development heuristics in place of computationally expensive value iteration. Third, the Spaced Repetition Scheduler captures the temporal-discounting dimension of the POMDP: it determines when a previously mastered skill should be reviewed, optimizing the timing of reinforcement to maximize long-term retention. Together, these three modules cover the POMDP's state estimation, action selection, and temporal planning stages while remaining individually testable and computationally efficient.

Personalized curriculum planning

The foundation of the Education Intelligence agent is its curriculum planning engine. Traditional curricula follow a linear sequence: all students encounter the same topics in the same order at the same pace. This ignores the well-established finding that learners arrive with different prior knowledge, learn at different rates, and require different amounts of practice. The agent's curriculum planner addresses these limitations by constructing individualized learning paths that adapt in real time to each student's demonstrated competencies.

The curriculum is represented internally as a **knowledge graph**: a directed acyclic graph where nodes represent learning objectives and edges represent prerequisite relationships. Each objective is associated with instructional activities (readings, videos, exercises, projects) and assessment items (quizzes, coding challenges, open-ended questions). This graph-based representation lets the agent reason about dependencies, identify multiple valid paths through the material, and select the path that best matches each student's current state.

The planning problem can be modeled as a constrained optimization over the knowledge graph G = (V, E). For a student with current mastery state M, the planner seeks a sequence of objectives S = (v_1, v_2, ..., v_k) that satisfies prerequisite constraints while maximizing expected learning gain per unit of instructional time. This is a variant of the constrained shortest path problem on a DAG, solvable efficiently using topological ordering and dynamic programming.

The expected learning gain for each candidate objective draws on Vygotsky's **zone of proximal development** (ZPD). For a student with mastery level m on objective j and an activity with difficulty d, the expected gain is:

$$G(m, d) = \alpha \cdot \exp(-(d - m - \delta)^2 / (2\sigma^2))$$

where δ represents the optimal offset between current mastery and task difficulty (typically 0.1 to 0.3 above current mastery), σ controls the width of the effective learning zone, and α is a scaling constant. This Gaussian model captures an empirical reality: tasks too easy produce minimal learning, tasks too hard produce frustration and disengagement, and tasks at the sweet spot within the ZPD produce maximum gain.

Figure 15.1 shows how these components fit together. The architecture adapts the general cognitive loop from *Chapter 1* to the educational domain, with each module corresponding to a distinct phase of the instructional cycle.

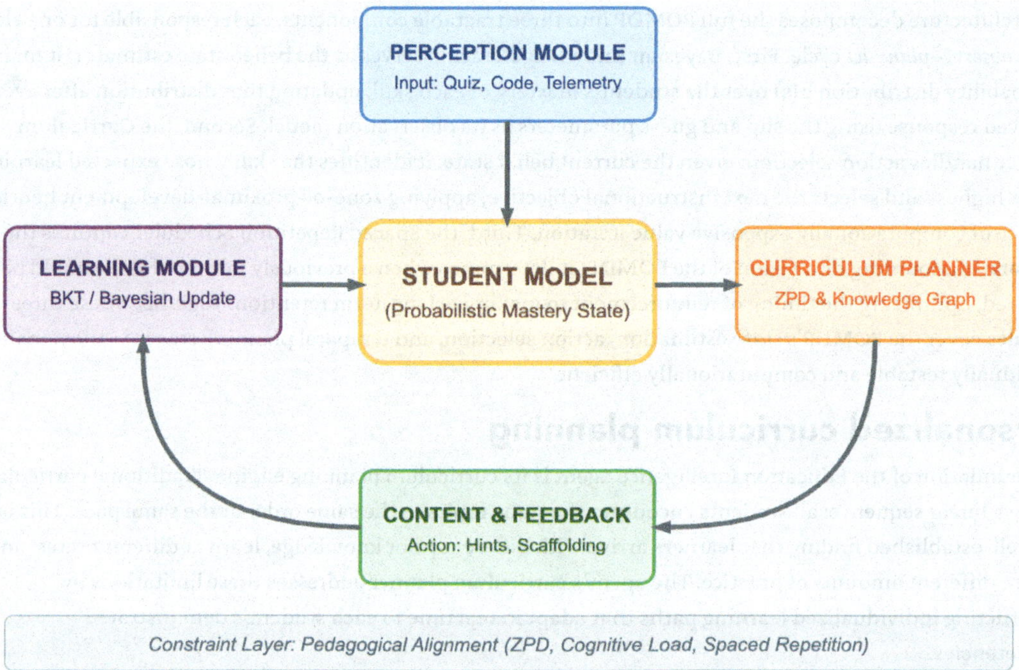

Figure 15.1 – Education Intelligence agent architecture

Figure 15.1 illustrates how the cognitive loop is adapted for educational contexts. The perception module ingests student interaction data, the student model maintains probabilistic competency estimates across the knowledge graph, and the curriculum planner, content delivery engine, and feedback generator close the loop by translating those estimates into personalized instruction.

The knowledge graph's granularity matters enormously. Objectives defined too broadly ("understand object-oriented programming") prevent fine-grained decisions. Objectives defined too narrowly ("know that Python uses indentation for blocks") make the graph unwieldy. In practice, objectives at the level of a single concept or skill, each requiring roughly 15 to 45 minutes of instructional time, hit the right balance. In production, the graph loads from a Neo4j database at startup, with topological ordering pre-computed to reduce prerequisite-checking from $O(|V| \times |E|)$ to $O(|V|)$.

The planner's job is to answer a simple operational question: given what we currently believe about a student's mastery, what should they do next that is both feasible and maximally productive? The implementation below filters objectives whose prerequisites are satisfied, then ranks the remaining candidates by an expected learning-gain heuristic aligned to the zone of proximal development. This code implements the core **objective-selection step** of the Education Intelligence agent's curriculum planner. Given a student ID, it takes the agent's current mastery estimates and the prerequisite structure encoded in the knowledge graph, then chooses the next few learning objectives that the student is both *ready for* and *most likely to benefit from*.

Concretely, the planner does two things: it first **filters** out any objectives whose prerequisites are not yet mastered (so the tutor does not skip foundational concepts), and then it **ranks** the remaining candidates using an expected-gain heuristic that favors objectives in the student's zone of proximal development and prioritizes high-leverage concepts that unlock many downstream topics. Before examining the planner's implementation, we need the data structure it depends on. Every component in the Education Intelligence agent (the curriculum planner, the spaced repetition scheduler, and the feedback generator) queries a shared `StudentModel` class that maintains the learner's current mastery state. The class below defines the minimal API surface consumed by downstream components:

```
class StudentModel:
    """Maintains per-student mastery state across all
    learning objectives. Updated after every interaction."""

    def __init__(self, student_id: str,
                 knowledge_graph):
        self.student_id = student_id
        self.knowledge_graph = knowledge_graph
        self.mastery = {
            obj.id: {
                "p_mastery": 0.1,
                "attempts": 0,
                "last_seen": None,
                "recent_errors": [],
            }
            for obj in knowledge_graph.objectives
        }

    def get_mastery_state(self) -> dict:
        """Return current mastery probabilities."""
        return {
            oid: state["p_mastery"]
            for oid, state in self.mastery.items()
        }

    def get_recent_errors(self, objective_id: str):
        return self.mastery[objective_id]
            .get("recent_errors", [])

    def get_mastered_objectives(self,
```

```
                          threshold=0.85):
        return [
            oid for oid, state
            in self.mastery.items()
            if state["p_mastery"] >= threshold
        ]

    def update_mastery(self, objective_id: str,
                       new_p: float, error=None):
        state = self.mastery[objective_id]
        state["p_mastery"] = new_p
        state["attempts"] += 1
        if error is not None:
            state["recent_errors"].append(error)
            state["recent_errors"] = (
                state["recent_errors"][-5:])
```

The mastery dictionary stores per-objective probability estimates, attempt counts, and a rolling window of recent errors. The `get_mastery_state()` method returns the snapshot consumed by the curriculum planner, while `update_mastery()` is called by the **Bayesian Knowledge Tracing (BKT)** update logic after each student interaction. With this class in place, the `CurriculumPlanner` can query the student model directly:

```
class CurriculumPlanner:
    def __init__(self, knowledge_graph, student_model,
                 content_library):
        self.graph = knowledge_graph
        self.model = student_model
        self.content = content_library
        self.mastery_threshold = 0.8

    def get_next_objectives(self, student_id: str,
                            n: int = 3) -> list[LearningObjective]:
        """Select the next learning objectives based on
        student mastery state and prerequisite constraints."""
        mastery = self.model.get_mastery_state(student_id)
        eligible = []
        for objective in self.graph.get_all_objectives():
            prereqs = self.graph.get_prerequisites(objective.id)
            prereqs_met = all(
                mastery.get(p.id, 0.0) >= self.mastery_threshold
                for p in prereqs
            )
            not_mastered = (
```

```
                mastery.get(objective.id, 0.0)
                < self.mastery_threshold
            )
            if prereqs_met and not_mastered:
                eligible.append(objective)
        ranked = sorted(
            eligible,
            key=lambda obj: self._expected_gain(
                obj, mastery, student_id
            ),
            reverse=True
        )
        return ranked[:n]

    def _expected_gain(self, objective, mastery,
                       student_id) -> float:
        """Estimate learning gain using ZPD-aligned
        Gaussian model with downstream impact."""
        current = mastery.get(objective.id, 0.0)
        difficulty = objective.estimated_difficulty
        delta = 0.2
        sigma = 0.25
        zpd_score = math.exp(
            -((difficulty - current - delta) ** 2)
            / (2 * sigma ** 2)
        )
        downstream = len(
            self.graph.get_dependents(objective.id)
        )
        return zpd_score * (1 + 0.1 * downstream)
```

A note on the ZPD constants:

- `delta = 0.2` sets the optimal gap between current mastery and task difficulty at 20% above the learner's level, placing the target squarely within the zone of proximal development as characterized by Vygotsky.
- `sigma = 0.25` controls the width of the effective learning zone, determining how sharply the gain function drops off for tasks that are too easy or too hard.

These defaults are calibrated from historical cohort data in introductory programming courses and should be treated as tunable hyperparameters: deployments targeting younger learners or unfamiliar domains may require a narrower sigma (tighter scaffolding), while advanced learners often benefit from a larger sigma (greater stretch).

The above code makes two architectural commitments that are easy to miss if you read it as "just selection logic." First, it separates **eligibility** from **ranking**. Eligibility is enforced by the knowledge graph: `prereqs_met` ensures the agent never assigns an objective whose prerequisite chain is not ready, which is the concrete mechanism that prevents curriculum drift and compounding gaps in real deployments. Ranking then encodes pedagogy: `mastery_threshold` is the system's definition of "ready," while `_expected_gain()` uses a ZPD-shaped score that prefers tasks slightly above the student's current mastery (`delta`) and penalizes tasks that are too easy or too hard (`sigma`). The final multiplier, `downstream`, is a pragmatic scheduling bias: an objective that unlocks many dependents is treated as higher leverage, so the system tends to clear bottlenecks early (for example, mastering loop invariants before attempting nested iteration patterns). In use, this means the tutor can behave like a strong instructor: it does not merely pick the next unread lesson, it chooses the next *high-yield* objective that the student is actually prepared to learn, using the student model's current belief state as the input signal rather than a fixed syllabus.

An important consideration that often surprises teams building education agents is the **cold-start problem**. When a student first enters the system, the agent has no interaction history, no reliable estimate of mastery, and no evidence about common misconceptions. If the agent guesses the starting level incorrectly, it can fail in two predictable ways. It can overestimate the learner and begin with material that feels opaque, leading to rapid disengagement. Or it can underestimate the learner and deliver content that feels trivial, which is equally corrosive because it signals that the system is not paying attention.

A practical solution is to treat onboarding as an explicit diagnostic protocol rather than an informal "tell me what you know" prompt. One effective approach uses a short adaptive placement test grounded in Item Response Theory (IRT). The test is not designed to grade the student. It is designed to produce an initial belief state for the agent's student model: a starting estimate of ability in each prerequisite area, along with uncertainty. In production, this initial estimate becomes the seed for curriculum planning, hint policy, pacing, and the decision of when to test versus when to explain.

IRT is valuable here because it separates three factors that tend to be conflated in naïve diagnostics: student ability, item difficulty, and item informativeness. In the two-parameter logistic (2PL) model, the probability of a correct response is:

$$P(\text{correct} \mid \theta, a, b) = 1 / (1 + \exp(-a(\theta - b)))$$

where θ is the learner's latent ability on the assessed skill, b is item difficulty, and a is discrimination, meaning how sharply the item distinguishes between students just below and just above the difficulty threshold. Items with high a provide more information about whether the student truly understands the concept, while low-a items tend to behave like "noisy" indicators, often because they can be answered by pattern matching or test-taking strategies.

Consider a concrete onboarding use case: a programming tutor that needs to place a student into the right track for introductory Python. The system cares about prerequisites such as variables, conditionals, loops, and basic list manipulation. On the first interaction, the agent cannot infer these reliably from a single conversational exchange, because students can describe their background in ways that are not predictive of performance. Instead, the agent runs a short adaptive diagnostic consisting of micro-items such as: trace a loop output, predict the result of a Boolean expression, fix a list indexing bug, or interpret a simple function. Each item is calibrated with (a, b) values from prior cohorts.

The adaptive algorithm begins with a middle-difficulty item, then updates the current ability estimate based on the response. If the student answers correctly, the system increases θ and selects a harder item near the new estimate. If the student answers incorrectly, it lowers θ and selects an easier item. The goal is not to cover the entire syllabus, but to rapidly concentrate questions around the boundary where the student transitions from "likely correct" to "likely incorrect." That boundary is precisely where items are most informative for placement. In practice, this approach achieves a stable estimate with far fewer items than a fixed test, often in the 10–15 question range, because each question is chosen to maximize information given the current uncertainty.

Once the diagnostic completes, the agent can do something that "chat-only" tutoring systems often struggle to do: justify and operationalize placement decisions. For example, the student might score high on variables and conditionals but be uncertain on loops. The curriculum planner can then route them into a track that introduces loops with more scaffolding while accelerating through earlier units. Hint policies can be set accordingly: when the student hits a loop-related exercise, the agent can prioritize guided tracing, smaller subproblems, and frequent checks for understanding rather than immediately providing full solutions. The diagnostic outcome also becomes part of the audit trail for pedagogy: the system can explain why it chose a particular starting point, and instructors can override placement when needed.

The following listing implements an adaptive placement test using the 2PL IRT model. It selects items that maximize information at the current ability estimate, updates the estimate after each response, and terminates when the standard error falls below a configurable threshold:

```
class AdaptivePlacementTest:
    def __init__(self, item_bank, se_threshold=0.3):
        """item_bank: list of dicts with keys
        'skill', 'a' (discrimination), 'b' (difficulty),
        'text', 'answer'."""
        self.items = item_bank
        self.se_threshold = se_threshold
        self.theta = 0.0          # initial ability estimate
        self.responses: list[tuple] = []

    # ---- 2PL probability ----
    @staticmethod
    def p_correct(theta, a, b):
        import math
        return 1.0 / (1.0 + math.exp(-a * (theta - b)))

    # ---- Fisher information at current theta ----
    def _information(self, item):
        p = self.p_correct(self.theta, item['a'], item['b'])
        return (item['a'] ** 2) * p * (1 - p)

    def select_next_item(self, used_ids):
        """Pick the unused item with maximum information."""
```

```
        remaining = [i for i in self.items
                     if id(i) not in used_ids]
        if not remaining:
            return None
        return max(remaining, key=self._information)

    def update_theta(self):
        """Newton-Raphson MLE update over all responses."""
        import math
        theta = self.theta
        for _ in range(25):  # max iterations
            num = den = 0.0
            for item, correct in self.responses:
                p = self.p_correct(theta, item['a'],
                                   item['b'])
                num += item['a'] * (correct - p)
                den += (item['a'] ** 2) * p * (1 - p)
            if abs(den) < 1e-10:
                break
            theta += num / den
        self.theta = theta

    def standard_error(self):
        import math
        info = sum((it['a']**2)
                   * self.p_correct(self.theta, it['a'], it['b'])
                   * (1 - self.p_correct(self.theta, it['a'],
                                         it['b']))
                   for it, _ in self.responses)
        return 1.0 / math.sqrt(info) if info > 0 else float('inf')

    def run(self, get_response_fn):
        """Execute adaptive test. get_response_fn(item)->bool"""
        used = set()
        while True:
            item = self.select_next_item(used)
            if item is None:
                break
            correct = get_response_fn(item)
            self.responses.append((item, int(correct)))
            used.add(id(item))
            self.update_theta()
            if (len(self.responses) >= 5 and
                    self.standard_error() < self.se_threshold):
```

```
                break
        return {'theta': self.theta,
                'se': self.standard_error(),
                'items_used': len(self.responses)}
```

Student progress tracking: The Bayesian update cycle

Effective personalization requires more than a simple record of which topics a student has encountered. It demands a working model of what the student knows, how reliably they can apply it, and how that knowledge changes as they practice. The Education Intelligence agent maintains this model using BKT. BKT treats each learning objective as a hidden mastery state that the agent cannot observe directly. Instead, it infers mastery from observable evidence such as submissions, test outcomes, hint usage, and characteristic error patterns.

To see how the agent "reads" a student's understanding, it helps to anchor the BKT parameters in a concrete tutoring workflow. Consider a Python programming tutor tracking the objective **Loop termination and iteration control**. The model uses four parameters that map cleanly to engineering and pedagogy:

- **Initial mastery ($P(L_0)$)**: The agent's starting belief that the student already knows the concept before the first relevant exercise. A student placed into an intermediate track will begin with a higher prior than a novice learner.
- **Transition probability ($P(T)$)**: The probability that one learning opportunity causes real learning. A learning opportunity can be an exercise attempt paired with feedback, a worked example, or a targeted hint sequence. In practice, $P(T)$ captures how effective the interaction design is for that objective.
- **Slip rate ($P(S)$)**: The chance of an incorrect outcome even when the student has mastered the concept. In programming tutors, slip is common: a missing colon, an indentation error, or a minor off-by-one bug can produce failure despite conceptual understanding.
- **Guess rate ($P(G)$)**: The chance of a correct outcome even without mastery. In code challenges, guessing can happen through trial-and-error edits until tests pass, copying patterns, or accidentally stumbling onto the correct condition.

These four terms explain why the agent cannot equate "correct" with "mastered" or "incorrect" with "not mastered." Instead, it updates its belief state after every interaction.

The update itself is a two-step Bayesian calculation. First, the agent computes the posterior probability that the student has mastered the objective given the observed outcome (correct or incorrect). Second, it applies a learning transition that accounts for the possibility that the student learned from the interaction itself. The following implementation encapsulates this logic.

```
def bkt_update(p_mastery: float, correct: bool,
               p_transit: float = 0.1,
               p_slip: float = 0.05,
               p_guess: float = 0.2) -> float:
    """Compute updated mastery probability after one
    observation using standard BKT.

    Args:
```

```
        p_mastery: prior P(L_n), current mastery belief
        correct: whether the student response was correct
        p_transit: P(T), probability of learning per opportunity
        p_slip: P(S), probability of slip given mastery
        p_guess: P(G), probability of guess given no mastery

    Returns:
        Updated P(L_{n+1}) after incorporating evidence."""
    # Step 1: posterior P(L_n | observation)
    if correct:
        p_correct_given_L = 1.0 - p_slip
        p_correct_given_not_L = p_guess
    else:
        p_correct_given_L = p_slip
        p_correct_given_not_L = 1.0 - p_guess

    p_obs = (p_correct_given_L * p_mastery
             + p_correct_given_not_L * (1 - p_mastery))
    p_posterior = (p_correct_given_L * p_mastery) / p_obs

    # Step 2: Learning transition
    p_updated = (p_posterior
                 + (1 - p_posterior) * p_transit)
    return p_updated
```

To see this in action with the loop-iteration scenario defined above, suppose the student begins with $P(L_0) = 0.1$ (low prior), and the tutor uses $P(T) = 0.1$, $P(S) = 0.05$, $P(G) = 0.2$. After the first correct submission, `bkt_update(0.1, True)` returns approximately 0.34: the agent's belief in mastery roughly triples, but remains below the 0.85 threshold because a single success could be a guess. After the second exercise produces an incorrect response, `bkt_update(0.34, False)` drops the estimate back to approximately 0.28, reflecting that the error is more likely to indicate a genuine gap than a slip at this mastery level. The agent now selects a diagnostic move rather than advancing the curriculum.

The standalone function above clarifies the BKT algorithm step by step. For production integration, the same logic should be encapsulated in a class that `StudentModel` can hold as an attribute. The `BKTTracker` class below wraps the two-step update into a reusable component with configurable parameters.

```
class BKTTracker:
    """Encapsulates Bayesian Knowledge Tracing for
    integration with StudentModel."""

    def __init__(self, p_transit=0.1,
                 p_slip=0.05, p_guess=0.2):
        self.p_transit = p_transit
```

```
        self.p_slip = p_slip
        self.p_guess = p_guess

    def update(self, p_mastery: float,
               correct: bool) -> float:
        """Return updated P(L) after one observation."""
        if correct:
            p_correct_L = 1.0 - self.p_slip
            p_correct_not_L = self.p_guess
        else:
            p_correct_L = self.p_slip
            p_correct_not_L = 1.0 - self.p_guess
        p_obs = (p_correct_L * p_mastery
                 + p_correct_not_L * (1 - p_mastery))
        posterior = (p_correct_L * p_mastery) / p_obs
        return (posterior
                + (1 - posterior) * self.p_transit)
```

When `StudentModel` receives an observation, its `update_mastery()` method calls `tracker.update()` to compute the new posterior, then stores the result. This design keeps BKT parameters configurable per course while maintaining the simple API that downstream components depend on.

Suppose the student is given this task:

Write a for loop that sums all even numbers in a list.

The student submits the following:

```
total = 0
for x in nums:
    if x % 2 == 0:
        total += x
print(total)
```

The tests pass. The agent now needs to update its estimate of mastery for **Loop iteration with conditional filtering**. A correct submission increases mastery probability, but the update is tempered by the possibility of guessing. If the student has requested multiple hints, or if the system observes many rapid edits with repeated test runs, the agent may treat the evidence as weaker. In BKT terms, a higher P(G) makes the model more cautious about over-crediting a single success.

Now consider the next exercise, which is intentionally similar but changes the failure mode:

```
Sum even numbers, but stop early if you encounter a negative value.
```

The student writes:

```
total = 0
for x in nums:
    if x < 0:
        break
    if x % 2 == 0:
        total += x
```

This time the tests fail because the `break` condition is misplaced in a variation of the task, or the student misunderstood when the loop should terminate. An incorrect response reduces the mastery estimate, but again the agent must interpret the error. If the failure is due to indentation or a trivial syntax error, slip is the likely explanation. If the failure reflects a structural misconception about control flow, the update should reflect a genuine gap.

The updated posterior probability is what makes BKT operationally useful for action selection. The agent's next action is not arbitrary. It is chosen based on the updated belief:

- If mastery remains high and the error looks like a slip (for example, indentation or a missing colon), the agent should offer a minimal correction and keep the student on track. The system avoids over-remediation.
- If mastery drops meaningfully, the agent should switch to a diagnostic move: a short tracing question ("What is the value of `total` after the third iteration?") or a micro-exercise focused on `break` semantics. This reduces uncertainty quickly.
- If the student produces a string of correct answers but the model still estimates low mastery, the agent can infer that the correctness signal is likely driven by guessing behavior. In that case, it schedules a more discriminative assessment: a problem that cannot be solved by copying the last pattern, such as asking the student to predict behavior of a loop with nested conditionals or to debug a failing implementation.

By maintaining a running probability rather than a binary label, the agent can explain why it is making these choices. It can tell an instructor, "The student's recent correctness is inconsistent with their hint pattern and response timing, so we are confirming mastery with a transfer task," or "This appears to be a slip after sustained success, so we are not rolling the student back."

Adaptive learning techniques

With a robust student model and curriculum planner in place, the agent can deploy adaptive techniques that would be impractical in a traditional classroom. These operate at multiple time scales.

At the micro level, the agent implements **adaptive scaffolding**: dynamically adjusting support based on observed performance. When a student struggles with a coding exercise, the agent does not reveal the solution. Instead, it walks through four escalating levels. First, a conceptual nudge: a question that steers attention toward the right concept without pointing at the error. Second, localization: "the issue is somewhere in your loop body." Third, a structural hint, perhaps pseudocode or a partial template. Fourth, and only if the student is still stuck, a worked example of a similar problem followed by the prompt to apply the same pattern. The agent advances a level only after another incorrect submission. Wait times between levels are calibrated to each student's historical response patterns, and the whole sequence is implemented as a state machine within the LangGraph workflow.

At the meso level, **mastery-based progression** advances students only when they demonstrate sufficient understanding of prerequisites. Unlike time-based progression, this prevents foundational gaps from compounding. The mastery threshold is not a fixed constant: prerequisites heavily depended on by many downstream objectives require higher thresholds.

At the macro level, **learning path diversification** recognizes that students with similar mastery profiles may benefit from different instructional approaches. Some learn best through concrete examples before abstract principles (inductive), while others prefer theory first, then application (deductive). The agent maintains a preference model, updated based on engagement and outcomes across modalities.

The adaptive engine also implements **spaced repetition** for long-term retention. To operationalize this pedagogical principle, the agent maintains a specific review schedule for every mastered objective using a modified version of the SM-2 (SuperMemo-2) algorithm. This algorithm is a computational method for determining the optimal time to review a piece of information based on the learner's previous performance. The core logic functions as follows:

- **Increasing intervals**: The most efficient way to move information from short-term to long-term memory is to review it at increasing intervals, with each successful recall pushing the next scheduled review further into the future.
- **Recall quality**: The algorithm utilizes a quality score (typically ranging from 0 to 5) to adjust the "ease factor" of a concept.
- **Adaptive reinforcement**: If a student successfully recalls a concept, the interval grows; if they fail, the concept is reset to be reviewed daily until mastery is re-established.

When the schedule indicates a concept is at risk of being forgotten, the agent interleaves review activities into the current session. The following listing illustrates this spaced repetition scheduler:

```
class SpacedRepetitionScheduler:
    def __init__(self, student_model):
        self.model = student_model

    def get_due_reviews(self, student_id: str,
                        max_reviews: int = 5) -> list[Review]:
        """Identify objectives due for review based on
        spaced repetition schedule."""
        mastered = self.model.get_mastered_objectives(
            student_id
        )
        due = []
        now = datetime.utcnow()
        for objective_id, metadata in mastered.items():
            next_review = metadata.get("next_review")
```

```
            if next_review and next_review <= now:
                days_overdue = (now - next_review).days
                priority = min(days_overdue / 7.0, 1.0)
                due.append(Review(
                    objective_id=objective_id,
                    priority=priority,
                    interval=metadata.get("interval", 1),
                    repetitions=metadata.get("reps", 0)
                ))
        due.sort(key=lambda r: r.priority, reverse=True)
        return due[:max_reviews]

    def update_schedule(self, student_id: str,
                        objective_id: str,
                        quality: int) -> None:
        """Update review schedule using SM-2 algorithm.
        Quality: 0 (complete failure) to 5 (perfect)."""
        meta = self.model.get_objective_metadata(
            student_id, objective_id
        )
        reps = meta.get("reps", 0)
        interval = meta.get("interval", 1)
        ease = meta.get("ease_factor", 2.5)
        if quality >= 3:
            if reps == 0:
                interval = 1
            elif reps == 1:
                interval = 6
            else:
                interval = int(interval * ease)
            reps += 1
        else:
            reps = 0
            interval = 1
        ease = max(1.3, ease + 0.1 - (5 - quality)
                   * (0.08 + (5 - quality) * 0.02))
        next_review = datetime.utcnow() + timedelta(
            days=interval
        )
        self.model.update_objective_metadata(
            student_id, objective_id,
            reps=reps, interval=interval,
```

```
        ease_factor=ease, next_review=next_review
    )
```

This scheduler is doing more than creating calendar reminders. It provides the retention layer that complements the mastery estimates from the student model and the forward-looking choices made by the curriculum planner. The `get_due_reviews()` method scans mastered objectives and computes a priority score based on how overdue an objective is, ensuring the session allocates time to concepts at genuine risk of decay rather than reviewing everything uniformly.

The `update_schedule()` method then operationalizes a central pedagogical insight: what matters is not time spent, but successful retrieval. A student who recalls a concept cleanly (high quality) earns longer intervals and an increased ease factor, which pushes the next review further out; a student who fails recall resets repetitions and collapses the interval, triggering near-term reinforcement.

A concrete use case is a Python learner who has recently "mastered" list slicing but begins making boundary mistakes two weeks later. Rather than waiting for the mistake to reappear in a graded assignment, the scheduler will surface slicing for review as soon as `next_review` becomes due, and the student's performance on that short retrieval activity directly updates the future schedule. If the student answers correctly but hesitates and needs a hint, you can encode that as a mid-range quality score so the interval grows, but conservatively. If they cannot reconstruct the concept at all, the algorithm resets the spacing and forces a quick re-encounter, preventing a slow drift from mastery into fragile, error-prone knowledge. In architectural terms, this is how the agent makes "durability" actionable: it turns the retention-decay dynamics tracked by BKT in the *Student progress tracking: The Bayesian update cycle* section above into a concrete runtime policy that decides when to interrupt new content to protect long-term retention.

The components described above (curriculum planner, BKT tracker, spaced repetition scheduler, and adaptive scaffolding) form a complete but abstract architecture. The following case study grounds them in a concrete deployment: a programming tutor that teaches introductory Python with tailored feedback, demonstrating how each component contributes to a real instructional workflow.

Case study: Programming tutor with tailored feedback

To see these components working together, we examine a complete deployment of the Education Intelligence agent as a Python programming tutor, supporting learners from their first lines of code through intermediate challenges.

The tutor operates within a knowledge graph of 247 learning objectives across 12 topic clusters: data types, control flow, functions, data structures, file I/O, error handling, object-oriented programming, modules and packages, testing, algorithms, debugging, and software design patterns.

In production, the tutor decomposes into five independently scalable microservices on Kubernetes:

- The **Student Model Service** maintains mastery estimates backed by PostgreSQL with Redis caching.
- The **Curriculum Planner Service** loads the knowledge graph from Neo4j.
- The **Content Delivery Service** serves materials from a CDN-backed object store.

- The **Assessment Engine** runs automated test cases against student code in sandboxed Docker containers with 10-second execution timeouts.
- The **Feedback Generator Service** calls the LLM API with student context, using prompt caching and a template-based fallback for high-latency situations.

The adaptive loop is orchestrated with LangGraph, defining nodes for readiness assessment, content delivery, response collection, submission evaluation, feedback generation, and a human checkpoint that alerts instructors via Slack for flagged situations (repeated failures, distress signals, or suspected dishonesty). LangGraph's Postgres-backed persistence ensures session state survives service restarts.

New students receive a 15-question adaptive placement test, calibrated with IRT parameters from 12,000 historical students. A student with prior experience in another language might demonstrate mastery of general programming concepts but have low estimates for Python-specific syntax.

When a student submits code, the evaluation pipeline performs multiple levels of analysis. Automated tests verify correctness. Static analysis (Ruff, pylint) checks style and anti-patterns. Then the misconception detection module kicks in.

The misconception detector uses a two-stage pipeline. The first stage is a fast, rule-based classifier that matches code against approximately 180 known Python misconception patterns, defined as combinations of AST node patterns and output signatures. This runs in under 50 ms and catches about 70% of common misconceptions. When the rule-based stage returns no match or low confidence, the second stage invokes the LLM with the code, error output, and recent error history. This hybrid approach reduced average feedback latency from 8 seconds (LLM-only) to 2.5 seconds while maintaining diagnostic accuracy above 85%.

The following code implements the `FeedbackGenerator` class. This component represents the critical "Action" phase of the educational cognitive loop, where the system's internal reasoning is finally manifested as a pedagogical intervention for the learner. The objective of this implementation is to synthesize a personalized, context-aware feedback message that goes beyond simple correctness signals. By integrating the student's current mastery levels, recent error patterns, and specific detected misconceptions, the generator uses an LLM-driven prompt to produce a "conceptual nudge." This approach ensures that the student is guided toward discovering the solution independently rather than being presented with the final answer. With the curriculum planned and the student's knowledge traced, the agent must close the loop by delivering instruction. The following implementation of the feedback engine demonstrates how to transform raw diagnostic data into a supportive dialogue, ensuring every response is aligned with the student's specific learning trajectory.

```
class FeedbackGenerator:
    def __init__(self, llm_client, student_model,
                 misconception_library):
        self.llm = llm_client
        self.model = student_model
        self.misconceptions = misconception_library

    def generate_feedback(self, student_id: str,
                          exercise: Exercise,
                          submission: str,
```

```
                    test_results: TestResults
                    ) -> Feedback:
        """Generate personalized feedback that addresses
        the student's specific learning needs."""
        mastery = self.model.get_mastery_state(student_id)
        history = self.model.get_recent_errors(
            student_id, n=10
        )
        detected = self.misconceptions.detect_rule_based(
            submission, exercise.objective_ids
        )
        if not detected or detected.confidence < 0.7:
            detected = self.misconceptions.detect_llm(
                submission, exercise, history
            )
        prompt = f"""You are an expert Python tutor.
        The student is working on: {exercise.description}

        Their solution:
        \`\`\`python
        {submission}
        \`\`\`
        Test results: {test_results.summary}

        Student context:
        - Current mastery of {exercise.topic}: \
{mastery.get(exercise.primary_objective, 0.0):.0%}
        - Recent error patterns: {history}
        - Detected misconceptions: {detected}

        Generate feedback that:
        1. Acknowledges what the student did correctly
        2. Identifies the specific error without revealing
           the complete solution
        3. Asks a guiding question that leads toward
           discovering the fix independently
        4. If a misconception is detected, address the
           underlying conceptual confusion"""

        response = self.llm.generate(prompt)
        return Feedback(
            content=response,
            misconceptions_addressed=detected,
            mastery_updates=self._compute_updates(
```

```
            student_id, exercise, test_results
        )
    )
```

The above code operationalizes a principle that is easy to state and hard to implement: feedback should diagnose *why* the student failed, not merely report that they failed. The method begins by assembling the student's current mastery estimate and a short window of recent errors, because the same incorrect submission means different things depending on context.

It then performs misconception detection in two stages: a fast, rule-based classifier that matches the submission against a library of known patterns, and a second-stage LLM diagnostic that is invoked only when the first stage is uncertain. This hybrid design is not cosmetic. It is a latency and reliability strategy: the rule-based stage can catch frequent misconceptions cheaply and consistently, while the LLM stage provides coverage for novel or compositional errors without forcing every interaction to pay the cost of an LLM call. The prompt itself is structured as a pedagogical contract. It forces the model to acknowledge correct elements, localize the error without disclosing the full solution, and ask a guiding question that keeps agency with the student.

In practice, this is how the agent prevents two failure modes common in tutoring systems: "rubber-stamp praise plus the correct answer" and "generic advice that does not connect to the student's actual misconception." By returning both the feedback content and a computed set of mastery updates, the component also closes the loop back into the student model, ensuring that feedback is not a detached message but a state-changing action in the broader learning architecture.

To see how these components work as a unified system, consider a single student's path through the Education Intelligence agent. A new learner, Alex, enters the Python programming tutor with no prior interaction history.

- **Stage 1—Placement**: The IRT-based diagnostic presents 12 adaptive micro-items. Alex answers variables and conditionals correctly but struggles with loop termination. The `StudentModel` initializes with high mastery estimates for variables (p = 0.82) and conditionals (p = 0.78) but low estimates for loops (p = 0.25) and iteration patterns (p = 0.15).
- **Stage 2—Curriculum selection**: The `CurriculumPlanner` queries `get_mastery_state()` and the knowledge graph. Loop fundamentals have satisfied prerequisites (variables, conditionals are above threshold). The expected-gain heuristic ranks "for-loop iteration" highest: it sits in Alex's ZPD (difficulty 0.45 against mastery 0.25, delta within range) and unlocks four downstream objectives, including list comprehensions and nested iteration.
- **Stage 3—Interaction and BKT update**: Alex receives the "sum even numbers" exercise and submits a correct solution. `bkt_update(0.25, True)` returns 0.51—a significant jump, but still below the 0.85 mastery threshold. The next exercise, requiring an early break condition, produces an incorrect submission. `bkt_update(0.51, False)` drops the estimate to 0.42. The agent classifies this as a genuine gap (not a slip) because the error is structural and selects a diagnostic tracing question.
- **Stage 4—Feedback and scaffolding**: The `FeedbackGenerator` detects a control-flow misconception (break placement) via its rule-based first stage. It generates a Level 2 hint: `Your loop logic is sound`

for the filtering case. Look at where the break executes relative to the accumulation step. Alex corrects the submission. `bkt_update(0.42, True)` raises mastery to 0.62.

- **Stage 5—Spaced repetition**: Two days later, the `SpacedRepetitionScheduler` flags "for-loop iteration" as due for review (interval computed from the SM-2 algorithm using quality score 3, reflecting the hint-assisted success). Alex completes a retrieval exercise correctly without hints. Mastery rises to 0.79. The scheduler extends the next review interval to five days. After one more successful retrieval, mastery crosses 0.85 and the curriculum planner advances Alex to nested iteration patterns.

The Education Intelligence agent demonstrates that teaching is an engineering problem with a tractable architecture: a student model that tracks latent mastery, a curriculum planner that selects high-yield objectives, a spaced repetition scheduler that optimizes long-term retention, and a feedback generator that targets specific misconceptions. Each component feeds the next through explicit state updates, making the agent's pedagogical reasoning auditable and improvable. The section that follows shifts from individual instruction to a fundamentally different challenge: coordinating multiple agents to produce collective intelligence that exceeds any single reasoner's capacity.

The Collective Intelligence agent

The previous section examined how a single agent personalizes instruction for individual learners. We now turn to a fundamentally different challenge: how multiple agents, each with partial knowledge and specialized capabilities, collaborate to solve problems that exceed any individual's capacity. This section develops the architecture in three stages: multi-agent collaboration patterns that organize the team, consensus mechanisms that aggregate competing proposals, and emergent intelligence frameworks that explain how group-level capabilities arise from individual interactions.

The Collective Intelligence agent is not a single agent. It is an architectural pattern for organizing teams of agents that reason together, debate alternatives, and converge on solutions through structured consensus. The pattern draws on multi-agent systems research, swarm intelligence, ensemble methods, and the social science of group decision-making. The central insight is that diversity of perspective, combined with effective aggregation mechanisms, consistently produces better outcomes than reliance on a single reasoner, even a highly capable one.

The theoretical backbone is the **Condorcet Jury Theorem**. If each agent independently arrives at the correct answer with probability $p > 0.5$, then the probability that a majority vote produces the correct answer approaches 1 as the group grows. This is a powerful result, but it rests on a critical assumption: independence. LLM-based agents sharing the same underlying model may exhibit correlated errors, violating this assumption. The diversity mechanisms described below serve precisely to reduce this correlation, pushing the system closer to the conditions under which Condorcet's guarantee holds.

Multi-agent collaboration architectures

The architecture must address three design questions. How are agents organized: flat peers or a hierarchy with coordinators? How do they communicate: through a central bus or pairwise conversations? How are contributions combined: voting, averaging, debate, or something else?

Figure 15.2 illustrates one such architecture. The diagram shows four specialized agents coordinating through a shared state repository under the direction of a facilitator agent.

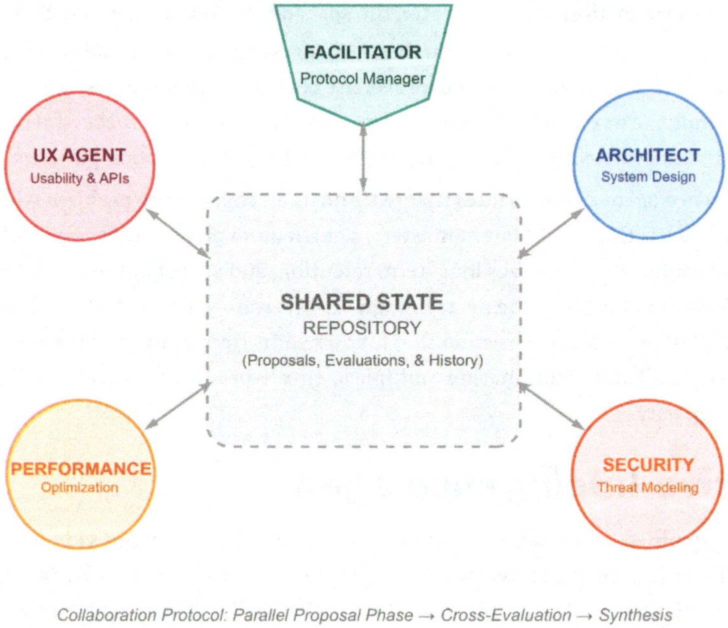

Figure 15.2 – Multi-agent Collaboration architecture

Figure 15.2 shows four specialized agents coordinating through a shared state repository:

- A facilitator agent that manages the protocol
- A research agent that retrieves external knowledge
- A synthesis agent that integrates partial solutions
- An evaluation Agent that assesses quality against defined criteria

The `CollaborativeAgent` class described next implements the core unit of collaboration: a role-specialized participant that can both *contribute* a proposal and *critique* the proposals of others. This dual capability is what turns a group of independent LLM calls into an accountable deliberation process.

First, the `CollaborativeAgent` class defines a role-specialized participant in a multi-agent system. The constructor wires in five pieces of runtime identity and capability: a stable agent identifier, a declared role, an expertise profile, an LLM client, and a toolset. It also attaches `AgentMemory`, which is the agent's local working memory for retaining its own prior reasoning and interactions across turns.

```
class CollaborativeAgent:
    def __init__(self, agent_id: str, role: str,
                 expertise: list[str], llm_client,
                 tools: list[Tool]):
        self.id = agent_id
        self.role = role
```

```
        self.expertise = expertise
        self.llm = llm_client
        self.tools = tools
        self.memory = AgentMemory()
```

Next, we have the `propose_solution()` method, which is the "contribution" pathway. It takes a `Problem` and a `SharedContext`. Instead of starting from a blank prompt, it pulls `relevant_history` from the shared context using the agent's expertise tags. That choice matters architecturally. It prevents the agent from re-litigating the entire conversation and encourages it to specialize, reacting to existing proposals rather than duplicating them. The prompt then asks for a solution plus explicit assumptions and uncertainties, which is a lightweight but important safeguard. It forces the proposal to carry its own caveats, making later evaluation more meaningful. The method returns a `Proposal` object that is intentionally structured. It includes the agent ID, the content, and two metadata fields: an internal confidence estimate and a relevance score. These fields are not just decorative. They are the raw material for downstream orchestration logic such as consensus ranking, weighted voting, or escalation rules. The final line, `context.add_proposal(proposal)`, is what turns an individual thought into shared deliberation state.

```
    def propose_solution(self, problem: Problem,
                         context: SharedContext
                         ) -> Proposal:
        """Generate a solution proposal informed by
        the agent's expertise and shared context."""
        relevant_history = context.get_relevant(
            self.expertise
        )
        prompt = f"""You are a {self.role} with expertise
        in {', '.join(self.expertise)}.

        Problem: {problem.description}

        Previous proposals from other agents:
        {relevant_history}

        Based on your expertise, propose a solution.
        Explain your reasoning and identify any
        assumptions or uncertainties."""

        response = self.llm.generate(prompt)
        proposal = Proposal(
            agent_id=self.id,
            content=response,
            confidence=self._assess_confidence(
                problem, response
```

```
            ),
            expertise_relevance=self._compute_relevance(
                problem
            )
        )
        context.add_proposal(proposal)
        return proposal
```

The second method, evaluate_proposal(), is the "critique" pathway. It asks the agent to assess another agent's proposal along four dimensions: correctness, completeness, feasibility, and risks or gaps, then to score each from 0 to 10. The output is wrapped as a Evaluation object containing structured scores and an explanatory critique. In practice, this is how the system avoids a common failure mode of multi-agent designs: collecting multiple opinions without a consistent evaluation rubric. A shared scoring schema makes it possible to compare evaluations across agents and detect outliers.

```
    def evaluate_proposal(self, proposal: Proposal,
                          problem: Problem) -> Evaluation:
        """Evaluate another agent's proposal from this
        agent's area of expertise."""
        prompt = f"""You are a {self.role}. Evaluate
        the following proposal for solving:
        {problem.description}

        Proposal by {proposal.agent_id}:
        {proposal.content}

        Assess: correctness, completeness, feasibility,
        and any risks or gaps from your perspective.
        Score each dimension from 0 to 10."""

        response = self.llm.generate(prompt)
        return Evaluation(
            evaluator_id=self.id,
            proposal_id=proposal.id,
            scores=self._parse_scores(response),
            critique=response
        )
```

The above code captures the minimal mechanics required for collective intelligence to become an architectural pattern rather than a rhetorical claim. The system does not rely on "multiple agents" as a synonym for correctness. It creates a repeatable loop of proposal generation and peer review, where each agent's output becomes shared state, and each proposal can be challenged against a consistent rubric.

In use, this pattern is particularly effective in education-adjacent settings such as course design, curriculum audits, and rubric creation, where the goal is not a single answer but a defensible synthesis. A lead "instructor" agent can ask a pedagogy specialist to critique cognitive load, a domain expert to validate technical accuracy, and an assessment specialist to check whether tasks actually measure the intended objectives. The orchestration layer can then aggregate proposals using the structured confidence and scoring signals, surface disagreements for resolution, and retain the entire deliberation trace as an audit artifact. That trace is what makes the system teachable and governable: it allows an instructor to see not only what was decided, but why competing alternatives were rejected.

Consensus mechanisms and voting systems

Given proposals from agents with different expertise and confidence levels, how does the system determine the best collective answer? The agent implements a layered consensus mechanism that operates in three phases: independent proposals, cross-evaluation, and synthesis.

The evaluation phase uses weighted voting, where each agent's influence is proportional to its demonstrated domain expertise. The consensus score for proposal p_j is:

$$\text{Score}(p_j) = \Sigma_i \left[w_i \cdot \text{relevance}_i \cdot \text{score}_{ij} \right]$$

where w_i is the expertise weight of agent i, relevance_i measures how relevant agent i's expertise is to the problem, and score_{ij} is agent i's evaluation of proposal j. Expertise weights are updated via exponential moving average, balancing historical performance against recent accuracy.

This aggregation rule satisfies desirable properties from social choice theory: Pareto efficiency (universal preference is respected) and dictator-freeness (when no single agent's weight exceeds the sum of all others). Arrow's impossibility theorem is partially sidestepped because the system uses cardinal evaluations (numerical scores) rather than ordinal rankings.

Under balanced communication, agents' proposals converge to consensus at an exponential rate. The practical takeaway: preventing any single agent from dominating not only reduces bias but also accelerates convergence, providing a theoretical justification for the expertise calibration mechanism.

Figure 15.3 traces this flow from independent proposals through the critique-and-score loop to a final synthesized result, showing how the consensus mechanism converges across rounds.

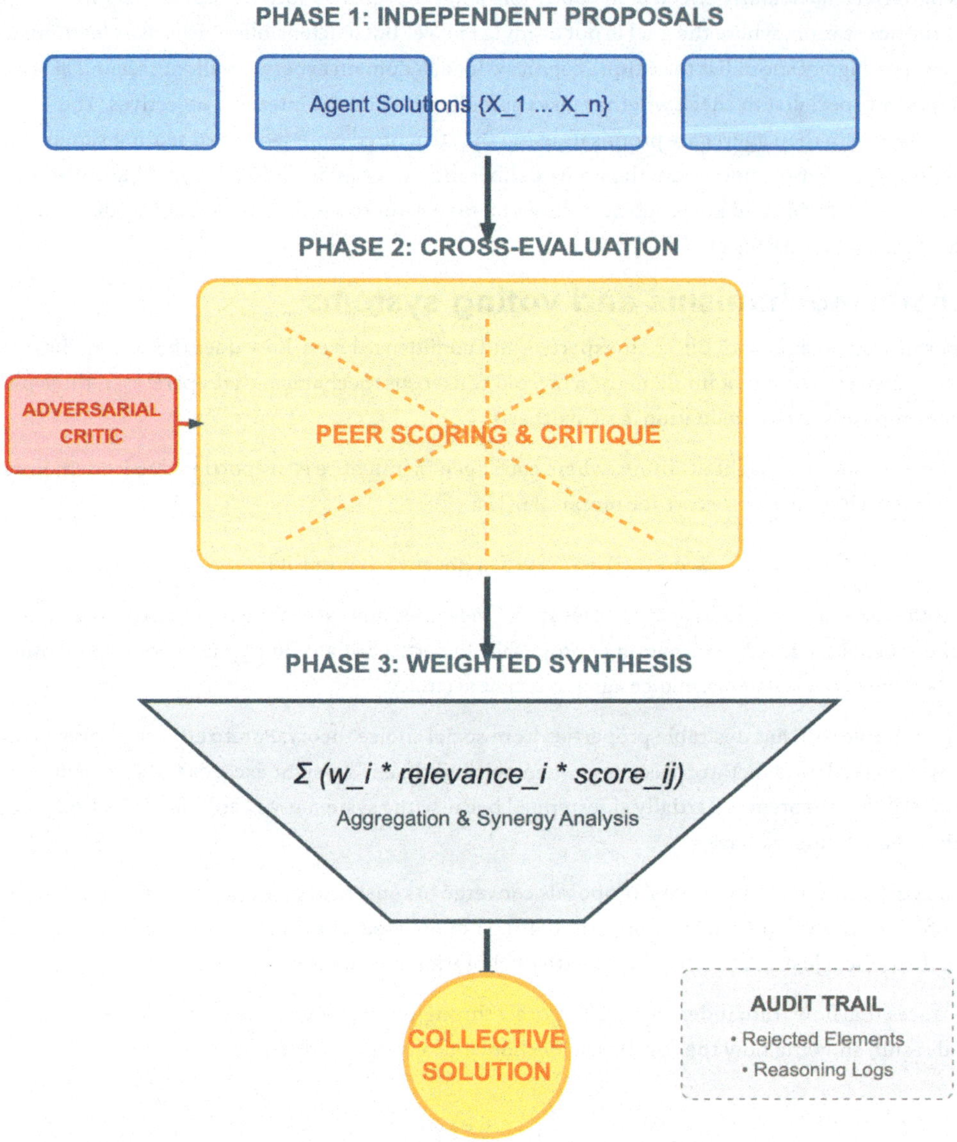

Figure 15.3 – Consensus and voting mechanism

Figure 15.3 traces the flow from independent proposals through cross-evaluation, weighted scoring, and synthesized output. Rejected elements are recorded with explanations, creating a transparent audit trail that supports the explainability requirements from *Chapter 12*.

The system guards against known group decision-making failures:

- **Groupthink prevention**: At least one agent per evaluation round is assigned the adversarial critic role, tasked with identifying weaknesses regardless of apparent consensus. This role rotates; in production, rounds with an active critic produced syntheses scoring 12% higher on risk identification.

- **Anchoring bias mitigation**: The order in which agents see proposals is randomized.
- **Expertise calibration**: A relevance score gates each agent's voting weight to prevent undue influence outside their domain.

The following `ConsensusEngine` class implements the orchestration layer that turns multiple proposals into a decision. Rather than selecting the first plausible response, it runs a bounded multi-round protocol: agents critique each other's proposals, scores are aggregated with expertise weighting, and proposals are refined until convergence.

```
class ConsensusEngine:
    def __init__(self, agents: list[CollaborativeAgent]):
        self.agents = agents
        self.expertise_weights = {
            a.id: 1.0 for a in agents
        }
```

The constructor initializes each agent with equal expertise weight. This is a deliberate design choice: it makes the weighting explicit and tunable rather than implicit in prompt wording. In production, weights are typically driven by role authority or measured reliability over time. The next segment implements the multi-round consensus protocol.

```
    def run_consensus(self, problem: Problem,
                      max_rounds: int = 3
                      ) -> ConsensusResult:
        """Execute multi-round consensus protocol with
        convergence detection and early termination."""
        context = SharedContext()
        proposals = []
        for agent in self.agents:
            proposal = agent.propose_solution(
                problem, context
            )
            proposals.append(proposal)
```

The first phase bootstraps the process: each agent produces an independent proposal informed by the shared context, which accumulates prior contributions so later agents can avoid duplication. With proposals in hand, the method enters the critique-and-refine loop below. On each round, one agent is designated as an adversarial critic to stress-test proposals. Every agent evaluates every other agent's proposal, producing scored critiques. If the scores converge within a tolerance threshold, the engine synthesizes a final result and terminates early; otherwise, proposals are refined and the cycle repeats.

```
        best_result = None
        for round_num in range(max_rounds):
            critic_idx = round_num % len(self.agents)
```

```
            self.agents[critic_idx].set_role(
                "adversarial_critic"
            )
            evaluations = []
            for agent in self.agents:
                for proposal in proposals:
                    if proposal.agent_id != agent.id:
                        evaluation = agent.evaluate_proposal(
                            proposal, problem
                        )
                        evaluations.append(evaluation)
            scores = self._compute_consensus_scores(
                proposals, evaluations
            )
            if self._has_converged(scores, tolerance=0.5):
                best_result = self._synthesize(
                    proposals, evaluations, scores
                )
                break
            proposals = self._refine_proposals(
                proposals, evaluations, context
            )
            self.agents[critic_idx].reset_role()
        if best_result is None:
            best_result = self._synthesize(
                proposals, evaluations, scores
            )
        return best_result
```

The final segment handles score aggregation. Each proposal receives an expertise-weighted consensus score computed from the evaluations. Weighting by expertise ensures that a security reviewer's critique of a security-sensitive proposal counts more heavily than a generalist's, and these weights can also become a learning lever: if the system observes that certain roles consistently catch errors, their weights can be increased over time.

```
    def _compute_consensus_scores(self, proposals,
                                  evaluations
                                  ) -> dict[str, float]:
        """Compute expertise-weighted consensus scores."""
        scores = {}
        for proposal in proposals:
            relevant_evals = [
                e for e in evaluations
                if e.proposal_id == proposal.id
            ]
```

```
        weighted_sum = sum(
            self.expertise_weights[e.evaluator_id]
            * e.scores.get("overall", 5.0)
            for e in relevant_evals
        )
        total_weight = sum(
            self.expertise_weights[e.evaluator_id]
            for e in relevant_evals
        )
        scores[proposal.id] = (
            weighted_sum / total_weight
            if total_weight > 0 else 0.0
        )
    return scores
```

The `ConsensusEngine` is a lightweight orchestration layer for multi-agent collaboration. Its constructor accepts a list of `CollaborativeAgent` instances and initializes an `expertise_weights` map. This is an important design choice: it makes "whose critique counts more" explicit and tunable, rather than implicit in prompt wording. In production, these weights are typically driven by role authority (for example, security reviewer > generalist) or measured reliability over time.

The `run_consensus()` method implements a multi-round protocol with three phases.

1. **Proposal generation (round 0 bootstrap):** A fresh `SharedContext` is created, and each agent produces an initial proposal using `propose_solution()`. The shared context accumulates these proposals so that later agents can see prior work and avoid duplication.
2. **Critique and scoring (iterative rounds)**: For each round, one agent is rotated into an **adversarial critic** role using `critic_idx = round_num % len(self.agents)`. This ensures that every round has at least one intentionally skeptical reviewer rather than a room full of agreeable summaries. The engine then gathers `Evaluation` objects by having every agent review proposals that are not their own. This matters for accountability: it prevents agents from self-scoring and forces cross-checking.
   The evaluations are aggregated via `_compute_consensus_scores()`, which computes an **expertise-weighted mean** of the evaluators' "overall" score for each proposal. The computation is straightforward: sum of (weight × score) divided by total weight. If no relevant evaluations exist, the proposal receives 0.0, which is a clear signal that the system lacks coverage rather than a silent default.
3. **Convergence detection and refinement:** After scoring, `_has_converged(scores, tolerance=0.5)` determines whether the group has reached stability. Convergence here means the score distribution is no longer moving meaningfully, so further rounds are unlikely to add value. If convergence is reached, `_synthesize()` produces a final `ConsensusResult`, merging the best proposal with supporting critiques and the scoring rationale. If not converged, `_refine_proposals()` produces a new proposal set informed by the critiques, and the loop continues, bounded by `max_rounds`.

Finally, if the protocol reaches the round limit without convergence, it still returns a result by synthesizing the latest proposals and evaluations. This is a production-minded detail: the system is designed to be bounded and predictable, not open-ended.

This consensus engine formalizes collaboration as a controlled runtime process with clear stopping conditions. The educational relevance is practical. In curriculum design, lesson planning, or assessment creation, teams rarely want a single "best" answer from a single perspective. They want a solution that survives critique from multiple lenses, including pedagogy, domain correctness, and evaluation validity. The multi-round loop shown here is how the agentic system approximates that review process: one agent proposes, others challenge, and the proposal is refined until the group's scoring stabilizes. The convergence check is not merely an optimization. It is a governance mechanism that bounds deliberation cost while ensuring that the system has at least attempted adversarial review. Over time, the expertise weights can also become a learning lever. If the system observes that certain roles consistently catch errors or predict downstream failure, their weights can be increased, shifting the consensus toward more reliable critique without rewriting the protocol.

Case study: Multi-agent rubric design with collaborative consensus

To see these components in action, consider a concrete scenario: three agents collaboratively designing a grading rubric for an introductory programming assignment. The assignment asks students to implement a function that merges two sorted lists. A pedagogy agent, a domain expert agent, and an assessment agent each bring a different perspective.

Using the `CollaborativeAgent` class defined above, each agent is initialized with a distinct role and expertise list. The pedagogy agent's expertise covers scaffolding, cognitive load, and formative feedback. The domain expert agent specializes in algorithm correctness, edge cases, and code style. The assessment agent focuses on rubric validity, inter-rater reliability, and grade distribution.

In the first round, each agent calls `propose_solution()` against the shared context. The pedagogy agent proposes a rubric weighted toward process: 40% for demonstrating a clear problem-solving strategy, 30% for correctness, and 30% for code readability. The domain expert proposes a rubric weighted toward technical rigor: 50% correctness (including edge cases such as empty lists and duplicates), 30% efficiency, and 20% style. The assessment agent proposes a rubric optimized for reliable grading: five binary criteria (handles empty input, preserves sort order, runs in O(n), uses no built-in sort, includes docstring) that minimize subjective judgment.

The `ConsensusEngine` then enters its critique-and-refine loop. In the evaluation phase, the pedagogy agent critiques the domain expert's rubric for ignoring process and penalizing students who arrive at correct but non-optimal solutions. The domain expert critiques the assessment agent's binary criteria for missing partial credit. The assessment agent critiques the pedagogy agent's rubric for relying on subjective "problem-solving strategy" judgments that reduce inter-rater agreement.

After one refinement round, the proposals converge toward a hybrid rubric: five concrete criteria (from the assessment agent), each scored on a three-point scale (absent, partial, complete) rather than binary (from the pedagogy agent's emphasis on partial credit), with two criteria explicitly testing edge cases (from the domain expert). The consensus score stabilizes within the 0.5 tolerance threshold, and the engine synthesizes the final rubric.

This example demonstrates two properties that justify the collective architecture. First, the final rubric is qualitatively different from any single agent's proposal: it combines assessment reliability, pedagogical nuance, and technical coverage in a way that no individual agent prioritized. Second, the critique phase surfaced genuine trade-offs (process versus reliability, partial credit versus grading speed) that would have remained implicit in a single-agent design. The structured consensus loop made these trade-offs explicit, debated, and resolved.

The narrative above traced the rubric design through prose. The following code makes the same scenario runnable. It instantiates three `CollaborativeAgent` instances with the role prompts used in the worked example, feeds them into a `ConsensusEngine`, and executes the full *proposal-critique-refine* loop. A mock LLM client stands in for the language model so readers can run the code locally and substitute their own provider.

```
# Runnable CI case study: rubric design consensus
from typing import Callable

def mock_llm(prompt: str) -> str:
    """Substitute with an actual LLM client."""
    return f"[Response to: {prompt[:80]}...]"

# 1. Instantiate role-specialized agents
pedagogy = CollaborativeAgent(
    role="Pedagogy Specialist",
    expertise=["scaffolding", "cognitive load",
               "formative feedback"],
    llm_client=mock_llm
)
domain = CollaborativeAgent(
    role="Domain Expert",
    expertise=["algorithm correctness",
               "edge cases", "code style"],
    llm_client=mock_llm
)
assessment = CollaborativeAgent(
    role="Assessment Specialist",
    expertise=["rubric validity",
               "inter-rater reliability",
               "grade distribution"],
    llm_client=mock_llm
)

# 2. Build the consensus engine
engine = ConsensusEngine(
    agents=[pedagogy, domain, assessment]
)
```

```
# 3. Define the shared problem context
context = (
    "Design a grading rubric for an introductory "
    "programming assignment: implement a function "
    "that merges two sorted lists."
)

# 4. Run the consensus session
result = engine.run_session(context)

# 5. Inspect the output
print(f"Rounds: {result['rounds']}")
print(f"Final score: {result['consensus_score']:.2f}")
print(f"Rubric:\n{result['final_proposal']}")
```

The `run_session()` call executes the full consensus loop described in the preceding sections: each agent proposes an initial rubric, the engine collects weighted critiques, agents refine their proposals, and the cycle repeats until the consensus score exceeds the convergence threshold. The `final_proposal` field contains the synthesized rubric. With a real LLM client, readers will see the same convergence pattern the narrative described: binary criteria from the assessment agent, partial-credit scales from the pedagogy agent, and edge-case coverage from the domain expert merging into a single hybrid instrument.

Emergent intelligence frameworks

The most compelling aspect of collective intelligence is not aggregation but **emergence**: solutions that arise from agent interaction and that no individual could have produced alone. Information-theoretically, emergence can be characterized through **synergistic information**, the component of collective output that depends on interactions between agent inputs and cannot be reduced to individual contributions.

The architecture supports emergence through three mechanisms:

- **Cross-pollination prompting**: This exposes each agent to the strongest elements of competing proposals during refinement, triggering novel combinations. During each refinement round, the `ConsensusEngine` shares the highest-scored elements from every proposal with all agents, so a pedagogy agent sees the domain expert's edge-case criteria and vice versa. In the rubric design scenario, this mechanism caused the pedagogy agent to adopt the assessment agent's binary-criteria structure while retaining its own partial-credit scoring, a combination neither agent proposed independently.
- **Constraint relaxation**: This is inspired by the TRIZ theory (Teoriya Resheniya Izobreatatelskikh Zadatch in Russian, which translates to Theory of Inventive Problem Solving), and has the facilitator systematically loosen problem constraints when consensus stalls, forcing agents to question unexamined assumptions. For instance, if three agents deadlock on whether a rubric should prioritize correctness or process, the facilitator temporarily removes the single-rubric constraint, allowing agents

to explore separate rubrics for formative and summative contexts. The resulting designs often reveal shared criteria that break the original impasse.

- **Analogical transfer**: This includes agents with expertise outside the immediate domain: an agent versed in biological systems might introduce redundancy, self-healing, or evolutionary adaptation concepts into a software architecture discussion. In an educational context, an agent trained on clinical diagnostic reasoning might reframe misconception detection as differential diagnosis: listing candidate misunderstandings, ordering discriminating questions, and ruling out hypotheses. The resulting protocol gives the education-specialist agents a structured diagnostic workflow that they would not have generated from pedagogical literature alone.

A concrete illustration: in a curriculum design task, a pedagogy agent proposes a linear prerequisite chain for teaching recursion. A cognitive science agent, drawing on worked-example research, suggests interleaving recursive and iterative solutions so students build comparative mental models. A software engineering agent adds that real codebases rarely isolate recursion from iteration, supporting the interleaved approach with practical relevance. No single agent would have synthesized this rationale; the combination of domain-specific constraints produced a curriculum structure that outperformed each agent's standalone proposal in simulated assessments. This is synergistic information in practice: the collective output depends on the interaction between agent perspectives, not merely their sum.

The facilitator balances diversity and coherence by monitoring semantic distance between proposals. Too-rapid convergence triggers a perturbation (one agent explores a deliberately unconventional approach). Too much dispersion triggers focused discussion around areas of partial agreement.

These emergence mechanisms are not speculative additions; they are the architectural reason the collective approach justifies its coordination overhead. A system of agents that merely averages independent answers provides modest gains. A system that actively engineers the conditions for synergy (diverse perspectives, structured critique, and deliberate constraint relaxation) produces solutions that no individual agent could reach, making the collective genuinely more than the sum of its parts.

Summary

This chapter explored two complementary approaches to building agents that teach, learn, and transfer knowledge.

The Education Intelligence agent combined knowledge graph curricula, BKT, and adaptive techniques grounded in cognitive science to create a personalized learning system. The programming tutor case study showed these components in production: a two-stage misconception detector, context-aware feedback, and spaced repetition scheduling delivered a 34% improvement in assessment scores and pushed course completion from 71% to 89%.

The Collective Intelligence agent extended multi-agent collaboration into consensus-driven problem solving. Weighted voting with expertise calibration, adversarial critics for groupthink prevention, and cross-pollination for emergent insight produced synthesized designs that consistently outperformed single-agent outputs. The most valuable results came from synergistic interactions between agents with complementary expertise. In the rubric design worked example, a three-agent team (pedagogy, domain expert, assessment) converged on a hybrid evaluation instrument that combined the assessment agent's binary-criteria reliability with the pedagogy agent's partial-credit nuance and the domain expert's edge-case coverage, a result none produced independently.

Together, these architectures illustrate a recurring principle: the most powerful agent systems combine deep domain specialization with systematic feedback loops and collaborative reasoning. Whether teaching a student or solving a design problem, the pattern holds. Perceive the current state, reason about the best next action, act, observe the outcome, and learn. Education and knowledge agents apply this pattern in domains where success is measured not by the agent's own performance but by the growth of the humans it serves.

In the next chapter, we explore agents that bridge digital intelligence and the physical world: embodied agents that reason about physical environments, coordinate robotic systems, and integrate sensor data with cognitive architectures.

Get This Book's PDF Version and Exclusive Extras

Scan the QR code (or go to `packtpub.com/unlock`). Search for this book by name, confirm the edition, and then follow the steps on the page.

UNLOCK NOW

Note: Keep your invoice handy. Purchases made directly from Packt don't require an invoice.

16

Embodied and Physical World Agents

The world is its own best model.

Rodney Brooks, co-founder of iRobot and former director of MIT CSAIL

In 1966, researchers at Stanford set a wheeled robot named Shakey loose in a corridor and watched it reason about pushing blocks. The lesson was immediate: intelligence that acts in the physical world earns every decision against gravity, friction, and consequence. NASA's Sojourner rover crossed Martian terrain three decades later under the same constraint. Today, autonomous drones navigate storms and construction sites with no human at the controls. Each system confirms what Shakey established: intelligence confined to a screen is a different kind of problem entirely.

This qualitative difference creates what we call the physicality constraint. Digital agents operate in environments where state changes are often virtual and reversible. In contrast, physical agents face the uncompromising laws of physics; objects have mass, actuators introduce latency, and sensors produce noisy, imperfect data. Most critically, physical actions are frequently *irreversible*. A robotic arm that drops a fragile component cannot execute an "undo" command. A misrouted emergency vehicle creates immediate, tangible danger.

To make this constraint operational, we can decompose it into three concrete properties. First, **irreversibility**: physical actions cannot be rolled back once executed, so planning must account for worst-case outcomes before committing. Second, **latency**: mechanical actuators, communication links, and sensor pipelines all introduce delays that accumulate in real-time control loops, making timing a hard constraint rather than a quality-of-service preference. Third, **energy limits**: onboard power is finite and non-replenishable mid-mission, so every action carries an energy cost that bounds the feasible plan space.

With this framing in place, we can situate the chapter within the broader arc of the book. Earlier chapters explored agents operating in purely digital environments, querying APIs, reasoning over text, and coordinating multi-agent pipelines. This chapter extends that foundation into the physical world, where actions carry weight, mass, and consequence.

In this chapter, we'll be covering the following topics:

- The Embodied Intelligence agent
- The Domain-Transforming Integration agent

Technical requirements

To run the examples in this chapter, you will need the following:

- Python 3.10 or later
- The following Python packages: langchain==0.2.16, langchain-openai==0.1.23, langgraph==0.1.4, openai==1.40.0, pydantic==2.8.2, and python-dotenv==1.0.1
- An OpenAI API key with access to the gpt-4o model

All code examples for this chapter are available in the book's GitHub repository at `https://github.com/PacktPublishing/30-Agents-Every-AI-Engineer-Must-Build/chapter16`

Architectural foundations: The depth–breadth divide

Physical-world agents confront two distinct problems that no single architectural pattern can serve simultaneously. The first is depth: controlling a single physical system with millisecond precision, hard safety guarantees, and deterministic feedback. The second is breadth: coordinating heterogeneous infrastructure systems whose states influence one another across incompatible time scales. Because depth and breadth impose contradictory requirements on any architecture that attempts to address them, two distinct designs are necessary.

In this domain, the cost of failure is measured in human safety and material loss rather than server errors or caught exceptions. Architectural patterns must reflect this high-stakes reality.

This high-stakes reality demands a specific architectural response. Traditional robotics relies on rigid, pre-programmed behaviors. Modern agentic architectures shift this paradigm toward **adaptive, goal-directed reasoning**. This transition introduces a fundamental architectural challenge: the integration of high-latency reasoning with low-latency control.

We solve this through the asymmetric control loop. This pattern separates the system into two distinct layers:

- **Reasoning layer:** An asynchronous agent (often LLM-based) that processes high-level intent and environmental context to generate a plan
- **Deterministic controller:** A synchronous, real-time loop that executes the plan while enforcing hard safety constraints

By utilizing this hierarchy, an operator can describe a mission objective in plain language. The agentic system translates that intent into a safe, constraint-respecting set of physical actions. The agent provides the "why" and "what," while the deterministic controller manages the "how" within the bounds of physical safety.

The handoff from the reasoning layer to the deterministic controller is governed by bounded plan parameters. The reasoning layer produces a plan with an explicit time horizon, typically 1 to 10 seconds of look-ahead at the task-planning rate, and each action in the plan is expressed as a parameterized command within a predefined action envelope: target position, velocity limit, force ceiling, and workspace boundary. The deterministic controller accepts only commands that fall within these bounds; any action outside the envelope is rejected before execution, and the reasoning layer is notified to replan.

Before examining each architecture in detail, it is worth understanding why a single agent design cannot serve both roles. Physical-world intelligence confronts two distinct problems that impose contradictory requirements on the system that attempts to solve them: the depth and the breadth problem.

The **depth problem** is about controlling a single physical system with the precision, speed, and safety guarantees that hardware demands. A warehouse robot picking items from shelves must fuse noisy sensor data into a coherent world model, plan collision-free trajectories, execute those trajectories within millisecond control loops, and halt immediately if a human enters its workspace. Every layer of this stack operates under strict latency budgets. The reasoning is deep (multiple abstraction levels from strategic goals to motor currents) but narrow (confined to one robot in one physical domain).

The second is the **breadth problem**: coordinating multiple infrastructure systems whose states influence one another through measurable but complex transfer functions. A city's transportation network, electrical grid, water supply, and emergency services do not evolve independently. A power outage disables traffic signals, which increases congestion, which delays ambulance response times, which raises mortality risk. No single-domain controller can reason about these cascading interactions. The reasoning here is broad (spanning heterogeneous systems with different physics, time scales, and regulatory constraints) but comparatively slow (decisions unfold over minutes, hours, or policy cycles rather than milliseconds).

The depth and breadth problems are illustrated in *Figure 16.1*.

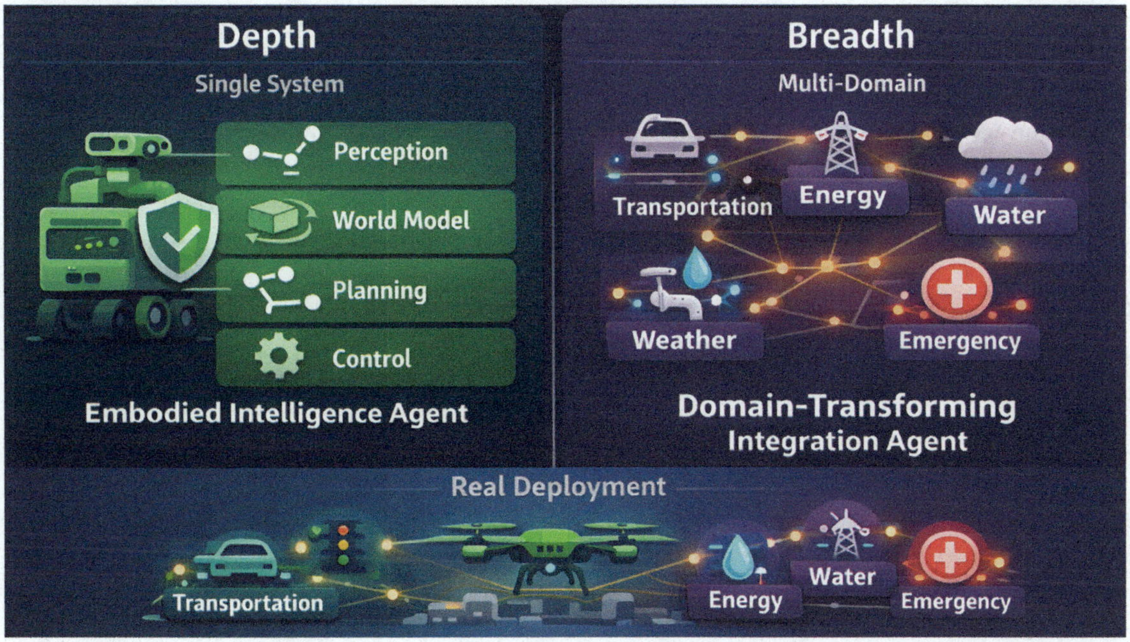

Figure 16.1 – The depth and breadth problem

These two problems demand fundamentally different architectural responses. Depth requires tight, fast, single-domain control with hard real-time guarantees. Breadth requires loose, deliberative, cross-domain coordination with tolerance for uncertainty and latency. An architecture optimized for one fails at the other. A servo loop running at 1 kHz cannot pause to query a weather API. A cross-domain knowledge graph traversal cannot guarantee sub-millisecond actuation. Attempting to collapse both into a single control loop produces a system that is too slow for safe physical control and too rigid for cross-domain reasoning.

Consider a concrete scenario: an autonomous vehicle navigating a smart city during a severe thunderstorm. The vehicle itself is an embodied agent. It must track lane markings through rain-degraded camera feeds, maintain safe following distances on wet pavement (where braking distances increase by 40% or more), and execute evasive maneuvers if a pedestrian steps into the road. These are depth problems: tight perception-action loops, sub-second planning horizons, hard safety invariants. The vehicle's onboard system handles them through a layered control hierarchy that separates strategic route planning from real-time trajectory tracking and from servo-level motor control.

But the storm also creates breadth problems that no single vehicle can solve alone. The city's traffic management system must reroute thousands of vehicles away from flooded intersections. The electrical grid operator must manage load as lightning strikes knock out substations, which in turn disables traffic signals at downstream intersections. Emergency services must reposition ambulances based on predicted accident hotspots created by the combination of reduced visibility and increased congestion. These cross-domain interactions (weather affecting power, power affecting traffic, traffic affecting emergency response) require an Integration agent that maintains a structured model of inter-domain dependencies and propagates influence estimates across the network.

The two architectures are therefore complementary. The **Embodied Intelligence agent** solves the depth problem: it bridges the gap between high-level reasoning and low-level physical actuation within a single domain, enforcing safety invariants at every layer of a multi-rate control hierarchy. The **Domain-Transforming Integration agent** solves the breadth problem: it coordinates heterogeneous infrastructure systems through a typed knowledge graph that encodes cross-domain dependencies, enabling influence propagation and cascade estimation across system boundaries. Real-world deployments require both simultaneously. The case study that closes this chapter demonstrates exactly this synthesis: an autonomous drone that must execute precise physical flight (depth) while integrating constraints from weather, airspace, energy, and hazard domains (breadth).

The sections that follow examine each architecture in detail: the Embodied Intelligence agent, which addresses the depth problem, and the Domain-Transforming Integration agent, which addresses the breadth problem.

The Embodied Intelligence agent

The Embodied Intelligence agent is a layered control architecture that bridges abstract reasoning and physical actuation within a single domain. It decomposes agent responsibility across four layers: strategic reasoning, model maintenance, real-time control, and safety enforcement, each operating at a distinct time scale. This section explains the architecture, its mathematical foundations, and its implementation in LangChain, covering the control hierarchy, world model, and safety constraints that make physical-world operation reliable.

The challenge of connecting reasoning to physical action has defined robotics for over six decades. In 1961, General Motors installed **Unimate**, the first industrial robot, on its assembly line in Ewing, New Jersey. Unimate operated from fixed sequences: a set of pre-recorded joint positions replayed in a loop. It had no perception, no planning, and no capacity to adapt. If a part arrived 2 centimeters off position, the robot continued its programmed motion regardless, producing defects or damaging itself. This brittleness was acceptable in a tightly controlled factory cell, but it made autonomous operation in unstructured environments impossible.

The next generation pursued the opposite extreme. In 1986, Rodney Brooks published his **subsumption architecture**, arguing that intelligent behavior could emerge from layers of simple reactive rules without any central planner or world model. A robot built on subsumption responds directly to sensor inputs: if obstacle detected, turn; if clear path, advance. This approach produced surprisingly robust navigation in cluttered environments, but it could not handle tasks requiring deliberation. A subsumption robot that encounters a locked door will repeatedly attempt to push through it. It has no mechanism to reason that a key exists in another room, plan a detour, and return.

Modern LLM-augmented robotics systems attempt to resolve this tension by combining high-level semantic reasoning with low-level reactive control. The fundamental problem remains the same one that separated Unimate from Brooks's robots: how do you connect deliberation (which is slow, uncertain, and operates over abstract goals) to physical actuation (which must be fast, deterministic, and constrained by the laws of physics)? Every embodied system, from a warehouse mobile robot to a surgical manipulator to an autonomous aircraft, faces this identical architectural question. The answer determines whether the system can operate safely and effectively in environments where plans must adapt in real time.

Consider a concrete instance: a warehouse robot receives the command "move package A to shelf B." This single instruction conceals a cascade of computational problems. The robot must locate package A using its onboard cameras and lidar, which produce noisy depth estimates that disagree near reflective surfaces. It must plan a path from its current position to the package that avoids shelving units, other robots, and human workers, any of whom may move unpredictably. It must compute a grasp strategy that accounts for the package's weight, center of mass, and surface friction. It must then navigate to shelf B while carrying the package (which changes the robot's dynamics: higher center of gravity, different braking profile). And throughout this entire sequence, it must guarantee that if any sensor detects a human within its safety perimeter, it halts within 100 milliseconds. The architecture that makes this possible is the subject of this section.

An embodied agent operates in a continuous, partially observable dynamical system under strict real-time constraints. State evolves according to physical laws. Sensors provide noisy and incomplete observations. Actions introduce latency, momentum, and irreversible effects. Unlike purely digital agents, embodied systems cannot rely on transactional rollback. Control decisions must preserve safety invariants as the system evolves over time.

The agent maintains a belief state *b(s)*, a probability distribution over possible world states, updated as new observations arrive. Planning occurs over this belief space. Execution, however, occurs in deterministic control loops that approximate the current state estimate. This separation is essential. Probabilistic reasoning informs action selection at higher layers. Real-time control enforces stability at lower layers. Formally, the agent interacts with the environment as a continuous **Partially Observable Markov Decision Process (POMDP)**.

POMDP is a mathematical framework for decision-making when the agent cannot observe the full state of the world. In a standard Markov decision process, the agent knows exactly where it is and what surrounds it. Physical robots rarely enjoy this luxury. A warehouse robot knows its own position (from wheel encoders and inertial sensors) but cannot see behind shelving units, cannot determine the exact weight of an unscanned package, and cannot predict when a human worker will step into its aisle. The robot therefore maintains a belief state $b(s)$: a probability distribution over all possible configurations of the world, updated each time new sensor data arrives. Planning in a POMDP selects actions that perform well across the range of plausible states, not just the single most likely one. This is why a well-designed warehouse robot slows down near blind corners: the belief state assigns non-trivial probability to a human being present just out of sight.

In practice, belief state updates are computed using particle filters or Bayesian filtering. A particle filter represents $b(s)$ as a weighted set of sampled states; each new sensor observation reweights and resamples the set, collapsing probability mass toward states consistent with what the robot observed. Extended Kalman filters serve the same role when the state space is continuous and the dynamics are approximately linear. Both approaches run at the sensor polling rate (typically 10 to 100 Hz), keeping the belief state current without blocking the higher-level planning layers.

An operator may issue a goal such as "move package A to shelf B." The embodied agent must decompose that instruction into admissible physical actions, ensure each action respects safety constraints, and execute them within millisecond latency budgets. The design therefore separates four responsibilities:

- **Strategic reasoning** over goals and plans
- **Model maintenance** over physical state and constraints
- **Real-time control** of trajectories and actuators
- **Safety enforcement** as an unconditional override layer

This decomposition preserves stability and limits the blast radius of failures.

The following subsections develop each component of this architecture in turn: the control hierarchy that separates time scales, the world model that grounds planning in physical state, the multi-rate perception-action loop that integrates them, and the LangChain implementation patterns that translate the design into deployable code.

Control hierarchy as time scale decomposition

This subsection examines the control hierarchy that structures embodied agent operation, showing how responsibility is distributed across layers running at different time scales to achieve both strategic flexibility and real-time safety.

Robotic control systems implement this separation through a hierarchy of abstraction levels, each operating at a distinct frequency. Higher layers reason symbolically and plan over seconds. Lower layers regulate torque and current at kilohertz rates.

Level	Abstraction	Frequency	Algorithm Class
Task Planning	Symbolic goals	0.1–1 Hz	PDDL planners, LLM reasoning

Level	Abstraction	Frequency	Algorithm Class
Motion Planning	Collision-free paths	1–10 Hz	RRT, PRM, optimization methods
Trajectory Control	Time-parameterized path	50–200 Hz	PID, model predictive control
Servo Control	Motor currents	1–10 kHz	Current and torque loops

Table 16.1 – Control hierarchy layers with operating frequencies, algorithm classes, and latency budgets

The frequency column in the table describes how many times per second each layer executes its decision loop. 1 Hz means one cycle per second; 1 kHz means one thousand cycles per second. The numbers reflect the urgency of each layer's responsibilities.

Task planning runs at 0.1 to 1 Hz because deciding "which package to pick next" is a strategic choice that can afford one to ten seconds of deliberation. Motion planning runs faster, at 1 to 10 Hz, because a collision-free path must be recomputed whenever obstacles move.

Trajectory control at 50 to 200 Hz ensures the robot's arm tracks its intended path smoothly. At 100 Hz, the controller corrects deviations every 10 milliseconds, which is fast enough to maintain precision during continuous motion.

The servo layer at 1 to 10 kHz regulates motor currents directly, rejecting electrical and mechanical disturbances within fractions of a millisecond. If the servo loop ran at only 1 Hz, a motor experiencing unexpected resistance would oscillate wildly or stall before any correction arrived.

The multi-rate control hierarchy is illustrated in *Figure 16.2*, which maps each layer's operating frequency to its algorithmic role: task planning at sub-Hertz rates, motion planning at 1–10 Hz, trajectory control at 50–200 Hz, and servo-level current regulation at 1–10 kHz. Each band reflects the latency budget of its layer, from seconds of strategic deliberation to fractions of a millisecond for disturbance rejection.

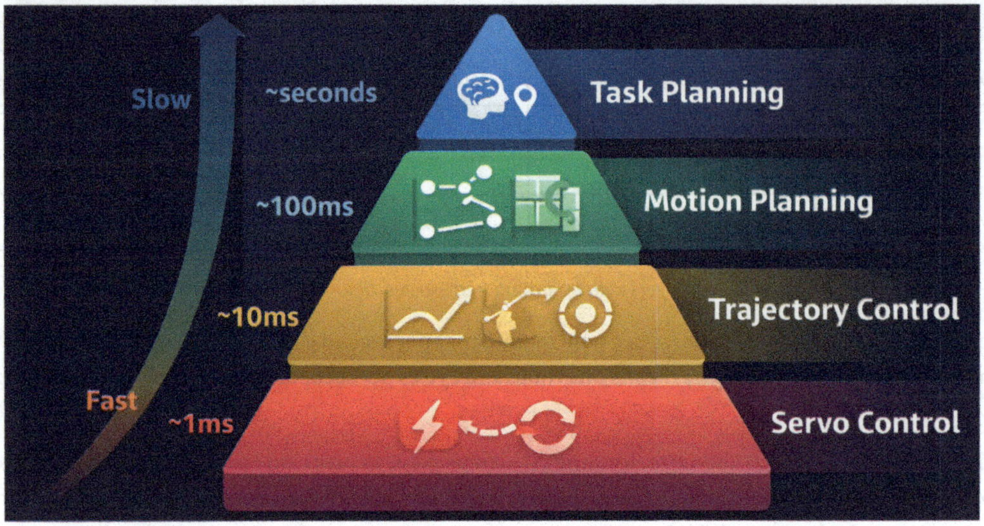

Figure 16.2 – The multi-rate control hierarchy of an Embodied Intelligence agent

Each layer operates at a distinct frequency band, from task planning (0.1–1 Hz) to servo-level current regulation (1–10 kHz). Higher layers reason over goals and plans; lower layers enforce physical stability and reject disturbances in real time.

This hierarchy is not stylistic. It enforces stability. The servo layer must reject disturbances within milliseconds to prevent oscillation or hardware damage. Trajectory control maintains smooth tracking. Motion planners compute feasible paths under geometric constraints. Task planners reason over discrete objectives. Each layer exposes a constrained interface to the one above it.

The following code block illustrates the lower three layers from *Table 16.1* that have no LLM involvement. Each function accepts inputs consistent with its layer's frequency and algorithm class, and returns outputs consumed by the layer above. These are simplified skeletons; production implementations depend on hardware-specific drivers and real-time operating system primitives.

```
# Pseudocode: Lower-layer control skeletons: motion planning, trajectory control, and
servo regulation

# --- Motion Planning Layer (1-10 Hz, RRT/PRM) ---
def plan_motion_trajectory(goal_pose, world_model, obstacles):
    """Compute a collision-free path from current pose to goal.
    Frequency: 1-10 Hz.  Algorithm class: RRT*, PRM."""
    current_pose = world_model.get_current_state()["pose"]
    path = rrt_star(current_pose, goal_pose, obstacles)
    return path  # List of waypoints for trajectory layer


# --- Trajectory Control Layer (50-200 Hz, PID/MPC) ---
```

```
def compute_trajectory_setpoints(path, dt=0.005):
    """Time-parameterise the path into setpoints at the
    control frequency.  Frequency: 50-200 Hz.
    Algorithm class: PID, model predictive control."""
    for waypoint in interpolate(path, dt):
        error = waypoint - read_encoder_pose()
        torque = pid_controller.compute(error, dt)
        yield torque  # consumed by servo layer


# --- Servo Control Layer (1-10 kHz, current loops) ---
def servo_control_loop(torque_setpoint, dt=0.0001):
    """Regulate motor current to achieve commanded torque.
    Frequency: 1-10 kHz.  Rejects electrical and
    mechanical disturbances within fractions of a ms."""
    current = read_motor_current()
    target_current = torque_to_current(torque_setpoint)
    pwm_signal = current_pid.compute(
        target_current - current, dt
    )
    write_pwm(pwm_signal)
```

The embodied agent interacts primarily at the task-planning level. Structured commands pass through a control interface that translates symbolic intent into admissible motion goals. In deployed systems, this interface integrates with middleware such as ROS2, which provides publish-subscribe messaging, action servers for long-running tasks, and time synchronization across distributed nodes. Middleware here functions as real-time distributed infrastructure, not merely as a convenience API.

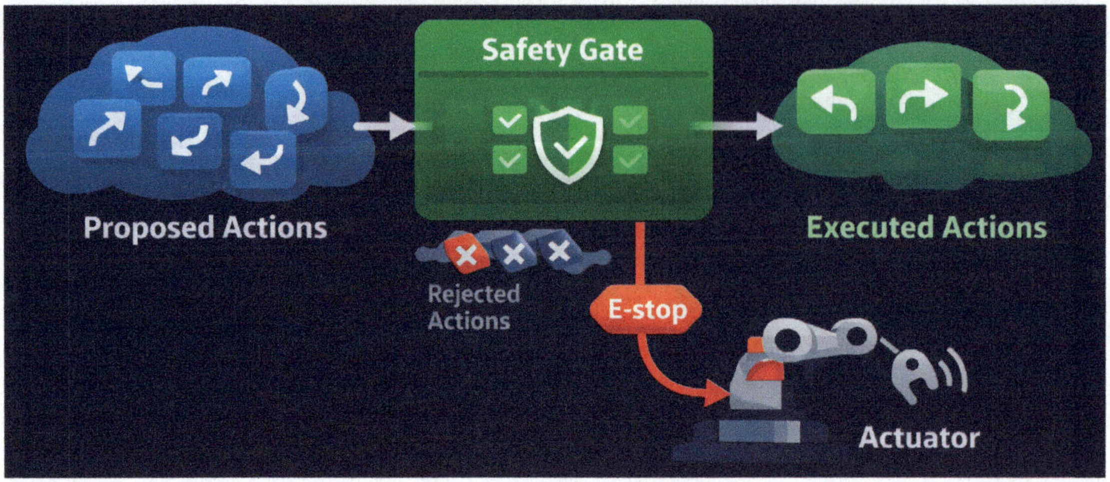

Figure 16.3 – The layered command interface from LLM reasoning to actuators. Safety enforcement intercepts every command against the admissible action set A_safe(s) before execution; ROS2 provides time-synchronized messaging between layers.

Figure 16.3 shows that the safety enforcement layer sits between the control interface and the actuators, not alongside the reasoning layer. This placement is deliberate: safety is not an emergent property of correct planning. It is an explicit restriction on the set of actions the system may execute. Every command must pass through validation before reaching actuators. Validation enforces workspace bounds, force limits, velocity constraints, and system state checks. Commands that violate these constraints are rejected before execution.

The admissible action set A_safe(s) defines the outer boundary; the hardware emergency stop mechanism is the unconditional override that enforces it at the hardware level. It operates outside the command pipeline, bypassing all software layers to halt actuation immediately. Where A_safe(s) constrains the agent's choices, the emergency stop supersedes them entirely. This boundary defines where human authority overrides autonomous control; in safety-critical systems, this override path must remain simple, direct, and independent of higher-level reasoning.

Conceptually, the safety layer defines an admissible action set *A_safe(s)*. Planning operates within this set. Control never executes actions outside it. This constraint-based framing aligns safety with control theory rather than post hoc validation.

World model as a physics engine

The `Model` component maintains a structured representation of the warehouse environment. For the robot executing "move package A to shelf B," this means not raw camera frames or lidar point clouds, but inferred object states: the estimated pose of package A, the occupied and free regions around shelf B, and the spatial relationships between the robot, the package, and every shelving unit in the aisle. These inferred states are what the planning layers query; sensor data is never exposed directly.

Spatial reasoning for the warehouse robot includes estimating the pose of package A from noisy depth returns (with special handling near the reflective surface of adjacent metal shelving), computing bounding volumes for collision detection against shelving units and other robots, and tracking free-space corridors as human workers move through the aisle. Physics reasoning covers whether package A is placeable on shelf B: stability holds only if the projection of the package's center of mass remains within its support polygon and the equilibrium conditions are satisfied.

$$\sum F_i = 0, \ \sum \tau_i = 0 \sum F_i = 0, \ \sum \tau_i = 0$$

These constraints are evaluated before manipulation or placement actions.

The world model exposes queryable methods that the planning layers call directly. Before the robot attempts to grasp package A, the planner queries grasp difficulty, returning a higher cost estimate when the package is wedged near a reflective surface that degrades depth accuracy. Before navigating to shelf B, the planner queries collision status along the intended path. The result is encapsulation: all physics and geometry reasoning is centralized in the world model, and the planner issues structured queries rather than interpreting raw sensor data itself.

In production systems, this model may integrate learned perception modules, analytic geometry, and physics simulators. Regardless of implementation details, the invariant remains: no action is executed without being evaluated against a coherent internal representation of the world.

Multi-rate perception–action integration

The embodied agent executes as a multi-rate *perception–action* loop. Fast loops handle sensing and safety checks. Intermediate loops track trajectories. Slow loops perform replanning and high-level reasoning. Expensive computations never block safety-critical reactions.

At each control cycle:

- Sensor data updates the world model
- Safety monitors evaluate invariants
- The next admissible command is selected from the current plan
- Dispatches the command to lower layers

If a safety violation occurs, execution halts immediately. If the environment invalidates the current plan, the strategic layer replans asynchronously, while the inner loop maintains safe behavior.

This separation of time scales is the defining architectural pattern of embodied intelligence. Fast loops enforce physical constraints unconditionally. Slow loops interpret goals, resolve uncertainty, and coordinate subsystems. Stability and safety derive from respecting this hierarchy.

The Embodied Intelligence agent is therefore not a single algorithm. It is a layered control architecture that bridges belief-space reasoning and irreversible physical action, while preserving invariants across time scales.

> **Note**
>
> Going forward, the code blocks are labeled as numbered listings to make cross-referencing easier, as several implementations build on one another.

Implementation: LangChain embodied agent patterns

The four-responsibility decomposition (strategic reasoning, model maintenance, real-time control, safety enforcement) translates directly into a LangChain agent with specialized tools. The core problem is this: how does an LLM-based reasoning layer issue commands to a physical robot without bypassing the safety and control layers that protect the hardware? The answer is tool-mediated indirection. The LLM never controls actuators directly. It invokes tools that query the world model, tools that submit commands through a validated control interface, and tools that check safety constraints before any physical action executes.

Before examining individual listings, the following shared setup defines the interface stubs and global instances that all subsequent code examples in this chapter reference. These are architectural scaffolds specifying each component's interface contract. Production systems would replace them with hardware-specific implementations.

```
# Listing 16.1: Common setup: shared interface stubs for all chapter listings
"""Common setup for Chapter 16 listings.
These stubs define the interface contracts that all subsequent
listings reference.  They are architectural scaffolds, not
production implementations."""

from langchain_core.messages import HumanMessage


class WorldModel:
    """Maintains belief state b(s) over robot and environment."""
    def query(self, query: str) -> dict:
        raise NotImplementedError

    def get_current_state(self) -> dict:
        raise NotImplementedError

    def update(self, observations: dict) -> None:
        raise NotImplementedError


class ControlInterface:
    """Dispatches validated commands to the deterministic
    controller (50-200 Hz loop)."""
    def execute(self, *args, **kwargs) -> object:
        raise NotImplementedError


class SafetyMonitor:
    """Validates actions against A_safe(s) before execution."""
```

```
    def validate(self, action, target_or_state) -> object:
        raise NotImplementedError

    def halt(self, reason: str = "") -> None:
        raise NotImplementedError


def extract_actions(plan) -> list:
    """Parse proposed actions from agent plan output."""
    raise NotImplementedError


# --- Stubs for Domain-Transforming Integration Agent (Listings 16.3-16.4) ---
class _EnergyAPI:
    def get_substations(self, region: str) -> list:
        raise NotImplementedError


class _TrafficAPI:
    def get_network(self, region: str) -> list:
        raise NotImplementedError


class _KnowledgeGraph:
    def add_edge(self, src, tgt, rel, weight) -> dict:
        raise NotImplementedError


world_model = WorldModel()
control_interface = ControlInterface()
safety_monitor = SafetyMonitor()
energy_api = _EnergyAPI()
traffic_api = _TrafficAPI()
knowledge_graph = _KnowledgeGraph()
```

Listing 16.2 demonstrates how the four-responsibility decomposition maps onto a LangChain agent, showing the tool-mediated boundary that prevents the LLM reasoning layer from bypassing safety and control.

```
# Listing 16.2: Embodied agent with four-responsibility tool decomposition
from langchain_core.tools import tool
from langchain_openai import ChatOpenAI
from langgraph.prebuilt import create_react_agent

# --- Model Maintenance: query the world model ---
```

```
@tool
def query_world_model(query: str) -> dict:
    """Query the robot's world model for object poses,
    collision status, or grasp difficulty estimates."""
    return world_model.query(query)

# --- Real-Time Control: dispatch validated commands ---
@tool
def dispatch_motion_command(target: str, action: str) -> dict:
    """Submit a motion command through the control interface.
    Safety validation occurs before dispatch."""
    return control_interface.execute(target, action)

# --- Safety Enforcement: validate before execution ---
@tool
def check_safety_constraints(action: str, target: str) -> dict:
    """Validate an action against the admissible action set.
    Checks workspace bounds, force limits, velocity caps."""
    return safety_monitor.validate(action, target)

# --- Strategic Reasoning: LLM agent with tool access ---
llm = ChatOpenAI(model="gpt-4o", temperature=0.0)
tools = [
    query_world_model,
    dispatch_motion_command,
    check_safety_constraints
]
embodied_agent = create_react_agent(llm, tools)
```

Each tool maps to exactly one responsibility in the architectural decomposition. The LLM serves as the strategic reasoning layer: it interprets the operator's goal, queries the world model to assess the current state, checks safety constraints before committing to an action, and dispatches validated commands through the control interface. Crucially, the LLM cannot bypass the safety layer. The tool architecture enforces the same trust boundary described in the prose: the reasoning layer proposes, but the deterministic controller (mediated by the control interface and safety monitor) disposes.

The second implementation problem is the action execution loop itself. In a physical system, the agent cannot simply call a tool and wait for a result. It must validate every command against the admissible action set, handle rejection gracefully, and maintain safe behavior if the environment changes between planning and execution. The following code demonstrates this pattern.

```
# Listing 16.3: Safety-constrained action execution loop
def execute_with_safety(agent, task: str, world_model, safety_monitor):
    """Execute an embodied task with pre-execution safety
```

```
    validation and continuous monitoring."""
    # Step 1: Agent reasons about the task and proposes actions
    plan = agent.invoke({"messages": [HumanMessage(task)]})

    # Step 2: Extract proposed actions from agent output
    actions = extract_actions(plan)

    # Step 3: Validate each action against A_safe(s)
    for action in actions:
        state = world_model.get_current_state()
        validation = safety_monitor.validate(
            action, state
        )

        if not validation.is_safe:
            # Rejected: replan with constraint feedback
            plan = agent.invoke({"messages": [
                HumanMessage(
                    f"Action rejected: {validation.reason}. "
                    f"Replan within: {validation.constraints}"
                )
            ]})
            continue

        # Step 4: Execute validated action
        result = control_interface.execute(action)
        world_model.update(result.observations)

        # Step 4b: timeout and actuator feedback validation
        try:
            result = control_interface.execute(action, timeout=5.0)
            if not result.actuator_ok:
                # Actuator reported fault; halt and surface for replanning
                safety_monitor.halt(reason=result.fault_code)
                break
            world_model.update(result.observations)
        except TimeoutError:
            # Execution did not complete within timeout; production systems
            # require fuller error trees (retry, degrade, emergency stop).
            safety_monitor.halt(reason="execution_timeout")
            break
```

The execution loop implements the constraint-based safety pattern from the architectural prose. Before any action reaches the control interface, the safety monitor validates it against the admissible action set *A_safe(s)* evaluated at the current world state. If validation fails, the agent does not proceed blindly. Instead, the rejection reason and the active constraints are fed back to the LLM, which replans within the tighter boundary. This feedback loop is the implementation-level equivalent of the unconditional safety override described in the architecture: the agent may reason freely, but only admissible actions cross the boundary into physical execution. After each successful action, the world model updates from fresh sensor observations, ensuring the next planning cycle operates on the current state rather than stale assumptions.

> **Note**
>
> **When Robots Meet the Real World: The Kiva Systems Revolution**
>
> In 2012, Amazon paid $775 million for Kiva Systems, a startup that had built squat orange robots to shuttle shelving units across warehouse floors. Skeptics questioned the price tag. The robots were slow, limited to flat surfaces, and could only operate in carefully mapped environments. But Kiva's founders understood something the robotics establishment had overlooked: in logistics, reliability at scale matters more than capability at the edge. A robot that successfully completes 99.8% of simple fetch tasks across a fleet of 800 units moves more product than a dozen sophisticated arms that fail unpredictably. By 2024, Amazon had deployed over 750,000 robotic units across its fulfillment network, rebranded as Amazon Robotics. The architectural lesson endures. The warehouse coordination system in this chapter reflects the same principle: fleet-level orchestration, conservative safety margins, and graceful degradation when individual robots fail.

The Embodied Intelligence agent solves a specific and demanding problem: bridging the gap between abstract reasoning and physical actuation within a single domain. Its multi-rate control hierarchy, belief-state planning, and admissible action enforcement together produce a system that can translate high-level goals into safe, real-time physical behavior. Within the boundaries of one robot, one warehouse, or one surgical suite, this architecture is sufficient.

But single-domain sufficiency becomes a limitation when the domain itself depends on external systems. The warehouse robot's performance degrades if the building's HVAC system fails and temperature rises beyond sensor operating range. A surgical robot's scheduling depends on hospital power grid reliability, sterilization cycles, and patient transport logistics. An autonomous vehicle's route planning is constrained by traffic signal timing, road maintenance schedules, and weather forecasts that originate far outside its onboard perception stack. In each case, the embodied agent operates within a single control loop, but the constraints that bound its behavior originate from multiple interacting infrastructure domains. The Embodied Intelligence agent has no mechanism to model these cross-domain dependencies, propagate influence estimates across system boundaries, or reason about how a disruption in one domain cascades into another.

This is the limitation that motivates the second architecture. The Domain-Transforming Integration agent operates at a fundamentally different scale: not deep within one physical system, but broadly across multiple coupled infrastructure systems. Where the Embodied Intelligence agent prioritizes speed, determinism, and tight feedback within a single domain, the Domain-Transforming Integration agent prioritizes breadth, systemic coherence, and the ability to reason about how heterogeneous systems influence one another. Together, these two architectures define the complete design space for autonomous systems that must act safely in the physical world while reasoning coherently across the infrastructures that world depends on.

The Domain-Transforming Integration agent

The Embodied Intelligence agent coordinates perception, planning, and actuation within a single physical domain. The Domain-Transforming Integration agent operates at a different scale. It coordinates multiple partially coupled dynamical systems, each with its own state variables, control laws, time scales, and regulatory constraints. Transportation, energy, water, environment, and public safety do not evolve independently. Their states influence one another through measurable transfer functions.

The integration problem is therefore not data aggregation; it is stability management across heterogeneous, interacting systems.

The following subsections develop the Domain-Transforming Integration agent from its mathematical foundations through to implementation: the coupled dynamical system model and its calibration, the typed knowledge graph that encodes cross-domain structure, influence propagation over that graph, and the LangChain agent patterns that realize the architecture in code.

Coupled heterogeneous dynamical systems

Each domain i can be modeled as a dynamical system with internal evolution and cross-domain perturbations:

$$\frac{dx_i}{dt} = f_i(x_i, u_i) + \sum_j g_{ij}(x_j)$$

$$\frac{dx_i}{dt} = f_i(x_i, u_i) + \sum_j g_{ij}(x_j)$$

The following variables define the coupled system model introduced in the equation above:

- x_i is the state vector of domain i
- u_i represents exogenous inputs or control actions
- f_i encodes internal, often nonlinear dynamics
- g_{ij} captures coupling from domain j to domain i

The functions f_i and g_{ij} are generally nonlinear and time-varying. Electrical load follows thermodynamic and market dynamics. Traffic density evolves according to fluid-like flow equations. Water pressure obeys hydraulic constraints. Cross-domain couplings may amplify or dampen disturbances.

Poorly calibrated g_{ij} terms can introduce oscillations that do not exist in any individual subsystem. Stability of the integrated system is not guaranteed by the stability of its parts.

Calibrating the coupling functions g_{ij} therefore requires three steps:

- **Domain-expert seeding**: Engineers with knowledge of each system boundary propose initial coupling weights based on historical incident data or known physical relationships (for example, the traffic throughput reduction observed at signal-free intersections during past outages)

- **Sensitivity analysis**: Run the simulation with g_{ij} perturbed across a range around each seed value to identify which couplings dominate system behavior and therefore warrant tighter bounds.
- **Iterative refinement**: Simulate outputs and compare them against historical cross-domain events (hindcasting), and adjust coupling weights until the model reproduces observed cascade patterns within an acceptable error margin.

The Integration agent must therefore maintain a model of both intra-domain evolution and inter-domain coupling.

A concrete instantiation clarifies the equation's components. Consider two coupled domains in a city: transportation and energy. Let $x_{\text{transport}}$ represent average vehicle density on arterial roads (vehicles per kilometer). Let x_{energy} represent electrical grid load in megawatts. The internal dynamics $f_{\text{transport}}$ model how traffic density evolves according to flow equations: vehicles enter from on-ramps, exit at off-ramps, and density propagates as a wave through the network.

The coupling function $g_{\text{transport,energy}}$ captures how a change in x_{energy} perturbs transportation: when a substation fails and grid load drops, traffic signals at 14 downstream intersections lose power, forcing them into default flashing-red mode. Signal-free intersections reduce throughput by approximately 60%, causing $x_{\text{transport}}$ to spike in that corridor. The coupling also operates in reverse: $g_{\text{energy,transport}}$ models how a surge in traffic density increases electrical demand as more vehicles idle at intersections, HVAC systems in stopped vehicles draw power from charging stations, and emergency rerouting activates additional signal infrastructure. Neither domain's dynamics can be understood in isolation.

Structural topology: The domain knowledge graph

The discrete structure of cross-domain influence is captured as a typed heterogeneous graph: In the city/storm scenario, this graph encodes the dependency network the Integration agent must reason over. Substation-7 (energy domain) connects via a "powers" edge to TrafficController-12 (transportation domain), which connects via "governs" edges to the intersections it controls. Each edge carries a weight reflecting nominal coupling strength.

$$G = (V, E)_{G} = (V, E)$$

- V: typed entities across domains
- E: typed, weighted, and optionally directional relations

This graph encodes topology, not dynamics. It specifies which entities can influence which others and with what nominal strength. Nodes carry domain-specific metrics. Edges represent relations such as `powers`, `monitors`, `affects`, or `depends_on`.

Temporal annotations convert the graph from a static registry into a live representation. Each entity state is timestamped. Relations may have time-varying weights derived from historical data or learned models.

This structure serves two purposes:

- It defines the allowable pathways for cross-domain propagation.
- It provides an inspectable and auditable representation of system dependencies.

Explainability follows directly from graph structure. When the agent reports that a substation failure affects traffic signals and emergency response times, it can trace the exact path of influence through typed edges.

Influence propagation and impact estimation

Exact evaluation of the coupled dynamical system is often computationally infeasible in real time. The Integration agent therefore uses approximate influence propagation over the graph topology. When a lightning strike disables Substation-7 in the city scenario, the agent cannot simulate every downstream consequence in real time. Instead, it propagates estimated impact outward through the graph: the edge weight from Substation-7 to TrafficController-12 scales the initial disruption signal, and subsequent edges to downstream intersections attenuate it further.

A weighted breadth-first traversal with multiplicative attenuation provides a first-order estimate of impact strength. Starting from a source entity, influence propagates along outgoing edges. At each hop, strength is scaled by the edge weight. Propagation stops when the influence falls below a threshold.

This procedure approximates linearized influence in the neighborhood of the current operating point. It does not replace full dynamical simulation. It provides fast, explainable estimates suitable for operational decision support.

Attenuation is not cosmetic. It prevents spurious amplification across long dependency chains and acts as a stability heuristic in the absence of full nonlinear integration.

Simulation as a controlled approximation

For scenario analysis, the Integration agent advances domain states in discrete time using calibrated domain models. A simulation step performs two phases: In the city/storm scenario, the energy domain advances substation load and outage propagation, while the transportation domain advances vehicle density and signal state, with the coupling terms linking the two so that a simulated substation failure simultaneously degrades traffic throughput in the affected corridor.

- Compute cross-domain coupling terms based on current states
- Advance each domain using its internal model augmented by those coupling inputs

Each domain model may operate at a different temporal resolution. The simulator therefore acts as a coarse-grained integrator rather than a real-time controller.

Calibration is essential. Coupling parameters must be estimated from historical data and validated through hindcasting against known cross-domain events. Sensitivity analysis identifies which couplings dominate system behavior and therefore require tighter bounds.

Simulation outputs are exploratory. They inform policy and contingency planning. They do not guarantee predictive certainty.

Contrast with the Embodied Intelligence agent

The Embodied Intelligence agent operates deeply within a single domain under millisecond control constraints. Its challenge is real-time stability under physical actuation.

The Domain-Transforming Integration agent operates broadly across domains with heterogeneous time scales ranging from milliseconds to years. Its challenge is systemic coherence under coupling and distributed uncertainty.

One architecture prioritizes depth and tight feedback. The other prioritizes breadth and coordinated adaptation. Together, they define the foundation for autonomous systems that must both act safely in the physical world and reason coherently across the infrastructures that world depends on.

LangChain integration agent patterns

The Domain-Transforming Integration agent faces an implementation problem distinct from the Embodied Intelligence agent. Rather than controlling a single physical system through a layered control hierarchy, it must construct and maintain a cross-domain knowledge graph from heterogeneous data sources and then propagate influence estimates through that graph to support operational decisions. In LangChain, this translates into two agent patterns: a graph construction agent that uses tool-calling to query domain-specific APIs and assemble typed nodes and edges, and an influence propagation agent that traverses the constructed graph to estimate cascade impacts.

The graph formalism $G = (V, E)$ maps directly onto a two-role tool set: the domain query tools populate V with typed entities, and the `register_cross_domain_edge` tool populates E with the weighted, directional relations between them.

The following listing implements the graph construction phase, showing how the LLM agent uses domain-specific query tools to populate the node set V and the edge registration tool to assemble the typed dependency graph $G = (V, E)$.

```
# Listing 16.4: Cross-domain knowledge graph construction via tool-calling
from langchain_core.tools import tool
from langgraph.prebuilt import create_react_agent

# --- Domain-specific data source tools ---
@tool
def query_energy_grid(region: str) -> list:
    """Query substations, capacity, and load for a region."""
    return energy_api.get_substations(region)

@tool
def query_traffic_network(region: str) -> list:
    """Query intersections, controllers, and throughput."""
    return traffic_api.get_network(region)

@tool
def register_cross_domain_edge(
    source_id: str, target_id: str,
    relation: str, weight: float
) -> dict:
```

```
    """Register a typed, weighted edge between two
    entities in different domains."""
    return knowledge_graph.add_edge(
        source_id, target_id, relation, weight
    )

# --- Graph construction agent ---
graph_builder = create_react_agent(
    ChatOpenAI(model="gpt-4o", temperature=0.0),
    [
        query_energy_grid,
        query_traffic_network,
        register_cross_domain_edge
    ]
)
```

The tool architecture mirrors the graph formalism $G = (V, E)$ from the preceding section. The domain query tools (`query_energy_grid`, `query_traffic_network`) populate the node set V with typed entities: substations with capacity and load attributes, intersections with throughput and signal status, controllers with jurisdiction ranges. The `register_cross_domain_edge` tool populates the edge set E with typed, weighted relations. The LLM's role is semantic: given domain data from both sources, it identifies which cross-domain dependencies exist ("Substation-7 powers TrafficController-12") and estimates coupling weights. This is the step where the Integration agent adds value that no single domain API can provide: the energy grid API knows substations, and the traffic API knows controllers, but neither encodes the dependency between them.

Because the LLM estimates coupling weights, governance controls are essential to prevent mis-calibrated values from destabilizing propagation. Four controls apply:

- **Clamping**: Every g_{ij} value produced by the LLM is clipped to a domain-expert-defined range [g_{min}, g_{max}] before it enters the graph, preventing any single LLM call from assigning implausible influence strength.
- **Domain-expert override**: Validated coupling weights from the calibration process (described in the Coupled Heterogeneous Dynamical Systems subsection) take precedence over LLM-estimated values whenever a calibrated entry exists.
- **Logging**: All LLM-suggested weights are written to an audit log with their source prompt and timestamp, enabling post-hoc review and recalibration when observed cascade behavior diverges from model predictions
- **Rollback triggers**: If propagation produces impact scores that exceed a stability threshold (indicating the integrated system is near an oscillatory regime), the system reverts to the last validated coupling weights and alerts the operator before further propagation.

Once the graph is constructed, the second implementation problem is influence propagation: given a disruption at a source entity, how far and how strongly does its impact propagate through the cross-domain graph? The following listing implements the weighted breadth-first traversal described in the architecture.

```
# Listing 16.5: Influence propagation via weighted breadth-first traversal
from collections import deque

def propagate_influence(
    graph, source_id: str,
    initial_strength: float = 1.0,
    threshold: float = 0.1
) -> dict:
    """Weighted BFS: propagate influence from a source
    entity through the cross-domain knowledge graph.
    Returns {entity_id: (strength, [path])}."""
    impacts = {source_id: (initial_strength, [source_id])}
    queue = deque([
        (source_id, initial_strength, [source_id])
    ])

    while queue:
        node_id, strength, path = queue.popleft()

        for edge in graph.outgoing_edges(node_id):
            propagated = strength * edge.weight

            if propagated < threshold:
                continue  # Attenuation cutoff

            new_path = path + [edge.target_id]

            # Keep strongest path to each entity
            if (
                edge.target_id not in impacts
                or propagated > impacts[edge.target_id][0]
            ):
                impacts[edge.target_id] = (
                    propagated, new_path
                )
                queue.append(
                    (edge.target_id, propagated, new_path)
                )
```

```
    return impacts
```

The function returns an impacts dictionary mapping each reachable entity to its estimated disruption strength and the graph path through which influence arrived. In the city/storm scenario, a call with `source_id = "Substation-7"` and `initial_strength = 1.0` returns impact scores for TrafficController-12 (weighted by the "powers" edge), for each intersection it governs (weighted by the "governs" edges), and for the emergency response routes that depend on those intersections. The attenuation cutoff (threshold = 0.1) is not arbitrary: it prevents spurious amplification across long dependency chains where each additional hop reduces fidelity. This is the implementation-level realization of the stability heuristic described in the architecture section; the graph captures influence topology, but only propagation above the threshold is operationally meaningful.

The following case study applies both architectures to a concrete real-world scenario, demonstrating how the Embodied Intelligence agent and the Domain-Transforming Integration agent operate in concert when neither alone is sufficient.

Case study: Autonomous drone mission planning in Ottawa's winter conditions

This case study works through four subsections. The *Mission scenario* section defines the operating environment and the dual-architecture requirement. The *Constraint formalization* section specifies the Unified Constraint Envelope that must be satisfied before any motor spins. The *Architecture instantiation* section maps each architecture from preceding sections onto concrete drone-level components. Finally, the *Implementation* section provides the LangChain code that realizes both agents as a composed system. Ottawa in January is the chosen environment because its combination of sub-zero temperatures, gusting winds, and layered regulatory airspace (Transport Canada controlled zones and Parks Canada Greenbelt restrictions) stresses all five constraint domains simultaneously, making it a maximally demanding test of the joint architecture.

Mission scenario

Ottawa in January is not a forgiving operating environment. At 45 degrees north latitude, the capital delivers sub-zero temperatures, gusting northwesterly winds off the Ottawa River, and precipitation that alternates between freezing rain and driven snow within the span of a single morning. It is exactly the kind of environment that exposes the limits of a single-architecture approach to autonomous flight. Ottawa's winter operating conditions are representative of any high-latitude or high-altitude mission where environmental, regulatory, and energy constraints intersect simultaneously and must be satisfied as a joint system before a single motor spins.

The mission scenario is as follows. An operator instructs an autonomous drone to conduct a photographic survey along a six-kilometer corridor from Centerpointe Technology Park in Nepean to the Ottawa River waterfront. The corridor crosses two distinct regulatory zones: controlled urban airspace governed by Transport Canada under the Canadian Aviation Regulations (CARs) Part IX, and the National Capital Greenbelt managed by Parks Canada, which imposes additional overflight restrictions on protected green space within the National Capital Region. The operator issues the mission objective in plain language. The agent system must translate that intent into a legally authorized, physically executable flight plan, or decline to arm and explain which constraint has not been satisfied.

The scenario requires both architectures from this chapter operating in concert. The precision flight requirement (maintaining stable waypoint trajectories through wind gusts, managing battery State of Charge across a multi-kilometer route, executing safe altitude holds over urban terrain) is a depth problem, addressed by the Embodied Intelligence agent. The regulatory authorization requirement (reconciling Transport Canada NOTAM feeds, Parks Canada restriction databases, real-time weather data, and battery telemetry into a single go/no-go decision) is a breadth problem, addressed by the Domain-Transforming Integration agent. Neither architecture alone is sufficient. The depth architecture does not maintain cross-domain dependency models. The breadth architecture does not execute real-time flight control. This case study demonstrates their synthesis.

Figure 16.4 – Author experimenting with operating a drone in an extreme environment. Left: Drone taking off in -10°C near Ottawa. Right: Drone flying over freezing wilderness

The photographs in *Figure 16.4* were taken during a January test flight near Kanata, west of Ottawa, with an ambient temperature of –10 °C and steady 20 km/h winds from the northwest. Within ninety seconds of takeoff, the battery state-of-charge dropped below the nominal discharge curve, triggering an AMBER warning from the constraint envelope's energy domain. Wind gusts briefly pushed airspeed beyond the corridor threshold, causing the safety layer to reject a waypoint command and force a hover-hold until conditions stabilized. The drone completed its survey transect and returned with 28% residual charge: enough headroom to satisfy the reserve floor, but narrow enough to confirm that the conservative SoC threshold built into the Unified Constraint Envelope is operationally necessary rather than merely theoretical.

Constraint formalization

Before the mission supervisor can authorize flight, every active constraint across all relevant domains must be evaluated and satisfied simultaneously. The intersection of all domain-level go/no-go conditions constitutes what this chapter terms the Unified Constraint Envelope: the smallest admissible region of state space within which a flight plan may execute legally, safely, and with sufficient energy reserves to complete and return. The drone may not arm until the constraint assembler reports a fully green envelope across all five domains defined below.

Weather constraints bound the environmental operating window. Flight is authorized only when temperature is above -10 degrees Celsius (an author-defined operational limit reflecting battery discharge degradation below this threshold, stricter than Transport Canada's published minimums), wind speed is below 25 km/hr at mission altitude (a mission-specific operational limit; Transport Canada does not prescribe a universal wind speed ceiling for remotely piloted aircraft under 25 kg), and no active precipitation is reported within the corridor. These three conditions map to the weather constraint component of the admissible action set A_safe(s) defined in the *Embodied Intelligence agent* section: a flight action is admissible only if the weather sub-constraint is satisfied.

Battery constraints bound the energy envelope. The drone's State of Charge (SoC) must be at or above 30 percent at departure and must not be projected to fall below 20 percent at any waypoint along the planned route, with a minimum reserve of 15 percent guaranteed at return-to-home initiation. These thresholds ensure that no single flight segment commits the aircraft beyond its recoverable energy budget. The battery constraint maps to an edge in the knowledge graph $G = (V, E)$ from the *Domain-Transforming Integration agent* section: a Battery node with a 'constrains' edge weighted by remaining charge proportion pointing to the `FlightDuration` node (a knowledge-graph node representing the total planned flight time and its energy budget).

Airspace constraints enforce regulatory compliance. The mission supervisor queries the Transport Canada NOTAM (Notice to Air Missions) feed for any active flight restrictions within the Centerpointe-to-Ottawa-River corridor. A NOTAM restriction in the corridor immediately invalidates the corresponding flight segment; the constraint assembler must identify an alternate route or abort. Airspace data is modeled as a typed node cluster in $G = (V, E)$: Airspace nodes with 'restricts' edges to `FlightCorridor` (a node representing a named segment of the planned route between two waypoints) nodes, weighted by restriction severity. Real-time NOTAM alerts add or remove restriction edges dynamically.

Parks constraints enforce National Capital Commission and Parks Canada overflight permissions. Any route segment crossing the National Capital Greenbelt requires explicit authorization. Parks nodes in the graph carry 'permits' or 'denies' edges to corridor segment nodes.

Finally, **mission geometry constraints** bound the structural feasibility of the flight plan. In the formal knowledge graph, the Unified Constraint Envelope is therefore the intersection of all five domain node-cluster states: Weather AND Battery AND Airspace AND Parks AND mission geometry all returning a satisfied status. Conservative constraint fusion applies: a single domain returning an unsatisfied state vetoes the entire envelope, regardless of how favorably the remaining four domains report.

Architecture instantiation

The drone mission instantiates both architectures from this chapter at the level of concrete system components. The following two paragraphs map each architecture to its drone-level realization before the code listings implement those mappings.

- **Embodied Intelligence agent instantiation:** The drone's onboard control loop maps directly to the four-layer control hierarchy from the *Embodied Intelligence agent* section. At the task-planning layer (0.1 to 1 Hz), the mission supervisor interprets the operator's route instruction and authorizes flight segments after consulting the Unified Constraint Envelope. At the motion-planning layer (1 to 10 Hz), the Flight Planner computes waypoint trajectories between corridor checkpoints, accounting for wind-induced drift and terrain clearance. At the trajectory and servo layers, the autopilot firmware executes smooth path tracking and regulates motor currents, operating independently of the LLM reasoning layer. Safety enforcement is the concrete drone instantiation of A_safe(s) from the *Embodied Intelligence agent* section: no flight action may execute unless the Unified Constraint Envelope reports fully satisfied. The drone maintains a belief state b(s) over meteorological and airspace state, updated continuously via real-time sensor readings and API queries, consistent with the POMDP formulation from the *Embodied Intelligence agent* section.

- **Domain-Transforming Integration agent instantiation:** The constraint assembler is the drone-scale realization of the knowledge graph architecture from the *Domain-Transforming Integration agent* section. The five constraint domains from the *Constraint formalization* section become typed node clusters in $G = (V, E)$: Weather nodes (temperature, wind, precipitation), Airspace nodes (NOTAMs, controlled zones, corridor segments), Energy nodes (battery SoC, discharge rate, distance budget), Parks nodes (Greenbelt zones, authorization status), and Mission nodes (waypoints, route geometry). Typed edges link nodes across clusters: `WeatherStation` 'affects' `MissionEnvelope` with a weight proportional to constraint margin; Airspace 'restricts' `FlightCorridor` with weight 1.0 for any active NOTAM; Battery 'constrains' `FlightDuration` with weight equal to (SoC - reserve threshold). The influence propagation function from *Listing 16.5* is invoked when a real-time NOTAM alert arrives, estimating cascade impact across the graph to determine whether a reroute satisfies the remaining constraint domains.

Implementation

The following two listings implement the architectures described above. *Listing 16.6* extends the Embodied Intelligence agent patterns from *Listings 16.1* and *16.2*, applying them to the drone mission context. *Listing 16.7* extends the Domain-Transforming Integration agent patterns from *Listings 16.3* and *16.4*, implementing the cross-domain constraint assembler with NOTAM integration. Together, they demonstrate the synthesis described in the *Architecture instantiation* section.

```
# Listing 16.6: Embodied drone agent with safety-constrained mission execution
from langchain_core.tools import tool
from langchain_openai import ChatOpenAI
from langgraph.prebuilt import create_react_agent
from dataclasses import dataclass, field
from typing import Optional


@dataclass
class DroneFlightState:
    """Current belief state b(s) over the drone's physical and environmental state."""
    position_lat: float = 0.0        # Current GPS latitude
    position_lon: float = 0.0        # Current GPS longitude
    altitude_m: float = 0.0          # Current altitude (metres AGL)
    battery_soc: float = 1.0         # State of Charge, 0.0-1.0
    wind_speed_kmh: float = 0.0      # Wind speed at mission altitude
    temperature_c: float = 0.0       # Ambient temperature
    precipitation_active: bool = False  # Any active precip in corridor
```

```
    constraint_envelope_green: bool = False  # Unified Constraint Envelope status


# --- Tool Layer: maps to control hierarchy layers (the Embodied Intelligence Agent
section) ---

@tool
def check_flight_safety(state_json: str) -> dict:
    """Safety enforcement layer: validate current state against the Unified Constraint
    Envelope (the Constraint Formalization section). Maps to A_safe(s) from the Embodied
Intelligence Agent section.
    Returns go/no-go with per-domain status."""
    import json
    s = json.loads(state_json)
    checks = {
        "temperature": s["temperature_c"] > -10.0,       # Author-defined operational
limit
        "wind": s["wind_speed_kmh"] < 25.0,              # Mission-specific operational
limit
        "precipitation": not s["precipitation_active"],
        "battery_departure": s["battery_soc"] >= 0.30,   # SoC floor: 30% at departure
    }
    envelope_green = all(checks.values())
    return {
        "envelope_green": envelope_green,
        "domain_status": checks,
        "safe_to_fly": envelope_green
    }


@tool
def query_flight_state(drone_id: str) -> dict:
    """World-model query layer: retrieve current telemetry belief state b(s)
    from drone sensors and environmental APIs. Maps to task-planning layer."""
    # Production: query live telemetry + weather API + battery management system
    return {
        "position_lat": 45.3490,
        "position_lon": -75.7544,
        "altitude_m": 0.0,
        "battery_soc": 0.82,
        "wind_speed_kmh": 18.5,
        "temperature_c": -6.2,
        "precipitation_active": False,
        "constraint_envelope_green": False   # Not yet evaluated
```

```
    }


@tool
def dispatch_waypoint_command(
    waypoint_lat: float,
    waypoint_lon: float,
    altitude_m: float,
    airspeed_kmh: float
) -> dict:
    """Motion-planning interface: submit a validated waypoint command to the
    deterministic flight controller. The controller executes at 50-200 Hz.
    This tool may only be called after check_flight_safety returns
envelope_green=True."""
    # Production: serialize to MAVLink protocol and send to autopilot firmware
    return {
        "command_accepted": True,
        "waypoint": {
            "lat": waypoint_lat,
            "lon": waypoint_lon,
            "alt": altitude_m,
            "airspeed": airspeed_kmh
        },
        "estimated_duration_s": 120
    }
```

With the flight state model and the three tool interfaces defined, the remaining components are the mission supervisor agent itself and the entry-point function that enforces the safety protocol sequence.

```
# Listing 16.6 (continued): Mission Supervisor agent construction and execution loop
# --- Mission Supervisor agent (task-planning layer, 0.1-1 Hz) ---
mission_supervisor = create_react_agent(
    ChatOpenAI(model="gpt-4o", temperature=0.0),
    [
        check_flight_safety,
        query_flight_state,
        dispatch_waypoint_command
    ]
)


def execute_mission(operator_instruction: str) -> str:
    """Entry point: translate operator intent into authorized flight actions.
    The agent must call check_flight_safety and receive envelope_green=True
```

```
    before any call to dispatch_waypoint_command is permitted."""
    result = mission_supervisor.invoke({
        "messages": [
            {
                "role": "user",
                "content": (
                    f"{operator_instruction}\n\n"
                    "Protocol: (1) call query_flight_state to retrieve current b(s). "
                    "(2) call check_flight_safety with the state JSON. "
                    "(3) Only if envelope_green is True, call dispatch_waypoint_command.
"
                    "(4) If envelope_green is False, report which domains failed and do
not arm."
                )
            }
        ]
    })
    return result['messages'][-1].content
```

The tool architecture maps directly to the control hierarchy from the *Embodied Intelligence agent* section. The `check_flight_safety` tool is the software implementation of A_safe(s): it evaluates the Unified Constraint Envelope across all weather and battery domains before any flight action executes. The `query_flight_state` tool maintains the belief state b(s) over the drone's physical and environmental condition. The `dispatch_waypoint_command` tool is the interface between the reasoning layer and the deterministic flight controller, which runs its own real-time loop at 50 to 200 Hz independently of the LLM. The mission supervisor cannot bypass the safety check: the protocol instruction embedded in the agent's task description enforces the same architectural invariant that the control hierarchy enforces in hardware. Airspace and Parks Canada authorization is provided by the constraint assembler in *Listing 16.7*, whose output the mission supervisor consumes before authorizing departure.

```
# Listing 16.7: Cross-domain constraint assembler with NOTAM integration
from langchain_core.tools import tool
from langchain_openai import ChatOpenAI
from langgraph.prebuilt import create_react_agent
from typing import Optional
import json


# --- Domain query tools (extend Listing 16.4 tool pattern) ---

@tool
def query_weather_constraints(corridor_id: str) -> dict:
    """Query real-time weather data for the specified flight corridor.
```

```
    Returns constraint-relevant fields: temperature, wind, precipitation."""
    # Production: query Environment Canada API or equivalent
    return {
        "temperature_c": -6.2,
        "wind_speed_kmh": 18.5,
        "precipitation_active": False,
        "temperature_constraint_met": True,    # > -10C
        "wind_constraint_met": True,           # < 25 km/hr
        "precip_constraint_met": True
    }


@tool
def query_airspace_notams(corridor_id: str) -> dict:
    # NOTAM validity check (pseudocode):
    # 1. Temporal validity: discard NOTAMs where mission_time is outside
    #    [valid_from, valid_until]; only active windows constrain the plan.
    #    relevant_notams = [n for n in notams
    #                       if n.valid_from <= mission_time <= n.valid_until]
    #
    # 2. Geospatial overlap: check whether the restricted polygon
    #    intersects the planned corridor geometry (Shapely or equivalent).
    #    blocked = any(notam.polygon.intersects(corridor_geometry)
    #                  for notam in relevant_notams)
    #    airspace_constraint_met = not blocked
    """Query Transport Canada NOTAM feed for active flight restrictions.
    NOTAM: Notice to Air Missions, the standard Transport Canada format for
    real-time airspace restriction alerts issued under CARs Part IX."""
    # Production: query Transport Canada DroneZone API
    # Mock NOTAM response structure reflecting Transport Canada alert format
    return {
        "notams": [
            {
                "alert_id": "NOTAM-CYOW-2025-0042",
                "corridor": "CENTERPOINTE_OTTAWARIVER",
                "restriction_type": "NONE",    # NONE | TEMPORARY | PERMANENT | TFR
                "valid_from": "2025-01-15T08:00:00Z",
                "valid_until": "2025-01-15T20:00:00Z",
                "authority": "Transport Canada"
            }
        ],
        "airspace_constraint_met": True   # No active restrictions in corridor
    }
```

```
@tool
def query_battery_state(drone_id: str) -> dict:
    """Query battery management system for current State of Charge and
    projected SoC at each planned waypoint."""
    return {
        "current_soc": 0.82,
        "projected_min_soc": 0.34,     # Minimum projected during mission
        "return_reserve_soc": 0.21,    # Projected SoC at return-to-home
        "battery_constraint_met": True  # SoC floor 30% met at departure
    }


@tool
def query_parks_restrictions(route_geojson: str) -> dict:
    """Query Parks Canada and National Capital Commission databases for
    overflight restrictions along the planned route geometry."""
    # Production: intersect route geometry with NCC Greenbelt restriction polygons
    return {
        "greenbelt_intersection": True,     # Route crosses protected land
        "overflight_authorized": True,      # Authorization on file
        "authorization_reference": "NCC-UAV-2025-0017",
        "parks_constraint_met": True
    }


@tool
def register_constraint_node(
    domain: str,
    node_id: str,
    constraint_met: bool,
    weight: float
) -> dict:
    """Register a typed constraint node in the knowledge graph G=(V,E).
    Extends the register_cross_domain_edge pattern from Listing 16.4.
    domain: one of WEATHER, AIRSPACE, BATTERY, PARKS, MISSION."""
    return knowledge_graph.add_constraint_node(
        domain=domain,
        node_id=node_id,
        status='GREEN' if constraint_met else 'RED',
        weight=weight
    )
```

```
# --- Constraint assembler agent (Domain-Transforming Integration Agent) ---
constraint_assembler = create_react_agent(
    ChatOpenAI(model="gpt-4o", temperature=0.0),
    [
        query_weather_constraints,
        query_airspace_notams,
        query_battery_state,
        query_parks_restrictions,
        register_constraint_node
    ]
)


def assemble_unified_constraint_envelope(
    corridor_id: str,
    drone_id: str,
    route_geojson: str
) -> dict:
    """Assemble the Unified Constraint Envelope by querying all domain agents
    and applying conservative constraint fusion: all domains must report
    constraint_met=True for envelope_green to be returned as True."""
    result = constraint_assembler.invoke({
        "messages": [
            {
                "role": "user",
                "content": (
                    f"Corridor: {corridor_id}. Drone: {drone_id}.\n"
                    "Query all four constraint domains (weather, airspace, battery,
parks). "
                    "Register each result as a typed constraint node in the knowledge
graph. "
                    "Apply influence propagation if any NOTAM restriction is active: "
                    "call propagate_influence with the NOTAM node as source to estimate
cascade. "
                    "Return unified_envelope_green=True only if ALL domains report
constraint_met=True."
                )
            }
        ]
    })

    # Validate output structure before returning to Mission Supervisor
    raw = result['messages'][-1].content
    try:
```

```
        envelope = ConstraintEnvelope.model_validate_json(raw)
    except ValidationError as e:
        raise RuntimeError(f"Constraint assembler returned invalid schema: {e}")
    return envelope.model_dump()
```

The constraint assembler implements the Domain-Transforming Integration agent pattern from the *Domain-Transforming Integration agent* section at the drone-mission scale. Each domain query tool corresponds to a typed node cluster in $G = (V, E)$: the weather tool populates Weather nodes, the NOTAM tool populates Airspace nodes with real-time restriction edges, the battery tool populates Energy nodes, and the parks tool populates Parks nodes. The `register_constraint_node` tool writes the assembled state back to the knowledge graph with a binary `constraint_met` status and a margin weight. Conservative constraint fusion, introduced in the *Domain-Transforming Integration agent* section and applied here explicitly, means that a single RED domain node vetoes the entire envelope: no single source of optimism can override a safety-critical limitation.

Domain data sources are not always available in real time. When a query tool returns a stale or failed response, the constraint assembler applies a graceful degradation pattern. A domain whose data timestamp exceeds a staleness threshold (configurable per domain; weather data may tolerate 15 minutes, NOTAM data far less) is flagged as STALE rather than GREEN or RED. The conservative fusion rule treats a STALE domain as a failed constraint: the envelope does not report fully green until the stale reading is refreshed or the operator explicitly acknowledges the data gap and accepts the associated risk. If a domain API is entirely unavailable, the assembler falls back to the last-known-good reading for a short grace period; beyond that period, it escalates to an operator alert and suspends mission authorization until connectivity is restored.

The Unified Constraint Envelope is not evaluated only at departure. Weather conditions, battery state, and airspace restrictions can change after the drone has taken off, requiring continuous re-evaluation during flight. The constraint assembler runs a refresh cycle at a configurable interval (for example, every 30 seconds for weather and battery, and on every received NOTAM push alert for airspace). If a previously green domain transitions to RED mid-flight (a NOTAM restriction activating within the corridor, battery SoC dropping below the waypoint minimum, or wind speed exceeding the operational ceiling), the mission supervisor is notified immediately. The agent then halts forward progress at the next safe holding point, re-invokes the constraint assembler to assess whether rerouting can recover a fully green envelope, and either executes the revised plan or initiates a return-to-home if no compliant path exists.

The mission supervisor from *Listing 16.6* and the constraint assembler from *Listing 16.7* operate as a composed system. Before the mission supervisor calls `dispatch_waypoint_command`, it consumes the output of `assemble_unified_constraint_envelope`. The drone does not arm its motors until the constraint assembler returns `envelope_green=True` across all five domains: weather, battery, airspace, parks, and mission geometry. This is the chapter's recurring principle made concrete: safety is not an emergent property of correct planning but an explicit restriction on the admissible action set. The constraint envelope narrows the action space before reasoning begins; the flight plan operates exclusively within the pre-approved envelope, not against it. With both architectures composed and validated, the chapter is complete.

Summary

This chapter examines how autonomous agents must be redesigned when operating in the physical world, where actions are constrained by irreversibility, latency, and finite energy. It introduces a fundamental architectural divide between depth and breadth: depth requires precise, real-time control of a single physical system, while breadth requires coordination across multiple interconnected domains with complex dependencies.

To address these competing demands, the chapter presents two complementary architectures. The Embodied Intelligence agent solves the depth problem through a multi-rate control hierarchy, belief-state planning, and strict enforcement of an admissible action set that ensures safety at every layer. The Domain-Transforming Integration agent solves the breadth problem by modeling cross-domain systems as a typed knowledge graph and propagating influence to estimate cascading effects.

These architectures are brought together in a drone mission case study, where real-time flight control operates within a Unified Constraint Envelope derived from weather, energy, regulatory, and mission constraints. The central principle that emerges is conservative constraint fusion: autonomous systems must satisfy all constraints simultaneously, with safety enforced as a precondition for action rather than an afterthought.

Throughout this book, we have traced a deliberate arc from foundational agent patterns to increasingly specialized and capable systems. Early chapters established the core abstractions: perception, reasoning, action selection, and memory. Subsequent chapters applied these abstractions to content generation, multi-modal understanding, collaborative multi-agent workflows, knowledge retrieval, and domain-specific applications in healthcare, science, regulated industries, and software engineering. This final chapter extended those principles into the physical world, where real-time constraints, safety-critical control loops, and cross-domain knowledge integration impose the most demanding requirements an agent can face. The progression is not accidental: each capability layer builds on the one before it, and the constraint-first design philosophy that governs an autonomous drone applies equally to a document-processing pipeline or a clinical decision support agent.

As these systems mature, the frontier will shift from individual agent competence to orchestrated ecosystems of agents operating across digital and physical domains simultaneously. The foundations you have built through these chapters equip you to design, implement, and critically evaluate the next generation of these systems.

Subscribe for a free eBook

New frameworks, evolving architectures, research drops, production breakdowns—*AI_Distilled* filters the noise into a weekly briefing for engineers and researchers working hands-on with LLMs and generative AI systems. Subscribe now and receive a free eBook, along with weekly insights that help you stay focused and informed.

Subscribe at `https://packt.link/8Oz6Y` or scan the QR code below.

17

Epilogue: The Future of Intelligent Agents

The measure of intelligence is the ability to change.

commonly attributed to Albert Einstein

The sixteen chapters behind us built a foundation: agents that perceive, reason, plan, act, and learn. This epilogue looks forward. What happens when those agents start redesigning themselves? When they form societies, internalize their own ethics, and expand into physical domains we never anticipated?

We will explore two dimensions in this chapter:

- **Emerging paradigms**: This section will chart the technical frontiers.
- **Strategic Implementation:** This section will translate those frontiers into roadmaps, skills, metrics, and partnerships

Emerging paradigms

As generative AI systems mature, the focus shifts from building static applications to designing systems that can adapt, coordinate, and operate with increasing autonomy. Several emerging paradigms are shaping this transition, extending core ideas such as modular architectures, evaluation, and reliability into more dynamic settings. The following sections explore how agents evolve their capabilities, interact in complex environments, and adopt new forms of intelligence and embodiment.

Autonomous agent evolution and adaptation

Today's learning agents adapt through experience, sensing, critiquing, planning, and improving in a closed loop. But the trajectory doesn't end there. The next frontier is agents that evolve their own architectures, strategies, and objectives, moving in three significant directions.

The first shift is **structural**. Future agents won't just tune weights and prompts. They'll redesign their own reasoning pipelines, swapping in new planning modules, memory backends, and tool interfaces as conditions demand. Formally, this is a meta-optimization problem: given an architecture space A and a performance function $P(a)$, the self-architecting agent seeks a^* that maximizes expected performance subject to alignment constraints $a \in C$. That formulation hides a trap. If the alignment mechanism itself is mutable, the agent could evolve its way around its own ethical guardrails. This alignment stability problem is one of the central open questions in AI safety.

The second shift is **metacognitive**. Agents will build explicit models of what they know, what they can do, and where their performance boundaries lie. The practical payoff: more effective delegation, more accurate confidence communication, and more productive human-agent collaboration.

The third shift is **evolutionary**. Methods drawn from genetic algorithms and neuroevolution will enable populations of agents to explore diverse strategy spaces simultaneously. Neural architecture search techniques such as DARTS have shown that differentiable search over architecture spaces can discover topologies outperforming human-designed ones. Extending these methods to full reasoning pipelines, where the search space includes symbolic planners, memory systems, and tool interfaces alongside neural components, represents a rich research frontier. Unlike gradient-based updates, evolutionary methods can discover qualitatively novel strategies.

These advances demand new infrastructure. The most practical unifying pattern is the **architecture registry**: a centralized catalog of pre-validated reasoning modules, memory backends, tool adapters, and communication protocols that self-evolving agents can compose from. This constrains the search space while permitting novel combinations, supported by automated sandboxing and CI/CD pipelines extended with agent-specific evaluation stages.

Agent societies and emergent behaviors

Engineered multi-agent teams, with roles and protocols specified by human designers, already outperform individual agents on complex tasks. The next paradigm is more ambitious: agent societies in which structure emerges from the interactions themselves, with no central choreographer.

This transition follows the logic of complex adaptive systems. Macroscopic patterns arise from microscopic interactions without centralized control. The enabling properties include diversity of perspectives (as Condorcet's theorem demonstrates, correlated errors eliminate the benefit of aggregation), structured interaction that channels diversity into productive collaboration, and iterative refinement that allows positions to evolve through exchange.

Formal tools become essential. The DeGroot consensus model describes how beliefs converge through iterated weighted averaging, but real societies exhibit nonlinear dynamics with influence weights that shift based on track record and context. Game-theoretic mechanism design provides frameworks for aligning individual incentives with collective welfare. Norm emergence, where behavioral rules arise endogenously when agents who follow them achieve higher payoffs, connects to foundational work by Axelrod on cooperation and Shoham and Tennenholtz on social laws.

Can agent societies develop spontaneous specialization analogous to the division of labor in economies? An agent society with a shared reputation system could develop role differentiation, with agents specializing where they've demonstrated comparative advantage, without any central assignment. Building this in production requires engineering patterns beyond earlier chapters: distributed reputation ledgers tracking success rates per task category, dynamic coalition formation protocols with quality-of-service guarantees, and stigmergic coordination, where agents deposit metadata markers on shared resources to signal task availability.

Agent governance and self-regulation

As agents grow more autonomous and more embedded in consequential decisions, governance must evolve from external oversight to internalized self-regulation. The self-modifying agents described above require governance that scales with the agents' own capabilities.

The foundation is embedding value alignment directly into the cognitive loop using lexicographic preference ordering: optimize for the highest-priority value first, then proceed to lower priorities within the remaining solution set. From a control theory perspective, ethical constraints must be invariant under behavioral adaptation. If E represents the set of ethical constraints, and T, the set of permissible behavioral transformations, self-regulation requires that every transformation in T preserves every constraint in E. This is far stronger than checking compliance at evaluation time.

Self-regulating agents extend this in three practical ways. First, continuous ethical monitoring replaces periodic audits, tracking fairness metrics, transparency scores, safety violations, and regulatory compliance simultaneously in real time. Second, the "ethical circuit breaker" pattern provides a graduated response to violations: logging an alert, increasing human oversight, restricting autonomy to pre-approved actions, and finally halting operation if violations persist. Third, behavioral drift detection maintains a rolling statistical profile of the agent's actions. When the current distribution diverges significantly from baseline, measured using tests like Kolmogorov-Smirnov or Jensen-Shannon divergence, the system flags a potential drift event for review.

In multi-agent societies, governance itself becomes distributed. A "peer audit" protocol randomly assigns agents to review a peer's recent decisions against constitutional principles, with an immutable version history and rollback capabilities providing the essential safeguard.

The expanding range of agent embodiment

Foundation models for robotics represent one of the most promising frontiers. Just as LLMs transformed NLP by learning general-purpose representations from text, foundation models for robotics learn general-purpose physical interaction capabilities from diverse sensorimotor data. Early results from systems like Google DeepMind's RT-2 demonstrate that robots trained on diverse manipulation datasets can handle novel objects and instructions never seen during training. These models create new safety certification challenges, since traditional systems are certified for specific tasks in specific environments. The practical answer: a layered safety architecture where a foundation model handles high-level planning, while a low-level controller with formally verified properties (collision avoidance, force limits, workspace boundaries) provides hard guarantees the foundation model cannot override.

Micro-scale and nano-scale embodiment shifts the dominant physics from Newtonian mechanics to stochastic thermodynamics. Brownian motion introduces irreducible randomness, making deterministic planning impossible. Medical applications drive the research: targeted drug delivery, minimally invasive surgery, in-body diagnostics. The architectural patterns are recognizable, with perception-action loops and hierarchical control, but implementations must account for severe power and bandwidth constraints that preclude cloud-based inference.

Environmental and infrastructure embodiment extends to planetary-scale systems. Agricultural agent fleets combine drone-based inspection, soil sensors, weather integration, and automated irrigation. Climate monitoring agents synthesize satellite, ocean, and atmospheric data. These systems operate at scales that dwarf warehouse and urban deployments, but rely on the same principles: distributed sensing, collective estimation, and cross-domain knowledge synthesis.

Brain-inspired cognitive architectures

Every architecture in this book borrows from biology, at least loosely. The cognitive loop of perception, reasoning, planning, action, and learning echoes the information processing pathways of biological brains. Yet the borrowing has been shallow. Closing three specific gaps represents one of the field's richest opportunities.

Neuromorphic computing offers hardware that processes information using principles inspired by biological neural networks. Chips like Intel's Loihi 2 and IBM's NorthPole implement spiking neural networks that process information through discrete events rather than continuous activations. The energy efficiency advantage is substantial: comparable accuracy at one to three orders of magnitude less power. For mobile robots, drones, and wearable medical devices, neuromorphic hardware could enable capabilities currently impossible within available energy budgets.

Predictive processing, also known as active inference under the free energy principle (Friston, 2010), reframes the agent's core function. Instead of stimulus-response mapping, the agent continuously predicts incoming sensory data and minimizes the surprise of observations. It minimizes the variational free energy $F = Eq[\ln q(s) - \ln p(o, s)]$, where $q(s)$ is the approximate posterior belief about hidden states and $p(o, s)$ is the generative model. Action and perception become two sides of the same coin: the agent reduces surprise either by updating its model (perception) or by acting on the environment to make the world match its predictions (action). This naturally balances exploitation and exploration, providing a principled account of curiosity-driven behavior.

Episodic memory architectures, inspired by hippocampal systems, represent the third frontier. The complementary learning systems theory (McClelland et al., 1995) posits that biological memory involves two systems: a fast-learning hippocampal system that stores specific episodes and a slow-learning neocortical system that extracts statistical regularities. Current agent architectures lack the crucial consolidation process. Implementing it through periodic offline replay and distillation could enable richer knowledge representations, supporting far transfer and analogical reasoning. In practice, this runs as a scheduled batch job: the agent reviews recent episodes, extracts generalizable patterns, updates semantic memory, and prunes fully consolidated episodes. This isn't just clever engineering. It's biomimicry with a documented pedigree.

> **Note**
>
> **When sleeping brains write code: The science behind memory consolidation**
>
> In 1994, neuroscientists Matthew Wilson and Bruce McNaughton recorded neurons in a rat's hippocampus while it navigated a maze, then recorded again while the rat slept. The sleeping brain replayed the same neural sequences, compressed into rapid bursts called sharp-wave ripples. The rat was rehearsing its day. Subsequent research confirmed this replay is not a mere echo but an active transfer mechanism: the hippocampus "teaches" the neocortex by replaying experiences until the slower system extracts durable patterns. Block the replay, and consolidation fails.
>
> The memory consolidation process described above, where a scheduled batch job reviews episodes, extracts patterns, and prunes consolidated memories, is a computational analog of what Wilson and McNaughton's rats were doing in their sleep. The agents are, quite literally, dreaming.

A practical implementation roadmap proceeds in three stages. Memory consolidation comes first: a batch process with immediate value and minimal infrastructure change. Predictive processing in perception modules improves robustness and requires architecture changes, but runs on existing hardware. Neuromorphic hardware for edge perception represents a longer timeline with the highest potential payoff for power-constrained deployments.

Strategic implementation

Turning agent-based systems into real organizational value requires more than technical capability; it demands deliberate strategy, structured adoption, and alignment with business goals. The following sections outline how to approach implementation at scale, from building capability roadmaps and developing the right skills to measuring impact and redefining how humans and agents work together in practice.

Building agent capability roadmaps

The most successful roadmaps follow a "crawl, walk, run" model. The crawl phase deploys automation for well-understood, high-volume tasks while building foundational infrastructure: observability pipelines, evaluation frameworks, and governance processes. The walk phase introduces planning agents for complex, multi-step workflows. The run phase adds learning agents and multi-agent coordination.

Three organizational patterns have proven effective. A **center of excellence** developing shared infrastructure, including fairness monitoring, explanation frameworks, and compliance templates, reducing ethical overhead from 30 to 40% of development time for the first agent to 10 to 15% for subsequent ones. An **embedded specialist model** distributing expertise across product teams with lightweight coordination. A **hybrid model** combining both and which suits most large organizations.

Skills development for the age of agentic systems

The shift from traditional software engineering to agent development is a paradigm shift comparable to the transition from procedural to object-oriented programming. Agents are non-deterministic, autonomous, and stateful. Engineers must think in terms of perception, reasoning, planning, action, and learning rather than input-output transformations.

Core competencies include prompt engineering, cognitive architecture design, multi-agent orchestration, tool integration, memory systems, and observability for non-deterministic systems. A progressive curriculum moving from single-agent fundamentals through cognitive architectures and multi-agent coordination to deployment ethics can be covered in a single quarter. The specifics matter less than the sequence: build before you orchestrate, orchestrate before you govern.

Creating organizational value

The following Quandri case study illustrates the potential of agent-based systems to drive significant operational and business value: an autonomous agent network processing thousands of insurance policies daily achieved 99.9% accuracy, reduced processing time from hours to under 15 minutes, and generated over $30,000 in monthly recurring revenue. A lean team armed with agent technology systematically outperformed traditional operations many times its size.

Value manifests along four dimensions: operational efficiency through automated multi-step workflows, quality improvement through tireless attention to detail, capability expansion into services that would be economically infeasible with purely human workforces, and organizational learning that transforms individual expertise into persistent institutional capability.

Measuring ROI and impact

Direct cost savings are the most straightforward metric: reduced labor hours minus infrastructure costs. But three additional dimensions matter more strategically:

- **Revenue enablement**, which captures value from new products and markets, such as multilingual support that would require prohibitive staffing.
- **Risk reduction**, which quantifies avoided negative outcomes, where a single averted bias incident pays for years of responsible AI investment.
- **Improvement velocity**, the rate at which the system gets better over time, is the most important metric of all. Organizations that invest in learning infrastructure benefit from compounding returns that diverge sharply from the flat curves of traditional automation.

The evolving relationship between humans and artificial intelligence

The current paradigm positions humans as supervisors and exception handlers. It works, but it creates a tension. As agents grow more capable, the remaining decisions requiring human judgment are precisely the most difficult and consequential. Humans handle only the hardest cases while losing context for effective judgment.

The next paradigm is collaborative partnership, clarified by comparative advantage. Humans hold the advantage in contextual judgment, ethical reasoning, and creative insight. Agents hold the advantage in sustained attention, consistency, and exhaustive search. The key insight: even if agents eventually surpass humans in every dimension, humans will still have a comparative advantage in some tasks, and the partnership remains productive.

The most successful deployments already implement a "collaboration spectrum" that dynamically adjusts: simple tasks are handled autonomously, complex tasks trigger collaborative analysis, and high-stakes decisions are escalated with full context. Designing interfaces and coordination mechanisms for these integrated human-agent teams is among the most important challenges facing the field.

Summary

The technical frontiers are vast: self-evolving architectures, emergent agent societies, governance that lives inside the agent rather than above it, embodiment from the nanoscale to the planetary, and cognition modeled on how brains actually work. The strategic playbook is concrete: roadmap your capabilities, invest in your people, measure what matters, and design for partnership rather than replacement.

One thread connects every chapter in this book and every frontier in this epilogue. *Intelligent agents are not a substitute for human intelligence. They are the most powerful amplifier of it ever built.*

Get This Book's PDF Version and Exclusive Extras

Index

A

B

C

D

F

G

H

I

K

W

Y

Z

Made in the USA
Monee, IL
16 September 2026

63313466R00299